THE LAW OF HEALTH CARE FINANCE AND REGULATION

THE LAW OF HEALTH CARE FINANCE AND REGULATION

Mark A. Hall
Fred D. and Elizabeth L. Turnage Professor of Law and Public Health
Wake Forest University

Mary Anne Bobinski
Dean and Professor of Law
University of British Columbia Faculty of Law

David Orentlicher
Samuel R. Rosen Professor of Law
Indiana University School of Law, Indianapolis

PUBLISHERS

1185 Avenue of the Americas, New York, NY 10036
www.aspenpublishers.com

Permissions
Aspen Publishers
1185 Avenue of the Americas
New York, NY 10036

Printed in the United States of America

1 2 3 4 5 6 7 8 9 0

ISBN 0-7355-5207-X

Library of Congress Cataloging-in-Publication Data

Hall, Mark A., 1955-
    The law of health care finance and regulation / Mark A. Hall, Mary Anne Bobinski, David Orentlicher.
        p. cm.
    Includes index.
    ISBN 0-7355-5207-X
    1. Medical care—Finance—Law and legislation—United States—Cases. I. Bobinski, Mary Anne. II. Orentlicher, David. III. Title.
KF3825.A7H35 2005
344.7303′21—dc22

                                                                2004046379

About Aspen Publishers

Aspen Publishers, headquartered in New York City, is a leading information provider for attorneys, business professionals, and law students. Written by preeminent authorities, our products consist of analytical and practical information covering both U.S. and international topics. We publish in the full range of formats, including updated manuals, books, periodicals, CDs, and online products.

Our proprietary content is complemented by 2,500 legal databases, containing over 11 million documents, available through our Loislaw division. Aspen Publishers also offers a wide range of topical legal and business databases linked to Loislaw's primary material. Our mission is to provide accurate, timely, and authoritative content in easily accessible formats, supported by unmatched customer care.

To order any Aspen Publishers title, go to *www.aspenpublishers.com* or call 1-800-638-8437.

To reinstate your manual update service, call 1-800-638-8437.

For more information on Loislaw products, go to *www.loislaw.com* or call 1-800-364-2512.

For Customer Care issues, e-mail *CustomerCare@aspenpublishers.com*; call 1-800-234-1660; or fax 1-800-901-9075.

Aspen Publishers
A Wolters Kluwer Company

To Larry C. Hall, Ph.D., for showing me the joys of an academic life.
—*M.A.H.*

To Holly, my best friend and life companion, and to my parents, for their encouragement.
—*M.A.B.*

To the memory of Prof. Herman I. Orentlicher, for his commitment to "neutral skepticism," rigorous standards, and, above all, decency.
—*D.O.*

To Bill Curran, for his guiding light.

Summary of Contents

Contents

2

■

Institutional Liability

4
■

Preface

This book contains the materials from *Health Care Law and Ethics* (6th ed. 2003) that are focused on health care organizations, finance, and regulation, with updates through August 2004 and substantial additional materials on selected topics. As the larger casebook enters its fifth decade, we pause to reflect on the remarkable metamorphosis of health care law from a subspecialty of tort law to a mushrooming academic and practice field whose tentacles reach into myriad scholarly disciplines and areas of substantive law. Each of the casebook's five prior editions reflects an important stage in this evolutionary growth. Health care law originated as a separate field of professional practice and academic inquiry during the 1960s, when the first edition of the casebook was published. Under the somewhat grandiose label of "medical jurisprudence," the primary focus at first was on medical proof in all kinds of criminal and civil litigation, on medical malpractice actions against physicians, and on public health regulation. The principal concern was how traditional bodies of legal doctrine and practice such as criminal, tort, and evidence law should apply in medical settings.

During the 1970s, bioethics became a major additional area of concern as a consequence of the right to die movement spawned by the *Quinlan* case and the focus on individual autonomy contained in the informed consent doctrine and the landmark decision on reproductive decisionmaking in Roe v. Wade. Law courses during this and earlier periods were taught under the heading of "law and medicine."

In the 1980s, economic and regulatory topics formed the third component of health care law, as exemplified by the increasing application of antitrust laws to the health care industry and the growing body of legal disputes under Medicare and

Medicaid. This newer dimension accelerated its growth into the 1990s with the spread of HMOs and other alternative delivery systems and the market restructuring that is now occurring. These newer topics found their way into courses described as "health law." New developments present continuing challenges to each of these areas of health care law and ethics. In the new millennium, genetics, bioterrorism, medical confidentiality, and financial conflicts of interest are examples of emerging issues that receive increased attention.

This path of development has resulted in an academic discipline defined more by an accretion of topics drawn from historical events than by a systematic conceptual organization of issues. Each of the four major branches—malpractice, bioethics, public health, and financing/regulation—stands apart from the others and is thought to be dominated by a distinct theme. The principal concern of malpractice law is quality of care; bioethics is concerned with individual autonomy; public health poses the rights of patients against the state; and the primary focus of financing and regulatory law is access to care and the cost of care. As a consequence, health care law has yet to become a truly integrated and cohesive discipline.[1] It is too much the creature of history and not of systematic and conceptual organization.

Our major ambition in the casebook is to remedy this state of disarray. This field has reached a stage of maturity that calls for stepping back and rethinking how all of its parts best fit together as a conceptual whole. In our view, that conceptual whole is best organized according to the fundamental structural relationships that give rise to health care law. These relationships are

1. the patient/physician relationship, which encompasses the duty to treat, confidentiality, informed consent, and malpractice;
2. state oversight of doctors and patients, which encompasses the right to die, reproductive rights, physician licensure, and public health; and
3. the institutions that surround the treatment relationship, encompassing public and private insurance, hospitals and HMOs, and more complex transactions and organizational forms.

We develop the traditional themes of quality, ethics, access, and cost throughout each of these three divisions. We also address cutting edge and controversial topics such as AIDS, genetics, managed care, and rationing, but not as discrete topics; instead, we integrate these recent developments within a more permanent, overarching organizational structure that is capable of absorbing unanticipated new developments as they occur.

In deciding which topics to present in each section and in what depth, our basic guide has been to focus on the attributes of the medical enterprise that make it uniquely important or difficult in the legal domain. Health care law is about the

---

[1] This disarray is reflected by the ongoing confusion over competing names for the field. Although "law and medicine" and "health care law" appear to signify the same topic, the first term is understood to mean older style malpractice subject matter and the second term is used to refer to newer economic and regulatory issues. Paradoxically, whereas "health care law" and "health law" might be thought to signify somewhat different fields—the latter not restricted to medical treatment and therefore encompassing public health issues—in fact they are taken to mean the same thing.

delivery of an extremely important, very expensive, and highly specialized professional service. If it were otherwise, this book would likely not exist. Some lawyers and scholars maintain that there is no unifying concept or set of ideas for health care law; instead, it is merely a disparate collection of legal doctrines and public policy responses, connected only by the happenstance that they involve doctors and hospitals in some way—much as if one had a course on the law of green things or the law of Tuesdays.[2] It would be far more satisfying to find one or more organizing principles that explain not only what makes the disparate parts of health care law cohere, but also why that coherence distinguishes health care law from other bodies of integrated legal thought and professional practice.

We believe those organizing principles can be found in the phenomenology of what it is to be ill and to be a healer of illness. These two human realities are permanent features that distinguish this field from all other commercial and social arenas. They permeate all parts of health care law, giving it its distinctive quality and altering how generic legal doctrine and conventional theories of government respond to its problems and issues. To capture this perspective in a phrase, it is one that David Wexler and Bruce Winnick first called "therapeutic jurisprudence," which views the law itself as a therapeutic agent. David Wexler & Bruce Winnick, Essays in Therapeutic Jurisprudence (1991). Health care law might still be worth studying even without these unique attributes of medical encounters, but it is much more engaging and coherent because of them. It is these attributes that give rise to an interrelated set of principles that justify classifying health care law as a coherent and integrated academic and professional discipline.

Accordingly, we stress the unique attributes of medical encounters throughout these materials by incorporating insights from other academic disciplines and theoretical perspectives. Behavioral disciplines such as psychology, sociology, and anthropology help to illuminate the nature of medical knowledge and the lived experience of illness, dependency, and trust as they occur in real-life medical encounters. Findings from health services research published in the health policy literature create a stronger empirical and theoretical base for exploring health care law, one that better exposes its broad social impact. Analytical disciplines such as economics and moral and political theory create the foundation for understanding developments in financing, regulation, and bioethics. And, the perspectives of feminist, communitarian, and critical race theory demonstrate the limitations of conventional analytical models and help us to understand how health care law must evolve to accommodate viewpoints and concerns that have been excluded in the past.[3]

[2] For a similar claim relating to cyberlaw, see Frank H. Easterbrook, Cyberspace and the Law of the Horse, 1996 U. Chi. Legal F. 207, 207-208 (1996).

[3] For additional discussion of the overall content of health care law and approaches to teaching in schools of law, medicine, management, and public health, see American Society of Law and Medicine Task Force on Health Law Curricula, Health Law and Professional Education, 63 U. Det. L. Rev. 245 (1985); George J. Annas, Health Law at the Turn of the Century: From White Dwarf to Red Giant, 21 Conn. L. Rev. 551 (1989); William J. Curran, Titles in the Medicolegal Field: A Proposal for Reform, 1 Am. J.L. & Med. 1 (1975); B.R. Grumet, Legal Medicine in Medical Schools: A Survey of the State of the Art, 54 J. Med. Educ. 755 (1979); Catherine J. Jones, Teaching Bioethics in the Law School Classroom: Recent History, Rapid Advances, the Challenges of the Future, 20 Am. J.L. & Med. 417 (1994); Jay Katz, Reflections on Teaching Law & Medicine, 25 Hous. L. Rev. 475 (1988); Peter Williams & William

In the first chapter, we have collected background and introductory readings that are relevant in a number of places throughout the book and to several different approaches to teaching the course. These are intended for teachers and students to draw on selectively when and where they see fit.

The death of Bill Curran, the original author of this casebook, left us with a considerable burden to shoulder. Although Prof. Curran was involved in the conceptual reorganization of these materials, he was unable to contribute to their selection and editing. Still, his presence is felt in every part of these materials through the inspiration of his mentoring, his friendship, and his vast body of work.

We intend that this book will continue to serve as more than a teaching tool, one that will prove useful as an ongoing resource for conducting research in health care law. To that end, we provide substantial bibliographic notes in each section. Also, we have created a dedicated World Wide Web site to serve this book: www.health-law.org. It contains interesting background materials, updates of important events since publication, additional relevant topics that were excluded due to space constraints, and links to other resources on the internet.

The following is a bibliography of resources and readings that relate to research in health care law generally. Additional bibliographic references that relate to health care finance and regulation can be found at page 363. See also Donald Caldwell, Jr., U.S. Health Law and Policy: A Guide to Current Literature (2d ed. 2001).

Treatises and Texts: Barry Furrow et al., Health Law (2d ed. 2001); Mark A. Hall, Ira Mark Ellman, and Daniel S. Strouse, Health Care Law and Ethics in a Nutshell (2d ed. 1999); Michael MacDonald et al., Treatise on Health Care Law; John H. Robinson, Roberta M. Berry & Kevin McDonnell eds., A Health Law Reader: An Interdisciplinary Approach (1999); World Health Organization, International Digest of Health Legislation.

Health Care Law Journals and Recurring Symposia: American Journal of Law and Medicine (Boston Univ.); Annals of Health Law (Loyola-Chicago); DePaul Journal of Health Care Law; Food, Drug and Cosmetic Law Journal; Health Law & Policy Abstracts (SSRN on-line journal); Health Matrix (Case Western Univ.); Houston Journal of Health Law & Policy; Journal of Contemporary Health Law and Policy (Catholic Univ.); Indiana Health Law Review (Indiana Univ.–Indianapolis); Journal of Health and Hospital Law (St. Louis Univ., AHLA); Journal of Health Care Law & Policy (Univ. Maryland); Journal of Law and Health (Cleveland-Marshall); Journal of Law, Medicine and Ethics (ASLME); Journal of Legal Medicine (So. Illinois Univ.); Medical Trial Technique Quarterly; Journal of Medicine and Law; St. Louis Univ. Law Journal; Seton Hall Law Review; Quinnipiac Health Law Journal; Whittier Law Review; Yale Journal of Health Policy, Law and Ethics.

Winslade, Educating Medical Students about Law and the Legal System, 70 Acad. Med. 777 (1995); Symposium, Teaching Health Law, 38 J. Leg. Educ. 485 (1988); Symposium, The Field of Health Law: Its Past and Future, 14 Health Matrix 1 (2004); Symposium, 6 J. Health Admin. Educ. 221 (1988); Kenneth R. Wing, Health Care Reform in the Year 2000: The View from the Front of the Classroom, 26 Am. J.L. & Med. 277 (2000); Thomas Mayo, The First Fifty Years: Health Law's Greatest Hit, 50 Syracuse L. Rev. 1261 (2000); American Health Care and the Law: We Need to Talk!, 19(4) Health Aff. 84 (July 2000).

Leading Medical, Industry, and Health Policy Journals: American Journal of Public Health; American Medical News (AMA); Health Affairs (published by Project Hope); Health Care Financing Review (HCFA); Health Services Research; Inquiry (published by the Blue Cross/Blue Shield Assoc.); Hospitals and Health Networks (AHA); Journal of the American Medical Association; Journal of Health Politics, Policy and Law; Medical Care; Milbank Memorial Fund Quarterly; Modern Healthcare; New England Journal of Medicine.

Computer Resources: BIOETHICSLINE (Georgetown Univ., Kennedy Institute of Ethics); HEALTH (based on Hospital Literature Abstracts); HEALTHLAWYER (AHA); LEXIS Health and Genmed libraries; MEDLINE (based on Index Medicus); WESTLAW HTH-TP (health texts and periodicals) database; and the Web site for this casebook, www.health-law.org, including its Related Websites page.

Health Law Societies, Digests, and Newsletters: ABA Forum on Health Law (newsletter); American College of Legal Medicine (Milwaukee; journal); American Society of Law, Medicine, and Ethics (Boston; two journals); BNA Health Law Reporter (D.C., weekly); American Health Lawyers Association (Washington, D.C.; monthly digest and newsletter, bimonthly journal); Specialty Law Digest: Health Care Law (monthly).

Acknowledgments

This manuscript could not have been prepared without the thoughtful advice of our colleagues who commented on drafts and gave us suggestions for revision (especially Bill Brewbaker, Seth Chandler, Judy Failer, Hank Greely, David Hyman, Eleanor Kinney, Jack Nelson, Mark Pescovitz, Phil Peters, and Dan Strouse), without the diligent help of those students and staff who assisted us over the past few years (Stephanie Ahrens, Chet Chea, Nathan Childs, Tyler Hall, Laura Hermer, David Higgins, Faith Long Knotts, James Martin, Kazumi I. Oka, Holli M. Palmer, and Jane Wooten), and without the superhuman patience of our families (who, curiously, wish to remain anonymous). Finally, we thank the authors and publishers who granted permission to use each of the excerpts of copyrighted material in these readings.

Mark A. Hall
Mary Anne Bobinski
David Orentlicher

September 2004

THE LAW OF HEALTH CARE FINANCE AND REGULATION

1

Introduction

The following three overview cases and the accompanying notes are intended to introduce issues and themes that are pursued in different parts of this book. You are not expected to retain their analyses and holdings at this point; you only need to get a sense of the range of topics that are covered in different courses that might be taught from this book.

The readings that follow these cases introduce background information and overarching perspectives that are important for understanding the legal issues developed throughout this book. Although lifted out of their respective contexts, we present them at the outset because they raise cross-cutting themes that cannot be cabined within a single chapter. Therefore, it will be necessary to revisit these readings from time to time throughout the course.

A. OVERVIEW CASES

■ IN RE BABY K
16 F.3d 590 (4th Cir. 1994)

WILKINS, Circuit Judge.

The Hospital instituted this action against Ms. H, Mr. K, and Baby K, seeking a declaratory judgment that it is not required under the Emergency Medical Treatment and Active Labor Act (EMTALA), 42 U.S.C.A. §1395dd (West 1992),[2]

---

[2] The Hospital also sought declaratory relief under §504 of the Rehabilitation Act of 1973 (Rehabilitation Act), 29 U.S.C.A. §794 (West Supp. 1993); the Americans with Disabilities Act of 1990 (ADA), 42 U.S.C.A. §§12101 et seq. (West 1993); the Child Abuse Prevention and Treatment Act (Child Abuse Act), 42 U.S.C.A. §§5101-5106h (West Supp. 1993); and the statutes and common

to provide treatment other than warmth, nutrition, and hydration to Baby K, an anencephalic infant. Because we agree with the district court that EMTALA gives rise to a duty on the part of the Hospital to provide respiratory support to Baby K when she is presented at the Hospital in respiratory distress and treatment is requested for her, we affirm.

I

Baby K was born at the Hospital in October of 1992 with anencephaly, a congenital malformation in which a major portion of the brain, skull, and scalp are missing. While the presence of a brain stem does support her autonomic functions and reflex actions, because Baby K lacks a cerebrum, she is permanently unconscious. Thus, she has no cognitive abilities or awareness. She cannot see, hear, or otherwise interact with her environment.

When Baby K had difficulty breathing on her own at birth, Hospital physicians placed her on a mechanical ventilator. This respiratory support allowed the doctors to confirm the diagnosis and gave Ms. H, the mother, an opportunity to fully understand the diagnosis and prognosis of Baby K's condition. The physicians explained to Ms. H that most anencephalic infants die within a few days of birth due to breathing difficulties and other complications. Because aggressive treatment would serve no therapeutic or palliative purpose, they recommended that Baby K only be provided with supportive care in the form of nutrition, hydration, and warmth. Physicians at the Hospital also discussed with Ms. H the possibility of a "Do Not Resuscitate Order" that would provide for the withholding of lifesaving measures in the future.

The treating physicians and Ms. H failed to reach an agreement as to the appropriate care. Ms. H insisted that Baby K be provided with mechanical breathing assistance whenever the infant developed difficulty breathing on her own, while the physicians maintained that such care was inappropriate. As a result of this impasse, the Hospital sought to transfer Baby K to another hospital. This attempt failed when all of the hospitals in the area with pediatric intensive care units declined to accept the infant. In November of 1992, when Baby K no longer needed the services of an acute-care hospital, she was transferred to a nearby nursing home.

Since being transferred to the nursing home, Baby K has been readmitted to the Hospital three times due to breathing difficulties. Each time she has been provided with breathing assistance and, after stabilization, has been discharged to the nursing home. Following Baby K's second admission, the Hospital filed this action to resolve the issue of whether it is obligated to provide emergency medical treatment to Baby K that it deems medically and ethically inappropriate. Baby K's guardian ad litem and her father, Mr. K, joined in the Hospital's request for a declaration that the Hospital is not required to provide respiratory support or other aggressive treatments. . . .

---

law of Virginia. In addressing these provisions, the district court concluded that a failure to provide respiratory support to Baby K because of her condition of anencephaly would constitute discrimination in violation of the ADA and the Rehabilitation Act but declined to rule on the application of the Child Abuse Act or Virginia law. Because we conclude that the Hospital has a duty to render stabilizing treatment under EMTALA, we need not address its obligations under the remaining federal statutes or the laws of Virginia.

II

Congress enacted EMTALA in response to its "concern that hospitals were 'dumping' patients [who were] unable to pay, by either refusing to provide emergency medical treatment or transferring patients before their emergency conditions were stabilized." Brooks v. Maryland General Hospital Inc., 996 F.2d 708, 710 (4th Cir. 1993). Through EMTALA, Congress sought "to provide an 'adequate first response to a medical crisis' for all patients," Baber v. Hospital Corp. of America, 977 F.2d 872, 880 (4th Cir. 1992), by imposing two duties on hospitals that have entered into Medicare provider agreements.

First, those hospitals with an emergency medical department must provide an appropriate medical screening to determine whether an emergency medical condition exists for any individual who comes to the emergency medical department requesting treatment. A hospital fulfills this duty if it utilizes identical screening procedures for all patients complaining of the same condition or exhibiting the same symptoms.

An additional duty arises if an emergency medical condition is discovered during the screening process. EMTALA defines an "emergency medical condition" as including:

> a medical condition manifesting itself by acute symptoms of sufficient severity (including severe pain) such that the absence of immediate medical attention could reasonably be expected to result in—
> (i)   placing the health of the individual . . . in serious jeopardy,
> (ii) serious impairment to bodily functions, or
> (iii) serious dysfunction of any bodily organ or part.

42 U.S.C.A. §1395dd(e)(1)(A).

When an individual is diagnosed as presenting an emergency medical condition:

> the hospital must provide either—
> (A) within the staff and facilities available at the hospital, for such further medical examination and such treatment as may be required to stabilize the medical condition, or
> (B) for the transfer of the individual to another medical facility in accordance with subsection (c) of this section.

42 U.S.C.A. §1395dd(b)(1).

The treatment required "to stabilize" an individual is that treatment "necessary to assure, within reasonable medical probability, that no material deterioration of the condition is likely to result from or occur during the transfer of the individual from a facility." 42 U.S.C.A. §1395dd(e)(3)(A). Therefore, once an individual has been diagnosed as presenting an emergency medical condition, the hospital must provide that treatment necessary to prevent the material deterioration of the individual's condition or provide for an appropriate transfer to another facility.

In the application of these provisions to Baby K, the Hospital concedes that when Baby K is presented in respiratory distress a failure to provide "immediate medical attention" would reasonably be expected to cause serious impairment of her bodily functions. Thus, her breathing difficulty qualifies as an emergency medical condition, and the diagnosis of this emergency medical condition triggers the duty of the hospital to provide Baby K with stabilizing treatment or to transfer her in accordance with the provisions of EMTALA. Since transfer is not an option available to the Hospital at this juncture,[5] the Hospital must stabilize Baby K's condition. . . .

III

. . . As the Hospital acknowledged during oral argument, Baby K resides at the nursing home for months at a time without requiring emergency medical attention. Only when she has experienced episodes of bradypnea or apnea[9] has Baby K required respiratory support to prevent serious impairment of her bodily functions. It is bradypnea or apnea, not anencephaly, that is the emergency medical condition that brings Baby K to the Hospital for treatment. . . . The Hospital does not allege that it would refuse to provide respiratory support to infants experiencing bradypnea or apnea who do not have anencephaly. Indeed, a refusal to provide such treatment would likely be considered as providing no emergency medical treatment. . . .

[The Hospital argues] that, in redressing the problem of disparate emergency medical treatment, Congress did not intend to require physicians to provide medical treatment outside the prevailing standard of medical care. The Hospital asserts that, because of their extremely limited life expectancy and because any treatment of their condition is futile, the prevailing standard of medical care for infants with anencephaly is to provide only warmth, nutrition, and hydration. Thus, it maintains that a requirement to provide respiratory assistance would exceed the prevailing standard of medical care. However, the plain language of EMTALA requires stabilizing treatment for any individual who comes to a participating hospital, is diagnosed as having an emergency medical condition, and cannot be transferred. . . . The Hospital has been unable to identify, nor has our research revealed, any statutory language or legislative history evincing a congressional intent to create an exception to the duty to provide stabilizing treatment when the required treatment would exceed the prevailing standard of medical care. We recognize the dilemma facing physicians who are requested to provide treatment they consider morally and ethically inappropriate, but we cannot ignore the plain language of the statute because "to do so would 'transcend our

---

[5] In order for a hospital to transfer a patient prior to stabilization, EMTALA requires: (1) the patient or a person acting on the patient's behalf to request a transfer in writing after being informed of the risks involved and the obligations of the hospital under EMTALA; or (2) a proper certification that the medical benefits expected from the transfer outweigh the risks involved. 42 U.S.C.A. §1395dd(c)(1). In addition, the transfer must meet the criteria for an appropriate transfer which include the requirement that a qualified receiving facility agree to accept that the patient and to provide appropriate medical treatment. 42 U.S.C.A. §1395dd(c)(1)(B), (c)(2). Since Ms. H objects to the transfer of Baby K, since the Hospital has not obtained a certificate that the benefits of a transfer would outweigh the medical risks involved, and since no qualified medical facility has agreed to accept Baby K, the requirements for transfer prior to stabilization have not been met. If Ms. H requests a transfer or the Hospital obtains a certification that the benefits of a transfer would outweigh the risks involved, and all of the requirements for an appropriate transfer are met, then the Hospital could, of course, transfer Baby K to another qualified medical facility prior to stabilization.

[9] Bradypnea is an "abnormal slowness of breathing." Dorland' Illustrated Medical Dictionary 230 (27th ed. 1988). In an infant who has established and sustained spontaneous breathing, apnea describes the cessation of respiration for more than 60 seconds. Id. at 112.

judicial function.' " *Baber*, 977 F.2d at 884. The appropriate branch to redress the policy concerns of the Hospital is Congress. . . .

IV

It is beyond the limits of our judicial function to address the moral or ethical propriety of providing emergency stabilizing medical treatment to anencephalic infants. We are bound to interpret federal statutes in accordance with their plain language and any expressed congressional intent. Congress rejected a case-by-case approach to determining what emergency medical treatment hospitals and physicians must provide and to whom they must provide it; instead, it required hospitals and physicians to provide stabilizing care to any individual presenting an emergency medical condition. EMTALA does not carve out an exception for anencephalic infants in respiratory distress any more than it carves out an exception for comatose patients, those with lung cancer, or those with muscular dystrophy—all of whom may repeatedly seek emergency stabilizing treatment for respiratory distress and also possess an underlying medical condition that severely affects their quality of life and ultimately may result in their death. Because EMTALA does not provide for such an exception, the judgment of the district court is affirmed.

Notes: Rationing, Justice, and the Doctor-Patient Relationship

1. *Introduction to Complexity*. How many different issues can you identify in the *Baby K* case? There are many problems raised by the case, most of which are not overtly addressed in the opinion. The complexity of health care issues is one of the major themes of this book. A wide range of philosophical debates and legal rules can be implicated by the facts (and frailties) of human biology. This creates a variety of lenses through which to view any case.

One method of studying the health care system is purely *descriptive*, looking at how health care providers and patients *actually* interact. How does the legal system respond to the problems created by biological frailty and the development of medical knowledge? Another focus is normative: How *should* providers and patients interact, and how *should* the legal system regulate health care relationships?

Under either the descriptive or the normative approach, health care interactions implicate one or more of four different sets of legal or ethical analysis. (1) We can look at the doctor-patient relationship in terms of legal duties and liabilities, focusing on whether the health care provider met her professional obligations to her patient under malpractice or fiduciary law. (2) We can also consider broader philosophical issues such as what is the proper realm of patient autonomy, and what is a provider's *moral* duty to act for the benefit of the patient ("beneficence"). (3) A medical case can also implicate broader societal issues, such as whether third-parties or the state in general has a stake in the treatment decision. This focus falls in the realm known as public health law, and implicates constitutional issues. (4) Finally, the medical encounter can be viewed through an organizational or economic lens, which focuses on who pays for the treatment and what institutional constraints are created by the setting in which treatment is provided. Can you identify how each of these four perspectives might be pertinent to *Baby K*?

Despite the variety of issues encountered in this book and the diversity of perspectives, there is a fundamental coherence to health care law. It lies in the fundamental nature of illness and the healing encounter. To use a common metaphor, imagine we are in a dark room with a mysterious object. We can use all of our other senses to determine the nature of the object: smell, taste, touch, etc. Although each person's sensory experiences might be very different, the fundamental nature of the object remains the same.

2. *What Really Happened in* Baby K? Baby K, whose name was Stephanie Keene, ultimately lived for two and a half years in a pediatric nursing facility. She died in the emergency room of Fairfax Hospital in Fairfax, Virginia—the same hospital in the *Baby K* case—after being taken there by ambulance for the sixth time. Her anencephaly had been diagnosed by ultrasound during the sixteenth week of her gestation, and her mother, Contrenia Harrell, decided to carry her to term, believing (according to press accounts) that " 'all life is precious' " and that God would guide Stephanie's life. Other local hospitals reportedly refused to accept a transfer of Baby K shortly after her birth.

Baby K's medical bills ultimately reached almost $1 million. They were covered in part by her mother's insurance with an HMO and in part by Medicaid. These financing systems are described in sections C.1 and C.3. They often do not pay the full costs of treatment. Nevertheless, hospital officials stated that the costs of Baby K's care were not a factor in the hospital's lawsuit. Even so, the hospital may have been thinking about the implications of the case for future patients, and the cost of caring for patients like Baby K are likely to be an issue for other hospitals as health insurers increasingly employ capitation rates for reimbursement, and as Medicare and Medicaid continue to limit their reimbursement rates.

The readings in section C.2 discuss the growing crisis over health care spending. Do any of these additional facts and speculations alter your instincts about who should make the treatment decision for a patient like Baby K? Do you think the insurers should have a stake in the decision? Would it be reasonable to tell Baby K's mother she can insist on treatment but not on payment, thereby remaining liable for the bills? If she still insisted on treatment, but the hospital knew she could never pay, should it still have to treat?

3. *A Medical Miracle?* Some might scoff at Ms. Harrell's reported belief in a medical miracle, but one may in fact have occurred here. As the court noted, anencephalic children generally do not live very long; fewer than 10 percent of such children survive more than a week. Baby K may be the longest lived child with anencephaly. Rather than a miracle, however, her length of life may indicate that the general lack of aggressive treatment for anencephalic children results in their actual lifespans being considerably shorter than their potential lifespans. The readings in section B.3 give more insight into why patients look to physicians for miracles, and how doctors decide what care is most beneficial.

4. *Unusual or Typical?* The *Baby K* case involves a fact situation that is the converse of the typical court case involving life-sustaining treatment. Such cases

usually involve physicians who insist on treatment over the objections of the patient or the patient's family. That is what happened in 1976 in the case of Karen Quinlan, the first "right-to-die" case, and in 1990 in the case of Nancy Cruzan, the first "right-to-die" case before the U.S. Supreme Court. Yet, the *Baby K* situation may become more typical as the result of greater pressures on physicians to limit medical costs. The care of dying patients is an obvious place to look for cost savings. Does this suggestion contravene our deeply treasured value of individual autonomy? Does this value hold the same force when society's resources are at stake? If care were terminated for Baby K, would the result be to force sacrifices by society's most vulnerable to benefit the comfortable or well-to-do? These perspectives are developed further in section D.2.

5. *The Court's Decision.* Do you agree with the majority's or the dissent's analysis of EMTALA? Note that, as the majority opinion indicates, EMTALA was passed in response to hospitals' refusing to provide care to patients who had neither insurance nor personal resources with which to pay for emergency care. Despite this legislative history, EMTALA has been interpreted to preclude refusals of emergency care on grounds other than the patient's inability to pay. Do you think Congress intended for EMTALA to require treatment of anencephalic children with ventilators? If Ms. Keene also had a cardiac defect that required open heart surgery to repair, and she were brought to the emergency room because of distress related to the heart condition, do you think the court would have required the hospital to perform the surgery? If not, then how can the court require the hospital to provide a ventilator for anencephalic children? Compare Bryan v. Rectors and Visitors of the University of Virginia, 95 F.3d 349 (4th Cir. 1996) (rejecting an EMTALA claim against hospital after physicians withheld resuscitative treatment from a hopelessly ill patient who suffered a heart attack and died).

Concerns about principle go both ways in this case. It is accepted practice to give anencephalic infants artificial nutrition and hydration through feeding tubes, as was done for Baby K. Is there any principled or practical distinction that justifies giving artificial feeding but refusing artificial breathing? If you can see such a distinction, should it be the sole province of physicians to apply, or is it a distinction that only patients and family can draw? See Chapter 2 for further discussion of this and other aspects of EMTALA and of patients' rights to decide.

As n.2 of the *Baby K* opinion indicates, the lower court found that withholding a ventilator would also violate the Rehabilitation Act of 1973 and the Americans with Disabilities Act of 1990. Both of these Acts prohibit discrimination against persons on account of their disabilities. As the court suggested, one could argue that Baby K was being denied treatment of her respiratory problems on account of her having the disability of anencephaly. Is this an appropriate way to characterize what was going on in the *Baby K* case? Why do you think the appellate court preferred to decide this case on the basis of an unlawful denial of emergency care rather than on the basis of unlawful disability discrimination?

6. *The Hospital's and the Physicians' Decision.* Inasmuch as the costs of Ms. Keene's care were fully reimbursed by the insurers, why do you suppose the hospital and the physicians were unwilling to provide emergency ventilatory treatment to Ms. Keene? After all, the treatment was life-sustaining, and it was clearly desired by Ms. Keene's mother. Do you think it was appropriate for the physicians to try to override the wishes of Ms. Keene's mother?

7. *Rationing Decisions*. This case is very much about the role of the courts in rationing health care. Was the majority correct to take a "hands off" attitude about the social policy implications of its decision? The precedent it set clearly makes it more difficult for health care providers to withhold care on the grounds that the care is not worth its cost. Are courts well situated to making decisions of this type? Are they better situated than legislatures? The need to ration medical resources is one of the themes that runs throughout this book. As introduced in section D.4, rationing entails two broad sets of inquiries: What substantive criteria should determine what type of care is provided or withheld? What procedural mechanisms should be used to make these decisions?

■ WICKLINE v. STATE
239 Cal. Rptr. 810 (Cal. Ct. App. 1986)

[Read the excerpt at page 137.]

Notes: Liability and Managed Care

1. *Holding Doctors Responsible for Their Mistakes*. Why do you suppose Mrs. Wickline chose not to sue her doctors? Did they deserve to be sued, in your opinion? If they had been, would they have been found liable? What standard of care did the court use to determine liability? What source of evidence was used to establish this standard and whether it was breached?

In addition to being sued in tort, several other legal and social mechanisms punish those who make medical mistakes or encourage them to do better. Consider briefly the structural differences among: licensing regulations, ethical sanctions, and market forces.

2. *Managed Care*. The process of utilization review used by Medi-Cal is widespread, both in government programs and under conventional private insurance. As described in section C.3, this is one of several techniques for saving money that are known more generally as "managed care." Other managed care techniques include restricting a patient's choice of physician and paying physicians in a manner that rewards them for economizing. Presently over half of privately insured people in the United States are covered under "alternative delivery systems" such as HMOs that employ some or all of these techniques.

3. *Medical Judgment*. Why did opinions vary so widely on the proper treatment of Mrs. Wickline (four vs. eight days postsurgery)? Is there supposed to be general agreement about medical questions of this nature? What nonmedical factors (other than money) might influence the decision when to send Mrs. Wickline home? Section B.2 offers additional explanation and discussion of medical decision-making.

4. *Medical Mistakes*. Why did things go so wrong, even prior to Mrs. Wickline's discharge from the hospital? Could anything have been done to avoid the bad course of events in the hospital? What systems should be in place to encourage doctors to do their best, and how much professional (not necessarily legal) accountability should there be when they fail to live up to perfection? Section B.3 explains

that physicians are subjected to much greater monitoring of the outcomes of their treatment than ever before.

5. *The Duty to Treat.* Is it realistic for the court to tell Mrs. Wickline's physicians that they have to continue treating her even if Medicaid reimbursement runs out? If she had no insurance to begin with, would they be required to accept her initially? If they are free to turn her away, would they be deterred from accepting her, knowing her insurance might not cover all the care that tort law might require? Should tort law demand less of doctors that treat patients with insufficient or no insurance?

■ FTC v. TENET HEALTH CARE CORPORATION
186 F.3d 1045 (8th Cir. 1999)

[Read the excerpt at page 536.]

Notes: Economics and Market Restructuring

1. *Market Turmoil.* Mergers and acquisitions are sweeping the health care industry, not only at the "horizontal" level depicted in this case (among hospitals), but also in a vertical dimension among hospitals, doctors, and insurers. These vertically integrated delivery systems raise a host of legal issues besides antitrust, cutting across wide swaths of corporate, tax, regulatory, and reimbursement law.

This market turmoil is being caused by the escalating forces of competition, brought on by employers', insurers', and the government's demands for holding down the costs of treatment. Which types of market restructuring are likely to foster competition? Which types are likely to hinder competition? Is competition ultimately a desirable force in health care delivery, or is it antithetical to the service mission of nonprofit hospitals and hostile to the quality of care? For further readings on the latter questions, see section D.3 and Chapter 3.F.2.

B. THE NATURE OF MEDICAL PRACTICE

The remainder of this chapter contains introductory and background materials that relate broadly to several or all portions of the book. The readings are diverse and introduce a wide range of challenging ideas and important information. You should read through the assigned parts at the outset, and then come back to individual excerpts as they become relevant to the discussion of particular legal topics in your course.

We begin with a description of the human condition of illness and the professional practice of medicine, since these are what distinguish health care law from other fields of legal study. It is essential throughout this book to have some appreciation of the impact that illness has on how people function, the intricacies of medical decisionmaking, and how doctors and patients interact. To focus your thoughts on these issues, reflect on your own experiences with medical care, and consider the following list of popular "misconceptions" (developed by Alain Enthoven). What observations and evidence emerge from these readings to rebut or qualify each of these commonly held notions?

1. The doctor should be able to know what conditions the patient has, to answer the patient's questions precisely, and to prescribe the right treatment. If the doctor isn't, that is incompetence or even malpractice.

2. For each medical condition, there is a "best" treatment. It is up to the doctor to know about that treatment and to use it. Anything else is unnecessary surgery, waste, fraud, or underservice.

3. Medicine is an exact science. Unlike 50 or 100 years ago, there is now a firm scientific base for what the doctor does. Standard treatments are supported by scientific proof of efficiency.

4. Medical care consists of standard products that can be described precisely and measured meaningfully in standard units such as "inpatient days," "outpatient visits," or "doctor office visits."

5. Much of medical care is a matter of life and death or serious pain or disability.

6. More medical care is better than less care.

7. People have no control over the timing of their need for medical care. Whatever care is needed is needed right away.

1. Doctors and Hospitals

■ HEALTH CARE PAST AND PRESENT
Robert Rhodes
Health Care Politics, Policy, and Distributive Justice:
The Ironic Triumph (1992)*

Death before the nineteenth century was an ever-looming presence in our ancestors' thoughts and a frequent visitor to their families. They feared it and had little control over it. Sudden death was as central to attitudes prior to the twentieth century as the cemetery was to every village and town. In disproportionate numbers, early death came to infants, but all ages and classes felt its sting in high proportion compared to modern times. In the 1640s, between one quarter and one third of all children of English peers and peasants died before the age of fifteen. . . .

Resignation and fatalism toward natural occurrences characterize preindustrial societies, just as a sense of self-direction and control characterize modern society. . . . Modern societies have faith that they can control the future. A futurist orientation allows for savings, capital formation, long periods of education, and life-styles that deny instant gratification for future health. Preindustrial conditions do not reward such faith. . . . Uncontrollable natural or supernatural forces took away life, and one needed to reconcile one's fate to the four horsemen of the apocalypse: disease, famine, pestilence, and drought.

The twentieth century represents perhaps the clearest triumph of science over fatalism. . . . The modern hospital, the professionalism of physicians and nurses, and effective pharmaceuticals, have dramatically altered mortality rates and improved the quality of life in postindustrial states.

THE RISE OF THE MODERN HOSPITAL

For those entering a hospital prior to 1900, the probability of treatment helping, rather than harming, would be less than fifty-fifty, and the odds would be considerably poorer prior to 1870. Today, we identify hospitals as technologic citadels of sophisticated medical practice. But their preindustrial origins were as religious and charitable institutions for the hopelessly sick and poor. They were places to comfort the indigent dying.

For the first three quarters of the nineteenth century, medical personnel were not in charge of hospitals. . . . In the main, hospitals at that time were places for the homeless poor and insane to die. The affluent classes were treated at home.

For a variety of reasons, however, hospitals became central to medical practice and education between 1870 and 1910.[6] . . .

THE MODERN PHYSICIAN

[T]he development of the medical profession parallels particular developments of the hospital. This is especially true of surgery, which enjoyed a dramatic increase of prestige and precision during this time. Technological advances played a major role in changing surgery. Before painkilling drugs, surgical methods in the first half of the nineteenth century depended upon powerful and swift physicians whose craft and tools were closer to the corner butcher. Mortality rates of about 40 percent followed amputation.

Three developments altered the brutality and mortality rates and allowed abdominal surgery, which was rarely performed prior to 1890. Dentist William Morton's demonstration of ether at Massachusetts General Hospital in 1846 ushered in a means of eliminating pain and allowed more careful and delicate surgery. Joseph Lister's discovery of antisepsis in 1867 gradually led to new procedures during surgery to prevent infection. However, antisepsis was poorly understood. Lister's technique was based on the use of carbolic acid spray, but his methods were adopted only over a long period of time. Fatal infections continued even after using the spray because antiseptic procedures were not followed carefully until after 1880. Soon, sterile procedures were properly followed and surgery rapidly expanded. Finally, the development of the X-ray in 1895, along with other diagnostic tools, opened the way for abdominal surgery for appendicitis, gallbladder, and stomach ulcers. Thoracic surgery and surgery of the nervous and cardiovascular systems developed in the early 1900s.

---

[6] Paul Starr, The Social Transformation of American Medicine 151 (1982).

TRIUMPH AND TRAGEDY

By 1950, the cliché a "medical miracle" had rich meaning. Infant mortality rates in the United States were fewer than 15 per 100,000 births, down from 300 or so per 100,000 at the turn of the century. Pneumonia, once whispered by medical staff who witnessed the suffering of the dying to be the "old man's relief," now was easily controlled with penicillin. Infectious diseases in particular dramatically declined in the first half of the twentieth century. Improvement in health was a triumph of modernity, and part of that triumph was a consequence of modern medicine. There is, however, much debate about the weight of medicine's contribution, compared to other modern factors. . . .

Our dramatic advances in health are also related to improved nutrition, lifestyle, and education, as well as to medical advancements. The literature of health care points, in particular, to . . . proper diet, minimal tension, absence of smoking or heavy drinking, daily exercise, and a life-style that provides low-risk factors for accidents. Advances in health and longevity are more closely tied to higher income, better diets, and especially greater education than to advances in medicine.

There are many important exceptions, of course. Pharmaceuticals have provided treatments at a very low price. . . . In particular, chemotherapeutic drugs have had a dramatic effect on reducing death. Vaccines have also been important. Smallpox, polio, and whooping cough have been virtually eliminated. . . .

Neonatology represents still another success story, reducing infant mortality rates by technologically advanced methods that maintain life for prematurely born infants. For the most part, however, the distinction in age/sex/mortality rates for industrial countries and preindustrial countries in the Third World today are not related to curative medicine or to technological advancement. They are related to environment, nutrition, income, and education. . . .

Yet, American perception of well-being is closely identified with medicine. Paradoxically, much of the public's present disenchantment with medicine is the consequence of this identification. Modern medicine has advanced to the frontiers of preserving life, but only by increasingly more expensive therapies and diagnoses to preserve life "on its margins." That is, additional expenditures and efforts to treat disease produce diminishing results in proportion to the effort. We are just beginning to learn that our scientific capacity to triumph over illness, physical anomalies, and death, on many occasions with medical miracles, brings with it a special brand of tragedy.

We have become totally modern. No more can we explain death and suffering as a consequence of fate. It is our medicine, or lack of it, that denies death and suffering. We know we must choose who receives scarce resources and who does not. No longer can we attribute to fate or to God the responsibility for making life-and-death decisions. Yet, these life-and-death decisions involve very expensive procedures and technologies and often contribute only marginally to extending life. Examples are well known and regularly make front-page newspaper drama: organ transplants, aggressive treatment of terminal patients, neonates under 750 grams, or long-term comatose patients.

These new choices challenge our basic values and frequently produce conflict. . . . Conflict is father to politics and law, and politics determines who gets what, when, and how. Conflict also forces moral reassessment of traditional attitudes and postures, including the justice question: "Who *should* get what, when and how."

How do we distribute health care? How should we? How does political power within the present economic system determine the distribution of health care? These questions obviously spill over the boundaries of economics, politics, sociology, law, medicine, history, and philosophy. In particular, looming over the politics of health care is a sense of the tragic, as well as the majestic. Tragedy points to human endeavors that are virtuous and honorable, yet carry the seeds of their own downfall. Our efforts to lessen the suffering and lengthen the lives of Americans through accessible, affordable, quality health care represent the best of our traditions and have been, on balance, an American success story. Sometimes we fall short in that effort because some group is unreasonably left behind in the political shuffle. The 37 million Americans who at the end of the 1980s had no health coverage represented such a group. At other times, our very success leads to exasperating dilemmas of bioethics and distributive justice that would cross the eyes of a Solomon. Our dilemma over public financing for costly organ transplants at the expense of other badly needed programs or continued aggressive treatment of comatose or terminally ill loved ones are poignant, modern examples. It is here where triumph merges with tragedy.

■ DOCTORS, PATIENTS, AND HEALTH INSURANCE: THE ORGANIZATION AND FINANCING OF MEDICAL CARE
Herman Miles Somers & Anne Ramsay Somers
1961

. . . The popular conception of the doctor-patient relationship is a mixture of fact and fancy. Until World War II the general practitioner family doctor was still in the majority. The one-to-one relationship of a personally chosen physician—where economic and other factors permitted any choice—with his patient was the most common form of medical practice. In big cities the doctor had an office, usually mahogany and leather, sparsely equipped with simple diagnostic aids, a few surgical tools, and some antiseptic drugs. But, especially in rural areas and suburbs, he was more often found in the homes of his patients doing his rounds, working at the bedside of the sick and injured. His black bag held almost all his equipment. His records were kept partly in a small notebook, mostly in his mind and heart. He appeared indefatigable, compassionate, and available wherever and whenever needed. . . .

This doctor of the past has been idealized in story, picture, and legend. . . . Despite its apparent anachronisms, the picture still appeals to people's sentiments—even to those fully aware of its use as a public relations device. It has the warmth and intimate concern that no hypodermic needle—no complex of steel and tubing—can replace, however effective they may be. Although medical miracles are now performed successfully between strangers, doctors and patients both believe that the absence of continuity, personal concern, and individual attention are detrimental to the best medical care. This is not without foundation.

The origin of the "traditional" doctor-patient relationship reaches deep into the past. From the beginning of medical history, the practicing physician has been part priest, part technician, part personal or family counselor. In early days, when medicine had very little in the way of scientific knowledge to rely on, it was inevitable that the subjective priestly element should be dominant. . . .

In modern times medicine has become more scientific. But the traditional reliance on mystical forces and a highly authoritarian doctor-patient relationship persists to a degree unknown in other contemporary human relations. . . . The relationship of citizen and state, of employer and employee, of teacher and pupil, parent and child, even of husband and wife, have undergone profound and acknowledged changes as a result of the technological and socio-economic trends of the past few centuries. But there is no general acknowledgment or acceptance of the significant change that has, in fact, been taking place in the doctor-patient relationship. Of the manifold and complex reasons, only a few of the more important can be noted here.

First and basic is the persistence—in spite of scientific progress—of large elements of uncertainty and fear regarding illness and medical care which are conducive to continued reliance on hope, faith, confidence and other subjective factors on the part of both doctor and patient. "Honor thy physician because of the need thou hast of him." So said Ecclesiastes to the Hebrews thousands of years ago. And still, today, patients yearn to have confidence in their doctors, to idealize them, to endow them with superhuman powers. Talcott Parsons, the Harvard sociologist, reconciles the use of such subjective factors—the use of "modern magic"—with the scientific basis of modern medicine by calling it a "functional bias."

> The basic function of magic is to bolster the self-confidence of actors in situations where energy and skill *do* make a difference but where, because of uncertainty factors, outcomes cannot be guaranteed. This fits the situation of the doctor, but in addition on the side of the patient it may be argued the *belief* in the possibility of recovery is an important factor in it. If from purely a technical point of view both the individual doctor and the general tradition are optimistically biased it ought to help. . . . Of course this argument must not be pressed too far.

As the boundaries of medical ignorance and uncertainty are pushed back, one would expect this resort to supra-scientific factors to decline, and, indeed, it has in the case of bacterial and other diseases where the cause and cure are clearly established. But the reduced role of subjective factors in the treatment of specific cases has been more than offset by an increasing interest in the role of the emotions in illness. A widespread increase in psychotherapy and psychosomatic medicine has renewed the emphasis on a personal doctor and a personal doctor-patient relationship of a type that permits knowledge of the "whole [person]." . . .

Moreover it is now widely believed that illness, *per se*, tends to create—even in the most intellectual of patients—an attitude of dependence, of "regression" to helplessness, and perhaps to childlike behavior. . . . In this state, confidence in the authority and benevolence of the doctor, as well as in his scientific knowledge and technical skill—the now-familiar "father-image"—is generally desired and often desirable.

Finally, there is the impenetrable mystery of death. The physician's relation to this event—however helpless he in fact may be—has endowed him, in the eyes of centuries of patients, with an aura of the mystery. To the extent that the physician identifies himself with this priestly role and takes on himself the burden associated therewith, or at least appears to do so through the gravity of his personal demeanor and behavior, his supra-scientific role continues to be respected and perpetuated, reinforcing in the eyes of individual patients and society at large his status as a dispenser of increasingly scientific medicine.

■ COMPETING SOLUTIONS: AMERICAN HEALTH CARE PROPOSALS AND INTERNATIONAL EXPERIENCE
Joseph White
1995

America's systems for delivering and paying for medical care are notably more complex than those of most other countries. Many doctors work in more than one hospital, making governance of medical staffs difficult; specialists are harder to coordinate because there are more of them; and the proliferation of forms of managed care means rapid change in patterns of gatekeeping and referral.

PHYSICIANS

American doctors go through extensive training to work long hours for high pay. The typical medical school program requires, after four years of college, four more years of "undergraduate" medical education. During the final two years, students receive some clinical training. Virtually all graduates then must complete some graduate medical education in order to be licensed to practice medicine. This education is obtained in residency programs, mainly in hospitals affiliated with medical schools. Normally only one year of residency (as an intern) is needed for licensure, but up to eight years (for neurosurgeons) may be required for certification as a specialist.

... Given the length of their training and the size of their debts, it is understandable that most physicians feel entitled to incomes that are much higher than those of most other Americans. ... [The median physician salary is about $170,000, roughly five times that of the average American worker. The range across specialties is broad. Pediatricians and general practitioners typically earn less than $150,000, common medical specialists (cardiology, dermatology, anesthesiology) are in the $200,000-$300,000 range, while heart surgeons and brain surgeons can earn well over $500,000. Some doctors earn substantially more from entrepreneurial activities such as medical patents and investments in various health care organizations.]

An unusually high proportion of American doctors are trained to specialize. Fewer than 10 percent of American doctors [call] themselves general practitioners (GPs), the standard term for primary care physicians. But because a specialist such as a family practitioner, internist, pediatrician, or obstetrician-gynecologist may be a person's regular physician, between 33 and 40 percent of physicians (depending on who is counting) are mainly primary care providers. [Specialists who receive several years of extra training and pass additional exams are designated as "Board Certified," meaning that they comply with voluntary, private standards set by the American Specialty Boards, which operate under the auspices of the AMA. At one time, board certification was relatively rare, but now the vast majority of new doctors obtain certification. About two dozen boards now exist, covering not only standard specialties but also areas of general practice such as family medicine and internal medicine.] . . .

Two-thirds of physicians practice in offices, the vast majority with admitting privileges to a hospital. Many practice in more [than one hospital] (for example, a nice suburban hospital for simple cases, and a high-tech academic medical center for difficult ones). Hospitals therefore must compete for admissions by making those physicians happy, such as by having the fanciest equipment. . . .

INSTITUTIONAL CARE

Long-term or chronic care, especially for the aged, is a complicated system on its own, and the potential expenses of long-term care are so great that it is highly unlikely that any reform will do much about it. [Therefore, the focus here is] on the costs of the current American health care system, of which one major component is hospital services for acute care.

The American supply of hospitals is dominated by private nonprofit hospitals—many owned by religious organizations. [About two-thirds] of hospital beds [are] provided by the nonprofits, 10 percent by the for-profit sector. The rest, just over a quarter of the beds, [are] in federal, state, or local facilities. It is hard to identify much difference between the behavior and efficiency of the for-profit and private nonprofits. If private institutions are more efficient, the savings go largely or entirely to investors.

Americans spend a great deal of money on hospitals: [about 40 percent] of all spending on patient care. But . . . the hospital is not as dominant a provider as it once was or still is in other countries. Hospitals and doctors tried to avoid regulation by moving care to ostensibly freestanding ambulatory care facilities. Examples include kidney dialysis units, and radiology group practices with close relations with hospitals. Some payers encouraged the shift, believing those facilities would be cheaper. . . .

Back in the traditional hospitals, the nature of care depends greatly on hospitals' relationships with doctors and medical schools, and on hospitals' catchment areas—the areas from which they get most of their patients. . . .

A suburban hospital can generally provide sophisticated care, such as cardiac bypass surgery, but it is not as likely to have clinical professors who are able to provide extremely specialized care for "interesting" cases. All hospitals want the most advanced equipment, but the academic medical centers must have it for research and training. These centers rely heavily on residents and interns for delivery of care and, most important, are likely to have a much lower-class population of patients.

Many of the [academic medical centers] are in inner cities. They are likely to have large outpatient departments to train the students (residents) and serve the local population, which feeds into the inpatient wards; the emergency room not only gets emergencies but also serves as an outpatient clinic for some for the population. All of this is the good news: If a major teaching hospital is in the inner city, then either a large and endowed institution or a state government pays for some care for the inner-city poor.

When local hospitals receive little funding for education, poor populations must frequently rely on a hospital financed by a strapped city or county budget. Such hospitals—for example, Cook County in Chicago, Boston City, and Charity in New Orleans—have interns and residents to do the work because of their relationship with a training program, but nowhere near the resources of a freestanding university hospital. All hospitals in the inner city try to convince Medicare that they deserve an extra subsidy for treating a poorer, less-insured, and often sicker population. The federal government calls these disproportionate share payments. One of the huge issues for American health care reform is what will happen to the academic medical centers and the remaining urban public hospitals if payment systems allow competing insurers to favor hospitals that are less expensive because they have lesser teaching and subsidy burdens.

Another major issue is how a bias toward specialized, high-technology medicine, created in part by how medical education is financed and how physicians are paid, is reinforced by arrangements for capital investment in American medicine. There are hardly any measures in place to prevent a "medical arms race" among hospitals that seek the most advanced technology in order to attract physicians and generate revenue. . . .

Because for years insurers would pay whatever physicians and hospitals billed, and hospitals relied on physicians to provide patients, hospitals competed for patients by having the best equipment, and insurers ended up paying for excess treatments and higher charges per treatment. At one time also physicians could refer patients to any specialist they wished, and patients could go directly to a specialist without referral.

The rise of managed care and of more aggressive bargaining by insurers has begun to change this basic pattern. Insurers have become more likely to refuse to approve a given service or to insist on a lower price. Hospitals still need to attract physicians by offering the best equipment, however, so they are caught between the demands of doctors and payers. Meanwhile insurers are limiting choice of and access to specialists by building closed panels, in which a person covered by a plan either cannot use or must pay a surcharge to use any provider who is not on special contract to the plan. A patient might find that her doctor of 20 years' standing is no longer part of her insurance plan; a physician might find that many of his patients can afford referral only to three nephrologists whom he does not know. One of the key issues in reform is whether these new restrictions on choice of physician are necessary.

■ DOCTORS, PATIENTS, AND HEALTH INSURANCE: THE ORGANIZATION AND FINANCING OF MEDICAL CARE
Herman Miles Somers & Anne Ramsay Somers
1961

[T]he conflict between [hospital] medical staff and [hospital] management has become both sharper and more open in recent years. The roots of this conflict—the basic dichotomy in hospital organization—go back to eighteenth century Britain and the establishment of the Anglo-American tradition of voluntary hospitals. There was no such dichotomy in medieval days when hospitals were operated, with little medical assistance, by monastic orders for the sick poor. There is generally no such duality in the major Continental hospitals which are usually run, with unquestioned authority, by full-time chiefs of medical services. The distinguishing feature of the Anglo-American voluntary hospital, however, has been its use by private physicians for private patients with little or no accompanying administrative or financial responsibility. . . .

Recent developments—the hospital's changing role, its increase in size, complexity, utilization, cost, and its greatly altered financial base—have intensified the inherent instability of this administrative structure. . . . Lay influences on hospital administration and policy are clearly increasing. Ultimate policy responsibility has always rested with lay trustees. Traditionally, they limited their oversight to balancing the books. With the tremendous increase in hospital costs, however, this single concern has led to increasing surveillance over the hospital's total functioning, including the organization of the medical staff. The hospital administrator, traditionally an untrained individual content to play a fairly subservient role and socially outranked by doctor and trustee alike, is being transformed into a professional with increasing self-confidence and authority. . . .

At the same time the hospital has become an indispensable workshop for the modern physician, who finds it virtually impossible to practice good medicine without hospital affiliation. The hospital is the center of his professional world, and he is acknowledged to be its key figure. Fully 40 percent of private physician income is now earned in the hospital. Naturally he wants "his" institution equipped with the latest scientific and technological facilities. But the doctor's relationship to the hospital is peculiarly ambiguous. As a rule he assumes neither administrative nor financial responsibility. Yet, in practice, his is the most powerful voice in the organization. He alone admits and discharges patients; he alone can diagnose, prescribe, and treat patients—still the chief purpose for which the hospital exists. With his high professional status, he may, in most hospitals, countermand administrative orders and defy lay authority with relative impunity. The result is the confusing duality that prevails today throughout the hospital system, public and private. . . .

It is sometimes proposed that hiring the medical staff on a salary or contract basis would increase the doctors' sense of responsibility for hospital administration and help clarify lines of accountability. It could integrate the administrative structure without restricting professional integrity. This is the general pattern in a few of the nation's best hospitals, such as the Henry Ford in Detroit and the Cleveland Clinic Hospital. Most of the profession is, however, vigorously opposed to such practice, alleging "hospital domination," "lay control," or the "corporate practice of medicine." Some hospitals have taken a middle road—employing full-time medical directors (this is frequently the practice in government hospitals) and in a few instances, full-time chiefs of medical services. This too is generally frowned on by physicians in private practice. . . .

Many hospital spokesmen, however, content themselves with pleading for physician cooperation in assuring some responsibility for hospital operations and costs. . . . But such recommendations are usually set in a purely hortatory context. It is not clear how such preachments are to influence the individual doctor. The "medical staff" of which he is a member is in most instances simply a term for the collectivity of physicians authorized to practice in a particular hospital. The staff can be as disciplinary an instrument as it chooses to be, but in most places it has chosen minimal responsibility. . . . By and large the staff still prefers not to interfere with the practices of the individual physician.

■ CLINICAL DECISION MAKING FROM THEORY TO PRACTICE
David M. Eddy
1996

Medical practice is in the middle of a profound transition. Most physicians can remember the day when, armed with a degree, a mission, and confidence, they could set forth to heal the sick. Like Solomon, physicians could receive patients, hear their complaints, and determine the best course of action. While not every patient could be cured, everyone could be confident that whatever was done was the best possible. Most important, each physician was free, trusted, and left alone to determine what was in the best interest of each patient.

All of that is changing. . . . Now physicians must deal with second opinions, precertification, skeptical medical directors, variable coverage, outright denials, utilization review, threats of cookbook medicine, and letters out of the blue chiding that Mrs. Smith is on two incompatible drugs. Solomon did not have to call anyone to get permission for his decisions. What is going on?

What is going on is that one of the basic assumptions underlying the practice of medicine is being challenged. This assumption is not just a theory about cholesterol, antiarrhythmia, or estrogens. This assumption concerns the intellectual foundation of medical care. Simply put, the assumption is that whatever a physician decides is, by definition, correct. The challenge says that while many decisions no doubt *are* correct, many are not, and elaborate mechanisms are needed to determine which are which. Physicians are slowly being stripped of their decision-making power.

Notes: Doctors and Hospitals

1. *History and Description.* For general histories and descriptions of the health care delivery system, see David Smith & Arnold Kaluzny, The White Labyrinth: A Guide to the Health Care System (2d ed. 1986); Harry A. Sultz & Kristina M. Young, Health Care USA: Understanding Its Organization and Delivery (2d ed. 1999). For more extensive historical accounts of the transformation of hospitals and their role in modern medicine, see Guenter B. Risse, Mending Bodies, Saving Souls: A History of Hospitals (1999); Charles Rosenberg, The Care of Strangers

(1987); David Rosner, A Once Charitable Enterprise (1982); Rosemary Stevens, In Sickness and in Wealth: American Hospitals in the Twentieth Century (1989).

2. *The Two-Headed Monster.* The unique structure of American hospitals, in which doctors are independent but essential to their financial well-being, has been described as "attractive as a two-headed monster" and as "stable as a three-legged stool." See H. L. Smith, Two Lines of Authority are One Too Many, 84 Modern Hosp. 59 (March 1955). This division of authority is mirrored throughout the organizational structure of the health-care system. For instance, hospitals, unlike any other business organization, are required by state licensure laws and private accreditation standards to have *two* sets of corporate bylaws, one for the hospital administration and a second for the medical staff. Similarly, health insurance traditionally pays hospitals separately from doctors, as reflected in the distinctions between Blue Cross (hospital insurance) vs. Blue Shield (physician insurance) and between Medicare Part A vs. Part B.

3. *Power Relationships in Medicine.* Medical sociologists and organizational theorists have produced a rich literature discussing the role of physicians within medical institutions. Leading examples are Eliot Freidson, Doctoring Together (1975); Eliot Freidson, Profession of Medicine (1970); Paul Starr, The Social Transformation of American Medicine (1982); David Young & Richard Saltman, The Hospital Power Equilibrium (1985); Jeffrey Harris, The Internal Organization of Hospitals: Some Economic Implications, 8 Bell J. Econ. 467 (1977); Mark Pauly & Michael Redisch, The Not-for-Profit Hospital as a Physicians' Cooperative, 63 Am. Econ. Rev. 87 (1973). For an exploration of how these insights illuminate a variety of legal doctrines and public policy debates, see Mark A. Hall, Institutional Control of Physician Behavior: Legal Barriers to Health Care Cost Containment, 137 U. Pa. L. Rev. 431 (1988) ("Because the law absorbs and reflects the values and relationships of traditional medicine, it has codified the ethic of professional dominance, effectively shielding physicians from the institutional influence contemplated by revolutionary changes in health care policy. . . . The principal reason our nation's emerging health care policy is in shambles is that policymakers have ignored the law's institutionalization of physician autonomy.").

2. The Nature of Medical Judgment

■ VARIATIONS IN PHYSICIAN PRACTICE: THE ROLE OF UNCERTAINTY*
David M. Eddy**
3 Health Affairs 74, No. 2 (Summer 1984)

. . . An analysis of procedure rates for Medicare patients in 13 large metropolitan areas in the United States showed that for more than half the procedures

**Dr. Eddy is a physician researcher, formerly on the faculty of Duke University, and now a consultant in Jackson Hole, Wyoming. The first paragraph is taken from a later work, Clinical Decision Making: From Theory to Practice (1996).

studied, the rates varied more than 300 percent between the areas with high and low rates. Another study that compared utilization rates in 16 large communities in four states found more than threefold differences between the highest and lowest rates for heart bypass, thyroid, and prostate surgery; fivefold differences for specific back and abdominal surgeries; sevenfold differences for knee replacements; and almost 20-fold differences for carotid endarterectomies. . . . In Vermont, the chance of having one's tonsils removed as a child are 8 percent in one community and 70 percent in another. In Iowa, 15 percent of the men younger than 85 years in one region have had prostatectomies compared with more than 60 percent in another. In Maine, the chance of hysterectomy by the age of 70 years varies across communities from less than 20 percent to more than 70 percent.[11] While some of the variations might be explained by differences in disease incidence, available resources, and patient preferences, it is impossible to explain all of them. . . .

Why do physicians vary so much in the way they practice medicine? At first view, there should be no problem. There are diseases—neatly named and categorized by textbooks, journal articles, and medical specialty societies. There are various procedures physicians can use to diagnose and treat these diseases. It should be possible to determine the value of any particular procedure by applying it to patients who have a disease and observing the outcome. And the rest should be easy—if the outcome is good, the procedure should be used for patients with that disease; if the outcome is bad, it should not. Some variation in practice patterns can be expected due to differences in the incidence of various diseases, patients' preferences, and the available resources, but these variations should be small and explainable.

The problem of course is that nothing is this simple. Uncertainty, biases, errors, and differences of opinions, motives, and values weaken every link in the chain that connects a patient's actual condition to the selection of a diagnostic test or treatment. This [reading] describes some of the factors that cause decisions about the use of medical procedures to be so difficult, and that contribute to the alarming variations we observe in actual practice. It examines the components of the decision problem a physician faces, and the psychology of medical reasoning, focusing in particular on the role of uncertainty. Finally, it suggests some actions to reduce uncertainty and encourage consistency of good medical practice.

Uncertainty creeps into medical practice through every pore. Whether a physician is defining a disease, making a diagnosis, selecting a procedure, observing outcomes, assessing probabilities, assigning preference, or putting it all together, he is walking on very slippery terrain. It is difficult for nonphysicians, and for many physicians, to appreciate how complex these tasks are, how poorly we understand them, and how easy it is for honest people to come to difference conclusions.

---

[11] Wennberg J. Dealing with medical practice variation: a proposal for action, Health Aff. 1984; 3:6.

DEFINING A DISEASE

If one looks at patients who are obviously ill, it is fairly easy to identify the physical and chemical disorders that characterize that illness. On the other hand, a large part of medicine is practiced on people who do not have obvious illnesses, but rather have signs, symptoms, or findings that may or may not represent an illness that should be treated. Three closely related problems make it difficult to determine whether or not a patient actually has a disease that needs to be diagnosed or treated.

One problem is that the dividing line between "normal" and "abnormal" is not nearly as sharp as a cursory reading of a textbook would suggest. . . .

A second problem is that many "diseases," at least at the time they are diagnosed, do not by themselves cause pain, suffering, disability, or threat to life. They are considered diseases only because they increase the probability that something else that is truly bad will happen in the future. . . .

The difficulty of defining a disease is compounded by the fact that many of the signs, symptoms, findings, and conditions that might suggest a disease are extremely common. If a breast biopsy were performed on a random sample of senior citizens, fully 90 percent of them could have fibrocystic disease. If obesity is a disease, the average American is diseased. By the time they reach seventy, about two-thirds of women have had their uteruses removed. . . .

Given these uncertainties about what constitutes a disease, it should not be surprising that there are debates about the definitions of many diseases, and when there is agreement about a definition, it is often blatantly and admittedly arbitrary. A quick review of the literature reveals multiple definitions of glaucoma, diabetes, fibrocystic disease of the breast, coronary artery disease, myocardial infarction, stroke, and dozens of other conditions. Morbid obesity is defined as 100 percent above the ideal weight. But what is "ideal," and why 100 percent? The lesson is that for many conditions a clinician faces, there is no clear definition of disease that provides an unequivocal guide to action, and there is wide room for differences of opinion and variations in practice. . . .

[E]ven when sharp criteria are created, physicians vary widely in their application of these criteria—in their ability to ask about symptoms, observe signs, interpret test results, and record the answers. The literature on "observer variation" has been growing for a long time. . . . A group of experts compiled 100 electrocardiogram tracings, 50 of which showed myocardial infarctions, 25 of which were normal, and 25 of which showed some other abnormality (according to the experts). These EKGs were then given to ten other cardiologists to test their diagnostic abilities. The proportion of EKGs judged by the ten cardiologists to show infarcts varied by a factor of two. If you had an infarct and went to physician A, there would be a 28 percent chance the physician would have missed it. If you did not have an infarct and went to physician B, there would be a 26 percent chance that physician would have said you had one. . . .

Thirteen pathologists were asked to read 1,001 specimens obtained from biopsies of the cervix, and then to repeat the readings at a later time. On average, each pathologist agreed with himself only 89 percent of the time (intraobserver agreement), and with a panel of "senior" pathologists only 87 percent of the time (interobserver agreement). Looking only at the patients who actually had cervical pathology, the intraobserver agreement was only 68 percent and the interobserver agreement was only 51 percent. The pathologists were best at reading more advanced disease and normal tissue, but were labeled "unsatisfactory" in their ability to read the precancerous and preinvasive stages.

Similar studies have been reported for the presence of clubbing of the fingers, anemia, psychiatric disease, and many other signs, symptoms, and procedures. Even if there were no uncertainty about what constitutes a disease and how to define it, there would still be considerable uncertainty about whether or not a patient has the signs, symptoms, and findings needed to fit the definition.

Selecting A Procedure

The task of selecting a procedure is no less difficult. There are two main issues. First, for any patient condition there are dozens of procedures that can be ordered, in any combination, at any time. The list of procedures that might be included in a workup of chest pain or hypertension would take more than a page, spanning the spectrum from simply asking questions, to blood studies, to X-rays. Even for highly specific diagnostic problems, there can be a large choice of procedures. For example, if a woman presents with a breast mass and her physician wants to know its approximate size and architecture, the physician might contemplate an imaging procedure. The choice could include mammography, ultra-sonography, thermography, diaphanography, computed tomography, lymphography, Mammoscan, and magnetic resonance imaging. A physician who chose mammography would still have to decide between xeromammography and film mammography, with several brands being available for the latter. There are about a dozen procedures that apply the principles of thermography. And why should a diagnostic workup be limited to one test? Why not follow a negative mammogram with a computed tomogram (or vice versa)? For the detection of colorectal cancer, a physician can choose any combination of fecal occult blood tests (and there are more than a dozen brands), digital examination, rigid sigmoidoscopy, flexible 30 cm sigmoidoscopy, flexible 60 cm sigmoidoscopy, barium enema (either plain or air contrast), and colonoscopy. These choices are not trivial. Most procedures have different mechanisms of action and a long list of pros and cons. Different brands of fecal occult blood tests have very different sensitivities and specificities, and film mammography and xeromammography differ in their radiation exposure by a factor of about four. These procedures are for relatively well-defined diseases; imagine the problems of selecting procedures to evaluate symptoms like fatigue, headache, or fever that can have about a dozen causes. . . .

In theory, much of the uncertainty just described could be managed if it were possible to conduct enough experiments under enough conditions, and observe the outcomes. Unfortunately, measuring the outcomes of medical procedures is one of the most difficult problems we face. The goal is to predict how the use of a procedure in a particular case will affect that patient's health and welfare. Standing in the way are at least a half dozen major obstacles. The central problem is that there is a natural variation in the way people respond to a medical procedure. Take two people who, to the best of our ability to define such things, are identical in all important respects, submit them to the same operative procedure, and one will die on the operating table while the other will not. Because of this natural variation, we can only talk about the probabilities of various outcomes—the probability that a diagnostic test will be positive if the disease is present (sensitivity), the probability that a test will be negative if the disease is absent (specificity), the probability that a treatment will yield a certain result, and so forth.

One consequence of this natural variation is that to study the outcomes of any procedure it is necessary to conduct the procedure on many different people, who are thought to represent the particular patients we want to know about, and then average the results. . . . Some diseases are so rare that, in order to conduct the ideal clinical trials, it would be necessary to collect tens of thousands, if not hundreds of thousands, of participants. A good example concerns the frequency of the Pap smear. One might wonder why the merits of a three-year versus one-year frequency cannot be settled by a randomized controlled trial. Because of the low frequency of cervical cancer, and the small difference in outcomes expected for the two frequencies, almost one million women would be required for such a study. . . .

Finally, even when the best trials are conducted, we still might not get an answer. Consider the value of mammography in women under fifty, and consider just one outcome—the effect on breast cancer mortality. Ignore for the time being the radiation hazard, false-positive test results, inconvenience, financial costs, and other issues. This is one of the best-studied problems in cancer prevention, benefiting from the largest (60,000 women) and longest (more than 15 years) completed randomized controlled trial, and an even larger uncontrolled study involving 270,000 women screened for five years in 29 centers around the country. Yet we still do not know the value of mammography in women under 50. The first study showed a slight reduction in mortality, but it was not statistically significant. The larger study suggested that mammography has improved since the first study, and that it is now almost as good in younger women as in older women, but the study was not controlled and we do not know if "almost" is good enough. Even for women over 50, where the first study showed a statistically significant reduction in breast cancer mortality (of about 40 percent at ten years), there is enough uncertainty about the results that no fewer than four additional trials have been initiated to confirm the results. These trials are still in progress.

Unable to turn to a definitive body of clinical and epidemiological research, a clinician or research scientist who wants to know the value of a procedure is left with a mixture of randomized controlled trials, nonrandomized trials, uncontrolled trials, and clinical observations. The evidence from different sources can easily go in different directions, and it is virtually impossible for anyone to sort things out in his or her head. Unfortunately, the individual physician may be most impressed by observations made in his or her individual practice. This source of evidence is notoriously vulnerable to bias and error. What a physician sees and remembers is biased by the types of patients who come in; by the decisions of the patients to accept a treatment and return for follow-up; by a natural desire to see good things; and by a whole series of emotions that charge one's memory. On top of these biases, the observations are vulnerable to large statistical errors because of the small number of patients a physician sees in a personal practice. . . .

Now assume that a physician can know the outcomes of recommending a particular procedure for a particular patient. Is it possible to declare whether those outcomes are good or bad? Unfortunately, no. The basic problem is that any procedure has multiple outcomes, some good and some bad. The expected reduction in chest pain that some people will get from coronary artery bypass surgery is accompanied by a splitting of the chest, a chance of an operative mortality, days in the hospital, pain, anxiety, and financial expense. Because the outcomes are multiple and move in different directions, tradeoffs have to be made. And making tradeoffs involves values.

Just as there is a natural variation in how each of us responds to a medical procedure, there is a variation in how we value different outcomes. The fact that General Motors alone produces more than 50 distinct models of automobiles, not to mention dozens of options for each model, demonstrates how tastes about even a single item can vary. Imagine the variation in how different people value pain, disability, operative mortality, life expectancy, a day in a hospital, and who is going to feed the dogs. . . .

[B]ecause decisions about procedures are typically made by physicians on behalf of their patients, the physicians must infer their patients' values, and keep them distinct from their own personal preferences. This raises the second problem, communication. It is difficult enough to assess one's own values about the outcomes of a complicated decision (think about switching jobs); consider having someone else try to learn your thoughts and do it for you. The room for error in communications can be appreciated by returning to the experiment in which four physicians asked 993 coal miners about cough, shortness of breath, pain, and sputum. The variation in their reports of responses to a simple question like, "Do you have a cough?" was large [from 150 to 300 percent variation in reporting the symptom present]; imagine a question like, "How do you feel about operative morality?"

PUTTING IT ALL TOGETHER

The final decision about how to manage a patient requires synthesizing all the information about a disease, the patient, signs and symptoms, the effectiveness of dozens of tests and treatments, outcomes and values. All of this must be done without knowing precisely what the patient has, with uncertainty about signs and symptoms, with imperfect knowledge of the sensitivity and specificity of tests, with no training in manipulating probabilities, with incomplete and biased information about outcomes, and with no language for communicating or assessing values. If each piece of this puzzle is difficult, it is even more difficult for anyone to synthesize all the information and be certain of the answer. It would be an extremely hard task for a research team; there is no hope that it could occur with any precision in the head of a busy clinician. Hence the wide variability in the estimates physicians place on the values of procedures.

[A] final example document[s] how difficult it is to combine information from many sources to estimate the value of a particular procedure. . . . A survey of 1,000 11-year-old schoolchildren in New York City found that 65 percent had undergone tonsillectomy. The remaining children were sent for examinations to a group of physicians and 45 percent were selected for tonsillectomy. Those rejected were examined by another group of physicians and 46 percent were selected for surgery. When the remaining children were examined again by another group of physicians, a similar percent were recommended for tonsillectomy, leaving only 65 students. At that point, the study was halted for lack of physicians.

CONSEQUENCES

The view of anyone who wants a close look at the consequences of different medical procedures is, at best, smoky. Some procedures may present a clear picture, and their value, or lack of it, may be obvious; putting a finger on a bleeding carotid artery is an extreme example. But for many, if not most medical procedures, we can only see shadows and gross movements. We usually know the direction in which various outcome measures can move when a medical activity is undertaken, but we typically do not know the probabilities they will move in those directions, or how far they will move. We certainly do not know how a particular individual will respond. Words like "rare," "common," and "a lot" must be used instead of "one out of 1,000," or "seven on a scale of one to ten."

There is also a strong tendency to oversimplify. One of the easiest ways to fit a large problem in our minds is to lop off huge parts of it. In medical decisions, one option is to focus on length of life and discount inconvenience, pain, disability, short-term risks, and financial costs. A physician can also draw on a number of simplifying heuristics. Anyone uncomfortable dealing with probabilities can use the heuristic, "If there is any chance of (the disease), the (procedure) should be performed." If one cannot estimate the number of people to be saved, one can use the heuristic, "If but one patient is saved, the effort is worthwhile." If one cannot contemplate alternative uses of resources that might deliver a greater benefit to a population, there is the heuristic, "Costs should not be considered in decisions about individual patients." There is a general purpose heuristic, "When in doubt, do it." Or as one investigator wrote, "An error of commission is to be preferred to an error of omission." Unfortunately, a large number of incentives encourage simplifications that lead to overutilization. It is time-consuming, mentally taxing, and often threatening to colleagues for a physician to undertake a deep analysis of a confusing clinical problem. A physician is less likely to be sued for doing too much than too little. Most physicians' incomes go up if they do more, and go down if they do less. Hospitals get to fill more beds and bill for more procedures, laboratories collect more money for services, and companies sell more drugs, devices, and instruments. The more that is done, the more the providers win. The losers are patients, consumers, and taxpayers—anyone who has to undergo a valueless procedure or pay the bill.

In the end, given all the uncertainties, incentives, and heuristics, a physician will have to do what is comfortable. If it is admitted that the uncertainty surrounding the use of a procedure is great, and that there is no way to identify for certain what is best, or to prove that any particular action is right or wrong, the safest and most comfortable position is to do what others are doing. The applicable maxim is "safety in numbers." A physician who follows the practices of his or her colleagues is safe from criticism, free from having to explain his or her actions, and defended by the concurrence of colleagues.

Notes: Medical Decisionmaking

1. *The Nature of Medical Judgment.* An even better sense of medical decision-making can be had from examining a range of particular medical cases. To some

extent, this is possible by reading the cases in this book, but for the most part the intricacies of the medical decisions are described in only an abbreviated fashion. A good example of one, full-length case discussion, which illustrates many of the dimensions of uncertainty of judgment described by David Eddy, is provided on the Web site for this book, www.health-law.org. For additional readings on the nature of medical judgment, see Jack Dowie & Arthur Elstein, Professional Judgment: A Reader in Clinical Decisionmaking (1988); Atul Gawande, Complications: A Surgeon's Notes on an Imperfect Science (2002); Kathryn Hunter, Doctors' Stories: The Narrative Structure of Medical Knowledge (1991); Steven Schwartz & Timothy Griffin, Medical Thinking: The Psychology of Medical Judgment and Decision Making (1986); Symposium, The Structure of Clinical Knowledge, 14 J. Med. & Phil. 103 (1989).

2. *Medical Terminology.* Prior editions of this book contained information about medical terminology, medical science, and anatomy. Lawyers who practice in this field must eventually acquire a fair amount of medical knowledge, and many law students enjoy learning something about a different profession's specialized vocabulary. Others see medical terminology as an obstacle to understanding what's really happening in these cases. We have chosen to cater to the latter group; our feeling is that if you end up working in this field, you will have plenty of opportunity to learn the terminology later. Here, when cases contain uncommon medical terms, we will define them for you. If we fail to do so, most terms used in this book are contained in better-quality general dictionaries. For those who want more specialized information, here is a sampling of various medical texts and treatises, some written especially for lawyers and others for medical professionals or for the lay public. **Medical Dictionaries:** Dorland's Illustrated Medical Dictionary; V. Slee et al., Slee's Health Care Terms (3d ed. 1996); Taber's Cyclopedic Medical Dictionary.

■ LAW AND MEDICINE
William J. Curran
1st ed. 1960

There may have been a time when doctors and lawyers had much in common, but today their environments are radically divergent and the problem of mutual understanding is a real one. The doctor is trained in a dynamic and experimental science, he is seeking truth in a physical world. He is steeped in the practical judgment, though he avoids generalization. The lawyer, on the other hand, lives within the generalities of the law. The courts apply justice through the advocacy system and seek truth through the burden of proof. When the doctor or other medical person comes into contact with the courts and lawyers, he is often mystified and is generally impatient with the conservatism of the courts in accepting the advances of science. The lawyer often does not seem to the doctor to be seeking truth, but only to place blame.

Most lawyers are Aristotelian in method, if not in philosophy. So are law students by the time they are seniors. That is to say, they work from settled principles on stated fact situations. While they are seeking the results of their deductive logic, their facts remain unchanged. This is not the case in science and in medicine.

The scientist seeks truth within the scientific method. The physician is also an experimentalist, an empiricist. At times, however, he does not like being called a scientist, particularly when he is treating a patient. Then he may prefer the title of artisan—but still an empirical artisan.

The failure to understand the basic difference in method between doctors and lawyers is often a stumbling block to greater cooperation between the two professions. It often leads the lawyer into error in presenting the medical issues in a legal action. It may seem obvious that a lawyer should understand the physician's methods as well as his conclusions. Yet, when the attorney accepts a case and prepares it for trial, he tends not to do this. If his client has a back injury, he is interested only in the doctor's conclusions in regard to that injury. He may study the basis for the physician's conclusions in regard to this case, but he rarely does anything more until the next case comes along when again he is interested only in *that* injury. . . .

■ PHYSICIANS VERSUS LAWYERS: A CONFLICT OF CULTURES
Daniel M. Fox*
AIDS and the Law (H. Dalton & S. Burris eds., 1987)

If we are to move in the direction of cooperation rather than conflict, we must understand the roots of the antagonism between the professions and the contemporary forces that threaten to deepen it.

I emphasize physicians' antagonism to lawyers, because I suspect that most lawyers are not normally antagonistic toward physicians. Physicians, on the other hand, believe they are being taken advantage of by lawyers who do not understand medicine or value it properly. They are, moreover, mortified because the conflict is usually displayed in public settings controlled by lawyers—court proceedings and legislative hearings.

The conflict between physicians and lawyers, though it is rooted in the modern history of the two professions, has become more intense in recent years as the authority most people accord to physicians has diminished. Some physicians accuse lawyers of helping to undermine public confidence in them by mindlessly pursuing malpractice litigation. Many attribute their rising premiums for malpractice insurance to the work of greedy and unscrupulous lawyers. Physicians often blame lawyers for the mass of regulations that burden them. In an astonishing display of professional bigotry, the new president of the Association of American Medical Colleges told a medical school graduating class in June 1986, "We're swimming in shark-infested waters where the sharks are lawyers."

To most physicians, adversarial proceedings are an ineffective and irrational method for resolving conflict. Where Anglo-American lawyers presume that a person accused of a crime is innocent until proven guilty in a court of law, physicians believe it is dangerous to make any presumption before examining

---

*Daniel Fox is widely known and published in the health care public policy field. He is the president of the Milbank Memorial Fund, and he previously held various positions in academics and government.

evidence. Similarly, most physicians do not understand the history or the logic of lawyers' claim that formalized conflict between plaintiffs and defendants in a courtroom or around a table resolves disagreements with reasonable equity and preserves social peace.

Physicians are trained to rely on two methods of addressing conflicts about data and their interpretation. The first method is the assertion of authority from the top of a hierarchy in which power is derived from knowledge. The second method is peer review-discussion to consensus among experts of roughly equal standing and attainment. Both methods, the hierarchical and the consensual, rest on the assumption that truth is best determined by experts. . . .

Note: Law vs. Medicine: A Culture Clash

Here are some additional perspectives on the differences and commonalities between doctors and lawyers:

> Doctors and lawyers are not alike, either by disposition, or by education, or in practice. Even though the basic objectives of our two professions are the same, namely, to serve society, the education and practice of each are worlds apart. . . . The adversary system squeezes the doctor into roles and settings with which he is unfamiliar and in which he is ineffective. . . . The adversary system, as effective as it may be in achieving justice, is clearly ineffective in establishing truth in medicine.

Charles G. Guild, III, M.D., Lawyers Doctors and Medical Malpractice: A Surgeon Reacts, *in* E. D. Shapiro et al., Medical Malpractice (2d ed. 1966).

> If a doctor were called on to treat typhoid fever he would probably try to find out what kind of water the patient drank, and clean out the well so that no one else could get typhoid from the same source. But if a lawyer were called on to treat a typhoid patient he would give him thirty days in jail, and then he would think that nobody else would ever dare to drink the impure water. If the patient got well in fifteen days, he would be kept until his time was up; if the disease was worse at the end of thirty days, the patient would be released because his time was out. As a rule, lawyers are not scientists. They think that there is only one way to make men good, and that is to put them in such terror that they do not dare to do bad.

Meyer Levin, Compulsion (1956) (taken from the defense attorney's closing argument to the jury).

For additional books and articles that illustrate differences of professional approach, ethical principles, and cultural values between lawyers and physicians (not necessarily with that intention in mind), see G. Annas, Judging Medicine (1988); C. Chapman, Physicians, Law and Ethics (1984); W. Curran, Law-Medicine Notes: Progress in Medicolegal Relations (1989); J. Katz, The Silent World of Doctor and Patient (1984); I. Kennedy, Treat Me Right: Essays in Medical Law and Ethics (1988); S. Law & S. Polan, Pain and Profit: The Politics of Malpractice (1978); D. Louisell & H. Williams, The Paenchyma of Law (1985); Peter D. Jacobson, Strangers in the Night: Law and Medicine in the Managed Care

Era (2002); William M. Sage, The Lawyerization of Medicine, 26 J. Health Pol. Pol'y & L. 1179 (2001); Alan A. Stone, Law's Influence on Medicine and Medical Ethics, 312 New Eng. J. Med. 310 (1985).

3. *Evidence-Based Medicine*

■ OVERSIGHT OF THE QUALITY OF MEDICAL CARE: REGULATION, MANAGEMENT, OR THE MARKET?*
Timothy Jost**
3 Ariz. L. Rev. 825 (1995)

The most important factor driving change has been an ever quickening reorganization of the health care industry, a reorganization that is becoming revolutionary rather than simply evolutionary in nature. The prevalence of the sole practitioner mode that dominated medical practice until the last two decades continues to decline as group practices and physicians employed by health care institutions or managed care organizations or allied with hospitals in integrated delivery systems become ever more common. The large health care corporation, whose power was long resisted by the medical profession, seems now to have carried the day.[83] Both institutions that provide health care, such as hospitals or nursing homes, and entities that pay for health care, including insurers or self-insured employers, have become much more interested in overseeing the work of the professionals who practice within them or whose care they purchase. The emergence of managed care organizations that both pay for and provide care, moreover, gives lay managers even greater control over medical practice.

In tandem with this change, and perhaps driven by it, has come a revolution in information processing. Developments in information processing technology in the second half of the twentieth century have dramatically enhanced the ability of the health care industry to collect, process, and analyze data. These advances create the possibility of engaging in analysis of the outcomes of health care processes.[87] Data describing large numbers of patients can be studied to determine the efficacy of alternative diagnostic and treatment modalities. This information in turn contributes to the construction of practice guidelines, which describe best

---

*Copyright © 1995 by the Arizona Board of Regents. Reprinted by permission.

**Newton D. Baker, Professor of Law, Washington and Lee University School of Law.

[83] This transformation was noted early on by Paul Starr, The Social Transformation of American Medicine 40-44 (1982), at 420-49 and Arnold S. Relman, The New Medical-Industrial Complex, 303 New Eng. J. Med. 963 (1980), and has continued at an accelerating pace. . . . It has also been noted in the legal literature, where some welcome it, Mark Hall, Institutional Control of Physician Behavior: Legal Barriers to Health Care Cost Containment, 137 U. Pa. L. Rev. 431 (1988), and others decry it, David Frankford, Creating and Dividing the Fruits of Collective Economic Activity: Referrals Among Health Care Providers, 89 Colum. L. Rev. 1861 (1989).

[87] See, e.g., Paul M. Ellwood, Shattuck Lecture—Outcomes Management: A Technology of Patient Experience, 318 New Eng. J. Med. 1549 (1988); Arnold Relman, Assessment and Accountability: The Third Revolution in Medical Care, 319 New Eng. J. Med. 1220 (1988).

practices. These practice guidelines can in some instances be reduced to algo-rithms that can be used to enable computer review of the quality of the practices of individual practitioners or institutions.[90] Outcome data can also be used to support pattern analysis, comparing the outcome of the care provided by indivi-dual practitioners or institutions with average or optimal practice as revealed by outcome analysis. . . .

[I]nformation processing technology and industry reorganization permit much greater oversight of health care by lay managers. Once it is possible to describe the quality of physician practices in terms that lay managers can apply or in algorithms that computers can manipulate, the genie is out of the bottle and physician dominance of quality oversight has been broken. In the last half-decade, health care institutions have begun to move from traditional physician-led quality assurance to a new management-led and data-driven philosophy of quality over-sight: continuous quality improvement or total quality management.

The continuous quality improvement or total quality management move-ment is based on quality improvement strategies developed in the industrial setting. The ideas of Demming, Juran, Schewhart and others had a significant impact on Japanese, and then American industrial production. Within the past few years these ideas have begun to be applied widely in health care as well.[99] . . .

The quality improvement philosophy is based on several principles: . . . Energy is better directed toward improving the system through which care is delivered than toward looking for "bad apples." Most quality deficiencies are caused by faulty systems, not by incompetents working within those systems. One can accomplish more, therefore, by raising the mean of the performance curve than by chopping off the tail. This emphasis on improving the average performance rather than punishing the bad actor is perhaps the clearest distinc-tion between quality improvement and traditional quality assurance, which has tended to be preoccupied with looking for "bad apples." This orientation gives quality improvement a more positive tone than quality assurance, thus making it more palatable to hospital employees and medical staff. It also results in a heavy emphasis on process and on systems. . . .

Any program directed at improving or assuring quality—be it private, public, or some combination of the two—will have to find a means to affect the behavior of individuals or institutions. A key question that must be answered, therefore, before turning to a consideration of the comparative strengths of various institutions that might address quality problems, is what levers are available to improve the quality of professional judgment and of health care production processes.

The first such lever is the generation and dissemination of informa-tion. . . . [H]owever, expectations as to what can be accomplished through data

---

[90] See William L. Roper et al., Effectiveness in Health Care: An Initiative to Evaluate and Improve Medical Practice, 319 New Eng. J. Med. 1197 (1988) (describing HCFA's interest in outcomes research).

[99] See, e.g., Donald M. Berwick et al., Curing Health Care: New Strategies for Quality Improvement (1991); Ellen J. Gaucher & Richard J. Coffey, Total Quality in Healthcare: From Theory to Practice (1993). . . .

collection and dissemination for influencing medical judgment should be modest. In the final analysis, medical practice cannot be reduced to statistics.

Second, . . . the culture of professionalism has played an important role in stimulating quality. The professional was a gentleman who rose above the crass concerns of merchants to dedicate himself to serving the needs of his patients with clear and undivided judgment. The concern that licensure boards have traditionally shown for professional ethics and for unprofessional conduct can be understood in part as an attempt to suppress normative error, and thus to sustain a culture in which quality was valued and promoted.

[Third,] . . . sanctions have a legitimate role, however marginal, in encouraging quality. Sanctions can be used to exclude from the market practitioners or institutions that totally lack the capacity to make appropriate professional judgments or to carry out effective production processes. Corrective or educative sanctions can improve the performance of those who have the basic capacity to do well but need information or direction. Punitive and deterrent sanctions may be appropriate for normative deficiencies that result in technical or judgment errors or for careless production processes. . . .

Fourth, incentives have an obvious role to play in encouraging quality. The market stimulates quality in other sectors of the economy by directing business toward those merchants who can deliver value for money. Incentives such as money, recognition, power, independence, or anything else of value can be used to encourage professionals or institutions to improve production processes or to be more attentive in making professional judgments and applying professional skills. . . .

Some commentators believe that the information processing revolution, aided by market restructuring, offers the promise of overcoming the traditional deficiencies of health care markets. If consumers have information about the comparative outcomes of professional care—it is contended—they can evaluate the quality of that care without needing to understand the professional judgments that produced those outcomes. If consumers possess comparative information about patient satisfaction with health care institutions, they need not understand the production processes that produced patient satisfaction in one institution or dissatisfaction in another. In the final analysis, we are told that if consumers can be given "report cards," the market will produce quality. But has the information revolution solved the market failures that originally justified regulation?

There are reasons to believe that it has not, or at least not totally. . . . The idea of comparison shopping for health care raises a host of methodological questions with respect to data collection and presentation. . . . [A] host of "noise" problems must be overcome. Outcomes data are meaningless or misleading unless they are adjusted for severity of illness, the presence of do not resuscitate orders or comorbidities, and other factors not under the control of providers. The history of the Health Care Financing Administration (HCFA) mortality surveys shows how devilishly difficult it can be both to adjust adequately for the host of exogenous factors that can affect mortality and to quell suspicions that attempted adjustments are not adequate. HCFA [now known as CMS] ultimately dropped its reporting because it determined that a high percentage of the lowest performing hospitals were institutions that served the poorest and most needy patients and because it could not solve intractable problems with its measurement methodology.[212] Similarly, California's outcome assessment program found that some of the state's most sophisticated hospitals rated poorly on outcome indices because they had been most aggressive in reporting complications of surgery to maximize Medicare Diagnosis Related Group reimbursement. Adjusting for risk, on the other hand, permits providers to play games with outcome reporting systems by inflating risk data about their patients, thus improving risk adjusted performance. . . . Adjusting for age, for example, may mask problems in treatment of the elderly. Finally, even if perfect risk adjustment could be achieved, some providers are still likely to appear as outliers simply because of random variation, a factor unlikely to be appreciated by consumers. . . .

How consumers will use the report card is also problematic. . . . If a report card covers a dozen plans or institutions, each with 50 quality measures, consumers would be dealing with 600 discrete bits of information—many of which might be continuous rather than binary variables—and a nearly infinite variety of combinations of variables. One potential result in this information-rich environment would be "information overload." Consumers might simply be overwhelmed by the quantity of information, and make choices randomly related to their actual optimal choice. . . .

The deficiencies of the market . . . ensure the existence of a continuing legitimate role for quality regulation. . . . The costs of government intervention point, however, to a limited rather than an expansive government role. . . . The task of professional regulation needs to be refocused on assuring initial and ongoing competency and the professionalism that supports it. Prevention of error should by and large be left to management, and accountability to consumers be assured through the market and through an independent ombudspersons' office responsible for investigating consumer complaints. All the resources of modern technology must then be brought to bear on the residual tasks of regulation.

Note: Outcomes and Effectiveness Assessment

The Information Revolution. Various aspects of the movement toward "evidence-based medicine" have generated a voluminous literature, some descriptive, some analytical, and some critical. For a sampling, in addition to the sources Timothy Jost cites, see Troyen A. Brennan & Donald M. Berwick, New Rules: Regulation, Markets and the Quality of American Health Care (1996); Michael L. Millenson, Demanding Medical Excellence (1997); Robert Dubois & Robert Brook, Assessing Clinical Decisionmaking: Is the Ideal System Feasible?, 25 Inquiry 59 (1988); David Frankford, Scientism and Economism in the Regulation of Health Care, 19 J. Health Pol. Pol'y & L. 773 (1994); Mark A. Hall et al., Measuring Medical Practice Patterns: Sources of Evidence from Health Services Research, 37 Wake Forest L. Rev. __ (2002); John V. Jacobi, Patients at a

---

[212] Jesse Green et al., Analyzing Hospital Mortality: The Consequences of Diversity in Patient Mix, 265 JAMA 1849, 1849-1853 (1991); Rolla Edward Park et al., Explaining Variations in Hospital Death Rates, 264 JAMA 484 (1990).

Loss: Protecting Health Care Consumers Through Data Driven Quality Assurance, 45 Kan. L. Rev. 705 (1997); Wendy Mariner, Outcomes Assessment in Health Care Reform: Promise and Limitations, 20 Am. J.L. & Med. 37 (1994); Lars Noah, Medicine's Epistemology: Mapping the Haphazard Diffusion of Knowledge in the Biomedical Community, 44 Ariz. L. Rev. 373 (2002); Sandra Tanenbaum, Knowing and Acting in Medical Practice: The Epistemological Politics of Outcomes Research, 19 J. Health Pol. Pol'y & L. 27 (1994); Sandra Tanenbaum, What Physicians Know, 329 New Eng. J. Med. 1268 (1993); Symposium, 17(4) Health Aff. (July-Aug. 1998); Symposium, 76 Milbank Q. 515 (1998); Symposium, Health Care Cost-Benefit and Cost-Effectiveness Analysis, 31 Medical Care JS1 (June 1993 Supp.). For studies that examine the impact of comparative outcomes measures such as report cards on actual consumer and provider behavior, see D. Mukamel & A. Mushlin, Quality of Care Information Makes a Difference, 36 Med. Care 945 (1998) (finding some impact); Mark Chassin, Achieving and Sustaining Improved Quality, 21(4) Health Aff. 40 (July 2002) (same); S. Mennemeyer et al., Death and Reputation: How Consumers Acted Upon HCFA Mortality Information, 34 Inquiry 117 (1997) (finding no impact). For a critique of the reliability and usefulness of physician report cards, see Timothy Hofer et al., The Unreliability of Individual Physician "Report Cards" for Assessing the Costs and Quality of Care of a Chronic Disease, 281 JAMA 2098 (1999) (finding that report cards "were unable to detect reliably true practice differences" and that their use "may foster an environment in which physicians can most easily avoid being penalized by avoiding . . . [more difficult patients who have not responded well to treatment]"); Comment, 29 Pepp. L. Rev. 585 (2002).

C. THE HEALTH CARE FINANCING AND DELIVERY SYSTEM

The readings in this section describe the economic and regulatory forces that shape how health care is delivered in the United States. All of us have some exposure to the world of medicine but few law students have reason to understand the intricacies of this financing and delivery system and how it has developed. This understanding is essential in a course that focuses on the full range of legal and public policy issues pertaining to the delivery and payment for medical care. Those issues have naturally taken shape according to the structural components and historical growth of the health care sector and its various institutions.

We begin with a rudimentary overview of the history of health insurance and of the principal events that have shaped its development. Included in this is a discussion of whether there is a "crisis" in American medicine. We finish with an introduction to more recent innovations such as HMOs. As you read through this alphabet soup of actors, institutions, and acronyms, rather than memorizing all the details, try to construct a coherent story line of how the health care sector took shape over time and how its various pieces interconnect at present. You don't need to master all the details now, for they will reemerge throughout the course, but it will be easier to remember them at the end if you have an initial framework to attach them to.

1. *Insurance and Regulation*

■ U.S. HEALTH CARE COVERAGE AND COSTS: HISTORICAL DEVELOPMENT AND CHOICES FOR THE [FUTURE]*
Randall R. Bovbjerg, Charles C. Griffin, & Caitlin Carroll**
21 J.L. Med. & Ethics 141 (1993)

American health policy today faces dual problems of too little coverage at too high a cost. Our combined system of private and public financing leaves about one seventh of the population without insurance coverage from any source. At the same time, the coverage Americans do have costs ever-larger shares of our country's productive capacity, well above what other countries pay and what many people, health plans, businesses, and governments want to pay. This "paradox of excess and deprivation"[2] results from the incremental approach the U.S. has taken to solving incompatible policy goals of widening health insurance coverage while trying to control costs and maintain a high level of quality. This essay examines the American record over the past 60 years in pursuing this incremental approach and draws from it lessons for the current effort to reform the system.

PRE-1929: ERECTING MEDICAL INFRASTRUCTURE AND ESCHEWING NATIONAL HEALTH INSURANCE

Neither medicine nor health coverage was very advanced prior to the Great Depression.[3] Accustomed to the medical miracles of the late twentieth century, one tends to forget that nineteenth century doctors could do little for patients, and hospitals were mainly charity wards where the poor went to die. Medical practice was totally unregulated, and competing theories of disease and treatment flourished. Antiseptic surgery developed only in the latter part of the century. At that same time, local, state, and national medical associations began to promote professional standards (of their own design) as well as the enactment of state licensure requirements. By 1912, it could be said that "for the first time in human history, a random patient with a random disease consulting a doctor chosen at random stands a better than 50/50 chance of benefitting from the encounter."[4]

---

* Reprinted with the permission of the American Society of Law, Medicine & Ethics. Updated by the editors of this book to reflect recent developments.

** The authors are, respectively, Senior Research Associate, Health Policy Center, The Urban Institute: Economist, The World Bank; and Research Assistant, The Urban Institute. Bovbjerg's name is pronounced "Boh-berg."

[2] Alain Enthoven and Richard Kronick, A Consumer-Choice Health Plan for the 1980s, 320 New Eng. J. Med. 29 (1989).

[3] Joseph A. Califano, Jr., America's Health Care Revolution: Who Lives? Who Dies? Who Pays? (New York: Random House, 1986); Paul Starr, The Social Transformation of American Medicine (New York: Basic Books, 1982); Edward Shorter, The Health Century (New York: Doubleday, 1987); Rosemary Stevens, In Sickness and in Wealth: American Hospitals in the Twentieth Century (New York: Basic Books 1989).

[4] This contemporaneous pronouncement came from Harvard Professor L. Henderson, calling the year 1912 "a Great Divide." Quoted in Richard Harris, A Sacred Trust (New York: New American Library, 1966), 5.

Table 1
The Rising Tide of Medical Costs: 1929-[2001]

Time period	Health care share of GDP at end of period (percent)	Annual growth in real health care dollars, per capita (percent)
1929	3.5	—
1929-1940	4.0	1.4
1940-1950	4.5	4.0
1950-1960	5.3	3.6
1960-1970	7.3	6.5
1970-1980	9.1	3.8
1980-1990	12.2	4.4
1990-2001	14.1	4.5

By the 1920s, today's familiar patterns of accreditation and licensure were set for medical education, medical practice, and hospitals. Doctors practiced almost exclusively as solo, office-based practitioners on a fee-for-service basis. Physicians treated their own patients in hospitals, rather than referring them to hospital-based specialists, often salaried, as in much of Europe. Community-based, voluntary hospitals were well established in most of the country, with not-for-profits dominant, basically serving as workshops for community physicians. Still, for most Americans, illness, injury, and early death were more to be suffered than helped by a doctor, much less insured against.

A good thing, too, for insurance coverage was virtually nonexistent, whether private or public. True, some private insurers were willing to write a kind of "health insurance," but only covering loss of income from disability, not physician or hospital bills. Historically, insurance theory—and commercial insurers—thought the term *health insurance* an oxymoron. The reason was that sickness, or more precisely, the use of medical services, was not believed to be an "insurable risk." . . .

Insurance may also have seemed less important because expenses for available care were not large relative to typical incomes. The average day in a hospital cost only a few dollars, and physicians did not charge—or earn—large amounts. . . . In short, in the era before health insurance, when patients themselves paid for almost all health care, the medical economy behaved much like the rest of the economy and was small relative to the whole. All together, the nation spent only about 3.5 percent of gross [domestic] product (GDP) on health care (Table 1).

1929-1940: ENTER HEALTH INSURANCE

Then came the birth of the "Blues," the true beginnings of health insurance as we now know it. . . . Blue Cross plans were organized by hospital associations, typically at the state level. The first Blues-style hospital plan started in 1934 with special New York enabling legislation. Very quickly, physicians followed suit, organizing their own Blue Shield plans, first for in-hospital surgical care, then for medical services as well. Blues plans had unique service areas, not competing with one another, and had strong ties to hospital associations and medical societies. . . .[8] By 1938, 1.4 million Americans were enrolled in 38 Blue Cross plans. Only after the hospitals and the Blues proved the market viable did ordinary insurers begin to write coverage for medical bills. . . .

These early Blues, followed by commercial plans, set the pattern for health coverage that still dominates U.S. health financing. Patients were given "free choice of provider" (able to use almost any provider, not limited to contracted doctors or hospitals), with relatively low out-of-pocket cost at the time of service. Providers received retroactive fee-for-service payment (not an advance salary, capitation, or contracted amount) for all services they deemed "medically necessary." Risk pooling and financing came from insurers acting as "third parties," at a remove both from patients (first parties) and from providers (second). . . .

At first, there was no cost problem, for when coverage reached few people, benefit and payment levels were low, and medical technology did not exist to provide very sophisticated care. There appears to have been virtually no appreciation for how expensive this mode of operation would ultimately prove to be.

Blues plans were publicly perceived to have a more social role than "ordinary" insurance. Their not-for-profit status, chartered as "hospital (and medical) service corporations," rather than as insurance companies, reflect this perception. . . . In hindsight, the Blues also reflected the economic and professional self-interest of medical providers, seeking to strengthen private practice, institutionalize fee-for-service billing, and promote fiscal and clinical independence from outside control. They helped strengthen providers as private entrepreneurs. . . .

THE 1940S [AND 1950S]: WORKPLACE GROUPS: GREAT LEAP FORWARD

Private health insurance took a great leap forward in the 1940s. The economy moved back to full employment, manufacturing surged, and urbanization accelerated. It became rather common for manufacturing workers, especially through unions, to seek group health coverage as a fringe benefit of employment. . . . The tax treatment of fringe benefits encouraged employment group coverage. IRS administrative decisions, later codified in the Internal Revenue Code of 1954, deemed such benefits taxable neither to employer nor employee. Hence, through workplace insurance, health services could be prepaid with pre-tax dollars, reducing the cost of private coverage by savings on tax otherwise due. As tax levels rose, this tax subsidy became a more valuable benefit. . . .

The federal government supplied some health services, but only to identifiably "federal" populations. For example, the armed services, veterans, and the merchant marine all had dedicated hospitals; and the Indian Health Service operated on reservations. Interestingly, federal coverage of these populations was achieved predominantly through direct service delivery operations rather than through the financing of purchases from private providers. At the local level, states and municipalities also ran some hospitals and medical clinics. Local institutions

---

[8] Odin W. Anderson, Blue Cross Since 1929 (Cambridge, MA: Ballinger Publishing Co., 1975); Sylvia Law, Blue Cross: What Went Wrong? (2d ed.) (New Haven: Yale University Press, 1976); Paul Starr, The Social Transformation of American Medicine (New York: Basic Books, 1982).

often specialized in tuberculosis or mental health care, but some also provided general acute care, notably cities' public general hospitals. Most hospital care, however, remained the province of not-for-profit community hospitals.

This era also brought heavier public subsidy to the mainly private suppliers of care. Immediately after the war, the federal Hill-Burton Act made available grants to expand and modernize hospital capacity, which had suffered during the war. Soon thereafter, federal grants were also made available for medical education. In addition, with the post-war enlargement of the National Institutes of Health, federal policy greatly expanded support for basic research. . . .

The 1950s brought health coverage to much of the middle class through a combination of private action and the tax subsidy. By 1960, over two thirds of Americans had private coverage, but over 55 percent of personal health spending still came from patients' own pockets rather than from insurance coverage. . . .

The beginnings of price increases were becoming visible, though without being considered a major problem. . . . As one example, the average hospital expense/day was only $7.98 in 1950, but rose to $16.46 in 1960. . . .

THE 1960s [AND 1970s]: ENTER BIG GOVERNMENT, INCREMENTALLY

The sixties were marked by further incremental expansion of coverage, with most attention paid to expansion of government-subsidized care for those omitted by private coverage (the poor, the frail, the aged) through the intervention of federal medical entitlement programs. The theory was that beneficiaries would be entitled to medical service. An emerging reality was that providers were entitled to collect what they wanted from government. The decade began with John F. Kennedy's newly activist leadership seeking a "New Frontier" that included federal medical coverage, at least for the elderly. Strong opposition came from fiscal conservatives and from medical interest groups, spearheaded by the AMA [American Medical Association], which supported voluntary private insurance. Opponents objected on the ground that "socialized medicine" would ultimately allow federal bureaucrats to control clinical decisions in medicine (as well as medical incomes). . . .

After President Lyndon B. Johnson's landslide victory in 1964, federally funded *Medicare* was enacted to provide conventional third-party coverage for the aged (those within the Social Security system and past retirement age) and the disabled (those unable to work). The program was patterned on the Blues, with automatic entitlement to Part A hospital coverage (parallel to Blue Cross) and voluntary enrollment in Part B physician and other coverage (Blue Shield). The state-federal *Medicaid* program was created, almost as an afterthought, to cover what one might call the "deserving" poor (basically those unable to work by virtue of age, blindness, or disability). Medicaid built on the Kerr-Mills precedent of state discretion operating within a federal set of rules. . . .

By virtue of the vastly increased public role in financing coverage as well as continued growth in private coverage, the pattern of U.S. health spending shifted markedly. Whereas in 1960 over half of total health spending was still met by patients' direct out-of-pocket payments, by 1970 the patient's share had dropped to only 35 percent, while the federal share doubled to over 20 percent. . . .

Medicare essentially adapted Blues' reimbursement principles to public payment; the prime objective was to give beneficiaries access to private providers. The program was created as a third party outside medical transactions, responsible for reimbursing hospitals for their "reasonable costs" retrospectively and physicians for their actual submitted bills. . . . Superimposing this public largesse on top of existing payment mechanisms favorable to providers understandably failed to promote cost-conscious tradeoffs between value and cost of services.

This decade of greatly subsidized demand and provider-driven payment spurred further hospital expansion and upgrading, as well as the entry of many new physicians, as manpower policy simultaneously responded to a perceived "physician shortage." Medical price rises became much larger than the general rate of inflation. Average hospital expense per day, for example, rose from $16.46 in 1960 to $53.95 in 1970. As one early-seventies commentator noted, the price of a hospital room in the early 1950s was about that of a good hotel, but by end of the 1960s, hospital prices had left hotels well behind. Usage of services also increased. . . .

Much of the 1960s growth was intentional, especially for serving the elderly and others previously without coverage. Such expansion continues to seem desirable from today's perspective. In hindsight, however, a key problem was not mere price increases and new benefits to encourage new services, but rather the "blank check" fashion in which expanded coverage was removed entirely from disciplined evaluation of the benefit obtained from new services. Neither public nor private payers made any attempt to signal *how much* new care was enough, either through payment rules and incentives or through explicit provisions about benefits or utilization of care. Medical "need" was once thought to set a natural limit on services; in fact, "need" is an expansive, not a limiting concept. All signals were for more of everything: scientific research and technological innovation, insurance benefits, and clinical services. Given free rein, medical care can expand enormously as we have since learned. Additional care can almost always offer some level of legitimate benefit to some patients. . . .

By the end of the 1960s, the basic patterns of U.S. health care delivery and financing were set: Private hospitals and physicians delivered most health care. Employers voluntarily provided private insurance to workers. Governments provided public insurance to those too old or unable to work (through public plans modelled on the private ones). All plans retrospectively reimbursed provider-set charges or costs. Each plan paid separately for its own financing, based on its own experience. Generous fee-for-service reimbursement encouraged even more services, with no built-in controls on price or utilization. . . .

[T]he 1970s became the first decade of "cost containment." Health prices were frozen (along with all others), then regulated by federal wage and price controls under President Nixon's "Economic Stabilization Program." Health controls were kept on for some months after others were lifted, and costs were effectively held down. Thereafter, inflation returned with a vengeance. There were so many manifestations of increased cost consciousness in the public sector that only the highlights can be mentioned. For example, a single 1972 omnibus bill strengthened federal health planning regulation, required utilization/quality review of Medicare hospitalizations, and limited the allowed annual growth of prevailing Medicare physician fees. Two years later, the National Health Planning Act required states, under threat of losing all federal health monies, to regulate hospital growth through certificates of need. Also in 1974, the HMO Act, sought reform reflecting a mix of regulation and market-oriented approaches. Many state governments also experimented with "prospective reimbursement" or hospital "rate setting" to control hospital costs, which were (and are) the largest share of health spending. In sharp contrast, the private sector response to rising costs was more muted. . . .

Costs continued to grow rapidly. The medical care CPI again outpaced the CPI for all items. Real medical spending outgrew real GDP by a factor of two, down slightly from the 1960s' two and a half. By 1980, health's share of GDP reached 9.1 percent (Table 1). . . .

THE 1980s: EVERY PLAN FOR ITSELF, AS COSTS RISE AND COVERAGE DROPS

The 1980s began with the self-consciously conservative administration of Ronald W. Reagan, who was philosophically committed to a limited federal role in health care. Still, there were expectations of an actively "pro-competitive" federal reform that would promote private coverage and private economizing. Academic and other theorists had developed such ideas, which were encouraged by the "privatizing" rhetoric of the new administration. . . . Probably the decade's most significant federal action came in 1983, when the administration and Congress collaborated in creating a Prospective Payment System (PPS) for inpatient hospital services under Medicare. In place of retrospective cost-based reimbursement, hospitals were to be paid fixed amounts per case, with rates set in advance for each of nearly 500 types of case, called "DRGs." Under this scheme, each institution is at financial risk for each case; a hospital earns no more for spending more and is able to keep the balance if it spends less. . . .

Some states experimented further with prospective payment for hospitals, either regulating only Medicaid rates or also covering most or all other payers. . . . Other states took market-oriented approaches: Arizona solicited competitive bids for HMO-like plans to cover its first-ever Medicaid program enrollees and California negotiated special hospital discounts for its Medicaid recipients' care through "selective contracting."

The private sector also showed new aggressiveness in attempting to contain costs during the 1980s. . . . Most significantly but with more difficulty, firms increasingly sought to move toward "managed care" and away from open-ended coverage of whatever services doctors and patients choose. Managed care includes not merely HMOs but also new entities called "PPOs" or other plans with limitations on what physicians and what services could be used. . . .

The U.S. has thus tried a mélange of different strategies for cost containment, both regulatory and market-oriented in nature. But all have been incremental (e.g., "managed care" for particular plans, administered prospective pricing for Medicare hospital payments) rather than system-wide (e.g., budgetary limits, restructured rules on insurance choice and pricing). And all have their weaknesses. . . . and powerful opponents.

With regard to health care coverage, the 1980s saw the first-ever drop in percentage of the population with coverage, driven by a drop in private health insurance coverage. For 1990, the total share of the population with private coverage dropped 5-10 percentage points. . . .

Many factors helped cause the decline in private coverage, but two were paramount: rising costs and declining insurance pooling. First, the continuing rise in health care costs has made insurance premiums too high to continue to attract new purchasers. . . . Second, risk pools have continued to disaggregate, as more and more firms self-insure and experience rating spreads to ever-smaller groups. This continuing trend means that firms with high-risk employees or a bad year of experience can no longer count on insurance to spread these costs. These problems are worst in the "small group" insurance market (often defined as under 50 or 25 employees). . . . Even those with large-group coverage fear for their coverage. Not only has corporate "downsizing" cost many employees their jobs, but cost-containment has led to sudden medical cutbacks as well. . . .

Some cost-containment efforts did help moderate the rate of growth in health spending, especially for hospital care. . . . Nonetheless, medical spending continued to grow rapidly. During the 1980s, real health care spending grew at 4.4 percent a year, over two and a half times as fast as real GDP, just as in the fast-growth 1960s. Health therefore consumed fully 12.2 percent of GDP in 1990, a total of $666 billion or about $2,566 per capita. . . .

[I]n the 1960s, U.S. health care spending was not far out of line with that of other developed countries, given the higher level of U.S. national income. Since then, especially in the 1980s, U.S. spending as a share of GDP has increased rapidly, whereas other countries' growth has been more controlled. Other developed countries all faced what they considered unacceptable cost increases in the 1970s and 1980s, but almost all implemented social limits on further growth, with significant success. The result is that the U.S. spends far more on health care than any other developed nation. . . .

ENTERING THE [NEW CENTURY]: OMINOUS TRENDS IN COST AND COVERAGE

Health spending is about to grow right off the charts, thanks to the magic of compound interest. The projections are truly staggering for policymakers worried about the federal deficit, workers' earnings, or international competitiveness—and these are not the worst-case scenarios, just extrapolations of current trends. For the year 2001, health spending reached 14.1 percent of GDP (Table 1), some $1.4 trillion or about $5,035 per capita, according to federal statisticians. . . . As disquieting as these statistics are, [this] century's "out years" (as budgeters call them) will be even worse: Health's share of GDP is projected to climb to some 17 percent in 2011, mostly paid by government. Such projections assume continuation of today's trends in price inflation, growth in utilization and intensity of services, growth and aging of the population, and other factors. Such numbers greatly inspire reformers. . . .

Where are we headed next? That is the subject of much discussion. . . . on Capitol Hill. . . . The political and practical backing for some change seems strong. But we end on a rather pessimistic note. This situation has existed before. Very high expectations attended earlier debates [on national health insurance], yet earlier reform plans all ended as incremental changes to the same basic system.

Recent experience shows, however, that a failure to fundamentally reform the system will only put off the day of reckoning, and not for long, as the tide of rising costs continues to erode the gains made over the last four decades. The underlying question is whether the current crisis will conquer the historic inertia of the payment system, which now nurtures a huge economic sector of politically active people. . . .

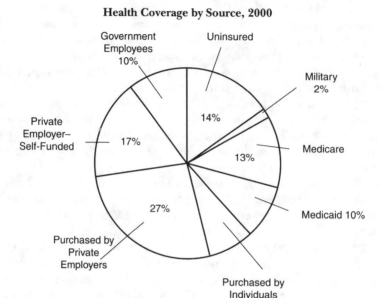

Health Coverage by Source, 2000

■ THE SAD HISTORY OF HEALTH CARE COST CONTAINMENT AS TOLD IN ONE CHART
Drew E. Altman and Larry Levitt
21(2) Health Affairs 9 (March 2002)*

What [this] Exhibit shows is that no approach our nation has tried, over the past thirty-five years, to control health costs has had a lasting impact. When Medicare and Medicaid passed in the mid-1960s, the new public programs took some of the burden of health spending off of the private sector, but only temporarily. By the late 1960s the rate of increase in private health spending per capita shot up. In the early 1970s wage and price controls had a dramatic impact on health care costs. But again, the impact was short-lived, and the rate of increase in private health spending rose dramatically after a few years. When President Jimmy Carter threatened tough cost containment regulation in the late 1970s, the health care industry organized what it called the "Voluntary Effort." The rate of increase in per capita private-sector health spending fell rapidly but then bounced back

* Reprinted with the permission of Project Hope.

Exhibit 1
**Annual Change in Private Health Spending Per Capita (Adjusted for Inflation),
1961–2001**

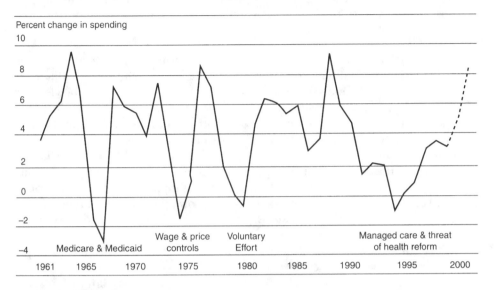

within a few years. Managed care and the threat of the Clinton health care reform plan appeared to have had a dramatic impact on the rate of increase in private health spending in the mid-1990s, but by the late 1990s it was on the rise again, reaching double-digit rates of increase by 2001. . . .

Some believe that we will not get a handle on health care costs as a nation until we are ready to make tough decisions about rationing medical care. An equally plausible scenario is that the apparent failure of all approaches reflects the American people's uncontainable desire for the latest and best health care, and that what we will do in the future is try small things that will work at the margin, complain a lot, but ultimately pay the bill.

2. The Crisis in Coverage and Spending

■ THE FUTURE OF THE AMERICAN HEALTH CARE SYSTEM

Henry T. Greely*
3 Stan. L. & Pol'y Rev. 16 (1991)

It was the best of times, it was the worst of times, it was the age of wisdom, it was the age of foolishness, it was the epoch of belief, it was the epoch of incredulity, it was

* Professor of Law, Stanford University.

the season of Light, it was the season of Darkness, it was the spring of hope, it was the winter of despair, we had everything before us, we had nothing before us, we were all going direct to Heaven, we were all going direct the other way—in short, the period was so far like the present period, that some of its noisiest authorities insisted on its being received, for good or for evil, in the superlative degree of comparison only.

Like Dickens's *ancien régime*, today's American medicine is a study in vivid contrasts. Infant mortality in the United States has just reached a record low; the revolution in genetics holds out the promise of unbelievably detailed knowledge of the human organism; successful surgery is performed on fetuses still in the womb; and hearts, livers, lungs, and bone marrow of others recall to life men and women otherwise doomed. Yet more than one American in eight has no health insurance coverage; . . . emergency rooms throughout the country are filled to overflowing, when they are not closing their doors for good; an American admitted to a hospital has better than one chance in about thirty of being injured there; and Americans living in the worst slums have life expectancies below those of the residents of some of the poorest countries in the world. American medicine is everywhere triumphant, but everywhere in rags. . . .

The coming crisis in the American health care system is amply illustrated [by] the problems in access, cost and quality that will make health policy the leading domestic policy issue of [our time]. The problem of access to health care is stated simply: An estimated [40] million Americans are not covered by any private or governmental health insurance plan. Although coverage is not the same as access, neither are the two divorced. People without health coverage are left to rely on hospital emergency rooms and, where available, public clinics for most of their care. Their access is rationed largely (and effectively) by inconvenience and waiting time. . . .

Cost of a service cannot be considered without also considering the quality of the service received. Measuring quality in health care is difficult, but two general problems, one actual and one perceived, are apparent in American medicine.

The actual problem is that health care is an uncertain science and the hospital a dangerous place. This commonplace truth recently took on renewed importance as the Harvard Medical Practice Study published its powerful review of the quality of medical care in New York hospitals. . . . Projecting the percentages across the country leads to the conclusion that about 1.5 million people are injured in hospitals by their medical care each year; about 400,000 of these people are injured by negligence. . . .

The perceived problem with quality is more subtle. Americans have longer—and healthier—life spans than ever before, but we do not *feel* healthy or well cared for. In the midst of unprecedented health, we perceive ourselves in unprecedented danger. Some of this may result from expectations that have outstripped reality; some may be from the frequent and frequently conflicting stories of new health threats—threats in food, water, air, and even in the imperceptible fluctuating electromagnetic fields of modern life. Each new study produces news stories, anxiety, and confusion.

Access, costs, and quality are all meaningless without some grounds for comparison, but medical comparisons are very difficult. Different countries deliver health care in different ways. What is satisfactory to one country's citizens and what is feasible in one country's political system may prove worthless in another's. Nonetheless, for whatever their value, we can make some comparisons. . . . [The United States spends 75 to 100 percent more per capita on health care than does Canada, France, Germany, and many northern European and Scandinavian countries, and 150 to 300 percent more per capita than England, Japan, Spain, and several other European countries.]

It is hard to know what those funds buy in terms of health because health is a product of so much more than medical care. Nevertheless, the casual observer can see no reason to believe that Americans are healthier than citizens of other rich countries; our life expectancy and infant mortality statistics show that, at least in some respects, we are less healthy.

In its technical brilliance, American health care is unsurpassed. Its best care would have seemed miraculous just a few years ago. But the bad side of American health care is very bad, and there is reason to think that it will get worse before it gets better. For one thing, the coming years will see a further increase in both the number of the elderly in the population and their percentage of the population. The growth will be particularly great among those over 85, the people most likely to make heavy use of the medical system. New technology, for which one can almost always read "expensive" new technology, continues to invade medicine. The HIV epidemic, though responsible for only about 1 percent of all American health care costs, will continue to increase pressure and cost in the system through at least the early years of the decade. And cost pressures on employers, on the states, and on the federal government will make it more and more tempting to cut health benefits, at the same time technical and statistical advances will make it easier to predict who will run up big medical bills.

An outside observer might conclude that America's greatest domestic problem over the next decade will be something other than health care—education, poverty, racism, crime, and the decaying infrastructure are some of the many possibilities. But, unlike those issues, the problems of the health system will soon reach a condition where the middle class will demand that something *must* be done. The nature and timing of the collapse cannot be predicted, but like the *ancien régime* a little more than 200 years ago, it is increasingly clear that the system cannot continue indefinitely.

■ WHY CONSERVATIVES DON'T TALK ABOUT AMERICA'S HEALTH SYSTEM
Democratic Study Group, U.S. House of Representatives
1991

Even though the United States devotes a far larger share of its GDP to health care than any other of the 23 industrialized countries, it does not rank similarly high in terms of the basic indicators of health status. Rather, the standing of the United States ranges from somewhere below the middle (life expectancy for women) to close to the bottom (infant mortality).

Despite our high level of health care spending, the United States ranks 21st out of the 23 industrialized countries in terms of infant mortality—ahead of only Portugal and Greece. . . . The United States ranks *18th* among the 23 industrialized countries in terms of life expectancy for males—again despite the high level of health care spending in the United States. . . . In 1987, life expectancy at birth for males in the United States was 71.5 years—about two years shorter than in Canada, about three years shorter than in Sweden, and more than four years shorter than in Japan.

Like infant mortality, life expectancy is also clearly linked to socioeconomic status, and there is a much lower male life expectancy (65.2 years) among the disproportionately poor black population in the United States. However, even the life expectancy for white males in the United States (72.2 years) is lower than the male life expectancy in 13 of the 23 industrialized countries (including such diverse countries as France, Greece, Australia, and Canada). . . .

For women, life expectancy in the United States ranks 15 out of 23. Countries with a higher female life expectancy than the United States include Spain, Greece, Canada, France, West Germany, and Sweden. . . .

While Americans are spending considerably more for health care than citizens of other industrialized countries—and may well be getting less for what we spend—it is nevertheless possible that Americans simply prefer the particular style of medicine and health care delivery that has developed in the United States. That is, we might be paying more than West Europeans, but getting in return a system with which we are satisfied.

A good indication of whether the level of satisfaction with the health care system is, in fact, higher in the United States than abroad is provided by . . . comparisons between attitudes in the United States and Canada. . . . [These] two nations have generally similar cultures and lifestyles but rather different health care systems (the Canadian system being a publicly funded program of universal health insurance [that spends about 30 percent less per capita]). . . .

[T]he level of satisfaction with health care services received was significantly higher in Canada than in the United States: 67 percent of Canadians stated they were *very* satisfied with the health care services they had received during the last year, compared to only 35 percent in the United States. Further, 18 percent of Americans surveyed were actually *dis*satisfied with the health care services they had received, while only 5 percent of Canadians were similarly dissatisfied. . . .

The data presented in this section suggest that the health care crisis in the United States is *not* the inevitable result of modern medicine. Rather, West European nations, Canada, and Japan all manage to spend significantly smaller fractions of their GDP on health care than the United States, while simultaneously providing broader access to health care than is available in this country.

Further, citizens of these other industrialized nations seem to receive at least as much (and generally more) health care services in the form of doctor visits and hospital stays as received by Americans. Overall health status in these other nations seems no worse (and generally better) than in the United States, and Western Europe appears to be ahead of the United States in addressing major health problems such as heart attacks and breast cancer.

■ DANGEROUS MEDICINE: A CRITICAL ANALYSIS OF CLINTON'S HEALTH PLAN
Doug Bandow*
1993

In his [1993] State of the Union speech the president stated that "our government will never again be fully solvent until we tackle the health-care crisis." . . . If one took his rhetoric seriously one would think that people were dying in droves due to inadequate medical care. . . . The theme of "crisis" has been repeated endlessly by Clinton aides, legislators, journalists, and analysts. Yet there is, demonstrably, no *crisis*. Problems, yes. Serious problems, yes. But a "crisis," no.

Indeed, if you become seriously ill, there is no better nation in which to become sick than the United States. America's death rate, perhaps the best measure of access to and quality of care, is among the lowest, and often *the* lowest, for most major illnesses. In some cases the differences are quite dramatic: You are twice as likely to die from a hernia or intestinal obstruction in Sweden than in the U.S., three times as likely to die from an ulcer in Great Britain than in America, and seven times as likely to die from prostate disease in Sweden than in the U.S.

This is not to say that American *health* is equal to that elsewhere. Infant mortality and life expectancy lag behind those of many other industrialized states, but that reflects serious social pathologies absent from many other nations. For example, the U.S. has many problems characteristic of Third World states in its inner cities. . . . [O]verall health figures are dramatically affected by America's high rates of homicide, drug use, and AIDS. . . . In short, if Americans survive to enter a nursing home, their life expectancy rises to the longest in the world. The fact that many do not survive is not a fault of the present health care system— nor will it be affected by health care "reform."

American medicine is particularly good at treating the injured and sick because it rewards research and innovation, and utilizes the latest medical techniques and technologies. The pharmaceutical industry, for instance, is one of America's most competitive businesses internationally. American companies have developed a larger share of significant new drugs than any other nation. These products actually reduce total health care costs by cutting the need for surgery and other expensive alternative procedures. Naturally, these products also save lives and ameliorate suffering for millions of people.

Compared to other nations the U.S. also makes available more high-tech devices and procedures . . . America has four times as many open-heart surgeries as Germany and six times as much radiation therapy and eight times as many magnetic resonance imaging [machines] as Canada. . . . American physicians, with a universe of modern technology at their fingertips, are the envy of the world's physicians. . . .

Still, the problems are real. Cost is the most obvious concern. Last year the nation spent. . . . 14 percent of gross national product, up from 13.2 percent in

---

*The author is a senior fellow at the Cato Institute, which is known for its libertarian and free market public policy positions.

1991. In the latter year the comparable percentages were 6.6 in Britain and Japan, 8.5 in Germany, and 9.1 in France. . . .

[S]pending/GDP ratios alone do not demonstrate the existence of a problem, let alone a crisis. There is no "right" amount of money to spend on health care and comparisons with other nations help little. Based on purchasing-power parities (rather than misleading exchange-rate measurements), America has the highest standard of living in the world: the U.S. gross domestic product per capita is more than 55 percent higher than that of Western Europe, 35 percent more than in Australia, 28 percent greater than in Japan, and 11 percent higher than in Canada. There is nothing strange, then, about Americans devoting an increasing share of their incomes on medical attention as they grow more prosperous. Surely there is at least as much justification for spending a marginal dollar on health as on a nicer car, more recreation, or another beer.

Notes: The Crisis in American Medicine

1. *The Perpetual Crisis*. American medicine has been declared to be in a "crisis" since at least the early 1960s. See Marion Sanders, The Crisis in American Medicine (1961). Can things really be all that bad if they've been like this so long? Another self-proclaimed iconoclast who doesn't think we are necessarily spending too much on health care is the highly-respected health economist Joseph P. Newhouse, An Iconoclastic View of Health Cost Containment, Health Aff., Supp. 1993, at 152. Economists David M. Cutler and Elizabeth Richardson claim that increased medical spending over the past several decades has produced increases in average health that are worth several times more than their aggregate costs. Your Money and Your Life: The Value of Health and What Affects It (NBER Working Paper No. 6895, Jan. 1999). See also Symposium, 22 (1) Health Aff. 1 (Jan. 2003).

Even if there is not a "crisis," there is still clearly a serious problem in American medicine. In case you're still not convinced, consider the following additional facts, opinions, and anecdotes (be sure to distinguish which is which).

> Medicine, like many other American institutions, suffered a stunning loss of confidence in the 1970s. Previously, two premises had guided government health policy: first, that Americans needed more medical care—more than the market alone would provide; and second, that medical professionals and private voluntary institutions were best equipped to decide how to organize those services. . . . In the 1970s this mandate ran out. The economic and moral problems of medicine displaced scientific progress at the center of public attention. Enormous increases in cost seemed ever more certain; corresponding improvements in health ever more doubtful. The prevailing assumptions about the need to expand medical care were reversed: The need now was to curb its apparently insatiable appetite for resources. In a short time, American medicine seemed to pass from stubborn shortages to irrepressible excess, without ever having passed through happy sufficiency.

Paul Starr, The Social Transformation of American Medicine 379 (1982).

America must start to laugh again. . . . My own contribution is to tell my friends about my recent hernia operation. I was in Greenwich Hospital for six hours, two of them for anesthesia and surgery. . . . Now, I ask my friends, what do you think the hospital bill came to—not the doctors' bills, I emphasize, but the hospital bill? Five hundred dollars, they guess. I prod them to go higher. A thousand? Three thousand? Then I let them have it: $11,450.46. . . . My friends respond with disbelief and rage. Eleven thousand dollars! As much as or more than a day care worker's annual salary, the price of a small car, a year's rent. We're talking here about cost-shifting—hospitals passing along the costs of the uninsured, underinsured and cut-rate (managed care) insured to traditional fee-for-service patients and their employers. For the same operation, Medicare, squeezed by Congress's cutbacks, pays the same hospital just $5,700; other insurance plans, including managed care, pay $5,000 to $10,000. . . .

Frederick Willman, My Solid Gold Hernia, N.Y. Times, Nov. 26, 1994.

Studies indicate that at least 25 percent of the money we spend on health care is wasted.[2] . . . Hospitals operate at an average of two-thirds of their capacity, with many at less than 50 percent. We have up to 400,000 excess hospital beds, at an unnecessary cost of up to $12 billion. We also suffer from excess technology. There are 10,000 mammography machines in operation, four times the number actually needed. . . . Millions of unnecessary procedures and tests are performed each year. Almost half the coronary bypasses, the majority of cesarean sections, and a significant proportion of many other procedures, such as pacemaker implants and carotid endarterectomies, are unnecessary or of questionable value. A former editor of the Journal of the American Medical Association is convinced that more than half of the forty million medical tests performed each day "do not really contribute to a patient's diagnosis or therapy." Doctors order many procedures and tests to protect themselves from potential medical malpractice liability. Some procedures are performed because doctors simply do not know the precise circumstances under which many procedures work. . . .

Joseph A. Califano, Rationing Health Care: The Unnecessary Solution, 140 U. Pa. L. Rev. 1525 (1992).

[T]hings have been rigged to dupe ordinary people into consistently voting against their true self-interest, thereby benefitting both industry interests and the upper middle class. . . . The consequence of the shell game in which costs are moved wherever employees/consumers/voters are not looking is that medical practice and health care plans are pervasively overregulated in the United States—that is, subject to legal prescriptions that make sense only because price tags have been generally removed. Several whole percentage points of the nation's GDP are thus diverted wastefully to health care from other uses.

Clark Havighurst, How the Health Care Revolution Fell Short, 65(4) Law & Contemp. Prob. 55, 79, 83 (Autumn 2002).

---

[2] See Robert H. Brook, Practice Guidelines and Practicing Medicine, 262 JAMA 3027, 3028 (1989).

Awe-inspiring medical technology has combined with egalitarian rhetoric to create the impression that contemporary medicine is highly effective. Undoubtedly, during the last generation, a limited number of specific procedures have become extremely useful. But where they are not monopolized by professionals as tools of their trade, those which are applicable to widespread diseases are usually very inexpensive and require a minimum of personal skills, materials, and custodial services from hospitals. In contrast, most of today's skyrocketing medical expenditures are destined for the kind of diagnosis and treatment whose effectiveness at best is doubtful.

Ivan Illych, Medical Nemesis 15 (1977).

In May of 2002, a panel of experts . . . released a report documenting . . . [that] the long-term uninsured face a twenty-five percent greater likelihood of premature death than do insured Americans. Institute of Medicine, Care Without Coverage (National Academy Press, Washington, D.C., 2002). . . . In sum, an estimated 18,000 Americans, six times the number killed in the attacks of September 11, die annually because they are uninsured. . . . The uninsured [also] . . . face, day by day, the risk of imminent financial disaster. Medical expenses are one of the leading causes of bankruptcy in the United States. Melissa B. Jacoby, Teresa A. Sullivan, and Elizabeth Warren, Rethinking the Debates Over Health Care Financing: Evidence from the Bankruptcy Courts, 76 New York University Law Rev. 387 (2001). . . . Lack of health insurance is among the greatest threats to financial security that Americans currently face.

Timothy Jost, Disentitlement: Health Care Entitlements and the Threats That They Face (2003).

There is no U.S. health care system. What we call our health care system is, in daily practice, a hodgepodge of historic legacies, philosophical conflicts, and competing economic schemes. Health care in America combines the tortured, politicized complexity of the U.S. tax code with a cacophony of intractable political, cultural, and religious debates about personal rights and responsibilities. Every time policymakers, corporate health benefits purchasers, or entrepreneurs try to fix something in our health care system, they run smack into its central reality: the primary producers and consumers of medical care are uniquely, stubbornly self-serving as they chew through vast sums of other people's money. Doctors and hospitals stumble their way through irresolvable conflicts between personal gain and ethical responsibilities; patients struggle with the acrimony and anguish that accompany life-and-death medical decisions; consumers, paying for the most part with everybody's money but their own, demand that the system serve them with the immediacy and flexibility of other industries; and health insurers are trapped in the middle, trying to keep everybody happy. A group of highly imaginative, energetic people armed with the world's largest Mark-n-Wipe board could not purposefully design a more complex, dysfunctional system if they tried. It is a $1.3 trillion per year fiasco narrated with moral shrillness and played out one competing anecdote after another.

J. D. Kleinke, Oxymorons: The Myth of a U.S. Health Care System 1 (2001).
   2. *More Facts and Figures.* One way to put health care spending in context is to compare it with total spending on other common consumables, as follows

(in billions, 1998): medical care = $1,032; food and tobacco = $907; housing = $856; household operation = $647; transportation = $647; recreation = $495. The following graph provides additional detail about historical spending levels for the health care sector.

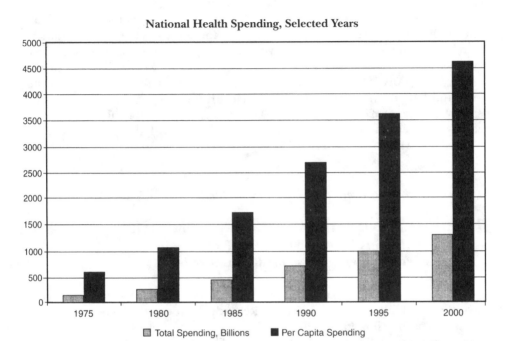

National Health Spending, Selected Years

For more readings that describe the evolution of the health care financing and delivery system and the various public policy problems it currently faces, see the series of articles in the New England Journal of Medicine starting with John K. Iglehart, The American Health Care System: Expenditures, 340 New Eng. J. Med. 70 (1999); Henry J. Aaron, Serious and Unstable Condition: Financing America's Health Care (1991); Paul J. Feldstein, Health Policy Issues: An Economic Perspective on Health Reform (1994); William Kissick, Medicine's Dilemmas: Infinite Needs versus Finite Resources (1994); Vincente Navarro, Dangerous to Your Health: Capitalism in Health Care (1993). A fascinating account of the early history of health insurance is Herman Somers & Anne Somers, Private Health Insurance, 46 Cal. L. Rev. 376, 508 (1958). For a comprehensive text on the politics of health policy, see Carol S. Weissert & Wm. G. Weissert, Governing Health: The Politics of Health Policy (1996).

There is seemingly an endless appetite for facts and figures about the U.S. health care delivery system. Those who wish more, or more recent, numbers can find them in the annual editions of the American Hospital Association's *Hospital Statistics,* in the annual reports of the Medicare Payment Advisory Commission (MedPac), in periodic issues of *Health Affairs* and on the Web pages for the U.S.

Census Bureau and the Centers for Medicare and Medicaid Services (CMS), which are linked to the Web page for this book, www.health-law.org.

3. *International Comparisons.* According to one analysis, the poor U.S. performance on aggregate health statistics is not due to major differences in health habits or lifestyles, since the United States ranks in the middle or toward the top in fat, alcohol, and cigarette consumption, and its health rankings remain low even when comparing only the white population and when excluding automobile deaths. Instead, this author argues that the lower U.S. rankings are due in large part to the relatively inadequate system of primary care physicians and the overuse of high-risk procedures. Barbara Starfield, Is U.S. Health Really the Best in the World?, 284 JAMA 483 (2000). Considering a broad range of indicators of health status and health care access, the World Health Organization ranked the U.S. health care system 37th in the world. For an insightful historical overview and analysis of international health comparisons, see Edward P. Richards, Past as Prolog, 66 UMKC L. Rev. 735 (1998).

3. Changes in Financing and Delivery Systems

■ MEDICARE AND THE AMERICAN HEALTH CARE SYSTEM: 1996 REPORT TO CONGRESS
Prospective Payment Assessment Commission

National health care expenditures . . . increased at more than twice the economywide rate of inflation since 1975. . . . Recently, however, the increase in health care spending has slowed. [From 1994-1999, spending per capita increased 3.5 percent each year adjusted for inflation.] . . . The recent changes in health care expenditure trends are due partly to pressure exerted by private payers. Employers that purchase coverage for employees and their dependents increasingly are demanding health insurance products that control their outlays yet preserve quality. This pressure has resulted in a shift toward managed care plans, which often have benefit packages that are similar to or more generous than traditional indemnity insurance, but at lower prices. Like indemnity offerings, managed care plans receive a premium for assuming the financial risk of providing a defined set of benefits for each person. Unlike traditional indemnity insurers, though, these plans attempt to constrain expenditures by playing an active role in the delivery of services. . . .

The most common managed care models are health maintenance organizations (HMOs), preferred provider organizations (PPOs), and point-of-service (POS) plans. In a traditional HMO plan, subscribers must receive their care from a limited group of providers. PPO and POS subscribers may not be subject to the same level of plan oversight as in HMOs: Generally they may go to any provider, but their out-of-pocket payments are lower if they choose participating providers that give the insurer discounted rates.

The number of people enrolled in managed care plans represents a significant share of the insured population. In 1995, 69 percent of employees in firms with 200 or more workers were in either an HMO (29 percent) or a PPO and POS plan (40 percent). . . .

Managed care plans use a variety of techniques to control their costs. First, they actively seek providers with lower-cost practice patterns and offer them a defined patient base in exchange for favorable payment rates. By limiting the number of providers or by creating strong financial incentives to choose certain ones, managed care plans influence which providers subscribers will use. Through this selective contracting, managed care plans can substantially affect providers' revenues. Plans' bargaining positions are strongest in areas with excess provider capacity. Providers that choose not to participate or that are not selected by the managed care plan may experience a decline in their patient volume.

In addition, managed care plans often use discounted fee-for-service rates to control their costs. They also use per case, per day, or per person payments to shift some of the financial risk of treating patients to providers. Per case or per day payments are generally made to hospitals, whereas per person payments are more often made to physicians, predominately primary care practitioners. These payment methods reward providers for delivering care efficiently, discouraging unnecessary service use.

A per person, or capitation, payment system is the most comprehensive way to shift financial risk to providers. Under capitation, providers receive a prepaid sum to furnish a defined set of services to a plan's enrollees. This creates a monetary incentive for physicians to limit patients' use of services (or encourage preventive services) because the physician receives the same payment regardless of the volume or intensity of care, or even if no care is provided at all. Many managed care plans also require primary care physicians to act as "gatekeepers" to specialty care or hospital services. Under these arrangements, the primary care physician must preauthorize any services a patient receives. While these physicians usually do not bear the full financial risk for the additional services, delegating the gatekeeping function enables managed care plans to use financial incentives to limit referrals. . . .

Hospitals are seeking alternative revenue streams by broadening the scope of services they offer and competing for patients with other types of providers. In 1985, about half the hospitals in the United States reported having an organized outpatient department, and outpatient services accounted for only 16.1 percent of all hospital revenue. By 1995, almost all hospitals had this capacity, and outpatient services represented 28.8 percent of total hospital revenue.

Similarly, a growing number of hospitals are venturing into the post-acute care market, where payments are still dominated by fee-for-service methods. Hospitals are developing skilled nursing facilities (SNFs) or are using acute care beds as swing beds to provide skilled nursing services. In addition, they are establishing their own rehabilitation units and home health agencies. . . .

Along with controlling their costs and seeking alternative revenue sources, hospitals are attempting to broaden (or maintain) their market share by securing a patient base through arrangements with other providers or managed care plans. Such arrangements have the potential to make overall service delivery more efficient and provide patients with a continuum of care. In 1994, for instance, 21 percent of community hospitals participated in health networks—groups of hospitals, physicians, other providers, insurers, or community agencies that coordinate and deliver a broad spectrum of services. Anecdotal evidence suggests that most hospitals have some type of arrangement, such as joint ventures or informal alliances, with other providers. Entering into arrangements with physicians is an increasingly popular strategy for hospitals. Such relationships can bolster a hospital's ability to secure managed care contracts. . . .

The long-term effects of the changing environment on hospitals are still unclear. . . . Hospitals traditionally have been viewed as the hub of the health care system and often have the capital reserves necessary to finance collaborations with other providers. Those that aggressively pursue such arrangements not only can improve their chances of being the hospital of choice for inpatient services, but also can exert more influence over medical practice decisions. In areas where managed care systems exert more control, however, hospitals may be viewed as cost centers with little input into delivery decisions.

PHYSICIANS

Historically, physicians determined not only which services would be provided, but where those services would be delivered. These decisions generally were made with little accountability for costs. Managed care is changing this. . . . One indication of the level of financial pressure physicians are facing is the trend in physician income. The annual growth in median net medical practice income fell from 8 percent in 1992 to 4 percent in 1993. In 1994, income dropped by 3.8 percent, the first decrease since the beginning of data collection in 1968.

Some physicians are responding to the intensified pressures by selling their practices to hospitals or managed care organizations, and becoming employees of those entities. In 1990, nearly 70 percent of physicians reported they were self-employed. By 1995, this share had dropped to 55 percent. . . .

Because physicians generate the demand for hospital services, they have leverage to assume a leadership role in arrangements with other providers. As health care funds become more and more limited, physicians—especially those who deliver primary care services—have an opportunity to play a larger part in deciding how those dollars will be distributed. . . .

■ THE HEALTH CARE REVOLUTION: REMAKING MEDICINE IN CALIFORNIA*
Barbara Marsh
L.A. Times, Aug. 31, 1995

To find out where the nation's health care system may be headed, ask anybody in San Diego. San Diegans know more than most Americans about managed care, which controls costs by limiting consumer choice. About two-thirds of insured San Diego residents were enrolled in health maintenance organizations last year—one of the highest levels in the country. "Every other major city and county in the country will be facing within five years the situation we are facing today," predicts Dr. Robert Ross, the county's health director. . . .

The system apparently pleases the healthy majority of consumers with access to doctors and hospitals at affordable prices. But those with unusual, chronic or serious illnesses often fail to benefit. Many San Diegans can't switch health plans because their employers offer only one. And consumers find it extremely difficult to fight a system that gives doctors financial incentives to minimize treatment. . . .

Surveys suggest that San Diegans generally are satisfied with their health care. . . . San Diegans were especially pleased with the quality of their care and the minimal paperwork involved. Eighty-five percent said they would recommend their doctor to a friend. . . .

Of course, managed care in San Diego—like elsewhere—isn't the result of a consumer revolt. It arose because employers threw up their hands at the rising costs of employee health care. In the late 1970s, an unusually active group of large employers—including defense and aerospace contractors, retailers, banks and local schools—got together to brainstorm ways to rein in double-digit increases in health benefits. The group even launched its own network of hospitals and physicians offering services at rates below traditional insurance plans. So employers couldn't have been more receptive when HMOs rushed into the market in the early 1980s. . . .

And many local hospitals, clinics, physicians and other providers have merged to form or align themselves with four vast systems that deliver managed care: HealthCare System, Scripps Health Corp., UCSD Healthcare and Kaiser. Experts predict more consolidation. . . .

Here as elsewhere, managed care has created an excess of specialist physicians. Many are fleeing San Diego for places still unpenetrated by HMOs. One day late in June, with a moving van parked outside his office, Dr. Steven Kotner fought back tears as he told how HMOs had lured away his patients with cheap insurance prices. "The majority would have stayed with me if they could," he says. His wife Andy, who managed his practice, defiantly lifts her chin to add, "They want us in Tennessee!"

Meanwhile, primary physicians, the workhorses of managed care, shoulder the patient burden. Dr. Laura Nathanson, a family practitioner in Encinitas, says it's tough to keep track of the terms of her patients' 18 different health plans. Her practice employs two staffers to keep up with the plans' ever-changing lists of approved providers, so patients won't get charged for services that aren't covered. When she's on call at night, Nathanson keeps three separate lists of approved test centers, hospitals and emergency rooms so she can direct patients to the right place. "I routinely tell patients, 'Don't go anywhere—even to Nordstrom's—unless you've had your visit authorized,' " she jokes. . . .

Consumer advocates say people here generally understand little about what they're buying when they join an HMO. Jeanne Ertle, executive director of San Diego Neighbor to Neighbor, a local activist group, says consumers don't carefully compare benefits, co-payments, or deductibles. "Ultimately, it's the bottom line," says Ertle. "Which one can they afford?" . . . So HMOs and managed care get mixed reviews from today's San Diegans. As the nation continues to wrestle with health care reform, the ambiguities will only deepen.

Managed care, for instance, has yet to tackle the problem of San Diego's growing population of uninsured residents. . . . Five years ago, Celia Martinez, who cares for a paralyzed invalid, says she applied for insurance through Kaiser's plan for individuals. The 63-year-old woman, who stands 5 foot 4 and weighs 200 pounds, says Kaiser refused to allow her to join because she weighs too much. Earlier this summer, Martinez broke her arm, couldn't work for six weeks—and found herself having to arrange a payment plan for the care she received through UCSD Medical Center. "When it comes to California, they don't help you," she says. "You don't get no help. Everything is pay, pay, pay." . . .

■ TRANSCRIPT OF INTERVIEW
WITH JAIME ROBINSON, Ph.D.*
Lehman Brothers Industry Expert Conference
Call Series
May 17, 2002

As we go into the new decade, the insurance industry is reevaluating whether it wants to be America's method of health care cost control. It's found that this is a very difficult and very unappreciated job. It appears to the public that there is a tradeoff between corporate profits and individual health care, which is a very, very bad image for the industry. The insurers now want to have a completely different image, which is helping the consumer make health care choices. . . .

I think the battle is over and the providers won. The health plans don't really want to get in there and second-guess doctor decision-making. That just proved to be a turf where the providers were very strong, and had the support of the patients and the regulators. . . . There is a lot of lousy medicine being practiced out there that the insurance companies could detect, and could clean up, but they could never convince anybody that they're doing it for the right reasons rather than simply for their own profits.

They've essentially abandoned that role. Increasingly they want to see themselves as a financial services company, like a Fidelity, [which manages investment funds for retirement accounts.] . . . Fidelity offer[s] a stock fund and a bond fund and a mixed fund and employees can allocate their savings across these however they want [with the help of] some decision support tools. . . . The health plans want to do that on the health plan side. "We have our PPO product and our HMO product and our Medical Savings Account product and we're not going to try to force people to pick one or the other. We're going to give them choices. We're going to give them information about the different products, about their prices, about access and about quality. We're going to give them Internet based decision support and tools, and we're going to let them choose. After that, what happens is between the patient and their doctor and their hospital. We, the insurance company, are not going to be responsible for that." . . .

One of the reasons that the insurance industry wants to get out of managed care and go back to being like the financial services industry is that it wants to stop

---

* Prof. Robinson is a health economist at the University of California at Berkeley. Reprinted with the permission of Prof. Robinson and Lehman Brothers.

being continually compared to the tobacco industry. It doesn't want to be the second most hated industry in America. The industry needs to re-brand itself as a consumer friendly decision support and information industry rather than something that's trying to save money for corporations.

Notes: Managed Care vs. Consumer-Directed Care

1. *Managed Care Is Here to Stay*. Despite fierce resistance by many doctors and some patients, managed care is here to stay, and, indeed, has become the dominant form of insurance. However, enrollment has shifted rather dramatically in recent years from tightly managed HMO plans to PPO and POS plans that give patients more options. Regardless of the form managed care takes, it raises a host of legal, ethical, and regulatory issues that are explored throughout this book. For now, consider these broad inquiries: Are you concerned that insurers are interfering with medical judgment by deciding what treatments to pay for? Would you be more comfortable with a regime that let physicians and patients decide for themselves, but rewarded physicians for saving money or punished them for being excessive? Or, is the answer to make patients pay much more out of pocket so that they regulate their own spending decisions?

2. *Consumer-Directed Care*. For a fuller account of Prof. Robinson's views, see The End of Managed Care, 285 JAMA 2622 (2001), where he observes:

> [The following] problems will plague a consumer-driven health care system. First, despite the widespread dissemination of information, . . . even the most sophisticated and Internet-enabled consumer . . . will face significant obstacles in understanding the quality and even the true price of health insurance and health care services. . . . [C]onsumers vary enormously in their financial, cognitive, and cultural preparedness to navigate the complex health care system. The new paradigm fits most comfortably the educated, assertive, and prosperous and least comfortably the impoverished, meek, and poorly educated. . . . Finally, the emerging era will make transparent and render difficult the redistribution of income from rich to poor that otherwise results from the collective purchasing and administration of health insurance.

The consumer-driven movement is occurring in several different ways. One is simply to *increase co-payments and deductibles* significantly, even for HMOs, which traditionally have imposed only minimal cost-sharing obligations on patients. The second is for employers to contribute only a fixed amount toward the cost of health insurance ("*defined contribution*") and let employees shop for whatever coverage they want, rather than pay for all or most of the cost of a group policy that the employer selects. A complementary approach is for the government to subsidize insurance through a *tax credit* that operates like a voucher. Third, insurers are adopting an approach to provider contracting known as "*tiered networks*":

> Health plans, employers and hospitals are returning to notions of preferred providers and health plans. . . . The basic notion involves dividing hospitals and groups of physicians so that even though all of them may be listed in that thick provider directory, not all are created equal. For example, a hospital may say that

10 of 12 hospitals in an area are on a preferred list. If an enrollee is admitted to one of those hospitals no co-payment or deductible is required. But if the same enrollee goes to one of the two local hospitals that are not on the preferred list ("affiliated hospitals"), they are required to pay a deductible or co-payment of anywhere from $100 to $400 per day. These arrangements are referred to as "tiering" of providers. . . . Under certain systems, [providers] may set their own price and decide for themselves whether they want to be in the low, medium or high tier. . . .

The move to tiering is partly a response to a change in the economic balance of power between health plans and providers. . . . In the early days of managed care, health plans did not contract with all hospitals and clinics. Instead, they offered a limited panel of providers the promise of more patients in exchange for discounted prices. Soon the sales people took over and decided that very broad provider networks were needed in order to match the competition, resulting in the extensive network overlap that now exists. . . . Many hospitals [then] used their newly found leverage to exit from [managed care] contracts. . . . By establishing tiers of providers, some health plans have returned to the old notion of identifying certain hospitals as preferred. At this point, that preference is based on pricing, although health plans say that they want to reach a point where tiering of hospitals and clinics would be based on measures of quality.

Allan Baumgarten, Tiering Approaches for Health Plans: Incentives and Information for Consumers (June 17, 2002). Other examples of increased consumerism are prescription drug manufacturers' much more aggressively advertising directly to consumers rather than only to physicians, and the wealth of medical and health insurance information now available on the Internet.

For a good overview of managed care generally, see Peter Kongstvedt, Managed Care: What It Is and How It Works (2d ed. 2002). For additional discussion of broad changes in the health care system, see Understanding Health System Change: Local Markets, National Trends (Paul B. Ginsburg & Cara S. Lesser eds., 2001).

3. *The Onslaught of Acronyms*. Regrettably, the health care field is overrun with acronyms. Since 1970 or so, no new institution or phenomenon seemingly can exist in medicine without being known primarily by its three-to-five-letter abbreviation. Most of the specialized organizational terms and acronyms you will encounter in these readings are collected and defined in the glossary at page 569 for convenient reference throughout the semester.

D. MORAL, ECONOMIC, AND POLITICAL THEMES

The remainder of this chapter addresses various analytical theories that give greater depth to our understanding of health care law and public policy. Most of these analytical frameworks spring from some branch of moral and political theory that addresses fundamental questions of social justice, such as how best to distribute scarce medical resources, and whose decision over medical treatment should govern when there is conflict. Necessarily, this must be a grab bag of somewhat disconnected lines of thought drawn from many different intellectual disciplines— primarily philosophy, economics, and political science. This is due to what Einer

Elhauge below calls the "paradigm pathology" of health care law: Although this field may have a core set of concerns, it lacks a dominant analytical mode. In classic fields of law such as contracts or torts, most people seem at least to be asking the same sorts of questions, even if they don't arrive at the same answers. Health care law has so many interdisciplinary, intellectual currents that courts and scholars sound at times like the mythical builders of the Tower of Babel. Some order can be brought to this melange of ideologies by categorizing different and competing "paradigms" of thought. As Clark Havighurst explains in the second reading in this section, the dominant paradigm in past decades has been professionalism, and this is the one to which all the contenders respond. Rather than attempt any neat packaging of the contenders, for they are still very untidy, try to identify which currents of thought are consistent with and opposed to the professionalism paradigm, and in what ways. Then, try to articulate how different paradigms would answer the fundamental questions of social justice mentioned above (who gets which resources, and who decides).

1. Competing Paradigms

■ ALLOCATING HEALTH CARE MORALLY*
Einer Elhauge**
82 Cal. L. Rev. 1449 (1994)

Health law policy suffers from an identifiable pathology. . . . [I]t employs four different paradigms for how decisions to allocate resources should be made: the market paradigm, the professional paradigm, the moral paradigm, and the political paradigm. . . . [R]ather than coordinate these decisionmaking paradigms, health law policy employs them inconsistently, such that the combination operates at cross-purposes.

This inconsistency results in part because, intellectually, health care law borrows haphazardly from other fields of law, each of which has its own internally coherent conceptual logic, but which in combination results in an incoherent legal framework and perverse incentive structures. In other words, health care law has not—at least not yet—established itself to be a field of law with its own coherent conceptual logic, as opposed to a collection of issues and cases from other legal fields connected only by the happenstance that they all involve patients and health care providers.

In other part, the pathology results because the various scholarly disciplines focus excessively on their favorite paradigms. Scholars operating in the disciplines of economics, medicine, political science, and philosophy each tend to assume that their discipline offers a privileged perspective. This leads them either to press their favored paradigm too far or to conceptualize policy issues solely in terms of what their paradigm can and cannot solve.

Instead, health law policy issues should be conceived in terms of comparative paradigm analysis. Such analysis focuses on the strengths and weaknesses of the various decisionmaking paradigms, determining which is *relatively* better suited to resolving various decisions, and then assigning each paradigm to the roles for which it is best suited. . . .

Luckily, this is a mode of analysis in which legal scholars, as cross-disciplinary generalists, have some plausible claim to comparative scholarly advantage. Unluckily, it is hard and arduous. Nevertheless, it offers the promise that health law scholars will provide insights into health policy that so far have been missed. In a field as intellectually new as modern health law, it should hardly be surprising that this task has only begun.

■ THE PROFESSIONAL PARADIGM OF MEDICAL CARE: OBSTACLE TO DECENTRALIZATION*
Clark C. Havighurst**
30 Jurimetrics J. 415 (1990)

The thesis of this article is that, despite all the organizational and financial changes that occurred in the health care sector in the 1980s, we still cannot fight the battle for efficiency effectively because we are saddled as a society with a particular paradigmatic conception of the medical care enterprise. The source of this paradigm is a deep-seated belief, long fostered by the medical profession, that medical care is not a commodity, that its characteristics are scientifically determined, and that decisions concerning it must be entrusted exclusively to professionals. That this paradigm is ideologically attractive and contains some significant kernels of truth simply complicates the problem of adapting it to accord with current economic realities.

The professional paradigm of the medical enterprise is a venerable one, stemming from the days early in this century when the medical profession rose to what sociologist Paul Starr has called a position of "cultural authority, economic power, and political influence."[8] Although its tenets are nowhere officially set down, some of them can be deduced from the profession's performance during the era when it exercised rather complete hegemony over health care and its financing. Judging from that experience, the profession's ideology has included the following themes:

- medical care should be evaluated only on the basis of safety and efficacy;
- cost considerations should not enter into medical decisionmaking because counting costs implies both a willingness to trade off a patient's welfare against other societal needs and a tolerance for differences based on ability to pay;
- decisions on the appropriate utilization of medical services should be based exclusively on scientific evidence and expert opinion;

** Professor of Law, Duke University.
[8] P. Starr, The Social Transformation of American Medicine 5 (1982).

- although patient preferences should be honored under the principle of informed consent, there is no similar urgency about giving people opportunities to express their preferences qua consumers, with cost differences in view; and
- professional norms alone should set the limits of a physician's judgment.

Under these general principles, the role of payers was long limited to ensuring that professional norms were followed, so that only care that was virtually useless or positively harmful was excluded. . . .

The professional paradigm derives much of its force from the egalitarian ideal in medicine—the belief that every citizen is entitled to medical care of the same quality and that "two-tier" medicine is unthinkable. Even though society has not seen fit to adopt an egalitarian policy by accepting either the heavy tax burden or the stringent rationing necessary to achieve it, the egalitarian ideal colors much thinking about medical care. Indeed, even in the absence of any actual legal or contractual entitlement, a powerful entitlement mentality must be confronted by anyone seeking to economize in the provision of health services. The professional paradigm generally supports this view of things, while the profession as a whole resists most of the measures that would be necessary to create an affordable, truly egalitarian system. There is here a marriage of convenience—between physicians' desires to resist infringements on their clinical freedom and a particularly extreme view of the requirements of social justice.

The scientific character of medicine has also provided vital support for the professional paradigm. Indeed, the success of the medical profession in establishing its scientific character in the early part of the century—in the Flexner Report,[9] for example—laid the groundwork for its claim of exemption from market forces and for its autonomy as a profession. Once medical care was viewed as the application of science to human problems rather than as a commercial service to be bought and sold in market transactions, the profession was able to resist most of the pressures that naturally arose and to head off, by effective lobbying or collective action, market developments that might have threatened its hegemony. . . .

Residues of the professional paradigm can be found in many places but are particularly significant in the legal system. Not only does the law tend to defer to the medical profession's presumed scientific authority on many points, but it is often administered with an egalitarian mentality that tends to define issues in terms of abstract rights. Indeed, the law frequently goes to great lengths to avoid appearing to concede that some persons might ever have a legal or even a contractual right to better medical care than someone else. This refusal to recognize the reality that some consumers might choose, or wish to choose, to purchase more or better health care than others—or have a lesser entitlement because of inability or unwillingness to pay—greatly complicates efforts to economize in the private sector. It also raises, perhaps inappropriately, the cost to government of providing for those who cannot support themselves. As long as the legal system does not acknowledge inequality or recognize efforts to escape the costly standards implicit in the professional/scientific/egalitarian paradigm, neither self-supporting

---

[9] A. Flexner, Medical Education in the United States and Canada (Carnegie Foundation for the Advancement of Technology, Bull. No. 4, 1910).

consumers nor taxpayers are in a good position to economize on health care by refusing to buy too much of a good thing.

2. Postmodern Critical Theory

■ SLAVERY, SEGREGATION AND RACISM: TRUSTING THE HEALTH CARE SYSTEM AIN'T ALWAYS EASY! AN AFRICAN AMERICAN PERSPECTIVE ON BIOETHICS*
Vernellia R. Randall
15 St. Louis U. Pub. L. Rev. 191 (1996)

. . . Just like the rest of America, the African American community is facing a number of bioethical issues including: abortion, disparate health status, racial barriers to access to health care, racial disparities in medical treatment, the Human Genome Project and genetic testing, organ transplantation, AIDS, physician assisted suicide and right to die, reproductive technology, and violence. Unlike the dominant American group, African Americans view these issues through an additional screen of fear and distrust. It is this fear and distrust that causes us to believe that the principles of bioethics: autonomy, beneficence, nonmaleficence, and justice, won't protect our community from mistreatment and abuse. . . .

African Americans have been experimented on without consent, thus violating the principle of autonomy. We have been treated and experimented on in ways which have caused us harm, thus violating the principles of nonmaleficence and beneficence. We have been given different treatment and provided different access to health care, thus violating the principle of justice. At best, the judgment in applying the articulated principles has been exercised fairly consistently in a manner which disadvantages and harms African Americans. . . .

Eurocentric bioethics focuses on the individual, ignoring the interests of others who are intimately affected, such as the family and the community. This focus on the individual is based on a philosophy that regards the self, and only the self, as the end per se. However, the African American perspective views this reliance on ethical egoism to be misplaced. African Americans believe that "it takes a whole village" to raise a child, and thus, at a minimum, African Americans view ethical egoism to be contradictory to the raising of healthy children. Furthermore, even as adults, none of us function as islands; we all must rely on others for, at a minimum, reaffirmation of our self-assessment.

Second, Eurocentric bioethics embraces Kantian ethics, which are antithetical to Afrocentric bioethics. Kantian ethics require universal norms and an impartial perspective, which is inattentive to relationships and community. Kantianism privileges abstract reasoning over virtue, character, and moral emotions. Kantian

---

* This article is reprinted with permission. Copyright © 1996, St. Louis University.
** Vernellia Randall is a Professor of Law at the University of Dayton School of Law. In addition to her legal training, Professor Randall has her B.S.N. and M.S.N. and worked for over a decade as a nurse.

ethics maintain that the only way we can morally constitute ourselves is by free and rational choice. It is the exclusivity of that claim that is troubling. African Americans believe that we morally constitute ourselves not only through free and rational choice but also through our parents and our community.

Third, Eurocentric bioethics tends to view the patient or research subject generically, without attention to race, gender, or insurance status. As a result, the development of laws and bioethical principles, discourse, and practices are informed by the values and beliefs of one group: white, middle-class, males.

Eurocentric bioethical principles such as autonomy, beneficence, and informed consent do not have the same force when viewed through the African American bioethical perspective of distrust. These principles leave considerable room for individual judgment by health care practitioners. The flaw of a principle-based paradigm is that very judgment. The application of the principles will be subject to other values held by the society. In a racist society (such as ours), the judgment is often exercised in a racist manner.

Thus, Eurocentric bioethics has adopted rules and has applied them with little, if any, concern for how race or other characteristics affect the working of the rules. In fact, numerous studies have documented a disparity between traditional bioethical practice and the needs of minority populations. For instance, African Americans notably differ from European Americans, both in their unwillingness to complete advance directives and in the desires expressed regarding life-sustaining treatment. Substantially more African Americans and Hispanics "wanted their doctors to keep them alive regardless of how ill they were, while more . . . whites agreed to stop life-prolonging treatment under some circumstances. . . ."

The implication for the African American community is the failure of bioethical problem-solving to take into consideration those factors important to solving problems in the African American community. Most of the problem-solving has been at odds with the affirmation of the African American individual and the African American community. In fact, for the most part, mainstream bioethicists have consistently neglected to comment on the social ills or injustices such as "the [African Americans'] enslavement, the injustices and discrimination they have suffered, the stereotyping of their language and culture, and their disadvantaged economic, political, educational, and health status." As a result of this lack of affirmation, or, this oppression, we are in danger of losing our own perspectives—our own gifts. . . .

African Americans face the health care system with anxiety, fear, and disaffection. Such anxiety, fear, and distrust will not be alleviated until bioethics constructs a practical, ethical approach to the anxiety and fear which would lead to community empowerment. Such a practical approach would require behaviors such as: reinstatement of community hospitals; assuring urban perinatal health care; encouraging traditional lay-midwifery; and reestablishing the extended family. However, such a practical approach must be based on not only on the traditional Eurocentric principles but also on:

- recognizing the needs of the community and not just the individual self;
- formulating bioethical and legal solutions involving both the family and the community;

- aggressively training health care providers and institutions about the African American perspective, thus making the barrier of distrust easier to overcome;
- eliminating the disparities in health status;
- aggressively reducing the existing disparities in health care delivery in the African American community.

■ THE COLONIZATION OF THE WOMB
Nancy Ehrenreich*
43 Duke L.J. 492 (1993)

Science has been called the religion of modern times, and probably only a fool would attempt to convince a reader, in the course of a law review article no less, that medicine, the form of science most widely used by the consuming public, is not "scientific." Yet that is what I must do here, for central to my argument is the notion that medicine is a hegemonic discourse—that it is laden with value choices and beliefs that masquerade as truth, nature, and biological "fact." My argument will be limited, however, to that part of medicine that deals with women and their reproductive processes, and I will not attempt to prove my point—a rather misguided effort anyway in an argument premised on profound skepticism about the notion of empirical proof itself—so much as to present a substantial amount of material suggestive of it. . . .

The scientific world view is accepted by scientists and laypeople alike. It is a belief system that denies its own reality as a world view, believing instead that it is a series of truths about knowing and controlling the unpredictable world we live in. . . . Through the use of the scientific method, it is thought, science can continually test and perfect the knowledge it acquires, moving ever closer to a "true" understanding of the world and the individuals who occupy it. . . . In the area of medicine, this theme of controlling nature is particularly evident. Technological advances have totally transformed what we mean by life and death, allowing tiny babies to survive and prosper after premature births and the elderly or those with permanent brain damage to exist (if not exactly "live") far beyond anything previously thought possible. Technology is extolled for enabling physicians to overcome "imperfections" in a woman's reproductive organs by removing eggs from ovaries, fertilizing them in petri dishes, and then returning them to the uterus. Physicians correct bad eyesight, replace torn ligaments, set broken bones, refashion hearts. Central to our notion of medicine is its role in controlling and transforming our bodies.

Upon examination, it can be seen that this view strongly associates science with many of the same terms that are traditionally associated with men; whereas, the opposite of science (anything that is unscientific) is associated with opposed and feminized terms. Science is thought to be an objective, neutral, rational, fact-based method of controlling nature, whereas non-"scientific" forms of knowledge are usually stigmatized as superstition and ignorance and thought to be based on

---

* Nancy Ehrenreich is a professor at the University of Denver College of Law.

subjective, biased, and emotional assessments of reality. Non-science is also clearly associated with women: the phrase "old wives' tale," for example, makes quite explicit the cultural equation between bad health care and women, simultaneously defining women's knowledge as nonscientific and dismissing it as erroneous. Moreover, women are seen not only as the source of dangerous medical advice but also as the sites of dangerous disease and decay. In short, . . . women are often treated as the prototypical embodiment of the natural world that science exists to control.

I can imagine many readers arriving at this point only to say, "So what? Medicine and science are, generally, objective and rational. Of course they are imperfect and will continually improve, but they are nevertheless as close as we can get to a neutral and accurate understanding of the world." Many recent writings, however, have fundamentally challenged that confidence in medical knowledge. . . .

[T]hings are actually much more complicated. I will start from the fundamental assumption, long accepted in the social sciences, that biological science is a product of culture, rather than an entity existing separate and apart from the world it attempts to know. In other words, the very categories through which medical scientists comprehend the world are themselves the product of the culture in which they live. Medicine is a social construct, rather than a set of "truths" about the world. To accept this premise is not to say that medicine is "wrong" or that it never works but that its understanding is partial, its truths contingent.

Applying this insight to the reproductive context, I will contend, therefore, that the field of obstetrics is not a domain in which experts use generally unchallengeable "facts" about human reproduction to facilitate the birthing process, but rather that it is an arena of struggle over the role(s) of women in society and indeed over the meaning of the word *woman*. Before turning to that broader point, however, I must first add one last piece of the picture of how Western dualisms operate in the realm of medicine by discussing how the reproductive process itself is perceived. . . .

As many writers have pointed out, medicine (as practiced in the United States) conceives of female reproductive processes, from menstruation to childbirth to menopause, as pathological, disease-like conditions that need to be controlled to prevent them from harming the women in whose bodies they occur (or, in the case of childbirth, the fetuses those women are carrying). . . . Childbirth itself is also seen as a dangerous, pathological, and unpredictable medical event. The role of the physician during labor is conceptualized, therefore, as imposing control and predictability on this process (and, hence, on the women through whom it is played out). Physicians "manage" the labor, performing various interventions to ensure that it proceeds along the lines of "normal" births, lines that are derived by averaging the wide range of patterns that labor actually follows among different women into a standardized set of "stages" with their own prescribed durations and symptomatology. In addition, successful childbirth has increasingly become equated with only the production of a "perfect" product, a child free of infection or disabilities. . . .

Protecting a fetus often entails imposing certain risks on the woman carrying it; a cesarean section, for example, is at least twice as likely as a vaginal birth to result in the death of the mother. Yet this risk becomes irrelevant if the cultural norm already prescribes that she be willing to sacrifice anything and everything for her children (born or unborn). Given that norm, it is easy for the doctor to either (1) assume that she is a good mother and therefore not consider her preferences very much during labor, on the assumption that she would want to sacrifice for her child, or (2) assume that she is a bad mother and therefore not consider her preferences very much during labor, on the assumption that she has no right to have them respected. . . .

In recent years, however, the medical model of reproduction has come under sustained attack by a burgeoning (at the beginning, primarily white) women's health movement. . . . [T]here are essentially three ways in which such sets of opposing terms are usually criticized. First, one can argue that the dualisms unfairly stereotype members of the low status group. That is, they are inaccurate: most white women are not passive, most African-Americans are not lazy, and so on. Those presenting a parallel challenge to the medical model claim that it unfairly stigmatizes alternative birthing approaches as less scientific or successful than traditional medicine. Second, one can argue that the dualisms elevate traits that are actually unenviable and socially destructive and disparage traits that are good and valuable. Thus, for example, relational feminists have contended that pure logic is not necessarily superior to intuitive understanding and that striving for self-sufficiency may be less laudable than recognizing human interdependence, and race theorists have suggested that contextual facts and narrative are as powerful conceptual tools as abstract analytics. In the reproductive context, this criticism takes the form of an effort to elevate alternative birthing strategies, arguing that they are actually better—both in terms of quality of care and in terms of human fulfillment—than the traditional approach.

The third critique of Western dualisms, and the one that is most important to my argument, alleges that the distinctions the dualisms draw are themselves incoherent. That is, in any particular instance, it will not be readily apparent whether an individual's reaction to her circumstances is rational or emotional, active or passive. What seems absolutely illogical to one person, for example, might indeed seem perfectly rational to another. Because of this indeterminacy of meaning, the act of labeling conduct as one or the other is facilitated by unstated (and perhaps unconscious) assumptions that reflect and reinforce power disparities in society. In other words, the dualisms do not represent or identify "real" differences in the world but rather serve as vehicles for the deployment of social power.

I mean two things by this assertion. First, the power to decide what is rational (or whatever) and what is not devolves upon those with power in the society at large. Because their visions of the world are those most often conveyed through societal institutions such as law, the media, and schools, it is their interpretations of a particular incident that will seem most "true." Second, that power to name, to interpret the world, legitimates the position of the dominant group to which it belongs as well as that group's oppression of others. The consistent application of the dominant terms of the dualisms to those in power and the devalued terms to a variety of "others" reinforces negative images of those others that then seem to justify their subordination. Relying on these insights, much of the critical feminist and critical race theory scholarship in the last several years has been directed at revealing the ways in which the dominant belief system's interpretation of the world prevents judges from seeing the behavior and concerns of women (of all colors) or people of color (of both sexes) as rational, responsible, and legitimate. . . .

II. LAW AND MEDICINE AS MUTUALLY LEGITIMATING DISCOURSES AND PRACTICES

. . . Legal authorities in general pay great deference to medical expertise. The most obvious example of this deference, of course, is the retention of a custom standard to define medical malpractice. . . . In the area of reproduction, this judicial deference to medical authority is particularly marked. . . . This judicial tendency to subsume women's interest in controlling their reproductive capacities within physicians' right to practice medicine reflects a similar attitude in the society at large. . . .

When considered in light of the sets of associations previously described, law's great deference to medicine is perhaps not surprising. . . . [L]aw is associated with many of the same traits as medicine. Both are thought to be neutral and objective pursuits, devoid of personal bias or subjective self-interest. Both are seen as coldly rational—as based on facts and rules, rather than opinions and values. Moreover, both are seen as controlling people: Whereas medicine controls their physical bodies, law controls the body politic, providing a peaceful means for resolving disputes that otherwise might dissolve into warfare. Put another way, medicine controls physical nature, whereas law avoids a social "state of nature." Finally, both fields are populated by elite white men who enjoy very comfortable incomes and high status. Given these affinities, judicial trust in the medical profession to make dispassionate and value-free decisions in individual cases is not surprising. . . .

Notes: Feminist and Critical Race Theory

1. *Constructive or Confrontational?* Some readers will find this style of analysis disturbing and threatening. Leslie Bender explains, however, that the aim of much critical analytical writing is to enlighten and sensitize:

> [T]here are many feminist analyses and perspectives, of which my arguments are only one. . . . Because many readers are unaware of the extensive writing and theorizing within feminism and from feminist premises about every kind of subject, they think feminist is a label meaning "political struggles for women's rights." Certainly feminist means that but it also means more. Some themes in feminist ethics are challenges to the values and conceptions of human natures and human interactions that dominate our current discourses in law, medicine, and ethics. Some feminist theorizing emphasizes the need to value and focus on care, compassion, responsiveness, responsibility, conversation, and communication, as well as learning to listen closely to others and to pay attention to others' needs, regardless of their differences from our own. I write in that tradition. Feminist ethics also challenges power structures and systemic biases in law and ethics that undervalue or disregard the perspectives and experiences of all women in differing ways and of men of subordinated statuses, whether subordinated by structures of race, class,

sexual identity, some other identity-based classification, or some combination thereof. Feminism seeks to reconstruct our understandings and practices in ways that more closely respond to the needs of those people in their daily lives . . . [and] dying processes.

A Feminist Analysis of Physician-Assisted Dying and Active Euthanasia, 59 Tenn. L. Rev. 519 (1992).

2. *Discrimination in Treatment.* Radical critiques of the medical establishment have considerable empirical as well as philosophical and political support. Researchers have demonstrated disturbing ethnic, gender, and socio-economic disparities in treatment patterns for patients with similar conditions. This discrimination can sometime take the form of the absolute denial of care. More often, treatments are not pursued aggressively for some patients as for others. See Leslie Laurence & Beth Weinhouse, Outrageous Practices: The Alarming Truth About How Medicine Mistreats Women (1994); Institute of Medicine, Unequal Treatment: Confronting Racial and Ethnic Disparities in Health Care (2002); U.S. Commission on Civil Rights, The Health Care Challenge: Acknowledging Disparity, Confronting Discrimination, and Ensuring Equality (Sept. 1999); Rene Bowser, Racial Profiling in Health Care: An Institutional Analysis of Medical Treatment Disparities, 7 Mich. J. Race & L. 80 (2001); Kevin Fiscella et al., Inequality in Quality: Addressing Socioeconomic, Racial, and Ethnic Disparities in Health Care, 283 JAMA 2579 (2000); Barbara Noah, Racial Disparities in the Delivery of Health Care, 35 San Diego L. Rev. 135 (1998); Symposium, 1 Yale J. Health Pol'y L. & Ethics (2001); Symposium, 40(1) Med. Care 1 (Supp. 2002). Sometimes, discrimination is more subtle, and is found in the patterns of communication between provider and patient. See Karen H. Rothenberg, Gender Matters: Implications for Clinical Research and Women's Health Care, 32 Hous. L. Rev. 1201, 1213-1214 (1996) (reporting studies that show male providers tend to interrupt female patients and that female patients report higher rates of being patronized than male patients). For a provocative challenge to this large body of evidence, claiming that it fails to account for legitimate factors that might explain patterns of disparate treatment, such as differing patient preferences, medical conditions, or prognoses, see Sally Satel, "PC" M.D.: How Political Correctness Is Corrupting Medicine (2001).

3. *Discrimination in Research.* The history of medical research reveals a disturbing pattern of discrimination against racial and ethnic minorities, women, and the poor. In this country, the Tuskegee experiments—in which researchers studied the long-term effects of infection with syphilis by withholding treatment from a group of African Americans males—provide a particularly vivid example of unethical conduct. See James H. Jones, Bad Blood (1993). Medical researchers also have discriminated against women. Researchers argued that excluding women was justified by the potential risks their research might present in the event of pregnancy, even if the women used birth control or were beyond child-bearing years. Researchers also argued that women did not make good research subjects because their biological differences might cloud the research findings.

Unfortunately, the routine exclusion of women from research trials meant that women with life-threatening illnesses might be denied access to potentially helpful experimental treatments. It also resulted in flawed research: If one believes the contention that female biology might alter research results, then excluding women from research must produce incomplete results. Finally, the exclusion of pregnant, or potentially pregnant, women from research (1) denies many women access to potentially helpful experimental treatments, (2) values fetal interests over maternal interests, and (3) means that new treatments will not have been proven to be safe for pregnant women or their fetuses. Widespread criticism of these practices has led to some significant congressional reforms, including a presumption that federally funded research would include subjects who were women and members of racial or ethnic minorities. See Rothenberg, supra.

4. *Outsider Jurisprudence*. Feminist critique, critical race theory, and critical legal studies are flourishing in health care law, as they are elsewhere in legal analysis. See, e.g., Symposium, Deconstructing Traditional Paradigms in Bioethics: Race, Gender, Class, and Culture, 15 St. Louis U. Pub. L. Rev. 183 (1996). Leading **critical legal scholars** are David Frankford and Gregg Bloche. Examples of their work include their Measuring Health Care: Political Fate and Technocratic Reform; 19 J. Health Pol. Pol'y & L. 647 (1994) (Frankford); Privatizing Health Care: Economic Magic to Cure Legal Medicine; 66 S. Cal. L. Rev. 1 (1992) (Frankford); The Invention of Health Law, 91 Cal. L. Rev. 247 (2003) (Bloche); Beyond Autonomy: Coercion and Morality in Clinical Relationships, 6 Health Matrix 229 (1996) (Bloche). Professors Vernellia Randall and Dorothy Roberts have been especially prominent scholars in **critical race theory**. See Vernellia Randall, Racist Health Care: Reforming an Unjust Health Care System to Meet the Needs of African-Americans, 3 Health Matrix 127 (1993); Dorothy E. Roberts, Killing the Black Body: Race, Reproduction, and the Meaning of Liberty (1997); Dorothy Roberts, Race and the New Reproduction, 47 Hastings L.J. 935 (1996); Dorothy Roberts, The Genetic Tie, 62 U. Chi. L. Rev. 209 (1995). See also Frank M. McClellan, Is Managed Care Good for What Ails You? Ruminations on Race, Age and Class, 44 Vill. L. Rev. 227 (1999); David B. Smith, Health Care Divided: Race and Healing a Nation (1999); African-American Perspectives on Biomedical Ethics (H. Flack & E. Pellegrino eds., 1992); "It Just Ain't Fair!" The Ethics of Health Care for African Americans (A. Dula & S. Goering eds., 1994). **Feminist critique** is multidisciplinary, but is especially rich with respect to reproductive issues. For a broad introduction, see articles published in Symposium, Feminist Bioethics, 26 J. Med. & Phil. 339 (2001); Symposium, New Perspectives on Women, Health & Law, 3 Texas J. Women and the Law 1-402 (1994). See also Susan M. Wolf, Feminism & Bioethics: Beyond Reproduction (1996); Leslie Bender, Teaching Feminist Perspectives on Health Care Ethics and Law: A Review Essay, 61 U. Cin. L. Rev. 1251 (1993); Feminist Perspectives in Medical Ethics (H. Holmes & L. Purdy eds., 1992); Mary Anne Bobinski & Phyllis Griffin Epps, Women, Poverty, Access to Health Care, and the Perils of Symbolic Reform, 5 J. Gender, Race, & Justice (2002); Lisa Ikemoto, The Fuzzy Logic of Race and Gender in the Mismeasure of Asian Women's Health Needs, 65 U. Cin. L. Rev. 799 (1997); Karen H. Rothenberg, New Perspectives for Teaching and Scholarship: The Role of Gender in Law and Health Care, 54 Md. L. Rev. 473 (1995); Tracey E. Spruce, The Sound of Silence: Women's Voices in Medicine and Law, 7 Colum. J. Gender & L. 239 (1998); Symposium, 9 Duke J. Gender L. & Pol'y 1 (2002).

3. Economics

■ **HEALTH PLAN***
  Alain Enthoven**
  1980

The fundamental strategic choice for public policy on health care costs is competition or regulation . . .

The choice between competition and regulation is a choice about the role of government. In the strategy of competition the government takes a much simpler and less intrusive role than in the regulatory approach. It seeks to set the basic framework of rules and incentives in such a way that the market (that is, the interaction of people making transactions in their own best interests) will produce the desired result. In the regulatory approach applied to health care, the government takes on a much more complex and demanding role, a role in which, in my view, it is bound to fail. In the regulatory approach government would leave today's cost-increasing incentives in place and then try to stop them from having their natural effect by direct detailed controls such as telling doctors how much they can charge for each service. In this approach direct controls are intended to substitute for rational economic incentives. In my view, the regulatory approach is like trying to make water run uphill, whereas in the competitive market approach the government is merely trying to channel the stream in its downhill course.

Procompetitive regulation is likely to be much simpler and more effective than direct controls on prices, capacity, and use of services, which act in opposition to the financial incentives. For in this case the basic incentives are pointing people in about the right direction. The regulators are attempting merely to modify the behavior of the regulated at the margin. . . .

On the other hand, under the regulatory approach, the regulators are attempting to make regulated entities behave in ways that are directly opposed to their financial interests, possibly even threatening their survival. Therefore, the incentive to attempt to bend, fight, or evade the regulations is much stronger. . . .

Regulation often raises costs to consumers. Regulators become responsible for the economic survival of the regulated. If they let a regulated entity fail, they will be blamed for denying society a needed service and for causing a loss of jobs. So they cannot force the regulated to sustain losses or even to live with less than some target rate of return on investment. So cost increases have to be "passed through" to consumers, and price controls become cost reimbursement, with all of its cost-increasing incentives.

Regulators are often "captured" by the regulated. They must get their information about the regulated industry from the regulated. The regulated firms hire high-priced lawyers and lobbyists who exert a constant pressure in their favor. The consumer interest in lower prices or better service is too diffused to allow for an effectively organized counterpressure. The formal procedures of regulation also make it very costly and time-consuming. This is especially true if there are many entities to be regulated, with many special circumstances to be considered, as is the case with physicians and hospitals. . . .

Competition, on the other hand, sets up an inexorable force for cost reduction. If company B can make a product of equal quality to company A's, but for less cost, it can sell it for a lower price and take the business away from company A. If company A cannot match the cost reduction, it will lose profits in the short run and risk being driven out of business in the long run. Survival demands that it cut costs. It has no regulators to appeal to for protection. . . .

Competition rewards innovation and often channels it in socially desirable directions. Fortunes are made on new products and services, so innovations that lead to better services or reduced costs are encouraged. Firms that do not match their competitors' innovations often do not survive.

Market economies are the most effective in improving productivity and raising living standards. There are good reasons for this. People accept efficiency improving changes such as closing unneeded plants or hospitals produced by impersonal market forces in the private sector. The people directly affected may not like them, but there is not much they can do about them. In the long run the whole economy benefits. But when such changes are imposed by government, those who would be harmed resist them, usually successfully, through legal and political action. . . .

In market systems producers and consumers adapt continuously and gradually to changing conditions, even in anticipation of future events. The expectation of higher gasoline prices in the future motivates people to buy cars with good mileage now. In regulatory systems the rules themselves create vested interests which make the rules very difficult to change. These factors make for great rigidity in regulated industries, in contrast to flexible adaptation in markets.

Government often responds to well-focused producer interests; competitive markets respond systematically, if imperfectly, to consumer interests. Voters base their choices on issues of decisive personal importance, on their pocketbooks if they see their livelihoods at stake. People specialize in production and diversify in consumption. To a dairy farmer, a rise in coffee prices is a minor irritant, but an increase in the price of milk (supported by government) is a "make-or-break" issue. People are therefore much more likely to pressure their representatives about the issues that affect their livelihoods than on their interests as consumers, and their companies and unions provide natural organizations for doing so. In competitive markets companies get their revenues from satisfied customers who have alternative choices. So in product and pricing decisions, business must seek to serve the desires of consumers. Thus the choice between a regulated and a competitive market system of health care services is a choice between service that responds mainly to the interests of providers or to those of consumers.

Regulation depends on coercion, on forcing people to behave in ways they consider opposed to their own best interests. The decentralized competitive market, on the other hand, leaves maximum freedom to individual providers and consumers consistent with achievement of society's purposes. As Charles Schultze put it:

Relationships in the market are a form of unanimous-consent arrangement. When dealing with each other in a buy-sell transaction, individuals can act voluntarily on the basis of mutual advantage. . . . Market-like arrangements not only minimize the need for coercion as a means of organizing society; they also reduce the need for compassion, patriotism, brotherly love, and cultural solidarity as motivating forces behind social improvement.

The development of these desirable virtues is more likely to be encouraged if we do not place too heavy a burden on people who practice them.

Moreover, the market encourages the pluralism and diversity that is valued by the American people. The regulatory approach works on the basis of uniform numerical standards. . . . [It thus tends to ignore individual differences in] a patient's needs, preferences, and lifestyle. Consider a woman who likes to ski and ride horseback and who has a partially detached retina in one eye. One ophthalmologist believes in an operation that does a minimum amount of "welding" (photocoagulation) and would minimize her loss of vision. Although that might satisfy the physician's criterion of technical excellence, it does not allow the woman to resume her athletic pursuits safely. Another ophthalmologist might propose to coagulate a complete circle around her retina. In this case the patient would lose some vision, but would have more of a guarantee that the retina will not detach again, and she could ski and ride again.

Patients suffering from severe angina pectoris (chest pain thought to be due to a lack of oxygen supply to the heart) pose another therapeutic dilemma. One doctor may recommend heart surgery; another, treatment with drugs such as nitroglycerine. For most such patients, there is no consensus among physicians today as to which is the best treatment. What is "best" in a particular case will depend on the values and needs of the patient, the skills of the doctor, and the other resources available. . . .

■ FOR-PROFIT ENTERPRISE IN HEALTH CARE*
Bradford H. Gray**
1986

The value questions about health care can be discussed under two broad categories—health care as an economic good and health care as a social good. . . . They are stated as polar extremes, although most observers probably accept the validity of some aspects of both sets. . . . One view emphasizes the attributes that health care shares with other goods and services that are offered and purchased in the marketplace. . . . A contrasting set of views opposes the idea that health care is properly seen as an economic good that is appropriately bought, sold, and disciplined by competitive forces in a marketplace. This view holds that health professionals and institutions should pursue the goals or ideals of applying

**The author is a sociologist who has worked in various academic, research, and public policy positions in the health care field. He is presently at the New York Academy of Medicine.

biomedical science on behalf of patients and to meet community needs, whether or not it is profitable to do so. Although the proper pursuit of such goals may often produce behavior that the market will reward, the behavior is not so motivated. This view holds that health care should be seen as a "social good," a conception that was more obviously applicable when infectious disease made an individual's misfortune a threat to his or her neighbors . . . and in an era when many people were dependent either on charity or public facilities (in distinction to public programs) for their medical care.

In this view, health care is a community service to which words such as caring and compassion and charity should apply—words that connote the family and the church, where the functions of caring for the sick once resided. The response to disease and disability should stem not from the fact that a market is created from peoples' misfortunes but from a humane response to their needs. The ideal is that the needs of the sick and unfortunate should be met by persons who, as a philosopher expressed it, are acting out of love rather than out of the expectation of gain. . . .

In this view it is quite appropriate to expect health care institutions and professionals to provide care to patients who are unable to pay. Ideally, perhaps, the funds required for such care should be raised by government through taxes; however, in the absence of such support, the institution's role is to provide needed service and to make up the resulting deficits however it can, including cross-subsidization from paying patients. Prices should be set to enable institutions to remain financially viable, not at whatever level the market might sustain.

The business orientation that is seen as a concomitant of for-profit health care also is regarded as a threat to the very ethos of health care. . . . [P]roviders will come to feel no shame in refusing to serve those who cannot pay, in declining to offer or provide needed services that cannot generate an acceptable economic return, in setting prices as high as the market will allow and doing whatever is necessary to maximize income, and in aggressively marketing services that may be unrelated to basic health needs but that generate profits (e.g., cosmetic surgery). It is thus feared that the move toward for-profit health care will affect the moral or ethical climate of health care. . . .

Adherents of the "social good" view also frequently point to some perverse effects of the marketplace—its stimulus to provide unnecessary services; . . . its eagerness to duplicate services without respect for community "need" if doing so serves competitive advantages; its alleged willingness to shade on aspects of quality when detection by customers is unlikely, as can happen in medical care; its emphasis on amenities, which are seen as the equivalent of packaging in other areas of merchandising. Critics see amenities as unrelated to quality in a basic functional sense. . . .

Although the two views of health care acknowledge the key role of the physician in the operation of the system, the social view emphasizes the fiduciary aspects of that role rather than the physician as entrepreneur or as customer, the object of the hospital's marketing efforts. The physician is seen as the translator of biomedical knowledge into practice, as the patient's agent, as motivated to identify needs and to do what is required, not to identify demand and satisfy it. It is felt that these key aspects of the physician's role can best be pursued in settings where profit is not the primary goal. . . . As [Paul] Starr put the argument,

The contradiction between professionalism and the role of the market is long-standing and unavoidable. Medicine and other professions have historically distinguished themselves from business and trade by claiming to be above the market and pure commercialism. In justifying the public's trust, professionals have set higher standards of conduct for themselves than the minimal rules governing the marketplace and maintained that they can be judged under those standards by each other, not by laymen. . . . [The] shift from clients to colleagues in the orientation of work, which professionalism demands, represents a clear departure from the normal role of the market.

In discussions of ideals that run counter to economic incentives, the question inevitably arises of the extent to which the behavior of physicians or health care institutions has actually conformed to ideals of altruism, service, and science. . . . Clearly, the highest ideals of medicine are not always fully realized in any sector of the health care system. . . . Jonsen has noted that [m]edical practice always involves a tension between altruism and self-interest. Ideals, even if imperfectly realized, may affect where the balance is struck, as may the way care is organized and paid for.

The contrasting views of health care as economic good and as social good involve a complex mix of values, assumptions, beliefs, and assertions. They underlie debates about many questions of health policy [and law]. . . .

Note: Markets vs. Regulation

Additional Readings. For additional readings on this debate, see Chapter 3.F. George J. Annas, Law, Medicine and the Market (1998); Competition in the Health Care Sector: Past, Present, and Future (W. Greenberg ed., 1978); Competitive Approaches to Health Care Reform (R. Arnould et al. eds., 1993); H. E. Frech, Competition and Monopoly in Medical Care (1996); Handbook of Health Economics (Anthony Culyer & Joseph P. Newhouse eds., 2000); Donald W. Light, The Restructuring of the American Health Care System, *in* Health Politics and Policy (T.J. Litman & L.S. Robins eds., 1997); M. Pauly, A Primer on Competition in Medical Markets, *in* Health Care in America (Frech & Zeckhauser eds., 1988); Thomas Rice, The Economics of Health Reconsidered (1998); Dwayne A. Banks et al., Cross-Subsidization in Hospital Care: Some Lessons from the Law and Economics of Regulation, 91 Health Matrix 1 (1999); Gregg Bloche, The Invention of Health Law, 91 Cal. L. Rev. 247 (2003); David Frankford, Privatizing Health Care: Economic Magic to Cure Legal Medicine, 66 S. Cal. L. Rev. 1 (1992); E. Ginzberg, The Grand Illusion of Competition in Health Care, 249 JAMA 1857 (1983); Russell Korobkin, The Efficiency of Managed Care "Patient Protection" Laws: Incomplete Contracts, Bounded Rationality, and Market Failure, 85 Cornell L. Rev. 1 (1999); P. Menzel, Economic Competition in Health Care: A Moral Assessment, 12 J. Med. & Phil. 63 (1987); B. Vladeck, The Market v. Regulation: The Case for Regulation, 59 Milbank Mem. Fund Q. 209 (1981); Symposium, Kenneth Arrow and the Changing Economics of Health Care, 26 J. Health Pol. Pol'y & L. 823 (2001); Symposium, 22 J. Health Pol. Pol'y & L. 382 (1997); Symposium, 7 Health Affairs (Summer 1988); Symposium, Competition in the Health Care Sector: Ten Years Later, 13 J. Health Pol. Pol'y & L. 223-364 (W. Greenberg ed., 1988); Symposium, Market-Oriented Approaches to Achieving Health Policy Goals, 34 Vand. L. Rev. 849 (1981).

4. Distributive Justice

■ UNCOMPENSATED HOSPITAL CARE: RIGHTS AND RESPONSIBILITIES*
Uwe Reinhardt**

While honest economists long ago despaired of developing an overarching theory of distributive justice, political philosophers continue to hammer away at the problem. The several distinct theories of distributive justice emerging from these efforts are elegant in their internal logic, and eminently stimulating even to a skeptic. In the end, however, that literature fails as a guide towards a universally acceptable principle of justice. On the contrary, it persuades one that there cannot possibly be such a principle. For however tight the internal logic of any particular philosopher's theory of justice may be, that logic is ultimately anchored on some overarching value for which that author claims primacy on purely subjective grounds. Collectively, the political philosophers writing on the subject teach us that justice, like beauty, rests in the eye of the beholder.

Libertarian philosophers, for example, elevate individual liberty to the status of the single, overriding social value to which all other values are subordinate, and which can never justly be traded off against any subordinate value. Implicit in the libertarian's concept of "liberty" is the tenet that the individual is entitled to dispose of his or her possessions as he or she sees fit. Extreme versions of the theory—articulated, for example, in Robert Nozick's Anarchy, State, and Utopia (1974)—hold that any governmental infringement on this presumed property right is ipso facto unjust. Thus, to tax one person's wealth in order to finance another person's health care is unjust, as is a policy that compels physicians or privately owned facilities to render health care to designated individuals. In the libertarian's credo, it is the health care provider's right to determine whom to serve and whom not to serve, and also what price to exact for health services rendered. Health care providers must find this a comforting credo.

Diametrically opposed to the libertarian credo are the various theories of distributive justice espoused by egalitarian philosophers. Egalitarian philosophers elevate "equal respect for all individuals" or "equality of opportunity" to the over-riding value of a just society to which all other values—among them individual liberty—are deemed subordinate. Equality of opportunity, argue these philosophers, requires as a minimum that all members of society have equal access to certain basic commodities, access to which determines an individual's range of

---

*This reading is excerpted from the first chapter of a book edited by T. Sloan, J. Blumstein & J. Perrin (1986). Reprinted with permission of Johns Hopkins University Press.

**The author, a professor of economics at Princeton University, is a prominent writer and speaker on health care public policy. His first name is pronounced "oo-veh."

opportunities and measure of self-respect. Health care, along with food, shelter, and education, is among these basic commodities.

The entitlements implicit in the egalitarian tenet seem rather open-ended, and as recent history in this country has shown, they certainly are. Egalitarians, however, do not glibly ignore resource constraints. They merely argue that, in the face of such constraints, need, rather than ability to pay, should be the basis for rationing. Clearly this theory of justice implies redistribution of the sort libertarians consider coercive and hence unjust.

One's own predilections aside, it is certainly no more logically compelling to let equal opportunity triumph completely over individual liberty than it is to do the reverse. Indeed, outside the ivory tower any prevailing sense of justice is apt to be an amalgam in which each of the pure theories is somewhat compromised. While purist philosophers may deplore such compromises, policymakers must not only countenance them but actively lead in forging the amalgam.

A remarkable and unique feature of American health policy has been its attempt to accommodate simultaneously both the egalitarian and the libertarian theories of justice in their extreme purity. No other nation in the industrialized West has been quite so bold, or quite so naive, as to attempt that feat. Ironically, no other nation finds itself, in the mid-1980s, with the unsolved problem of uncompensated indigent care at the center stage of its health policy debate. There appears to be a causal link between schizoid thinking on the ethical plane and impotence at the level of policy.

Throughout the postwar period, and possibly even earlier, our policies on the distribution of health care have been firmly rooted in the egalitarian credo: It has been a widely shared notion that health care in the United States should be distributed on the basis of medical need rather than ability to pay. Furthermore, with appeal to the overarching principle of "equal respect for all individuals," it has generally been held (at least in public debate) that the nation should aim for equality in the process of health care—that there should be equity in the so-called amenities accompanying the delivery of health care, including the travel and wait time during access and the degree of free choice among providers. Politicians of all ideological stripes have supported these tenets (at least none has openly questioned them), and health care providers have endorsed them as well.

Cynics may argue that no one seriously entertained these lofty maxims and that they were recited by politicians mainly for public consumption. Some glaring remaining inequalities in access to health care may be cited to buttress that case. But a fair reading of health legislation during the 1960s and 1970s should persuade even a skeptic that public policy in those years was motivated by a genuine desire to move the country closer to an egalitarian distribution of health care. By the end of the 1970s, few policy analysts and even fewer public officials still questioned the proposition that access to all medically necessary and technically feasible health care on equal (process) terms is one of an American citizen's basic rights.

The pursuit of an egalitarian health care system is, of course, not a uniquely American phenomenon. Most other industrialized nations have shared that goal, and some of them seem to have been rather more successful than have we in approaching it. A uniquely American phenomenon, however, has been the endeavor to extract an egalitarian distribution of health care from a delivery system still firmly grounded in libertarian principles.

To be sure, our health care delivery system does not measure up in all respects to a libertarian's dream. Some individual liberties are being compromised by government for the sake of quality control, and even the staunchest defenders of the libertarian credo, America's physicians, have from time to time enlisted the government's coercive power to protect their economic turf through occupational licensing. We share such infringements with other modern societies. But in no other modern society espousing egalitarian principles for the distribution of health care have physicians and hospitals been quite so free as they have in the United States to organize their facilities as they see fit, to practice medicine as they see fit, and to price their services as they see fit. In these realms, libertarian principles have prevailed, and every legislative attempt to compromise them for the sake of cost control or greater equity in distribution has, until very recently, been beaten back successfully, with overt appeals to the libertarian credo. "If you want an egalitarian distribution of health care," providers have said, "we endorse it heartily, and we shall do our best to bring it about—but for a fee, and we want that fee to be reasonable as we define that term."

Libertarian and egalitarian purists wrestle with one another in any democratic society. The politician's task, as noted earlier, is to fashion from this struggle a sustainable social compromise. It is on that count that American health policy has performed poorly relative to other democracies. For, in seeking to cater to both extremes among notions of distributive justice, American policymakers have bestowed upon the nation a maze of public health programs that make a Rube Goldberg contraption appear streamlined by comparison.

There has been extraordinarily generous public health insurance coverage for some services and for some individuals—replete with completely free choice of providers by patients and with virtually open-ended reimbursement formulas for providers, . . . entitlements that have, on occasion, bordered on handing providers the key to the public treasury. . . . Yet, attempts to curb that flow of public funds into private treasuries have always been decried and, until very recently, rejected as an intolerable, regulatory infringement on private liberties.

Congressional respect for this peculiar conception of "liberty" naturally carried the danger of turning any federal health program into a fiscal hemorrhage. Too timid to prevent that outcome through controls on providers, our politicians have pursued the next logical policy to contain public health budgets: They simply have left glaring gaps in health insurance coverage, particularly for the near poor and the unemployed (whose health insurance coverage typically ceases with employment). . . . [O]ne would be hard put to identify any other industrialized society today that would still visit upon an unemployed worker's family, already down on its luck in so many material and emotional ways, the added anxiety and potential real hardship of going without health insurance coverage. It happens only in America.

It has become fashionable to attribute our long-standing failures in this area to a streak of meanness in the American character. Having lived both outside and inside this nation, I do not accept that interpretation. The special genius of nations who have long settled these problems lies not in their citizens' superior character, but lies, as noted, in a political process capable of forging a more stable ethical foundation for their health care systems. In all of these nations, the providers of health care enjoy fewer liberties than do their American counterparts. But in addition, a good many of these countries—for example, the United Kingdom, West Germany, France, Switzerland, and Holland—have been rather more tolerant of some degree of tiering in their health systems than have the champions of egalitarianism in the United States. Perhaps the time has come for Americans, too, to debate more openly—and without the customary rancor and slander—just what are the essential ingredients of a just health care system.

Note: Social Justice

Broad theories of social justice relevant to health care delivery are pursued further in Chapter 3.A. For additional readings, see Norman Daniels, Donald Light & Ronald Caplan, Benchmarks of Fairness for Health Care Reform (1996); Larry Palmer, Law, Medicine and Social Justice (1989); Kevin P. Quinn, Viewing Health Care as a Common Good: Looking Beyond Political Liberalism, 73 S. Cal. L. Rev. 277 (2000).

■ PATIENT POWER: SOLVING AMERICA'S HEALTH CARE CRISIS
John C. Goodman & Gerald L. Musgrave
1992

The potential demand for health care is virtually unlimited. Even if there were a limit to what medical service can do (which, over time, there isn't), there is an almost endless list of ailments that can motivate our desire to spend. About 83 million people suffer from insomnia, 70 million have severe headaches, 32 million have arthritis, 23 million have allergies, and 16 million have bad backs. Even when the illnesses are not real, our minds have incredible power to convince us that they are.

Consider the case of an 80-year-old man who suffered from the condition of "slowing down." Despite the physician's counsel that the condition was perfectly normal at age 80, the patient and his wife went on a literal shopping spree in the medical marketplace. As the physician explained to the *New York Times*:

> A few days ago the couple came in for a follow-up visit. They were upset. At their daughter's insistence they had gone to an out-of-town neurologist. She had wanted the "best" for her father and would spare no (Medicare) expense to get it. The patient had undergone a CAT scan, a magnetic resonance imaging, a spinal tap, a brain-stem evoke potential and a carotid duplex ultrasound. No remediable problems were discovered. The Medicare billing was more than $4,000 so far; . . . they were emotionally exhausted by the experience and anxious over what portion of the expenses might not be covered by insurance. I have seen this Medicare madness happen too often. It is caused by many factors, but contrary to public opinion, physician greed is not high on the list. I tried to stop the crime, but found I was just a pawn in a ruthless game, whose rules are excess and waste. Who will stop the madness? . . .

■ MAKING MEDICAL SPENDING DECISIONS: THE LAW, ETHICS, AND ECONOMICS OF RATIONING MECHANISMS*
Mark A. Hall

When we are ill, we desperately want our doctors to do everything within their power to heal us, regardless of the costs. Medical technology has advanced so far, however, that literal adherence to this credo for every human frailty would consume much more than our country's entire economic output,[1] and, in the process, cause economic collapse. . . . Any workable system for financing and delivering health care must face the fundamental problem of how best to allocate limited medical resources among competing beneficial uses. Someone, somewhere must decide which items of potential medical benefit are not worth the cost. . . .

It is sometimes thought that medical advances will eventually reduce medical spending by making people fundamentally healthier, but this assumption is equally flawed. Medical needs are inherently limitless because aging and illness are a permanent feature of the human condition. Much beneficial medical care results in people living to an older age where they are more frail and succumb to more chronic and expensive diseases. This does not mean we should suppress these innovations, only that the drive to conquer all forms of illness is ultimately doomed to failure. The course of history over this century demonstrates that, as medicine advances, so do both medical needs and medical spending.

For these various reasons, most policy analysts recognize that rationing in some form is desirable and inevitable. Every spending decision is necessarily a rationing decision simply because resources devoted to one person or one use are not available for someone or something else. If wants are limitless and resources are finite, it is impossible to maintain that rationing is avoidable in all its forms.

We have always rationed health care resources on a massive scale, only according to irrational and unjust principles.[12] Presently, we ration health care by denying it to those unfortunate individuals who lack insurance either because their employer does not provide it or because their level of poverty has not yet fallen to the desperate level required for Medicaid eligibility.[13] At the same time, we heavily subsidize health insurance for the upper and middle classes through a regressive tax policy that excludes from an employee's income the value of insurance premiums contributed by employers. Moreover, for those who are fully insured, we devote vast resources to save lives and restore health once an illness

---

[1] The U.S. gross domestic product per capital is about $23,000. To see how easy it would be to spend this amount each year on maximal health care, consider that it costs about this same amount on average simply to incarcerate a prisoner (not counting the costs of building new prison space). See also Lamm, R. D., "Rationing of Health Care: Inevitable and Desirable," 140 U. Pa. L. Rev. 1511, 1512 (1992) ("[A] French study asked how much it would cost to give all the health care that is 'beneficial' to each citizen. The answer was five-and-one-half times the French gross national product.").

[12] Fuchs, V.R., "The 'Rationing' of Medical Care," 311 New Eng. J. Med. 1572 (1984); Rosenblatt, R.E., "Rationing 'Normal' Health Care: The Hidden Legal Issues," 59 Texas L. Rev. 1401-1420 (1981).

[13] In 1992, the poverty line for a family of four was $14,335. Medicaid eligibility often is set at less than half the poverty level and, in some states, may be set at less than one-quarter the federal poverty level.

or accident occurs, but we spend only microscopic amounts in comparison on basic safety, health education, and health prevention measures. . . .

The haphazard and unprincipled basis on which rationing presently occurs effectively rebuts another argument," raised by critics of rationing, namely, that rationing should occur only under numerous, morally demanding conditions that presently do not exist. These critics impose unattainably Utopian prerequisites to rationing, such as developing ethically unassailable and scientifically valid rationing criteria, insisting on their strict egalitarian application throughout all strata of society, and first eliminating all wasteful spending, both within medicine and elsewhere in society. These demands ignore the fact that any systematically thought-out rationing scheme, however flawed, is far superior to the thoughtless and inhumane way in which many uninsured people are now treated. A more considered form of resource allocation is the first step, not the last, toward social equity and broad-based reform.[16] Only with some better approach to rationing will minimally acceptable access to health care become affordable for everyone.

Despite these many powerful arguments, it is still controversial to speak in terms of rationing health care. In order to avoid drawing the fire of those who oppose any use of this term, I will instead lean towards the more neutral terminology of resource allocation or spending decisions. I will not entirely refrain from the "R" word, however. Its emotional baggage can help to dramatize the pervasive necessity of making medical spending decisions. Despite their differing emotional content, both rationing and allocation can fairly be used in the generic sense that refers to either implicit or explicit denial of marginally beneficial medical treatment out of consideration for its cost. . . .

[R]egardless of the overall structure of a health care financing and delivery system, [w]hether it is regulatory or competitive, public or private, we are plagued by two basic issues: (1) Who should decide what care is not worth the costs, and (2) what criteria of benefit should be used to make this determination? The second of these problems is the one that has received more attention to date. Numerous volumes have been written on questions such as whether the short supply of transplantable organs should be distributed based simply on random draw or who has been waiting the longest, or instead based on elaborate concepts of medical need or medical benefit.[23] This literature also gives extensive thought to routine medical technologies. It explores whether medical resources generally should be rationed according to age or instead according to some more quantitative formula for effectiveness or value. Others before me have debated at length whether

---

[16] See generally Callahan, D., "Rationing Health Care: Will it be Necessary? Can it be Done Without Age or Disability Discrimination?," 5 Issues in Law & Med. 353 (1989); Callahan, D., "Meeting Needs and Rationing Care," 16 Law Med. & Health Care 261 (1988).

[23] The leading general discussions are found in AMA Council in Ethical and Judicial Affairs, "Ethical Considerations in the Allocation of Organs and Other Scarce Medical Resources Among Patients," 155 Archives Internal Med. 29 (1995); Blank, R.H., Rationing Medicine (1988); Churchill, L.R., Rationing Health Care in America: Perceptions and Principles of Justice (1987); Kilner, J.F., Who Lives? Who Dies?: Ethical Criteria in Patient Selection (1990); Winslow, G.R., Triage and Justice (1982). An early general discussion is contained in Note, "Scarce Medical Resources," 69 Colum. L. Rev. 620 (1969). The most recent treatment is the cogent and comprehensive analysis by Elhauge, E., "Allocating Health Care Morally," 82 Cal. L. Rev. 1449 (1994). For a thorough discussion of rationing criteria used commonly throughout society, see generally Elster, J., Local Justice: How Institutions Allocate Scarce Goods and Necessary Burdens (1992).

medical benefit should be defined by the number of lives saved, the length of life, the quality of life, or some more intermediate goal such as diagnostic certainty, and whether judgments about people's social worth can be prevented from tainting these concepts.

These are tremendously fascinating and important questions deserving of continuing inquiry, but they avoid what I see as a more fundamental question: Who should be the rationing decisionmaker? . . . [M]edical sociologist David Mechanic [f]irst articulated that health care spending decisions can be made through three fundamentally different mechanisms. Cost-sensitive treatment decisions can be made by patients, by physicians, or by third parties—primarily private and governmental insurers but also various regulatory or review organizations. Elsewhere in our economy, cost/benefit trade-offs are usually made through the purchasing decisions of individual consumers. For example, nutrition resources are allocated at both the macro and micro levels through the aggregation of countless individual decisions of how much food to buy, of what quality, and from what source. This simple market mechanism is not generally available or desirable for health care because of the unpredictability of illness and the complexities of medical judgment. . . . [W]e purchase insurance rather than pay out of pocket because we want to protect ourselves from the uncertain costs of health care and the anxiety of making spending decisions under the strain of serious illness. Moreover, even without insurance, patients make few of their medical decisions themselves because the complexity of treatment compels us to delegate extensive authority to our doctors. . . .

Insurers, either private or governmental, can make medical spending decisions through cost-sensitive rules about what treatment they will pay for. Until recently, this has seldom happened, but in 1994 Oregon became the first state to attempt explicit rule-based rationing for all of medicine. Oregon ranked over 600 condition-treatment pairings (e.g., surgery for appendicitis) according to their medical effectiveness, for purposes of allocating limited Medicaid funding. Elsewhere in this country, efforts are under way to develop a host of much more detailed and nuanced clinical practice guidelines, which could also serve as rule-based tools for third-party resource allocation. In addition to insurers' payment rules, spending decisions can be imposed by other parties who are similarly outside the doctor-patient relationship. Courts, citizen groups or other ideal democratic processes, and physician administrators who review the work of treating doctors are each able to set limits or give directions on how medical resources are spent. . . .

The third fundamental alternative for allocating medical spending authority is for physicians to incorporate cost considerations into their clinical judgment. Authorizing physicians to make cost/benefit trade-off decisions at the bedside differs from centralized, rule-based rationing because it individualizes spending decisions to the circumstances of each patient, and it operates through professional incentives rather than bureaucratic authority. Bedside rationing, however, fundamentally compromises physicians' role-based ethic, which . . . traditionally requires doctors to provide all care that offers any benefit, regardless of its cost. Physician bedside rationing is rendered even more controversial by the use of financial incentives to motivate doctors' performance. . . .

As can be seen from this summary, most of this book is taken up with what Edward Rubin terms a "microanalysis of social institutions," one that seeks to assess the relative strengths, weaknesses, and characteristics of alternative mechanisms for allocating health care resources, drawing from both political economics and social theory. . . . Accordingly, I will not be wedded to a particular analytical framework or ideological perspective. I will undertake a pragmatic analytical critique, one that seeks to clarify for each rationing mechanism its basic rationale, its inherent limits, the evidence supporting both views, the potential for harm or manipulation, and the accommodations needed to make it work.

Notes: Health Care Rationing; Institutional Analysis

1. Other aspects of rationing, which is perhaps the most important health care policy issue of our times, are explored in Chapters 3.D and 3.D.3. See the footnotes above for cites to several multidisciplinary sources. See also Einer Elhauge, The Limited Regulatory Potential of Medical Technology Assessment, 82 Va. L. Rev. 1525 (1996); David Eddy, Health System Reform: Will Controlling Costs Require Rationing Services?, 272 JAMA 324 (1994); Rand Rosenblatt, Rationing "Normal" Health Care: The Hidden Legal Issues, 59 Tex. L. Rev. 1401 (1981); 60 Tex. L. Rev. 919 (1982); James Blumstein, Rationing Medical Resources: A Constitutional, Legal, and Policy Analysis, 59 Tex. L. Rev. 1345 (1981); 60 Tex. L. Rev. 899 (1982).

2. *Comparative Institutional Analysis.* The approach Mark Hall takes to analyzing health care rationing is known as "comparative institutional analysis" or as "legal process theory." It is an approach that is well suited to analyzing numerous legal and public policy issues, in health care and elsewhere, and so it is employed throughout this book. Its focus is not so much on what the correct answer is, but on what are the best (or least worst) institutions and processes for arriving at an answer. This approach compares the strengths and weakness of various institutions and processes within the judicial system, the private sector, the public sector, the nonprofit sector, and professional groups, among others. An excellent example of institutional choice analysis applied to problems in health policy is Russell Korobkin, The Efficiency of Managed Care "Patient Protection" Laws: Incomplete Contracts, Bounded Rationality, and Market Failure, 85 Cornell L. Rev. 1 (1999). See also Ezekiel Emanuel, Choice and Representation in Health Care, 56 Med. Care Res. & Rev. 1 (1999). See generally Neil Komesar, Imperfect Alternatives: Choosing Institutions in Law, Economics and Public Policy (1995); Edward Rubin, The New Legal Process, The Synthesis of Discourse, and the Microanalysis of Institutions, 109 Harv. L. Rev. 1393 (1996).

2

Institutional Liability

A. THE DUTY TO TREAT

Ordinarily, the patient-provider relationship is a consensual one to which both parties must agree. Therefore, an individual physician may, generally speaking, refuse to accept patients for any reason or for no reason. The same is true to a lesser extent for hospitals, but they may not turn patients away in emergencies until they have at least stabilized the patient's condition. While historically a physician's freedom to turn away patients found its limitations primarily in the law, the growth of formal arrangements between managed care health plans and physicians means that a provider's obligation to treat is being increasingly defined by the private agreements among the patient, insurance plan, and provider. The following materials explore the origins of, and limits on, this freedom of contract between providers and patients.

■ HURLEY v. EDDINGFIELD
59 N.E. 1058 (Ind. 1901)

BAKER, Justice.

The appellant sued appellee for $10,000 damages for wrongfully causing the death of his intestate. The court sustained appellee's demurrer to the complaint, and this ruling is assigned as error.

The material facts may be summarized thus: At and for years before decedent's death appellee was a practicing physician at Mace, in Montgomery county, duly licensed under the laws of the state. He held himself out to the public as a general practitioner of medicine. He had been decedent's family physician. Decedent became dangerously ill, and sent for appellee. The messenger informed appellee of decedent's violent sickness, tendered him his fee for his services, and stated to him that no other physician was procurable in time, and that decedent relied on him for attention. No other physician was procurable in time to be of any use, and decedent did rely on appellee for medical assistance. Without any reasons whatever, appellee refused to render aid to decedent. No other patients were requiring appellee's immediate service, and he could have gone to the relief of decedent if he had been willing to do so. Death ensued, without decedent's fault, and wholly from appellee's wrongful act. The alleged wrongful act was appellee's refusal to enter into a contract of employment. Counsel do not contend that, before the enactment of the law regulating the practice of medicine, physicians were bound to render professional service to every one who applied. The act regulating the practice of medicine provides for a board of examiners, standards of qualification, examinations, licenses to those found qualified, and penalties for practicing without license. The act is a preventive, not a compulsive, measure. In obtaining the state's license (permission) to practice medicine, the state does not require, and the licensee does not engage, that he will practice at all or on other terms than he may choose to accept. Counsel's analogies, drawn from the obligations to the public on the part of innkeepers, common carriers, and the like, are beside the mark. Judgment affirmed.

■ WILMINGTON GENERAL HOSPITAL v. MANLOVE
174 A.2d 135 (Del. 1961)

SOUTHERLAND, Chief Justice.

This case concerns the liability of a private hospital for the death of an infant who was refused treatment at the emergency ward of the hospital. The facts are these:

On January 4, 1959, Darien E. Manlove, the deceased infant, then four months old, developed diarrhea. The next morning his parents consulted Dr. Hershon. They asked whether the medicine they had for him was all right and the doctor said that it was. In the evening of the same day Mrs. Manlove took the baby's temperature. It was higher than normal. They called Dr. Hershon, and he prescribed additional medication (streptomycin), which he ordered delivered by a pharmacy.

Mrs. Manlove stayed up with the child that night. He did not sleep. On the morning of January 6th the parents took the infant to Dr. Hershon's office. Dr. Thomas examined the child and treated him for sore throat and diarrhea. He prescribed a liquid diet and some medicine. . . .

On the morning of January 7th (a Wednesday) [the infant's] temperature was still above normal—102. Mr. and Mrs. Manlove determined to seek additional medical assistance. They knew that Dr. Hershon and Dr. Thomas were not in their offices on Wednesdays, and they took their infant to the emergency ward of the Wilmington General Hospital.

There is no real conflict of fact as to what occurred at the hospital. The parents took the infant into the reception room of the Emergency Ward. A nurse was on duty. They explained to the nurse what was wrong with the child, that is, that he had not slept for two nights, had a continuously high temperature, and that he had diarrhea. Mr. Manlove told the nurse that the child was under the care of Dr. Hershon and Dr. Thomas, and showed the nurse the medicines prescribed. The nurse explained to the parents that the hospital could not give treatment because the child was under the care of a physician and there would be danger that the medication of the hospital might conflict with that of the attending physician. The nurse did not examine the child, take his temperature, feel his forehead, or look down his throat. The child was not in convulsions, and was not coughing or crying. There was no particular area of body tenderness.

The nurse tried to get in touch with Dr. Hershon or Dr. Thomas in the hospital and at their offices, but was unable to do so. She suggested that the parents bring the baby Thursday morning to the pediatric clinic.

Mr. and Mrs. Manlove returned home. Mrs. Manlove made an appointment by telephone to see Dr. Hershon or Dr. Thomas that night at eight o'clock. At eight minutes past three o'clock in the afternoon the baby died of bronchial pneumonia. . . .

It was assumed by both parties below that the hospital was a private hospital and not a public one—that is, an institution founded and controlled by private persons and not by public authority. The trial court disagreed, finding a quasi-public status in the receipt of grants of public money and tax exemptions. . . . Hence, the court concluded, liability may be imposed on the defendant in an emergency case.

We are compelled to disagree with the view that the defendant has become a public (or quasi-public) hospital. It is admitted (although the record does not show it) that it is privately owned and operated. We find no dissent from the rule that such a hospital is a private hospital, and may, at least in the absence of control by the legislature, conduct its business largely as it sees fit. . . .

Moreover, the holding that the receipt of grants of public money requires the hospital to care for emergency cases, as distinguished from others, is not logical. Why emergency cases? If the holding is sound it must apply to all the hospital services, and that conclusion, as we shall see, is clearly unsound. . . .

We are of opinion that the defendant is a private and not a public hospital, in so far as concerns the right of a member of the public to demand admission or treatment. What, then, is the liability of a private hospital in this respect?

Since such an institution as the defendant is privately owned and operated, it would follow logically that its trustees or governing board alone have the right to determine who shall be admitted to it as patients. No other rule would be sensible or workable. Such authority as we have found supports this rule. "A private hospital owes the public no duty to accept any patient not desired by it, and it is not necessary to assign any reason for its refusal to accept a patient for hospital service." 41 C. J. S. Hospitals §8, p.345. . . .

. . . Does that rule apply to the fullest extent to patients applying for treatment at an emergency ward? . . .

It may be conceded that a private hospital is under no legal obligation to the public to maintain an emergency ward, or, for that matter, a public clinic. But the maintenance of such a ward to render first-aid to injured persons has become a well-established adjunct to the main business of a hospital. If a person, seriously hurt, applies for such aid at an emergency ward, relying on the established custom to render it, is it still the right of the hospital to turn him away without any reason? In such a case, it seems to us, such a refusal might well result in worsening the condition of the injured person, because of the time lost in a useless attempt to obtain medical aid. Such a set of circumstances is analogous to the case of the negligent termination of gratuitous services, which creates a tort liability. Restatement, Law of Torts, "Negligence," §323. . . .

As above indicated, we are of opinion that liability on the part of a hospital may be predicated on the refusal of service to a patient in case of an unmistakable emergency, if the patient has relied upon a well-established custom of the hospital to render aid in such a case. . . .

Applying this rule here, we inquire, was there an unmistakable emergency? Certainly the record does not support the view that the infant's condition was so desperate that a layman could reasonably say that he was in immediate danger. The learned judge indicated that the fact that death followed in a few hours showed an emergency; but with this we cannot agree. It is hindsight. And it is to be noted that the attending physician, after prescribing for the child one morning before, did not think another examination that night or the next morning was required. If this case had gone to the jury on the record here made, we would have been required to hold that it was insufficient to establish liability. We cannot agree that the mere recitation of the infant's symptoms was, in itself, evidence of an emergency sufficient to present a question for the jury. Before such an issue could arise there would have to be evidence that an experienced nurse should have known that such symptoms constituted unmistakable evidence of an emergency. . . .

The possibility that the case might turn on additional evidence respecting the matters we have touched upon was not considered either by the court or counsel. In the circumstances we think the case should go back for further proceedings. We should add, however, that if plaintiff cannot adduce evidence showing some incompetency of the nurse, or some breach of duty or some negligence, his case must fail. Like the learned judge below, we sympathize with the parents in their loss of a child; but this natural feeling does not permit us to find liability in the absence of satisfactory evidence.

For the reasons above set forth the order denying summary judgment is affirmed, without approving the reasons therefor set forth in the court's opinion.

■ SOPHIE'S CHOICES: MEDICAL AND LEGAL RESPONSES TO SUFFERING
Lois Shepherd*
72 Notre Dame L. Rev. 103 (1996)

[U]nprecedented claims to rights based on the avoidance of suffering are being made and recognized in courts and legislatures. The basis of such appeals

* Law professor at Florida State University. Reprinted with permission. Copyright © 1996, Notre Dame Law Review, University of Notre Dame. The editors and Aspen Law Books are required to state that they bear any responsibility for any errors that may have occurred in reprinting or editing this excerpt.

is a belief that the suffering imposed by nature need not be tolerated and that such suffering instills in the suffering individual a right to relief. Suffering thus becomes a sufficient condition for a right. There need be no tortfeasor nor any societally caused harm, nor any inequality for a suffering individual (or such individual's advocate) to claim relief. . . . In such instances the basis of the rights espoused is the principle that people should not be required to suffer when the means are available to end or altogether avoid such suffering. . . .

I think we can look at a number of possible reasons why there is pressure to talk about and recognize rights based in suffering. . . . [W]e appear to be developing a collective conscience, a shared empathy, and a feeling of responsibility for the welfare of others, especially in matters of health. As this collective conscience develops in a country whose jurisprudence gives great deference to individual rights, there is a developing sense that in matters of social welfare we have certain rights. These certain "positive" rights are rights *to* certain goods or services, rather than simply rights to non-interference with respect to obtaining such goods or services. This plays out in the health care arena in an incrementally emerging right to health care. This right emerges in those situations when our collective conscience cannot turn away—when the suffering is acute and visible—such as when a patient arrives at the emergency room in need of immediate attention. . . .

[C]hanges in the legal culture reflect a heightened public awareness and appreciation of others' suffering. This may be due, in part, to the fact that historical distinctions between public and private have blurred, so that, according to Hannah Arendt, the two realms "constantly flow into each other like waves in the never-resting stream of the life process itself."[155] Concerns that were originally and exclusively the province of the family, where the necessary tasks for the survival of life took place, have become a "collective" concern. We are now a "collective of families economically organized into the facsimile of one super-human family." . . .

In the collective conscience, we share not only a growing awareness of the suffering, and especially the visible suffering, of others, but a growing sense of responsibility to help others avoid avoidable suffering. We find conceptual support for this heightened social responsibility in such theories as the feminist ethic of care. The ethic of care requires attending to responsibilities and relationships, rather than attending to rights and fairness (the ethic of justice). Rather than learning and then applying abstract principles, such as equality, reciprocity, and property rights that have universal applicability (since all are grounded in an ethic of justice), an individual or society acting under the ethic of care would seek responses that are appropriate to the particular case.

Much of the recent work on the ethic of care is an outgrowth of Carol Gilligan's 1982 work, *In a Different Voice*, in which she presents her empirical findings that women and men tend to reason about moral problems from different approaches. . . . Gilligan writes:

> The moral imperative that emerges repeatedly in interviews with women is an injunction to care, a responsibility to discern and alleviate the "real and recognizable trouble" of this world. For men the moral imperative appears as an injunction

---

[155] Hannah Arendt, The Human Condition 33 (1958).

to respect the rights of others and thus to protect from interference the rights to life and self-fulfillment.

Whether there are gender differences in moral reasoning or not, . . . we continue to move along the path of a collective conscience in matters of health. [T]he responsibility we feel for the care of others becomes duty, and in the language of advocacy for recognition and adherence to that duty, we see constant recourse to the familiar language of rights. To give proper weight to a concern within our rights-based constitutional framework, there is pressure to . . . create new, unprecedented expectations of rescue-like behavior.

■ WIDEMAN v. SHALLOWFORD COMMUNITY HOSPITAL
826 F.2d 1030 (11th Cir. 1987)

HILL, Circuit Judge.

This case presents the novel question of whether a county government's alleged practice of using its emergency medical vehicles only to transport patients to certain county hospitals which guarantee the payment of the county's medical bills violates a right protected by the federal constitution. We hold that such a practice, even if proved, would not violate any established constitutional right. . . .

I. BACKGROUND

The facts underlying this case are undeniably tragic. On April 12, 1984, Toni Wideman, who at the time was four months pregnant, began experiencing abdominal pain. She called her obstetrician, Dr. John Ramsey, who instructed her to come immediately to Piedmont Hospital. Ms. Wideman called the 911 emergency telephone number in DeKalb County and requested an ambulance to take her to Piedmont. Three employees of the DeKalb County Emergency Medical Service (EMS) responded to this call. Ms. Wideman claims that she again informed the EMS employees to take her to Piedmont where her doctor was waiting, but they refused and, instead, took her against her wishes to Shallowford Community Hospital. After a substantial delay, during which the attending physician at Shallowford spoke by phone with Dr. Ramsey, Ms. Wideman was transferred to Piedmont. At that point, however, Dr. Ramsey was unable to stop her labor, and Ms. Wideman gave birth to a premature baby, named Ebony Laslun Wideman, who survived for only four hours. . . .

. . . It seems that both parties, as well as the district court, have assumed that the alleged policy violates a cognizable constitutional right, which the plaintiffs characterize as their right to the provision of essential medical treatment and services by the county.[3] However, . . . the proper resolution of this case requires

---

[3] The constitutional right alleged by the plaintiffs arguably may be characterized as the much more specific right to the medical care and services of their choice. Ms. Wideman was provided with medical care in this case; indeed, she was rushed to a hospital in an ambulance provided by the county. Her claim appears to be that she should have been able to direct the ambulance wherever she wanted to

us first to determine whether the Constitution grants a right to medical care and treatment in these circumstances. . . .

III.A. EXISTENCE OF A CONSTITUTIONAL RIGHT TO ESSENTIAL MEDICAL CARE

Beginning from the broadest prospective, we can discern no general right, based upon either the Constitution or federal statutes, to the provision of medical treatment and services by a state or municipality. If such a right exists at all, it must derive from the Fourteenth Amendment's due process clause, which forbids a state to deprive anyone of life, liberty or property without due process of law. The due process clause, however, has traditionally been interpreted as protecting certain "negative liberties," i.e., an individual's right to be free from arbitrary or discriminatory action taken by a state or municipality. This circuit has recognized the "well established notion that the Constitution limits the actions the states can take rather than mandating specific obligations." Bradberry v. Pinellas County, 789 F.2d 1513, 1517 (11th Cir. 1986). . . .

Two Supreme Court decisions dealing with access to abortions also support our conclusion that there is no general right to medical care or treatment provided by the state. In Maher v. Roe, 432 U.S. 464 (1977), two indigent women brought suit challenging a Connecticut regulation prohibiting the funding of abortions that were not medically necessary. The plaintiffs argued under the Fourteenth Amendment that the state regulation impinged on their constitutional right to an abortion, as recognized in Roe v. Wade, 410 U.S. 113 (1973). The Court upheld the state regulation, concluding that *Roe* did not declare an unqualified constitutional right to an abortion; rather, that case declared a woman's right to be protected from unduly burdensome interference with her freedom to decide whether to terminate her pregnancy. Significantly, in reaching this result, the Court noted that "the Constitution imposes no obligation on the states to pay the pregnancy-related medical expenses of indigent women, or indeed to pay any of the medical expenses of indigents." *Maher*, 432 U.S. at 469 (footnote omitted).

The Court's subsequent decision in Harris v. McRae, 448 U.S. 297 (1980), reinforced the constitutional distinction between requiring the state to provide medical services and prohibiting the state from impeding access to such services. The plaintiffs in *Harris* challenged the constitutionality of the Hyde amendment, which denied public funding for certain medically necessary abortions, as violating their due process liberty interest in deciding whether to terminate a pregnancy. The Supreme Court held that although the liberty protected by the due process clause prohibits unwarranted government interference with freedom of choice in the context of certain personal decisions, "it does not confer an entitlement to such funds as may be necessary to realize all the advantages of that freedom." . . . More recently, the Court has interpreted *Maher* and *Harris* as standing for the

---

go. For purposes of our analysis, however, we shall consider the plaintiffs' alleged constitutional right as they have characterized it.

proposition that, "as a general matter, the state is under no constitutional duty to provide substantive services for those within its border." Youngberg v. Romeo, 457 U.S. 307, 317 (1982).

Several court of appeals decisions have addressed the issue of whether a state or municipality has a duty under the Fourteenth Amendment to provide various protective services to its citizens. Almost without exception, these courts have concluded that governments are under no constitutional duty to provide police, fire, or other public safety services. . . .

B

That there exists no such general right to the provision of medical care and services by the state, however, does not end our inquiry. Both the Supreme Court and various circuit courts have indicated that the existence of a "special custodial or other relationship" between an individual and the state may trigger a constitutional duty on the part of the state to provide certain medical or other services. In these special circumstances, the state's failure to provide such services might implicate constitutionally protected rights.

For example, the Supreme Court has held that the Eighth Amendment prohibition against cruel and unusual punishments, applicable to the states via the Fourteenth Amendment, requires states to provide medical care for those whom it is punishing by incarceration. . . . Similarly, the Court has held that an involuntarily committed mental patient retains . . . a clear Fourteenth Amendment right "to adequate food, shelter, clothing, and medical care." *Youngberg*, 457 U.S. at 315 . . .

Following this rationale, a constitutional duty can arise only when a state or municipality, by exercising a significant degree of custody or control over an individual, places that person in a worse situation than he would have been had the government not acted at all. Such a situation could arise by virtue of the state affirmatively placing an individual in a position of danger, effectively stripping a person of her ability to defend herself, or cutting off potential sources of private aid. The key concept is the exercise of coercion, dominion, or restraint by the state. . . .

In the present case, we conclude that DeKalb County did not exercise a degree of coercion, dominion, or restraint over Ms. Wideman sufficient to create a "special relationship," . . . The county did not force or otherwise coerce her into its ambulance; it merely made the ambulance available to her, and she entered it voluntarily. Ms. Wideman's physical condition at the time might have required her to seek immediate medical help, and that need might have induced her to make use of the service provided by the county, hoping that she could convince the EMS employees to take her where she wanted to go. Her physical condition, however, cannot be attributed to the county. . . . Therefore, the county was under no affirmative constitutional duty to provide any particular type of emergency medical service for her. . . .

. . . Because the Constitution does not require municipalities to provide any emergency medical services at all, it would be anomalous indeed to hold them liable for providing limited services which happen to be less extensive than a particular citizen may desire. . . .

Notes: The Differing Obligations of
Physicians and Hospitals;
Hospitals as Quasi-Public Facilities

1. *The "No Duty" Rule.* As the *Hurley* court suggests, physicians are not obligated to provide care to a particular patient unless they have agreed to do so. A standard characterization of this principle appears in Oliver v. Brock, 342 So. 2d 1, 3 (Ala. 1976):

> A physician is under no obligation to engage in practice or to accept professional employment, but when the professional services of a physician are accepted by another person for the purposes of medical or surgical treatment, the relation of physician and patient is created. The relation is a consensual one wherein the patient knowingly seeks the assistance of a physician and the physician knowingly accepts him as patient. The relationship between a physician and patient may result from an express or implied contract, either general or special, and the rights and liabilities of the parties thereto are governed by the general law of contract. . . . 61 Am. Jur. 2d, Physicians, Surgeons, and Other Healers, §96.

This "no duty" rule is consistent with tort law's normal "Good Samaritan" doctrine, which does not require individuals, even professionals, to come to the aid of strangers in distress. A physician's *ethical*, as opposed to legal, duty is somewhat more demanding, however. The American Medical Association's Principles of Medical Ethics state that a "physician shall, in the provision of appropriate patient care, except in emergencies, be free to choose whom to serve. . . ." Council on Ethical and Judicial Affairs, Code of Medical Ethics: Current Opinions with Annotations xii (2002-2003). Why couldn't this ethical pledge be converted into an implied promise that physicians make to the public at large? See William E. May, Medical Ethics: Code and Covenant or Philanthropy and Contract?, 5(6) Hastings Ctr. Rep. 29 (1975). Doesn't the public rely on physicians as much as they do on hospital emergency rooms? Consider especially Dr. Eddingfield's status as the plaintiff's family physician. Despite these qualms, *Hurley* is still thought to state the prevailing law for physicians.

2. *Triggering a Treatment Relationship.* A physician's complete freedom to refuse treatment exists only if a treatment relationship has not been initiated. We discuss below what actions constitute the initiation of treatment; but here, the fact that Dr. Eddingfield may have treated Mr. Hurley in the past did not suffice, because the law considers treatment relationships to coincide with "spells of illness." Thus, once a patient recovers from an illness or stops seeking treatment, a new treatment relationship must be formed in order to invoke a duty of continuing treatment. Consider how this issue might come out differently when the patient receives medical care from a health maintenance organization (HMO). In this regard, see O'Neill v. Montefiore Hospital, 202 N.Y.S.2d 436 (App. Div. 1960) (patient died of a heart attack after calling his HMO's on-call physician from a nearby hospital emergency room and allegedly being told to see his primary care physician in the morning); see also Hand v. Tavera, discussed at pages 93-94.

3. *The Hospital's Duty.* Despite the reluctance of the *Manlove* court to find a duty to treat, it is considered a groundbreaking case in that it paved the way for other courts to make more definitive findings of hospital liability for the refusal of emergency care. See, e.g., Stanturf v. Sipes, 447 S.W.2d 558 (Mo. 1969) (hospital may be liable for refusing to treat frostbite victim who could not post $25 deposit); Mercy Medical Center v. Winnebago County, 206 N.W.2d 198 (Wis. 1973) ("It would shock the public conscience if a person in need of medical emergency aid would be turned down at the door of a hospital"); but see Campbell v. Mincey, 413 F. Supp. 16 (N.D. Miss. 1975) (no obligation of hospital emergency room to care for pregnant woman in labor). Many states impose a requirement of open emergency rooms by statute or regulation. See Waxman & Dorn, States Take the Lead in Preventing Patient Dumping, 22 Clearinghouse Rev. 136 (1988). See generally Karen Rothenberg, Who Cares? The Evolution of the Legal Duty to Provide Emergency Care, 26 Hous. L. Rev. 21 (1989); Jeffrey E. Fine, Note, Opening the Closed Doors: The Duty of Hospitals to Treat Emergency Patients, 24 Wash. U. J. Urb. & Contemp. L. 123 (1983); Annot., 11 A.L.R. Fed. 683 (1972).

How do you explain the fact that hospitals have a duty to provide emergency care to all who seek it while physicians are under no such obligation? Arguably, it does not make sense to expect physicians to be available at all times, while hospitals can reasonably be expected to always have someone staffing their emergency rooms. But what about just expecting physicians to be available during their regular office hours for emergencies? Can't doctors factor into their scheduling the possibility of emergencies? Don't they in fact already do that? Is part of the issue that physicians may not necessarily have the expertise for any emergency patient that comes though the door? Suppose the physician is a dermatologist and is confronted with a cardiac emergency. Is there anything the doctor reasonably could do besides call 911?

Hospitals, too, may be able to limit their obligation according to their capacity or expertise. Suppose a hospital has no emergency room because it specializes in elective surgeries. Or suppose the emergency room is full? When this happens, hospital emergency departments often place themselves on "drive-by" status, which means they alert ambulances not to stop there. One court held this was permissible in the case of a child who consequently suffered brain damage, even though the hospital had treated the child many times in the past and had encouraged his parents to pass up other closer hospitals and come there if he had serious problems. Davis v. Johns Hopkins Hospital, 622 A.2d 128 (Md. 1993).

4. *The Meaning of Reliance.* Why is the *Manlove* reliance theory limited to just emergency care? Observe the court's reasoning that "such a refusal [of treatment] might well result in worsening the condition of the injured person, because of the time lost in a useless attempt to obtain medical aid." Presumably, this is true only in a very serious or "unmistakable" emergency. It might be possible, however, to argue for other types of reliance. Suppose, for instance, that a prospective patient chose to live in the community because of the presence of a hospital, and it would thereby frustrate his or her reliance if the hospital could deny care in nonemergencies as well as emergencies. Absent such a showing, patients may have only psychological reliance but no *detrimental* reliance in the sense of a material change in one's position for the worse.

Where reliance is detrimental, shouldn't the patient have to demonstrate actual reliance in the particular case, rather than reliance being assumed? The *Manlove* court appeared to treat only the detriment part as requiring proof, not the psychological expectation. Should we presume that patients always legitimately expect emergency rooms to be open to them? Consider, for instance, Guerrero v. Copper Queen Hospital, 537 P.2d 1329 (Ariz. 1975), which found that a hospital in a border town owned by a local mining company had a duty to accept two severely burned Mexican children whose family lived across the border.

5. *Physicians "On Call."* *Hurley* and *Manlove* appear consistent because one is about doctors and the other is about hospitals. But does it make sense for hospitals to have a duty to accept emergency patients if the doctors who work there are free to refuse treatment? Courts have resolved this problem by holding that a doctor who is "on call" for a hospital emergency room voluntarily undertakes the hospital's greater duty of care. The leading decision is Hiser v. Randolph, 617 P.2d 774 (Ariz. 1980). At 11:45 P.M. one night, Bonita Hiser came to the emergency room at Mojave County General Hospital in a semi-comatose condition arising out of an exacerbation of her juvenile onset diabetes. Along with the seven other doctors in the area, Dr. Randolph took turns as the on-call physician for the emergency room, a duty for which he was paid $100 per 12-hour shift, and he was on call when Mrs. Hiser came to the hospital. When the emergency room nurse called Dr. Randolph, he refused to come in. He claimed this was because he lacked the expertise to treat diabetes, but there was also evidence that his refusal was based on personal animosity toward Mrs. Hiser or the fact that Mrs. Hiser's husband was a lawyer. Mrs. Hiser died because of the delay in treatment. The court found that Dr. Randolph breached his duty of care arising from his status as an on-call physician. According to the court,

> the obviously intended effect of the [hospital's] bylaws and rules and regulations was to obligate the emergency room doctor "on call" to provide emergency treatment to the best of the doctor's ability to any emergency patient of the hospital. Under these circumstances, the lack of a consensual physician-patient relationship before a duty to treat can arise has been waived by the signatory doctors.

But see Childs v. Weis, 440 S.W.2d 104 (Tex. Ct. App. 1969) (physicians on emergency call were under no specific duty to see all patients who presented themselves to the emergency room).

A similar analysis is possible for HMO physicians. See St. Charles v. Kender, 646 N.E.2d 411 (Mass. Ct. App. 1995) (HMO subscriber is a third-party beneficiary of an HMO's contracts with its physicians; contract was breached when physician failed to return patient's calls for an appointment). In Hand v. Tavera, 864 S.W.2d 678 (Tex. Ct. App. 1993), Lewis Hand went to the Humana Hospital (Village Oaks) emergency room because of a three-day headache. He also had high blood pressure, and his medical history revealed that his father had died of an aneurysm. The emergency room physician was able to control Mr. Hand's blood pressure and headache temporarily with medication but ultimately concluded that Mr. Hand should be admitted to the hospital. Hospital admissions required the approval of another physician under the Humana Health Care Plan, so the emergency room physician called Dr. Robert Tavera, the physician responsible that evening for authorizing admissions of Humana patients. Dr. Tavera decided that Mr. Hand should be treated as an outpatient. A few hours after returning home, Mr. Hand suffered a stroke. The trial court granted Dr. Tavera summary judgment on the ground that no patient-physician relationship had been formed, but the appellate court held that a patient-physician relationship existed by virtue of Mr. Hand's membership in the Humana Health Care Plan and Dr. Tavera's designation "as the doctor acting for the Humana plan that night." As the court observed, "Hand paid premiums to Humana to purchase medical care in advance of need . . . and Tavera's medical group agreed to treat Humana enrollees in exchange for the fees received from Humana. In effect, Hand had paid in advance for the services of the Humana plan doctor on duty that night, who happened to be Tavera, and the physician-patient relationship existed."

6. *The Quasi-Public Status of Hospitals.* Another basis for imposing a duty to treat, distinct from the reliance theory, is the assertion that physicians or hospitals owe duties to the public at large simply by virtue of their having chosen to become licensed health care providers. It is a version of this argument that the *Hurley* court rejects with the cryptic comment that "analogies, drawn from the obligations to the public on the part of innkeepers, common carriers, and the like, are beside the mark." In ancient common law, certain occupations and businesses were considered to be "common callings," meaning that they could not turn away customers without a good reason. Innkeepers and public transport ("common carriers") were the classic examples. The reasons for these heightened public service duties were the importance of the service, the monopoly status of the business, and the support it received from the government. See Charles Burdick, The Origin of the Peculiar Duties of Public Service Companies, 11 Colum. L. Rev. 514, 616, 742 (1911); O. W. Holmes, Jr., Common Carriers and the Common Law, 13 Am. L. Rev. 40 (1879). In modern times, these "businesses affected with a public interest" are the public utilities (electric, phone, trains, etc.), and common law duties of public service have been supplanted by overt government regulation. This body of common law has therefore become somewhat archaic, but it is still sometimes invoked against trade associations or labor unions that refuse membership. See generally, Comment, Judicial Intervention in Admission Decisions of Private Professional Associations, 49 U. Chi. L. Rev. 840 (1982); Developments, Judicial Control of Actions of Private Associations, 76 Harv. L. Rev. 983 (1963).

In Chapter 4, we will see that this body of law has been used to characterize hospitals as "quasi-public" facilities for purposes of giving *physicians* rights of access to their medical staffs. Considering that patients are the ultimate customers for whom public benefit is intended, shouldn't this analogy have even more application to them? It would be ironic indeed to insist on physician access but deny patient access. Nevertheless, the *Manlove* court rejected this view. In other states, more recent decisions have been more receptive to the quasi-public characterization. For instance, in Thompson v. Sun City Community Hospital, 688 P.2d 605 (Ariz. 1984), the court found that a cause of action exists against a hospital that stabilized a patient with a severed artery and then transferred him for financial reasons. The court based the duty to treat on the general public policy embodied in hospital licensing regulations and private accreditation standards. Also, in Payton v. Weaver, considered at page 157, the court suggested in dictum that this public service theory could be used to impose a community-wide obligation on kidney dialysis centers to share the burden of treating an unwanted disruptive patient. Cf. A.J.G. Priest, Possible Adaptation of Public Utility Concepts in the Health Care Field, 35 Law & Contemp. Probs. 839 (1970).

7. *The Private Status of Physicians.* Reconsider the situation of physicians. Why shouldn't medical practice by physicians be considered a "common calling" or a quasi-public service? Indeed, it turns out that, in fifteenth-century English law, physicians were included on the list of common callings along with blacksmiths and other important professions. Perhaps today the missing ingredient is that a physician rarely has a local monopoly; usually there are several in town. But not always. One court found a common law duty to treat where the sole physician practice group in town refused to accept a patient who had filed a complaint against one of the doctors in the group. Leach v. Drummond Medical Group, 192 Cal. Rptr. 650 (Cal. Ct. App. 1983).

In a few state statutes, regulatory law imposes some limited duties on physicians to provide care for patients. In Massachusetts, for instance, physicians, as a condition of being licensed, must agree to charge Medicare patients no more than Medicare's "reasonable charge." This has been held not to violate the constitutional rights of physicians. Dukakis v. Massachusetts Medical Society, 815 F.2d 790 (1st Cir. 1987).

8. *Paying vs. Indigent Patients.* Perhaps this body of law is not more developed because doctors and hospitals rarely turn away patients who can pay. For patients who cannot pay, the public service theory is usually no help, since the common law never required common callings to serve people for free. Only the reliance theory reaches this result, but it is restricted to severe emergencies, those in which the patient is worse off for having made a futile attempt to secure service. Only in Arizona have courts used a public service theory to impose a duty to treat patients who cannot pay, and there too the duty is limited to emergency care. (Should it be?)

9. *Enforcement of Public Rights.* For patients who cannot pay, regulatory law places hospitals under somewhat greater duties than the common law to treat both emergency and nonemergency patients, but these public law duties are limited and are not enforceable by individual patients. The federal Hill-Burton Act (42 U.S.C. §291) requires hospitals who have received construction grants under the Act to provide 3 percent of the their care to indigent patients for 20 years. See James Blumstein, Court Action, Agency Reaction: The Hill-Burton Act as a Case Study, 69 Iowa L. Rev. 1227 (1984); Kenneth Wing, The Community Service Obligation of Hill-Burton Health Facilities, 23 B.C. L. Rev. 577 (1982). Construction funding under the Act ceased a number of years ago, however, so few hospitals are still under this obligation, and even when the law was in effect individual patients could not easily enforce it. See generally AHA v. Schweiker, 721 F.2d 170 (7th Cir. 1983); Rand E. Rosenblatt, Health Care Reform and Administrative Law: A Structural Approach, 88 Yale L.J. 243 (1978).

Another source of relevant law is charitable tax exemption. Nonprofit hospitals are considered to be "charities" that are exempt from property and income tax. Part of this charitable status includes an obligation to treat some patients for free. As discussed in Chapter 4.B.2, federal law restricts this free-care obligation to emergency patients, as do most states, but a few states are beginning to require hospitals to devote a certain percentage of their overall services to patients who cannot pay. Once again, however, this is a community service obligation owed to the public at large, not to individual patients, and so it cannot be enforced very easily by private action. See Simon v. Eastern Kentucky Welfare Rights Association, 426 U.S. 26 (1975) (indigent patients lack standing to challenge the IRS's interpretation of charitable hospital's free care obligation under federal tax law). Finally, the Joint Commission on Accreditation of Healthcare Organizations (JCAHO) private accreditation standards require hospitals to accept patients without regard to "source of payment," but this is interpreted to mean accepting all patients with some source of payment (e.g., not turning away Medicaid patients) rather than a duty to accept patients who cannot pay.

This leaves us with the following patchwork of laws: for physicians, no common law duty to treat, even in emergencies. For hospitals: (1) a common law duty to treat emergency patients regardless of payment, but only in severe emergencies; (2) common law and regulatory duties to treat all patients who can pay; but (3) no enforceable duty to treat nonemergency or mild emergency patients who cannot pay. This set the stage for enactment of a new federal statute, the Emergency Medical Treatment and Active Labor Act (EMTALA), discussed in the *Burditt* case at page 98.

Notes: Moral and Constitutional Rights to Health Care

1. *Moral Rights to Treatment.* The discussion of legal rights to treatment surely must be informed by how our society views moral rights to health care. While Lois Shepherd argues that we are evolving toward a more caring community (page 87), what message does society send when the law limits the right to treatment so narrowly as to encompass only serious emergencies? Does the emergency care limitation suggest that we are trying to limit care to the most compelling needs and to avoid people demanding too much care (emergencies being thought of as unpredictable). This might be seen as a partial embodiment of the "rescue principle" discussed in Chapter 3.D.1, which declares that the strongest ethical demand in medicine is to help those in greatest need. In this regard, the moral dimension of medicine is stronger than in any other commercial arena, because there is no equivalent requirement that grocers, restaurants, or hotels provide their services for free to people in dire straits. What justifies this distinction? Is it that if food and housing were available on demand, it would be too easy to abuse the privilege? But what kinds of incentives for patients does a right only to emergency care generate? Is the reluctance of the courts to find even broader rights to health care a reflection of the difficulty in deciding who to hold responsible for vindicating these rights?

The moral issue can also be debated from a broader, social perspective. So far, we have thought only about whether patients have a right to demand treatment from particular doctors and hospitals. Even where they do not have these private rights, perhaps they have a claim to a more public right, one that society as a whole owes to provide minimally decent health care to all. Arguments to this effect are explored in Chapter 3. We currently recognize this claim to basic social support for education and to a more limited extent for food and housing. But for health care, there is no national safety net. Medicaid coverage provides health insurance for the poor, but less than half of those living in poverty are eligible. Almost 47 million Americans have no health insurance of any kind. Perhaps this social inequity is politically and morally sustainable only because private hospital emergency rooms exist as a last resort for those without insurance. Could it be, then, that the heightened private law duties of hospitals have weakened our nation's public law commitment to health care access? See Mark A. Hall, The Unlikely Case in Favor of Patient Dumping, 28 Jurimetrics 389 (1988). For an argument that private law duties tend to undermine voluntary charity, see Richard Epstein, Mortal Peril: Our Inalienable Right to Health Care? (1997).

2. *Positive vs. Negative Liberty.* If there is a moral right to health care generally, it is clearly not vindicated as a substantive due process right by the U.S. Constitution. *Wideman* is a classic statement of the principle that the Bill of Rights embodies primarily negative, not positive, liberties, that is, it is concerned mainly with freedoms from government imposition, not rights to government assistance. Thus, the Constitution becomes relevant to health care when the government bans treatment choices or forces treatment, but not when it simply declines to assist in obtaining treatment. In this regard, the U.S. Constitution differs markedly from constitutional models in Europe.

Wideman was followed by an important Supreme Court opinion confirming its general analysis in this regard. In DeShaney v. Winnebago County Department of Social Services, 489 U.S. 189 (1989), the Court held that no constitutional violation occurred in a case where a child was left with permanent brain damage when a state social services agency failed to intervene aggressively enough to prevent child abuse. The state had received several reports of severe beatings by the father. The Court reaffirmed "that the due process clauses generally confer no affirmative right to governmental aid," and it reasoned that the state agency had not assumed a "special relationship" with the child by virtue of having made some ineffectual efforts to protect him since the agency did nothing to make him more vulnerable to the danger. See also Archie v. Racine, 847 F.2d 1211 (7th Cir. 1988) (en banc) (§1983 action not maintainable for city rescue service's negligent failure to dispatch ambulance; no constitutional right to treatment exists).

3. *Institutional Responsibilities of Mental Hospitals.* An exception to this negative liberty principle exists for individuals over whom the state has control, and it has generated significant litigation with respect to mental hospitals. An early, highly influential decision addressing the constitutional right to treatment in the context of state institutionalization is Judge Frank Johnson's remarkable order taking direct charge over the administration of Alabama's state mental hospital because of its persistent failure to provide any meaningful form of treatment. Wyatt v. Stickney, 325 F. Supp. 781 (M.D. Ala. 1971), 344 F. Supp. 373 (M.D. Ala. 1972). See also O'Connor v. Donaldson, 422 U.S. 563 (1975) (civil commitment to psychiatric hospital invalid without treatment); Comment, Wyatt v. Stickney and the Right of Civilly Committed Mental Patients to Adequate Treatment, 86 Harv. L. Rev. 1282 (1973). In Thomas S. v. Morrow, 781 F.2d 367 (4th Cir. 1986), the court found a constitutional duty to provide "clinically adequate community mental health services" in order to ensure the availability of a

least restrictive means of treatment for patients that would otherwise have to be involuntarily committed.

Prisoners are another class of persons who gain certain rights to health care by virtue of their confinement. There, the rights rest also in the Eighth Amendment's prohibition against cruel and unusual punishment.

4. *Equal Protection.* In Maher v. Roe, 432 U.S. 464, 469-470 (1977), discussed in *Wideman*, the Court identified another possible source of a constitutional duty to treat: "The Constitution imposes no obligation on the states to pay . . . any of the medical expenses of indigents. But when a state decides to alleviate some of the hardships of poverty by providing medical care, the manner in which it dispenses benefits is subject to constitutional limitations." For example, in Memorial Hospital v. Maricopa County, 415 U.S. 250 (1974), the Court struck down Arizona's requirement of a year's residence in a county as a condition of receiving nonemergency medical care at county expense as infringing on the right to travel. Might a state be subject to an equal protection attack for funding some procedures but not others? See Doe v. Colautti, 592 F.2d 704 (3d Cir. 1978) (finding no violation of the equal protection clause when Pennsylvania's medical assistance program provided less generous benefits for psychiatric care than for general medical care).

5. *Legislative Mandates.* In Harris v. McRae, 448 U.S. 297 (1980), another abortion funding case discussed in *Wideman*, the Court addressed a nonconstitutional theory for compelling government funding of health care. States that participate in Medicaid are, generally speaking, required to fund most medically necessary forms of treatment. Beal v. Doe, 432 U.S. 438, 444 (1977). Although *McRae* found this statutory requirement to be inapplicable to abortions, in other cases the medical necessity mandate has proved to be an effective tool for obtaining Medicaid coverage. Ellis v. Patterson, 859 F.2d 52 (8th Cir. 1988) (requiring reasonable funding once a state decides to provide coverage for liver transplants); Rush v. Parham, 625 F.2d 1150 (5th Cir. 1980) (requiring funding for sex change operations in certain circumstances). However, there is no statutory requirement that Medicaid be funded at a level sufficient to cover all people who need it. See Chapter 3 for additional discussion.

■ BURDITT v. U.S. DEPARTMENT OF HEALTH AND HUMAN SERVICES
934 F.2d 1362 (5th Cir. 1991)

REAVLEY, Circuit Judge.

Hospitals that execute Medicare provider agreements with the federal government pursuant to 42 U.S.C. §1395cc must treat all human beings who enter their emergency departments in accordance with the Emergency Medical Treatment and Active Labor Act (EMTALA), 42 U.S.C. §1395dd. Hospitals and responsible physicians found to have violated EMTALA's requirements are subject to civil money penalties. [This case is an appeal by Dr. Burditt of a $20,000 fine assessed against him by the Department of Health and Human Services. EMTALA also provides for a private cause of action, with prevailing plaintiffs entitled to monetary damages from the offending hospital and appropriate equitable relief. Damages may not be recovered from physicians in a private cause of action, however.] . . .

I.A. FACTS

Mrs. Rosa Rivera arrived in the emergency room of DeTar Hospital in Victoria, Texas at approximately 4:00 P.M. on December 5, 1986. At or near term with her sixth child, she was experiencing one-minute, moderate contractions every three minutes and her membranes had ruptured. Two obstetrical nurses, Tammy Kotsur and Donna Keining, examined her and found indicia of labor and dangerously high blood pressure. Because Rivera had received no prenatal care, and had neither a regular doctor nor means of payment, Kotsur telephoned Burditt, who was next on DeTar's rotating call-list of physicians responsible for such "unaligned" obstetrics patients. Upon hearing Rivera's history and condition, Burditt told Kotsur that he "didn't want to take care of this lady" and asked her to prepare Rivera for transfer to John Sealy Hospital in Galveston, Texas, 170 miles away. Burditt agreed to call back in five to ten minutes.

Kotsur and Keining told the nursing supervisor, Jean Herman, and DeTar's administrator, Charles Sexton, of their belief that it would be unsafe to transfer Rivera. When Burditt called back, Keining told him that, according to Sexton's understanding of hospital regulations and federal law, Burditt would have to examine Rivera and personally arrange for John Sealy to receive her before he could legally transfer her. Keining asked Burditt for permission to start an intravenous push of magnesium sulfate as a precaution against convulsive seizures. Burditt told Keining to begin administering this medication only if Rivera could be transported by ambulance. . . .

Burditt arrived at approximately 4:50 to examine Rivera. He confirmed her blood pressure to be the highest he had ever seen, 210/130, and he assumed that she had been hypertensive throughout her pregnancy. As the experienced head of DeTar's obstetrics and gynecology department, Burditt knew that there was a strong possibility that Rivera's hypertension would precipitate complications which might kill both Rivera and her baby. He also knew that the infants of hypertensive mothers are at higher-than-normal risk of intrauterine growth retardation. He estimated that Rivera's baby was six pounds—less than normal weight—and arranged her transfer to John Sealy, a perinatal facility better equipped than DeTar to care for underweight infants. . . .

At approximately 5:00, Herman showed Burditt DeTar's guidelines regarding EMTALA, but he refused to read them. Burditt told Herman that Rivera represented more risk than he was willing to accept from a malpractice standpoint. Herman explained that Rivera could not be transferred unless Burditt signed a DeTar form entitled "Physician's Certificate Authorizing Transfer." Burditt asked for "that dang piece of paper" and signed his name under the following:

> I have examined the patient, _____, and have determined that, based upon the information available to me at this time, the medical benefits reasonably expected from the provision of appropriate medical treatment at another medical

facility outweigh the increased risks to the patient's medical condition from effecting [the] transfer. The basis for my conclusion is as follows: _____

Burditt listed no basis for his conclusion and remarked to Herman that "until DeTar Hospital pays my malpractice insurance, I will pick and choose those patients that I want to treat."

Burditt then went to care for another unaligned patient, Sylvia Ramirez, while the nurses arranged Rivera's transfer. They found another obstetrical nurse, Anita Nichols, to accompany Rivera to John Sealy. Burditt returned to the nurses' station and stayed there from 5:30 to 6:18. He never again examined Rivera or asked about her medical condition, though he inquired several times about the status of her transfer. Burditt delivered the Ramirez baby at 6:22. Afterward, Nichols told him the results of her examination of Rivera and informed him that the ambulance had arrived. Based exclusively on Nichols' statements, Burditt concluded that Rivera's condition had not changed since his examination two hours before. Burditt did not reexamine Rivera though he saw her being wheeled to the ambulance. He did not order any medication or life support equipment for Rivera during her transfer.

Nichols delivered Rivera's healthy baby in the ambulance approximately 40 miles into the 170-mile trip to John Sealy. She directed the driver to nearby Ganado Hospital to get a drug called pitocin to staunch Rivera's bleeding. While there, Nichols telephoned Burditt, who ordered her to continue to John Sealy despite the birth. Instead, per Rivera's wishes, Nichols returned Rivera to DeTar, where Burditt refused to see her because she failed to proceed to John Sealy in accordance with his instructions. Burditt directed that Rivera be discharged if she was stable and not bleeding excessively. A DeTar official pressed Burditt to allow Dr. Shirley Pigott to examine Rivera. Rivera stayed at DeTar under Pigott's care for three days and left in good health. . . .

II.A.1. SCREENING

Because Rivera presented herself to DeTar's emergency department and a request was made on her behalf for care, EMTALA required DeTar to

> provide for an *appropriate* medical screening examination *within the capability of the hospital's emergency department* to determine whether or not an emergency medical condition . . . exists or to determine if the individual is in active labor. . . .

42 U.S.C. §1395dd(a) (emphasis added). The parties agree that DeTar appropriately screened Rivera and discovered that she had an "emergency medical condition"—severe hypertension—within the meaning of 42 U.S.C. §1395dd(e)(1).[3]

[3] EMTALA defines "emergency medical condition" as

a medical condition manifesting itself by acute symptoms of sufficient severity (including severe pain) such that the absence of immediate medical attention could reasonably be expected to result in—
    (A) placing the patient's health in serious jeopardy,
    (B) serious impairment to bodily functions, or
    (C) serious dysfunction of any bodily organ or part.

42 U.S.C. §1395dd(e)(1) (Supp. IV 1987).

II.A.2. EMERGENCY MEDICAL CONDITION AND ACTIVE LABOR

Patients diagnosed with an "emergency medical condition" or "active labor" must either be treated or be transferred in accordance with EMTALA. Burditt claims that Rivera received all of the care that she was due under EMTALA because he stabilized her hypertension sufficiently for transfer and she was not in active labor when she left DeTar for John Sealy.

II.A.2.a. Unstable Emergency Medical Condition

Rivera's blood pressure was 210/130 at 4:00 and 5:00. This was the last reading known to Burditt before he facilitated her transfer. Nurses also measured her blood pressure as 173/105 at 5:30, 178/103 at 5:45, 186/107 at 6:00, and 190/110 at 6:50. Experts testified that Rivera's hypertension put her at high risk of suffering serious complications, including seizures, heart failure, kidney dysfunction, tubular necrosis, stroke, intracranial bleeding, placental abruption, and fetal hypoxia. This is substantial, if not conclusive evidence that Rivera entered and exited DeTar with an emergency medical condition.

Burditt argues that he fulfilled EMTALA's requirements with respect to Rivera's hypertension by "stabilizing" it, or

> provid[ing] such medical treatment of the condition as may be necessary to assure, within reasonable medical probability, that no material deterioration of the condition is likely to result from [a] transfer. . . .

42 U.S.C. §1395dd(e)(4)(A). He claims that the magnesium sulfate that he ordered for Rivera has an antihypertensive effect that complements its primary anticonvulsive purpose.

Development of any of the possible complications could have killed or seriously injured Rivera, her baby, or both, and thus would constitute a "material deterioration" under 42 U.S.C. §1395dd(e)(4)(A). Any deterioration would "result" from transfer in that Rivera would have received better care for any complication at DeTar than in the ambulance. Thus, Burditt could not have stabilized Rivera unless he provided treatment that medical experts agree would prevent the threatening and severe consequences of Rivera's hypertension while she was in transit. [The HHS appeals board] could properly disregard Burditt's testimony and accept that of all other testifying experts in holding that Burditt provided no such treatment, and thus did not stabilize Rivera's emergency medical condition. . . .

II.A.2.b. Active Labor

EMTALA defines "active labor" as labor at a time when

> (B) there is inadequate time to effect safe transfer to another hospital prior to delivery, or
> (C) a transfer may pose a threat [to] the health and safety of the patient or the unborn child.

42 U.S.C. §1395dd(e)(2)(B)-(C). This statutory definition renders irrelevant any medical definition of active labor. . . .

Burditt challenges the ALJ's finding that, at approximately 5:00, there was inadequate time to safely transfer Rivera to John Sealy before she delivered her baby. Dr. Warren Crosby testified that, based on Burditt's own examination results, Rivera would, more likely than not, deliver within three hours after Burditt [made the decision to transfer her to] John Sealy. . . . Burditt does not challenge [the] conclusion that the ambulance trip from DeTar to John Sealy takes approximately three hours. We therefore hold that [the HHS appeals board] properly concluded that Rivera was in active labor under 42 U.S.C. §1395dd(e)(2)(B).

The ALJ also found that Rivera was in active labor under clause C at the time Burditt examined her. There is always some risk of a vehicular accident in transit, so transfer always "may" pose a threat to the health and safety of the patient or fetus. . . . We believe that Congress intended clause C to extend EMTALA's . . . protection to women in labor who have any complication with their pregnancies regardless of delivery immanency. Because better medical care is available in a hospital than in an ambulance, whether a transfer "may pose a threat" under 42 U.S.C. §1395dd(e)(2)(C) depends on whether the woman in labor has any medical condition that could interfere with the normal, natural delivery of her healthy child. Under the statutory language, a woman in labor is entitled to EMTALA's . . . protections upon a showing of possible threat; it does not require proof of a reasonable medical probability that any threat will come to fruition. . . .

The record overwhelmingly confirms that Rivera's hypertension could have interfered with a normal delivery, and she was thus in active labor under 42 U.S.C. §1395dd(e)(2)(C). . . .

II.A.3. TREAT OR TRANSFER

Upon discovery of active labor or an emergency medical condition, EMTALA usually requires hospitals to treat the discovered condition. Under certain circumstances, however, EMTALA allows hospitals to transfer patients instead of treating them. 42 U.S.C. §1395dd(b)(1)(B). . . . [The court went on to find that Burditt had not satisfied the requirements under EMTALA for a transfer before stabilization. Under EMTALA, transfer is permitted if the patient requests transfer *or* the physician has certified in writing that the medical benefits of transfer outweigh the increased risks to the patient. In addition, the receiving hospital must be capable of providing the needed treatment and must have agreed to accept the transfer. Finally, the transfer must occur with appropriate personnel and transportation, including appropriate life support measures. While Burditt had obtained consent from John Sealy before the transfer, he had not reasonably concluded that the benefits of transfer outweighed the risks nor had he arranged for the transfer with appropriate personnel and transportation.]

II.C. EMTALA's CONSTITUTIONALITY

As his final attempt to escape [liability], Burditt claims that EMTALA effects a public taking of his services without just compensation in contravention of the Constitution's Fifth Amendment.

Assuming *arguendo* that professional services constitute property protected by the takings clause, Burditt has not shown that EMTALA effects a taking. EMTALA imposes no responsibilities directly on physicians; it unambiguously requires hospitals to examine and stabilize, treat, or appropriately transfer all who arrive requesting treatment. Its provision for sanctions against physicians who knowingly violate its requirements is merely an enforcement mechanism that does not alter its explicit assignment of duties.

Governmental regulation that affects a group's property interests "does not constitute a taking of property where the regulated group is not required to participate in the regulated industry." Whitney v. Heckler, 780 F.2d 963, 972 (11th Cir.), *cert. denied*, 479 U.S. 813 (1986).

Two levels of voluntariness undermine Burditt's taking assertion. Only hospitals that voluntarily participate in the federal government's Medicare program must comply with EMTALA. Hospitals must consider the cost of complying with EMTALA's requirements in deciding whether to continue to participate in the Medicare program.

Second, Burditt is free to negotiate with DeTar or another hospital regarding his responsibility to facilitate a hospital's compliance with EMTALA. Thus, physicians only voluntarily accept responsibilities under EMTALA if they consider it in their best interest to do so. Accordingly, Burditt's claim under the takings clause is without merit. . . .

Notes: The Federal Patient Dumping Statute

1. *Historical Background.* Congress passed the Emergency Medical Treatment and Active Labor Act (EMTALA) as part of the Consolidated Omnibus Reconciliation Act of 1986 (COBRA), in response to the perception that state law was too weak to prevent widespread patient dumping. While EMTALA, or COBRA, has worked better than previous legal efforts, in part because of the private right of action, there are still concerns that patient dumping persists at unacceptable levels. One scholar argues, however, that

> EMTALA is a virtual catalogue of how to get a statute wrong. First, generalize from unrepresentative anecdotal evidence in identifying the problem. Draft the statute sloppily, and leave the most important words undefined or defined too broadly. Finance the resulting open-ended entitlement with an unfunded mandate imposed on private parties. . . . [Design the enforcement system] to reward the wrong people. Finally, apply the statute even after the world on which it depended has vanished. Any one of these problems would be bad enough in isolation, but their combined effect is devastating to the interests EMTALA was intended to protect.

David A. Hyman, Dumping EMTALA: When Bad Laws Happen to Good People (1998) (not yet published). As you read the following notes, see if you can determine why someone might reach such a conclusion. Nevertheless, Prof. Hyman acknowledges that

> the statute is wildly popular across the entirety of the political spectrum and among such disparate interest groups as physicians, advocates for the poor, [academics,] and consumer groups. Unlike many reforms, EMTALA does not create a new administrative bureaucracy; it does not favor the interests of the well-connected against the less fortunate; its on-budget costs are modest; and it seems to be no more intrusive than is absolutely necessary to accomplish its objectives.

David A. Hyman, Patient Dumping and EMTALA: Past Imperfect/Future Shock, 8 Health Matrix 29 (1998). For further discussion of these and other aspects of EMTALA, see David A. Ansell & Robert L. Schiff, Patient Dumping: Status, Implications, and Policy Recommendations, 257 JAMA 1500 (1987); Andrew Jay McClurg, Your Money or Your Life: Interpreting the Federal Act Against Patient Dumping, 24 Wake Forest L. Rev. 173 (1989); Karen Rothenberg, Who Cares? The Evolution of the Legal Duty to Provide Emergency Care, 26 Hous. L. Rev. 21 (1989); Lawrence E. Singer, Look What They've Done to My Law, Ma: COBRA's Implosion, 33 Hous. L. Rev. 113 (1996); Annot., 104 A.L.R. Fed. 166 (1991).

2. *Screening and Stabilizing.* EMTALA creates two distinct duties. First, the duty to screen patients is triggered by their arrival at the hospital, and it ceases if it is determined they are not in what the statute defines as an "emergency" condition. Second, if they are in an emergency condition, then the hospital must stabilize them. (The statutory requirements are similar for patients in active labor.) Most litigation has arisen at the first stage, in cases where patients claim the hospital failed entirely to evaluate or recognize their emergency condition. But that is not our main concern here. Our concern is, if there clearly is an emergency, how far does the duty to treat extend? Do hospitals have to perform bypass surgery after they halt a heart attack? Although *Burditt* found that "stabilizing" care was not rendered in that case, what about other typical situations? Consider whether the outcome would be any different under EMTALA than it was under this state law decision: Joyner v. Alton Ochsner Medical Foundation, 230 So. 2d 913 (La. Ct. App. 1970) (auto accident victim did not "require immediate admission" after stabilizing care was rendered, despite "multiple deep facial lacerations, a possible head injury, traumatic damage to the teeth and multiple bruises and contusions of the body, resulting in considerable loss of blood"). Consider whether the duty to treat under EMTALA is as strong as it is under this state law decision: Thompson v. Sun City Community Hospital, 688 P.2d 605 (Ariz. 1984) (a cause of action exists against a hospital that stabilized a patient with a severed artery and then transferred him for financial reasons). Is the federal statute any more demanding than the *Manlove* reliance theory? See generally M. Hall, The Unlikely Case in Favor of Patient Dumping, 28 Jurimetrics J. 389 (1990) ("In the great majority of cases, the federal standard will do nothing to prevent patient dumping. . . . Even for those patients who do require stabilization prior to transfer, the federal law will result only in a delay in the transfer."); Wing & Campbell, The Emergency Room Admission: How Far Does the "Open Door" Go?, 65 U. Det. L. Rev. 119 (1985).

According to the Eleventh Circuit, the stablilization requirement of EMTALA applies only when a hospital discharges a patient or transfers the patient to another hospital. Harry v. Marchant, 291 F.3d 767 (11th Cir. 2002) (en banc). See also Bryan V. Rectors and Visitors of the University of Virginia, 95 F.3d 349, 352 (4th Cir. 1996) (also observing that the stabilization requirement of EMTALA is defined in terms of transfer or discharge).

3. *The Patient's Indigency.* While the passage of EMTALA was motivated by concerns about private hospitals "dumping" indigent or uninsured patients on public hospitals, the statutory language imposes no requirement that patients show that they were denied emergency services because of indigency or lack of insurance. See 42 U.S.C. §1395dd(a) ("if any individual . . . comes to the emergency

department . . . , the hospital must provide for an appropriate medical screening examination within the capability of the hospital's emergency department"). Accordingly, courts have generally held that it is irrelevant why a person did not receive an appropriate screening exam or, if an emergency was identified, why a person did not receive stabilizing care before discharge or transfer. As one court observed, "[EMTALA] applies to any and all patients, not just to patients with insufficient resources." Brooker v. Desert Hosp. Corp., 947 F.2d 412, 415 (9th Cir. 1991). *Accord* Summers v. Baptist Medical Center, 91 F.3d 1132 (8th Cir. 1996); Gatewood v. Washington Healthcare Corp., 933 F.2d 1037, 1040 (D.C. Cir. 1991).

The Supreme Court addressed the motive question in the context of EMTALA's stabilization requirement and rejected any need to show an improper motive. Roberts v. Galen of Virginia, Inc., 525 U.S. 249 (1999). The Court "express[ed] no opinion" on the need to show an improper motive for a claim of inappropriate medical screening.

Perhaps the most controversial extension of EMTALA beyond economic discrimination occurred in the *Baby K* case. In In re Baby K, 16 F.3d 590 (4th Cir. 1994), parents of an anencephalic child sought ventilatory treatment of their child during periodic bouts of respiratory distress. After the second of three such episodes, the hospital sought judicial permission to withhold the ventilator when the child next came to the emergency room. In the view of the hospital, it was medically and ethically inappropriate to ventilate the child given her limited life expectancy, her total absence of consciousness, and the futility of treatment at improving her condition. According to the hospital, the only appropriate treatment for the child was the treatment "it would provide other anencephalic infants—supportive care in the form of warmth, nutrition, and hydration." The court rejected the hospital's argument. It observed that EMTALA requires stabilizing treatment in the event of a medical emergency, and the child's respiratory distress met EMTALA's definition of a medical emergency. If there was to be an exception for "futile" care under EMTALA, Congress would have to write that exception into the statute. The court's opinion in *Baby K* is presented in Chapter 1.

The *Baby K* decision raises serious questions about the ability of society to contain health care costs. If the hospital in the case could not deny a ventilator to an anencephalic child, how could any emergency medical care be withheld on the ground that its high costs were not justified by its minimal benefit? Is there a distinction between the economic or other discrimination prohibited by EMTALA and the denial of care that results when a hospital is concerned about the limits of society's resources?

Perhaps in recognition of these concerns, the Fourth Circuit limited the impact of *Baby K* two years later. In Bryan v. Rectors and Visitors of the University of Virginia, 95 F.3d 349 (4th Cir. 1996), an EMTALA claim was brought on behalf of a patient who died of a heart attack after her physicians decided that "no further efforts to prevent her death should be made." Twenty days before the heart attack, the patient had been admitted to the hospital in respiratory distress. Eight days before the heart attack, apparently because of the hopelessness of the patient's condition, her physicians decided to withhold further life-sustaining treatment, including cardiopulmonary resuscitation, in the event of a cardiac arrest. When she suffered her heart attack, no efforts were made to prevent her death. According to the court, there was no EMTALA violation because EMTALA "was intended to regulate the hospital's care of the patient only in the immediate aftermath of the act of admitting her for emergency treatment and while it considered whether it would undertake longer-term full treatment or instead transfer the patient to a hospital that could and would undertake that treatment." Id. at 352.

4. *Preventive Dumping.* There has been concern that hospitals would try to evade their EMTALA obligations by dumping patients before they reach the emergency room. For example, when called by a paramedic or emergency medical technician who is transporting a patient by ambulance, the emergency room staff might direct the ambulance to another hospital. Early cases suggested that hospitals would have considerable freedom to prevent patients from reaching the emergency room. See Miller v. Medical Center of Southwest Louisiana, 22 F.3d 626 (5th Cir. 1994) (hospital not liable under EMTALA for refusing to accept the transfer of a patient who needed specialized emergency care beyond the capabilities of the transferring hospital); Johnson v. University of Chicago Hospitals, 982 F.2d 230 (7th Cir. 1992) (hospital not liable for diverting an ambulance to another hospital).

Subsequent amendment of the EMTALA regulations and case law interpreting the amendment have limited the ability of hospitals to engage in preventive dumping. Under one regulation, patients have come to the hospital's emergency room for purposes of EMTALA once they have reached any part of the hospital's property, including a hospital-owned ambulance service. 42 C.F.R. §489.24(b) (2002) (applied in Hernandez v. Starr County Hospital District, 30 F. Supp. 2d 970 (S.D. Tex. 1999)). The same regulation permits hospitals to divert non-hospital-owned ambulance services if the emergency department "does not have the staff or facilities to accept any additional emergency patients." 42 C.F.R. §489.24(b). The Ninth Circuit has interpreted this provision to mean that a hospital violates EMTALA when it diverts a non-hospital-owned ambulance in the absence of an inability to provide treatment for the patient. Arrington v. Wong, 237 F.3d 1066 (9th Cir. 2001). See Caroline J. Stalker, Comment, How Far Is Too Far?: EMTALA Moves from the Emergency Room to Off-Campus Entities, 36 Wake Forest L. Rev. 823 (2001).

Note that there is some ambiguity to §489.24(b). Although the regulation seems to limit the ability of hospitals to divert non-hospital-owned ambulances, it also states that "[a]n individual in a non-hospital-owned ambulance off hospital property is not considered to have come to the hospital's emergency department even if a member of the ambulance staff contacts the hospital by telephone or telemetry communications and informs the hospital that they want to transport the individual to the hospital for examination and treatment."

A related question is whether patients must come to the emergency department, as opposed to other parts of the hospital, to trigger EMTALA. As indicated, under 42 C.F.R. §489.24(b), EMTALA is triggered when a patient is anywhere on the hospital's property. Thus, a First Circuit decision emphasizes the point that a hospital's duty to stabilize before transfer applies to any patient in the hospital, "regardless of how that person enters the institution or where within the walls he may be when the hospital identifies the problem." Lopez-Soto v. Hawayek, 175 F.3d 170, 173 (1st Cir. 1999) (holding that EMTALA applies when a pregnant woman is admitted to the maternity ward and taken to the operating room for a cesarean section, and her infant is born with respiratory distress and needs emergency care).

5. *Dumping After Admission to the Hospital.* Courts disagree as to whether EMTALA's stabilzation requirement continues to apply once the patient has been admitted to the hospital. Cases have arisen in which patients were admitted to the hospital for treatment and, after a few or more days of treatment, been transferred to another hospital or discharged before their illness was fully treated. Some courts have concluded that the obligation to stabilize persists throughout the patient's hospitalization. See Thornton v. Southwest Detroit Hospital, 895 F.2d 1131 (6th Cir. 1990); Lee v. Alleghany Regional Hospital Corporation, 778 F. Supp. 900 (W.D. Va. 1991); Smith v. Richmond Memorial Hospital, 416 S.E.2d 689 (Va. 1992).

Other courts have concluded that the stabilization requirement ceases upon the patient's admission to the hospital. Bryan v. Rectors and Visitors of the University of Virginia, 95 F.3d 349, 352 (4th Cir. 1996); James v. Sunrise Hospital, 86 F.3d 885 (9th Cir. 1996); Bryant v. Adventist Health Systems/West, 289 F.3d 1162 (9th Cir. 2002). Note that in *Bryan* and *Bryant*, the courts were deciding about the stabilization requirement for care rendered during the patient's hospital stay and not in the context of a transfer or discharge. Hence, it is not surprising that the courts were especially concerned about converting state malpractice claims into federal EMTALA claims. See note 6, infra, this page.

In a final rule that took effect on November 10, 2003, the Centers for Medicare and Medicaid Services took the position that a hospital's obligations cease once the patient has been admitted to the hospital as an inpatient.

6. *Appropriate Medical Screening.* In interpreting EMTALA's requirement of an "appropriate medical screening examination," courts have recognized an important tension between ensuring access to emergency care for all persons and creating a federal cause of action for charges of malpractice in the emergency room. If a person is sent home from the emergency room after a physician wrongly concludes that there is no serious health problem, the mistaken diagnosis may reflect either the negligent provision of care or the purposeful denial of care. A hospital trying to evade its EMTALA obligations might do so by giving undesired patients short shrift when screening them. At the same time, patients who have been injured by malpractice may try to bring their claim under both state tort law and federal EMTALA law, thereby increasing their potential recovery, gaining access to a federal forum and its quicker judgments, and increasing its bargaining power with the hospitals by virtue of the latter's possible loss of its participation in Medicare. EMTALA claims are often appended to state tort claims when people sue for injuries allegedly caused by inadequate emergency care. Singer, supra, 33 Hous. L. Rev. at 118 & n.22.

Courts have consistently stated that EMTALA cannot be used to bring claims for medical malpractice, and they have tried to distinguish between a denial of care and the negligent provision of care by looking at whether the hospital screened the patient in the same way it screens similarly situated patients. As the D.C. Circuit explained, the issue is whether the hospital "conform[ed] its treatment of a particular patient to its standard screening procedures. . . . [A]ny departure from standard screening procedures constitutes inappropriate screening." Gatewood v. Washington Healthcare Corporation, 933 F.2d 1037, 1041 (D.C. Cir. 1991).

Similarly, the Fourth Circuit has stated that EMTALA's screening requirement is designed to prevent "disparate treatment." Vickers v. Nash General Hospital, Inc., 78 F.3d 139, 143 (4th Cir. 1996). Hospitals are obligated only to "apply uniform screening procedures to all individuals coming to the emergency room." In re Baby K, 16 F.3d 590, 595 (4th Cir. 1994). *Accord* Summers v. Baptist Medical Center, 91 F.3d 1132, 1138 (8th Cir. 1996); Repp v. Anadarko Municipal Hospital, 43 F.3d 519, 522 (10th Cir. 1994); Holcomb v. Monahan, 30 F.3d 116, 117 (11th Cir. 1994). The Sixth Circuit has adopted a similar standard, although there is some suggestion in the court's discussion that the departure from the hospital's standard screening procedures must have resulted from some invidious motive like bias against the patient on the basis of "race, sex, politics, occupation, education, personal prejudice, drunkenness, spite . . . distaste for the patient's condition (e.g., AIDS patients). . . ." Cleland v. Bronson Health Care Group, Inc., 917 F.2d 266, 271–272 (6th Cir. 1990). Even if the Sixth Circuit requires some invidious motive, would it ever be difficult to find a bias lurking that would be unacceptable under the *Cleland* standard?

Despite the courts' admonition that EMTALA does not create a federal malpractice cause of action, it is impossible to escape that result. Do you see how a requirement that hospitals provide all patients with their standard screening procedures amounts to requiring that the hospitals provide nonnegligent care? See Demetrios G. Metropoulos, Note, Son of COBRA: The Evolution of a Federal Malpractice Law, 45 Stan. L. Rev. 263 (1992).

As the preceding discussion indicates, courts have interpreted the requirement of an appropriate screening examination as an equal treatment right rather than an entitlement right. But isn't EMTALA a statute that grants an entitlement rather than a right of equal treatment? Is there a way to define appropriate screening examination as an entitlement without turning it even more clearly into the equivalent of nonnegligent care?

B. HOSPITAL LIABILITY

While most doctors are well insured, some are not; and even those who are do not always make the most attractive targets for suit. Moreover, many medical errors do not result from physicians' mistakes. Therefore, plaintiffs are sometimes eager to hold the institutions in which physicians practice responsible for bad medical outcomes. There are two prominent institutions: hospitals and insurers, especially HMOs. These targets of suit entail both unique theories of liability and unique defenses against liability, which the follow sections explore.

You will learn shortly that two distinct theories of liability have emerged: vicarious and direct. In the former, the institution is held strictly liable for acts of negligence by member physicians, based on the physician's relationship with the institution. Observe how this branch of liability takes shape according to differences in how types of physicians are connected with hospitals. Direct liability, the second branch, depends on showing some wrongdoing by the institution's management with respect to physician competence and patient care. Here, the issue is what responsibility is it realistic to assign to lay managers with respect to clinical matters? Overarching this development of legal doctrine is an evolution in judicial and public attitudes about the role that institutions play in the delivery of health care. This change has occurred both with respect to hospital liability and in the migration of liability from hospitals to HMOs. To set these materials in their historical context, then, we begin with a now outmoded, but still seminal decision.

■ SCHLOENDORFF v. SOCIETY OF NEW YORK HOSPITAL
105 N.E. 92 (N.Y. 1914)

CARDOZO, J.

In the year 1771, by royal charter of George III, the Society of the New York Hospital was organized for the care and healing of the sick. During the century and more which has since passed, it has devoted itself to that high task. It has no capital stock; it does not distribute profits; and its physicians and surgeons, both the visiting and the resident staff, serve it without pay. Those who seek it in search of health are charged nothing if they are needy, either for board or for treatment. The well-to-do are required by its by-laws to pay $7 a week for board, an amount insufficient to cover the per capita cost of maintenance. Whatever income is thus received is added to the income derived from the hospital's foundation, and helps to make it possible for the work to go on. The purpose is not profit, but charity. . . .

To this hospital the plaintiff came in January, 1908. She was suffering from some disorder of the stomach. She asked the superintendent or one of his assistants what the charge would be, and was told that it would be $7 a week. She became an inmate of the hospital, and after some weeks of treatment, the house physician, Dr. Bartlett, discovered a lump, which proved to be a fibroid tumor. He consulted the visiting physician, Dr. Stimson, who advised an operation. The plaintiff's testimony is that the character of the lump could not, so the physicians informed her, be determined without an ether examination. She consented to such an examination, but notified Dr. Bartlett, as she says, that there must be no operation. She was taken at night from the medical to the surgical ward and prepared for an operation by a nurse. On the following day ether was administered, and, while she was unconscious, a tumor was removed. Her testimony is that this was done without her consent or knowledge. She is contradicted both by Dr. Stimson and by Dr. Bartlett, as well as by many of the attendant nurses. For the purpose of this appeal, however, since a verdict was directed in favor of the defendant, her narrative, even if improbable, must be taken as true. Following the operation, and, according to the testimony of her witnesses, because of it, gangrene developed in her left arm, some of her fingers had to be amputated, and her sufferings were intense. She now seeks to charge the hospital with liability for the wrong.

Certain principles of law governing the rights and duties of hospitals, when maintained as charitable institutions have, after much discussion, become no longer doubtful. It is the settled rule that such a hospital is not liable for the negligence of its physicians and nurses in the treatment of patients. Hillyer v. St. Bartholomew's Hospital, [1909] 2 K.B. 820. This exemption has been placed upon two grounds. The first is that of implied waiver. It is said that one who accepts the benefit of a charity enters into a relation which exempts one's benefactor from liability for the negligence of his servants in administering the charity. The hospital remains exempt, though the patient makes some payment to help defray the cost of board. Such a payment is regarded as a contribution to the income of the hospital, to be devoted, like its other funds to the maintenance of the charity. The second ground of the exemption is the relation subsisting between a hospital and the physicians who serve it. It is said that this relation is not one of master and servant, but that the physician occupies the position, so to speak, of an independent contractor, following a separate calling, liable, of course, for his own wrongs to the patient whom he undertakes to serve, but involving the hospital in no liability, if due care has been taken in his selection. On one or the other, and often on both of these grounds, a hospital has been held immune from liability to patients for the malpractice of its physicians. The reasons that have led to the adoption of this rule are, of course, inapplicable where the wrong is committed by a servant of the hospital and the sufferer is not a patient. It is therefore also a settled rule that a hospital is liable to strangers—i.e., to persons other than patients—for the torts of its employees committed within the line of their employment.

In the case at hand, the wrong complained of is not merely negligence. It is trespass. Every human being of adult years and sound mind has a right to determine what shall be done with his own body; and a surgeon who performs an operation without his patient's consent commits an assault, for which he is liable in damages. This is true, except in cases of emergency where the patient is unconscious, and where it is necessary to operate before consent can be obtained. The fact that the wrong complained of here is trespass, rather than negligence, distinguishes this case from most of the cases that have preceded it. . . . [The plaintiff] had never waived the right to recover damages for any wrong resulting from this operation, for she had forbidden the operation. In this situation, the true ground for the defendant's exemption from liability is that the relation between a hospital and its physicians is not that of master and servant. The hospital does not undertake to act through them, but merely to procure them to act upon their own responsibility. . . .

The wrong was not that of the hospital; it was that of physicians, who were not the defendant's servants, but were pursuing an independent calling, a profession sanctioned by a solemn oath, and safeguarded by stringent penalties. If, in serving their patient, they violated her commands, the responsibility is not the defendant's; it is theirs. There is no distinction in that respect between the visiting and the resident physicians. Whether the hospital undertakes to procure a physician from afar, or to have one on the spot, its liability remains the same. . . .

It is true, I think, of nurses, as of physicians, that, in treating a patient, they are not acting as the servants of the hospital. The superintendent is a servant of the hospital; the assistant superintendents, the orderlies, and the other members of the administrative staff are servants of the hospital. But nurses are employed to carry out the orders of the physicians, to whose authority they are subject. The hospital undertakes to procure for the patient the services of a nurse. It does not undertake, through the agency of nurses, to render those services itself. The reported cases make no distinction in that respect between the position of a nurse and that of a physician and none is justified in principle. If there are duties performed by nurses foreign to their duties in carrying out the physician's orders, and having relation to the administrative conduct of the hospital, the fact is not established by this record, nor was it in the discharge of such duties that the defendant's nurses were then serving. The acts of preparation immediately preceding the operation are necessary to its successful performance, and are really part of the operation itself. They are not different in that respect from the administration of the ether. Whatever the nurse does in those preliminary stages is done, not as the servant of the hospital, but in the course of the treatment of the patient, as the delegate of the surgeon to whose orders she is subject. The hospital is not chargeable with her knowledge that the operation is improper any more than with the surgeon's.

If, however, it could be assumed that a nurse is a servant of the hospital, . . . [w]as she to infer from the plaintiff's words that a distinguished surgeon intended to mutilate the plaintiff's body in defiance of the plaintiff's orders? Was it her duty, as a result of this talk, to report to the superintendent of the hospital that the ward was about to be utilized for the commission of an assault? I think that no such interpretation of the facts would have suggested itself to any reasonable mind. The preparation for an ether examination is to some extent the same as for an operation. The hour was midnight, and the plaintiff was nervous and excited. . . . There may be cases where a patient ought not to be advised of a contemplated operation until shortly before the appointed hour. To discuss such a subject at midnight might cause needless and even harmful agitation. About such matters a nurse is not qualified to judge. She is drilled to habits of strict obedience. She is accustomed to rely unquestioningly upon the judgment of her superiors. No woman occupying such a position would reasonably infer from the plaintiff's words that it was the purpose of the surgeons to operate whether the plaintiff forbade it or not. I conclude, therefore, that the plaintiff's statements to the nurse on the night before the operation are insufficient to charge the hospital with notice of a contemplated wrong. . . .

The conclusion, therefore, follows that the trial judge did not err in his direction of a verdict. A ruling would, indeed, be an unfortunate one that might constrain charitable institutions, as a measure of self-protection, to limit their activities. A hospital opens its doors without discrimination to all who seek its aid. It gathers in its wards a company of skilled physicians and trained nurses, and places their services at the call of the afflicted, without scrutiny of the character or the worth of those who appeal to it, looking at nothing and caring for nothing beyond the fact of their affliction. In this beneficent work, it does not subject itself to liability for damages, though the ministers of healing whom it has selected have proved unfaithful to their trust.

Notes: Hospital Liability; Charitable and Governmental Immunity

1. Is Justice Cardozo's rejection of hospital liability as absolute as it first appears? What about the qualification, "if due care has been taken in [the doctor's] selection"? What if the court were more demanding about the nurse's duty to speak up? Compare these potential theories of liability with those introduced in the

modern landmark case of Darling v. Charleston Community Hospital, excerpted at page 121.

2. *Charitable Immunity*. The rule of charitable immunity was subjected to an increasing number of exceptions—distinguishing between paying and nonpaying patients, patients and strangers, and administrative versus professional acts—until it eventually crumbled. The leading decision is President of Georgetown College v. Hughes, 130 F.2d 810 (D.C. Cir. 1942), which observed that charitable hospitals could simply purchase insurance to protect themselves from economic catastrophe. The gist of this changed attitude is best captured in a colorful dissent by the renowned Pennsylvania Justice Musmanno in Michael v. Hahnemann Medical College and Hospital of Philadelphia, 172 A.2d 769 (Pa. 1961):

> Hospitals then were little better than hovels in which the indigent were gathered for the primitive cures available. The wealthy and the well-to-do were cared for in their homes. The hospital or infirmary was more often than not part of the village parish. Charity in the biblical sense prevailed. And if it happened that some poor mortal was scalded by a sister of mercy, who exhausted from long hours of vigil and toil, accidentally spilled a ladle of hot soup on a hand extended for nourishment, there was no thought of lawsuits against the philanthropists who made the meager refuge possible. But if, following such a mishap, litigation should have been initiated in the courts, it is not difficult to understand why judges would be reluctant to honor such a complaint, convinced on the basis of humanity, that an enterprise utterly devoid of worldly gain should be exempt from liability. A successful lawsuit against such a feeble structure might well have demolished it and have thus paralyzed the only helping hand in the world of unconcern for the rag-clothed sick and the crutchless disabled.
>
> The situation today is quite different. Charitable enterprises are not housed in ramshackly wooden structures. They are not mere storm shelters to succor the traveler and temporarily refuge those stricken in a common disaster. Hospitals today, to a large extent, are mighty edifices, in stone, glass and marble. They maintain large staffs, they use the best equipment that science can devise, they utilize the most modern methods of helping themselves to the noblest purpose of man, that of helping one's stricken brother. But they do all this on a business basis, and properly so. . . . And if the hospital is a business for the purpose of collecting money, it must be a business for the purpose of meeting its obligations. . . .

Despite this shift in attitude, a number of states retain a version of charitable immunity in statutes that limit the amount of recovery against nonprofit hospitals or charities generally to anywhere from $10,000 to $500,000. See Note, The Quality of Mercy: "Charitable Torts" and their Continuing Immunity, 100 Harv. L. Rev. 1382 (1987). See generally Charles Tremper, Compensation for Harm from Charitable Activity, 76 Cornell L. Rev. 401 (1991); Annot., 25 A.L.R. 4th 517 (1983).

3. *Governmental Immunity*. Public hospitals might also claim governmental immunity under the common law concept that "the king can do no wrong." See, e.g., Withers v. University of Kentucky, 939 S.W.2d 340 (Ky. 1997) (university hospital is a "state agency" immune from suit). Most states, however, have abrogated governmental immunity to some degree by statute, as has the federal government. This abrogation is often limited, though, to "ministerial" or "proprietary"

functions, thus preserving many of the same arcane distinctions that arose under charitable immunity and the *Schloendorff* rule. See, e.g., Moser v. Heistand, 681 A.2d 1322 (Pa. 1996) (immunity exists only for suits based simply on physician error, not for suits based on failures in administration that result in physician error). See generally John Akula, Sovereign Immunity and Health Care: Can Government Be Trusted?, 19(6) Health Aff. 152 (Dec. 2000). Substantial immunity is still common in many states for psychiatric hospitals, and full immunity is still preserved for injuries suffered during the course of active military duty. See Feres v. United States, 340 U.S. 135 (1950). In sharp contrast, Veterans Administration (VA) hospitals are subject by statute to a form of strict liability, without regard to negligence. See Brown v. Gardner, 513 U.S. 115 (1994).

4. *Subsequent Developments in Vicarious Liability.* The refusal to apply ordinary principles of respondeat superior even to employed nurses gave way in later decades to a rule that held the hospital responsible for "administrative" errors, in contrast with errors in medical judgment. What resulted was a string of arcane distinctions and inconsistent decisions concerning such routine medical acts as administering medication, giving injections, and applying casts. For instance, giving a blood transfusion to the wrong patient was considered "administrative," whereas giving the wrong blood to the right patient was labeled an error of medical judgment. See generally Bing v. Thunig, 143 N.E.2d 3 (N.Y. 1957). As will be seen in the next case, these cracks in hospitals' liability armor eventually led to the outright reversal of *Schloendorff* by *Bing*. The modern issue, then, becomes how does standard respondeat superior apply to physicians who are not, strictly speaking, employees.

On the modern status of hospital liability generally, see James Smith, Hospital Liability; Mary Bertolet & Lee Goldsmith, Hospital Liability: Law and Practice; Aspen Hospital Law Manual.

■ ADAMSKI v. TACOMA GENERAL HOSPITAL
579 P.2d 970 (Wash. Ct. App. 1978)

REED, Acting Chief Judge.
. . . On January 9, 1974, plaintiff injured his finger while playing basketball. According to plaintiff the bone had broken and was protruding from a gash on the palmar surface of the finger. Plaintiff, aided by a friend, forced the bone back into position, applied a crude splint, covered the wound with a makeshift bandage and continued the game. Later that evening he presented himself for treatment at the emergency room of Tacoma General. . . . [T]he physician in charge, Dr. Tsoi . . . irrigated, debrided and cleansed the wound with saline solution and the cut was closed completely with nylon sutures and bandaged. [Because Dr. Tsoi did not realize the bone had been exposed, he did not sufficiently treat the wound for a deep infection. After plaintiff contacted a series of nurses and other doctors, the wound was reopened and cleaned three days later at another hospital, and the finger eventually healed properly.] . . .

Plaintiff brought this action for damages against Dr. Tsoi, Tacoma Emergency Care Physicians, Inc., P.S. (TECP), a group of physicians who had contracted with Tacoma General, and Tacoma General, alleging as to the latter that (1) Dr. Tsoi was negligent in his diagnosis and treatment, (2) Dr. Tsoi was acting as the Hospital's agent, and (3) the Hospital's nurse-employees were negligent.

Tacoma General moved for summary judgment in its favor, asserting it could not be held liable for Dr. Tsoi's negligence upon the theory of respondeat superior because the doctor was not acting as its agent (employee-servant). Tacoma General argued the doctor was an independent contractor over whose actions it neither had nor exercised any right of control. . . .

According to the [] supporting documents, on January 1, 1973 the Hospital contracted with TECP, a group of five licensed physicians, among them Dr. Tsoi, to furnish emergency room physicians on a 24-hour basis. The contract specifically classifies the emergency room doctors as "independent contractors" and not "agents or employees" of the Hospital. The agreement further provided inter alia that (1) Tacoma General alone is to bill patients for the fees of the physicians, who agree to charge going rates; (2) the Hospital undertakes to collect from the patient, by suit if necessary; (3) Tacoma General guarantees TECP $10,000 per month; (4) after certain deductions TECP is to be credited with 85 percent of all doctor fees collected, less the $10,000 guaranty; the Hospital retains 15 percent for its collection services; (5) the emergency room doctors must be members of Tacoma General's staff and may not carry on a private practice in Pierce County, although they are not prohibited from (a) providing emergency room service to other hospitals, (b) assisting private physicians with surgery upon request, (c) teaching medical subjects and (d) providing medical laboratory consulting services; (6) emergency room physicians are precluded from utilizing the emergency room as a "source of private practice"; (7) if TECP desires to furnish a physician other than one of the five named in the contract, Tacoma General's Board must first consent; (8) Tacoma General and TECP will each procure and maintain "professional liability, negligence, errors and omissions, and public liability" policies with limits of $1 million.

On this record, the trial court concluded that Dr. Tsoi was an independent contractor and not an employee of the Hospital, and thus refused to hold the Hospital liable on a respondeat superior theory. . . .

We have found no Washington cases addressing the problems inherent in the application of the doctrine of respondeat superior to the hospital-physician relationship. Tacoma General argues that the ordinary rules of agency must be applied and that if this is done, Dr. Tsoi must be held to be an independent contractor for whose negligent acts the Hospital is not responsible. . . . Tacoma General points out that nowhere in its contract with TECP does it reserve the right to exercise any control over the actual medical treatment rendered to its emergency room patients. Rather, Tacoma General argues, the only contract requirement is that the doctors must be members of Tacoma General's staff and conform to the usual and accepted professional and ethical standards of conduct.

The experience of the courts has been that application of hornbook rules of agency to the hospital-physician relationship usually leads to unrealistic and unsatisfactory results, at least from the standpoint of the injured patient. Consequently, we have seen a substantial body of special law emerging in this area; the result has been an expansion of hospital liability for negligent medical acts committed on its premises.

For many years the majority of courts followed the rule espoused by Tacoma General and held that physicians, because of their skill and training in a highly technical field, were not subject to control by hospital lay boards and thus could not be servants or employees in the sense required by the doctrine of respondeat superior. Rather, physicians were classified as independent contractors with the result that the hospitals in which they labored could not be held vicariously liable for their medical mistakes. . . . The rationale of *Schloendorff* was followed in many jurisdictions until the decision in Bing v. Thunig, 143 N.E.2d 3 (N.Y. 1957). In a masterful opinion by Judge Fuld, the New York court rejected Cardozo's "professional skill" theory of immunity as being out of step with the times. In essence, the *Bing* court reasoned that other highly skilled professionals were not being excluded from application of the rule of respondeat superior and no valid reason existed for excluding medical practitioners per se. Judge Fuld stressed that hospitals had become more than just a place for physicians to bring their patients for treatment; that, in fact, the hospital itself renders care and treatment through its facilities and employees. In holding the hospital responsible for the negligence of its nurses, Judge Fuld stated:

> The conception that the hospital does not undertake to treat the patient, does not undertake to act through its doctors and nurses, but undertakes instead simply to procure them to act upon their own responsibility, no longer reflects the fact. Present-day hospitals, as their manner of operation plainly demonstrates, do far more than furnish facilities for treatment. They regularly employ on a salary basis a large staff of physicians, nurses and internes, as well as administrative and manual workers, and they charge patients for medical care and treatment, collecting for such services, if necessary, by legal action. Certainly, the person who avails himself of "hospital facilities" expects that the hospital will attempt to cure him, not that its nurses or other employees will act on their own responsibility.

Once again the majority of courts chose to follow the New York court's lead and embraced the *Bing* concept that, in certain cases the doctrine of respondeat superior may serve to render a hospital liable for the negligent acts of the medical personnel who deliver its service to its patients. Since *Bing*, the principal difficulty encountered by the courts has been in determining in which cases to apply the rule of vicarious liability. Application of the traditional right of control test has not solved the problem because the governing body of a hospital never actually exercises, nor can it exercise, much control over a physician's medical decisions and his actual treatment of patients, even when he is clearly an employee of the hospital, such as an intern or resident.

Even before *Schloendorff* and *Bing*, however, the California court, in Brown v. La Societe Francaise de Bienfaisance Mutuelle, 138 Cal. 475, 71 P. 516 (1903) applied the doctrine of respondeat superior to the hospital-physician relationship because (1) the patient in the case sought treatment primarily from the hospital, and (2) the hospital paid the doctor a salary. It is on the basis of the "Brown formula" that many courts now regularly hold hospitals liable for the negligence of their interns and resident physicians.

Conversely, where the patient contacts his personal physician and is by him admitted to a hospital for treatment, and the doctor looks directly to the patient for his fees, the courts uniformly treat the physician as an independent contractor. Such a holding results in a refusal to impose vicarious liability upon the hospital for the physician's medical mistakes even though they may occur on hospital premises.

The *Brown* formula does not, however, cover all the possible variations of the hospital-doctor-patient relationship; the most troublesome situation has been that where the patient, not having contacted his personal physician, presents himself at the hospital for treatment and is there provided with or referred to a physician, usually a specialist, who is neither an intern, resident or other salaried employee of the hospital. The courts generally look to all of the facts and circumstances to determine if the hospital and doctor enjoy such a "significant relationship" that the rule of respondeat superior ought to apply.[1] . . . In such cases, it should make no difference that the physician is compensated on some basis other than salary or that he bills his patient directly. These are artificial distinctions, the efficacy of which has long since disappeared and to the perpetuation of which we do not subscribe.

An example of the more enlightened approach is found in . . . Beeck v. Tucson General Hospital, 18 Ariz. App. 165, 500 P.2d 1153 (1972). [There] a summary judgment in favor of the hospital was reversed, the appellate court finding the relationship between the hospital and the physician in charge of its radiology department was that of employer-employee. Even though the doctor and his partner contracted to staff the department and were compensated by a percentage of revenues rather than by salary, the court found a significant relationship between hospital and doctor and applied the doctrine of respondeat superior. In support of its holding, the Arizona court noted the following pertinent facts: (1) the hospital billed for the radiologist's services; (2) the doctors received no other compensation; (3) the doctors agreed generally not to engage in private practice; (4) the doctors were solely responsible for operation of the department; (5) the doctors provided their own insurance coverage; (6) the doctors were to comply with the policies, rules and regulations of the hospital and the American Osteopathic Association; (7) the contract term was five years, terminable upon 120 days' written notice; (8) the hospital owned all the equipment and office supplies and provided the supporting technicians; (9) the patient had no choice in selecting a radiologist, the hospital having made that choice for her. The court noted that . . . the doctor was employed for an extended period of time; and he performed a service which was "a inherent function of the hospital, a function without which the hospital could not properly achieve its purpose." Finally, the fact that Mrs. Beeck had signed a document acknowledging that all those performing services for her, including the radiologist, were independent contractors, and

[1] The term "significant relationship" is suggested in Cunningham, The Hospital-Physician Relationship: Hospital Responsibility for Malpractice of Physicians, 50 Wash. L. Rev. 385 (1975), wherein the author opines that the courts, without saying so, appear to be working toward an "enterprise tort," with the inquiry being addressed solely to whether the tort occurred within the scope of the "hospital enterprise" which is defined as "any service, medical or otherwise, the hospital purports to provide the patient."

not employees or agents of the hospital, gave the Arizona court little pause: "Unless the radiologist were actually an independent contractor the clause reciting him to be so is of no effect." . . .

In Schagrin v. Wilmington Medical Center, Inc., 304 A.2d 61 (Del. S. Ct. 1973) . . . [the] court appears to fasten on a nondelegable duty to the public which was assumed by the hospital when it, although not required by law to do so, elected to staff and maintain emergency room services as part of its total hospital enterprise.[5]

Turning to the case before us it can readily be seen that . . . Dr. Tsoi was performing "an inherent function of the hospital, a function without which the hospital could not properly achieve its purpose," Beeck v. Tucson General Hospital, i.e., he was an integral part of the total hospital function or enterprise. Clearly, when one considers all the facts and circumstances of the relationship between Tacoma General and its emergency room physicians, a substantial and genuine issue arises as to whether that relationship is that of principal and agent. It was error to resolve this issue by summary judgment.

Moreover, where a physician is found not to be the actual agent of the hospital, the latter may still be held responsible for his departures from good medical practice under the so-called holding out or ostensible agent theory. Restatement (Second) Agency §267, p.578 (1958) sets forth the rule as follows: "One who represents that another is his servant or other agent and thereby causes a third person justifiably to rely upon the care or skill of such apparent agent is subject to liability to the third person for harm caused by the lack of care or skill of the one appearing to be a servant or other agent as if he were such." . . .

In Howard v. Park, 37 Mich. App. 496, 195 N.W.2d 39 (1972), the defendant clinic referred a little girl patient to an independent doctor for removal of a leg cast using a "vibrating wheel." The patient sustained severe cuts and sought damages from the clinic. The *Howard* court found the clinic liable on ostensible agency grounds. The court noted that (1) treatment took place in the clinic; (2) the clinic chose the physician; and (3) the clinic billed on its stationery for the physician's charges. The court refused to adopt a requirement that the patient must inquire as to the treating doctor's status in order to entertain a reasonable belief he was the hospital's employee. . . .

Tacoma General argues, however, that there can be no "ostensible agency" or agency by estoppel as it is sometimes called, in the absence of proof of an "affirmative misrepresentation" of Dr. Tsoi's status. . . . On the contrary, a "holding out" or representation may arise when the hospital acts or omits to act in some way which leads the patient to a reasonable belief he is being treated by the hospital by one of its employees.

---

[5] . . . [T]he Washington State Board of Health has adopted rules and regulations . . . [that] require a licensed hospital to provide emergency care services in accordance with the community's needs and the hospital's capabilities. . . . One requirement is that there must be a physician responsible for the services, whose functions and responsibilities are subject to the medical direction of the hospital. It could thus be argued that Washington state has imposed upon hospitals a duty to provide emergency care services to the public and that they cannot shift the responsibility by contract. This concept was neither developed nor argued at either the trial court level nor in this court on appeal.

In the instant case, a jury could find that Tacoma General held itself out as providing emergency care services to the public. A jury could find that plaintiff reasonably believed Dr. Tsoi was employed by the Hospital to deliver that emergency room service. It appears plaintiff was not advised to the contrary and, in fact, he believed he was being treated by the Hospital's agent; in addition, the written instructions provided him after surgery could reasonably be interpreted as an invitation to return for further treatment if plaintiff could not contact his personal physician. The form bearing this instruction also carried the title "Tacoma General Hospital Emergency Care." Clearly, when the facts before the trial court and the fair inferences therefrom are viewed in a light most favorable to plaintiff, a jury could find that the emergency room personnel were "held out" as employees of the Hospital. It was error, therefore, not to submit this issue to the jury. . . .

For this and the other reasons we have outlined, summary judgment was an inappropriate method of disposing of plaintiff's claims.

Notes: Hospital Vicarious Liability

1. *Hospital Control.* Is it consistent with the corporate practice of medicine doctrine to hold a hospital responsible for the professional mistakes of its agent-physicians? The corporate practice of medicine doctrine holds that it is illegal for corporations to subject physicians to the control of lay management because this would constitute the unlicensed practice of medicine. If respondeat superior liability is premised on the principal's control of an agent's actions, how can it coexist with this prohibition of corporate control of physicians? One leading decision, issued with respect to an HMO, found it necessary to declare the corporate practice of medicine doctrine "totally abolished" in order to hold the HMO vicariously liable for an employed physician's mistake. Sloan v. Metropolitan Health Council of Indianapolis, 516 N.E.2d 1104 (Ind. Ct. App. 1987). The court also reasoned, consistent with other decisions, that respondeat superior does not require actual control but merely a finding that the negligent acts occurred within the course and scope of employment. Otherwise, hospitals could not be held responsible for employed nurses, or airlines for employed pilots. Perhaps based on this thinking, other courts have not found it necessary to abolish the corporate practice of medicine doctrine in order to hold hospitals liable for physicians' errors. See, e.g., McDonald v. Hampton Training School for Nurses, 486 S.E.2d 299 (Va. 1997) (vicarious liability attaches even though hospital does not control actual medical judgment).

2. *"Captain of the Ship."* One hospital defense against vicarious liability that still remains is the "captain of the ship" or borrowed servant doctrine. The effect of this doctrine is not only to hold physicians (usually surgeons) responsible for subordinate doctors and nurses, but sometimes also to relieve the hospital from vicarious responsibility. This occurs when a hospital employee's negligent acts are directed or supervised by a physician who is not an agent of the hospital; then, the independent physician can be found to have temporarily "borrowed" the hospital's employee. Courts usually find that the hospital and the physician in charge share the employee and therefore share liability. See, e.g., Tonsic v. Wagner,

329 A.2d 497 (Pa. 1974). However, courts sometimes hold the doctor solely liable if he instructs the nurse to do an act that contravenes hospital policy. See, e.g., Hoffman v. Wells, 397 S.E.2d 696 (Ga. 1990). See also Restatement (Second) of Agency §227.

3. *Indemnification Agreements.* The principles of vicarious liability introduced here apply to other medical institutions than just hospitals. Materials below explore for instance how vicarious liability applies to HMOs. Earlier, it was observed that physician practice groups or clinics can be held liable as an entity for the negligence of one of their members. It is possible in all of these circumstances, however, to reallocate liability among the parties through the use of indemnification agreements. These agreements do not alter the rights of the injured patient, but they do affect which of several joint tortfeasors can seek contribution or indemnification from the others. Negotiating these indemnification agreements is a major aspect of contract drafting, especially in managed care settings.

4. *Adamski* introduces three concepts of vicarious liability: actual agency (which includes simple employment); ostensible agency; and nondelegable duty (also known as enterprise liability). The third of these is discussed below and at page 121. The first two tend to blend together based on the facts and circumstances of the arrangement. Which facts and circumstances mentioned in *Adamski* and the cases it cites are most relevant to actual agency? Which are most relevant to ostensible agency? How could an arrangement be structured to avoid the first characterization? What techniques would help to avoid the second characterization? Do you agree that the informed consent form is irrelevant to both characterizations? What about signs in the ER waiting room or physicians wearing identification badges?

5. *Facts and Circumstances.* In contrast with the facts-and-circumstances test applied in *Adamski*, most courts in recent years have held that emergency room physicians are subject to a jury finding of ostensible agency regardless of the specifics of the arrangement with the hospital. The courts' reasoning is reflected in the following cases: Gilbert v. Sycamore Municipal Hospital, 622 N.E.2d 788 (Ill. 1993) (hospital advertising itself as offering quality care contributes to the impression that doctors work for the hospital); Hardy v. Brantley, 471 So. 2d 358 (Miss. 1985) (emergency room patient is not in a position to inquire into the specifics of his doctor's contractual arrangements with the hospital); Simmons v. Tuomey Regional Medical Center, 533 S.E.2d 312 (S.C. 2000) (patient did not specifically choose any of the emergency room physicians that treated her). Where ostensible agency is applied outside the classic emergency room setting to hospital-based specialists such as radiologists and anesthesiologists, courts continue to be somewhat more open to argument both ways, depending on the facts and circumstances. Compare Milliron v. Francke, 793 P.2d 824 (Mont. 1990) (providing radiologist with office, equipment, personnel, and billing is not sufficient to establish agency relationship; in a rural setting, it is understood this is necessary to maintain adequate staffing; with Sword v. NKC Hospitals, 714 N.E.2d 142 (Ind. 1999) (anesthesiologist could be found to be an apparent agent of a hospital that "aggressively marketed its services to the public . . . [as] 'the most technically sophisticated birthplace in the region'" and touted the "'full

availability of a special anesthesiology team, experienced and dedicated exclu-
sively to OB patients'"). See generally H. Ward Classen, Hospital Liability for
Independent Contractors: Where Do We Go From Here?, 40 Ark. L. Rev. 469
(1987); J. D. Ingram, Liability of Medical Institutions for the Negligence of
Independent Contractors Practicing on their Premises, 10 J. Contemp. Health
L. & Pol'y 221 (1994).

6. *Office-Based Physicians.* Do you think the ostensible agency doctrine could
apply to specialists who are not entirely hospital based, such as surgeons or consultants referred by a patient's primary care physician? So far, courts have not gone
this far, but at least one has opened the possibility of holding hospitals vicariously
liable even for physicians who maintain an office-based practice. In Kashishian v.
Port, 481 N.W.2d 277 (Wis. 1991), the patient's personal physician admitted her to
a teaching hospital for cardiac evaluation and called in a member of the medical
school to perform a surgical procedure, which went awry. The court sent the case
against the hospital back for trial, holding that "the plaintiff's contact with a private personal physician [is not] necessarily inconsistent with the hospital having
held out specialists and/or consultants as its apparent agents. . . . [T]he doctrine of
apparent authority is not limited to the emergency room context, [n]or is it limited
to situations where a patient enters the hospital without a personal attending
physician." At present, this is a distinctly minority position, but some courts appear
willing to expand vicarious liability to any situation where "a patient seeks treatment from a hospital and not from a particular physician of the patient's
choosing." Syracuse v. Diao, 707 N.Y.S.2d 570 (App. Div. 2000) (allowing case
to go to trial where a patient simply called a specialized surgery center to request
an appointment but did not ask for a particular physician).

7. *Reliance.* Ordinarily, the ostensible agency doctrine requires a showing that
the injured party detrimentally relied on the representation of agency. If reliance
is applied in a strict "but-for" causation fashion, it is impossible to show because few
patients assert that they would have declined medical treatment at that institution
if they had known the doctors were really independent contractors. Accordingly, a
few courts have held that ostensible agency does not exist even in the classic
emergency room situation. Albain v. Flower Hospital, 553 N.E.2d 1038 (Ohio
1990), overruled in Clark v. Southview Hospital & Family Health Center, 628
N.E.2d 46 (Ohio 1994). Most courts, however, have applied the reliance requirement in more psychological terms, holding that it is sufficient that the patient
subjectively relied on the hospital to render the treatment and expected the doctors to be employees. See, e.g., *Clark*; *Sword*. Under this test, it is not necessary to
show any alteration in the plaintiff's behavior on account of the hospital's holding
out. This is consistent with Restatement (Second) of Torts §429, which unlike its
agency law counterpart, does not require explicit reliance. What justifies this lib-
eralization of tort doctrine? Perhaps it is an indication that courts are moving
toward per se enterprise liability, at least for certain classes of hospital-based physicians—those who patients believe the hospital selects for them.

8. *Enterprise Liability.* The enterprise liability concept referred to briefly in
Adamski (see n.1) would hold hospitals automatically liable for all acts of negligence
within their walls, regardless of the specifics of actual or apparent agency, that is,
even if the doctor is conceded to be an obvious independent contractor. The
rationale is one of nondelegable duty, namely, that the public policy supporting

hospital responsibility is so strong that, as a matter of law, the hospital may not avoid responsibility by delegating the function to an independent contractor. The classic example is an airline that attempts to shield itself from liability by retaining pilots as independent contractors.

So far, this nondelegable duty concept has been applied in only a few cases and only to emergency room care. The leading case is Jackson v. Power, 743 P.2d 1376 (Alaska 1987). Based on hospital licensing statutes and Joint Commission accreditation standards, the court observed that the hospital had assumed a duty to ensure adequate emergency room services. The court then concluded that a hospital "may not shield itself from liability by claiming that it is not responsible for the results of negligently performed health care when the law imposes a duty on the hospital to provide that health care. . . . We simply cannot fathom why liability should depend upon the technical employment status of the emergency room physician who treats the patient." Is this reasoning necessarily limited to emergency room care? To hospital-based physicians? So far, this is as far as courts have taken it. Other courts have refused to adopt the nondelegable duty doctrine at all. E.g., Baptist Memorial Hospital System v. Sampson, 969 S.W.2d 945 (Tex. 1998).

9. *The Next Stage.* Falling between vicarious liability for some physicians and enterprise liability for all physicians is a position known as "direct institutional liability," in which hospitals are held liable even for acts of independent physicians, but only if the hospital management breached a duty of care owed directly to patients with respect to selecting or supervising the physician. That theory of liability is thought to have been introduced by the next case. See if you can discern in this case a major shift in liability, or instead whether its holding rests on a more conventional application of vicarious liability. To the extent it presages a new duty of hospitals, precisely what is the content of that duty?

■ DARLING v. CHARLESTON COMMUNITY MEMORIAL HOSPITAL
211 N.E.2d 253 (Ill. 1965), cert. denied, 383 U.S. 946 (1966)

SCHAEFER, Justice.

. . . On November 5, 1960, the plaintiff, who was 18 years old, broke his leg while playing in a college football game. He was taken to the emergency room at the defendant hospital where Dr. Alexander, who was on emergency call that day, treated him. Dr. Alexander, with the assistance of hospital personnel, applied traction and placed the leg in a plaster cast. A heat cradle was applied to dry the cast. Not long after the application of the cast plaintiff was in great pain and his toes, which protruded from the cast, became swollen and dark in color. They eventually became cold and insensitive. On the evening of November 6, Dr. Alexander "notched" the cast around the toes, and on the afternoon of the next day he cut the cast approximately three inches up from the foot. On November 8 he split the sides of the cast with a Stryker saw; in the course of cutting the cast the plaintiff's leg was cut on both sides. Blood and other seepage were observed by the nurses and others, and there was a stench in the room, which one witness said was the worst he had smelled since World War II. The plaintiff remained in Charleston Hospital until November 19, when he was transferred to Barnes Hospital in

St. Louis and placed under the care of Dr. Fred Reynolds, head of orthopedic surgery at Washington University School of Medicine and Barnes Hospital. Dr. Reynolds found that the fractured leg contained a considerable amount of dead tissue which in his opinion resulted from interference with the circulation of blood in the limb caused by swelling or hemorrhaging of the leg against the construction of the cast. Dr. Reynolds performed several operations in a futile attempt to save the leg but ultimately it had to be amputated eight inches below the knee.

The evidence before the jury is set forth at length in the opinion of the Appellate Court and need not be stated in detail here. The plaintiff contends that it established that the defendant was negligent in permitting Dr. Alexander to do orthopedic work of the kind required in this case, and not requiring him to review his operative procedures to bring them up to date; in failing, through its medical staff, to exercise adequate supervision over the case, especially since Dr. Alexander had been placed on emergency duty by the hospital, and in not requiring consultation, particularly after complications had developed. Plaintiff contends also that in a case which developed as this one did, it was the duty of the nurses to watch the protruding toes constantly for changes of color, temperature and movement, and to check circulation every ten to twenty minutes, whereas the proof showed that these things were done only a few times a day. Plaintiff argues that it was the duty of the hospital staff to see that these procedures were followed, and that either the nurses were derelict in failing to report developments in the case to the hospital administrator, he was derelict in bringing them to the attention of the medical staff, or the staff was negligent in failing to take action. Defendant is a licensed and accredited hospital, and the plaintiff contends that the licensing regulations, accreditation standards, and its own bylaws define the hospital's duty, and that an infraction of them imposes liability for the resulting injury.

The defendant's position is stated in the following excerpts from its brief:

> It is a fundamental rule of law that only an individual properly educated and licensed, and not a corporation, may practice medicine. . . . Accordingly, a hospital is powerless under the law to forbid or command any act by a physician or surgeon in the practice of his profession. . . . A hospital is not an insurer of the patient's recovery, but only owes the patient the duty to exercise such reasonable care as his known condition requires and that degree of care, skill and diligence used by hospitals generally in that community. . . . Where the evidence shows that the hospital care was in accordance with standard practice obtaining in similar hospitals, and Plaintiff produces no evidence to the contrary, the jury cannot conclude that the opposite is true even if they disbelieve the hospital witnesses. . . . A hospital is not liable for the torts of its nurse committed while the nurse was but executing the orders of the patient's physician, unless such order is so obviously negligent as to lead any reasonable person to anticipate that substantial injury would result to the patient from the execution of such order. . . . The extent of the duty of a hospital with respect to actual medical care of a professional nature such as is furnished by a physician is to use reasonable care in selecting medical doctors. When such care in the selection of the staff is accomplished, and nothing indicates that a physician so selected is incompetent or that such incompetence should have been discovered, more cannot be expected from the hospital administration.

The basic dispute, as posed by the parties, centers upon the duty that rested upon the defendant hospital. That dispute involves the effect to be given to . . . hospital regulations adopted by the State Department of Public Health under the Hospital Licensing Act, to the Standards for Hospital Accreditation of the American Hospital Association, and to the bylaws of the defendant. . . .

> The conception that the hospital does not undertake to treat the patient, does not undertake to act through its doctors and nurses, but undertakes instead simply to procure them to act upon their own responsibility, no longer reflects the fact. Present-day hospitals, as their manner of operation plainly demonstrates, do far more than furnish facilities for treatment. They regularly employ on a salary basis a large staff of physicians, nurses and internes, as well as administrative and manual workers, and they charge patients for medical care and treatment, collecting for such services, if necessary, by legal action. Certainly, the person who avails himself of "hospital facilities" expects that the hospital will attempt to cure him, not that its nurses or other employes will act on their own responsibility. (Fuld, J., in Bing v. Thunig (1957), 2 N.Y.2d 656, 163 N.Y.S.2d 3, 11, 143 N.E.2d 3, 8.)

The Standards for Hospital Accreditation, the state licensing regulations and the defendant's bylaws demonstrate that the medical profession and other responsible authorities regard it as both desirable and feasible that a hospital assume certain responsibilities for the care of the patient.

We now turn to an application of these considerations to this case. . . . [W]e need not analyze all of the issues submitted to the jury. Two of them were that the defendant had negligently:

> 5. Failed to have a sufficient number of trained nurses for bedside care of all patients at all times capable of recognizing the progressive gangrenous condition of the plaintiff's right leg, and of bringing the same to the attention of the hospital administration and to the medical staff so that adequate consultation could have been secured and such conditions rectified; . . .
>
> 7. Failed to require consultation with or examination by members of the hospital surgical staff skilled in such treatment; or to review the treatment rendered to the plaintiff and to require consultants to be called in as needed.

We believe that the jury verdict [against the hospital] is supportable on either of these grounds. On the basis of the evidence before it the jury could reasonably have concluded that the nurses did not test for circulation in the leg as frequently as necessary, that skilled nurses would have promptly recognized the conditions that signalled a dangerous impairment of circulation in the plaintiff's leg, and would have known that the condition would become irreversible in a matter of hours. At that point it became the nurses' duty to inform the attending physician, and if he failed to act, to advise the hospital authorities so that appropriate action might be taken. As to consultation, there is no dispute that the hospital failed to review Dr. Alexander's work or require a consultation; the only issue is whether its failure to do so was negligence. On the evidence before it the jury could reasonably have found that it was. . . .

Judgment affirmed.

■ JOHNSON v. MISERICORDIA COMMUNITY HOSPITAL
301 N.W.2d 156 (Wis. 1981)

COFFEY, Justice.

. . . This action arose out of a surgical procedure performed at Misericordia by Dr. Salinsky on July 11, 1975, in which he unsuccessfully attempted to remove a pin fragment from Johnson's right hip. During the course of this surgery, the plaintiff's common femoral nerve and artery were damaged causing a permanent paralytic condition of his right thigh muscles with resultant atrophy and weakness and loss of function. . . .

[T]he jury found that Salinsky was negligent with respect to the medical care and treatment he afforded the plaintiff and attributed 20 percent of the causal negligence to him and 80 percent to the hospital. . . . [T]he only facts material to this review are those connected with Misericordia Hospital in appointing Dr. Salinsky to the medical staff with orthopedic privileges.

The record establishes that Misericordia was formerly . . . a nursing home known as Downtown Nursing Home, Inc. Subsequently, . . . all of the nursing home services were discontinued and the name "Misericordia Community Hospital" was adopted. The hospital known as Misericordia Community Hospital was not and has not been accredited by the Joint Commission on Accreditation of Hospitals. . . .

Dr. Salinsky applied for orthopedic privileges on the medical staff. In his application, Salinsky stated that . . . his privileges at other hospitals had never "been suspended, diminished, revoked, or not renewed." In another part of the application form, he failed to answer any of the questions pertaining to his malpractice insurance. . . .

Mrs. Jane Bekos, Misericordia's medical staff coordinator (appointed April of 1973), testifying from the hospital records, noted that Salinsky's appointment to the medical staff was recommended by the then hospital administrator, David A. Scott, Sr., on June 22, 1973. Salinsky's appointment and requested orthopedic privileges, according to the hospital records, were not marked approved until August 8, 1973. This approval of his appointment was endorsed by Salinsky himself. Such approval would, according to accepted medical administrative procedure, not be signed by the applicant but by the chief of the respective medical section. Additionally, the record establishes that Salinsky was elevated to the position of Chief of Staff shortly after he joined the medical staff. However, the court record and the hospital records are devoid of any information concerning the procedure utilized by the Misericordia authorities in approving either Salinsky's appointment to the staff with orthopedic privileges, or his elevation to the position of Chief of Staff.

Mrs. Bekos, testified that . . . she failed to contact any of the references in Salinsky's case. . . . Further, Mrs. Bekos stated that an examination of the Misericordia records reflected that at no time was an investigation made by anyone of any of the statements recited in his application. . . .

Dr. A. Howell, the hospital's medical director, stated that the hospital did not have a functioning credentials committee at this time, and therefore the executive committee . . . assume[d] the responsibility of evaluating and approving applications for medical staff privileges. . . . [T]he minutes of [the June 21st] meeting list Salinsky as an attending member of the defendant's medical staff at the meeting despite the fact that Salinsky's application for staff privileges had neither been recommended for approval, nor approved by the committee as of this date. . . .

At trial, the representatives of two Milwaukee hospitals, . . . gave testimony concerning the accepted procedure for evaluating applicants for medical staff privileges. Briefly, they stated that the hospital's governing body, i.e., the board of directors or board of trustees, has the ultimate responsibility in granting or denying staff privileges. However, the governing board delegates the responsibility of evaluating the professional qualifications of an applicant for clinical privileges to the medical staff. The credentials committee (or committee of the whole) conducts an investigation of the applying physician's or surgeon's education, training, health, ethics and experience through contacts with his peers in the specialty in which he is seeking privileges, as well as the references listed in his application to determine the veracity of his statements and to solicit comments dealing with the applicant's credentials. Once the credentials committee (or committee of the whole) has conducted their investigation and reviewed all of the information bearing on the applicant's qualifications, it relays its judgment to the governing body, which, as noted, has the final appointing authority.

The record demonstrates that had the executive committee of Misericordia, in the absence of a current credentials committee, adhered to the standard and accepted practice of investigating a medical staff applicant's qualifications and thus examined Salinsky's degree, postgraduate training, and contacted the hospitals referred to in his application, it would have found, contrary to his representations, that he had in fact experienced denial and restriction of his privileges, as well as never having been granted privileges at the very same hospitals he listed in his application. This information was readily available to Misericordia, and a review of Salinsky's associations with various Milwaukee orthopedic surgeons and hospital personnel would have revealed that they considered Salinsky's competence as an orthopedic surgeon suspect, and viewed it with a great deal of concern. . . .

[W]e hold that a hospital has a duty to exercise due care in the selection of its medical staff. . . . [O]ur holding is supported by the decisions of a number of courts from other jurisdictions. See . . . Annot., 51 A.L.R.3d 981 (1973). These cases hold that a hospital has a direct and independent responsibility to its patients, over and above that of the physicians and surgeons practicing therein, to take reasonable steps to (1) insure that its medical staff is qualified for the privileges granted and/or (2) to evaluate the care provided. . . .

The resolution of the issue of whether the hospital was negligent in granting Salinsky orthopedic surgical privileges and appointing him to its medical staff depends on whether Misericordia exercised that degree of care and skill as the average hospital exercises in selecting its medical staff. Applying this standard to the facts of this case, Johnson was only required to show that the defendant did not exercise reasonable care (that degree of care ordinarily exercised by the average hospital) to determine whether Salinsky was competent. . . . Therefore, the trial court's instruction that the hospital was required to exercise reasonable care in the granting of medical staff privileges and that reasonable care "meant that degree of care, skill and judgment usually exercised under like or similar circumstances by the average hospital," was proper.

Turning to the plaintiff's proof requirements, since the procedures ordinarily employed by hospitals in evaluating applications for staff privileges are not within the realm of the ordinary experience of mankind, we agree with the ruling of the appellate court that expert testimony was required to prove the same. . . .

There was credible evidence to the effect that a hospital, exercising ordinary care, would not have appointed Salinsky to its medical staff. Mr. Harden, administrator for Family Hospital, testified a hospital governing board with knowledge that an applicant for medical staff privileges had his orthopedic surgical privileges revoked at one hospital, on the recommendation of a panel of three orthopedic surgeons, and that his orthopedic privileges at another hospital were confined to simple operative procedures, would not, on the basis of this information, have granted him surgical privileges in that speciality. Dr. Sam Neeseman stated that a hospital's credentials committee, with knowledge of such events would not, in the exercise of ordinary care, have approved the applicant's request for orthopedic privileges. . . . Thus, the jury's finding of negligence on the part of Misericordia must be upheld as the testimony of Mr. Harden and Dr. Neeseman constituted credible evidence which reasonably supports this finding. . . .

[A]lthough [a hospital] must rely on the medical staff and in particular the credentials committee (or committee of the whole) to investigate and evaluate an applicant's qualifications for the requested privileges, . . . this delegation of the responsibility to investigate and evaluate the professional competence of applicants for clinical privileges does not relieve the governing body of its duty to appoint only qualified physicians and surgeons to its medical staff and periodically monitor and review their competency. . . . The facts of this case demonstrate that a hospital should, at a minimum, require completion of the application and verify the accuracy of the applicant's statements, especially in regard to his medical education, training and experience. Additionally, it should: (1) solicit information from the applicant's peers, including those not referenced in his application, who are knowledgeable about his education, training, experience, health, competence and ethical character; (2) determine if the applicant is currently licensed to practice in this state and if his licensure or registration has been or is currently being challenged; and (3) inquire whether the applicant has been involved in any adverse malpractice action and whether he has experienced a loss of medical organization membership or medical privileges or membership at any other hospital. The investigating committee must also evaluate the information gained through its inquiries and make a reasonable judgment as to the approval or denial of each application for staff privileges. The hospital will be charged with gaining and evaluating the knowledge that would have been acquired had it exercised ordinary care in investigating its medical staff applicants. . . . This is not to say that hospitals are insurers of the competence of their medical staff, for a hospital will not be negligent if it exercises the noted standard of care in selecting its staff.

Notes: Hospitals' Direct Liability; Risk Management Programs

1. *Direct vs. Vicarious Liability. Darling* is undoubtedly the most significant hospital liability case over the past 50 years. It is frequently referred to as a landmark decision in the field of hospital liability because it placed at least some degree of direct responsibility on the hospital for the maintenance of an acceptable standard of care of patients. Direct or "corporate" liability contrasts with vicarious liability in that it imposes on hospitals a duty of care owed directly to patients with respect to medical judgment. Conventional forms of direct liability entail primarily administrative, not medical, functions such as maintaining safe premises, sterile equipment, and adequate rules and regulations. *Darling* is recognized as extending direct corporate liability to substandard medical care rendered by independent doctors. Hospitals thus can be found liable for some act of negligence on their part with respect to patient care decisions made by independent doctors; vicarious liability, on the other hand, attaches regardless of the degree of hospital care but only when doctors are actual or apparent agents.

2. Darling's *Progeny*. Consider whether the *Darling* court actually intended to announce a new theory of liability. How else could the case have been reasoned, using principles from the previous case and notes? Commentators have observed that *Darling* achieved its status largely by virtue of the importance that academic commentators and subsequent decisions attached to it, and the vocal reaction of hospitals and physicians. The leading commentator was health law professor Arthur Southwick, in The Hospital's New Responsibility, 17 Clev.-Marshall L. Rev. 146 (1968); and The Hospital as an Institution—Expanding Responsibilities Change its Relationship with the Staff Physician, 9 Cal. W. L. Rev. 429 (1973). For additional commentary, see T. Hardy, When Doctrines Collide: Corporate Negligence and Respondeat Superior when Hospital Employees Fail to Speak Up, 61 Tul. L. Rev. 85 (1986); A. Hornstein, Damned If You Do, Damned If You Don't: Hospital Liability for Physicians' Malpractice, 64 Neb. L. Rev. 689 (1985); Comment, The Emerging Trend of Corporate Liability: Courts' Uneven Treatment of Hospital Standards Leaves Hospitals Uncertain and Exposed, 47 Vand. L. Rev. 535 (1994). See generally Annot., 62 A.L.R.4th 692 (1988).

3. *Enterprise Liability and the Balance of Power.* What reaction to *Darling* would you expect from the medical profession and the hospital industry? Surprisingly, *Darling* was openly embraced by hospitals but vehemently attacked by physicians. It greatly influenced the standards of the Joint Commission and virtually became the official philosophy of the American Hospital Association. The AMA's reaction to the *Darling* decision was immediate and negative. In considering why this would be so, consider what *Darling* signals about the power relationship between hospitals and physicians. Would it be fair to impose hospital responsibility for patient care without allowing hospital authority? In its comment on the case in 12 Citation 82 (1965), the AMA said, "The effect of this decision is unfortunate since it appears to place a hospital in a position where it must exercise control over the practice of medicine by physicians on its attending staff in order to avoid liability. This is apt to encourage control of the practice of medicine by persons who are not licensed physicians."

A similar reaction occurred in 1992 when the Clinton health care reform task force aired an idea for medical malpractice reform known as exclusive enterprise liability. As discussed at page 149, exclusive enterprise liability would change existing law in two ways: (1) it would hold hospitals and HMOs vicariously liable for all negligent injuries caused by any member physician, regardless of status or contractual relationship with the institution; and (2) the institution would be solely liable, letting doctors entirely off the hook. Surprisingly, the hospital industry was interested in this idea but the AMA vehemently opposed it, causing the Clinton administration to quickly back away. Even though the AMA was clamoring for relief from medical malpractice, it viewed this proposal for abolishing physician liability as a Trojan Horse because of its implications for the relative power balance between doctors and medical institutions. Despite this hostility, some HMOs, most teaching hospitals, and virtually all government hospitals implement a de facto form of exclusive enterprise liability in which the institution pays for the physicians' malpractice insurance (usually as part of its own self-insured retention fund), defends all suits, and pays all judgments for claims arising from treatment at the institution. See generally Kenneth Abraham & Paul Weiler, Enterprise Liability and the Evolution of the American Health Care System, 108 Harv. L. Rev. 381 (1994); Frances Miller, Malpractice Liability and Physician Autonomy, 342 Lancet 973 (1993); William Sage, Kathleen Hastings & Robert Berenson, Enterprise Liability for Medical Malpractice and Health Care Quality Improvement, 20 Am. J.L. & Med. 1 (1994).

4. *Duty to Supervise and Nursing Negligence. Darling* and its progeny identify two forms of hospital negligence with respect to physicians: negligent selection and retention, and negligent supervision. The first of these, which is developed in Johnson v. Misericordia Community Hospital, is much less controversial. Observe that it was recognized in passing even in *Schloendorff*, supra. It entails reviewing physicians' competency and performance history before admission to the medical staff and periodically (typically every two years) thereafter.

The duty to supervise, in contrast, assumes *contemporaneous* supervision of daily treatment decisions *as they are made.* Several subsequent decisions have alluded to this duty of contemporaneous supervision, but few have squarely imposed it, distinct from the duty of care in selection and retention. Indeed, subsequent decisions in Illinois have expressly disavowed any such duty arising from *Darling*. See Pickle v. Curns, 435 N.E.2d 877 (Ill. App. Ct. 1982). Courts have reasoned that it would constitute bad medical practice and unlawful interference with the physician-patient relationship for lay administrators to actively review treatment decisions. See, e.g., Gafner v. Down East Community Hospital, 735 A.2d 969 (Me. 1999); Jensen v. Archbishop Bergan Mercy Hospital, 459 N.W.2d 178 (Neb. 1990); Albain v. Flower Hospital, 553 N.E.2d 1038 (Ohio 1990). See generally E. Hollowell, Does Hospital Corporate Liability Extend to Medical Staff Supervision?, 10 L. Med. & Health Care 225 (1982); Note, 17 Wake Forest L. Rev. 309 (1981).

Other courts, however, have rather explicitly imposed such a duty, at least in dictum. See, e.g., Bost v. Riley, 262 S.E.2d 391 (N.C. Ct. App. 1980); Thompson v. Nason Hospital, 591 A.2d 703 (Pa. 1991). Usually, these are cases of gross negligence in which the departure from medical standards is so blatant that it is possible to attribute to hospital administrators constructive knowledge of the error in progress. One route for attributing this knowledge is through nurses, under the logic that, at some point, nurses should object to or call to a superviser's attention treatment that is going extremely badly. Because nurses are hospital employees, this theory essentially holds hospitals vicariously liable for nurses' failure to speak up or intervene. See Strubhart v. Perry Memorial Hospital, 903 P.2d 263 (Okla. 1995); Koeniguer v. Eckrich, 422 N.W.2d 600 (S.D. 1988); T. Hardy, supra, 61 Tul. L. Rev. 86 (1986) (the test under *Darling* should be "whether in a given situation a reasonable, prudent nurse would have spoken up about a physician's negligence"). Is this explanation consistent with the facts in *Darling*? Is it consistent with the practical realities of the doctor-nurse relationship? Recall Justice Cardozo's treatment of this very same theory of liability in *Schloendorff*, supra.

   5. *Risk Management.*

   The newly created role in hospitals of "risk manager" marks the official recognition of a role that has become central to the way hospitals are run. Their role is clearly defined . . . "to avoid or minimize potential legal, and hence, financial loss for the health care provider." Although they may fulfill several different administrative functions, . . . I contend that current risk management practices in hospitals have risen to a pitch of near hysteria. They embody actions that are unprecedented in their intrusiveness into the doctor-patient relationship and are unethical in violating the rights of patients. . . . The typical responses of risk managers are wildly overactive. If people in ordinary life were to act in accordance with the minuscule probabilities on which risk management bases its decisions, we would all be in a constant state of paralysis. . . . Hospital administrators have refused to permit competent adult patients to reject burdensome treatment even when physicians concur with the patient's wish. It is not uncommon for administrators to request that a court order be obtained whenever there is a shred of doubt (which almost always exists) about what the law says. Where it was once physicians who overtreated patients because they believed it was their moral obligation to continue therapy, it is now hospital administrators and risk managers who more often insist on overtreatment out of fear of medical-legal liability. It is not a great exaggeration to view risk managers as enemies of patients. . . .

   Who are these risk managers, and what is the origin of their role in the hospital? Some risk managers have law degrees, but most do not. Some are nurses who rose to the rank of supervisor and then moved into hospital administration, often after obtaining a master's degree. Others come from the ranks of hospital administrators, some with a degree in hospital or business administration. More rare are individuals with an advanced degree in a field such as sociology, and still others made their career in health planning or administration and were around long before the occupation of risk manager was invented. Large medical centers typically have an office of risk management in addition to in-house counsel. The staff of lawyers works together with risk management both in devising hospital policies that affect patients and in dealing with individual cases in which anyone suspects that there may be a risk of some sort.

   The overall movement can be traced back to the late 1960s and early 1970s, when efforts were begun in industrial and other workplaces to reduce the costs of liability payments by underwriters and insurance companies. The trend widened, and in the 1980s risk management offices began to be established in hospitals . . . to deal with concerns about possible liability arising out of incident reports in the hospital: a patient falling out of bed, a visitor slipping in a puddle of water in the corridor, an inadvertent injury to a patient in the course of treatment. . . . The original worries about legal liability have now expanded to encompass everything that might place the hospital in a bad light. Risk managers are now charged with the task of minimizing risks other than those of liability. They look out for the projected risks of bad publicity, the actions of a disgruntled employee, or the possible political ramifications of a medical decision or hospital policy. . . . Even when the patient has no family, and there is no one around who would sue the hospital, risk management is brought into the case. One of the peculiar features of this situation is the nearly automatic response by many physicians to call risk management whenever the slightest uncertainty is voiced about an ethical matter or vaguely perceived to have legal implications. . . .

Ruth Macklin, Enemies of Patients (1993). Does this account confirm the fears of the AMA about the consequences for physicians of exposing hospitals to liability?

Hospitals are now required to have risk management programs by Joint Commission accreditation standards, and, in a few states, by hospital licensing laws. Risk management programs are now common also in nursing homes and HMOs. On their structure and content generally, see American Society for Healthcare Risk Management, Risk Management Handbook for Health Care Facilities (1990); J. Orlikoff & A. Vanagunas, Malpractice Prevention and Liability Control for Hospitals (1988); G. Troyer & S. Salman, Handbook of Health Care Risk Management (1986); B. Youngberg, Essentials of Hospital Risk Management (1990). One empirical study found that most risk management activities had no discernible effect on malpractice claims against hospitals. L. Morlock & F. Malitz, Do Hospital Risk Management Programs Make a Difference?, 54 Law & Contemp. Probs. 1 (Spring 1991).

6. *Informed Consent Liability.* One form of physician supervision for which courts have been especially reluctant to impose hospital liability is the duty to obtain informed consent. One might suppose that it easily falls within the hospital's administrative functions to ensure that patients have signed the proper paperwork before major operations are conducted, especially since nurses usually have a central role in obtaining informed consent. Most courts, however, hold that informed consent is solely the responsibility of the physician because the delicate considerations of what exactly to tell the patient and when are matters "particularly calling for the exercise of medical judgment." Fiorentino v. Wenger, 280 N.Y.S.2d 373 (N.Y. 1967); Valles v. Albert Einstein Medical Center, 805 A.2d 1232 (Pa. 2002) (no liability even for employed physician because "a medical facility cannot maintain control over this aspect of the physician-patient relationship"). But see Campbell v. Pitt Co. Memorial Hospital, 352 S.E.2d 902 (N.C. Ct. App. 1987) (hospital has a duty where its own internal policies require the nurse to ensure that informed consent is obtained from obstetrics patients).

7. *Self-Imposed Standards.* The hospital licensing regulations, accreditation standards, and hospital bylaws referred to in the *Darling* opinion contained statements such as the following:

[Regulations]

The [hospital] board [of directors] shall be responsible for the maintenance of proper standards of professional work in the hospital and shall require that the medical staff function in conformity with reasonable standards of competency. . . .

[Accreditation Standards]

Maintaining high standards of medical care will depend upon the character of the [medical] staff and the effectiveness of its organization to carry out the following duties: 1. Selection of those recommended for staff appointments and hospital privileges. 2. Constant analysis and review of the clinical work done in the hospital. . . . It is the duty of the hospital [medical] staff through its chiefs of service and Executive Committee to see that members of the staff do not fail in the matter of calling consultants as needed.

[Medical Staff Bylaws]

The purpose of this organization shall be to insure that all patients admitted to the hospital or treated in the outpatient department receive the best possible care.

Another important aspect of the court's holding is that standards such as these, to which the hospital subscribed or was bound, can be introduced as evidence, but not conclusive proof, of the customary standard of administrative care that prevails in the hospital industry. Is the effect of these standards to make a hospital strictly liable for any mistakes that doctors make? How would you revise these standards in order to perform their intended function in these various legal documents while at the same time moderating their liability effect?

8. *Hospital Custom.* Most courts hold hospitals to a national standard of care in selecting medical staff members. Would a similar locality standard be more appropriate? Consider the history and accreditation status of Misericordia Community Hospital, which was a very small hospital with relatively few medical staff. Under the national standard, are these factors relevant to the "like or similar circumstances" qualifier? See Note, Johnson v. Misericordia Community Hospital: Corporate Liability of Hospitals Arrives in Wisconsin, 1983 Wis. L. Rev. 453 (arguing that the *Misericordia* standards are too demanding for some hospitals). Observe, though, that the duty to fully investigate physicians' credentials is greatly eased now that hospitals can obtain records of past malpractice lawsuits and disciplinary actions by other hospitals from the National Practitioner Data Bank.

Hospital negligence cases are not as dependent on expert witnesses as are physician negligence cases, despite the *Johnson* court's holding on this point. Once the issue of physician negligence is established, issues of administrative care and proper oversight are subject to the "reasonable person" standard. Other courts sometimes hold that these issues are subject to commonsense understanding. If you were on a jury, would you consider a hospital negligent if it approved a physician who had been sued for malpractice three times in the past five years? If he had lost or settled two of the three suits for substantial amounts? Empirical studies show that physicians who have lost even small claims against them are more likely to pay on a malpractice claim in the near future, but these odds are increased only by 3 percent. See L. Smarr, Malpractice Claims: Does the Past Predict the Future?, 272 JAMA 1453 (1994).

9. *Medical Staff Committees.* Observe the brief discussion at the end of *Johnson* concerning the legal effect of the hospital's delegating the task of medical staff credentialing to members and committees of the medical staff. Recall that medical staff members are, generally speaking, not agents of the hospital. Therefore, could a hospital not claim in a typical case, where it merely follows the medical staff's recommendation, that it is not responsible for their sloppiness or poor judgment? Assume the hospital board has no way to know that the medical staff did a poor job or made a bad decision. This defense does not work for two reasons: (1) Although medical staff members are independent contractors in their medical status as practicing doctors, they are agents of the hospital in their administrative status while sitting on medical staff committees. Therefore, ordinary respondeat superior applies to their committee mistakes. (2) The duty to screen medical staff members is considered nondelegable. See Joiner v. Gonzales, 186 S.E.2d 307 (Ga. Ct. App. 1971).

Distributing liability in the opposite direction, would it be possible to hold medical staff members individually liable for doing a poor job in evaluating an applicant? Alternatively, could the medical staff be held liable as an entity? One court has answered "yes," holding that the medical staff can be sued as an unincorporated association, in which case, if one member were found negligent, all 141 could be held jointly and severally responsible. Corleto v. Shore Memorial Hospital, 350 A.2d 534 (N.J. Super. 1974). In practice, physicians are not individually exposed since hospitals usually assume responsibility for liability arising from medical staff review activities. See generally W. Isele, The Hospital Medical Staff: Its Legal Rights and Responsibilities (1984); J. Horty & D. Mulholland, The Legal Status of the Hospital Medical Staff, 22 St. Louis U. L.J. 485 (1978).

10. *Puzzles to Ponder.* In *Johnson*, the jury found Dr. Salinsky negligent. Is this necessary to hold the hospital liable for its own negligence? If a hospital negligently admits a bad doctor to the medical staff, shouldn't it be liable for any injury the doctor causes, under the notion that the hospital's negligence is distinct from the doctor's? This question seems to never have been addressed directly by the courts. Uniformly, they find hospital negligence only where the doctor is also negligent. The best explanation for this limitation is one of proximate cause. A hospital's negligent screening of a physician is not sufficiently proximate to a patient's injury, even if it literally causes the injury, unless the injury results from the physician's own negligence as well.

Another doctrinal puzzle is whether hospitals who negligently credential a physician are liable to patients who are injured off premises in the doctor's private office. Although standard foreseeability and but-for causation tests would appear to be met, most courts hold that hospitals are liable only for injuries to hospital patients, even where the plaintiff can prove she relied on the hospital credentials in selecting the doctor. Again, the notion appears to be one of proximate cause, influenced by older notions of privity of contract. See Insinga v. LaBella, 543 So. 2d 209 (Fla. 1989) (no hospital liability for giving admitting privileges to a person masquerading as a physician, where injury occurred outside hospital); Pedroza v. Bryant, 677 P.2d 166 (Wash. 1984) (no hospital liability for negligence in prenatal care even though plaintiff had delivered her seven previous children at that hospital and she died at the hospital). But see Copithorne v. Framingham

Union Hospital, 520 N.E.2d 139 (Mass. 1988) (hospital duty extends to medical staff member who drugged and raped patient in her home). Should it make any difference if the doctor practices in a hospital-owned and leased medical office building right next door? What if the hospital owns an HMO which the doctor and patient belong to?

C. MANAGED CARE LIABILITY

We turn now to a new form of institution, one that combines medical delivery with medical financing. When confronted with HMOs' institutional liability, courts quickly applied the same structure of analysis that had developed for hospitals. Because HMOs differ in important respects from hospitals, however, the result of this analysis may not be the same. In the following materials, consider how different types of managed care entities and arrangements should be treated under the various theories and branches of no liability, vicarious liability, and direct liability.

■ BOYD v. ALBERT EINSTEIN MEDICAL CENTER
547 A.2d 1229 (Pa. Super. Ct. 1988)

OLSZEWSKI, Judge:

This is an appeal from the trial court's order granting summary judgment in favor of defendant/appellee, Health Maintenance Organization of Pennsylvania (hereinafter HMO). Appellant asserts that the trial court erred in granting the motion for summary judgment when there existed a question of material fact as to whether participating physicians are the ostensible agents of HMO. For the reasons stated below, we reverse the grant of summary judgment.

The facts, as averred by the parties in their pleadings and elicited through deposition testimony, reveal that at the time of her death, decedent and her husband were participants in the HMO. HMO is a medical insurance provider that offers an alternative to the traditional Blue Cross/Blue Shield insurance plan.[1] Decedent's husband became eligible for participation in a group plan provided by HMO through his employer. Upon electing to participate in this plan, decedent and her husband were provided with a directory and benefits brochure which listed the participating physicians. Restricted to selecting a physician from this list, decedent chose Doctor David Rosenthal and Doctor Perry Dornstein as her primary care physicians.

In June of 1982, decedent contacted Doctor David Rosenthal regarding a lump in her breast. Doctor Rosenthal ordered a mammogram to be performed which revealed a suspicious area in the breast. Doctor Rosenthal recommended

---

[1] A Health Maintenance Organization is an organized system of health care which provides or arranges for a comprehensive array of basic and supplemental health care services. These services are provided on a prepaid basis to voluntarily enrolled members living within a prescribed geographic area. Responsibility for the delivery, quality and payment of health care falls to the managing organization—the HMO.

that decedent undergo a biopsy and referred decedent to Doctor Erwin Cohen for that purpose. Doctor Cohen, a surgeon, is also a participating HMO physician. The referral to a specialist in this case was made in accordance with the terms and conditions of HMO's subscription agreement.[2]

On July 6, 1982, Doctor Cohen performed a biopsy of decedent's breast tissue at Albert Einstein Medical Center. During the procedure, Doctor Cohen perforated decedent's chest wall with the biopsy needle, causing decedent to sustain a left hemothorax. Decedent was hospitalized for treatment of the hemothorax at Albert Einstein Hospital for two days.

In the weeks following this incident decedent complained to her primary care physicians, Doctor David Rosenthal and Doctor Perry Dornstein, of pain in her chest wall, belching, hiccoughs, and fatigue. On August 19, 1982, decedent awoke with pain in the middle of her chest. Decedent's husband contacted her primary care physicians, Doctors Rosenthal and Dornstein, and was advised to take decedent to Albert Einstein Hospital where she would be examined by Doctor Rosenthal. Upon arrival at Albert Einstein emergency room, decedent related symptoms of chest wall pain, vomiting, stomach and back discomfort to Doctor Rosenthal. Doctor Rosenthal commenced an examination of decedent, diagnosed Tietz's syndrome,[3] and arranged for tests to be performed at his office where decedent underwent X-rays, EKG, and cardiac ioenzyme tests.[4] Decedent was then sent home and told to rest.[5]

During the course of that afternoon, decedent continued to experience chest pain, vomiting and belching. Decedent related the persistence and worsening of these symptoms by telephone to Doctors Rosenthal and Dornstein, who prescribed, without further examination, Talwin, a pain medication. At 5:30 that afternoon decedent was discovered dead in her bathroom by her husband, having expired as a result of a myocardial infarction.

Appellant's complaint and new matter aver that HMO advertised that its physicians and medical care providers were competent, and that they had been evaluated for periods of up to six months prior to being selected to participate in the HMO program as a medical provider. The complaint further avers that decedent and appellant relied on these representations in choosing their primary care physicians. The complaint then avers that HMO was negligent in failing to

> qualify or oversee its physicians and hospital who acted as its agents, servants, or employees in providing medical care to the decedent nor did HMO of Pa. require

[2] Doctor Rosenthal admitted in his deposition that HMO limited specifically the doctors to whom decedent could have been referred.

[3] Tietze's Syndrome is an inflammatory condition affecting the costochondral cartilage. It occurs more commonly in females, generally in the 30 to 50 range.

[4] HMO avers that decedent was returned to the doctor's office for testing because it was more comfortable and convenient for her. Appellant, however, asserts that the tests were performed in the doctor's office, rather than the hospital, in accordance with the requirements of HMO whose primary interest was in keeping the medical fees within the corporation.

[5] Appellant contends that Doctor Rosenthal acted negligently in ordering the tests to be performed in his office when decedent exhibited symptoms of cardiac distress. The safer practice, avers appellant, would have been to perform the tests at the hospital where the results would have been more quickly available. Appellant further contends that, despite Doctor Rosenthal's diagnosis of Tietz's Syndrome, the nature of the tests he ordered indicates that he was concerned about the possibility of a heart attack.

its physicians, surgeons and hospitals to provide adequate evidence of skill, training and competence in medicine and it thereby failed to furnish the decedent with
competent, qualified medical care as warranted.

Finally, appellant's new matter avers that HMO furnished to its subscribers documents which identify HMO as the care provider and state that HMO guarantees
the quality of care.

Appellant's theory of recovery before the trial court was primarily one of
vicarious liability under the ostensible agency theory. See Capan v. Divine
Providence Hospital, 287 Pa. Super. 364, 430 A.2d 647 (1980). In granting defendant HMO's motion for summary judgment, the trial court found that plaintiff/
appellant had failed to establish either of the two factors on which the theory of
ostensible agency, as applied to hospitals in *Capan*, is based. On appeal, appellant
contends that the evidence indicates that there exists a question of fact regarding
whether HMO may be held liable under this theory. . . .

The group master contract provides that HMO "operates a comprehensive
prepaid program of health care which provides health care services and benefits to
Members in order to protect and promote their health, and preserve and enhance
patient dignity." HMO was incorporated in 1975 under the laws of Pennsylvania
and converted from a nonprofit to a for-profit corporation in 1981. HMO is based
on the individual practice association model (hereinafter IPA), which means that
HMO is comprised of participating primary physicians who are engaged in part in
private practice in the HMO service area. Under the plan, IPA contracts with HMO
to provide medical services to HMO members. IPA selects its primary and specialist physicians and enters into an agreement with them obligating the physician
to perform health services for the subscribers of HMO.

The primary physician's role is defined as the "gatekeeper into the health
care delivery system." "An HMO member must consult with his primary physician
before going to a specialist and/or the hospital." If the primary physician deems it
necessary, he arranges a consultation with an HMO participating specialist, which
constitutes a second opinion. "Basically, with the primary physicians 'screening'
the members' illnesses, excessive hospitalization and improper use of specialists
can be reduced."

Member-patients use a physician directory and choose a conveniently located
office of a participating primary physician. HMO members will only receive reimbursement from nonparticipating providers when the condition requiring
treatment was of an immediate nature. Determinations of immediacy are made
by the HMO quality assurance committee. In any event, persons desiring emergency nonprovider benefits must notify HMO or their primary physician of the
emergency within 48 hours and must give written proof of the occurrence within
ninety days after service is rendered. . . .

Primary physicians are paid through a mechanism termed "capitation."
Capitation is an actuarially determined amount prepaid by HMO to the primary
physician for each patient who has chosen his office. The dollar amount is based
upon a predetermined rate per age group. The primary physicians are paid 80
percent of the capitation amount and the remaining 20 percent is pooled by IPA
and goes back into a pooled risk-sharing fund as a reserve against specialty referral
costs and hospital stays. Each primary care office has its own specialist fund and

hospital fund established by allocating a predetermined amount each month for each member who has chosen that primary care office. The surplus from the specialist fund is returned to the primary care office. The hospital fund, however, is governed by a hospital risk/incentive-sharing scheme which anticipates a number of inpatient days per members per year. If the actual hospital utilization is less than anticipated, the HMO and IPA each receive 50 percent of the savings. IPA must place the savings in the Special IPA risk-sharing account and must use the funds to offset losses resulting from unanticipated physician costs. If utilization is greater than anticipated, IPA is responsible for 50 percent of the loss up to the amount of uncommitted funds in the Special IPA risk sharing account. . . .

HMO asserts that because the theory of ostensible agency has been applied in Pennsylvania only to the relationship between hospitals and independent contractor physicians, the theory is not appropriate in the instant situation. We emphasize, however, that when this court introduced the concept of ostensible agency to this Commonwealth in *Capan*, supra, we based that decision in large part upon "the changing role of the hospital in society [which] creates a likelihood that patients will look to the institution" for care. Because the role of health care providers has changed in recent years, the *Capan* rationale for applying the theory of ostensible agency to hospitals is certainly applicable in the instant situation. . . .

We find that the facts indicate an issue of material fact as to whether the participating physicians were the ostensible agents of HMO. HMO covenanted that it would "[provide] health care services and benefits to Members in order to protect and promote their health. . . ." "HMOPA operates on a direct service rather than an indemnity basis." Appellant paid his doctor's fee to HMO, not to the physician of his choice. Then, appellant selected his primary care physicians from the list provided by HMO. Regardless of who recommended appellant's decedent to choose her primary care physician, the fact remains that HMO provides a limited list from which a member must choose a primary physician. Moreover, those primary physicians are screened by HMO and must comply with a list of regulations in order to honor their contract with HMO.

Further, as mandated by HMO, appellant's decedent could not see a specialist without the primary physician's referral. As HMO declares, the primary physician is the "gatekeeper into the health care delivery system." "An HMO member must consult with his primary physician before going to a specialist and/or the hospital." Moreover, appellant's decedent had no choice as to which specialist to see. In our opinion, because appellant's decedent was required to follow the mandates of HMO and did not directly seek the attention of the specialist, there is an inference that appellant looked to the institution for care and not solely to the physicians; conversely, that appellant's decedent submitted herself to the care of the participating physicians in response to an invitation from HMO. See comment (a), Restatement (Second) Agency §267. . . .

We conclude, therefore, that the trial court erred when it granted HMO's motion for summary judgment on the ground that the participating physicians were not the ostensible agents of HMO. . . .

McEwen, Judge, concurring.

I concur in the result reached by the majority since the author, after a very careful analysis of the issues presented in this appeal, reaches the quite basic principle that issues of material fact may not be resolved by summary judgment.

I write only because it appears to me that the learned trial court improperly resolved by summary judgment the basic factual issue of whether the literature, in which HMO "guaranteed" and "assured" the quality of care provided to its subscribers, had been distributed to appellant or to other subscribers of HMO.

It might also be mentioned that while the court was understandably uncertain as to the theories upon which plaintiff was proceeding,[1] it appears that the amended complaint of plaintiff does contain factual averments supporting a breach of warranty claim.

■ WICKLINE v. STATE
239 Cal. Rptr. 810 (Cal. Ct. App. 1986)

ROWEN, Associate Justice.

[Lois Wickline, who was treated under California's Medicaid program (known as "Medi-Cal"), sued the State, but not her physician, for negligently causing her premature discharge from the hospital, resulting in complications that eventually necessitated amputation of her right leg. Wickline alleged that her premature discharge was the fault of Medi-Cal's erroneous withholding of its authorization for her continued hospitalization.] This is an appeal from a judgment for plaintiff entered after a trial by jury. For the reasons discussed below, we reverse the judgment.

Principally, this matter concerns itself with the legal responsibility that a third party payor, in this case, the State of California, has for harm caused to a patient when a cost containment program is applied in a manner which is alleged to have affected the implementation of the treating physician's medical judgment. . . .

I

Responding to concerns about the escalating cost of health care, public and private payors have in recent years experimented with a variety of cost containment mechanisms. We deal here with one of those programs: The prospective utilization review process.

At the outset, this court recognizes that this case appears to be the first attempt to tie a health care payor into the medical malpractice causation chain and that it, therefore, deals with issues of profound importance to the health care community and to the general public. For those reasons we have permitted the filing of amicus curiae briefs in support of each of the respective parties in the matter to assure that due consideration is given to the broader issues raised before this court by this case. . . .

---

[1] The trial court noted in its opinion that

the gravamen of plaintiff's complaint is that HMO of PA guaranteed or warranted the quality of care provided. . . . Plaintiff's theory of recovery . . . is not entirely clear. A reading of the complaint suggests Plaintiff is proceeding upon grounds of corporate liability. However, in his answer to the motion of HMO of PA for summary judgment, plaintiff contends HMO of PA is vicariously liable through ostensible agency.

Early cost containment programs utilized the retrospective utilization review process. In that system the third party payor reviewed the patient's chart after the fact to determine whether the treatment provided was medically necessary. If, in the judgment of the utilization reviewer, it was not, the health care provider's claim for payment was denied.

In the cost containment program in issue in this case, prospective utilization review, authority for the rendering of health care services must be obtained before medical care is rendered. Its purpose is to promote the well recognized public interest in controlling health care costs by reducing unnecessary services while still intending to assure that appropriate medical and hospital services are provided to the patient in need. However, such a cost containment strategy creates new and added pressures on the quality assurance portion of the utilization review mechanism. The stakes, the risks at issue, are much higher when a prospective cost containment review process is utilized than when a retrospective review process is used.

A mistaken conclusion about medical necessity following retrospective review will result in the wrongful withholding of payment. An erroneous decision in a prospective review process, on the other hand, in practical consequences, results in the withholding of necessary care, potentially leading to a patient's permanent disability or death.

II

Though somewhat in dispute, the facts in this case are not particularly complicated. In 1976, Wickline, a married woman in her mid-40's, with a limited education, was being treated by Dr. Stanley Z. Daniels (Dr. Daniels), a physician engaged in a general family practice, for problems associated with her back and legs. Failing to respond to the physical therapy type of treatment he prescribed, Dr. Daniels had Wickline admitted to Van Nuys Community Hospital (Van Nuys or Hospital) in October 1976 and brought in another physician, Dr. Gerald E. Polonsky (Dr. Polonsky), a specialist in peripheral vascular surgery, to do a consultation examination. Peripheral vascular surgery concerns itself with surgery on any vessel of the body, exclusive of the heart.

Dr. Polonsky examined plaintiff and diagnosed her condition as arteriosclerosis obliterans with occlusion of the abdominal aorta, more generally referred to as Leriche's Syndrome. . . .

According to Dr. Polonsky, the only treatment for Leriche's Syndrome is surgical. In Wickline's case her disease was so far advanced that Dr. Polonsky concluded that it was necessary to remove a part of the plaintiff's artery and insert a synthetic (Teflon) graft in its place.

After agreeing to the operation, Wickline was discharged home to await approval of her doctor's diagnosis and authorization from Medi-Cal for the recommended surgical procedure and attendant acute care hospitalization. It is conceded that at all times in issue in this case, the plaintiff was eligible for medical benefits under California's medical assistance program, the "Medi-Cal Act," which is more commonly referred to as Medi-Cal. (Welf. & Inst. Code, §§14000 et seq., 14000.4.)

As required, Dr. Daniels submitted a treatment authorization request to Medi-Cal, sometimes referred to as form "161," "MC-161" or "TAR." In response to Dr. Daniels' request, Medi-Cal authorized the surgical procedure and 10 days of hospitalization for that treatment.

On January 6, 1977, plaintiff was admitted to Van Nuys by Dr. Daniels. On January 7, 1977, Dr. Polonsky performed a surgical procedure in which a part of plaintiff's artery was removed and a synthetic artery was inserted to replace it. Dr. Polonsky characterized that procedure as "a very major surgery."

Later that same day Dr. Polonsky was notified that Wickline was experiencing circulatory problems in her right leg. He concluded that a clot had formed in the graft. As a result, Wickline was taken back into surgery, the incision in her right groin was reopened, the clot removed and the graft was resewn. Wickline's recovery subsequent to the two January 7th operations were characterized as "stormy." She had a lot of pain, some spasm in the vessels in the lower leg and she experienced hallucinating episodes. On January 12, 1977, Wickline was returned to the operating room where Dr. Polonsky performed a lumbar sympathectomy.

A lumbar sympathectomy is a major operation in which a section of the chain of nerves that lie on each side of the spinal column is removed. The procedure causes the blood vessels in the patient's lower extremity to become paralyzed in a wide open position and was done in an attempt to relieve the spasms which Wickline was experiencing in those vessels. Spasms stop the outflow of blood from the vessels causing the blood to back up into the graft. Failure to relieve such spasms can cause clotting.

Dr. Polonsky was assisted in all three surgeries by Dr. Leonard Kovner (Dr. Kovner), a board certified specialist in the field of general surgery and the chief of surgery at Van Nuys. Dr. Daniels was present for the initial graft surgery on January 7, 1977, and for the right lumbar sympathectomy operation on January 12, 1977.

Wickline was scheduled to be discharged on January 16, 1977, which would mean that she would actually leave the hospital sometime before 1 p.m. on January 17, 1977. On or about January 16, 1977, Dr. Polonsky concluded that "it was medically necessary" that plaintiff remain in the hospital for an additional eight days beyond her then scheduled discharge date. Drs. Kovner and Daniels concurred in Dr. Polonsky's opinion.

Dr. Polonsky cited many reasons for his feeling that it was medically necessary for plaintiff to remain in an acute care hospital for an additional eight days, such as the danger of infection and/or clotting. His principal reason, however, was that he felt that he was going to be able to save both of Wickline's legs and wanted her to remain in the hospital where he could observe her and be immediately available, along with the hospital staff, to treat her if an emergency should occur.

In order to secure an extension of Wickline's hospital stay, it was necessary to complete and present to Medi-Cal a form called "Request for Extension of Stay in Hospital," commonly referred to as an "MC-180" or "180." . . .

At Van Nuys, Patricia N. Spears (Spears), an employee of the hospital and a registered nurse, had the responsibility for completing 180 forms. In this case, as requested by Dr. Polonsky, Spears filled out Wickline's 180 form and then presented it to Dr. Daniels, as plaintiff's attending physician, to sign, which he did, in compliance with Dr. Polonsky's recommendation. All of the physicians who testi-fied agreed that the 180 form prepared by Spears was complete, accurate and adequate for all purposes in issue in this matter.

Doris A. Futerman (Futerman), a registered nurse, was, at that time, employed by Medi-Cal as a Health Care Service Nurse, commonly referred to as an "on-site nurse." . . .

Futerman, after reviewing Wickline's 180 form, felt that she could not approve the requested eight-day extension of acute care hospitalization. While conceding that the information provided might justify some additional time beyond the scheduled discharge date, nothing in Wickline's case, in Futerman's opinion, would have warranted the entire eight additional days requested and, for those reasons, she telephoned the Medi-Cal Consultant. She reached Dr. William S. Glassman (Dr. Glassman), one of the Medi-Cal Consultants on duty at the time in Medi-Cal's Los Angeles office. The Medi-Cal Consultant selection occurred randomly. As was the practice, whichever Medi-Cal Consultant was available at the moment took the next call that came into the office. . . .

After speaking with Futerman on the telephone, Dr. Glassman rejected Wickline's treating physician's request for an eight-day hospital extension and, instead, authorized an additional four days of hospital stay beyond the originally scheduled discharge date. . . .

After review of Wickline's 180 form, Dr. Glassman testified that the factors that led him to authorize four days, rather than the requested eight days, was that there was no information about the patient's temperature which he, thereupon, assumed was normal; nothing was mentioned about the patient's diet, which he then presumed was not a problem; nor was there any information about Wickline's bowel function, which Dr. Glassman then presumed was functioning satisfactorily. Further, the fact that the 180 form noted that Wickline was able to ambulate with help and that whirlpool treatments were to begin that day caused Dr. Glassman to presume that the patient was progressing satisfactorily and was not seriously or critically ill. . . .

In essence, respondent argues, Dr. Glassman based his decision on signs and symptoms such as temperature, diet and bowel movements, which were basically irrelevant to the plaintiff's circulatory condition for which she was being treated and did not concern himself with those symptoms and signs which an ordinary prudent physician would consider to be pertinent with regard to the type of med-ical condition presented by Wickline.

Complying with the limited extension of time authorized by Medi-Cal, Wickline was discharged from Van Nuys on January 21, 1977. Drs. Polonsky and Daniels each wrote discharge orders. At the time of her discharge, each of plaintiff's three treating physicians were aware that the Medi-Cal Consultant had approved only four of the requested eight-day hospital stay extension. While all three doctors were aware that they could attempt to obtain a further extension of Wickline's hospital stay by telephoning the Medi-Cal Consultant to request such an extension, none of them did so. . . .

At trial, Dr. Polonsky testified that in the time that had passed since the first extension request had been communicated to Medi-Cal, on January 16th or 17th, and the time of her scheduled discharge on January 21, 1977, Wickline's condi-tion had neither deteriorated nor become critical. In Dr. Polonsky's opinion no new symptom had presented itself and no additional factors had occurred since the original request was made to have formed the basis for a change in the Medi-Cal Consultant's attitude regarding Wickline's situation. In addition, he stated that at the time of Wickline's discharge it did not appear that her leg was in any danger.

Dr. Polonsky testified that at the time in issue he felt that Medi-Cal Consultants had the state's interest more in mind than the patient's welfare and that that belief influenced his decision not to request a second extension of Wickline's hospital stay. In addition, he felt that Medi-Cal had the power to tell him, as a treating doctor, when a patient must be discharged from the hospital. Therefore, while still of the subjective, noncommunicated, opinion that Wickline was seriously ill and that the danger to her was not over, Dr. Polonsky discharged her from the hospital on January 21, 1977. He testified that had Wickline's condition, in his medical judgment, been critical or in a deteriorating condition on January 21, he would have made some effort to keep her in the hospital beyond that day even if denied authority by Medi-Cal and even if he had to pay her hospital bill himself. . . .

All of the medical witnesses who testified at trial agreed that Dr. Polonsky was acting within the standards of practice of the medical community in discharging Wickline on January 21, 1977. . . .

Wickline testified that in the first few days after she arrived home she started feeling pain in her right leg and the leg started to lose color. In the next few days the pain got worse and the right leg took on a whitish, statue-like marble appearance. Wickline assumed she was experiencing normal recovery symptoms and did not communicate with any of her physicians. Finally, when "the pain got so great and the color started changing from looking like a statue to getting a grayish color," her husband called Dr. Kovner. It was Wickline's memory that this occurred about the third day after her discharge from the hospital and that Dr. Kovner advised Mr. Wickline to give extra pain medicine to the plaintiff.

Thereafter, gradually over the next few days, the plaintiff's leg "kept getting grayer and then it got bluish." The extra medication allegedly prescribed by Dr. Kovner over the telephone did not relieve the pain Wickline was experiencing. She testified that "by then the pain was just excruciating, where no pain medicine helped whatsoever." Finally, Wickline instructed her husband to call Dr. Kovner again and this time Dr. Kovner ordered plaintiff back into the hospital. Wickline returned to Van Nuys that same evening, January 30, 1977, nine days after her last discharge therefrom. . . .

Attempts to save Wickline's leg through the utilization of anticoagulants, antibiotics, strict bed rest, pain medication and warm water whirlpool baths to the lower extremity proved unsuccessful. On February 8, 1977, Dr. Polonsky amputated Wickline's leg below the knee because had he not done so "she would have died." The condition did not, however, heal after the first operation and on February 17, 1977, the doctors went back and amputated Wickline's leg above the knee. . . .

In Dr. Polonsky's opinion, to a reasonable medical certainty, had Wickline remained in the hospital for the eight additional days, as originally requested by him and her other treating doctors, she would not have suffered the loss of her leg. . . .

Dr. Polonsky testified that in his medical opinion, the Medi-Cal Consultant's rejection of the requested eight-day extension of acute care hospitalization and his authorization of a four-day extension in its place did not conform to the usual medical standards as they existed in 1977. He stated that, in accordance with those standards, a physician would not be permitted to make decisions regarding the care of a patient without either first seeing the patient, reviewing the patient's chart or discussing the patient's condition with her treating physician or physicians.

III

From the facts thus presented, appellant takes the position that it was not negligent as a matter of law. Appellant contends that the decision to discharge was made by each of the plaintiff's three doctors, was based upon the prevailing standards of practice, and was justified by her condition at the time of her discharge. It argues that Medi-Cal had no part in the plaintiff's hospital discharge and therefore was not liable even if the decision to do so was erroneously made by her doctors. . . .

As to the principal issue before this court, i.e., who bears responsibility for allowing a patient to be discharged from the hospital, her treating physicians or the health care payor, each side's medical expert witnesses agreed that, in accordance with the standards of medical practice as it existed in January 1977, it was for the patient's treating physician to decide the course of treatment that was medically necessary to treat the ailment. It was also that physician's responsibility to determine whether or not acute care hospitalization was required and for how long. Finally, it was agreed that the patient's physician is in a better position than the Medi-Cal Consultant to determine the number of days medically necessary for any required hospital care. The decision to discharge is, therefore, the responsibility of the patient's own treating doctor.

Dr. Kaufman testified that if, on January 21, the date of the plaintiff's discharge from Van Nuys, any one of her three treating doctors had decided that in his medical judgment it was necessary to keep Wickline in the hospital for a longer period of time, they, or any of them, should have filed another request for extension of stay in the hospital, that Medi-Cal would expect those physicians to make such a request if they felt it was indicated, and upon receipt of such a request further consideration of an additional extension of hospital time would have been given.

Title 22 of the California Administrative Code §51110, provided, in pertinent part, at the relevant time in issue here, that: "The determination of need for acute care shall be made in accordance with the usual standards of medical practice in the community."

The patient who requires treatment and who is harmed when care which should have been provided is not provided should recover for the injuries suffered from all those responsible for the deprivation of such care, including, when appropriate, health care payors. Third party payors of health care services can be held legally accountable when medically inappropriate decisions result from defects in the design or implementation of cost containment mechanisms as, for example, when appeals made on a patient's behalf for medical or hospital care are arbitrarily ignored or unreasonably disregarded or overridden. However, the physician who complies without protest with the limitations imposed by a third party payor, when his medical judgment dictates otherwise, cannot avoid his ultimate responsibility for his patient's care. He cannot point to the health care payor as the liability scapegoat when the consequences of his own determinative medical decisions go sour.

There is little doubt that Dr. Polonsky was intimidated by the Medi-Cal program but he was not paralyzed by Dr. Glassman's response nor rendered powerless to act appropriately if other action was required under the circumstances. If, in his medical judgment, it was in his patient's best interest that she remain in the acute care hospital setting for an additional four days beyond the extended time period originally authorized by Medi-Cal, Dr. Polonsky should have made some effort to keep Wickline there. He himself acknowledged that responsibility to his patient. It was his medical judgment, however, that Wickline could be discharged when she was. All the plaintiff's treating physicians concurred and all the doctors who testified at trial, for either plaintiff or defendant, agreed that Dr. Polonsky's medical decision to discharge Wickline met the standard of care applicable at the time. Medi-Cal was not a party to that medical decision and therefore cannot be held to share in the harm resulting if such decision was negligently made.

In addition thereto, while Medi-Cal played a part in the scenario before us in that it was the resource for the funds to pay for the treatment sought, and its input regarding the nature and length of hospital care to be provided was of paramount importance, Medi-Cal did not override the medical judgment of Wickline's treating physicians at the time of her discharge. It was given no opportunity to do so. Therefore, there can be no viable cause of action against it for the consequences of that discharge decision. . . .

V

This court appreciates that what is at issue here is the effect of cost containment programs upon the professional judgment of physicians to prescribe hospital treatment for patients requiring the same. While we recognize, realistically, that cost consciousness has become a permanent feature of the health care system, it is essential that cost limitation programs not be permitted to corrupt medical judgment. We have concluded, from the facts in issue here, that in this case it did not.

For the reasons expressed herein, this court finds that appellant is not liable for respondent's injuries as a matter of law. That makes unnecessary any discussion of the other contentions of the parties.

Notes: Managed Care Liability

1. *The Components of Managed Care.* Managed care is a term that applies broadly to a wide variety of arrangements that restrict the generosity of traditional health insurance. Managed care (1) restricts choice of physicians through networks and gatekeepers, (2) alters discrete treatment decisions through utilization review and prior authorization requirements, and (3) creates cost-constrained financial incentives through capitation payments and risk-sharing pools. Each of these components has distinct liability implications and can exist separately from the

others. For instance, "managed indemnity" insurance does (2) but not (1) or (3), simply by adding utilization review to traditional insurance. Preferred provider organizations (PPOs) do (1) but not (3), and may do (2) but not necessarily. HMOs are the fullest embodiment of managed care because they incorporate all three components. In analyzing these cases and others that are likely to arise in the future, however, be sure to think individually about each of these components and observe how they might arise in a variety of different institutional forms. For general comprehensive commentary and analysis, see Haavi Morreim, Holding Health Care Accountable (2001); Gail Agrawal & Mark Hall, What If You *Could* Sue Your HMO? Managed Care Liability beyond the ERISA Shield, _____ St. Louis U. L.J. _____ (2003); Diana Bearden & Bryan Maedgen, Emerging Theories of Liability in the Managed Health Care Industry, 47 Baylor L. Rev. (1995); B. Furrow, Managed Care Organizations and Patient Injury: Rethinking Liability, 31 Ga. L. Rev. 419 (1997); Clark Havighurst, Vicarious Liability: Relocating Responsibility for the Quality of Medical Care, 26 Am. J.L. & Med. 7 (2000); Peter Jacobson & Neena Patil, Managed Care Litigation: Legal Doctrine at the Boundary of Tort and Contract, 57 Med. Care Res. & Rev. 440 (2000); Bryan A. Liang, Patient Injury Incentives in Law, 17 Yale L. & Pol'y Rev. 1 (1998); Vernelia Randall, Managed Care, Utilization Review, and Financial Risk Shifting: Compensating Patients for Health Care Cost Containment Injuries, 17 U. Puget Sound L. Rev. 1 (1993); Gary T. Schwartz, Medical Malpractice, Tort, Contract and Managed Care, 1998 U. Ill. L. Rev. 885; Joanne B. Stern, Bad Faith Suits against HMOs: Finally, a Breakthrough, 20 Whittier L. Rev. 313 (1998); David L. Trueman, Managed Care Liability Today: Laws, Cases, Theories, and Current Issues, 33 J. Health L. 191 (2000).

2. *HMO Immunity.* In a few jurisdictions, HMOs are immune from suit for negligent treatment, in some states by statute and in one state formerly by court decision. Williams v. Good Health Plus, Inc., 743 S.W.2d 373 (Tex. Ct. App. 1987), resonates with hospital decisions early in the century by holding that an HMO logically cannot be held liable because the corporate practice of medicine doctrine prevents it from controlling physicians' treatment decisions. That decision has since been overturned by statute, however. Comment, 30 Tex. Tech. L. Rev. 1227 (1999). Economist Patricia Danzon is one who argues for HMO immunity under the theory that holding physicians individually liable is sufficient, unless the HMO agrees by contract to assume liability. Patricia M. Danzon, Tort Liability: A Minefield for Managed Care, 24 J. Leg. Stud. 491 (1997). See also Richard A. Epstein & Alan O. Sykes, The Assault on Managed Care: Vicarious Liability, Class Actions, and the Patient's Bill of Rights, 30 J. Leg. Stud. 625 (2002). Do you agree?

3. *Vicarious Liability.* There are two basic types of HMOs, with several permutations. The HMO type in *Boyd* was an Independent Practice Association (IPA), which is composed of a large contractual network of physicians who maintain practices in their own offices and see patients with many different types of insurance. For decisions similar to *Boyd*, see Schleier v. Kaiser Foundation Health Plan, 876 F.2d 174 (D.C. Cir. 1989); Dunn v. Praiss, 606 A.2d 862 (N.J. Super. Ct. App. Div. 1992). An agency relationship is much easier to establish with the other type of HMO, a staff or group model, in which a smaller number of physicians work exclusively for a single HMO in a centralized clinic. What about a PPO (preferred

provider organization) or POS (point of service) plan with an open network in which patients are encouraged to stay with the designated physicians but are free to go outside the network and select any doctor they want by paying a higher deductible or copayment? What about a closed network that is very large but has no gatekeeping restrictions, i.e., patients can see anyone they want when they want, but only within the network? See generally Comment, Managed Health Care: HMO Corporate Liability, Independent Contractors, and the Ostensible Agency Doctrine, 15 J. Corp. L. 535 (1990).

How might an IPA HMO alter its structure or operations to avoid the attribution of agency and vicarious liability? See Chase v. Independent Practice Ass'n, 583 N.E.2d 251 (Mass. App. Ct. 1991) (vicarious liability rejected where HMO contract stated the IPA only "arranged for" services but did not provide services directly); Jones v. U.S. Healthcare, 723 N.Y.S.2d 478 (App. Div. 2001) (an HMO "cannot be held vicariously liable for defendant doctors' and hospital's alleged malpractice in discharging plaintiff and her baby prematurely, where the . . . Group Master Contract, membership card and Member Handbook clearly state that doctors and hospitals participating in defendant's health care program are independent contractors"). But see Petrovich v. Share Health Plan, 719 N.E.2d 756 (Ill. 1999) (exculpatory language in insurance documents does not control if the patient didn't actually read or understand the documents). Because IPAs are now the dominant form of HMOs, and because HMO lawyers have widely adopted these techniques, the working assumption among both plaintiff's and defense lawyers is that HMOs generally cannot be held vicariously liable simply by virtue of forming a network and requiring gatekeeping. This is also confirmed in several of the state managed care liability statutes discussed on the next page. See Gail Agrawal & Mark Hall, What If You *Could* Sue Your HMO? Managed Care Liability beyond the ERISA Shield, 47 St. Louis U. L.J. 235 (2003).

4. *HMO Direct Liability.* The focus of *Boyd* is vicarious liability, but HMOs have also been held to the same type of direct corporate liability ushered in by Darling v. Charleston Community Memorial Hospital, page 121. Recall that for hospitals, direct corporate liability takes two basic forms: a duty of care in the selection of physicians, and a duty of care in the contemporaneous supervision of physicians. The former is readily applicable to HMOs as well. Several courts have held that they have the same obligation hospitals do to review the credentials and competency of physicians that they select for their network. See, e.g., McClellan v. Health Maintenance Organization, 604 A.2d 1053 (Pa. Super. Ct. 1992). HMOs are required under their own accreditation standards to engage in a hospital-like credentialing process, and increasingly they are required to do so by state regulation as well. Nevertheless, many managed care networks accept virtually "any willing provider," that is, anyone with a license who agrees to the network's payment terms. A "Dear Doctor" letter sent by one PPO to California physicians stated "Welcome to the PPO network. You are now part of a carefully selected panel of more than 300 hospitals and 21,000 physicians." Robert A. Berenson, Beyond Competition, 16 Health Aff., No. 2, at 171, 175 (1997). Some states require by statute that HMOs accept any qualified provider. Does either voluntary or mandatory nonselectivity undermine the basis for a duty of care in selection?

Recall that the second branch of *Darling*—the duty of contemporaneous supervision—is highly controversial with respect to hospitals and is accepted in only a very limited fashion in most jurisdictions because it doesn't make sense to require hospital administrators to actively intervene in medical treatment decisions. Is the case for an HMO's duty to supervise any stronger? Even if there is no such mandatory duty, however, consider whether HMOs have voluntarily assumed such a duty through their utilization review function. Is this not the essential point of *Wickline*, that when insurance companies choose to intervene in treatment decisions, they assume a duty of care in doing so? Accord Shannon v. McNulty, 718 A.2d 828 (Pa. Super. Ct. 1998) ("When . . . an insurer interjects itself into the rendering of medical decisions affecting a subscriber's care it must do so in a medically reasonable manner").

To remove any doubt about this issue, about a dozen states have adopted statutes that hold insurers liable for personal injuries caused by negligent or inappropriate administration of health insurance benefits. See Agrawal & Hall, supra; Note, 74 Temp. L. Rev. 507 (2001). There is considerable doubt, however, whether these statutes can legally apply to employer-provided health insurance, due to the federal preemption doctrine discussed in the following case. Controversy over adopting this liability principle as a matter of federal law has been a major stumbling block in Congress's deliberations over the managed care patient "bill of rights."

5. Wickline's *Holding*. The precise holding or nonholding of *Wickline* has been a source of considerable confusion, both in the courts and among lawyers and commentators. This confusion is due in part to the unusual tactical decision by the plaintiff's lawyer not to sue the treating physicians. As a result, the plaintiff was able to use the treating physicians as experts for her side, but the physicians were unwilling to indict themselves by testifying that the four-day stay fell below a minimally acceptable standard of care. Without such testimony, the court was forced to find no liability. Without any basis in the clinical evidence for finding anyone liable, much of what the court said about the competing responsibilities of physicians and insurers was rendered dictum.

Nevertheless, *Wickline* is still the seminal case on the issues it addresses. In trying to make sense of what the opinion means for future disputes, distinguish these two issues: (1) whether insurers are potentially on the liability hook for making bad coverage decisions and (2) whether physicians are off the liability hook when insurers are at fault. Realize it is possible to answer "yes" to (1) and no to (2); in other words, both can be held liable at the same time. Others sometimes interpret *Wickline* to mean, however, that the doctor's ultimate responsibility absolves the insurance company from blame. The most prominent instance of this reading of *Wickline* is a subsequent California decision, Wilson v. Blue Cross of Southern California, 271 Cal. Rptr. 876 (Cal. Ct. App. 1990). There, a psychiatric patient committed suicide after being released from the hospital when his private insurer stopped paying for his hospitalization benefits due to lack of medical necessity. The court found it necessary to distinguish and disapprove *Wickline* in order to allow the case to be tried against the insurer under a negligence theory. Is anything in *Wickline* opposed to such a holding? For a sampling of the extensive commentary on these two cases, see John Blum, An Analysis of Legal Liability in Health Care Utilization Review and care management, 26 Hous. L. Rev. 191 (1989); Comment, Health Care Utilization Review: Potential Exposures to Negligence Liability, 52 Ohio St. L.J. 1289 (1991).

Under *Wickline*, could insurer liability be imposed based not only on the substance of the utilization review decision, but also based on the process. What flaws were present in Medi-Cal's UR process? How feasible would it be to improve on that process?

If insurers can be found liable for negligent failures to approve necessary care, can they also be held accountable for negligent approvals of harmful care?

6. *Bringing Liability and Payment into Sync.* Does the potential liability under *Wickline* make sense from the physician's perspective? Physicians complain that it is unfair to hold them responsible for failing to provide treatment that insurance will not pay for. What realistic options did Mrs. Wickline's physicians have? How might the tort standard of medical appropriateness be brought more into sync with the insurance standard? One possibility is by referring to the law of abandonment, which allows physicians to terminate care in certain circumstances if they give proper notice and an opportunity to locate another physician. Whether lack of payment is a permissible reason to give this notice has not yet clearly been decided.

7. *Few Cases but Big Verdicts.* One reason for the lack of clarity about the respective responsibilities of physicians and insurers is that there have been surprisingly few cases like *Wickline* and *Wilson* with decisions on the merits. This suggests that perhaps in practice insurers rarely deny coverage for care that is required by the minimal standard of medical practice. The paucity of suits may also be due to the preemption of state law by the federal ERISA statute, discussed in the next case. Others attribute the favorable malpractice record of staff model HMOs like Kaiser to their detailed programs of malpractice prevention and physician monitoring and to the availability of a grievance process for dissatisfied patients. William Curran & George Moseley, The Malpractice Experience of Health Maintenance Organizations, 70 Nw. U. L. Rev. 69 (1975). These characteristics typically do not exist, however, in the broad network model HMOs that currently prevail in the market. Further explanation for the small number of suits comes from a recent empirical study, which reports that plaintiffs' lawyers are reluctant to name health insurers in medical malpractice suits since this greatly complicates the litigation and is usually unnecessary given the fact that the treating physician is "on the hook" in any event (for reasons explained in *Wickline*). Also, plaintiffs' lawyers report seeing few or no cases where harm results from health insurers' refusing to pay for treatment that physicians request. Agrawal & Hall, supra.

Although there have been few successful cases against health insurers, when plaintiffs have succeeded, they sometimes win very large punitive damages awards, in the range of $50 million to $100 million. For instance, in Fox v. Health Net, a California jury awarded $77 million in punitive damages (plus $12 million compensatory) against an HMO that had refused to pay for an innovative cancer treatment, which the surviving family claimed resulted in the patient's death. This was eclipsed by the $120 million verdict in Goodrich v. Aetna U.S. Healthcare, $116 million of which were punitive damages. Like Fox, the Goodrich verdict was based on an HMO's reluctance to authorize expensive, state-of-the-art treatment for terminal cancer that it considered to be experimental. Similarly, an Ohio court awarded $30 million against a Blue Cross insurer for failing to pay for cancer treatment (Dardinger v. Athem, 2002 WL 31895279 (Oh. 2002)), and a Florida jury awarded $80 million against Humana for terminating coverage for a special therapy program for a child with cerebral palsy, although this verdict was subsequently set aside for improper instructions and evidence. Humana Health Ins. Co. v. Chipps, 802 So. 2d 492 (Fla. Dist. Ct. App. 2001).

Does this track record of very few successful verdicts, but some that are extremely large, create appropriate incentives for plaintiffs to sue? Is it likely to send appropriate deterrence signals to health insurers? Does the few number of suits suggest a need to remove barriers to suing health plans? Would a "floodgate" of litigation threaten the viability of the managed care industry or of its core cost-containment practices? For discussion from various perspectives, see the literature cited in note 1; David Studdert et al., Expanded Managed Care Liability: What Impact on Employer Coverage?, 18(6) Health Aff. 7 (Dec. 1999).

8. *Financial Incentives.* Another potential basis for direct liability against HMOs and managed care arrangements is the use of financial incentives to encourage physicians to economize. An insurer might avoid the entire issue of liability for second guessing medical judgment by paying doctors in a way that encourages them to economize in their own clinical decisionmaking. Using *Wickline*'s notion of "defects in the design or implementation of cost containment mechanisms," is it possible nevertheless to argue that some financial incentives are too strong per se, or that in practice they caused a physician to err? Consider by analogy the suits in the 1990s against Domino's Pizza for pressuring its deliverers to drive too fast. Financial incentives might also lead to claims for punitive damages or for breach of fiduciary duty in medical malpractice cases against physicians.

9. *Breach of Contract.* The *Boyd* concurrence suggests that HMO liability might also be based on a contractual or quasi-promissory theory, such as warranty or fraud. Is there a difference between the nature of the promises an HMO makes and those made by typical hospitals or doctors? Professor Brewbaker argues that, because HMOs, unlike hospitals, sell medical services, they undertake an implied warranty of quality which, as with doctors, promises nonnegligent care. Therefore, he argues that HMOs should be automatically liable for any negligent care delivered under their auspices, regardless of whether they fall under the theories of liability devised for hospitals. Wm. Brewbaker, Medical Malpractice and Managed Care Organizations: The Implied Warranty of Quality, 60 Contemp. Probs. 117 (Spring 1997).

10. *Employer Liability.* If insurers can be held liable for lack of care in selecting physicians and supervising treatment decisions, how about employers who construct their own managed care plans? Many large employers eliminate the "middle man" by contracting directly with hospitals and physicians on a self-insured basis. In doing so, an employer may either "rent a network," that is, contract with an existing network of providers, or it might form its own network. In either event, is it plausible to impose the same type of managed care liability on employers as on the insurers they have ousted? If such liability existed under state law, it would likely be preempted for reasons addressed in the following case. For discussion, see Dana M. Muir, Fiduciary Status as an Employer's Shield: The Perversity of ERISA Fiduciary Law, 2 Univ. Pa. J. Lab. & Emp. L. 391 (2000).

11. *Exclusive Enterprise Liability.* The furthest extension of the concepts of enterprise liability developed for hospitals, HMOs, and other forms of managed

care would be to hold a network of hospitals, doctors, and insurers exclusively liable at the highest institutional level for any medical mistake that occurs within any component part. If the health care delivery system were to move toward and "integrated delivery system" structure, commentators have speculated whether these networks should or will be the final point of liability focus. So far, most networks are only loosely formed contractual affiliations in which the parties (hospitals, doctors, and insurers) agree on a nonexclusive basis to market their services collectively to employers or other insurers. Does this entail sufficient integration, coordination, selection, and supervision to justify imposition of enterprise liability? Consider whether it is feasible for integrated delivery systems to influence the quality of care if these affiliations are nonexclusive, that is, if doctors and hospitals belong to several such networks? See generally K. Abraham & P. Weiler, Enterprise Medical Liability and the Choice of the Responsible Enterprise, 20 Am. J.L. & Med. 29 (1994); Clark C. Havighurst, Making Health Plans Accountable for the Quality of Care, 31 Ga. L. Rev. 587 (1997); Karen A. Jordan, Managed Competition and Limited Choice of Providers: Countering Negative Perceptions through a Responsibility to Select Quality Network Physicians, 27 Ariz. St. L.J. 875 (1995); William Sage, Enterprise Liability and the Emerging Managed Care Health Care System, 60(2) Law & Contemp. Probs. 159 (Spring 1997); Comment, Tort Liability of Integrated Health Care Delivery Systems: Beyond Enterprise Liability, 29 Wake Forest L. Rev. 305 (1994).

12. *Class Action Suits.* A group of prominent plaintiffs' lawyers, known as the REPAIR Team, flush from their victories over tobacco companies, have recently brought large class action suits against the major national HMOs, using RICO, the federal white-collar crime statute. This avoids the problems caused by federal preemption under the ERISA statute, discussed in the next case, because ERISA preempts only state law. (This strategy is suggested by Humana, Inc. v. Forsyth, 114 F.3d 1467 (9th Cir. 1999), which allowed a class action suit under RICO based on allegations that an insurer committed fraud by calculating subscribers' copayments based on providers' list prices rather than on the discounted prices it had negotiated with providers.) These new class actions allege that HMOs systematically misrepresent how generous they are in making coverage decisions, and fail to disclose utilization review restrictions and methods of physician payment. These nondisclosures are also alleged to violate fiduciary principles under the ERISA statute itself. An additional set of class actions have been brought by physicians, using a variety of state common law theories, as well as the federal statutes, to claim various economic injuries under their contracts with HMOs.

So far, the only federal appellate decision has dismissed the RICO claims based on the absence of any cognizable damages. The plaintiffs claimed only that, due to managed care practices, their insurance policies had a lower market value than their employers paid for them, not that they had suffered any *actual* denial of services. Maio v. Aetna, 221 F.3d 472 (3d Cir. 2000). However, a lower court ruling has indicated that various legal theories may be viable, under both RICO and ERISA, especially when the claims are brought by physicians rather than patients. In re Managed Care Litigation, 135 F. Supp. 1253 (S.D. Fla. 2001). For analysis, see Kathy Cerminara, Taking a Closer Look at the Managed Care Class Actions, 11 Annals Health L. 1 (2002); Clark Havighurst, Consumers Versus Managed

Care: The New Class Actions, 20(4) Health Aff. 2 (July 2001); David Studdert &
Troyen Brennan, 342 New Eng. J. Med. 280 (2000). See generally Kathy
Cerminara, The Class Action Suit as a Method of Patient Empowerment in the
Managed Care Setting, 24 Am. J.L. & Med. 7 (1998).

Problem: Enterprise Liability

Mike Mulligan is administrator of Marcus Welby Hospital, a large facility in a
metropolitan area. Mary Anne is the local lawyer. Mike has a plan to protect the
hospital from the erosion of business that has resulted from managed care contracts taking more and more patients into the larger facilities nearby. Mulligan's
plan is for the hospital to form its own managed care network. Mulligan would like
to include as many of the local physicians as possible in the network. (Assume this is
legal under antitrust law.) The network will then sell HMO type insurance to local
residents. The revenue premiums will be split 50/50 between the hospital and the
doctors, with the physician half going mostly to the primary care physicians. These
primary care physicians will act as gatekeepers for hospitalization decisions, referrals to specialists in town, and referrals to larger hospitals for more complex care.

Mulligan consults Mary Anne about advice on the liability implications of this
plan. The hospital has been named in a number of suits recently, and he is concerned at the formation stage about what new liability exposure the network will
create and what steps are possible to manage or reduce that exposure. Taking the
position of Mike Mulligan, how desirable would each of the following alternative
ideas be from a business or practical perspective? Taking the position of Mary
Anne, how desirable would each be from a legal perspective?

1. Automatically accept into the network any doctor with medical staff privileges at the hospital.
2. In contracting with doctors, insist on an indemnification clause that
   requires them to compensate the hospital for any paid claims that arise
   from the doctor's own fault.
3. Agree to purchase malpractice insurance for network physicians, defend
   any claims brought by patients, and pay for any resulting liability. Consider
   this option both for hospital-based care only and for all medical care.
4. Increase the size and authority of the risk management department,
   school them in the techniques of quality assurance and "total quality management," and impose a passel of practice guidelines that cover liability-
   sensitive areas of medicine.
5. Write insurance contracts so as to notify subscribers that network physicians are independent contractors. Post similar statements in doctors'
   waiting rooms, at hospital entrances, on hospital admission forms, and
   on informed consent forms. Review stationery, billing forms, and uniform
   dress to avoid creating the unintended impression of an agency relationship between the hospital and network physicians.
6. Have the risk management department and Mary Anne review all advertising and marketing materials to eliminate any statements that might
   create an expectation or image of receiving quality care.

7. Write insurance contracts so as to specifically promise an "adequate level of care, consistent with the coverage provided by this insurance and within the standards of care that prevail in other, similar locations in this state."

◼ AETNA HEALTH INC. v. DAVILA
543 U.S. ___ (2004)

Justice THOMAS delivered the opinion of the Court.

In these consolidated cases, two individuals sued their respective HMOs for alleged failures to exercise ordinary care in the handling of coverage decisions, in violation of a duty imposed by the Texas Health Care Liability Act (Texas Act). We granted certiorari to decide whether the individuals' causes of action are completely pre-empted by the . . . Employee Retirement Income Security Act of 1974 (ERISA). . . .

[Davila was covered by Aetna through his employer, and Calad was covered by CIGNA through her husband's employer.] Respondents both suffered injuries allegedly arising from Aetna's and CIGNA's decisions not to provide coverage for certain treatment and services recommended by respondents' treating physicians. Davila's treating physician prescribed Vioxx to remedy Davila's arthritis pain, but Aetna refused to pay for it. Davila did not appeal or contest this decision, nor did he purchase Vioxx with his own resources and seek reimbursement. Instead, Davila began taking Naprosyn, from which he allegedly suffered a severe reaction that required extensive treatment and hospitalization. [Editors' note: The Court fails to mention that Davila nearly died from bleeding ulcers and that, although Vioxx is much more expensive than Naprosyn, it has fewer side effects relating to bleeding ulcers.]

Calad underwent surgery, and although her treating physician recommended an extended hospital stay, a CIGNA discharge nurse determined that Calad did not meet the plan's criteria for a continued hospital stay. CIGNA consequently denied coverage for the extended hospital stay. Calad experienced postsurgery complications forcing her to return to the hospital. She alleges that these complications would not have occurred had CIGNA approved coverage for a longer hospital stay.

[In separate state-court suits,] respondents . . . argued that petitioners' refusal to cover the requested services violated their "duty to exercise ordinary care when making health care treatment decisions," and that these refusals "proximately caused" their injuries. Petitioners removed the cases to Federal District Courts, arguing that respondents' causes of action fit within the scope of, and were therefore completely pre-empted by, ERISA. . . . The United States Court of Appeals for the Fifth Circuit consolidated their cases with several others raising similar issues. . . . After examining the causes of action available under [ERISA], the Court of Appeals determined that respondents' claims could possibly fall under . . . §502(a)(1)(B), which provides a cause of action for the recovery of wrongfully denied benefits. . . . [However, the court ruled that this case does not fall under ERISA because] respondents "are not seeking reimbursement for benefits denied them," but rather request "tort damages" arising from "an external, statutorily imposed duty of 'ordinary care.'" . . .

II

Congress enacted ERISA to "protect . . . the interests of participants in employee benefit plans and their beneficiaries" by setting out substantive regulatory requirements for employee benefit plans and to "provid[e] for appropriate remedies, sanctions, and ready access to the Federal courts." 29 U.S.C. §1001(b). The purpose of ERISA is to provide a uniform regulatory regime over employee benefit plans. To this end, ERISA includes expansive pre-emption provisions, see ERISA §514, which are intended to ensure that employee benefit plan regulation would be "exclusively a federal concern." ERISA's "comprehensive legislative scheme" includes "an integrated system of procedures for enforcement." . . . As the Court said in Pilot Life Ins. Co. v. Dedeaux, 481 U.S. 41, 107 S. Ct. 1549, 95 L. Ed. 2d 39 (1987):

> [T]he detailed provisions of §502(a) set forth a comprehensive civil enforcement scheme that represents a careful balancing of the need for prompt and fair claims settlement procedures against the public interest in encouraging the formation of employee benefit plans. The policy choices reflected in the inclusion of certain remedies and the exclusion of others under the federal scheme would be completely undermined if ERISA-plan participants and beneficiaries were free to obtain remedies under state law that Congress rejected in ERISA. "The six carefully integrated civil enforcement provisions found in §502(a) of the statute as finally enacted . . . provide strong evidence that Congress did *not* intend to authorize other remedies that it simply forgot to incorporate expressly."

Therefore, any state-law cause of action that duplicates, supplements, or supplants the ERISA civil enforcement remedy conflicts with the clear congressional intent to make the ERISA remedy exclusive and is therefore pre-empted. . . . It follows that if an individual brings suit complaining of a denial of coverage for medical care, where the individual is entitled to such coverage only because of the terms of an ERISA-regulated employee benefit plan, and . . . if an individual, at some point in time, could have brought his claim under ERISA §502(a) . . . then the individual's cause of action is completely pre-empted by ERISA. . . .

III

The only action [Davila] complained of was Aetna's refusal to approve payment for Davila's Vioxx prescription. Further, the only relationship Aetna had with Davila was its partial administration of Davila's employer's benefit plan. Similarly . . . Calad contests only CIGNA's decision to refuse coverage for her hospital stay. . . . It is clear, then, that respondents complain only about denials of coverage promised under the terms of ERISA-regulated employee benefit plans. Upon the denial of benefits, respondents could have paid for the treatment themselves and then sought reimbursement through a §502(a)(1)(B) action, or sought a preliminary injunction. . . .[2]

---

[2] Respondents also argue that the benefit due under their ERISA-regulated employee benefit plans is simply the membership in the respective HMOs, not coverage for the particular medical

Respondents contend, however, that the complained-of actions violate legal duties that arise independently of ERISA or the terms of the employee benefit plans at issue in these cases. Both respondents brought suit specifically under the Texas Act, alleging that petitioners "controlled, influenced, participated in and made decisions which affected the quality of the diagnosis, care, and treatment provided" in a manner that violated "the duty of ordinary care." . . . The Texas Act does impose a duty on managed care entities to "exercise ordinary care when making health care treatment decisions," and makes them liable for damages proximately caused by failures to abide by that duty. However, if a managed care entity correctly concluded that, under the terms of the relevant plan, a particular treatment was not covered, the managed care entity's denial of coverage would not be a proximate cause of any injuries arising from the denial. Rather, the failure of the plan itself to cover the requested treatment would be the proximate cause.[3] More significantly, the Texas Act clearly states that "[it] . . . create[s] no obligation on the part of the health insurance . . . entity to provide to an insured or enrollee treatment which is not covered by the health care plan of the entity." Hence, . . . interpretation of the terms of respondents' benefit plans forms an essential part of their [state law] claim, and [state law] liability would exist here only because of petitioners' administration of ERISA-regulated benefit plans. Petitioners' potential liability under the Texas Act in these cases, then, derives entirely from the particular rights and obligations established by the benefit plans. . . . [R]espondents bring suit only to rectify a wrongful denial of benefits promised under ERISA-regulated plans, and do not attempt to remedy any violation of a legal duty independent of ERISA. . . .

[T]he Court of Appeals found significant that respondents "assert a tort claim for tort damages" rather than "a contract claim for contract damages," and that respondents "are not seeking reimbursement for benefits denied them." But, distinguishing between pre-empted and non-pre-empted claims based on the particular label affixed to them would "elevate form over substance and allow parties to evade" the pre-emptive scope of ERISA simply "by relabeling their contract claims as claims for tortious breach of contract." . . . In [previous Supreme Court cases finding preemption], the plaintiffs all brought state claims that were labeled either tort or tort-like. . . .

Respondents also argue—for the first time in their brief to this Court—that the Texas Act is a law that regulates insurance, and hence that ERISA §514(b)(2)(A) saves their causes of action from pre-emption.[4] This argument is unavailing. . . . ERISA §514(b)(2)(A) must be interpreted in light of the congressional intent to create an exclusive federal remedy in ERISA §502(a). Under ordinary principles of conflict pre-emption, then, even a state law that can arguably be characterized as

---

treatments that are delineated in the plan documents. Respondents did not identify this possible argument in their brief in opposition to the petitions for certiorari, and we deem it waived.

[3] To take a clear example, if the terms of the health care plan specifically exclude from coverage the cost of an appendectomy, then any injuries caused by the refusal to cover the appendectomy are properly attributed to the terms of the plan itself, not the managed care entity that applied those terms.

[4] ERISA §514(b)(2)(A) reads, as relevant: "[N]othing in this subchapter shall be construed to exempt or relieve any person from any law of any State which regulates insurance, banking, or securities."

"regulating insurance" will be pre-empted if it provides a separate vehicle to assert a claim for benefits outside of, or in addition to, ERISA's remedial scheme.

IV

Respondents, their *amici*, and some Courts of Appeals have relied heavily upon Pegram v. Herdrich, 530 U.S. 211 (2000), in arguing that ERISA does not pre-empt or completely pre-empt state suits such as respondents'. . . . *Pegram* cannot be read so broadly. In *Pegram*, the plaintiff sued her physician-owned-and-operated HMO (which provided medical coverage through plaintiff's employer pursuant to an ERISA-regulated benefit plan) and her treating physician, both for medical malpractice and for a breach of an ERISA fiduciary duty. The plaintiff's treating physician was also the person charged with administering plaintiff's benefits; it was she who decided whether certain treatments were covered. We reasoned that the physician's "eligibility decision and the treatment decision were inextricably mixed." We concluded that "Congress did not intend [the defendant HMO] or any other HMO to be treated as a fiduciary to the extent that it makes mixed eligibility decisions acting through its physicians." . . .

[I]t was essential to *Pegram*'s conclusion that the decisions challenged there were truly "mixed eligibility and treatment decisions," *i.e.*, medical necessity decisions made by the plaintiff's treating physician *qua* treating physician and *qua* benefits administrator. Put another way, the reasoning of *Pegram* "only make[s] sense where the underlying negligence also plausibly constitutes medical maltreatment by a party who can be deemed to be a treating physician or such a physician's employer." Cicio v. Does, 321 F.3d 83, 109 (C.A.2 2003) (Calabresi, J., dissenting in part). Here, however, petitioners are neither respondents' treating physicians nor the employers of respondents' treating physicians. Petitioners' coverage decisions, then, are pure eligibility decisions, and *Pegram* is not implicated. . . .

Justice GINSBURG, with whom Justice BREYER joins, concurring.
. . . [This] decision is consistent with our governing case law on ERISA's preemptive scope. I therefore join the Court's opinion. But, with greater enthusiasm . . . I also join "the rising judicial chorus urging that Congress and [this] Court revisit what is an unjust and increasingly tangled ERISA regime." DiFelice v. AETNA U.S. Healthcare, 346 F.3d 442, 453 (C.A.3 2003) (Becker, J., concurring). Because the Court has coupled an encompassing interpretation of ERISA's preemptive force with a cramped construction of the "equitable relief" allowable under §502(a)(3), a "regulatory vacuum" exists: "[V]irtually all state law remedies are preempted but very few federal substitutes are provided."

A series of the Court's decisions has yielded a host of situations in which persons adversely affected by ERISA-proscribed wrongdoing cannot gain make-whole relief [because] "there is a stark absence in [ERISA] itself and in its legislative history of any reference to an intention to authorize the recovery of extracontractual damages" for consequential injuries. . . . [F]resh consideration of the availability of consequential damages under §502(a)(3) is plainly in order. See 321 F.3d, at 106, 107 (Calabresi, J., dissenting in part) ("gaping wound" caused by the breadth of preemption and limited remedies under ERISA, as interpreted by this Court, will not be healed until the Court "start[s] over" or Congress "wipe[s] the slate clean"); *DiFelice*, 346 F.3d, at 467 ("The vital thing . . . is that either Congress or the Court act quickly, because the current situation is plainly untenable."); Langbein, What ERISA Means by "Equitable": The Supreme Court's Trail of Error in *Russell, Mertens,* and *Great-West*, 103 Colum. L. Rev. 1317, 1365 (2003). . . . The Government notes a potential amelioration. . . . [It] suggests that the Act, as currently written and interpreted, may "allo[w] at least some forms of 'make-whole' relief." . . . As the Court points out, respondents here declined the opportunity to amend their complaints to state claims for relief under §502(a). . . . But the Government's suggestion may indicate an effective remedy others similarly circumstanced might fruitfully pursue.

"Congress . . . intended ERISA to replicate the core principles of trust remedy law, including the make-whole standard of relief." *Langbein*, 1319. I anticipate that Congress, or this Court, will one day so confirm.

Notes: ERISA Preemption

1. *Damages Under ERISA.* Under ERISA, patients who are wrongly denied health insurance benefits can recover compensation only for the costs of treatment, but not for consequential damages, pain and suffering, wrongful death, or punitive damages. Corcoran v. United Healthcare, Inc., 965 F.2d 1321 (5th Cir. 1992), dramatically illustrates the hardship caused by this restriction in available remedies. There, a woman miscarried late in her pregnancy, due, she alleged, to the HMO's refusal to authorize hospitalization for pregnancy complications. The court limited her potential remedies under ERISA to an order for treatment or compensation for treatment costs. But, because the fetus had died, these remedies were meaningless. This restriction of damages is much more severe even than that imposed by ordinary contract law. Therefore, it is important to note the concurring Justices' argument in *Davila* that this limitation can and should be revisited.

The majority in *Davila* appears to think the outcome makes perfect sense according to congressional intent. Legislative history discussed in Chapter 3.C, however, reveals that Congress wrote ERISA primarily with pension benefits in mind, and long before managed care health insurance existed. Do you see why limiting damages to the costs of treatment might have made a lot more sense under traditional insurance? Assuming, as the concurrence argues, that ERISA's remedies no longer make sense for managed care insurance, whose responsibility is it to fix the problem: Congress's or the courts'? See Andrews-Clarke v. Travelers Insurance Co., 948 F. Supp. 49 (D. Mass. 1997) ("Although the [failure of the utilization reviewer to approve hospitalization for a deeply troubled alcoholic who later committed suicide] is extraordinarily troubling, even more disturbing to this Court is the failure of Congress to amend a statute that, due to the changing realities of the modern health care system, has gone conspicuously awry from its original intent. Does anyone care? Do you?"). In 2001, each chamber of Congress approved different versions of a "patients' bill of rights," discussed in Chapter 3.B, which would have amended ERISA to allow tort damages against health insurers, but differences between the two bills were never reconciled.

2. *ERISA terminology* is obscure and confusing. Essentially, an ERISA "plan" exists any time an employer pays for health insurance. If the employer simply purchases health insurance, then technically there may be a distinction between the "plan," which is the decision to purchase, and the insurance, which is the contracted-for benefit. Would it be possible, using this distinction, to argue that ERISA preempts only suits against employers for failing to provide insurance, but not suits against insurers for failing to provide the benefits covered by the insurance? Observe how the *Davila* Court avoids this issue in footnote 2 of the opinion, but a few lower courts have adopted this position. See, e.g., Washington Physicians Service Ass'n v. Gregoire, 147 F.3d 1039 (9th Cir. 1998) ("The mere fact that many [employers] choose to buy health insurance for their [employees] does not cause a regulation of health insurance automatically to 'relate to' any employee benefit plan—just as a decision to buy an apple a day for every employee, or to offer employees a gym membership, does not cause all state regulation of apples and gyms to 'relate to' employee benefit plans."). But see Hotz v. Blue Cross & Blue Shield of Massachusetts, 292 F.3d 57, 59-60 (1st Cir. 2002) ("Although the [employer plan/insurance plan] distinction is linguistically possible, it would mean that numerous past ERISA suits brought to secure payment for medical services from third-party providers under ERISA plans lacked a legal basis."). See generally Russell Korobkin, The Failed Jurisprudence of Managed Care, and How to Fix It: Reinterpreting ERISA Preemption, 51 UCLA L. Rev. 457 (2003).

Regardless, ERISA preemption would still apply to situations in which the employer self-insures, that is, pays for health care directly out of its own funds. In that case, ERISA clearly preempts state law liability against the employer.

3. *Which Claims Are Preempted?* The end of the *Davila* opinion briefly alludes to ERISA's effect on more conventional medical malpractice claims that arise under managed care insurance. Lower court decisions clarify the following: ERISA clearly does not apply to a malpractice claim against only the treating physician for a medical mistake that is unaffected by health insurance. Likewise, courts usually find no preemption if a plaintiff attempts to hold a health insurer vicariously liable for a treating physician's mistake. Pacificare of Oklahoma v. Burrage, 59 F.3d 151 (10th Cir. 1995); Rice v. Panchal, 65 F.3d 637 (7th Cir. 1995). This helps to explain *Davila*'s reference to the fact that the plaintiffs' physicians in that case were not employees of the health plans.

The law is unsettled, however, when there is a medical treatment mistake and the plaintiff attempts to hold the insurer *directly* responsible because it selected bad physicians or influenced their treatment decisions. This is similar to the situation in Pegram v. Herdrich, 530 U.S. 211 (2000), which is discussed in *Davila* and excerpted in Chapter 3.E.3. There, the patient claimed that her doctor was influenced by profit distributions from the HMO and that this financial tie violates ERISA fiduciary standards. In the course of rejecting that claim under ERISA, the Court noted that the patient was free to pursue her claim in state court in the form of a medical malpractice suit. This strongly suggests that direct liability actions against HMOs for care provided by treating physicians are not preempted by ERISA, even after *Davila*.

In short, courts must distinguish between tort claims based on insurance coverage decisions, which are preempted, and medical malpractice liability, which is not preempted. In drawing this line, many lower courts have followed a rule of thumb that distinguishes between claims based on the *quantity* of care and those based on its *quality*. See, e.g., Bauman v. U.S. Healthcare, Inc., 193 F.3d 151 (3d Cir. 1999); Dukes v. U.S. Healthcare, 57 F.3d 350 (3d Cir. 1995). The *Davila* case makes no reference to this concept, however. Instead, it focuses on whether the insurer or the treating physician made the critical decision. Is that distinction likely to be sufficiently clear in most cases? What about situations in which the treating physician is employed full time by an HMO, and the HMO instructs the physician that a particular treatment option is not approved, for instance, that women should not remain in the hospital longer than 48 hours following normal childbirth? That might be regarded as a quantity decision based on the insurance policy's medical appropriateness criteria, or it might be regarded as a form of direct HMO liability for interfering with physicians' ability to make good treatment decisions. Does *Davila* resolve which is the correct characterization?

One further complication: if it is possible to find an agency relationship between the HMO and the treating physician, should it matter that the HMO is not the physician's employer? Isn't the critical factor whether or not the physician agreed with, or acquiesced in, the HMO's decision? In *Davila*, the HMO refused to pay for treatments the physicians ordered, but, in many other cases, physicians may not order treatment they know the HMO won't pay for or that will cost the physician money under the HMO's payment incentives. Shouldn't patients be able to blame the HMO, at least in part, when this happens? In such cases, should *Davila* apply?

There is a very large academic literature discussing these issues, but at the moment, it all predates *Davila*, so it is of only limited use in predicting the future course of judicial rulings in this area.

4. *Medicare Preemption*. Preemption issues might also arise under Medicare, which has a restrictive set of remedies for beneficiaries. One important ruling held that Medicare's administrative review process does not preempt a state tort action against a private HMO that contracted to deliver Medicare services. McCall v. Pacificare of California, Inc., 21 P.3d 1189 (Cal. 2001).

3

Health Care Financing and Reform

The organization of health care law can be thought of in terms of concentric rings. At the center is the core treatment relationship between physician and patient. Outside this core are various external interests that might affect individual medical decisions. This book looks at the financial and institutional arrangements that surround the treatment relationship. This chapter explores who pays for medical care, and under what terms. The next chapter explains the structure of medical facilities and how they relate to member physicians and to each other. It also examines the most complex layer in this set of rings: the emerging interconnections among insurers, facilities, and physicians as the marketplace for health care delivery undergoes rapid and fundamental transformation.

The dominant themes are political and economic: as our society struggles to solve the problems that confront the health care financing and delivery system, should we rely primarily on a market model that treats medicine as a consumer good, or on a social model that looks to regulatory governmental intervention to correct the perceived failures of the marketplace? This theme is introduced in Chapter 1.D.3, and is developed in more depth below, especially in Chapter 3.F.2.

A. SOURCES OF HEALTH INSURANCE

Our fragmented system of paying for health care makes it difficult to cover comprehensively all of the complex legal regimes created by the many different sources of insurance. Rather than dividing the world of insurance into public vs. private, and conventional vs. managed care, we have chosen to organize this chapter around the generic issues that affect all sources of insurance: who is eligible, what services are covered, how is insurance regulated, how are disputes resolved, and how are doctors and hospitals paid? Along the way, it will be necessary, however, to learn whether answers to these questions differ according to the particular source of insurance. Therefore, we begin with a description of the entire, complex financing system.

1. The Right to Health Care

■ UNCOMPENSATED HOSPITAL CARE: RIGHTS AND RESPONSIBILITIES
Uwe Reinhardt

[Read the excerpt at page 75.]

■ THE RIGHT TO A DECENT MINIMUM OF HEALTH CARE*
Tom L. Beauchamp & James F. Childress**

The history of the right to health care has been characterized more by political rhetoric than by careful analysis. The primary question has been whether the government should be involved in health care allocation and distribution, rather than leaving these matters to the marketplace. Libertarians insist that all rights to social goods based on enforced beneficence violate the principle of respect for autonomy. Society has often allowed this libertarian-supported rule of ability to pay to determine the distribution of health goods and services, but we will argue that this rule should not be allowed to serve as our only principle of distributive justice.

Two main arguments support a right to health care: (1) an argument from collective social protection and (2) an argument from fair opportunity. The first argument focuses on the similarities between health needs and other needs that have conventionally been protected by government. Threats to health are relevantly similar to threats presented by crime, fire, and polluted environments. The latter threats are conventionally resisted by collective actions and resources.

... If government has an obligation to provide one type of essential service, then it must have an obligation to provide another.... However, ... these public programs pertain to social goods, such as public health, whereas health care is largely a matter of the individual's private good....

A second argument buttresses this first argument by appealing to the fair-opportunity rule. From this perspective, the justice of social institutions is gauged by their tendency to counteract lack of opportunity caused by unpredictable bad luck and misfortune over which the person has no meaningful control. Insofar as injury, disability, or disease creates profoundly significant disadvantages and

---

*This excerpt is from Principles of Biomedical Ethics (4th ed. 1994).
**Kennedy School of Ethics at Georgetown University, and University of Virginia, respectively.

reduces agents' capacity to function properly, justice is done if societal health care resources are used to counter these morally arbitrary, disadvantaging effects and to restore to persons a fair chance to use their capacities.[43] ...

This general guideline of fair opportunity suggests a path for giving content to the idea of a decent minimum of health care and for setting priorities in the allocation of resources. ... The rule of fair opportunity asserts that collective moral obligations exist to provide health care at the level needed for persons to receive as fair a chance in life as possible.

Even if the arguments we have presented for a moral right to health care are rejected on grounds that justice does not support this right, a legal right or entitlement to health care can be supported on a different moral basis such as compassion and beneficence. ... According to the "enforced beneficence argument," as Allen Buchanan terms it, beneficent citizens who do not believe that the needy have a right to health care would still establish certain health programs for the needy while coercively requiring those with the resources to sustain the programs.[45] ... If the goals are sufficiently fundamental and important, coercion can be morally justified to fulfil the goals independent of the existence of rights.

A directly related argument from societal beneficence focuses on the expression of social virtue and excellence in public policies, with an emphasis on creating a morally worthy society with which citizens can identify. This communitarian approach concentrates on compassion for victims of the various lotteries of life. Themes from this approach echo in the influential report of the President's Commission for the Study of Ethical Problems in Medicine and Biomedical Research on Securing Access to Health Care (1983): "The depth of a society's concern about health care can be seen as a measure of its sense of solidarity in the face of suffering and death. ... A society's commitment to health care reflects some of its most basic attitudes about what it means to be a member of the human community."

THE SCOPE OF THE RIGHT TO HEALTH CARE

Apart from the contest between libertarian and nonlibertarian views of justice, an intractable, and ultimately the most important, problem is how to specify the entitlements and limits established by a right to health care. Two broad views have attracted wide contemporary support: a right to equal access to health care and a right to a decent minimum of health care. Both rely on egalitarian premises. The former represents a strong egalitarian perspective of equal access to all bona fide health care resources. The latter incorporates only a weak egalitarian point of view, viz., equal access to fundamental health care resources. ... The societal obligation can be discharged at various levels, but the decent-minimum approach entails acceptance of [a] two-tiered system of health care: enforced social coverage for basic and catastrophic health needs (tier 1), together with voluntary private coverage for other health needs and desires (tier 2). ...

---

[43] Norman Daniels, Just Health Care (1985).

[45] Allen Buchanan, The Right to a Decent Minimum of Health Care, *in* President's Commission for the Study of Ethical Problems in Medicine and Biomedical and Behavioral Research, Securing Access to Health Care, vol. 2, esp. p.234.

Although some parties will be distressed to learn that the standard is "decent" care rather than "optimum" care, only the former can be justified in a socially funded policy. When we later . . . discuss explicit health policies such as the pioneering Oregon health plan, we will see that it is unrealistic to expect a higher level than adequate care. Rationing will also be an essential part of the process. Otherwise priorities cannot be set and maintained.

This proposal has the advantage of holding out the potential for compromise among libertarians, utilitarians, communitarians, and egalitarians, because it incorporates some moral concerns stressed by each of these theories. It guarantees basic health care for all on a premise of equal access, while allowing unequal additional purchase by individual initiative and contract. It mixes private and public forms of distribution, and it affirms collective as well as free-market methods of delivering health care. . . .

Despite these attractions, the decent-minimum proposal has proved difficult to explicate and implement. . . . Those who promote access to a decent minimum or adequate level of care usually do not specify where to set limits on expenditures for health care that confer precise entitlements. . . . [This] raises problems of whether society can fairly, consistently, and unambiguously devise a public policy that recognizes a right to care for primary needs without creating a right to exotic and expensive forms of treatment, such as liver transplants costing over $200,000 for what many deem to be marginal benefits in quality-adjusted life-years. More importantly, the model is purely programmatic until society defines what decent minimum means in operational terms. This task is, we believe, the major problem confronting health policy in the United States today.

Notes: The Right to Health Care

1. *The Right to Health Care.* Consider these additional perspectives on whether there is a moral or social right to health care, and what that right might be:

> There is a moral right to health care, but not of the sort often claimed. It is a right grounded not in purchasing power, merit, or social worth, but in human need. The right to health care finds its rationale in a social concept of the self, in a sense of common humanity, and in a knowledge of common vulnerability to disease and death. The right begins in a recognition that we all fall ill and are susceptible to disability and death. That is our nature and, whatever cultural variations there may be . . ., the root awareness we have of this is not an invention but a discovery. Second, while some illnesses are self-induced diseases generally are not the sort of things which are distributed by merit. We are all very likely to incur needs for health care for which we are not responsible and which are, in many instances, unforseeable. Third, health care . . . is effective. Ill health is, in sum, the sort of thing which is universally experienced, but unevenly distributed, over which we have little control or predictive powers and for which there is frequently effective help. A just society is one in which the right to health care is based on the elemental fact of human need. . . . A more complete statement of a right to health care is as follows: *A right to health care based on need means a right to equitable access based on need alone to all effective care society can reasonably afford.* [The author defines "need alone" to mean that a person's entitlement to health care depends on the person's need for care, the person's race, wealth, status, or other social attributes.]

Larry R. Churchill, Rationing Health Care in America 90-94 (1987) (emphasis in original).

> [P]ermitting a noticeably lower tier of services for the poor can be based on respect for poor persons' own preferences. If poor, I will rationally and knowledgeably prefer to spend less on preserving health and saving life than if I am well off. Especially in choosing whether to cover and pay for statistically expensive, marginally beneficial procedures, lower income people will properly choose differently. To flatten out these differences through uniform health services *without* changing the basic distribution of income rides roughshod over poor people's preferences for the only lives they have to live. If wider injustice is the problem, it should be attacked by redistributing economic resources generally, not by restricting the choices of the poor when those choices are plausibly rational within their real life context.

Paul T. Menzel, Some Ethical Costs of Rationing, 20 L. Med. & Health Care 57, 62-63 (1992).

> [T]he United States [has] never really come close to forging the chain of public policies necessary to empower consumers to purchase health care according to their respective needs and circumstances. . . . [W]here other nations have more or less arranged their health carrrre systems so that those who want more or better care than is suitable for the median citizen must pay more for it, the United States has structured things so that lower- and middle-income premium payers bear heavy burdens so that the elite classes can continue to enjoy the style of health care to which they are accustomed.

Clark Havighurst, How the Health Care Revolution Fell Short, 65(4) Law & Contemp. Prob. 55, 77-78, 89 (Autumn 2002).

> Treating access to scarce medical resources as a matter of entitlement rather than as a matter of contingent market transactions may communicate an implied proposition about the value of life and the worth and nonfungibility of individual persons. . . . Other things being equal, . . . treating disease (or person) X and not disease (or person) Y seems unprincipled and incomprensible. The taint of irrationality casts the value of life in doubt.

Michael Shapiro, On Not Watering all the Flowers: Regulatory Theory and the Funding of Heart Transplantation, 28 Jurimetrics 21 (1987).

It is also possible to construct an argument in favor of a uniform right to a single level of care based on essentially pragmatic concerns. One version goes like this: Social programs work only when they have the weight of the politically powerful behind them. While a right to treatment theoretically might require only a right of the poor to funding for basic medical care, history tells us that rights given only to the powerless fair poorly, that the powerless do much better when their fate is tied to the fate of the more powerful in society. The elderly poor, for example, have fared much better under Medicare, which covers all of the elderly, than have the nonelderly poor under Medicaid, which covers only the poor. Similarly, Social Security, a benefit system for all, has survived budgetary concerns much better than the welfare system. For another attempt at a different pragmatic argument, see Einer Elhauge, Allocating Health Care Morally, 82 Cal. L. Rev. 1449 (1995). For additional discussions of the moral foundation and meaning of the right to health care, see Norman Daniels, Just Health Care 27-29 (1985); Timothy Jost, Disentitlement: Health Care Entitlements and the Threats That They Face (1993); President's Commission for the Study of Ethical Problems in Medicine and Biomedical and Behavioral Research, Securing Access to Health Care (1983); Andre Hampton, Markets, Myths, and a Man on the Moon: Aiding and Abetting America's Flight from Health Insurance, 52 Rutgers L. Rev. 987 (2000); Kevin P. Quinn, Viewing Health Care as a Common Good: Looking Beyond Political Liberalism, 73 S. Cal. L. Rev. 277 (2000); Note, Universal Access to Health Care, 108 Harv. L. Rev. 1323 (1995); Symposium, 60 Brook. L. Rev. 1 (1994); and the excerpt by Ronald Dworkin at page 238.

■ THE UNITED STATES: BREAKTHROUGHS AND WASTE
Uwe E. Reinhardt*
17 J. Health Pol. Pol'y & L. 637 (1992)

[T]here does not exist in the United States a genuine national health policy.... The [resulting] complexity... can be illustrated by trying to ascertain the political locus of fiscal responsibility for the treatment of a particular diseased organ of a particular American individual: If the organ belongs to a person 65 years or older, the responsibility lies with the federal government for at least a part of the expenses, as the patient will then be covered by the federal Medicare program for the aged.... If the organ belongs to a person younger than 65, ... it may be the state's fiscal responsibility if that person is sufficiently poor to qualify for the particular state's Medicaid program (a threshold that varies substantially across the United States). If the treatment of the organ is not the responsibility of the state, it may be the fiscal responsibility of a county, failing which, the responsibility lies with the individual him- or herself. If the organ is an uninsured child's and the child's parents are either poor or indifferent to the child's plight, its treatment will sometimes be regarded as nobody's responsibility....

■ UNITED STATES v. MILLIGAN
17 F.3d 177 (6th Cir. 1994)

KEITH, Circuit Judge.
[This case is an appeal from convictions for criminal fraud in connection with obtaining medical services under false pretenses.]... In July 1990, Benny Milligan ("Milligan") performed janitorial work at the Martin-Marietta plant in New Orleans, Louisiana, which manufactured external fuel tanks for the National Aeronautic and Space Administration's ("NASA") space shuttle. He received health insurance subsidized by NASA, with Connecticut General Insurance Company as

*Professor of Economics, Princeton University.

the provider. In return for a minimal deductible and premium, the health insurance plan provided complete coverage to Milligan and his family. James McElveen ("McElveen"), a commercial painter, had no health insurance.

On Sunday, July 8, 1990, Milligan, his wife Tamara, McElveen [and friends] ...travelled to a waterfall on the Natchez Trace. [They were drinking heavily.] As the group approached the waterfall, McElveen accidentally ran off an embankment obscured by overgrown bushes and trees and fell 30 feet. Because he was unconscious and bleeding profusely, McElveen's friends carried him up the hill, and drove him to the hospital. McElveen, whose pallor was grey and lips blue, cried and moaned, but did not speak.

Upon arrival at Lewis Community Hospital ("LCH"), Milligan ran into the hospital and stated he needed assistance for an accident victim. He identified the victim as [himself,] "Benny Milligan."...McElveen's friends [engaged in this subterfuge because they] questioned whether he would receive medical care if he was uninsured. [One of the friends] stated she had seen news reports of hospitals evicting uninsured patients....

Believing McElveen required spinal surgery outside his expertise, Dr. Moore referred McElveen to Vanderbilt University Medical Center ("VUMC")....Dr. Devito discussed treatment options, his recommendations, and the risks of surgery with McElveen. After the discussion, McElveen signed treatment and operative consent forms [in his friend's name,] "Benny Milligan."...McElveen's surgical procedure involved two surgeons, several assistants, and lasted about six hours. [It cost about $40,000, most of which Milligan's insurance paid.]...

The jury rejected the defendants' necessity defense and convicted them of mail and wire fraud. We agree....The defense of necessity is not applicable when one has a choice of several courses of action....Here, the defendants had the choice to reveal McElveen's uninsured status and request treatment, and they failed to pursue this alternative. The choice was not foreclosed, because each of the treating facilities had policies requiring treatment of uninsured patients.

The defendants nonetheless argue the health care system reserves the best medical services for the insured and relegates uninsured patients to marginal care. Thus, according to the defendants, had they not concealed his uninsured status, McElveen would not have received the necessary treatment. Here, however, defendants have not satisfied a second component of the necessity defense...—that [they] cease the criminal offense as soon as a safe opportunity arises...by revealing their deception once McElveen's condition stabilized. [Instead], after others discovered the deception, the defendants failed to come forward and explain their dilemma and chose instead to deny their fraud....These lies converted an unplanned reaction to a desperate situation into a fraudulent scheme and conspiracy to avoid payment of medical bills....

Appellants next argue...the health care providers suffered no loss because they claim they would have rendered the same care to McElveen regardless of insurance status or inability to pay. According to defendants, this loss would have occurred regardless of the fraud....Although the hospitals admit they would have serviced McElveen absent insurance, we are not prepared to hold McElveen was entitled to free health care. McElveen made no arrangements to pay for his care and the fraud deprived the hospitals the opportunity to arrange an alternative payment schedule for the services.

Thirty-seven million Americans, or 16.6 percent of the nonelderly population, are without health insurance. Eighty-three percent of the uninsured are either employed (often as low-wage workers, like McElveen) or children. More than two in five are minorities. To many Americans, rising health care costs make the purchase of insurance prohibitively expensive. This court does not suggest that health based on wealth is a wise policy. We sympathize with those forced into bankruptcy merely because they become ill.

This court, however, cannot condone defrauding hospitals with policies sympathetic toward the uninsured. . . . In 1991, hospitals provided $13.4 billion worth of medical care to Americans without compensation. Many hospitals have shouldered the injustices of a sick health care system by providing health care without compensation. These institutions should not be punished by allowing persons who consciously defraud health care providers to receive more lenient sentencing, thereby encouraging uninsured individuals to cheat the hand which heals them. Such a holding would discourage warmhearted contributions by unnecessarily exposing them to unfettered abuse. . . .

2. *Private Health Insurance*

■ U.S. HEALTH CARE COVERAGE AND COSTS: HISTORICAL DEVELOPMENT AND CHOICES FOR THE [FUTURE]
Randall R. Bovbjerg, Charles C. Griffin & Caitlin Carroll
21 J.L. Med. & Ethics 141 (1993)

[Read the excerpt at page 35. Also, look at the pie chart following the article, at page 42, and the transcript of the interview with Prof. Robinson at page 56.]

■ PAYING FOR HEALTH CARE*
Thomas Bodenheimer & Kevin Grumbach**
272 JAMA 634 (1994)

At the center of the debate over health system reform in the United States lies the decision of how to pay for health care. Health care financing in the United States evolved to its current state as a series of social interventions. Each intervention solved a problem but in turn created its own problems requiring further intervention. In this article, we discuss the historical process of health care financing as solution-creating-new-problem-requiring-new-solution. [As summarized in the table], the four basic modes of paying for health care are out-of-pocket payment, individual private insurance, employment-based group private insurance, and government financing. These four modes can be viewed both as an historical progression and as a categorization of current health care financing....

Sources of Health Care Financing in [2003] as a Pecentage of Payments and of Population[2]

Source of Payment	Percentage of Total Payments
Out-of-pocket	17
Individual private insurance	5
Employment-based private insurance	30
Government financing	43
Total	95[3]

Source of Coverage	Percentage of Population
Uninsured	14
Individual private insurance	8
Employment-based private insurance	54
Government	24
Total	100

OUT-OF-POCKET PAYMENTS

Fred Farmer broke his leg in 1892. His son ran 4 miles to get the doctor who came to the farm to splint the leg. Fred gave the doctor a couple of chickens to pay for the visit. Fred Farmer's great-grandson, who is uninsured, broke his leg in [2002]. He was driven to the emergency department where the physician ordered an X-ray and called in an orthopedist who placed a cast on the leg. Mr. Farmer was charged [$700].

In the 19th century, people like Fred Farmer paid physicians and other health care practitioners in cash or through barter.... Americans purchase most consumer items, from VCRs to haircuts, through direct out-of-pocket payments. Why has direct out-of-pocket payment been relegated to a lesser role in health care? Economists such as [Kenneth] Arrow[4] have discussed some of the problems with treating health care as a typical consumer item.

---

[2] For out-of-pocket payments, the percentage of expenditures is greater than the percentage of the uninsured population, because out-of-pocket dollars are paid not only by the uninsured but also by the insured and Medicare populations in the form of deductibles, copayments, and uncovered services. Because private insurance tends to cover healthier people, the percentage of expenditures is far less than the percentage of population covered. Public expenditures are far higher per population, because the elderly and disabled are concentrated in the public Medicare and Medicaid programs.

[3] Total expenditures total only 95 percent; philanthropy and other private flunds account for the other 5 percent.

[4] Arrow KJ. Uncertainty and the welfare economics of medical care. Am. Econ. Rev. 1963;53:941-973.

First, whereas a VCR is a luxury, the great majority of Americans regard health care as a basic human need.... If health care is a basic human need, then people who are unable to afford health care must have a payment mechanism available that is not reliant on out-of-pocket payments.

Second, although the purchase and price of VCRs are relatively predictable (i.e., people can choose whether or not to buy them, and the price is known), the need for and cost of health care services is unpredictable. Most people do not know if or when they may become severely ill or injured or what the cost of care will be.... The unpredictability of many health care needs makes it difficult to plan for these expenses. The medical costs associated with serious illness or injury usually exceed a middle-class family's savings.

Third, unlike purchasers of VCRs, consumers of health care may have little idea what they are buying at the point of needing care.

> Jenny develops acute abdominal pain and goes to the hospital to purchase a remedy for her pain. The physician tells her that she has acute cholecystitis or a perforated ulcer and recommends hospitalization, abdominal sonogram, and upper endoscopy. Will Jenny, lying on a gurney in the emergency department and clutching her abdomen with one hand, use her other hand to leaf through her Textbook of Internal Medicine to determine whether she really needs these services, and should she have brought along a copy of Consumer Reports to learn where to purchase them at the cheapest price? ...

For these reasons, among others, out-of-pocket payments are flawed as a dominant method of paying for health care services. Because direct purchase of health care services became increasingly difficult for consumers and was not meeting the needs of hospitals and physicians for payment, health insurance came into being....

INDIVIDUAL PRIVATE INSURANCE

[Private health insurance can be purchased individually or through groups. Most private health insurance is obtained on a group basis as a fringe benefit of employment. Because of the transaction costs of marketing and administering health insurance to individuals, as well as the tax advantages described below of employment-based group insurance, individual health insurance covers less than 10 percent of the U.S. population.]

EMPLOYMENT-BASED PRIVATE INSURANCE

Betty Lerner and her schoolteacher colleagues paid $6 per year to Prepaid Hospital in 1929. Ms. Lerner suffered a heart attack and was hospitalized at no cost. The following year Prepaid Hospital built a new wing and raised the teachers' prepayment to $12.

Rose Riveter retired in 1961. Her health insurance premium for hospital and physician care, formerly paid by her employer, had been $25 per month. When she called the insurance company to obtain individual coverage, she was told that premiums at age 65 years cost $70 per month. She could not afford the insurance and wondered what would happen if she became ill.

The development of private health insurance in the United States was impelled by the increasing efficacy and cost of hospital care. Hospitals became places not only in which to die, but also in which to get better. Many patients, however, were unable to pay for hospital care, which meant that hospitals were unable to attract customers.

In 1929, Baylor University Hospital agreed to provide up to 21 days of hospital care to 1,500 Dallas, Tex, schoolteachers such as Betty Lerner, if they paid the hospital $6 per person per year. As the depression deepened and private hospital occupancy in 1931 decreased to 62 percent, similar hospital-centered private insurance plans spread. These plans (anticipating more modern health maintenance organizations) restricted care to a particular hospital. The American Hospital Association built on this prepayment movement and established statewide Blue Cross hospital insurance plans allowing free choice of hospital....

[I]n 1939 the California Medical Association established the first Blue Shield plan to cover physician services. These plans, controlled by state medical societies, followed Blue Cross in spreading across the nation.[5]

In contrast to the consumer-driven development of health insurance in European nations, U.S. health care coverage was initiated by health care providers seeking a steady source of income. Hospital and physician control over the "Blues," a major sector of the health insurance industry, guaranteed that reimbursement would be generous and that cost control would remain on the back burner.

The rapid growth of private insurance was spurred by an accident of history. During World War II, wage and price controls prevented companies from granting wage increases but allowed the growth of fringe benefits. With a labor shortage, companies competing for workers began to offer health insurance to employees such as Rose Riveter as a fringe benefit. After the war, unions picked up on this trend and negotiated for health benefits. The results were dramatic. Enrollment in group hospital insurance plans increased from 12 million in 1940 to 101 million in 1955.

Under employer-sponsored health insurance, employers usually pay all or part of the premium that purchases health insurance for their employees. However, the flow of money is not so simple. The federal government views employer-premium payments as a tax-deductible business expense. Moreover, the government does not treat the health insurance fringe benefit as taxable income to the employee, even though the payment of health insurance premiums for employees could be interpreted as a form of employee income. Because each premium dollar of employer-sponsored health insurance results in a reduction in taxes collected, the federal government is in essence subsidizing employer-sponsored health insurance. This subsidy is enormous, estimated at $75 billion in 1991. [It is also highly regressive, since it provides the least benefit to people in the lowest tax brackets.]

[5] Starr P. The Social Transformation of American Medicine. New York, N.Y.: Basic Books (1982); Law SA. Blue Cross: What Went Wrong? New Haven, Conn.: Yale University Press (1974).

The growth of employer-sponsored health insurance attracted commercial insurance companies to the health care field to compete with the Blues for customers. The commercial insurers changed the entire dynamic of health insurance. The new dynamic—which applies to both individual and employment-based health insurance—was called "experience rating."

> Healthy Insurance Company insures three groups of people: (1) a young, healthy group of bank managers; (2) an older, healthy group of truck drivers; and (3) an older group of coal miners with a high rate of chronic illness. Under experience rating, the Healthy Insurance Company sets its premiums according to the experience of each group in using health care services. Since the bank managers rarely use health care, each pays a premium of $100 per month. Because the truck drivers are older, their risk of illness is higher than that of the bankers and their premium is $300. The miners, who have high rates of black lung disease, are charged a premium of $500. The average premium income for the Healthy Insurance Company is $300 per member per month.
> Blue Cross insures the same three groups and needs the same $300 per member per month to cover health care plus administrative costs for, these groups. Blue Cross sets its premiums by the principle of "community rating." For a given health insurance policy, all subscribers in a community pay the same premium. The bank managers, truck drivers, and mine workers all pay $300 per month.

Health insurance provides a mechanism to distribute health care more in accordance with human need rather than exclusively on the basis of ability to pay. To achieve this goal, health insurance contains a subsidy—a redistribution of funds from the healthy to the sick—that helps pay the health care costs of those unable to purchase services on their own. . . .

Experience rating is far less redistributive than community rating. Within each group, those who become ill are subsidized by those who remain well. But looking at groups as a whole, healthier groups (bank managers) do not subsidize high-risk groups (mine workers). Thus, the principle of health insurance, to distribute health care more in accordance with human need rather than exclusively on the basis of ability to pay, is diluted by experience rating.[11]

In their early years, Blue Cross plans set insurance premiums by the principle of community rating. Commercial insurers, on the other hand, used experience rating as a weapon to compete with the Blues. Under experience rating, commercials such as the Healthy Insurance Company could offer less expensive premiums to low-risk groups such as bank managers, who would naturally choose a Healthy Insurance Company commercial plan at $100 over the Blue Cross plan at $300. Experience rating helped commercial insurers overtake the Blues in the private-insurance market. . . .

Many commercial insurers would not market policies to such high-risk groups as mine workers, who would then be left to Blue Cross. To survive the competition from the commercials, Blue Cross had no choice but to seek younger and healthier groups by abandoning community rating and reducing the premiums for those groups. In this way, most Blue Cross and Blue Shield plans

---

[11] Light DW. The practice and ethics of risk-rated health insurance. JAMA 1992; 267:2503-2508.

switched to experience rating. Without community rating, older and sicker groups became less and less able to afford health insurance. . . .

The most positive aspect of health insurance—that it assists people with serious illness to pay for their care—has also become one of its main drawbacks: the difficulty of controlling costs in an insurance environment. Under direct purchase, the "invisible hand" of each individual's ability to pay holds down the price and quantity of health care. Yet a well-insured patient, for whom the cost of care causes no immediate fiscal pain, will use more services than someone who must pay for care out-of-pocket. In addition, health care providers can increase fees far more easily if a third party is available to foot the bill; recall the case of Betty Lerner in which Prepaid Hospital doubled its premium in one year.

Health insurance, then, was a social intervention attempting to solve the problem of unaffordable health care under an out-of-pocket payment system; but its capacity to make health care more affordable created a new problem. If people no longer had to pay out-of-pocket for health care, they would use more health care, and if health care providers could charge insurers rather than patients, they could more easily raise prices—especially if the major insurers (the Blues) were controlled by hospitals and physicians. The solution of insurance fueled the problem of rising costs. As private insurance became largely experience rated and employment based, Americans who were low income, chronically ill, or elderly found it increasingly difficult to afford private insurance.

GOVERNMENT FINANCING

In 1984, Rose Riveter developed colon cancer. Because of the enactment of Medicare in 1965, she was no longer uninsured. However, her Medicare premium, hospital deductible, physician copayments, short nursing-home stay, and uncovered prescriptions cost her $2,700 the year she became ill with cancer.

Employer-sponsored private health insurance grew rapidly in the 1950s, helping working Americans and their families afford health care. However, two groups in the population received little or no benefit: the poor and the elderly. The poor were usually unemployed or employed in jobs without the fringe benefit of health insurance; they could not afford insurance premiums. The elderly, who needed health care the most and whose premiums had been partially subsidized by community rating, were hit hard by the tilt toward experience rating. In the late 1950s, less than 15 percent of the elderly had any health insurance. Only one thing could provide affordable care for the poor and the elderly: tax-financed government health insurance.

The government entered the health care financing arena long before the 1960s through such public programs as municipal hospitals and dispensaries to care for the poor and state-operated mental hospitals. Only with the 1965 enactment of Medicare (for the elderly) and Medicaid (for the poor) did public insurance paying for privately operated health care services become a major feature of American health care.

Medicare Part A is a hospital insurance plan for the elderly financed largely through Social Security taxes from employers and employees. Medicare Part B insures the elderly for physicians' services and is paid for by federal taxes and monthly premiums from the beneficiaries. Medicaid is a program run by the states and funded from federal and state taxes that pays for the care of a portion of the population below the poverty line. Because Medicare has large deductibles, copayments, and gaps in coverage, many Medicare beneficiaries also carry supplemental ("Medigap") private insurance or Medicaid. . . .

The advent of government financing improved financial access to care for some people but in turn aggravated the problem of rising costs. Over time, as costs rose, access declined: Medicaid cutbacks pushed low-income people out of the program, and uncovered services under Medicare left the elderly increasingly unable to pay for prescriptions and long-term care. At the same time, the rising costs of private insurance were placing coverage out of the fiscal reach of more and more employers. . . .

The United States is now deliberating on a new solution to these financing problems, a solution that will undoubtedly beget its own problems. Plans for reforming health insurance in the United States may be characterized by how they propose to rearrange the four basic modes of financing. The plan drafted by the Heritage Foundation, Washington, D.C., for example, emphasizes individually purchased private insurance and increased reliance on out-of-pocket payments. Other proposals call for expansion of employment-based financing of private insurance. Single-payer plans would make government financing the dominant mode of payment. . . .

Notes: Uninsured Patients; Insurance Fraud; Patient Cost-Sharing

1. *Your Insurance.* What kind of health insurance do you and your family have? Obtain a copy or make inquiries to find out how much you would be liable for out-of-pocket if each of the following happened to you: (1) A simple broken arm during an intramural league soccer game. Cost: $200 doctor's fees, $50 medication, $200 facility charge. (2) Acute appendicitis, requiring an appendectomy. Cost: $1,000 doctor's fees, $200 medication, and $2,000 hospital charge. (3) A major trauma like that in the *Milligan* case.

If an injury occurs as the result of a car accident or an occupational hazard, the medical costs may be covered by automobile insurance or by a worker's compensation scheme rather than by conventional health insurance.

2. *Uninsured Patients.* The extent to which James McElveen could have insisted on free care based on the hospitals' tax exemption, on their receipt of federal (Hill-Burton) construction grants, or on a federal statute that prevents "patient dumping" is explored in Chapters 2.A and 4.B.3. Some states and counties reimburse private hospitals for their costs of treating indigent patients in emergencies, but the standards for demonstrating indigency are usually stringent. But see Sioux Valley Hospital Association v. Lake Co., 533 N.W.2d 161 (S.D. 1995) (state statute requires county to reimburse hospital for emergency care whenever patient can't afford to pay the bill). A few states used to maintain compensation pools funded by an earmarked tax on hospital services, but now only Maryland does so. See generally Symposium, 16 Health Affairs No. 4 (Aug. 1997). Where this

public compensation is not available, private hospitals are forced to fund uncompensated care by "cost-shifting," that is, by charging paying patients more. The difficulty they face in doing so is that large insurers, both public and private, increasingly are insisting that this padding be removed from the hospital bills they pay. This forces hospitals to inflate charges only for their paying customers with the least market clout—those covered by small insurers or who pay out-of-pocket. As one typical example, a teaching hospital might charge an uninsured patient twice as much for childbirth as it receives from an HMO that has negotiated a discount, and three times as much as it receives from Medicaid.

3. *Public Hospitals.* In addition to seeking charity care from the private hospitals where he was treated, McElveen might have gone to a public hospital. Most larger municipalities (cities or counties) maintain at least one publicly owned hospital that will treat anyone, regardless of their ability to pay. What are the inadequacies of such a system? First, it does not exist in all locations. Second, it is focused on hospital care for acute or emergency conditions and so overlooks chronic illnesses, outpatient services, and preventive care. See A. Bindmin & K. Grumbach, America's Safety Net: The Wrong Place at the Wrong Time?, 268 JAMA 2426 (1992) (uninsured patients have significantly higher rates of "avoidable" hospitalization, for conditions such as asthma, congestive heart failure, and premature or high-risk delivery). Many cities also have publicly funded clinics that provide outpatient and preventive services, especially for indigent children and expectant mothers, but this network has even larger holes than the public hospital system. Finally, where they do exist, public hospitals are generally underfunded and so they offer care that is often perceived as inferior. Several prominent suits attempting to force municipalities to better fund their public hospitals have achieved only moral victories due to jurisdictional obstacles. See Greater Washington D.C. Area Council of Senior Citizens v. District of Columbia Government, 406 F. Supp. 768 (D.D.C. 1975) (finding that inadequate conditions and substandard care at public hospital violated city's duty, but holding that the court had no power to mandate increased government expenditures); Evelyn V. v. Kings County Hospital Center, 819 F. Supp. 183 (E.D.N.Y. 1993) (public hospital's level of service may violate state and federal statutes, but potential patients do not have a cause of action in federal court to order compliance); Tailfeather v. Board of Supervisors, 48 Cal. App. 4th 1223 (Cal. 1996) (county not obligated to adopt formal standards specifying maximum waiting times for indigents' receipt of medical care). See generally John V. Jacobi, Mission and Markets in Health Care: Protecting Essential Community Providers for the Poor, 75 Wash. U. L.Q. 1431 (1997); Michael Jacobs, When Antitrust Fails: Public Health, Public Hospitals, and Public Values, 71 Wash. L. Rev. 899 (1996); J. Kassirer, Our Ailing Public Hospitals, 333 New Eng. J. Med. 1348 (1995); Sidney D. Watson, Health Care in the Inner City: Asking the Right Question, 71 N.C. L. Rev. 1647 (1993).

Public hospitals and clinics are also operated by the federal government for Native Americans (the Indian Health Service), military personnel, and veterans (VA hospitals). See Comment, Health Care for Indigent American Indians, 20 Ariz. St. L.J. 1105 (1989); M. Hall ed., Health Care Corporate Law: Financing and Liability, Chapter 3 (1993).

4. *The Family's Obligation to Pay.* Although various sources for indigent care exist, including hospitals' own charity care, indigence does not legally excuse

a hospital patient from paying. Hospitals once readily wrote off delinquent accounts as bad debts, but they now pursue them more aggressively. Moreover, hospitals are entitled under the common law "necessaries" doctrine to seek payment from a patient's spouse or parent (for minor patients). Recent cases have reexamined the modern application of the necessaries doctrine in order to consider situations of separation and in view of the constitutional obligation to make the doctrine reciprocal between male and female spouses. See Forsyth Memorial Hospital v. Chisholm, 467 S.E.2d 88 (N.C. 1996) (separation does not excuse husband's obligation to pay for wife unless hospital had actual notice at the time); Connor v. Southwest Florida Regional Medical Center, 668 So. 2d 175 (Fla. 1995) (refusing to extend necessaries doctrine to both wife and husband and instead choosing to overturn doctrine entirely).

5. *Health Insurance Fraud.* Fraudulent or abusive billing practices under public and private health insurance is estimated to cost tens of billions of dollars each year. This is a matter of sufficient national concern that recent federal legislation makes insurance fraud a federal crime and creates a coordinated enforcement effort that has led to a vast increase in the number of prosecutions and settlements (more than $1 billion per year by one estimate). The primary target is providers rather than patients. For instance, false billing under Medicaid has been rampant for years. Consider the following:

> Nursing facilities represent convenient resident "pools" and make it lucrative for unscrupulous persons to carry out fraudulent schemes. The [Office of Inspector General (OIG)] has become aware of a number of fraudulent schemes . . . by which health care providers, including medical professionals, inappropriately bill Medicare and Medicaid for the provision of unnecessary services and services which were not provided at all. . . . Some examples follow: One physician improperly billed $350,000 over a two-year period for comprehensive physical examinations of residents without ever seeing a single resident. A psychotherapist working in nursing facilities manipulated Medicare billing codes to charge for three hours of therapy for each resident when, in fact, he spent only a few minutes with each resident. . . . The OIG has learned about podiatrists whose entire practices consist of visits to nursing facilities. Noncovered routine care is provided, e.g., toenail clipping, but Medicare is billed for . . . toenail removals, a service that is covered but not frequently or routinely needed. . . . Investigators discovered one resident for whom bills were submitted claiming a total of 11 toenail removals.

DHHS Office of Inspector General, Special Fraud Alert: Fraud and Abuse in the Provision of Services in Nursing Facilities (1996). For an extensive description and analysis of Medicaid fraud and its prosecution, see Paul Jesilow, Henry Pontell & Gilbert Geis, Prescription for Profit: How Doctors Defraud Medicaid (1993). Remarkably, these researchers found that most doctors accused or convicted of Medicaid fraud believed they were doing nothing wrong because they were merely manipulating the complex bureaucratic rules of an underfunded public system in order to do what was right for their patients and earn a living wage. Indeed, similar types of manipulation are commonplace under private insurance, even by respected doctors, who exaggerate or fudge diagnoses in order to obtain coverage for treatment they think is proper but that is not actually insured. Victor G. Freeman et al., Lying for Patients: Physician Deception of Third-Party Payers,

159 Arch. Intern. Med. 2263 (1999); Matthew K. Wynia et al., Physician Manipulation of Reimbursement Rules for Patients: Between a Rock and a Hard Place, 283 JAMA 1858 (2000). For instance, a doctor might classify an annual check-up as an office visit for a cold, or he might classify a 15-minute visit as an "extended" office visit. Do these actions deserve felony treatment? For additional discussion of civil and criminal fraud in public and private insurance, see Pamela Bucy, Health Care Reform and Fraud by Health Care Providers, 38 Vill. L. Rev. 1003 (1993); Pamela Bucy, Civil Prosecution of Health Care Fraud, 30 Wake Forest L. Rev. 693 (1995); Michael K. Sparrow, License to Steal: Why Fraud Plagues America's Health Care System (1999); Symposium, 51 U. Ala. L. Rev. 1 (1999); Symposium, 3 Quinnipiac Health L.J. 1 (2000); Symposium, 43 St. Louis L. Rev. 1 (1999); Chapter 4.E.

The recent upsurge in federal prosecution of fraud under Medicare has led to an outcry of protest by physicians and hospitals over abuse of prosecutorial powers. Using the federal False Claims Act, prosecutors maintain that incorrect billings under Medicare, or even poor quality of care, constitute criminal fraud. Providers complain that prosecutors are seizing on technical noncompliance with immensely complex Medicare rules and paperwork requirements and relying on vague and ambiguous standards of illegality. Rather than challenge these prosecutions in court, however, they usually agree to settle, sometimes for very large amounts in the tens or hundreds of millions of dollars, to avoid risking the legal and public consequences of being found guilty of criminal fraud. For detailed commentary and debate, see David Hyman, Health Care Fraud and Abuse: Market Change, Social Norms, and "The Trust Reposed in the Workmen," 30 J. Legal tud. 531 (2002) (with commentary by Roger Feldman and Arti Rai); Timothy Jost & S.L. Davies, The Empire Strikes Back: A Critique of the Backlash against Fraud and Abuse Enforcement, 51 Ala. L. Rev. 239 (1999); Joan H. Krause, Health Care Providers and the Public Fisc: Paradigms of Government Harm under the Civil False Claims Act, 36 Ga. L. Rev. 121 (2001); Joan H. Krause, Medical Error as False Claim, 27 Am. J.L. & Med. 181 (2001); Joan H. Krause, "Promises to Keep": Health Care Providers and the Civil False Claims Act, 23 Cardozo L. Rev. 1363 (2002); Dayna Matthew, An Economic Model to Analyze the Impact of False Claims Act Cases on Access to Healthcare for the Elderly, Disabled, Rural and Inner-City Poor, 27 Am. J.L. & Med. 439 (2001); Dayna Matthew, Tainted Prosecution of Tainted Claims: The Law, Economics, and Ethics of Fighting Medical Fraud under the Civil False Claims Act, 76 Ind. L.J. 525-589 (2001); Gordon E. Rountree, Health Care Providers and Fraud Investigations: What Can You Do When the Government Changes the Rules in the Middle of the Game?, 8 Ann. Health L. 97 (1999); William M. Sage, Fraud and Abuse Law, 282 JAMA 1179 (1999).

6. *Social vs. Private Insurance.* Economists would take issue with Bodenheimer & Grumbach's assertion that medical expenses fit the classic model for insurable costs. See e.g., Alain Enthoven, Health Plan (1980), excerpted at page 70. These economists observe that conventional casualty insurance such as life, fire, and liability is designed for unpredictable, high-cost events but that most people's medical expenses are highly predictable and affordable out-of-pocket. Therefore, for most of us, private health insurance functions more like a financing or pre-payment mechanism than as true insurance. Employer-provided health insurance has proven popular nonetheless, both because of the tax break and also because of

the appearance that someone else is paying. Moreover, group insurance spreads medical costs across a pool of subscribers such that the relatively healthy subsidize the relatively sick, so it serves a redistributive as well as a payment function. This is most obvious in the case of "social insurance" programs like Medicare and Medicaid, which are financing mechanisms in which society as a whole constitutes the group. Whether to conceive of medical benefits coverage as classic private insurance that is marketed like any other commodity, or instead as a financing mechanism for a fundamental social service, lies at the heart of many of the controversies explored in these notes, such as how comprehensive health insurance should be, whether insurers should be allowed to pick and choose among subscribers, and whether health insurance should be community rated.

Notes: Access to Private Health Insurance

1. *Preexisting Conditions.* Experience rating is not the only method by which insurers adjust for subscribers' relative health risk. There are a variety of techniques for what is known generically as "medical underwriting." These also include considering whether to accept the subscriber or employer group at all, and excluding coverage for high-cost conditions. For instance, insurers commonly exclude from coverage any conditions that subscribers have at the time of enrollment (so-called preexisting conditions) under the reasoning that this encourages people to buy insurance while they are still healthy; after all, someone whose house is burning cannot buy fire insurance. Interpreting these preexisting condition exclusions has generated significant litigation focusing on what constitutes a new versus continuing condition and whether patients were aware of their condition when they signed up. See, e.g., Bullwinkel v. New England Mutual Life Insurance Co., 18 F.3d 429 (7th Cir. 1994) (breast lump discovered before policy was preexisting, even though it had not been diagnosed as cancer until after effective date of policy); Sapp v. Paul Revere Life Insurance Co., 28 F.3d 108 (9th Cir. 1994) (AIDS is preexisting where infection was discovered prior to insurance, even though no symptoms were experienced until after). See generally, J. Franco, Undermining the Protection of Health Insurance: The Preexisting Condition Clause, 30 New Eng. L. Rev. 833 (1996); T. Williams, "Going Bare": Insurance and the Pre-existing Condition Problem, 15 J.L. & Com. 575 (1995).

2. *Medical Underwriting.* Insurers who will accept only healthy subscribers are known as "cherry pickers" or "cream skimmers." The motivation to avoid high-risk subscribers becomes more obvious in view of the fact that most medical expenses are concentrated in a small number of people. On average, only 4 percent of people in any insurance pool generate 50 percent of its claims expenses, while 20 percent of enrollees generate 80 percent of claims. An insurer will obviously benefit by avoiding a portion of the 4 or 20 percent. Bad risks can be avoided either openly, by examining medical records and conducting medical exams, or indirectly, by selective advertising or by adjusting benefits to discourage the sick and attract the healthy. For instance, one HMO was accused of putting its enrollment office on the third floor of a building without an elevator, and another tried to attract healthy elderly subscribers by holding square dances.

3. *Small Group Market Reforms.* These problems are more severe for individual subscribers and small groups because each policy covers only one or a few people; therefore, purchasing decisions are driven much more by the individuals' health characteristics than by group averages. As a result, small employers often have a more difficult time finding insurance or they face premiums that are much higher than for large group insurance. To correct this imbalance, insurance regulation has tightened up considerably on the extent to which insurers can engage in various forms of medical underwriting for small groups. Many states require a modified form of community rating for small groups. A 1997 federal statute known as the Health Insurance Portability and Accountability Act (HIPAA) limits the length of time group insurers can exclude preexisting conditions, and it requires open enrollment (that is, accepting all applicants) and automatic renewal for groups.

> Opponents of the Clinton plan [for comprehensive reform and universal coverage] had stressed during the debates the value of incremental reforms, such as portability of benefits, increased community rating, and decreased use of pre-existing condition exclusions. After the demise of the Clinton plan, some legislators, notably Senators Nancy Kassebaum and Edward Kennedy, continued to talk about incremental reforms. In 1997, a hodge-podge of such incremental reforms and other provisions passed under the name of the Health Insurance Portability and Accountability Act. HIPAA eventually took the form of an election year "Christmas tree" bill. Among other things, HIPAA [requires new federal rules on privacy of medical information, creates a demonstration project for "medical savings accounts,"] amends the fraud and abuse laws, changes the rules on previous disposition of assets by Medicaid patients, gives tax preferences to promote long term care insurance, and encourages state insurance pools for the medically uninsurable. Its most important changes fall into four major areas.
>
> First, HIPAA seeks to provide "portability" by making full employer-provided coverage available to more employees of large employers. It does not, in fact, allow a worker covered at one employer to take that coverage to another employer, but makes it harder for the second employer to deny coverage. The Act restricts the pre-existing condition limitations that employers can apply. An employer is no longer allowed to exclude coverage for pre-existing conditions indefinitely; in most cases, such a limitation is restricted to no more than 12 months. In addition, employees and their families are usually able to carry their "credit" toward a pre-existing condition limitation from one employer to another, unless there is a lengthy break in employment. Thus, if an employee with a pre-existing condition such as diabetes has been subject to a twelve month pre-existing condition limitation for diabetes-related coverage at one employer and then moves to another employer, the second employer cannot limit her coverage for that condition. In addition, the Act specifically excludes genetic predispositions from being treated as pre-existing conditions.
>
> Second, HIPAA seeks to make small-employer coverage more available. It requires that insurers offering small group insurance (defined as 50 or fewer workers) accept every small employer or individual who applies for coverage. It also generally requires insurers to renew any such coverage. Employers who offer health insurance must cover all eligible employees; they cannot exclude any employees from participation in health plans because of health status, medical condition, claims experience, medical history, genetic information, or several other characteristics. They are forbidden from charging different premiums to

or making different contributions on behalf of their employees based on health status.

Third, the Act provides that insurers selling in the individual market must generally offer coverage to, and accept enrollment from, any individual who was previously covered by group insurance for at least 18 months. The individual coverage may not contain any pre-existing condition exclusions and must also generally be renewed at the option of the insured person....

Many of the provisions of HIPAA share the important characteristic of being less than meets the eye. The portability provisions may relieve "job lock" for people who have, or whose covered family members have, serious pre-existing conditions, but only if they choose to move to another job with health benefits. Those provisions give no help to an employee who is moving from an employer that provides coverage to one that does not. The provisions concerning small groups force insurers to offer and renew coverage to small employers, but do not restrict, in any way, the price they charge, either initially or on renewal. Individually underwritten coverage must be offered to all those previously covered by employers regardless of health status, but, again, there are no limitations on the price to be charged.... Various HIPAA provisions may prove useful for some people, but the Act's overall effect on the health care system is minimal.

Henry Greely, The Regulation of Private Health Insurance, *in* Health Care Corporate Law: Formation and Regulation (Mark Hall ed., Supp. 1999). For other analyses and descriptions of HIPAA, see Colleen Medill, HIPAA and Its Related Legislation: A New Role for ERISA in the Regulation of Private Health Care Plans?, 65 Tenn. L. Rev. 485 (1998); Jack Rovner, Federal Regulation Comes to Private Health Care Financing, 7 Ann. Health L. 183 (1998); Symposium, Making a Federal Case out of Health Care, 22 Cato J. 1 (2002). See generally John V. Jacobi, The Ends of Health Insurance, 30 U.C. Davis L. Rev. 312 (1997).

The main problem with mandating community rating or other "incremental" health insurance reforms is that, absent more fundamental reform, people cannot be forced to purchase insurance. These reforms would also raise prices for many healthy subscribers. Therefore, more people may opt out of the insurance market, thereby only accelerating its disintegration. Accordingly, these insurance reforms are, for the most part, limited to small employer groups because it is not considered feasible to extend them to individual purchasers or to large groups. For individuals, eliminating medical underwriting would create too great a risk of "adverse selection" (that is, buying insurance on the way to the hospital). For larger groups, these restrictions are either considered unnecessary or likely to cause them to drop out of the insurance market by deciding to self insure (i.e., funding their workers' health benefits directly rather than purchasing insurance).

See generally M. Hall, Reforming Private Health Insurance (1994); M. Hall, Reforming the Health Insurance Market for Small Businesses, 326 New Eng. J. Med. 565 (1992).

4. *Finding Individual Insurance.*

If you...have any type of illness [and don't have employer-sponsored insurance],...you might be shut out of the health-insurance market.... This group includes the self-employed, employees of small firms that don't offer medical insurance, people between jobs, young adults moving off their parents' policies, widowed or divorced people who have lost their spouse's group coverage, and people who retire early and lose their group health coverage before they're 65 and old enough for Medicare. . . . Needing to buy your own health insurance makes you one of the unwanted children of the insurance marketplace. Consider the case of Carolyn Weaver, who, . . . in 1992, bought her own health-insurance policy . . . with a deductible of $500. The policy cost $1,665 a year and because a test revealed that Weaver had a blood factor that might lead to rheumatoid arthritis, it excluded coverage for arthritis and for most diseases of the spine. Shortly after Weaver got the policy, [the insurer] hiked her premiums almost 64 percent, attributing the increase to the higher cost of medical care. Premiums kept rising and Weaver had to increase her deductible to $5,000, to afford the policy. By this year, because of Weaver's advancing age (she is now 63) and rising health-care costs, the annual premium had reached $18,500. The final straw: [the insurer] has canceled her coverage because it is leaving the individual-health-insurance market. Weaver has been scouring the market for new insurance, but because other health problems have developed, she has had a tough time finding a carrier willing to insure her at a price she can afford. . . .

Few insurance carriers want to insure people like Weaver. . . . Many companies avoid writing policies in the individual market, or, when they do write them, they devise strategies that limit the company's risk and the consumers' ability to obtain coverage for the care they need. . . . The good deals often vanish when people get sick or injured and begin to file claims. . . .

Most individual policies are medically underwritten. That means carriers look closely at an applicant's medical record and turn down people whose conditions pose too much risk. Most companies deny coverage to people with serious conditions such as cancer, diabetes, coronary artery disease, or multiple sclerosis. But they may also turn down applicants with ailments like hay fever and ear infections. To underwriters, covering people with medical problems is like insuring a burning house. . . . Recently, [researchers] asked 19 insurance companies and HMOs in 8 cities to consider what they told them were seven hypothetical applicants who had a variety of mild and serious health conditions. More than one-third of the applications were rejected. Only 10 percent were offered "clean" coverage, without exclusions or surcharges.

The Perils of Buying Your Own Policy, Consumer Rep., Sept. 2002.[*] See also Symposium, 21(6) Health Aff. 12 (2002).

Two avenues are open to individuals who can't find insurance on their own. In about a dozen states, Blue Cross is required to sell individual policies on an open enrollment basis. In about two dozen other states, the insurance industry maintains a "high risk pool" where individuals cannot be turned down. In both instances, premiums are capped at about 200 percent of market averages, with insurers absorbing any excess costs. Obviously, many individuals still have difficulty affording health insurance even at these subsidized rates.

5. *The Fairness of Community Rating.* Is there an ethically compelling case in favor of community rating? One principle of justice would say that people with poor health should have greater, not lesser, access to health care. See Bryan Ford,

---

the Uncertain Case for Market Pricing of Health Insurance, 74 B.U. L. Rev. 109 (1994); David Light, The Practice and Ethics of Risk-Related Health Insurance, 267 JAMA 2503 (1992); Deborah Stone, The Struggle for the Soul of Insurance, 18 J. Health Pol. Pol'y & L. 287 (1993). However, another principle of justice might say that people like James McElveen who deliberately engage in risky behavior should not be allowed to force those who do not to pay their extra costs of insurance. How much of medical costs do you speculate are caused by voluntary behaviors? Which of these behaviors should be "punished" with higher insurance premiums or tolerated as legitimate life-style choices? Consider each of the following: smoking, eating meat, obesity, having children, drinking while pregnant, failing to exercise regularly, hang gliding. See Robert Schwartz, Life Style, Health Status, and Distributive Justice, 3 Health Matrix 195 (1993).

6. *Genetic Discrimination.* The problems of risk segmentation and risk rating are expected to multiply geometrically as a consequence of rapidly expanding genetic knowledge. At some point in the not-too-distant future, it may be possible at birth to know each person's medical and personality predispositions throughout life. Even short of that, should knowledge of specific genetic traits be used by insurers in their medical underwriting decisions? Several states have banned the use of genetic test results by health and life insurers. See Richard A. Bornstein, Genetic Discrimination, Insurability and Legislation: Closing of the Legal Loopholes, 4 J.L. & Pol'y 551 (1996); Eric Holmes, Solving the Insurance/ Genetic Fair/Unfair Discrimination Dilemma in Light of the Human Genome Project, 85 Ky. L.J. 503 (1997); Karen Rothenberg, Genetic Information and Health Insurance: State Legislative Approaches, 23 J.L. Med. & Health Care 23 (1995) (summarizing statutes). Doesn't this just force insurers to use more inexact proxies for genetic information, such as family history? Consider the fate of a person who now can't get health insurance because of a family history of a late-onset disease, but whose genetic tests show he is actually *free* of the genetic defect. Perhaps these laws should prohibit the use of genetic information gained from *any* source, including medical or family history. But, is there any reason to give special protection to genetic conditions as distinct from environmentally acquired health problems such as AIDS or a car accident? See M. Hall, Insurers' Use of Genetic Information, 37 Jurimetrics 13 (1996) (summarizing the debate and its voluminous commentary); Symposium, 149 U. Pa. L. Rev. 1439 (2001) (point/counterpoint).

Does genetic predisposition to a disease constitute a "preexisting condition" potentially excluded from insurance coverage? Recent federal legislation says "no," but if this is so, does genetic predisposition also fail to qualify as an "illness or condition" necessary for health insurance to cover the treatment? One state court held that genetic predisposition to cancer does constitute an "illness or condition" and therefore a prophylactic hysterectomy is covered. Katskee v. Blue Cross/Blue Shield of Nebraska, 515 N.W.2d 655 (1994).

7. *Severing Employment and Insurance.* The primary difficulty created by an employment-based insurance system is that insurance ceases or changes when a worker loses or switches jobs. A complex array of regulatory concepts, known as portability, conversion, and continuation, attempt to deal with this problem. As noted above, the federal law called HIPAA allows people to switch to a new employer policy when they change jobs, without undergoing a new waiting period

("portability"), as long as they do not drop coverage for more than two months. HIPAA also requires insurers to "convert" group coverage to individual coverage for people who leave the group, but this comes at a greatly increased cost. In a 1985 law known as "COBRA," Congress required group insurers to give departing employees and their dependents the option to "continue" their group coverage (rather than convert to individual coverage) at essentially the same price, only to be paid by the employee rather than the employer. This continuation right extends for only 18 to 36 months, depending on the circumstances of termination. 29 U.S.C. §1161. See Geissal v. Moore Med. Corp., 524 U.S. 74 (1998) (COBRA benefits are available even if the worker has coverage available in another group through a spouse's job); Note, You're Sick? You're Fired! The Case for Eliminating COBRA's Gross Misconduct Exception, 80 Minn. L. Rev. 197 (1995).

This combination of protections still leaves a number of problems. People with employer-sponsored insurance often are stuck with the particular policy an employer selects for the group. People who buy their own insurance do not receive the same tax breaks as employer-sponsored insurance, and the current tax deduction is highly regressive since it gives the most support to people with the greatest income. Also, as people move between jobs and in and out of the workforce, they can still fall through various cracks in the regulatory system. Therefore, proposals are now circulating to de-couple health insurance from employment. This could occur in several ways, to a greater or lesser degree. One idea, known as "defined contribution," is for employers to give employees a fixed budget the employees can use to shop for insurance anywhere they want, rather than an employer's paying for a benefit plan the employer selects. A second approach is to provide a tax credit (rather than deduction) to anyone who purchases health insurance, whether or not insurance comes as a job benefit. See Grace-Marie Arnett ed., Empowering Health Care Consumers through Tax Reform (1999); Jon R. Gabel, Job-Based Health Insurance, 1977-1998: The Accidental System under Scrutiny, 18(6) Health Aff. 62 (Dec. 1999); Symposium, 38(2) Inquiry 175 (Summer 2001); Symposium, 18(6) Health Aff. (Dec. 1999).

These proposals have renewed debate over the merits of employer-based insurance. What dangers do you see in unraveling group purchasing arrangements? What advantages are there? For a defense of employer-based insurance, see Dayna Matthew, Controlling the Reverse Agency Costs of Employer-Based Health Insurance, 31 Wake Forest L. Rev. 1037 (1996); David A. Hyman & Mark A. Hall, Two Cheers for Employment-Based Health Insurance, 2 Yale J. Health Pol'y L. & Ethics 23 (2002). For a thorough analysis of the economic impact of health benefits on wages and corporate profitability, see Mark V. Pauly, Health Benefits at Work (1998).

8. *The Road to Nowhere?* Is America's unique combination of public and private insurance regulated by federal and state rules brilliant, or a nightmare? Is this a structure worth building on, or is it unsustainable in the long run? Here is one provocative viewpoint:

> Ironically, by maintaining a largely private health insurance system aimed at limiting the reach of government regulation, we reap ever more complex regulation to compensate for the inadequacies of that very system. Oddly, too, there is evidently a political consensus favoring the kind of piecemeal regulation that nobody really

likes, but no political majority favors more streamlined basic reform.... The actual experience of the tens of millions of Americans who lack consistent coverage defies neat legislative categorization. Often they move chaotically in and out of employ-ment and in and out of insurance.... The more the regulations try to address every contingency, the worse the bureaucratic morass becomes, but the more details are left out, the more people fall through the cracks. One can imagine sick people without health insurance being caught in an endless maze of paper trails and bureaucratic appeals....

Out of frustration with the gaps in insurance, we are superimposing ever more baroque regulatory overlays.... [Existing law] creates a convoluted, expen-sive regulatory apparatus. The technicalities are bewildering.... Each [new enactment] necessitates an explicit interpretation of what is exempt and how reg-ulation is to be shared; it requires ever more elaborate attention to contingencies, ever more prudent lawyering, and evermore pages in the Federal Register....

[In] a universal system,... everyone is in one group. Hence, there is no regulatory need to resolve issues of continuity and eligibility, let alone intermin-able certifications, appeals, and adjudications.... There are no questions of rate-banding, cross-subsidies, guaranteed issues, or permissible exclusions for various categories of applicants and conditions, and no lawyers, lobbyists, and consumer advocates tilting with regulators over such arcana. But the United States continues to resist a universal system, because adopting one would mean giving too large a role to government.

Robert Kuttner, The Kassebaum-Kennedy Bill: The Limits of Incrementalism, 337 New Eng. J. Med. 64 (1997). See also J. D. Kleinke, Oxymorons: The Myth of a U.S. Health Care System at xii (2001) ("almost any fix for what ails the U.S. health care system, be it a private market initiative or act of public legislation, every 'solution' an entrepreneur or politician can dream up, runs headlong into the utter complexity of the system, the uncanny ability of those working in it to defend their precious turf against the solution, and the constant disconnect between what people in health care say they are going to do and what they actually end up doing.... The long view of our industry's history shows that health care is not changing so much as running in place, faster and faster, consuming more and more dollars as it tries to 're-engineer' itself out of its own realities."); and see another excerpt from this same book at page 221.

An excellent collection of articles surveying various proposals to expand private coverage through additional incremental reforms is in Symposium, 38 Inquiry 87 (2001). For an argument that we are evolving in fits and starts toward a comprehensive system of social insurance, see John V. Jacobi, The Ends of Health Insurance, 30 U.C. Davis L. Rev. 312 (1997). For a survey of future direc-tions, see Stuart Altman et al., eds., The Future U.S. Healthcare System: Who Will Care for the Poor and Uninsured? (1998).

Notes: Patient Cost-Sharing

1. *The "Consumer-Directed" Movement.* It is widely accepted that "the main cause of the unnecessary and unjustified increase in costs is the complex of irrational economic incentives inherent in the system of... what are called 'third-party' payors." A. Enthoven, Health Plan 16 (1980). This is why many market-oriented

reformers would restrict the existing scope of health insurance in order to encourage patients to pay more out-of-pocket. John Goodman & Gerald Musgrave, Patient Power: Solving America's Health Care Crisis (1992); Regina Herzlinger, Market-Driven Health Care (1997). Greatly increasing patients' sensitivity to costs is expected to force doctors and hospitals to become more price competitive. At the same time, greater use of Internet resources can help patients become better informed consumers of health care. See Arti K. Rai, Reflective Choice in Health Care: Using Information Technology to Present Allocation Options, 25 Am. J.L. & Med. 387 (1999).

Patients can be more cost-sensitive about treatment options in a variety of ways, which are loosely referred to as "consumer-directed" health plans. One approach, which some employers are beginning to embrace, is simply to increase substantially the co-payment and deductible amounts, to produce what is known as "catastrophic" insurance. "Catastrophic" refers to insurance that kicks in only after a patient has incurred a very large expense, for instance, after paying out of pocket the first $5,000 in a year. A less popular approach is known as "bare bones" insurance, which may cover more initial expenses but quickly maxes out when catastrophic levels are reached. See Victor Fuchs, What's Ahead for Health Insurance in the United States?, 323 New Eng. J. Med. 1822 (2002); Jason S. Lee & Laura Tollen, How Low Can You Go? The Impact of Reduced Benefits and Increased Cost Sharing, 21(4) Health Aff. 1 (July 2002); James C. Robinson, Renewed Emphasis on Consumer Cost-Sharing in Health Insurance Benefit Design, 21(3) Health Aff. 16 (May 2002).

Another idea is to couple catastrophic coverage with a "savings account" that is tax-sheltered, or is subsidized by employers. Money in this account can be used only for medical expenses but is used at the patient's discretion, and unused funds can be rolled forward to future years. Originally called medical savings accounts (MSAs), these are now being called health savings accounts (HSAs) or other variants. The primary legal issue is whether contributions to these accounts will be excluded from income taxation. Legislation passed in 1997 permitted this on a limited trial basis, but a 2002 IRS ruling and the 2004 Medicare Modernization Act greatly expanded the potential use of HSAs.

These proposals have been opposed on several grounds. They are thought likely to aggravate the segmentation of risk pools since they are most attractive to younger, healthier, and wealthier subscribers. Regina Jefferson, Medical Savings Accounts: Windfalls for the Healthy, Wealthy & Wise, 48 Cath. U. L. Rev. 685 (1999). Therefore, they have the potential to pull the most desirable subscribers out of comprehensive insurance, making things increasingly difficult for those who remain. Also, patient cost sharing may not save as much money and instill as much cost consciousness as proponents advocate. This is likely for two reasons that distinguish health care from other consumer products. First, even catastrophic insurance would continue to cover the majority of medical spending, thereby insulating it from consumer-driven pressures. Although most people's health expenses would fall below a $5,000 deductible each year, most health care spending (60-70 percent) is devoted to the small percentage of people who would exceed the deductible, since their expenses can be truly catastrophic. See M. Berk & A. Monheit, The Concentration of Health Care Expenditures, Revisited, 20(2) Health Aff. 9 (Mar. 2001).

Second, even for the portion of spending that patients do control, it is questionable whether they will be willing to make independent cost/benefit trade-off decisions at the point of treatment, or how wisely they will decide. Most people follow their physicians' advice about what care they need, and physicians are motivated to recommend all care that will produce any benefit, pretty much regardless of cost. It is an open question whether patients scrutinize this advice and make informed decisions if they are subjected to much great cost-sharing, but one prominent research study suggests they won't. In the 1970s, the RAND Corporation conducted extensive controlled study of the effects of placing patients under varying degrees of financial responsibility for their care. The results reveal that cost-sharing indeed has a striking effect on utilization: A catastrophic insurance plan that required the patient to pay 95 percent of the first $1,000 successfully reduced expenditures 31 percent relative to zero out-of-pocket costs, with no discernible differences in health status for most patients. But the lowest-income participants under the cost-sharing plans scored noticeably worse on several measures of health status than did low-income participants under the free plan. Further analysis revealed that most of the cost savings came from patients' reducing their initial visits to their doctors, and that patients cut back both on necessary and unnecessary visits. Once they saw their doctors, patients who paid mostly out of pocket incurred about the same costs as those who paid nothing out of pocket. Joseph Newhouse et al., Free for All? Lessons from the RAND Health Insurance Experiment (1993). These findings suggest that people in general do not make objectively wise medical spending decisions without the advice of their doctors, but once they consult their doctors, they are inclined to follow medical advice regardless of the financial cost to them (within the $1,000 limit that was studied). It is uncertain whether this would still hold true in a different environment where cost-sharing is much more widespread and where much better information is available through the Internet. For additional and more detailed analysis of this entire debate, see Mark A. Hall, Patient Spending Decisions, *in* Making Medical Spending Decisions (1997).

2. *Why Insurance Is Desirable.* Reducing the scope of health insurance in order to increase patient cost-sharing assumes that insurance causes medical markets to behave irrationally. Bruce Vladeck, the past head of CMS, offers a particularly well-stated attack of this fundamental premise in The Market v. Regulation: The Case for Regulation, 59 Milbank Mem. Fund Q. 209 (1981):

> The current argument for greater competition in the health care sector is based on the initial assumption that health care markets are distorted because of the wide prevalence of insurance.... But the advocates of increased competition seldom go the further step: inquire just why it is that there is so much health insurance around.... Consumers have sought the kinds of health insurance they have, not because they wish to act irrationally in the aggregate economic sense, but precisely because they don't wish to be forced to make rational trade-offs when they are confronted with medical care consumption decisions. No matter how we draw our curves or shape our abstract arguments, the elemental fact is that medical care is about living and dying, something considered by many to be of a rather different character from the purchase of tomatoes. The primary characteristic of most consumers of medical care most of the time is that they are scared. They are scared of dying, or disfigurement, or permanent disability; and these are serious matters. It

is hardly fair to expect any of us to make rational decisions about matters of such import. As a society, we may be prepared to pay a substantial economic premium to insulate people from having to make such decisions.

See Chapters 1.D.3 and 3.F.2 for additional discussion of whether medicine should be governed by the same economic principles as other markets.

3. Public Insurance Programs

■ MEDICAID: PAST SUCCESSES AND FUTURE CHALLENGES
Jane Perkins
12 Health Matrix 7 (2002)*

I. INTRODUCTION

Since its enactment as [Title XIX] of the Social Security Act in 1965, Medicaid has been an entitlement program for beneficiaries and states. Individuals who meet Medicaid eligibility requirements have a legal right to have payments made to their providers for the covered services they need....States have an open-ended entitlement to receive federal matching payments for all state spending on covered services. The federal payments do not come without strings attached, however, as States must implement their Medicaid programs consistent with minimum federal requirements.

Medicaid covers one in seven people, more than any other public or private insurer in America, including Medicare.[2] The program is the health care safety net for the poor, the elderly, and people with disabilities....Despite its importance, Medicaid faces serious threats. After a period of slow growth, Medicaid spending is expected to increase in the coming years, particularly for people with disabilities and the elderly. These demands could be compounded by recession-driven increases in eligibility. To complicate matters, Medicaid does not have a wealth of political support behind it. Tied at its inception to the receipt of public benefits, the program has never shaken its stigma as a welfare program. Medicaid may become a target of legislative and judicial decision makers who are seeking to curb program spending and others who see the Medicaid entitlement as antithetical to their concepts of states' rights and a reduced federal role....

II. OVERVIEW OF THE MEDICAID PROGRAM RULES

Over its thirty-five year history, Medicaid has been expanded, restricted, and modified—all too often as part of eleventh-hour congressional compromises. Not surprisingly then, Medicaid is complex, confounding, and in the words of one

*Legal Director, National Health Law Program, Chapel Hill, N.C. Copyright © 2002 Health Matrix: The Journal of Law-Medicine; Jane Perkins.
[2] Kaiser Comm'n on Medicaid and the Uninsured, Henry J. Kaiser Family Found., Medicaid: A Primer 2 (Mar. 2001), www.kff.org/content/2001/2248/2248.pdf.

judge, "almost unintelligible to the uninitiated." Moreover, given the breadth of options available to the States for implementing Medicaid, there is great variation from state to state in terms of administration, eligibility, benefits, delivery systems, and provider payment.

Administration of the Medicaid program at the federal level is the responsibility of the Centers for Medicare and Medicaid Services (CMS), of the United States Department of Health and Human Services.[5] . . . Each State is required to have in effect a comprehensive, written state plan for medical assistance that has been approved by the federal government. The plan describes who is eligible for Medicaid, what services are covered, and how the program is administered. . . . The federal matching payments to states for Medicaid covered services can vary from 50% to 83% of the total expenditures, with poorer per capita income states receiving higher federal payments. . . . Medicaid [is] the single largest source of federal funding to the states, accounting for nearly 40% of all federal grants-in-aid to the states.

A. MEDICAID ELIGIBILITY—FITTING INTO A CATEGORY

An individual is not eligible for Medicaid simply because he or she is poor. Rather, individuals must fit into [one of four] recognized eligibility categories: . . . children and their caretakers, pregnant women, the elderly, and people with disabilities. For example, States must cover children under age six whose family incomes are below 133% of the federal poverty level, and children between ages six and nineteen whose family incomes are below the federal poverty level. In most states, individuals who are receiving Supplemental Security Income (SSI) on the basis of disability also automatically qualify for Medicaid. . . . States have the option of covering the medically needy—persons who fit into a federal public benefit program category, such as SSI, but whose income or resources are above the eligibility levels for the benefit program. Such individuals qualify for Medicaid once their income, minus incurred medical expenses, is less than the State's medically needy income level. . . .

In addition to fitting within an eligibility group, an individual must meet financial criteria by having limited income and resources.[27] The individual must have the appropriate immigration status, in most cases U.S. Citizenship.[28] Finally, the person must be a resident of the state where they are applying for Medicaid benefits. Given the strict eligibility requirements, it is not surprising that . . . Medicaid cover[s] only 37% of non-elderly Americans with incomes below the federal poverty level.[29]

B. SERVICES—STRUCTURED TO THE COVERED POPULATIONS' NEEDS

Under federal law, States must provide coverage for certain services and may choose to cover other types of services when needed by program beneficiaries.

---

[5] Until July 1, 2001, CMS was known as the Health Care Financing Administration or HCFA.

[27] For example, possession of a car with an equity value of $1,500, or less at state option, makes an applicant ineligible for Medicaid.

[28] Most immigrants . . . are barred from receiving full-scope Medicaid benefits for at least five years.

[29] [In 2002, the federal poverty level was an income of roughly $8,500 for a single person, plus $3,000 for each additional family member.—EDS.]

States can impose "nominal" co-payments on services, typically prescriptions and physician visits. However, given that Medicaid is serving low-income populations, many beneficiaries and services are exempt from cost sharing, including children and youth, pregnant women, nursing home residents, emergency services, family planning services, and hospice services.

Included in the mandatory benefit package that is available to most beneficiaries are: inpatient and outpatient hospital services, physician services, laboratory and x-ray services, family planning services, federally qualified health center services, nurse-midwife services, and pediatric nurse-practitioner services. States must also cover home health services for any individual who is eligible to receive nursing facility services.... There are twenty-three optional services that States can choose whether to cover for adults, including prescription drugs [and] dental services.... [According to regulations,] "each service must be sufficient in amount, duration, and scope to reasonably achieve its purpose." For example, while a State can limit coverage of inpatient hospital days to, for example, twenty-one days per year, it should not be able to limit these services to one day per year....

States also have substantial flexibility to decide how they will deliver services to Medicaid beneficiaries and how providers will be paid. Traditionally, States have set provider participation rules and paid providers who choose to participate a fee for each service rendered. Over the last fifteen years, however, Medicaid has shifted dramatically toward managed care delivery that emphasizes prepaid or discounted services and utilization controls, such as prior authorization requirements before providers can render services. Over half of all Medicaid beneficiaries [are] enrolled in managed care....

III. MEDICAID'S DIVERSE PROGRAMS

While it is treated as a single program, Medicaid is really four separate programs, each with populations, services, and expenditures that differ from one another. These four programs are: a long-term care program for the elderly and people with disabling and chronic health needs, a "Medigap" program for elderly and disabled individuals who cannot afford Medicare cost sharing, a children's health program, and a provider support program that helps assure the viability of the public health infrastructure serving Medicaid and low-income patients. Each of these programs is described below.

Medicaid's coverage of long-term care services is a key difference between Medicaid and other public and private insurers. Medicaid is the largest single purchaser of long-term care services for the elderly and non-elderly people with disabilities in the United States.[30] In 1998, Medicaid funded almost half of the total nursing home expenditures and nearly 40% of total long-term care

---

[30] Medicare, the federally funded and administered program for the elderly and persons with disabilities would seem a logical choice for the long-term care "program"; however, Medicare coverage is focused on acute services and long-term care services are limited.... [C]ommercial insurers generally have avoided the long-term care market and, while coverage is growing, quality policies are often affordable only to middle and upper income persons who do not qualify for Medicaid.

expenditures in the United States. Long-term care services represent 42% of total Medicaid spending....

Elderly persons and people with a wide range of disabilities qualify for long-term care services, including individuals with physical impairments, mental health conditions, cerebral palsy, cystic fibrosis, Down's syndrome, autism, and HIV/AIDS.... State Medicaid agencies must apply special eligibility rules to individuals who are entering a nursing home and who have a spouse living at home. These rules allow couples to protect some of their income and resources for the at-home spouse, thus allowing the institutionalized spouse to qualify for Medicaid sooner and preventing the at-home spouse from becoming impoverished by the institutionalized spouse's ongoing nursing home bills....

One of the Medicaid program's primary beneficiary groups is children under age twenty-one. In 1998, Medicaid covered one-fourth of the children in America. Over 50% of Medicaid beneficiaries were children and youth—about twenty-one million children. Another 21% of program beneficiaries (over eight million people) were adult caretakers with children. Even though children and their caretakers represent about three fourths of the Medicaid population, they account for only 25% of program spending.... [31]

Medicaid's fourth "program" acts as a major financial support system for a wide range of health care providers who serve low-income people and people with disabilities. Medicaid is a "vendor payment program," meaning that payments are made directly to health care providers, not patients.... Some providers are more dependent on Medicaid than others—nursing homes, community health centers, and disproportionate share hospitals (DSHs) that serve a disproportionate number of Medicaid and other low-income people. For example, Medicaid covers 33% of patients using community health centers and more than 35% of patients using public hospitals....

IV. MEDICAID'S SUCCESSES

Medicaid has achieved a remarkable number of significant successes that, unfortunately, often go unacknowledged. For over three decades, Medicaid has offered insurance coverage to millions of people who would otherwise be uninsured because they cannot afford to pay for private insurance, their employers do not offer insurance, or their chronic health conditions have deemed them uninsurable by the commercial marketplace. Currently, Medicaid covers 26.1% of the elderly, 40.1% of all children, and 20% of persons with disabilities in America....

Medicaid's positive influences go beyond lowering the ranks of the uninsured, however. The program has improved and protected public health. For example, Medicaid has helped the United States provide near-universal protection against debilitating, communicable childhood diseases. In 1993, the Medicaid Act was amended and the Vaccine for Children program enacted.... Medicaid has also played a major role in reducing infant mortality rates through a series of expansions during the 1980s to enroll infants and children for ambulatory care services and pregnant women for prenatal care services. Medicaid's coverage rules

---

[31] In 1998, Medicaid spending averaged $1,225 per child, compared to $11,235 for each elderly beneficiary and $9,558 for each disabled beneficiary.

have also been targeted to allow States to address such public health concerns as HIV/AIDS and tuberculosis. Women can now enroll in Medicaid to obtain treatment for breast and cervical cancer.

Medicaid has provided essential services for people with disabilities that are not generally available through private health insurance coverage. Private health insurance, rooted in the workplace, was not designed to cover people with chronic, disabling conditions. Thus, the benefit packages offered by private insurers are geared toward acute care services and "rehabilitation," that return the insured to their previous level of functioning. By contrast, the benefits package offered by Medicaid includes coverage of long-term care services and services which help maximize functioning, such as home health services, durable medical equipment, prosthetic devices, and personal care attendant services.

Though not exclusively designed for working individuals, Medicaid coverage has also created work incentives. For example, thirty-five states and the District of Columbia have chosen to offer medically needy programs that allow individuals to spend down their excess income and become eligible for Medicaid, thus eliminating arbitrary income cut-offs that would discourage individuals from working. Since 1999 States also have been able to continue Medicaid coverage of people with disabilities who return to work. Without Medicaid, these individuals would risk losing health insurance coverage and experience long waiting periods for private insurance through their workplace. . . .

V. MEDICAID'S CHALLENGES

Despite its unquestionable successes, Medicaid faces serious challenges. Of particular concern is whether Medicaid will remain an entitlement program. . . . In past sessions, Congress has considered making Medicaid a capped annual allocation to the states, known as a "block grant." . . . With increasing demands expected on the health care delivery system from a population that is aging and increasingly disabled, the question becomes, what can be done to assure needed care while also keeping spending in check?

The Bush administration has announced . . . a program to increase States' flexibility to operate their Medicaid programs by waiving provisions of the Federal Medicaid Act. [This] ostensibly is designed to grant States rapid approval of requests that have as their goal coverage of currently uninsured populations in the state whose incomes are below 200% of the federal poverty level—for the most part, childless adults and near-poor children. To accomplish this, however, a State cannot increase the amount of federal money currently spent on or allocated to the State for its Medicaid program. To meet this requirement for "budget neutrality," the States will be given unprecedented ability to reduce coverage of optional eligibility groups, alter the benefit package for currently-covered optional eligibility groups and for the expansion group, and to impose increased cost sharing on these groups. . . .

[This] initiative could undermine Medicaid's existence as an entitlement program. Caps on enrollment are allowed; therefore, for the populations affected by the cap, Medicaid will not be an open-ended entitlement. Moreover, States will be allowed to expand coverage to uninsured groups through Medicaid or another program, the State Children's Health Insurance Program (SCHIP).

SCHIP currently allows States to expand coverage to uninsured near-poor children by expanding the Medicaid program or by establishing a separate program, typically with more limited benefits and, according to Congress, minus the legal entitlement for beneficiaries. By implementing [a] waiver through a separate program, States can seek to avoid providing beneficiaries with a legally enforceable right to the covered benefits. . . .

There are [also] complex activities underway in the federal judiciary that are garnering scant public attention but that could have an enormous effect on the rights of poor people and people with disabilities. . . . [C]ourts are determining whether beneficiaries have an individual private right of action when eligibility and services are not provided as required by the Federal Medicaid Act. . . . While the Medicaid Act does not expressly provide for such a private right of action, the courts have long recognized that a civil rights statute, 42 U.S.C. §1983, expressly authorizes private enforcement.[32] . . .

VI. CONCLUSION

Over [the Medicaid program's] thirty-five year history, . . . health care providers who serve Medicaid patients have come to depend on the program's provider payments, [and] states are heavily reliant on the program's open-ended entitlement to federal funding. . . . Over the next five years, Medicaid will face significant pressures . . . from some policy makers and members of the judiciary who see beneficiary "entitlement" as a dirty Medicaid word (and who react particularly to the entitlement's association with lawsuits to enforce federal requirements). However, decisionmakers who take aim at the Medicaid entitlement should think twice. Indeed, the entitlement brings with it the legal right to enforce the statutory requirements that are placed on the states. However, the entitlement is what makes Medicaid an insurance program—the key factor that allows an individual to know that coverage will be there when health care is needed and a health care provider to know that payments will be made when services are delivered.

■ THE AMERICAN HEALTH CARE SYSTEM: MEDICARE*
John K. Iglehart**
327 New Eng. J. Med. 1467 (1992)

Six times in the 20th century, America has flirted unsuccessfully with national health insurance legislation—the provision of medical care to all citizens. Instead, policymakers have allowed subsidies to finance part of private health insurance by exempting employer-paid premiums from taxation. The government has also provided or funded services for groups deemed particularly vulnerable or entitled to them—Native Americans, migratory workers, other categorically defined poor

---

[32] Wilder v. Virginia Hospital Ass'n, 496 U.S. 498, 522 (199); [Westside Mothers v. Haveman, 289 F.3d 852 (6th Cir. 2002)].

*Excerpted with permission of the publisher. Copyright © 1992, Massachusetts Medical Society.
**The author is the founding editor of *Health Affairs*, the leading health policy journal.

people, veterans of military service, the permanently disabled, people with end-stage renal disease, and all elderly people. Medicare, which provides the nation's elderly with ready access to short-term medical services, represents the most ambitious dimension of this strategy of incrementalism.... From an international perspective, it is a peculiar institution; no other nation has compulsory health insurance for its elderly citizens alone....

Enacted in 1965 after a debate that spanned decades, the Medicare law symbolized the continuing struggle over defining the government's role in America's predominantly private system of health care.... The American Medical Association (AMA) bitterly opposed the measure because of its probable intrusion into clinical practice. To appease the AMA, the law's preamble expressly prohibited any federal "supervision or control over the practice of medicine or the manner in which medical services are provided." Although these words remain in the law, they have long been ignored....

Like America's social security program, Medicare's hospital-financing scheme is grounded in the principle of social insurance. That is, employees make mandatory contributions as defined in law to dedicated trust funds during their working years, with the promise of receiving benefits (income or services) after they retire. This concept was popularized in the later 1800s by German Chancellor Otto von Bismarck, who constructed German's national health insurance plan around it. The principle applies only to Medicare's hospital trust fund. Medicare's other major component, supplemental medical insurance, was modeled after traditional indemnity coverage....

As an enterprise, Medicare's scope is daunting, although the [Centers for Medicare and Medicaid Services (CMS), formerly the] Health Care Financing Administration (HCFA), which oversees the program, is remarkably small, given the expenditures it manages.... Medicare's estimated outlay of $[217] billion in [2000] overshadowed the budgets of all of America's private corporations and most of the world's nations. The program has virtually created whole new medical enterprises (kidney-dialysis centers, home health companies, and the suppliers of medical equipment for home use) that flourish as the result of a congressional decision to add a benefit. In [2000] the private insurers with whom Medicare contracts to administer the program [known as "fiscal intermediaries"] paid [more than 900] million claims to some 600,000 physicians and medical suppliers....

Currently, [40] million people are eligible to receive medical benefits financed by Medicare: [34.4] million who are over the age of 65 [and worked in a job for ten years that paid payroll taxes], [5.5] million who are permanently disabled, and some 165,000 who have end-stage renal disease. Medicare's end-stage renal disease program is unique; it is the only instance in which a diagnosis provides the basis for Medicare benefits for persons of all ages. It is also the classic example of how government operates as the virtual single payer for a private medical service.

BENEFITS

Medicare's covered benefits apply mostly to the treatment of patients with acute illnesses. Although chronic conditions are addressed, the supportive long-term care often needed by patients with such conditions is not generally covered despite a perceived need. Medicare also does not pay for . . . routine foot, hearing, vision, and dental care. As a consequence of the original compromise that stitched together several disparate bills, Medicare is divided into two parts: Part A is hospital insurance, and all eligible elderly beneficiaries are automatically enrolled. Part B is supplemental medical insurance, and enrollment is voluntary, although the vast majority of elderly beneficiaries sign on. The compulsory nature of Part A is a key feature of social insurance. This part of Medicare finances inpatient hospital services, care in a skilled-nursing facility for continued treatment or rehabilitation after hospitalization, home health care services, and hospice care for the terminally ill. Under Part A, Medicare pays for all reasonable expenses, minus a deductible amount [$812 in 2002], for the first 60 days in each benefit period. For days 61 to 90 a daily coinsurance payment [$203 in 2002] is also charged. Since the repeal of the Medicare Catastrophic Coverage Act of 1988, there has been no cap on beneficiaries' out-of-pocket liability.

Part B pays for physicians' services and outpatient hospital services, including emergency room visits, ambulatory surgery, diagnostic tests, laboratory services, outpatient physical therapy, occupational-therapy and speech-pathology services, and durable medical equipment. Generally, Part B does not pay for routine physical examinations, preventive care, or services not related to the treatment of illness or injury. Under Part B, Medicare pays 80 percent of the approved amount (according to a fee schedule, reasonable charges, or reasonable costs) for covered services in excess of an annual deductible of $100. . . .

[A new Part C, called Medicare + Choice or Medicare Advantage, was created in 1998 and expanded in 2004. It allows people to receive full Medicare coverage (combining parts A and B) by electing from several alternative financing models, including HMOs.]

Medicare pays for about half the average elderly person's medical bill, a proportion that has remained reasonably constant over the years. . . . To protect beneficiaries against larger increases in their out-of-pocket costs, the HCFA has encouraged doctors to become participating physicians and thereby accept assignment (defined as 80 percent of the fee-schedule amount, less any unmet deductible) as payment in full. The encouragement takes three forms: fee-schedule amounts are 5 percent higher for participating physicians, claims are paid more expeditiously, and Medicare carriers publish directories of participating physicians for free distribution. No additional charges, known as balance-billing charges, may be levied by participating physicians directly on beneficiaries. [Nonparticipating physicians may not charge more than 15 percent above the fee schedule.] . . . Because Medicare does not provide complete insurance coverage for its eligible population, about 75 percent of its elderly beneficiaries obtain supplementary packages [known as Medigap insurance] from private insurers or through their previous employers. . . .

Most of those who require medical care receive far more from Medicare than they contributed in payroll taxes. For example, a couple retiring, with one wage earner who had paid average Medicare taxes [for 25 years,] . . . the present value of future Part A benefits is estimated to be . . . more than ten times the amount they paid into the trust fund. For Part B, retirees receive benefits that average four times their premiums. . . .

PAYMENT

When Medicare was enacted, the program embraced the methods of payment advocated at the time by hospitals and physicians, in an effort to win their support. Thus, Medicare agreed to pay hospitals the reasonable costs they incurred in providing services to eligible beneficiaries and agreed to reimburse physicians on a fee-for-service basis, using the "customary, prevailing, and reasonable" method. . . . As medical costs continued to soar well beyond the rate of inflation in the 1980s, Congress acted twice to reduce the discretion previously enjoyed by hospitals and physicians to establish their own prices, subject to various constraining factors imposed by government. In 1983, Congress authorized the creation of Medicare's prospective payment system for hospitals. The policy required Medicare to fix prices in advance on a cost-per-case basis, using as a measure 467 diagnosis-related groups [DRGs]. Through the 1983 law, Congress changed what was paid for, who determined the price, and how that price would be calculated and thereby reduced the growth rate of the program's expenditures for inpatient hospital care. . . . [CMS has since developed] a method of pay for hospital outpatient services on a prospective basis. . . .

More recently (in 1989), Congress directed [CMS] to pay physicians according to a fee schedule based on a resource-based relative-value scale [RB-RVS]. . . . Congress authorized the creation of a uniform fee schedule for some 7,000 medical procedures . . . in the belief that diagnostic and surgical procedures [by specialists were being overpaid while] evaluation and management [services by primary care physicians were being underpaid]. The Physician Payment Review Commission estimated that by 1996 fees paid to generalist physicians would be 39 percent higher than they would have been under the previous payment method, whereas those paid to thoracic surgeons and ophthalmologists would be 35 and 25 percent lower, respectively. . . .

THE FUTURE

Medicare achieves its highest marks from the millions of elderly beneficiaries who depend on the program to pay for a substantial portion of their medical care, but surveys of public opinion also show wide-spread support for it among people under 65 [as well]. . . . [Nevertheless], given its rapid rate of growth, [Medicare] will remain at the center of government efforts to trim the massive budget deficit. [Previously,] budget-cutting exercises exacted most of their toll from providers, and they remain a prime target now. But providers are scarcely prepared to be the sole stakeholders who accept sacrifice. The only other real options are raising taxes on the general population, reducing Medicare benefits, or asking the elderly to pay more on some income-related basis. However, elected politicians of almost every stripe have shown no disposition to embrace any of these unpopular approaches, suggesting by their inaction that we can somehow have it all. That is indeed a fanciful formula for the future. . . .

Notes: Medicare and Medicaid; Long-Term Care Insurance

1. Medicare was enacted as Title XVIII of the Social Security Act; Medicaid constitutes Title XIX. The Centers for Medicare and Medicaid Services (CMS)

(formerly the HCFA), which administers both Medicare and Medicaid, is part of the Department of Health and Human Services. Under Medicare, day-to-day administrative tasks such as reviewing and paying claims for treatment are contracted out to private insurance companies, which are referred to as "carriers" or "fiscal intermediaries." Medicaid is administered mostly by individual state agencies. Other good overviews can be found at Timothy Jost, Disentitlement: Health Care Entitlements and the Threats That They Face (1993); Timothy Jost, Governing Medicare, 51 Admin. L. Rev. 39 (1999); John Iglehart, The American Health Care System: Medicaid, 340 New Eng. J. Med. 403 (1999); John Iglehart, The American Health Care System: Medicare, 340 New Eng. J. Med. 327 (1999); Medicaid Symposium, 45 St. Louis U. L.J. 1 (2001); Medicaid Symposium, 22 Health Care Fin. Rev. 1 (2000); Medicaid Symposium, 22(1) Health Aff. 1 (Jan. 2003); Maxwell Mehlman & Karen Visocan, Medicare and Medicaid: Are They Just Health Care Systems?, 29 Hous. L. Rev. 835 (1992). The most widely-used source for detailed knowledge about Medicare and Medicaid is the CCH treatise by that name. For historical and political accounts, see Judith M. Feder, Medicare: The Politics of Federal Hospital Insurance (1977); Theodore R. Marmor, The Politics of Medicare (2d ed. 1999); Herman & Anne Somers, Medicare and the Hospitals: Issues and Prospects (1967).

2. *Overlapping and Supplemental Coverage.* Most Medicare recipients choose to purchase supplemental Medigap insurance. Also, because some elderly people continue to work past 65, and some have working spouses, many Medicare recipients are covered by private insurance as well. This overlay of insurance from different sources creates the additional legal complexity of determining who is the primary insurer. The same problem can arise apart from Medicare, when two spouses have employer-provided private insurance. As between overlapping private insurers, this is known as the "coordination of benefits" problem, and it is usually resolved through state regulation that requires the two insurers to split the medical bills. When Medicare is involved, however, the federal statute declares that private insurance coverage must be exhausted before Medicare pays anything. Litigation has focused on whether Medicare can recoup from private insurers payments that it now discovers it erroneously made years ago, even though the private insurer who should have paid never received any claim for payment at the time. See Health Insurance Association of America v. Shalala, 23 F.3d 412 (D.C. Cir. 1994) (striking down portions of Medicare's "secondary payer program" but sustaining most of its aspects).

A related complexity, but one that applies mainly to private insurers, arises when a subscriber who suffers an injury is reimbursed for medical costs both by health insurance and by a tort recovery. Most insurance contracts give the health insurer a right of subrogation to recoup payments covered by a tort award, but many states have antisubrogation statutes that limit or nullify these clauses. The concern is that many tort awards are lump sum negotiated settlements that cannot easily be apportioned between medical costs and pain and suffering. When the insurance in question is self-funded by an employer, however, ERISA has been found to preempt these state anti-subrogation statutes. McInnis v. Provident Life & Accident Insurance Co., 21 F.3d 586 (4th Cir. 1994).

3. *Balance Billing.* Observe the differences between Medicare and Medicaid concerning what physicians are allowed to charge patients beyond the program's

payment. Medicaid allows no extra charges, and so physician participation is much lower. Medicare originally allowed unlimited extra charges, but has successively restricted this freedom. Physicians can always collect their 20 percent copayment, based on the Medicare fee-schedule, but Medicare encourages "participating physicians" to forgo the extra 15 percent that the law allows by "taking assignment," that is, by agreeing to accept only the Medicare fee in exchange for more prompt and direct payment. Currently, over three-quarters of physicians do so. Hospitals and other facilities are not allowed to charge any amount above the prescribed Medicare fees.

Some states have stepped in to require physicians to accept Medicaid patients or to prohibit them from charging Medicare patients more (that is, a ban on "balance billing"). For the most part, these laws have been upheld as constitutional and consistent with the federal statutes. See, e.g., Dukakis v. Massachusetts Medical Society, 815 F.2d 790 (1st Cir. 1987); Downhour v. Somani, 85 F.3d 261 (6th Cir. 1996). In a related decision, the Supreme Court upheld Maine's requirement that pharmaceutical companies doing business with its state Medicaid program must give equivalent discounts to uninsured residents of the state. Pharmaceutical Research and Manufacturers of America v. Walsh, 538 U.S. 644 (2003).

Some physicians have attempted a number of techniques to circumvent restrictions on excess billing. One, known as "private contracting," has patients agree to pay entirely out of pocket and not submit to Medicare for reimbursement. Out of fear that this would allow physicians to selectively coerce their patients to go without Medicare benefits, Congress in 1997 prohibited these private agreements unless the physician forgoes any Medicare payment from all patients for at least two years. United Seniors Ass'n v. Shalala, 182 F.3d 965 (D.C. Cir. 1999). This produced an outcry from the AMA over denying patients and physicians the freedom to contract outside Medicare, but so far the law has not been amended. See generally Symposium, Medicare Private Contracting (The "Kyl" Amendment), 10 Health Matrix 1 (2000). More recently, physicians have adopted a different tactic, which is to charge a substantial fee of several thousands of dollars a year in addition to Medicare billings, for "boutique" or "concierge" services such as 24-hour direct access through cell phones or pagers and a promise to greatly limit the number of patients a physician sees in order to have more time for each patient. The legality of this arrangement is still in doubt, with physicians claiming this does not violate balance billing rules since the extra payments are for administrative or non-Medicare-covered services. What about the ethics of these boutique practices? Proponents argue this allows physicians to regain control of their professional lives and to establish the type of personal and holistic medical practice that has long since disappeared. Critics say this is elitist and exploitative. See Troyen A. Brennan, Luxury Primary Care: Market Innovation or Threat to Access?, 346 New Eng. J. Med. 1165 (2002).

4. *Medicaid/Medicare Managed Care.* Managed care has thrived under Medicaid but stalled under Medicare. Under Medicaid, the two most notable examples are Tennessee (whose program is called TennCare) and Arizona (whose program acronym is AHCCCS ("access")). Program details vary quite a bit, but the gist is for the state to selectively contract, based on competitive bidding, with a number of health plans structured as HMOs. Each Medicaid recipient is then required to select a primary health plan, which receives a capitation payment.

Most of these demonstration projects apply only to the AFDC component of Medicaid, but states are beginning to expand managed care to cover the elderly and disabled SSI recipients. Since 1997, federal "waivers" are no longer required for states to implement Medicaid managed care. Various descriptions and reviews of Medicaid managed care innovations can be found in Bruce Babbitt & Jonathan Rose, Building a Better Mousetrap: Health Care Reform and the Arizona Program, 3 Yale J. Reg. 243 (1986); John Iglehart, Medicaid and Managed Care, 332 New Eng. J. Med. 1727 (1995); James F. Blumstein & Frank A. Sloan, Health Care Reform through Medicaid Managed Care: Tennessee (TennCare) as a Case Study and a Problem, 53 Vand. L. Rev. 125 (2000); Sidney D. Watson, Commercialization of Medicaid, 45 St. Louis U. L.J. 53 (2001); Note, 110 Harv. L. Rev. 751 (1997); Symposium, 15 Health Aff. (Fall 1996); Symposium, 22 J. Health Pol. Pol'y & L. 687 (1997). For historical discussions of the criteria and process for obtaining federal waivers, see Vernelia Randall, Section 1115 Medicaid Waivers: Critiquing the State Applications, 26 Seton Hall L. Rev. 1055 (1996). Judith Rosenberg & David Zorig, Managing Medicaid Waivers: Section 1115 and State Health Care Reform, 32 Harv. J. Legis. 545 (1995).

The Medicare + Choice program enacted in 1998 has encountered some stumbling blocks in its implementation. Its purpose is to offer Medicare enrollees a wide variety of private insurance alternatives to traditional Medicare, in order to stimulate managed care cost savings. Originally projected to reach a third of Medicare enrollees, Medicare + Choice covers less than half of that, almost entirely in HMOs. None of the other alternative financing arrangements (such as medical savings accounts or provider-sponsored plans) took hold. Regulators have encountered two problems: explaining all the complex choices in a manner that most Medicare enrollees can understand, and designing payment rules that avoid rewarding insurers simply for enrolling healthier members. Also, many of the largest national HMOs have withdrawn from Medicare, claiming insufficient payments and burdensome regulation, despite significant increases in Medicare payments to participating HMOs. On balance, the program has cost rather than saved money by attracting a disproportionate number of healthier people whom traditional Medicare could have covered for less than it paid the private health plans. As one observer has summarized, so far Medicare has succeeded in reducing costs only in the old-fashioned way, through regulated prices but not by promoting more private market competition. Timothy Jost, Disentitlement: Health Care Entitlements and the Threats That They Face (1993). Nevertheless, in the 2004 Medicare Modernization Act, Congress sought to revitalize Medicare managed care under the name "Medicare Advantage," by increasing payments even more to private health plans that accept Medicare beneficiaries.

For more about Medicare managed care, see Nancy-Ann DeParle, As Good as It Gets? The Future of Medicare + Choice, 27 J. Health Pol. Pol'y & L. 495 (2002); Symposium, 18(1) Health Aff. 1 (Jan./Feb. 1999); Marsha Gold, Medicare + Choice: An Interim Report Card, 20(4) Health Aff. 120 (July 2001); Louis F. Rossiter, Understanding Medicare Managed Care (2001).

5. *Medicare Reform.* When Medicare was first enacted, Part A was projected to cost only $9 billion a year in 1990. It actually cost $60 billion. Government actuaries failed to anticipate the continuing inflationary effects of Medicare's generous

payment methods, the increased demand for medical services that resulted from making health insurance much more widespread, and the expanded life expectancy of the elderly. See Steven Hayward & Erik Peterson, The Medicare Monster, Reason, Jan. 1993, at 19. Major reforms are needed to save the program from immediate bankruptcy, but the future is even more ominous. The aging of the baby-boom generation will greatly reduce ratio of workers to retirees from the current 4:1 to only 2:1 by 2060. Presently, reform ideas focus on moving Medicare enrollees into managed care plans, but it is clear that, eventually, Medicare will require either radical increases in funding or radical reductions in benefits. See Theodore Marmor & Gary McKissick, Medicare's Future: Fact, Fiction and Folly, 26 Am. J.L. & Med. 225 (2000); Marilyn Moon, Medicare, 344 New Eng. J. Med. 928 (2001); Symposium, 26 J. Health Pol. Pol'y & L. 1 (2001); Symposium, 22 Health Care Fin. Rev. 1 (2000); Symposium, 18 (1) Health Aff. 1 (Jan./Feb. 1999).

6. *Long-Term Care.* This chapter focuses on conventional medical insurance for hospitals and doctors and so neglects the sources of financing for long-term care insurance that covers nursing homes and home health care. The appropriate source and financing for this type of insurance will be one of the most pressing public health policy issues through at least the turn of the century. Two developments are accelerating the rate at which long-term care is increasing its portion of the nation's health care budget: the aging of the baby-boom generation and increasing life expectancy. Private insurance for nursing homes is not very extensive because of its costs. Its costs are high because most people don't consider purchasing it until they anticipate needing it. Mark Pauly, The Rational Nonpurchase of Long-Term-Care Insurance, 98 J. Pol. Econ. 153 (1990). The principal fallback is Medicaid, which requires the elderly to impoverish themselves. Various financial planning techniques are possible for sheltering assets from Medicaid "spend down" rules, but Congress is steadily curbing these techniques. For instance, Medicaid now counts assets that the patient transferred as long as 36 months ago, that are owned jointly by the patient's spouse, or that are in a revocable trust. 42 U.S.C. §1396p. Congress also made it a criminal offense for lawyers or financial advisers to counsel clients in avoiding restrictions. See generally Hal Fliegelman & Debora Fliegelman, Giving Guardians the Power to do Medicaid Planning, 32 Wake Forest L. Rev. 341 (1997); Note, 4 Elder L.J. 459 (1996); Symposium, 31 McGeorge L. Rev. 703 (2000); Symposium, 1 Quinnipiac Health L.J. 113 (1997); Symposium, 19 Nova L. Rev. 533 (1995).

Policy analysts are exploring a number of options for making private financing of nursing homes more feasible (such as "reverse mortgages" and "continuing care retirement communities") or for devising innovative hybrids between public and private financing. See generally M. Cohen et al., Financing Long-Term Care: A Practical Mix of Public and Private, 17 J. Health Pol. Pol'y & L. 403 (1992); Marshall Kapp, Options for Long-Term Care Financing, 42 Hastings L.J. 719 (1991); Joshua M. Wiener et al., Federal and State Initiatives to Jump Start the Market for Private Long-Term Care Insurance, 8 Elder L.J. 57 (2000); Symposium, 19(3) Health Aff. (May 2000); Symposium 4 J. Health Care L. & Pol'y 159 (2001); The coverage of home health care is somewhat more extensive under private insurance and Medicare because it is seen as an inexpensive alternative to hospital or institutional care. See generally S.M. Weitzman, Legal and Policy Aspects of Home Care Coverage, 1 Ann. Health L. 1 (1992).

Note: The New Medicare Prescription Drug Coverage Law

On December 8, 2003, President Bush signed into law the Medicare Prescription Drug, Improvement, and Modernization Act of 2003, H.R. 1. This is the most significant change to the Medicare program since its inception in 1965. The major provisions are:

- Effective in 2006, there will be a new Part D of Medicare that provides outpatient prescription drug coverage.
- Part C of Medicare (also called Medicare + Choice), which provides HMO and other private managed care options for Medicare enrollees, is renamed "Medicare Advantage." Payments to private health plans are increased to be the same as Medicare fee-for-service costs.
- Beginning in 2010, Medicare will begin to experiment with giving beneficiaries financial incentives to enroll in private health plans such as HMOs or PPOs, by accepting competitive bids from these plans and passing on to beneficiaries a portion of any savings from bids that are lower than the average, risk-adjusted cost for standard Medicare coverage.
- Starting in 2006, Part B premiums will be based in part on income ("means tested"). After phase-in, those earning $200,000 or more will pay three times more than those earning $80,000 or less, with a sliding scale between these two points.
- Medical Savings Accounts (MSAs), which are discussed at page 183, are made more generous and are renamed Health Savings Accounts (HSAs). These are tax-advantaged accounts that non-Medicare people can use to pay for health care costs not covered by insurance, if they have a high-deductible ("catastrophic") insurance policy.

The following government report provides useful background for understanding the new Part D Prescription Drug Benefit, whose details are discussed below. See also Symposium, 23(1) Health Affairs 1 (Jan. 2004); Symposium, 20(2) Health Aff. 1 (Mar. 2001); Symposium, 19(2) Health Aff. 1 (Mar. 2000).

■ ISSUES IN DESIGNING A PRESCRIPTION DRUG BENEFIT FOR MEDICARE CONGRESSIONAL BUDGET OFFICE
October 2002

One of lawmakers' highest health related priorities [in recent years has been] adding a prescription drug benefit to Medicare. Although that program gives older Americans broad insurance coverage for many health needs, it provides only limited coverage of drugs not dispensed during a hospital stay. That gap in coverage has become increasingly significant as prescription drugs have assumed greater importance in the treatment of disease and as spending for outpatient prescription drugs has soared.

Designing a Medicare drug benefit is a complex task, however. The competing goals for such a benefit mean that policymakers must make trade offs (such as between broad coverage or widespread enrollment and cost). They must consider many different design elements and how those elements might interact. And they must try to avoid various problems that arise in creating such a benefit. Ultimately, the choices that designers make will affect not only the cost of the benefit but a host of other factors, such as demand for and prices of prescription drugs, spending by other federal and state programs, and how various parts of the market for health insurance operate....

Although most Medicare beneficiaries use some prescription drugs, that spending is concentrated among a relatively small part of the Medicare population: people with chronic conditions requiring long term drug therapy. Only 17 percent of Medicare beneficiaries will spend more than $5,000 on prescription drugs in 2005, CBO estimates, but their combined spending will make up nearly 54 percent of total drug expenditures by Medicare beneficiaries that year.

Roughly one quarter of Medicare beneficiaries have no prescription drug coverage.... Thus, they must pay all of their drug costs out of pocket. The other three quarters obtain drug coverage as part of a plan that supplements Medicare's benefits. But those supplemental plans differ greatly in the extent of coverage they provide.... Medicare beneficiaries who lack drug coverage tend to be people in the low to middle part of the income distribution. People with higher income are more likely to have employment based plans or individually purchased medigap policies (which charge high premiums for drug coverage).... Proposals that would target Medicare drug coverage toward low to middle income beneficiaries who are not eligible for Medicaid would concentrate new federal spending on those least likely to have drug coverage now. Broad based proposals, by contrast, would tend to replace coverage that three fourths of beneficiaries now get from private and nonfederal sources with Medicare funded coverage....

HOW COMPREHENSIVE WILL THE BENEFIT BE?

The most important factor determining the cost of a Medicare drug benefit is the scope and structure of its coverage. Choices about coverage include:

- The deductible amount—whether coverage begins with an enrollee's first dollar of drug spending in a given year or after the deductible amount is reached
- Cost-sharing rates—what part of the cost of a prescription is the responsibility of the enrollee
- The benefit cap—the level of spending beyond which the enrollee must pay the full cost of each prescription; and
- The catastrophic stop-loss amount—the level of spending beyond which the enrollee pays little or nothing for prescriptions.

The possible variations on those choices are endless. Some combinations could produce Medicare drug benefits unlike anything available in the private sector today. For example, [the new Medicare drug benefit has] a hole in coverage: a spending level between the benefit cap and the stop-loss amount at which enrollees would have no drug coverage. Employment-based drug plans almost never include such holes.

The benefit structure would affect the cost of the Medicare drug program not only directly but also indirectly, through the out-of-pocket expenses it would require of enrollees. For instance, benefits with low cost-sharing rates would encourage those enrollees who were newly shielded from paying the full cost of a prescription to use more—and more expensive—drugs.

HOW WILL THE BENEFIT BE ADMINISTERED?

Almost all of the recent proposals for a Medicare drug benefit envision using organizations such as pharmacy benefit managers (PBMs) to administer the benefit—an approach that is common in the private sector. Critical choices, however, are the number of such organizations that would serve a region, the restrictions they would be subject to, the basis on which they could compete for enrollees, and whether they would assume any insurance risk (that is, be liable for any costs that were not fully covered by enrollees' premiums or federal reimbursements).

In examining prescription drug proposals, CBO has concluded that certain administrative features offer the greatest opportunity to control federal costs and total spending on outpatient prescription drugs. Those features are allowing benefit managers to employ the full array of cost-management tools now available to private-sector drug plans, forcing benefit managers to compete among themselves for enrollees' business, and making managers assume financial risk for delivering benefits.... [Cost management] tools include formularies (lists of drugs that a health plan will cover) and related approaches that steer demand to preferred drugs [and] networks of pharmacies.... All of those tools, to one degree or another, work by influencing physicians' or consumers' choices about what drug to prescribe or where to fill a prescription. In addition, requiring benefit managers to assume some insurance risk for the benefits they pay out and allowing multiple entities to compete for enrollees on the basis of premiums and reimbursements would give managers a greater incentive to hold down spending.

However, the savings from those features would be partly offset by plan's marketing costs. Competition [among private drug plans] would introduce additional expenses associated with marketing to and enrolling Medicare beneficiaries, which would not arise if a single plan administered the drug benefit in each region. Competing plans would have to provide specific information about their plans to beneficiaries. If plans were also responsible for enrolling people and collecting their premiums, the cost of carrying out those administrative functions would be higher than under a single-plan system....

Even the most effective benefit management, however, would not keep the prices of some drugs from rising under a Medicare drug benefit. By raising the limit on consumers' willingness or ability to pay for covered drugs, a generous drug benefit would make newly insured patients more tolerant of high prices. With such a benefit, if a manufacturer developed a unique drug whose target population consisted mainly of Medicare beneficiaries, it could raise the drug's price (or, if the drug was new, enter the market with a high launch price). Preventing very high prices for such drugs would be difficult apart from imposing direct price controls or threatening to deny or delay coverage of the drug—actions that could increase uncertainty about the market for new drugs and thus discourage investment in pharmaceutical research and development.

ADVERSE SELECTION

A stand-alone prescription drug benefit could be especially prone to the insurance-market phenomenon known as adverse selection, in which people who expect to have higher-than-average costs disproportionately enroll in an insurance plan....Adverse selection is a problem because it undermines the purpose of insurance, which is to spread financial risks among a wide pool of people....The main way to prevent adverse selection into the drug program would be to encourage as many people as possible to enroll. The government could do that through a number of approaches:

- Requiring One-Time Enrollment. A "choose it or lose it" policy would boost enrollment because even healthy Medicare beneficiaries might be worried enough about developing an expensive medical condition someday that they would enroll in the drug benefit if they had only one chance to do so.
- Subsidizing the Program to a Large Extent. Broad federal subsidies would mean that even fairly healthy people would be likely to get more in benefits than they paid in premiums.
- Risk-Rating Premiums. Adjusting the premiums that enrollees would pay according to their risk of high drug spending would encourage healthier people to enroll because their costs would be lower....

It is possible that only one plan or even no plans would participate in the drug program in some [regions]. Without multiple plans in a region, the full benefits of competition would not be realized. If that happened, the government might have to provide its own public plan as a fallback in those areas ... to ensure a competitive program nationwide. Fallback plans would be very vulnerable to... adverse selection in any region where there was also a [private] plan. If the fallback plan was less aggressive than [private] plans in managing costs, the government could end up paying more, on average, in areas requiring such direct intervention.

Notes: Medicare Part D, Prescription Drug Benefit

1. *The Devil Is in the Details.* Like Part B, the new Part D prescription drug benefit will be voluntary, i.e., Medicare-eligible individuals choose whether or not to enroll and pay a subsidized premium. Unlike Part B, however, Prescription Drug Plans (Rx Plans) will be offered primarily by competing private companies, such as insurance companies, HMOs, and pharmacy benefit managers. The government would directly offer a drug benefit plan only if fewer than two private Rx Plans are not available in a geographic region. Significantly, the premiums for private Part D plans will be set by private insurers and will vary from region to

region. This is in marked contrast to the Medicare Part B premium, which is the same nationwide. The government will subsidize 75 percent of the Part D premium for most Medicare beneficiaries, but will pay 100% of the premium for low-income beneficiaries (135% of federal poverty level) who are not covered by another source such as Medicaid. Payments to health plans will be adjusted for health status and insurance risk, to counter adverse selection.

The private companies offering Rx Plans will submit plan designs and premium bids to the government for approval. The most recent estimates by the Congressional Budget Office are that the monthly premium for a standard Rx Plan will be $35 per month; however, standard plan premiums offered to individuals in 10-50 regions of the United States will vary between companies and across regions. Furthermore, Rx Plans may offer "alternate" plan designs that are "actuarially equivalent" (or better) and for which premiums may also vary.

Thus, when the new Medicare drug benefit is implemented in 2006, retirees will face the following dizzying array of alternatives:

- An Rx Plan-provided "standard" benefit plan design
- An Rx Plan-provided "alternate" benefit plan design
- A Medicare Advantage HMO or PPO plan that includes prescription drug coverage
- A government-underwritten "fallback plan" if fewer than two Rx Plans are offered in a geographic area

In order to provide marketing information to seniors, private companies will be given the names and addresses of Medicare beneficiaries.

The standard Part D coverage will have a $275 deductible and then pay for 75 percent of drug costs up to $2,250 a year. Then, coverage ceases until total costs reach $3,600 (the "doughnut hole"), at which point 95 percent of drug costs are paid. These dollar thresholds increase each year at the same rate as Medicare's overall costs for the program. The deductibles, co-payments, and gap in coverage are lowered or eliminated for people who are below 150 percent of the federal poverty level.

The legislation prohibits the government from regulating or negotiating drug costs. Instead, costs will be whatever drug companies charge, subject to negotiation by the private Rx Plans. Rx Plans may also adopt "formularies" that require the use of generic drugs and that refuse to cover more expensive drugs when less expensive ones are equally effective, but beneficiaries may appeal these restrictions in individual cases of medical necessity.

To encourage employers to continue providing drug coverage to retired workers, employers who do so will receive a subsidy for paying the costs of a qualifying drug plan. However, the law prohibits any coverage that pays for the deductibles and co-payments in the standard plan.

2. *The Opposition.* Opponents of this new law fall into several camps. Some believe the law is too generous and costly by offering drug benefits to all Medicare recipients rather than targeting only those who need this benefit the most. Others believe the law is too stingy because of the "doughnut hole" in coverage and because there is no cap on the total amount of drug costs a person could incur. Another point of criticism is prohibiting the government from using its purchasing

power to negotiate lower prices. The strongest opposition comes from those who opposed the move toward delivering Medicare benefits through private insurance companies.

✦3. *Handwriting on the Wall.* This law has two elements that indicate how Congress might be inclined to reform other parts of Medicare in the future. ✦First, some benefits are means-tested for the first time. ✦Second, there is a move away from a defined entitlement to a set of governmental benefits and toward a structure that subsidizes beneficiaries' purchase of private benefits.

B. INSURANCE AND HMO REGULATION

This section addresses whether and how various forms of health care financing and delivery should be regulated by state insurance laws. Even though the first case is 60 years old and no longer states current law, the issues it confronts remain alive today in only a slightly different form. As you read this case, consider what objectives state insurance regulation is designed to accomplish and how these goals fit with modern organizational forms and arrangements such as HMOs and IDSs.

■ JORDAN v. GROUP HEALTH ASS'N
107 F.2d 239 (D.C. Cir. 1939)

RUTLEDGE, Associate Justice.

... [T]he Superintendent of Insurance for the District [of Columbia]... contends that Group Health is... a health or accident insurance company within the meaning of §653 of the D.C. Code[4]... [and] that it is carrying on its operations illegally and without complying with the requirements of these statutes....

Group Health['s]... corporate objects, summarized, are to provide, without profit to the corporation, for medical services, preventive and curative, surgery, hospitalization, and medical and surgical supplies, exclusively for members of Group Health and their dependents.... There are two classes of membership, family membership and individual membership. For the latter, dues are $2.20 monthly; for the former, $3.30....

In return for the monthly dues, Group Health undertakes to arrange for [both preventive and curative] medical and surgical services to be rendered by independent practitioners, not full-time staff members,[6] either at the clinic maintained by Group Health or, if necessary, at the home of the member or the hospital where

---

[4] ... Section 653 of the D.C. Code defines "health, accident, and life insurance companies or associations," prohibits them from transacting business unless they possess certain assets as a capital or guarantee fund, and provides for licensing and examinations by the superintendent Section 646 requires insurance organizations to file copies of charter, articles of incorporation or association, and certificates of authority to do business with the superintendent. Section 647 requires the filing of annual statements of financial condition; ... §652 requires the superintendent to see that insurance companies or associations possess the assets required by law or by charter. The Revenue Act of 1937 ... imposes a percentage tax on net premium receipts, dues, et cetera....

[6] The physicians apparently devote only a portion of their time to the work of Group Health, the remainder being devoted to private practice, although it seems to be contemplated that some physicians will give full time to the work. They receive fixed annual compensation, paid in monthly installments, not specific fees for each treatment or case....

the patient may be. Hospitalization is by arrangement with established independent hospitals....

The physicians and hospitals look solely to Group Health for their compensation as to the services it undertakes to arrange for. Nor is the cost of service rendered to an individual member limited by or apportioned to his contributions. For $26.40 a year, an individual member may receive much, little or no service. In effect the plan is one by which the members by making regular, limited payments receive service and supplies in variable degrees according to their needs, within specified limitations....

The effect of the agreement or arrangement is to make available to members, if they wish to receive them, the services of the physicians contracted for by Group Health; but it is specifically provided that (1) Group Health cannot and will not regulate or control the physician in his work—he is left free, in fact required, to exercise his own judgment entirely independently as to diagnosis and treatment;...(4) the Medical Director may determine the extent of the services which will be available to members in each individual case;...(7) finally, Group Health assumes no liability, if for any reason it becomes unable to procure any or all such services when called upon to do so, or to indemnify the member for failure of the physician to keep his agreement or perform it properly, and its only obligation in such a case is "to use its best efforts to procure the needed services from another source."...

It is unnecessary for us to attempt formulation of an all-inclusive or exclusive definition of insurance or of indemnity, or to distinguish them sharply. While the basic concepts are not identical and each has varied legal usages, they have common and primary elements which are controlling here. Fundamentally each involves contractual security against anticipated loss. Whether the contract is one of insurance or of indemnity there must be a risk of loss to which one party may be subjected by contingent or future events and an assumption of it by legally binding arrangement by another.... Hazard is essential and equally so a shifting of its incidence.... Insurance also, by the better view, involves distribution of the risk, but distribution without assumption hardly can be held to be insurance. These are elemental conceptions and controlling ones. How are they to be applied to Group Health's...service to the sick or injured?

Here certainly is risk, hazard which has descended. But has it been shifted to or assumed by Group Health? On this question the exact nature of its obligation becomes important. Does it assume the risk, or contract to bear the member's loss when it falls? Is it obligated to pay, in cash or in kind, to him or to another for his benefit or for that of a beneficiary designated by him the amount by which he is damaged or any amount? Unless the bylaws are to be discarded and ignored entirely, there can be only one answer. The agreement is not to pay to the member or to any one else the amount of loss which is caused to him. True, the physician receives his salaried compensation. But he receives no more and no less because of the falling of the loss.... [I]n an inaccurate, nontechnical sense, he, rather than Group Health, is the one more nearly analogous to an insurer. If incidence of illness in the group is light, so is his work; if heavy, so is his labor up to the maximum of his contract. In either case his compensation is the same. Nor is the burden of Group Health increased normally by the falling of particular losses. Its obligation to the physician remains the same. That to particular members is not at all affected by the volume of illness in the group whether great or small. As a matter of good faith, of fulfilling moral expectations, in epidemic conditions it undoubtedly would expand the arrangements for service temporarily, so far as its resources would permit. Sizable increase in membership would cause it likewise to enlarge the number of physicians under contract, so as to make the service generally and normally available. But this would not expand the obligation or the liability to any particular member. In any event, whatever the emergency or the experience, it undertakes not to supply the service, or see or guarantee that it is supplied, or be responsible for the failure to supply it or to do so properly, but only to "use its best efforts" to secure similar service from another source.... The contract is, in fact, unique. It does not fit neatly into established categories of "agency," "guaranty," "insurance," "indemnity" and the like....

Although Group Health's activities may be considered in one aspect as creating security against loss from illness or accident, more truly they constitute the quantity purchase of well-rounded, continuous medical service by its members.... Its primary purpose is to reduce the cost rather than the risk of medical care; to broaden the service to the individual in kind and quantity; to enlarge the number receiving it; to regularize it as an everyday incident of living, like purchasing food and clothing or oil and gas, rather than merely protecting against the financial loss caused by extraordinary and unusual occurrences, such as death, disaster at sea, fire and tornado. It is, in this instance, to take care of colds, ordinary aches and pains, minor ills and all the temporary bodily discomforts as well as the more serious and unusual illnesses.... There is, therefore, a substantial difference between contracting in this way for the rendering of service, even on the contingency that it be needed, and contracting merely to stand its cost when or after it is rendered....

[O]bviously it was not the purpose of the insurance statutes to regulate all arrangements for assumption or distribution of risk. That view would cause them to engulf practically all contracts, particularly conditional sales and contingent service agreements.... The question turns, not on whether risk is involved or assumed, but on whether that or something else to which it is related in the particular plan is its principal object and purpose.[26] ... With differences such as have been pointed out, the application of statutory regulations designed to fit the one to the operations of the other could not be other than incongruous, or fatal to the cooperative. It would result, not in regulation, but in destruction of the organization....

We think these conclusions are sustained by the authorities which are pertinent.... Those to which we have been referred are favorable to the view we take, none to the contrary.[30] ... [This] becomes the more evident when the purpose and

---

[26] "Care must be taken to distinguish mere contracts to render service on the happening of a contingency from true contracts of insurance.... The cases have failed to declare a satisfactory rule for distinguishing between the two types of agreements, but it would seem that the contract should not be classed as insurance if the paramount purpose in its formation was to be the rendition of the services rendered.... However, it should be insurance if the chief purpose of the agreement is the protection against the risk involved." 3 U. of Pittsburgh L. Rev. 250, 251 and notes 7-12 (1936). See also 52 Harv. L. Rev. 809, 814 n.37 (1939)....

[30] The closest approach, where litigation has been prolific, is found perhaps in the cases relating to burial associations, in which of course the element of contingency, the lack of regularized service, and the opportunity as well as the practice of trading on credulity and fear are much greater. Death strikes only once.... [T]hough the majority of the cases classify such arrangements as insurance, [t]hey are clearly not in point here ... as the obligation assumed is a definite and binding one to supply the service. Many of them also involve businesses operating for profit, frequently in the disguise of a "nonprofit,

nature of many of the statutory requirements are considered, particularly those relating to the maintenance of reserves or "guarantee funds" and to the regulation of investments and financial operations. The object of these is protection of the insured and thus of the public against the insurer.... Such requirements can have meaning, purpose and useful effect only in relation to definite and binding obligations as to which, in their absence, there is danger of default.... It is not the function or purpose of Group Health to pile up vast accumulations of capital to await the needs of a distant day; it is rather to keep a steady flow of funds, with as small a margin as possible, running from patient to physician as nearly contemporaneously with the reverse flow of service from physician to patient as can be.... To require it to maintain a guarantee fund of $25,000 or of $100,000, in accordance with the provisions of §653, would be to divert funds from its primary purpose and keep them in idleness to no end of security for its members....

　　　Appellant visualizes serious consequences for the effective regulation of insurance activities from a decision such as we have reached. We do not share his concern. Experience to date with consumer cooperatives, organized and limited in their activities, management and membership as in Group Health, has not shown that they are susceptible to the abuses feared. If they or others should appear, measures for their control should be enacted by the legislature, not prescribed through judicial expansion of existing statutes designed for other organizations' activities and abuses.

■ THE HEALTH CARE REVOLUTION: REMAKING MEDICINE IN CALIFORNIA
Barbara Marsh
Los Angeles Times, August 31, 1995

[Read the excerpt at page 55.]

■ TRANSCRIPT OF INTERVIEW WITH JAIME ROBINSON, Ph.D.
Lehman Brothers Industry Expert Conference Call Series
May 17, 2002

[Read the excerpt at page 56.]

---

association," which is in fact an adjunct of an undertaking concern.... Apart from the conflicts as to ... burial associations, the courts divide squarely on servicing plate glass windows with replacement of broken glass, ... [and on] [c]leaning bicycles, repairing and replacing them when damaged accidentally or stolen.... [R]egardless of this confusion, most, if not all, of the cases are distinguishable from the present one—some in many features such as predominance of the risk element over all others, absence of cooperative interest and action, profit-seeking, open or disguised—but all by the definite assumption of contractual liability for the risk involved....

The following case addresses issues relating to federal preemption of state regulation, which are dealt with in more depth in the following section. The case is included here because it introduces a more modern perspective on the status and regulatory treatment of HMOs.

■ RUSH PRUDENTIAL HMO v. MORAN
122 S. Ct. 2151 (2002)

SOUTER, J., delivered the opinion of the Court, [which was split 5-4].

Illinois's Health Maintenance Organization Act provides... a right to independent medical review of certain denials of benefits. The issue in this case is whether the statute... is preempted by the Employee Retirement Income Security Act of 1974 (ERISA), 29 U.S.C. §1001 *et seq.,* [which is addressed in the next section]. We hold it is not....

Debra Moran is a beneficiary under [an employee welfare benefit] plan, sponsored by her husband's employer.... As the [insurance policy] explains, Rush contracts with physicians "to arrange for or provide services and supplies for medical care and treatment" of covered persons. Each covered person selects a primary care physician from those under contract to Rush, while Rush will pay for medical services by an unaffiliated physician only if the services have been "authorized" both by the primary care physician and Rush's medical director.

In 1996, when Moran began to have pain and numbness in her right shoulder, Dr. Arthur LaMarre, her primary care physician, unsuccessfully administered "conservative" treatments such as physiotherapy. In October 1997, Dr. LaMarre recommended that Rush approve surgery by an unaffiliated specialist, Dr. Julia Terzis, who had developed an unconventional treatment for Moran's condition. Although Dr. LaMarre said that Moran would be "best served" by that procedure, Rush denied the request and, after Moran's internal appeals, affirmed the denial on the ground that the procedure was not "medically necessary." Rush instead proposed that Moran undergo standard surgery, performed by a physician affiliated with Rush.

In January 1998, Moran made a written demand for an independent medical review of her claim.... When Rush failed to provide the independent review, Moran sued in an Illinois state court to compel compliance with the state Act. Rush removed the suit to Federal District Court, arguing that the cause of action was "completely preempted" under ERISA, [a federal statute that regulates pension plans and other employee fringe benefits].

While the suit was pending, Moran had surgery by Dr. Terzis at her own expense and submitted a $94,841.27 reimbursement claim to Rush. Rush treated the claim as a renewed request for benefits and began a new inquiry to determine coverage. The three doctors consulted by Rush said the surgery had been medically unnecessary. Meanwhile, the federal court remanded the case back to state court..., [and] the state court enforced the state statute and ordered Rush to submit to review by an independent physician. The doctor selected was a reconstructive surgeon at Johns Hopkins Medical Center, Dr. A. Lee Dellon. Dr. Dellon decided that Dr. Terzis's treatment had been medically necessary, based on the definition of medical necessity in Rush's Certificate of Group Coverage, as well as his own medical judgment. Rush's medical director, however, refused to concede that the surgery had been medically necessary, and denied Moran's claim in January 1999.... The Court of Appeals for the Seventh Circuit reversed.... Because the decision of the Court of Appeals conflicted with the Fifth Circuit's treatment of a similar provision of Texas law in Corporate Health Ins., Inc. v. Texas Dept. of Ins., 215 F.3d 526 (2000), we granted certiorari. We now affirm.

II

To "safeguar[d]...the establishment, operation, and administration" of employee benefit plans, ERISA...contains an express preemption provision that ERISA "shall supersede any and all State laws insofar as they may now or hereafter relate to any employee benefit plan...." A saving clause then reclaims a substantial amount of ground with its provision that "nothing in this subchapter shall be construed to exempt or relieve any person from any law of any State which regulates insurance, banking, or securities." The "unhelpful" drafting of these antiphonal clauses occupies a substantial share of this Court's time. [See Chapters 2.C and 3.C.]...

As a law that "relates to" ERISA plans, [the Illinois statute] is saved from preemption only if it also "regulates insurance." Rush insists that the Act is not such a law.... [I]n deciding whether a law "regulates insurance" under ERISA's saving clause, we start with a "common-sense view of the matter."... Rush contends that seeing an HMO as an insurer distorts the nature of an HMO, which is, after all, a health care provider, too. This, Rush argues, should determine its characterization, with the consequence that regulation of an HMO is not insurance regulation within the meaning of ERISA.

The answer to Rush is, of course, that an HMO is both: it provides health care, and it does so as an insurer. Nothing in the saving clause requires an either-or choice between health care and insurance...[I]t would ignore the whole purpose of the HMO-style of organization to conceive of HMOs without their insurance element.... The HMO design goes beyond the simple truism that all contracts are, in some sense, insurance against future fluctuations in price, R. Posner, Economic Analysis of Law 104 (4th ed. 1992), because HMOs actually underwrite and spread risk among their participants, a feature distinctive to insurance.

So Congress has understood from the start, when the phrase "Health Maintenance Organization" was established and defined in the HMO Act of 1973, 42 U.S.C. §300 et seq. The Act was intended to encourage the development of HMOs as a new form of health care delivery system, and when Congress set the standards that the new health delivery organizations would have to meet to get certain federal benefits, the terms included requirements that the organizations bear and manage risk.... This congressional understanding that it was promoting a novel form of insurance was made explicit in the Senate Report's reference to the practices of "health insurers to charge premium rates based upon the actual claims experience of a particular group of subscribers," thus "raising costs and diminishing the availability of health insurance for those suffering from costly illnesses." The federal Act responded to this insurance practice by requiring qualifying

HMOs to [use community rating], and it was because of that mandate "pos[ing] substantial competitive problems to newly emerging HMOs" that Congress authorized funding subsidies [for qualifying HMOs]. . . .

This conception has not changed in the intervening years. Since passage of the federal Act, States have been adopting their own HMO enabling Acts, and today, at least 40 of them, including Illinois, regulate HMOs primarily through the States' insurance departments, see Aspen Health Law and Compliance Center, Managed Care Law Manual, although they may be treated differently from traditional insurers, owing to their additional role as health care providers, see, e.g., Alaska Ins. Code §21.86.010 (health department reviews HMO before insurance commissioner grants a certificate of authority); Ohio Rev. Code Ann. §1742.21 (health department may inspect HMO). Finally, this view shared by Congress and the States has passed into common understanding. . . . While the original form of the HMO was a single corporation employing its own physicians, the 1980s saw a variety of other types of structures develop even as traditional insurers altered their own plans by adopting HMO-like cost-control measures. See Weiner & de Lissovoy, Razing a Tower of Babel: A Taxonomy for Managed Care and Health Insurance Plans, 18 J. of Health Politics, Policy and Law 75, 83 (Spring 1993). The dominant feature is the combination of insurer and provider, and "an observer may be hard pressed to uncover the differences among products that bill themselves as HMOs, [preferred provider organizations (PPOs)], or managed care overlays to health insurance." Managed Care Law Manual, *supra*. . . . Rush cannot checkmate common sense by trying to submerge HMOs' insurance features beneath an exclusive characterization of HMOs as providers of health care. . . .

On a second tack, Rush . . . [argues] that an HMO is no longer an insurer when it arranges to limit its exposure, as when an HMO arranges for capitated contracts to compensate its affiliated physicians with a set fee for each HMO patient regardless of the treatment provided. Under such an arrangement, Rush claims, the risk is not borne by the HMO at all. . . . The problem with Rush's argument is . . . that capitation contracts do not relieve the HMO of its obligations to the beneficiary. The HMO is still bound to provide medical care to its members, and this is so regardless of the ability of physicians or [other] third-part[ies] to honor their contracts with the HMO. . . .

Nor do we see anything standing in the way of applying the . . . general state definition of HMO [to] include a contractor that provides only administrative services for a self-funded plan. Rush points out that the general definition of HMO under Illinois law includes not only organizations that "provide" health care plans, but those that "arrange for" them to be provided. . . . Rush hypothesizes a sort of medical matchmaker, bringing together [employers] and medical care providers; even if the latter bear all the risks, the matchmaker would be an HMO under the Illinois definition. . . . Even on the most generous reading of Rush's argument, however, it boils down to the bare possibility (not the likelihood) of some overbreadth in the application of [the Illinois statute] beyond orthodox HMOs. . . . In sum, . . . HMOs have taken over much business formerly performed by traditional indemnity insurers and they are almost universally regulated as insurers under state law. . . . Thus, the Illinois HMO Act is a law "directed toward" the insurance industry, and [so is saved from ERISA preemption]. . . .

■ HEALTH MAINTENANCE ORGANIZATIONS*
*Michele M. Garvin***

This [reading] provides an overview of the health maintenance organization (HMO) model of care and the federal and state legal issues relating to HMO product development and operations. Unlike the traditional separation among hospitals, physicians, and insurers, HMOs combine the financing and delivery of care into a single integrated system. As a result of its hybrid role, an HMO faces legal and regulatory issues relating both to its "insurance" or financing function, and to its "provider" or delivery function.

HMO CHARACTERISTICS AND CONCEPT

At the end of [2000], over [80] million Americans, or roughly [28] percent of the United States population, received their health care through HMOs. While HMOs are currently considered to be part of the mainstream health care system and the cornerstone of various "managed competition" health care reform proposals, HMOs were a virtually unknown concept 20 years ago. [T]he term *HMO* emerged in the early 1970s, [but] its predecessor, the prepaid group practice model, has been in existence for a much longer period of time.... Federal policy and law during the 1970s and 1980s promoted HMOs as an alternative to traditional insurance. While government promotion of HMOs was essential in overcoming legal and market barriers to HMO growth, the long-term success of HMOs has been based on their ability to control medical costs and to manage care. HMOs have been able to attract members away from traditional health insurance plans by passing along cost savings in the form of lower premiums or expanded benefits.

The term *health maintenance organization*, first used by health policy analysts Paul Ellwood and Walter McLure in the 1970s, refers broadly to an organized prepaid health care system. HMOs are designed to deliver health care in exchange for predetermined monthly or minimal payments. Because they retain any leftover money, HMOs have an incentive to keep people well—thus the term *health maintenance....*

...HMO members are "locked-in" to the HMO provider panel, i.e., health services are covered only if HMO members receive care from the HMO's closed network of participating providers.... The "lock-in" feature of the traditional HMO model distinguishes HMOs from preferred provider organizations (PPOs) and HMO "point of service" (POS) plans. While PPO and POS products do not restrict the delivery of care to a specific provider network, these plans provide financial incentives (e.g., reduced payment or increased benefit coverage) to members to seek care from participating network providers....

In the contemporary scene, an organizer of an HMO faces [two] major decisions: what delivery system will be used in providing medical services to its

---

*This is an excerpt from Chapter 1 of Health Care Corporate Law: Managed Care (M. Hall & W. Brewbaker eds., 1996).
**Health law attorney, Ropes & Gray, Boston MA.

members, . . . and whether the HMO will seek federal qualification for any of its products. . . .

HMO MODEL TYPES

HMOs employ four basic organizational structures: the staff model, the group model, the independent practice association or "IPA" model, and the network model. In 1995, roughly 11 percent of HMO members were enrolled in staff model HMOs; 20 percent in group models; 50 percent in IPAs; and 19 percent in network models.

The main differences among the four models of HMO delivery structure arise out of variations in the plan's financial relationship with its participating physicians. Under the staff model, participating physicians are employees of the HMO and are paid a salary. . . .

Under the group practice model, the HMO contracts with an independent physician group practice and generally pays the group a monthly fixed per capita amount (capitation payment) for each HMO enrollee who selects a physician affiliated with the group as his or her primary care physician. The individual physicians are either employed by, or under contract with, the group.

In the IPA model, the HMO contracts either directly with individual physicians in independent practice, or with one or more associations of physicians in independent practice, and/or with one or more multi-specialty group practices. In those cases where an association represents the physicians, the association is generally organized as a non-profit corporation, although in some cases it may be organized as a stock corporation with physician shareholders. In either case, the corporation is referred to as an "Independent Practice Association" or "IPA." IPAs may be formed to facilitate contracting with a number of competing managed care plans or may be organized specifically for the purpose of participating in one particular plan. . . .

The IPA model differs from the staff and group models in several respects. It generally preserves fee-for-service physician reimbursement by paying participating providers according to a fixed fee schedule. However, the fee schedule is typically accompanied by a risk-sharing arrangement. Most commonly, a percentage of physician fees is withheld from payments otherwise due and is returned only if budgeted utilization goals are met. Because IPA physicians retain a significant fee-for-service practice, IPAs are generally slower than other forms of HMOs to adopt managed care principles. They seldom own their own facilities, with most physician members working out of solo or small shared office practices. . . .

A final model of HMO organization is emerging as a result of the recent pressure on hospitals to form closer affiliations with physicians on their medical staffs. The "joint venture" HMO model typically involves either the formation of a separate physician-hospital organization (PHO) that contracts with the HMO or a three-way contractual arrangement among a hospital, its staff physicians and the HMO. The physicians may participate in the venture either directly or through an IPA. The HMO generally pays the joint venture either on a capitated basis or under a premium-sharing arrangement. The extent to which the joint venture entity may assume financial risk directly will vary depending on state HMO and insurance laws. . . .

STATE HMO ENABLING ACTS AND LICENSURE REQUIREMENTS

State enabling statutes[2] authorize and regulate the establishment and operation of HMOs. These laws generally set forth rules governing HMO formation and licensure, benefit requirements, obligations to enrollees, quality assurance standards, financial solvency requirements, marketing and advertising requirements, and ongoing reporting and compliance obligations. In addition, state HMO laws confer specifically enumerated powers on both HMOs and on the state agency charged with their regulation.

Under many state HMO statutes, the commissioner of insurance and the commissioner of public health have dual jurisdiction over HMO operations, with the insurance commissioner exercising primary authority. Where dual jurisdiction exists, the department of public health usually regulates the HMO's quality assurance programs and medical components as well as certificate of need compliance.

JURISDICTION OVER RISK-BEARING NETWORKS

Increasingly, states are limiting the degree of financial risk that providers and provider networks may assume. For example, an individual provider that accepts capitated payments from an HMO assumes the risk that the care he or she must deliver will cost more than the capitation payments. Similarly, an intermediary, such as a physician hospital organization or an IPA, that contracts with an HMO on a capitated or other fixed price basis bears the risk that it will be unable to meet its obligations to participating providers. Under the laws of some states, entities that assume financial risk for the provision of health care services may technically be engaged in the business of insurance requiring licensure as either an insurance company or an HMO.

Capitation payments to providers are generally regarded as less problematic than arrangements with intermediaries because the risk that an intermediary will go bankrupt and leave providers completely uncompensated is removed. Even so, some states regulate capitated provider arrangements heavily. A Maryland attorney general's opinion, for example, found that a provider that accepted capitation payments was engaged in the business of insurance and was subject to licensure as an insurer. [A number of states] have developed specific licensure requirements for provider-based delivery systems that accept financial risk. The National Association of Insurance Commissioners [see n.2 supra] is also developing risk-based capital requirements for capitated delivery systems. Other states require HMOs to oversee the financial solvency of physicians or IPAs that accept risk and to develop solvency plans for these groups. California has recently enacted legislation limiting the amount of risk that capitated physicians may assume for services not directly provided by the physician in connection with point of service plans. . . .

For licensure purposes, some state regulators distinguish between entities that contract with licensed HMOs and indemnity insurers and those that enter

---

[2] Twenty-seven states have enacted HMO legislation based in whole or in part on the Model Health Maintenance Organization Act [developed by the National Association of Insurance Commissioners (NAIC). This is an advisory group composed of each state's chief insurance regulator.]. Most other states have enacted some other version of HMO enabling legislation.

into arrangements with self-insured employers. For example, the Ohio Department of Insurance permit[ed] HMOs and indemnity insurers to capitate PHOs because a regulated entity that is authorized by statute to accept risk is involved. In comparison, a PHO that enters into a capitated arrangement directly with an employer must be licensed as an insurer because all of the risk is transferred from the employer to the PHO....

FEDERAL QUALIFICATION

After several years of debate, Congress enacted the Health Maintenance Organization Act of 1973, which was intended to encourage the development of HMOs.... [I]t substantially reduced the then-existing legal and financial barriers to HMO development in three important ways. First, it provided for federal financial assistance, making available federal grants, contracts, loans and loan guarantees to HMOs that met certain qualification requirements ("federally qualified HMOs").... Next, the Act established the so-called dual choice requirement. Under this provision, any employer with 25 or more employees that provided employer-sponsored health insurance was required to make available at least one federally qualified HMO of each model type. The dual choice requirement expired in 1995....

...An HMO's status as federally qualified means that it has voluntarily complied with standards provided in the federal...Act and is thus entitled to certain benefits and privileges. With the elimination of the federal loans program and other federal benefits, the advantages of federal qualification may no longer outweigh the administrative burdens and product restrictions imposed by the HMO Act. However, many employers and consumers still consider federal qualification an important standard.

To become a qualified plan, an HMO must (1) offer a comprehensive minimum benefit package, (2) meet certain financial standards, (3) have a quality assurance system in place, (4) not impose preexisting condition limitations on members accepted for enrollment or refuse to re-enroll a member on the basis of health care status, (5) have grievance procedures, and (6) comply with community rating requirements.... In addition, federally qualified HMOs were required to offer preventive care and early childhood care benefits that were substantially more generous than those covered by the typical indemnity package at the time the Act was passed. Thus, HMOs were able to compete effectively on the basis of both benefits and price in the employer group market....

Prior to the 1988 Amendments, the federal HMO Act was perceived by employers and some HMOs as inhibiting new product development, primarily because of the benefit and rating requirements it imposed, but also because physician services could be provided by out-of-plan physicians only in emergencies or out-of-service area situations. The 1988 HMO Act Amendments allowed HMOs to begin offering both qualified and nonqualified plans as separate lines of business within the same legal entity. In addition, they permitted 10 percent of physician services to be delivered by out-of-network physicians.

As HMO market penetration increased, employers complained that, rather than saving money, HMOs were increasing overall health care costs. Employers observed that the employees selecting the HMO option tended to be younger and healthier than those selecting indemnity coverage. Because indemnity premiums are traditionally based on the claims experience of the covered population, many employers found themselves paying an increasingly higher premium for the indemnity group. In certain situations, the indemnity group represented a sicker population with a higher overall utilization of health care services than the HMO group. Moreover, employers did not realize a cost-savings attributable to the favorable claims experience of the healthy HMO population since HMO premiums were community-rated. In response to these concerns, the 1988 Amendments permitted federally qualified HMOs to adjust the community rate prospectively based on the group's anticipated utilization of health care, thus rewarding groups with more favorable utilization. . . .

CURRENT HMO REGULATORY ENVIRONMENT

HMOs are no longer an experiment in health care competition and cost-containment, but are instead part of the health care industry mainstream. As such, federal and state regulators are focusing increasingly on HMOs' financial solvency. As more people enroll in HMOs, there is greater potential for market disruption in the event of an insolvency. Moreover, as the health products offered by HMOs and indemnity carriers become increasingly similar, the justification for applying different regulatory standards has become less obvious. Further, states are reassessing utilization review practices and provider risk-sharing methodologies to ensure that HMOs or risk sharing providers do not inappropriately deny covered benefits and necessary care to HMO members in an effort to control costs.

Similarly, as HMO members have come to represent a greater portion of the insured population in a particular market, decisions to exclude certain providers from participation in the HMO's network have attracted increased attention. With many employers discontinuing indemnity options, providers without HMO contracts may be hard pressed to continue operating, and some employees may be concerned that their ability to continue to receive treatment from a particular provider or to choose a provider is being threatened. As a consequence, providers and consumers have sought passage of mandated provider or mandated benefit laws, so-called any provider (or freedom of choice) laws [which require HMOs to include any provider in their network who is willing to accept the HMO's standard payment and contracting terms], and fair contracting standards.

Notes: Regulation of Health Insurance, HMOs, and PPOs

1. *Components of Insurance Regulations.* As n.4 in *Jordan* outlines, the main requirements of traditional state insurance regulation are to maintain large capital reserves for solvency protection and to pay taxes on insurance premiums. States also regulate how insurers invest their funds, the content of insurance policies, the rates insurers charge, and whether insurers engage in fair business practices. See generally R. Jerry, Understanding Insurance Law (2d ed. 1996).

2. *Traditional Health Insurance.* Considering the reasoning in *Jordan,* how well do even conventional indemnity health plans fit the classic casualty insurance mold? Isn't health insurance mostly just a pooled financing mechanism for

predictable medical expenses rather than protection against unexpected catastrophic illness or injury? In short, is health insurance more like automobile liability insurance or more like the financing of automobile maintenance, purchase, and repair?

3. *Managed Care Entities.* HMOs and other "alternative delivery systems" embody to varying degrees the three main components of "managed care": restriction of providers; utilization review; and cost-containment financial incentives. For additional description, particularly of how the "gatekeeping" function affects consumers' access to specialists and hospitalization, see sections 3.D.2 and 3.E.3.

4. *Capitation Payments.* The most important difference between HMOs and traditional insurance is how providers are paid. Payment to both physicians and hospitals increasingly is taking the form of complex capitation and "withhold" formulae rather than simple salary:

> Here's how capitation typically works. Say an HMO has 100 enrollees, each covered by a $100 monthly premium. First, the HMO subtracts $20 from each premium to cover its administrative expenses—and pad its profits. It divide the remaining $80 equally between a physician group and a hospital. Of the doctors' $40 payment per member per month, $10 goes to the enrollee's primary care physician. The other $30 is pooled to cover specialty and inpatient care. Half of the doctors' entire capitated payment, $20, is set into a risk pool... to pay specialists for care as it occurs. Most groups reimburse specialists on a... modified fee-for-service basis, although some groups pay specialists on a capitated basis. The remaining $10 goes into a reserve to cover any unexpectedly high inpatient- or specialty-care costs. [Money left in these pools at year end is returned to the primary care physicians as a bonus, and the physicians make up any deficits.]...
>
> [The hospital's portion would amount to $48,000 per year (100 × $40 × 12).] In most capitated environments, the hospital could expect... 25 [in]-patient days per 100 enrollees. Given a cost of $1,000 per day, inpatient stays would eat up $25,000 of the hospital's risk pool. Outpatient care would account for another $12,000 of the pool, and out-of-area care $1,000 more. Thus the hospital figures on annual costs of $38,000 against a risk pool of $48,000. The hospital generally splits the resulting $10,000 bonus with the medical group as a reward to doctors for controlling utilization. Conversely, utilization could surge, saddling the hospital with annual expenses of $60,000. This deficit is also split with doctors, who pay for the loss out of the reserve pool they've established for inpatient care.

J. Johnsson, The Whys and Wherefores of Capitation, Am. Med. News, Dec. 6, 1993, at 31. See also T. Bodenheimer & K. Grumbach, Capitation or Decapitation: Keeping Your Head in Changing Times, 276 JAMA 1025 (1996); M. Gold et al., A National Survey of Arrangements Managed-Care Plans Make with Physicians, 333 New Eng. J. Med. 1670 (1995).

5. *HMO History and Legal Obstacles.* Precursors of HMOs can be traced all the way into the nineteenth century, mainly as industry-sponsored health clinics for employees. The most prominent early example is Kaiser-Permanente, which was started in the Pacific Northwest by industrialist Henry J. Kaiser in the 1940s to serve the many employees of his different companies. Blue Cross in its origins could also be characterized as an HMO since it was started during the Great Depression by a single hospital attempting to market its services through a prepaid

enrollment fee. Even today, the conventional Blues plans resemble HMOs in that they contract directly with providers rather than simply indemnifying subscribers. This structural similarity with HMOs is close enough that Blue Cross/Blue Shield enabling statutes proved to be another legal stumbling block for HMOs. Because the Blues were at first run by the medical profession and the hospital industry, state statutes usually required any nonprofit entity that sold comprehensive medical services on a prepaid basis to be controlled by hospitals and to include all providers in the community. Several courts declared these laws to be an unconstitutional delegation of public power because they gave the private medical establishment veto authority over HMO formation. See, e.g., Group Health Insurance v. Howell, 202 A.2d 689 (N.J. 1964). See Comment, Prepayment Health Care Plan Enabling Acts—Are Their Restrictive Features Constitutional?, 7 Duq. L. Rev. 125 (1968). HMOs were also hampered by the application of the corporate practice of medicine doctrine discussed in Chapter 4.B.1.

Following Group Health's victory in *Jordan*, it had to fight yet another legal battle, this time all the way to the U.S. Supreme Court. Fearing the effects of prepaid medicine on physician autonomy, the D.C. Medical Society organized a boycott of Group Health by threatening to expel its physicians from the medical society and from hospital medical staffs. The Supreme Court sustained a criminal indictment against the local medical society and the AMA under the antitrust laws. AMA v. United States, 317 U.S. 519 (1943).

Although HMOs often prevailed in these and other court challenges to their legal authority, the burden of defending against these pervasive inhibiting statutes and overcoming the persistent hostility of local providers deterred the formation of HMOs in many states until the modern enabling legislation. See generally R. Holley & R. Carlson, The Legal Context for the Development of Health Maintenance Organizations, 24 Stan. L. Rev. 644 (1972); Developments, The Role of Prepaid Group Practice in Relieving the Medical Care Crisis, 84 Harv. L. Rev. 887 (1971). Even then, HMOs continued to face the same opposition from physicians that was displayed in prior generations. Under market pressures, this hostility has given way to resigned acceptance in some parts of the country and open embrace in others. See John Iglehart, Physicians and the Growth of Managed Care, 331 New Eng. J. Med. 1167 (1994). See generally Lawrence Brown, Politics and Health Care Organization: HMOs as Federal Policy (1983).

6. *Modern HMO Regulation. Jordan* is included here primarily for its historical importance and to consider the fundamental nature of health insurance. Its precise holding is now legally moot due to the modern enabling statutes mentioned in *Rush Prudential*, which regulate both the insurance and the medical care of functions of HMOs. Typical are requirements that HMOs engage in provider credentialing, conduct quality assurance reviews, have an adequate array of physicians in their networks, and maintain various consumer protections such as grievance procedures.

7. *Consumer Protection, Provider Protection, or Industry Self-Regulation?* The modern HMO and PPO enabling statutes are sometimes criticized for continuing to impose restrictive policies under the disguise of consumer protection. As Professor Greaney explains, "Virtually every state has some law or administrative regulation that may impede bargaining or restrict an insurer's ability to channel patients to low-cost providers." T. Greaney, Competitive Reform in Health

Care: The Vulnerable Revolution, 5 Yale J. Reg. 179, 187 (1988). For instance, PPO "enabling acts" sometimes contain obstructive provisions that require PPOs to limit payment differentials between preferred and outside providers to the 20 to 25 percent range. A particularly controversial provision of these laws are "any willing provider" statutes mentioned by Garvin, which require HMOs to include any provider in their network who is willing to accept the HMO's standard payment and contracting terms. On the wisdom of any willing provider legislation, see Jill A. Marsteller et al., The Resurgence of Selective Contracting Restrictions, 22 J. Health Pol. Pol'y & L. 1133 (1997); Comment, 27 Cumb. L. Rev. 199 (1997); Comment, 45 U. Kan. L. Rev. 557 (1997). See generally Charles Weller, "Free Choice" as a Restraint of Trade in American Health Care Delivery and Insurance, 69 Iowa L. Rev. 1351 (1984).

Another round of debate over the proper bounds of state regulation has been provoked by an AMA legislative initiative known as the "Patient Protection Act," which the HMO industry characterizes as an "anti-managed care backlash." This initiative resulted in major enactments in 45 states. The legislation contains a multitude of provisions, many of which might be characterized as both patient protection and provider protection. In addition to the independent review process described in *Rush Prudential,* examples include (1) giving subscribers more information about how HMOs work (prohibiting so-called gag clauses), (2) requiring HMOs to include a PPO-type option that allows subscribers to go outside the network, (3) giving physicians procedural protections when they are excluded from the network, (4) requiring HMOs to pay for emergency care if a "prudent layperson" would have thought it was necessary to go to an emergency room; (5) allowing patients with chronic illness to have direct access to specialists, or women to have direct access to obstetricians, without going through the gatekeeping system, and (6) mandating minimum coverage provisions such as at least two days in the hospital following childbirth (prohibiting so-called drive-through deliveries). Frank A. Sloan & Mark A. Hall, Market Failures and the Evolution of State Regulation of Managed Care, 65(4) Law & Contemp. Probs. 169 (2002). The HMO industry responded with a call for voluntary adoption of various patient rights. President Clinton proposed federal legislation in 1998 based primarily on the consensus measures endorsed by the industry, but, as this edition went to press, Congress has not yet acted. The major stumbling block is the inability to agree on whether to impose tort liability on health plans for injuries caused by wrongful denial of coverage.

Commentaries, such as the following, see these laws as part of a more widespread and deep-seated "backlash" against the overreaching of managed care and market forces in health care:

> The managed care backlash represents the first stirrings of resistance to the profound uprooting and the destruction of [health care's market-based] transformation. The essential message of all the horror stories told by patients is the anguish of abandonment. The howl of doctors, nurses, and other caregivers is moral revulsion at the callousness they are forced to enact. Backlash is a cold shudder against the market paradigm, which taken to its logical endpoint as managed care seems to be doing, respects no human bonds, shows no mercy, and has no use for kindness, loyalty, and other moral qualities of community.

Deborah Stone, Managed Care and the Second Great Transformation, 24 J. Health Pol. Pol'y & L. 1213 (1999). For more on the managed care backlash, see Thomas Bodenheimer, The HMO Backlash: Righteous or Reactionary?, 335 New Eng. J. Med. 1601 (1996); Symposium, 24 J. Health Pol. Pol'y & L. 873-1257 (1999); Symposium, 16(6) Health Affairs 1 (Dec. 1997). Prof. Stone goes on to criticize these laws for catering to the interests of people with insurance and diverting attention from the plight of those with no insurance. A similar point is made by Prof. Havighurst, from the other end of the political spectrum. In a provocative essay, he argues that patient protection legislation is being driven by social "elites"—the portion of the public that is "most aware, affluent, influential, and politically active," supported by special interests such as physicians. Therefore, the standards set by this legislation "are designed to suit the preferences of the privileged minority and the interests of health care providers, thereby denying ordinary people the freedom to spend their limited incomes in ways that maximize their welfare." He sees this body of regulation as one of several "mechanisms through which the expensive tastes of upper middle class consumers are invisibly subsidized by persons with either lower expectations or less ability to command attention to their health problems." He concludes:

> It is especially objectionable for academic experts and self-styled "consumer advocates" claiming to represent the interests of all consumers to support the use of the judicial system and state power to deny fellow citizens alternative kinds of health care that would better meet their respective needs—not only for health care but for other things as well. To satisfy their own needs (including their need to demonstrate their symbolic aspirations for others), the political majority, other special interests, and elite movers and shakers of health policy are content to design things so that lower-income consumers have only a Hobson's choice—either pay the high cost of upper-middle-class medical care or go without any health coverage at all.

Clark Havighurst, The Backlash against Managed Health Care: Hard Politics Make Bad Policy, 34 Ind. L. Rev. 398 (2001).

Both sides of the debate over these laws are well represented in a series of articles: in favor of these laws, by Marc Rodwin, in 26 Seton Hall L.J. 1007 (1996), 32 Hous. L. Rev. 1319 (1996), and 15 Health Aff. 110 (1996); and against them, by David Hyman, in 73 S. Cal. L. Rev. 221 (2000), 78 N.C. L. Rev. 5 (1999), and 43 Vill. L. Rev. 409 (1998). See generally The Challenge of Regulating Managed Care (John E. Billi & Gail B. Agrawal eds., 2001); Eugene DeClercq & Diana Simmes, The Politics of "Drive-Through Deliveries," 75 Milbank Q. 175 (1997); Barry Furrow, Regulating the Managed Care Revolution: Private Accreditation and a New System Ethos, 43 Vill. L. Rev. 361 (1998); Russell Korobkin, The Efficiency of Managed Care "Patient Protection" Laws: Incomplete Contracts, Bounded Rationality, and Market Failure, 85 Cornell L. Rev. 1 (1999); Wendy K. Mariner, Standards of Care and Standard Form Contracts: Distinguishing Patient Rights and Consumer Rights in Managed Care, 15 J. Contemp. Health L. & Pol'y 1 (1998); Michael Misocky, The Patients' Bill of Rights: Managed Care under Siege, 15 J. Contemp. Health L. & Pol'y 57 (1998); Wm. Sage, Regulating through Information: Disclosure Laws and American Health Care, 99 Colum. L. Rev. 1701 (1999); Comment, 28 Cap. U. L. Rev. 685 (2000).

8. *The Federal HMO Act.* Similar concerns have been expressed about the obstructive effects of the federal HMO Act. Although it does not impose overt regulation on HMOs, the financial and legal benefits of "federal qualification" made compliance a practical necessity until recently. As Clark Havighurst explains, the result may have been to slow rather than spur the market strength of HMOs:

> HMO supporters fall into two distinct camps, with widely varying perceptions of the HMO and its role. The first camp, typified by proponents of the HMO Act, values HMOs as a model health care system, providing a large population with comprehensive services of good quality and plowing savings from efficiency in resource use back into improved accessibility, better care, and more extensive services.... To those who hold this view, the HMO model is a promising way to improve the quality of care and to extend more health care to people, particularly those whose health needs have not been well served....
>
> The other camp of HMO supporters responds to all of the positive quality and access benefits of the HMO, but sees as the cardinal virtue its cost consciousness and its consequent potential for restoring effective price competition, as well as quality competition, in the market for health services.... Supporters of HMOs as a new competitive force do not seek to obtain subsidies for them so much as to obtain freedom of entry and a market test from which might emerge a mixed system of fee-for-service providers and HMOs of many kinds, some emphasizing comprehensiveness and high quality and others offering somewhat lower quality, but adequate, care at less cost.

Clark C. Havighurst, Health Maintenance Organizations and the Health Planners, 1978 Utah L. Rev. 123. See generally Symposium, Is the Managed Care Revolution Finished?, 65(4) Law & Contemp. Probs. 1 (Autumn 2002).

Opponents of the new wave of state regulation enforcing patients' rights claim that these laws attempt to force HMOs to behave like traditional indemnity insurers. However, many or most of these provisions are ones that HMOs themselves had adopted, under market pressures or after finding that various cost-management strategies were not effective. See R. A. Dudley & H. S. Luft, Managed Care in Transition, 344 New Eng. J. Med. 1087 (2001); James C. Robinson, The End of Managed Care, 285 JAMA 2622 (2001). Robinson argues provocatively that because managed care has failed to meet market demands, the next generation of cost containment techniques will focus on greatly increased cost-sharing by patients.

9. *HMO Regulation of Provider Groups.* Although state HMO enabling acts eventually resolved the legal issue presented in *Jordan,* Garvin explains that the same issue is now being faced by provider groups that accept capitation or other forms of at-risk payment. Garvin gives several examples of state rulings on whether these risk-bearing provider groups constitute insurance companies or HMOs, thus subjecting them to solvency regulation. If so, then the capital requirements of forming such groups are vastly increased. Garvin points to one proposed compromise, adopted in Ohio and other states, which is to regulate providers when they assume insurance risk directly from employers but not when they contract "downstream" from other regulated entities. Another important distinction is whether providers are capitated mainly for services they render themselves, or instead

whether providers accept "global" capitation for a full range of medical services. Although the former can be viewed as a service contract that puts the provider at risk primarily just for time and effort, global capitation makes the provider financially obligated to purchase services from others that they are unable to render directly. Some states regulate only the latter type of capitation contracts. For additional discussion, see Edward B. Hirshfeld et al., Structuring Provider-Sponsored Organizations: The Legal and Regulatory Hurdles, 20 J. Leg. Med. 297 (1999); National Ass'n of Insurance Commissioners, The Regulation of Health Risk-Bearing Entities (Dec. 1996), reprinted at 6 BNA Health L. Rep. 73 (1997); Allison Overbay & Mark Hall, Insurance Regulation of Providers that Bear Risk, 22 Am. J.L. & Med. 361 (1996); Symposium, 23 Am. J.L. & Med. 449 (1997).

10. *ERISA Preemption.* These emerging issues are complicated even more by ERISA preemption. As discussed in more detail in the next section, ERISA broadly preempts any state law that relates to employee benefits, unless the state is regulating the business of insurance. *Rush Prudential* appears to hold that most types of state regulation meet the definition of insurance regulation, but one can never be sure how ERISA will be interpreted. Prior to *Rush Prudential,* several circuit courts had ruled that ERISA preempts state any-willing-provider laws. See Note, 101 Colum. L. Rev. 1107 (2001). However, in Kentucky Association of Health Plans v. Miller, 538 U.S. 329 (2003), the Supreme Court upheld the power of states to enact any-willing-provider statutes, under ERISA's insurance regulation savings clause.

11. *Empirical Evidence.* Deciding whether HMOs are the monsters or messiahs of medicine, and the appropriate degree of regulation or encouragement, should be influenced not only by their potential for harm but also by empirical findings on their actual performance. The following notes discuss these findings, first looking at cost containment, and then at quality of care.

12. *Do HMOs Save Money?* The cost containment record of HMOs has been rather subdued. They have succeeded in lowering hospitalization costs appreciably—as much as 40 percent in staff/group model HMOs—without a corresponding increase in outpatient costs. Robert Miller & Harold Luft, Managed Care Plan Performance Since 1980: A Literature Synthesis, 271 JAMA 1512 (1994). These cost savings have been largely absorbed, however, by the increased coverage benefits of HMOs. As a result, throughout the 1980s, HMOs engaged in what is known as "shadow pricing": tracking their prices close to traditional indemnity insurance so that prices increase at about the same rate. During the 1990s, competition from HMOs became much more aggressive in some parts of the country (notably California and Minnesota) such that they offered not only lower premiums but also experienced a lower rate of premium growth. Some markets saw substantial (5 to 10 percent) *declines* in HMO premiums and drastic new reductions (30 to 50 percent) in the use of hospitals. Skeptics responded, however, that HMOs achieved lower prices more through "biased" or "favorable" selection than through real efficiencies. HMOs are thought to attract relatively younger and healthier subscribers because their financial incentives and restrictions on choice of provider are unattractive to patients with chronic illnesses and established provider relationships, which causes "adverse selection" against traditional insurance. Consequently, lower HMO premiums may reflect simply an artificially lower-risk pool of subscribers. Fred Hellinger, Selection Bias in

HMOs: Analysis of Recent Evidence, 9 Health Care Fin. Rev. 55 (Winter 1987). The actual extent of this biased selection effect is still very much a subject of dispute, since the lower deductibles and copayments common in HMOs also tend to attract subscribers who expect substantial medical expenses. One recent study concluded that HMOs are cheaper than traditional indemnity insurance, but about half the difference is an artifact of HMOs attracting healthier people, and the other half is due to HMOs paying lower prices to hospitals and physicians, not to HMOs delivering less care. Daniel Altman et al., Enrollee Mix, Treatment Intensity, and Cost in Competing Indemnity and HMO Plans, National Bureau of Economic Affairs Working Paper No. W7832 (Aug. 2000).

In any event, HMOs are no longer showing impressive price advantages over other kinds of insurance, nor are they offering substantially more generous insurance. Instead, they are beginning to look increasingly like PPOs, with similar levels of cost-sharing but more options to go outside the network or to move within the network without gatekeeping controls. Traditional unrestricted indemnity insurance has all but disappeared from the market, except under Medicare and Medicaid. See Jon R. Gabel et al., Job-Based Health Insurance in 2001, 20(5) Health Aff. 180 (Sept. 2001). One disenchanted former executive in the managed care industry has this to say about the trajectory of HMOs:

> Conventional wisdom has it that managed care has failed to live up to all but its most brutal promises. Left in the rubble are bewildered consumers, disappointed employers, enraged patients, embittered physicians, and a raft of lawsuits. . . . What once looked like a permanent reduction in health insurance premiums—thanks to a onetime round of severe price competition among managed care organizations—turned out to be an anomaly, a momentary pause in their inevitable rise. . . . In the final analysis, most "managed care" really was "managed cost" all along—but it failed to accomplish even that goal, and the U.S. health care system is worse off for the experiment.
>
> Although it is easy and occasionally fun to pick on the bad manners and various hypocrisies of managed care, it is also unfair. The nation's managed care organizations were asked to do a job that simply cannot be done. . . . As a society, we expected managed care to fix, in a few short years, the disaster in slow motion that is the U.S. health care system. We asked large, organizationally complex insurance companies to reform a century's worth of self-serving professional habits, rein in ever-expanding consumer and patient demands, and fix dysfunctional economic behaviors—all while answering to the taskmasters on Wall Street every quarter. . . . Most of us believed that these insurance companies could do well financially by doing good medically. We were wrong.

J. D. Kleinke, Oxymorons: The Myth of a U.S. Health Care System, at xi (2001).

13. *Do HMOs Harm Quality?* "Reversing the financial incentives in the provision of health care would be dangerous to patients. . . . Incentives for economy can also be incentives for no care or inferior care. . . . The danger that HMOs will provide inferior care is particularly acute when the organization is a profit-making one, when the physician's compensation is based on a percentage of profit rather than a fixed salary, . . . when HMO enrollees have no alternative means of obtaining medical care, and when the HMO population is exclusively poor or aged." Sylvia Law, Blue Cross: What Went Wrong? 108-109 (2d ed. 1976). One notorious

instance of HMO abuse occurred with the California Medicaid program's experimental use of an HMO option in the early 1970s. Many of these Medicaid HMOs gave little or no care to enrollees and eventually declared bankruptcy after siphoning off large amounts of their revenue to related for-profit organizations. See David Chavkin & Anne Treseder, California's Prepaid Health Plan Program: Can the Patient be Saved?, 28 Hastings L.J. 685 (1977). Also discussing the problems of HMO underservice, particularly in government programs, see George Anders, Health Against Wealth: HMOs and the Breakdown of Medical Trust (1996); John V. Jacobi, Canaries in the Coal Mine: The Chronically Ill in Managed Care, 9 Health Matrix 79 (1999); Carol Jimenez, Medicare HMOs: A Consumer Perspective, 26 Seton Hall L. Rev. 1195 (1996).

Naturally, there is another side to the story. One reason for optimism about the quality of HMO care is that

> there are countervailing pressures against any tendencies to over-economize. Physicians face the threat of a malpractice suit. . . . Incentives for keeping the subscriber population healthy can be built into the method of rewarding physicians. And competition among pre-paid group practice plans, or between such plans and alternative delivery systems, also limits any potential trend toward unduly low hospitalization rates. Yet the strongest force militating against excessive economizing is the strongly imbued norms of practicing good medicine under conditions of strict professional review.

Developments, supra, 84 Harv. L. Rev. at 926. The HMO industry has developed its own, self-reported measures of quality to assist employers and subscribers in making wise insurance purchasing decisions. These "quality report cards," described at page 30, provide statistics in a comparable format about matters such as the rates of mammography and childhood immunizations, five-year survival rates after cancer, and patient satisfaction. How much confidence do you have that competitive forces will spur HMOs to improve their performance measures? Enough that you think they should be essentially self-regulated for the quality of medical outcomes, like hospitals? Would you expect these measures to be geared more to patients' interest in quality, or employers' interest in cost? See John V. Jacobi, Patients at a Loss: Protecting Health Care Consumers Through Data Driven Quality Assurance, 45 Kan. L. Rev. 705 (1997); William M. Sage, supra, 99 Colum. L. Rev. 1701.

A large and elaborate study by RAND confirmed that low-income enrollees are especially vulnerable in HMOs; those who were sick at the start of the study did worse (under some but not most measures of health status) than comparable patients in fee-for-service insurance. Joseph Newhouse et al., Free For All? Lessons from the RAND Health Insurance Experiment (1993). For most people, however, numerous studies have shown that patient satisfaction and the quality of care overall are as high or higher in HMOs as elsewhere. See id.; Peter Franks & Carolyn Clancy, Gatekeeping Revisited—Protecting Patients from Overtreatment, 327 New Eng. J. Med. 424 (1992); Joseph Gottfried & Frank A. Sloan, The Quality of Managed Care: Evidence from the Medical Literature, 65(4) Law & Contemp. Probs. 103 (2002); Robert Miller & Harold Luft, HMO Plan Performance Update: An Analysis of the Literature, 1997-2001, 21(4) Health Aff. 1 (July 2002); James D. Reschovsky & Peter Kemper, Do HMOs

Make a Difference?, 36 Inquiry 374 (2000); Symposium, 30 J. Leg. Stud. 527 (2001). The focus of research and concern now is whether patients do as well in HMOs when the patients are those who suffer from serious chronic illnesses that require ongoing expensive treatment, or from rare conditions that require unusually expensive drugs or special expertise that is not available in the established network.

HMO Regulation Quiz

The following questions can be answered simply and clearly by those who understand this complex area. See how you do.

1. Which of these is the better argument that, in the absence of explicit regulation, physician groups that are paid global capitation are not subject to general state insurance regulation?
   a. These groups are engaged primarily in the delivery of health care services.
   b. These groups do not bear substantial financial risk.
2. True or false:
   a. All HMOs must comply with the federal HMO Act.
   b. The main concern of both federal and state HMO regulation is financial solvency.
3. Which kinds of patients in HMOs are most vulnerable to poor quality of care?

C. ERISA PREEMPTION

Although the next case addresses a state statute governing a narrow aspect of health insurance, its focus is actually intended to be on the broad implications of the Employee Retirement Income Security Act of 1974, a federal statute better known as ERISA, which preempts state regulation. Although ERISA law appears quite technical and perhaps incidental to our main inquiry, it has vast importance for the structure of the health care market and the proper role of state and federal oversight. As one health law scholar has noted, "Although in its text 'hospital' appears only once and 'physician' not at all, ERISA may be the most important law affecting health care in the United States." William Sage, "Health Law 2000": The Legal System and the Changing Health Care Market, 15 Health Aff., No. 3, at 9 (Fall 1996).

As you read the first case, pay careful attention to what purpose ERISA serves, and how its complex preemption provisions are crafted and interpreted. The second case then clarifies what, if any, substantive regulation ERISA imposes in place of state oversight. Before you begin, read carefully the following statutory language that defines the scope of preemption:

> (a) Except as provided in subsection (b) of this section, the provisions of [ERISA] shall supersede any and all state laws insofar as they may now or hereafter relate to any employee benefit plan. . . .

(b) (2)(A) Except as provided in subparagraph (B), nothing in [ERISA] shall be construed to exempt or relieve any person from any law of any state which regulates insurance, banking, or securities. (B) Neither an employee benefit plan... nor any trust established under such a plan shall be deemed to be an insurance company or other insurer, bank, trust company, or investment company or to be engaged in the business of insurance or banking for purposes of any law of any State purporting to regulate insurance companies, insurance contracts, banks, trust companies, or investment companies. ...

(c) For purposes of this section, the term *state law* includes all laws, decisions, rules, regulations, or other state action having the effect of law, of any state.

Section 514 of ERISA, 29 U.S.C. §1144.

■ AMERICAN MEDICAL SECURITY, INC. v. BARTLETT
111 F.3d 358 (4th Cir. 1997)

NIEMEYER, Circuit Judge.

...This case presents the tension between Maryland's effort to guarantee through its regulation of insurance that employee benefit plans offer at least 28 state-mandated health benefits, and Congress' preemption, through ERISA [the Employee Retirement Income Security Act of 1974] of any state regulation that "relates to" an employee benefit plan.

ERISA is a comprehensive federal statute regulating [primarily private pension plans, but also covering other employee fringe benefit plans], including plans maintained for the purpose of providing medical or other health benefits for employees. To assure national uniformity of federal law, ERISA broadly preempts state law and assures that federal regulation will be exclusive. Section 514(a) provides that ERISA "shall supersede any and all state laws insofar as they may now or hereafter relate to any employee benefit plan" as defined by ERISA. The courts have interpreted this clause broadly to carry out Congress' purpose of displacing any state effort to regulate ERISA plans. See, e.g., FMC Corp. v. Holliday, 498 U.S. 52, 58 (1990) ("The preemption clause is conspicuous for its breadth"); Shaw v. Delta Airlines, Inc., 463 U.S. 85, 98 (1983) ("The section's preemptive scope [is] as broad as its language"). Thus, any law that "relates to" a plan is preempted by §514(a). ...

Although ERISA's preemptive scope is broad, the "savings clause" explicitly saves from ERISA's preemption those state laws that regulate insurance. See 29 U.S.C. §1144(b)(2)(A). At the same time, however, the "deemer clause" provides that state insurance laws are not saved from preemption if they deem an employee benefit plan to be an insurance company in order to regulate it. See 29 U.S.C. §1144(b)(2)(B); see also Pilot Life Ins. Co. v. Dedeaux, 481 U.S. 41, 45, 107 S. Ct. 1549, 95 L. Ed. 2d 39 (1987). Thus, a preempted law is saved from preemption if it regulates insurance, ... but at bottom, state insurance regulation may not directly or indirectly regulate self-funded ERISA plans. Accordingly, although plans that provide benefits in the form of insurance may be indirectly regulated through regulation of that insurance, plans that are self-funded or self-insured may not themselves be regulated as insurance companies even if the self-funded or self-insured plan purchases stop-loss insurance to cover losses or benefits payments beyond a specified level....

[Plaintiffs in this declaratory judgment action include three] Maryland employers sponsoring self-funded employee health benefit plans subject to ERISA. Each has purchased stop-loss insurance...to cover their plans' benefit payments above an annual $25,000-per-employee level, known as the "attachment point."...The employee benefit plans sponsored by these three Maryland employers contained substantially fewer benefits than the 28 mandated by Maryland for health insurance policies regulated by the Maryland Insurance Commissioner. The benefit plans sponsored by these Maryland employers did not, for example, include benefits for skilled nursing facility services, outpatient rehabilitative services, and certain organ transplants, all of which are mandated for inclusion in Maryland health insurance policies....

Stop-loss insurance provides coverage to self-funded plans above a certain level of risk absorbed by the plan. It provides protection to the plan, not to the plan's participants or beneficiaries, against benefits payments over the specified level.... Stop-loss insurance is thus akin to "reinsurance" in that it provides reimbursement to a plan after the plan makes benefit payments.

The state of Maryland regulates health insurance, requiring that health insurance policies afford at least 28 specified benefits.[2] Apparently not wishing to be subject to state-mandated health benefits, insurance companies and their ERISA plan clients have entered into arrangements under which plans self-fund benefits and purchase stop-loss insurance to insure themselves against benefits paid beyond designated attachment points.... [B]y absorbing a minimal amount of initial risk and insuring the remainder through stop-loss insurance, plans are able to provide health benefits of a kind or at a level different from what state law requires of [regulated] health insurance.

Recognizing that such arrangements bypass Maryland's regulations for health insurance and intending to prevent such arrangements, the Maryland Insurance Commissioner adopted regulations that require plans to absorb the risk of at least the first $10,000 of benefits paid to each beneficiary.... Justifying the regulation and explaining how low attachment points permit self-funded ERISA plans to bypass state mandates, the Insurance Commissioner stated in his order: "...The goal is obvious: As policies become available with attachment points lower than many deductibles, it became an increasingly attractive option to 'self-insure' a health plan, but to continue to shift the majority of the risk to the insurance carrier by purchasing 'stop loss' coverage." The regulations [that plaintiffs seek to declare invalid] accordingly provide that any stop-loss

---

[2] [Included in this list are: "(4) Inpatient mental health and substance abuse services...up to a maximum of 25 days per covered person per year in a hospital or related institution;...(10) Mammography services for persons ages 40 to 49 once every other calendar year, and for ages 50 and above once per calendar year;...(16) Chiropractic services up to 20 visits per condition per year; (17) Skilled nursing facility [and home health] services as an alternative to medically necessary inpatient hospital services up to a maximum of 100 days per year; (18) Infertility [and family planning] services...; (19) Nutritional services for the treatment of cardiovascular disease, diabetes, malnutrition, cancer, cerebral vascular disease, or kidney disease up to a maximum of six visits per year per condition; (20) Autologous and nonautologous bone marrow, cornea, kidney, liver, heart, lung, heart/lung, pancreas, and pancreas/kidney transplants;...(25) Pregnancy and maternity services, including abortion; (26) Generic prescription drugs...; (27) Controlled clinical trials....]

insurance policy with a specific attachment point below $10,000 is deemed to be a health insurance policy for purposes of Maryland's health insurance regulations and must therefore contain mandated benefits. . . .

In summary, on one side of the issue before us, the Maryland Insurance Commissioner seeks to take advantage of his right under ERISA's savings clause to regulate the business of insurance. And on the other side, the insurance companies seek to take advantage of ERISA's preemption and deemer clauses to remove self-funded plans from the reach of state insurance regulation.

III

We begin the analysis with the question of whether Maryland's regulations "relate to" ERISA employee benefit plans and thus whether they fall within ERISA's preemptive scope. A regulation relates to an employee benefit plan when it has a "connection with or reference to such a plan." *Shaw*, 463 U.S. at 96-97. The Maryland Insurance Commissioner wisely concedes that the regulations at issue do "relate to" ERISA plans. . . .

Even though Maryland's regulations relate to ERISA plans, they nevertheless may be saved from preemption if they constitute a law that "regulates insurance." . . . In determining whether a state law is one that "regulates insurance," it is not enough that it operate only on insurance companies or insurance policies. The regulation must regulate the business of insurance in the sense that the object of its regulation (1) "has the effect of transferring or spreading a policyholder's risk"; (2) "is an integral part of the policy relationship between the insurer and the insured"; and (3) "is limited to entities within the insurance industry." Metropolitan Life Insurance Co. v. Massachusetts, 471 U.S. 724, 743 (1985). [That decision held that a state may, consistent with ERISA, require health insurers to include certain mandated mental health benefits in policies they sell to employers.]

In this case, the Maryland Insurance Commissioner can well argue with respect to the first *Metropolitan Life* factor that the setting of attachment points allocates risk. Higher attachment points burden plans with more risk while lower attachment points increase insurance company risk. The Commissioner might also be able to argue successfully on the second *Metropolitan Life* factor that the regulations address a practice integral to the insured-insurer relationship. . . . This factor is, however, complicated by the fact that the intended, stated, and actual effect of the regulations is to reach the relationship between ERISA plans and their participants who are not parties to the insurance contract. The third *Metropolitan Life* factor is complicated in the same way. Although the state's regulation of attachment points is limited to entities in the insurance industry, the stated purpose of the regulations is also to reach the [employer]-participant relationship, a relationship which is outside the insurance industry. . . .

We recognize that the regulations are carefully drafted to focus directly on insurance companies issuing stop-loss insurance and not on the employee benefit plans themselves. . . . The state asserts a need for this regulation because, in its absence, the loophole would allow every self-funded plan to provide coverage for fewer health benefits than state law mandates for health insurance policies. It argues that absorbing a minimal risk is simply a sham to circumvent state insurance regulation, the area carved out by ERISA in which states may act. But in seeking to address this perceived loophole, the state in fact ends up regulating self-funded employee benefit plans that are exclusively subject to ERISA. In seeking to require self-funded plans to offer coverage consistent with state insurance law, Maryland crosses the line of preemption.... By aiming at the [employer]-participant relationship, Maryland law violates the ERISA provision that no ERISA plan "shall be deemed to be an insurance company... for purposes of any law of any state purporting to regulate insurance companies [or] insurance contracts." 29 U.S.C. §1144(b)(2)(B).

The state's fear that [employers] will circumvent state regulation and offer citizens too few health benefits is understandable. But to state that fear reveals that Maryland is really concerned, not with the business of insurance and its coverage of risks, but with the benefits that ERISA plans can choose to provide their participants and beneficiaries. No matter how understandable this concern may be, only Congress may address it, not the state of Maryland through its insurance regulations.... If a self-funded plan insured by stop-loss insurance having an attachment point of $5,000 provided no benefit for organ transplants, the regulations would either raise plan costs by including unwanted, state-mandated insurance coverage for organ transplants or convert the self-funded plan into a fully insured plan contrary to its preference. These effects impermissibly intrude on the relationship between an ERISA plan and its participants and beneficiaries....

When ERISA preempted state law relating to ERISA-covered employee benefit plans, it may have created a regulatory gap, but Maryland is without authority to fill that gap....

■ McGANN v. H & H MUSIC CO.
946 F.2d 401 (5th Cir. 1991)

GARWOOD, Circuit Judge.
...McGann, an employee of H & H Music, discovered that he was afflicted with AIDS in December 1987. Soon thereafter, McGann submitted his first claims for reimbursement under H & H Music's group medical plan...issued by General American, the plan insurer, and informed his employer that he had AIDS. McGann met with officials of H & H Music in March 1988, at which time they discussed McGann's illness. Before the change in the terms of the plan, it provided for lifetime medical benefits of up to $1,000,000 to all employees.

In July 1988, H & H Music informed its employees that...benefits payable for AIDS-related claims [are limited] to a lifetime maximum of $5,000.[3] No limitation was placed on any other catastrophic illness. H & H Music became self-insured under the new plan and General American became the plan's administrator. By January 1990, McGann had exhausted the $5,000 limit on coverage for his illness.

---

[3] Other changes included increased individual and family deductibles, elimination of coverage for chemical dependency treatment, adoption of a preferred provider plan and increased contribution requirements.

In August 1989, McGann sued H & H Music ... and General American under §510 of ERISA, which provides, in part, as follows:

> It shall be unlawful for any person to discharge, fine, suspend, expel, discipline, or discriminate against a participant or beneficiary for exercising any right to which he is entitled under the provisions of an employee benefit plan, ... or for the purpose of interfering with the attainment of any right to which such participant may become entitled under the plan. ...

29 U.S.C. §1140. ...

[I]n order to survive summary judgment McGann must make a showing sufficient to establish that a genuine issue exists as to defendants' specific intent to retaliate against McGann for filing claims for AIDS-related treatment or to interfere with McGann's attainment of any right to which he may have become entitled.[4]

Although we assume there was a connection between the benefits reduction and either McGann's filing of claims or his revelations about his illness, there is nothing in the record to suggest that defendants' motivation was other than as they asserted, namely to avoid the expense of paying for AIDS treatment ... no more for McGann than for any other present or future plan beneficiary who might suffer from AIDS. McGann concedes that the reduction in AIDS benefits will apply equally to all employees filing AIDS-related claims and that the effect of the reduction will not necessarily be felt only by him. ... He does not challenge defendants' assertion that their purpose in reducing AIDS benefits was to reduce costs.

Furthermore, McGann has failed to adduce evidence of the existence of "any right to which [he] may become entitled under the plan." The right referred to in the second clause of §510 is not simply any right to which an employee may conceivably become entitled, but rather ... *promised benefits*.

McGann's allegations show no promised benefit, for there is nothing to indicate that defendants ever promised that the $1,000,000 coverage limit was permanent. The H & H Music plan expressly provides: "Termination or Amendment of Plan: The Plan Sponsor may terminate or amend the Plan at any time or terminate any benefit under the Plan at any time." ... To adopt McGann's contrary construction of this portion of §510 would mean that an employer could not effectively reserve the right to amend a medical plan to reduce benefits respecting subsequently incurred medical expenses, as H & H Music did here, because such an amendment would obviously have as a purpose preventing participants from attaining the right to such future benefits as they otherwise might do under the existing plan absent the amendment. But this is plainly not the law, and ERISA does not require such "vesting" of the right to a continued level of the same medical benefits once those are ever included in a welfare plan. ... McGann's claim cannot be reconciled with the well-settled principle

---

[4] We assume, for purposes of this appeal that the defendants' knowledge of McGann's illness was a motivating factor in their decision to reduce coverage for AIDS-related expenses, that this knowledge was obtained either through McGann's filing of claims or his meetings with defendants, and that McGann was the only plan beneficiary then known to have AIDS.

that Congress did not intend that ERISA circumscribe employers' control over the content of benefits plans they offered to their employees....

ERISA does not broadly prevent an employer from "discriminating" in the creation, alteration or termination of employee benefits plans; thus, evidence of such intentional discrimination cannot alone sustain a claim under §510. That section does not prohibit welfare plan discrimination between or among categories of diseases. Section 510 does not mandate that if some, or most, or virtually all catastrophic illnesses are covered, AIDS (or any other particular catastrophic illness) must be among them. It does not prohibit an employer from electing not to cover or continue to cover AIDS, while covering or continuing to cover other catastrophic illnesses, even though the employer's decision in this respect may stem from some "prejudice" against AIDS or its victims generally. The same, of course, is true of any other disease and its victims. That sort of "discrimination" is simply not addressed by §510. Under §510, the asserted discrimination is illegal only if it is motivated by a desire to retaliate against an employee or to deprive an employee of an existing right to which he may become entitled. The district court's decision to grant summary judgment to defendants therefore was proper. Its judgment is accordingly affirmed.

Notes: ERISA Preemption; Mandated Benefits

1. *Does Any Law Not "Relate to" Employee Benefits?* When it was first enacted in 1974, ERISA law was the province of highly specialized tax attorneys. The general legal community only slowly came to realize the tremendous importance of ERISA preemption for health care law and policy. Owing to the broad "relates to" language,[1] the potential sweep of ERISA preemption is limited only by the bounds of one's imagination. In these materials, ERISA preemption has major impact primarily in three places (in addition to here): (1) malpractice actions against HMOs, Chapter 2.C; (2) contract claims for the denial of payment under health insurance, Chapter 4.D.2; and (3) state attempts to require employers to offer health insurance, page 344. But, ERISA preemption is capable of cropping up almost anywhere. Consider, for instance, whether the following are potentially preempted: physicians' contract actions against managed care plans that drop them from their networks; taxation of firms that assist self-insured employers in administering their health benefits; state laws that limit health insurers' or employers' subrogation rights when employees' tort awards include medical expenses. The answer to each is "potentially, yes" (with certain qualifications). See S. Law & B. Ensminger, Negotiating Physicians' Fees: Individual Patients or Society?, 61 N.Y.U.L. Rev. 1, 80-81 (1986) ("in this judicially constructed Alice in Wonderland

---

[1] This is somewhat an oversimplification, because ERISA preemption actually stems from two independent statutory sources, one explicit and the other implied. These materials focus on the explicit preemption language in section 514 of the Act, which affects primarily regulatory measures. However, courts have recognized an even stronger form of preemption, called complete preemption, emanating from section 502 (29 U.S.C. §1132), which gives the federal courts exclusive jurisdiction over actions to enforce rights under ERISA plans. Section 502 is the basis preempting the tort and contract actions discussed in Chapters 2.C and 4.D.2. Unlike the regulatory preemption in section 514, there is no "insurance savings clause" for the judicial preemption in section 502.

world, any state seeking to regulate insurers' arrangements with physicians or providers must be prepared to litigate claims of ERISA preemption").

In recent years, courts have begun to adopt a more limited interpretation of "relates to." The most notable example comes from New York State Conference of Blue Cross & Blue Shield Plans v. Travelers Insurance Co., 514 U.S. 645 (1995), which held that ERISA does not preempt a New York statute that requires hospitals to collect surcharges from patients covered by commercial insurers, but not from patients insured by Blue Cross & Blue Shield plans. These surcharges were used to reimburse hospitals for the costs of treating patients without insurance. Blue Cross patients were not charged because Blue Cross' premiums were already more expensive than commercial insurers, due to Blue Cross' policy of accepting both healthy and sick subscribers. The plaintiffs in *Travelers* argued that the New York statute was preempted by ERISA because it "make[s] the Blues more attractive (or less unattractive) as insurance alternatives and thus ha[s] an indirect economic effect on choices made by insurance buyers, including ERISA plans." The Supreme Court disagreed, holding that statutes that have "only an indirect economic effect on the relative costs of various health insurance packages" available to ERISA plans are not preempted by ERISA. The Court emphasized, though, that it still supports a broad reading of "relates to":

> [W]e do not hold today that ERISA preempts only direct regulation of ERISA plans, nor could we do that with fidelity to the views expressed in our prior opinions on the matter. We acknowledge that a state law might produce such acute, albeit indirect, economic effects, by intent or otherwise, as to force an ERISA plan to adopt a certain scheme of substantive coverage . . . and that such a state law might indeed be preempted under §514. But as we have shown, New York's surcharges do not fall into [that] category; they affect only indirectly the prices of insurance policies, a result no different from myriad state laws in areas traditionally subject to local regulation. . . .

In a subsequent decision, the Court found no preemption even though the financial assessment was imposed directly on clinics owned and operated by self-insured employers, since the tax applied generally to all health care facilities and did not target those sponsored by employers. DeBuono v. NYSA-ILA Medial and Clinical Services Fund, 520 U.S. 806 (1997). A possible maneuver that would greatly reduce the scope of ERISA preemption would be to focus more precisely on what is meant by an employee benefit "plan." If "plan" means only the employer's promise to purchase insurance, and not the insurance plan itself, ERISA might be construed to preempt only laws that target employers, not those that target insurers or other businesses. For instance, following the *American Medical Security* decision, Maryland legislators re-enacted the same law but with language that directs it only to insurers who sell stop-loss policies, and not to employers. Whether this avoids ERISA preemption is still unresolved. A few lower courts have adopted this position, but it has not yet been addressed by the Supreme Court. See, e.g., Washington Physicians Service Ass'n v. Gregoire, 147 F.3d 1039 (9th Cir. 1998) ("The mere fact that many [employers] choose to buy health insurance for their [employees] does not cause a regulation of health insurance automatically to 'relate to' any employee benefit plan—just as a decision to buy an apple a day for every employee, or to offer employees a gym membership, does not cause all state regulation of apples and gyms to 'relate to' employee benefit plans."). Cf. UNUM Life Insurance Co. of America v. Ward, 526 U.S. 358 (1999) (using a broad construction of ERISA's "relates to" clause in holding that ordinary common law rules of agency and contract interpretation relate to employer-sponsored disability insurance).

For further discussion of the possible implications of *Travelers,* see J. Brown, ERISA and State Health Care Reform: Roadblock or Scapegoat?, 13 Yale L. & Pol'y Rev. 339 (1995) (detailed analysis of which laws are preempted or not); Catherine Fisk, The Last Article about the Language of ERISA Preemption?, 33 Harv. J. Leg. 35 (1996) (criticizing the method of statutory interpretation applied to ERISA preemption); Karen Jordan, *Travelers Insurance:* New Support for the Argument to Restrain ERISA Preemption, 13 Yale J. Reg. 163 (1996) (detailed analysis of *Travelers* and its effects on contract and tort claims). See generally Donald T. Bogan, Protecting Patient Rights Despite ERISA: Will the Supreme Court Allow States to Regulate Managed Care?, 74 Tul. L. Rev. 951 (2000); Margaret Farrell, ERISA Preemption and Regulation of Managed Health Care, 23 Am. J.L. & Med. 251 (1997); Jana K. Strain & Eleanor D. Kinney, The Road Paved with Good Intentions: Problems and Potential for Employer-Sponsored Health Insurance under ERISA, 31 Loy. U. Chi. L.J. 29 (1999).

2. *The Insurance Savings Clause.* Broad ERISA preemption was intended to ensure uniform federal regulation of employee benefits. However, ERISA imposes substantive regulation primarily only on *pension* benefits, not on *welfare* benefits such as health insurance. For the latter, *McGann* illustrates that ERISA creates virtually no federal regulation to replace state oversight. Thus, but for the insurance savings clause discussed in *American Medical Security,* the health insurance industry would be virtually free from all state or federal law of any kind for the vast bulk of its business, namely, the portion sold as employee coverage. It appears that Congress did not realize it was creating such a regulatory vacuum, but subsequent lobbying by vested interests has precluded any alteration of the status quo. Daniel Fox & Daniel Schaffer, Health Policy and ERISA: Interest Groups and Semiprotection, 14 J. Health Pol. Pol'y & L. 239 (1989); Leon Irish & Harrison Cohen, ERISA Preemption: Judicial Flexibility and Statutory Rigidity, 19 U. Mich. J.L. Ref. 109, 111 (1985).

The extent of the legal void created by ERISA preemption depends on the scope of the insurance savings clause, which restores state authority. The three-point test applied in *Metropolitan Life,* which is discussed in *American Medical Security,* pinpoints only the most central core of insurance practice—risk spreading—and only when that practice relates directly to the policy holder. These two limitations exclude a broad array of important activity. In Group Life & Health Insurance Co. v. Royal Drug, 440 U.S. 205 (1979), the Court held that an insurance company's setting the amount it is willing to pay a health care provider does not constitute the business of insurance because it fails to meet either prong of the test. Similarly, in Union Labor Life Insurance Co. v. Pireno, 458 U.S. 119 (1981), the Court excluded from the business of insurance the process of verifying insurance claims, because it occurs only after risk has been transferred.

More recent decisions, however, have taken a more relaxed approach to this issue, one that uses a "commonsense" test for what is insurance regulation, a test that does not require that all three parts of the McCarran-Ferguson test be applied in a strict or rigid fashion. For instance, Rush Prudential HMO v. Moran, 122 S. Ct. 2151 (2002), found that a state law that permits an administrative appeal of HMOs' denial of coverage does regulate insurance even though it does not necessarily affect the aspect of insurance that "spreads a policyholder's risk." In Kentucky Ass'n of Health Plans v. Miller, 538 U.S. 329 (2003), the Supreme Court made a "clean break" from its previous reliance on the three-part McCarran-Ferguson definition of insurance regulation. Instead, it adopted the following two-part test to capture the ordinary meaning of insurance regulation: "First, the state law must be specifically directed toward entities engaged in insurance.... Second... the state law must substantially affect the risk pooling arrangement between the insurer and insured." See also UNUM Life Insurance Co. of America v. Ward, 526 U.S. 358 (1999) (common law rules regarding interpretation of insurance contracts regulate insurance if they are unique to insurance). For commentary, see Comment, 68 U. Chi. L. Rev. 223 (2001).

3. *Self-Insured Employers and the "Deemer Clause."* Although the *McGann* court does not stress this fact, H & H Music's conversion of its health benefits plan to a self-insured basis was critical to its success in court, because of the effect this has under ERISA of preempting state regulation. Most states, including Texas, require insurers to cover AIDS treatment on the same basis as other catastrophic diseases. Otherwise, it would be too easy for private insurers to slough off their highest cost subscribers onto the state Medicaid program. Although these laws clearly fall under the insurance savings clause (review the *Metropolitan Life* precedent discussed in *American Medical Security*), the "deemer clause" prevents them from being applied to self-insured employers. This sweeping preemption has encouraged more large employers to self-insure for health benefits. As a result, almost half of privately insured people are not protected by any form of regulation, state or federal. For additional discussion of the deemer clause and the complications created by stop-loss coverage, see K. Caster, The Future of Self-Funded Health Plans, 79 Iowa L. Rev. 413 (1994); J. Lenhart, ERISA Preemption: The Effect of Stop-Loss Insurance on Self-Insured Health Plans, 14 Va. Tax Rev. 615 (1995); Charles D. Weller, The Secret Life of the Dominant Form of Managed Care: Self-Insured ERISA Networks, 6 Health Matrix 305 (1996); Note, ERISA's Deemer Clause and the Question of Self-Insureds: What's a State to Do?, 67 Wash. U. L.Q. 291 (1989).

Elsewhere in its opinion, the court in *American Medical Security* clarified that ERISA does not bar states from regulating the solvency of insurers that sell stop-loss or reinsurance coverage. Solvency regulation of insurance falls squarely within the traditional boundaries of traditional statute authority, which is protected by ERISA's insurance savings clause. This raises the additional question of whether states can regulate hospitals and doctors that contract directly with employers on terms that mimic insurance. A self-funded employer, rather than purchasing reinsurance, might shift its risk to providers through capitation contracts. In such a case, most states believe they can regulate the providers for solvency to the extent providers are paid on an at-risk basis but not to the extent of their fee-for-service contracts. This position still remains largely untested in the courts, however.

4. *Mandated Insurance Benefits.* Notice the range of benefits that Maryland mandates private health insurance cover. Which of these mandated benefits are

compelled by broad public policy concerns, and which are open to criticism as responses to pressure from particular interest groups? The argument against these mandates is that state legislatures too easily succumb to special interest lobbying by provider groups, thereby increasing the costs of health insurance overall and pricing more people out of the market. Recall from the discussion above that, although states can force insurers to increase coverage, they cannot force employers to purchase it. One study estimated that, if all mandated coverage provisions were removed, 16 percent more small employers would purchase coverage. Jon Gabel & Gail Jensen, The Price of State Mandated Benefits, 26 Inquiry 419 (1989). However, another study refutes this finding, J. Gruber, State-Mandated Benefits and Employer-Provided Health Insurance, 55 J. Pol. Eco. 433 (1994), and when this was actually attempted in state demonstration projects, few small employers in fact took the bait because they found the cheap, "bare bones" coverage was not attractive enough. Families USA, No Sale: The Failure of Barebones Insurance (July 1993).

The same tensions exist at the federal level. In the Health Insurance Portability and Accountability Act of 1997, Congress struggled with how to make private health insurance more comprehensive and available, without making it less affordable. One provision of the Act requires that larger employers, including for the first time self-insured employers, who offer mental health benefits do so on parity with other benefits. Employers are not required to offer mental health benefits, but if they do so, those benefits cannot be subject to lower annual or lifetime limits than medical benefits. Out of concern that this might prompt employers to drop mental health coverage altogether, however, the law exempts employers for whom this mandate would result in increasing insurance costs more than 1 percent. See Brian Shannon, Paving the Path to Parity in Health Insurance Coverage for Mental Illness, 68 U. Colo. L. Rev. 63 (1997).

5. *Accidental Federalism.* Is there any sense or logic in the complicated pattern of state versus federal jurisdiction over the various aspects of health care finance and delivery covered so far in this chapter? Consider not only ERISA but also the HIPAA legislation discussed at pages 177 and 180, which regulates how insurers offer coverage to small businesses but not how this coverage is priced, and which creates a uniform federal law for privacy of medical information, among other things. For heroic attempts to make sense of, or improve on, all of this, see John D. Blum, Overcoming Managed Care Regulatory Chaos through a Restructured Federalism, 11 Health Matrix 327 (2001); Richard A. Briffault & Sherry Glied, Federalism and the Future of Health Care Reform, in Gregg Bloche, ed., *The Privatization of Health Care Reform* 49-81 (2003); Eleanor D. Kinney, Clearing the Way for an Effective Federal-State Partnership in Health Reform, 32 U. Mich. J.L. Rev. 899 (1999); Karen Pollitz et al., Early Experience with "New Federalism" in Health Insurance Regulation, 19(4) Health Aff. 7 (July 2000).

6. *A Path Through the Maze.* Let us recapitulate the complex analysis required to answer an ERISA preemption question: (1) ERISA's preemption clause is extremely broad because so many state laws "relate to" employee benefits. (2) The insurance savings clause would reinstate most relevant state regulation, except for the fact that it sometimes gives a narrow construction. And, (3) regardless, for reasons just explained, self-insured health benefits may never be subjected

to state regulation. The confusion surrounding this complicated scheme and the meaning of its various parts has deterred states from asserting more aggressive regulatory jurisdiction, even where that might be possible to do.

ERISA Preemption Quiz

The following questions are supposed to have clear, settled answers for those who understand this complex law. See how you do:

Due to ERISA preemption, are any of the following true? Why or why not?

a. States may not force employers to purchase insurance.
b. States may not require self-insured employers to cover mental health services.
c. States may not regulate the rates that hospitals charge (i) insurers and HMOs, or (ii) self-insured employers.

D. HEALTH INSURANCE COVERAGE

In the previous section, we made the transition from looking at who is covered by what types of insurance, to looking at which benefits are covered. This section explores the latter topic in much greater depth. We start by examining whether it is desirable or permissible to exclude some medical conditions or treatments by assessing which medical needs are most demanding and what treatments work the best. The public policy focus here is on how insurance contracts or statutes might be rewritten, and the legal focus is on disability discrimination. Then, we go on to look at how to interpret and apply insurance contracts and statutes once they are adopted, and how to appeal coverage denials.

As you read this section, realize that, in a world of limited resources, insurance cannot pay for all beneficial medical care that anyone might need. The problem, then, is which approach to limiting insurance benefits makes the most sense, and whether discrimination law allows sensible health care public policy to emerge from either market or political forces.

1. Rationing and Discrimination

■ **ALEXANDER v. CHOATE**
469 U.S. 287 (1985)

Justice MARSHALL delivered the opinion of the Court.

... Faced in 1980-1981 with projected state Medicaid costs of $42 million more than the state's Medicaid budget of $388 million, the directors of the Tennessee Medicaid program decided to institute a variety of cost-saving measures. Among these changes was a reduction from 20 to 14 in the number of inpatient hospital days per fiscal year that Tennessee Medicaid would pay hospitals on behalf of a Medicaid recipient. Before the new measures took effect, respondents, Tennessee Medicaid recipients, brought a class action for declaratory and injunctive relief in which they alleged, inter alia, that the proposed 14-day limitation on inpatient coverage would have a discriminatory effect on the handicapped. Statistical evidence, which petitioners do not dispute, indicated that in the 1979-1980 fiscal year, 27.4 percent of all handicapped users of hospital services who received Medicaid required more than 14 days of care, while only 7.8 percent of nonhandicapped users required more than 14 days of inpatient care.

Based on this evidence, respondents asserted that the reduction would violate §504 of the Rehabilitation Act of 1973 ... [which] provides: "No otherwise qualified handicapped individual ... shall, solely by reason of his handicap, be excluded from the participation in, be denied the benefits of, or be subjected to discrimination under any program or activity receiving Federal financial assistance." 29 U.S.C. §794. . . .

[The] major thrust of respondents' attack was directed at the use of any annual limitation on the number of inpatient days covered, for respondents acknowledged that, given the special needs of the handicapped for medical care, any such limitation was likely to disadvantage the handicapped disproportionately. . . . [T]he Medicaid programs of only ten states impose such restrictions.[4] Respondents therefore suggested that Tennessee follow these other states and do away with any limitation on the number of annual inpatient days covered. Instead, argued respondents, the state could limit the number of days of hospital coverage on a per-stay basis, with the number of covered days to vary depending on the recipient's illness (for example, fixing the number of days covered for an appendectomy); the period to be covered for each illness could then be set at a level that would keep Tennessee's Medicaid program as a whole within its budget. . . .

The first question the parties urge on the Court is whether proof of discriminatory animus is always required to establish a violation of §504 and its implementing regulations, or whether federal law also reaches action by a recipient of federal funding that discriminates against the handicapped by effect rather than by design. . . . Discrimination against the handicapped was perceived by Congress to be most often the product, not of invidious animus, but rather of thoughtlessness and indifference—of benign neglect. . . . For example, elimination of architectural barriers was one of the central aims of the Act, yet such barriers were clearly not erected with the aim or intent of excluding the handicapped. . . .

At the same time, the position urged by respondents—that we interpret §504 to reach all action disparately affecting the handicapped—is also troubling. Because the handicapped typically are not similarly situated to the nonhandicapped, respondents' position would in essence require each recipient of federal funds first to evaluate the effect on the handicapped of every proposed action that might touch the interests of the handicapped, and then to consider alternatives for achieving the same objectives with less severe disadvantage to the handicapped. The formalization and policing of this process could lead to a wholly unwieldy administrative and adjudicative burden. . . .

---

[4] As of 1980 the average ceiling in those states was 37.6 days. Six states also limit the number of reimbursable days per admission, per spell of illness, or per benefit period.

To determine which disparate impacts §504 might make actionable,...[we must strike] a balance between the statutory rights of the handicapped to be integrated into society and the legitimate interests of federal grantees in preserving the integrity of their programs: While a grantee need not be required to make "fundamental" or "substantial" modifications to accommodate the handicapped, it may be required to make "reasonable" ones....

[A]n otherwise qualified handicapped individual must be provided with meaningful access to the benefit that the grantee offers. The benefit itself, of course, cannot be defined in a way that effectively denies otherwise qualified handicapped individuals the meaningful access to which they are entitled; to assure meaningful access, reasonable accommodations in the grantee's program or benefit may have to be made. In this case, the 14-day limitation will not deny respondents meaningful access to Tennessee Medicaid services or exclude them from those services.

The new limitation does not invoke criteria that have a particular exclusionary effect on the handicapped; the reduction, neutral on its face, does not distinguish between those whose coverage will be reduced and those whose coverage will not on the basis of any test, judgment, or trait that the handicapped as a class are less capable of meeting or less likely of having. Moreover, it cannot be argued that "meaningful access" to state Medicaid services will be denied by the 14-day limitation on inpatient coverage; nothing in the record suggests that the handicapped in Tennessee will be unable to benefit meaningfully from the coverage they will receive under the 14-day rule.[22] The reduction in inpatient coverage will leave both handicapped and nonhandicapped Medicaid users with identical and effective hospital services fully available for their use, with both classes of users subject to the same durational limitation....

To the extent respondents further suggest that their greater need for prolonged inpatient care means that, to provide meaningful access to Medicaid services, Tennessee must single out the handicapped for more than 14 days of coverage, the suggestion is simply unsound. At base, such a suggestion must rest on the notion that the benefit provided through state Medicaid programs is the amorphous objective of "adequate health care." But Medicaid programs do not guarantee that each recipient will receive that level of health care precisely tailored to his or her particular needs. Instead, the benefit provided through Medicaid is a particular package of health care services, such as 14 days of inpatient coverage. That package of services has the general aim of assuring that individuals will receive necessary medical care, but the benefit provided remains the individual services offered—not "adequate health care."[23]...

Section 504 does not require the state to alter this definition of the benefit being offered simply to meet the reality that the handicapped have greater medical needs. To conclude otherwise would be to find that the Rehabilitation Act requires states to view certain illnesses, i.e., those particularly affecting the handicapped, as

---

[22] The record does not contain any suggestion that the illnesses uniquely associated with the handicapped or occuring with greater frequency among them cannot be effectively treated, at least in part, with fewer than 14 days' coverage. In addition, the durational limitation does not apply to only particular handicapped conditions and takes effect regardless of the particular cause of hospitalization.

[23] ...[W]e express no opinion on whether annual limits on hospital care are in fact consistent with the Medicaid Act....

more important than others and more worthy of cure through government subsidization. Nothing in the legislative history of the Act supports such a conclusion. Cf. Doe v. Colautti, 592 F.2d 704 (3d Cir. 1979) (state may limit covered-private-inpatient-psychiatric care to 60 days even though state sets no limit on duration of coverage for physical illnesses). Section 504 seeks to assure evenhanded treatment and the opportunity for handicapped individuals to participate in and benefit from programs receiving federal assistance. The Act does not, however, guarantee the handicapped equal results from the provision of state Medicaid, even assuming some measure of equality of health could be constructed....

We turn next to respondents' alternative contention...that all annual durational limitations discriminate against the handicapped because (1) the effect of such limitations falls most heavily on the handicapped and because (2) this harm could be avoided by the choice of other Medicaid plans that would meet the state's budgetary constraints without disproportionately disadvantaging the handicapped. Viewed in this light, Tennessee's current plan is said to inflict a gratuitous harm on the handicapped that denies them meaningful access to Medicaid services....

On the contrary, to require that the sort of broad-based distributive decision at issue in this case always be made in the way most favorable, or least disadvantageous, to the handicapped, even when the same benefit is meaningfully and equally offered to them, would be to impose a virtually unworkable requirement on state Medicaid administrators. Before taking any across-the-board action affecting Medicaid recipients, an analysis of the effect of the proposed change on the handicapped would have to be prepared. Presumably, that analysis would have to be further broken down by class of handicap—the change at issue here, for example, might be significantly less harmful to the blind, who use inpatient services only minimally, than to other subclasses of handicapped Medicaid recipients; the state would then have to balance the harms and benefits to various groups to determine, on balance, the extent to which the action disparately impacts the handicapped. In addition, respondents offer no reason that similar treatment would not have to be accorded other groups protected by statute or regulation from disparate-impact discrimination.

It should be obvious that administrative costs of implementing such a regime would be well beyond the accommodations that are required....As a result, Tennessee need not redefine its Medicaid program to eliminate durational limitations on inpatient coverage, even if in doing so the State could achieve its immediate fiscal objectives in a way less harmful to the handicapped....

■ WILL CLINTON'S PLAN BE FAIR?
Ronald Dworkin*
New York Review of Books, Jan. 13, 1994

Some critics deny that health-care rationing is really necessary: They argue that if the waste and greed in the American health-care system were eliminated, we

---

*Professor of Law, New York University.

could save enough money to give men and women all the medical treatment that could benefit them. But...the greatest contribution to the rise in medical costs in recent decades has been the availability of new, high-tech means of diagnosis, like magnetic resonance imaging and new and very expensive techniques like organ transplants and, on the horizon, monoclonal-antibody treatment for cancer....Many politicians and some doctors say that much of the new technology is "unnecessary" or "wasteful." They do not mean that it provides no benefit at all. They mean that its benefit is too limited to justify its cost, and this is an argument for rationing, not an argument that rationing is unnecessary....So we cannot...avoid the question of justice: What is "appropriate" medical care depends on what it would be unfair to withhold on the grounds that it costs too much. That question has been missing from the public debate....

For millennia doctors have paid lip service, at least, to an ideal of justice in medicine which I shall call the rescue principle. It has two connected parts. The first holds that life and health are, as René Descartes put it, chief among all goods: Everything else is of lesser importance and must be sacrificed for them. The second insists that health care must be distributed on grounds of equality: that even in a society in which wealth is very unequal and equality is otherwise scorned, no one must be denied the medical care he needs just because he is too poor to afford it. These are understandable, even noble, ideals. They are grounded in a shared human understanding of the horror of pain, and, beyond that, of the indispensability of life and health to everything else we do. The rescue principle is so ancient, so intuitively attractive, and so widely supported in political rhetoric, that it might easily be thought to supply the right standard for answering questions about rationing....

In past centuries, however, there was not so huge a gap between the rhetoric of the rescue principle and what it was medically possible for a community to do. But now that science has created so many vastly expensive forms of medical care, it is preposterous that a community should treat longer life as a good that it must provide at any cost—even one that would make the lives of its people barely worth living....

The rescue principle does have something helpful, though negative, to say about the other question of justice, which is how health care should be distributed. It says that if rationing is necessary, it should not be done, as it now largely is in the United States, on the basis of money. But we need more positive advice: What should the basis of rationing be? The egalitarian impulse of the principle suggests that medical care should be distributed according to need. But what does that mean—how is need to be measured? Does someone "need" an operation that might save his life but is highly unlikely to do so? Is someone's need for life-saving treatment affected by the quality his life would have if the treatment were successful? Does the age of patient matter—does someone need or deserve treatment less at 70 than a younger age? Why? How should we balance the need of many people for relief from pain or incapacity against the need of fewer people for life-saving care? At one point the procedures of an Oregon commission appointed to establish medical priorities ranked tooth-capping ahead of appendectomy, because so many teeth can be capped for the price of one operation. Why was that so clearly a mistake? We need a different, more helpful statement of ideal justice....

[A] more satisfactory ideal of justice in health care [is] the "prudent insurance" ideal. We should allocate resources between health and other social needs, and between different patients who each need treatment, by trying to imagine what health care would be like if it were left to a free and unsubsidized market [under transformed social conditions in which people were better informed and wealth was distributed more equitably]....We can speculate about what kind of medical care and insurance it would be prudent for most Americans to buy, for themselves, ...and we can use those speculations as guidelines in deciding what justice requires now—in deciding, for example, which medical tests and procedures are "necessary and appropriate."...Of course, any judgment about what most prudent people would do is subject to exceptions: some people have special preferences, and would make very different decisions from those many other people would....But it seems fair to construct a mandatory coverage scheme on the basis of assumptions about what all but a small number of people would think appropriate, allowing those few who would be willing to spend more on special care to do so, if they can afford it, through supplemental insurance....

HEALTH CARE RATIONING AND DISABILITY RIGHTS
Philip G. Peters, Jr.*
70 Ind. L.J. 491 (1995)

...Any criterion suggested for rationing health care will be controversial. The stakes are high and no popular or ethical consensus has emerged. But allocation decisions are omnipresent and their continuation is inevitable....Americans have never been willing to pay for all the health care that is of any conceivable benefit, nor are they likely to do so in the future. Unfortunately, the existing mechanisms for deciding who receives what care are blunt and often irrational or unfair, reflecting the influence of wealth, employment, habit, cost, and power....Common sense tells us to give priority to services that do the most good. As a result, an approach which would eliminate only the least beneficial or least cost-effective treatments has considerable potential appeal. It offers both the promise of maximizing health care outcomes from limited resources and the surface allure of scientific objectivity and nonpartisan neutrality....

But rationing the least effective care has a dark side beneath its veneer of objectivity. Any health care allocation scheme which attempts to maximize health care outcomes by giving priority to the most effective treatments has the potential to disfavor disabled patients and others, such as the elderly and the frail, whose quality of life is most impaired or whose conditions are most resistant to cure. As a result, the use of effectiveness criteria to allocate health resources may be challenged as violating society's commitment to equality in general, and to protection of those with the greatest need in particular.

The resolution of this conflict between efficiency and equality has dramatic implications for health policy....It arises whenever effectiveness or

*Ruth L. Hulston Professor of Law, University of Missouri-Columbia.

cost-effectiveness is used by health care providers or insurers to determine which treatments to provide or insure. Those instances range from bedside decisions by clinicians to macroallocation decisions by benefit plans about coverage of conditions such as AIDS, infertility, or mental illness. In each setting, allocations based on medical utility have the potential to disfavor some patients on the basis of their disability....

I. [EFFECTIVENESS MEASURES AND THE OREGON EXPERIMENT]

Health economists have worked for decades on methodologies for calculating both the effectiveness and the cost-effectiveness of health care expenditures.[11] Originally utilized to compare the value of different treatments for the same disease, these methods were later used to compare the cost-effectiveness of treatments for different diseases. Cost-effectiveness calculations have the appeal of incorporating outcomes research, patient preferences, and expected costs into a rational and potentially sophisticated scheme for maximizing health care outcomes from the available resources....

Theoretically, at least, calculating the effectiveness of a medical service is relatively straightforward. This calculation involves both an estimate of the likely outcomes and an assignment of value to those outcomes. The value assigned to an outcome is determined by the impact which the treatment is expected to have on a patient's quality of life. That value is then adjusted to reflect the probability and duration of the expected benefit.[12] The product of this calculus is a single unit which expresses the number and quality of additional years that the treatment is likely to confer. These outcome units have been called both Quality-Adjusted Life Years ("QALYs") and Well Years....

The theoretical value of these calculations cannot be overstated. They provide a common unit of measurement which permits treatments for different diseases to be compared on the basis of their expected benefit or their cost-effectiveness.[16] Using QALYs or their equivalents, comparisons can be made

---

[11] The history of Quality-Adjusted Life Years ("QALYs") is briefly described in John La Puma, Quality-Adjusted Life Years: Ethical Implications and the Oregon Plan, 7 Issues L. & Med. 429, 433-434 (1992) (expanding upon John La Puma & Edward F. Lawlor, Quality-Adjusted Life-Years: Ethical Implications for Physicians and Policymakers, 263 JAMA 2917 (1990)). American researchers initially derived the methodology from operations research in engineering and mathematics, using it in the health care setting to measure the tradeoff between survival and quality of life that is implicated by some treatment choices such as conservative care versus aggressive care. See id. The British, most notably Alan Williams, then borrowed the concept as a way of suggesting priorities in their national health care system....More recently, QALYs have been calculated for a number of treatments in the United States....

[12] ...Milton C. Weinstein & William B. Stason, Foundations of Cost-Effectiveness Analysis for Health and Medical Practices, 296 New Eng. J. Med. 716, 718-719 (1977).

[16] ...John Rawles includes several helpful illustrations of comparisons based on cost-effectiveness:

> For example, a patient with severe arthritis of the hip who is unable to work and is in severe distress scores a quality of life of 0.7.... His expectation of life of ten years is reduced to seven quality adjusted life years. Successful hip replacement, by eliminating disability and distress, restores 3 QALYs to his total, at an average cost of pounds sterling 750 per QALY.
>
> Another example is a patient with renal failure undergoing renal dialysis twice a week in hospital for a year. He is unable to work and suffers moderate distress with a quality of life

between such disparate treatments as AZT, autologous bone marrow transplants, infertility treatments, mammography screening, early CT scans for head pain, and heroic care for patients in persistent vegetative states. . . .

As the health economist David Hadorn has emphasized, reliable cost-effectiveness data will help health care providers minimize human suffering to the maximum extent possible with the resources society allocates to health care.[17] . . . Current insurance and clinical practices often make the same kinds of calculations regarding treatment value and cost, albeit in a more intuitive manner. . . . QALYs can help improve the process, making it more rational and, therefore, more just. . . .

QALYs may also help health decisionmakers to avoid what David Eddy has called "rationing by meat ax." By excluding the least effective treatments for conditions that ordinarily are covered by insurance, savings could be generated to fund more comprehensive coverage of treatments for conditions such as mental health that are typically excluded or restricted. Blanket restrictions on treatments for infertility or mental health, for example, could be replaced by narrower exclusions of only those treatments which are least effective.

In addition, the exclusion of whole groups of uninsured persons from programs such as Medicaid could be replaced by the exclusion of marginally effective care. Oregon, for example, replaced a Medicaid system in which a six-year-old child was eligible when a seven-year-old was not, in which pregnant women had coverage but other women did not, and in which single adults with children were covered but those without children or with a spouse were excluded. In its place, the state has instituted a system [described below] that provides protection for [all people below the poverty line] by prioritizing the treatments covered.[24] . . . This explicit attention to the difficult choices is in marked contrast to current practices, such as those of physicians who use neutral terms such as "futility" to mask intuitive judgments about the value of treatment to the patient. . . .

But measurement of medical effectiveness also presents serious methodological and ethical problems which must be surmounted before its use expands. The methodological problems arise both from the difficulty of obtaining adequate data about outcomes, benefits, and costs and also from predictable issues of study design. Problems of this kind contributed to the failure of Oregon's initial attempt to prioritize medical treatments entirely on the basis of net benefit. . . .

In order to calculate a treatment's medical effectiveness, analysts must estimate its probable outcome and then place a value on that outcome. Both steps could disfavor disabled patients. When outcomes are taken into account, patients

of 0.9. However, hemodialysis is life-saving, so every year adds 0.9 to the number of QALYs he would otherwise enjoy, at a cost of pounds sterling14000 per QALY.

John Rawles, Castigating QALYs, 15 J. Med. Ethics 143, 144-145 (1989).

[17] David C. Hadorn, Setting Health Care Priorities in Oregon: Cost-Effectiveness Meets the Rule of Rescue, 265 JAMA 2218, at 2225 (1991) (describing the original Oregon methodology and the modifications undertaken before submission to the federal government for approval). . . .

[24] Norman Daniels, Is the Oregon Rationing Plan Fair?, 265 JAMA 2232 (1991); David M. Eddy, What's Going on in Oregon?, 266 JAMA 417, 419 (1991). Compare the approach of Missouri, which spent nearly $1 million keeping Nancy Cruzan alive in a persistent vegetative state, while providing Medicaid for only 40 percent of its citizens below the poverty level. Leonard M. Fleck, Just Health Care Rationing: A Democratic Decisionmaking Approach, 140 U. Pa. L. Rev. 1597, 1611 (1992).

with preexisting disabilities, such as diabetes, cancer, or pulmonary disease, could be disfavored because they often have more difficulty fighting unrelated illnesses (comorbidity) than patients who are otherwise healthy.[36] For example, diabetes reduces the probable effectiveness of some treatments for serious heart ailments. Unchecked alcoholism, another disability, could interfere with the success of organ transplantation. . . .

In addition, seriously disabled patients could be disfavored when values are placed on treatment outcomes. For example, QALY use disfavors lifesaving care for patients who are expected to be disabled after treatment, because saving the life of a disabled person with an impaired quality of life will theoretically generate fewer quality-adjusted life years than saving the life of a person whose quality of life after treatment would be better. . . .

The chance that disabled patients will fare unfavorably in QALY calculations is further accentuated by the risk that the scales used to measure quality of life will unfairly underestimate the quality of life of disabled persons. This was precisely the federal government's criticism of the Oregon quality of life measurements. Yet, until the Oregon plan was submitted for federal government approval, no public attention had been called to the discriminatory potential of prioritization on the basis of medical effectiveness. Although the Oregon plan was vilified on other grounds (principally that only poor people would be asked to make sacrifices to help fund an expansion of health care coverage for other poor people),[43] virtually no public debate on disability rights had occurred. As a result, the Bush administration's rejection of the plan because of discrimination against patients with disabilities surprised most observers and caused some speculation that the administration had simply used the disability rights issue to derail a proposal which it found objectionable for other reasons. . . .

Oregon's initial ranking of treatments in May, 1990, was based on a pure cost-effectiveness analysis, but problems with that list[44] induced the Oregon

---

[36] See, e.g., David C. Hadorn, The Problem of Discrimination in Health Care Priority Setting, 268 JAMA 1454, 1457-1458 (1992) (noting poorer outcomes commonly associated with de facto disabilities such as severe diabetes or cancer); David Orentlicher, Rationing and the Americans with Disabilities Act, 271 JAMA 308, 310 (1994) (recognizing that patients with pulmonary disease are poor candidates for coronary bypass surgery). In another example, an HMO denied payment for a $170,000 liver transplant requested by an e-antigen positive hepatitis-B patient due to the high rate of reinfection of e-antigen positive patients and the liver shortage. Barnett v. Kaiser Found. Health Plan, Inc., Health Care Facility Mgmt. (CCH) ¶22,594 (N.D. Cal. 1993). The HMO's eight-member advisory board had concluded that transplantation was not an appropriate medical treatment for the patient's condition. The federal district court ruled that the HMO had not abused its discretion in considering this factor, even though transplantation might be the patient's only chance of survival. The disability rights laws were apparently not addressed.

[43] See, e.g., Alexander M. Capron, Oregon's Disability: Principles or Politics?, Hastings Ctr. Rep., Nov.-Dec. 1992, at 18, 19; Charles J. Dougherty, Setting Health Care Priorities: Oregon's Next Steps, Hastings Ctr. Rep., May-June 1991, at Supp. 1; Michael J. Garland, Justice, Politics and Community: Expanding Access and Rationing Health Services in Oregon, 20 L. Med. & Health Care 67, 69, 74-77 (1992); Hadorn, Setting Health Care Priorities, supra n.17, at 2224; Paul T. Menzel, Some Ethical Costs of Rationing, 20 L. Med. & Health Care 57, 62 (1992); W. John Thomas, The Oregon Medicaid Proposal: Ethical Paralysis, Tragic Democracy, and the Fate of a Utilitarian Health Care Program, 72 Or. L. Rev. 47, 51-52, 127-128 (1993).

[44] . . . In David Eddy's view, Oregon's inability to estimate accurately either costs or benefits precluded reliance on its initial list. Categories of services and outcomes were defined too broadly. For example, "trouble speaking" could range from mild lisp to mutism. Duration of treatment benefits was poorly differentiated. Cost data were incomplete or inaccurate. And the list generated serious

Health Services Commission to abandon that list and produce another one in April, 1991, using a more intuitive, multifactorial methodology. Nonetheless, considerations of effectiveness continued to play a crucial role . . . at three junctures. First, the Commission divided all treatments into one of seventeen different categories and then ranked these categories. A sampling of the categories illustrates the methodology: "acute fatal, treatment prevents death with full recovery" (ranked #1); "maternity care" (#2); "acute fatal, treatment prevents death without full recovery" (#3); "comfort care" (#7); "acute nonfatal, treatment causes return to previous health state" (#10); and "infertility services" (#15). These rankings gave priority to treatments which produced complete cures over those which ordinarily produce only partial recovery. In this way, the Commission retained a blunt measure of effectiveness in its ranking process. The Commission also considered cost-effectiveness as one of many factors used to create and rank these categories.

Second, the Commission used QALYs to rank treatments within the 17 categories.[51] Third and finally, the Commissioners reviewed the resulting list and adjusted some of the rankings using their "professional judgments and their interpretation of the community values." The Commissioners imposed a "reasonableness" test upon themselves, taking into account effectiveness and cost along with other factors such as public health impact, incidence of condition, and social costs. The result was a ranking of 709 treatments of which 587 were to be funded in the first year. . . .

[T]he Department of Health and Human Services ("HHS") announced that Oregon had been denied a waiver [of the usual Medicaid coverage requirements] because its plan violated the Americans with Disabilities Act ("ADA"). . . . HHS specifically identified two instances in which disabilities had been impermissibly taken into account: (1) the ranking of alcoholic cirrhosis of the liver (#690) below

---

doubts whether the values assigned to treatment outcomes, especially lifesaving treatments, had been accurately measured. David M. Eddy, Oregon's Methods: Did Cost-Effectiveness Analysis Fail?, 266 JAMA 2135 (1991); David M. Eddy, Oregon's Plan: Should It Be Approved?, 266 JAMA 2439 (1991).

Counter-intuitive rankings resulted from these problems. Reportedly, "burn over large areas of the body" scored the same as an "upset stomach." Michael Astrue, then-general counsel of the Department of Health and Human Services, was startled that treatments for ectopic pregnancies and appendicitis were ranked below some dental caps and splints for temporomandibular joint disorder. Michael J. Astrue, Pseudoscience and the Law: The Case of the Oregon Medicaid Rationing Experiment, 9 Issues L. & Med. 375, 379 (1994); see also Hadorn, Setting Health Care Priorities, supra n.17, at 2219 (suggesting that the results were the "inevitable consequence" of cost-effectiveness analysis). . . . Unwillingness to accept the implications of cost-effectiveness analysis, especially for the prioritization of noncritical care over life-extending care, may also partially explain the adverse reaction to this list. . . .

[51] Benefits were measured using Dr. Robert M. Kaplan's Quality of Well-Being ("QWB") sale. Using the results of a random telephone poll of 1,001 Oregon households in which respondents were asked to rank 23 symptoms and 6 levels of functional impairment, the Commission assigned a value to various states of health, such as requiring a wheelchair or having severe burns. The benefits associated with each treatment were then calculated by using the values for the various outcomes provided by the telephone survey and weighting those values to reflect the probability of their occurrence. Expected outcomes were ascertained by polling practitioners. Outcomes (such as death or return to former health) were estimated five years after treatment. Net benefit (QWB) scores were derived by comparing the QWB score without treatment to the QWB score with treatment. The Commission multiplied the expected QWB by the duration of the benefit (thereby obtaining a measure of quality-adjusted life years or QALYs). In most cases, duration was the patient's life expectancy.

other cirrhoses (#366) and (2) the ranking of extremely low birth weight babies (#708) below heavier babies (#22).

Oregon denied that it had violated the ADA, but nevertheless complied with HHS's demands. Approval was not granted until Oregon had eliminated quality of life data from its formal methodology and had abandoned the separate classification of alcoholic cirrhosis and low birth weight babies. In addition, the newly elected Clinton administration insisted that Oregon no longer disfavor infertility treatments. In March, 1993, the Oregon Commission approved a new list which was based first on mortality and then, as a tie-breaker, on cost considerations. It was then adjusted by the Commission to reflect community values, such as a preference for preventive services and a dislike for medically ineffective care. The plan took effect on February 1, 1994.

This exchange between Oregon and the federal government has dramatic implications for health policy. Oregon's capitulation has cast a shadow over similar endeavors by other states. In its wake, considerable confusion exists about the permissible role of effectiveness in allocating health resources.... Alexander Morgan Capron, an ... advocate of rationing, was ... dire in his assessment. "As some form of rationing is an inevitable part of all health insurance," he concluded, "the ADA roadblock to rational prioritization of services by their expected benefit should be of grave concern to us all."[70]

Was the federal government correct? Exactly what limits do the disability rights laws place on the use of effectiveness criteria? Answering these questions requires a basic understanding of the disability rights laws.

II. FEDERAL DISABILITY RIGHTS LAW

A. THE BASIC PARADIGM

Two federal statutes protect disabled individuals from improper discrimination in health care decisionmaking: The Rehabilitation Act of 1973 and the more recent Americans with Disabilities Act of 1990 ("ADA").... Although the ADA is much more detailed than the Rehabilitation Act and the wording of the various titles of the ADA are slightly different, the basic paradigm of the two federal laws protecting disability rights can be briefly summarized. Section 504 of the Rehabilitation Act bars discrimination by any program receiving federal financial assistance or any executive agency against an "otherwise qualified" individual with a disability "by reason of her or his disability." The ADA extends this prohibition against discrimination "on the basis of" disability to state programs and private entities that do not receive federal funding.[74]

Federal law defines disabled persons as individuals who have a "physical or mental impairment which substantially limits a major life activity," "who have a record of such an impairment," or who are "regarded as having such an impairment." The regulations list examples such as blindness, mental retardation, emotional illness, cancer, heart disease, and HIV infection....

[70] Capron, supra note 43, at 20.
[74] See 42 U.S.C. §12101(a)(14).

Because functional impairment may affect a person's qualifications for some benefits, the laws governing disability rights permit consideration of a person's disability if the condition legitimately affects that person's ability to meet the essential eligibility requirements. This basic structure is quite different from civil rights legislation governing race because race is presumed to be irrelevant.

While acknowledging that disabilities are sometimes relevant, Congress also recognized that their consideration would often result in the exclusion of disabled persons who could become qualified with modest modifications of policies or practices. To prevent this, Congress required that a reasonable effort be made to accommodate the needs of disabled persons before concluding that they are ineligible. By conferring on people with disabilities this right to affirmative assistance, Congress endorsed, at least in a limited way, an egalitarian approach to distributive justice which allocates extra resources for those persons with the greatest need.[83] . . . To summarize this basic paradigm, a disabled person is qualified to receive health benefits or services if, with reasonable accommodation, she is able to meet the "essential" or "necessary" eligibility criteria. . . .

When the issue is joined, as it was in Oregon, the statutory terms *essential* and *necessary* seem sufficiently elastic to permit courts to consider whether medical utility is a permissible basis for disfavoring disabled patients. In effect, courts would be deciding whether the objective of maximizing health outcomes is an "essential" program objective within the meaning of the equal opportunity laws. . . . HHS did exactly this in responding to the Oregon waiver request. . . . While the legal status of rationing based on effectiveness is still uncertain, underwriting exclusions based on anticipated cost have express congressional sanction. In the ADA, Congress authorized benefits plans to engage in "the legitimate classification of risk."[97] As a result, plans remain free to consider how various disabilities influence a person's risk of death or illness. This exclusion permits risk-bearing health plans (but not necessarily practicing physicians) to consider the anticipated cost of treating various disabilities. However, the statutory exemption for underwriting practices does not appear to sanction the use of QALYs or other measures of a given treatment's effectiveness. Unlike restrictions based on underwriting risks, eligibility restrictions based on effectiveness are not based on the risk of subscriber illness and its predicted cost. They are based, instead, on predicted outcomes. Patients whose care is relatively ineffective are not necessarily any more costly or financially risky than other

[83] As federal district court Judge Devine poignantly observed, this provision charts a course between the extremes of no assistance for overcoming disabilities (social Darwinism) and unlimited assistance. Garrity v. Gallen, 522 F. Supp. 171, 207 (D.N.H. 1981). . . . See Wendy E. Parmet, Discrimination and Disability: The Challenges of the ADA, 18 L. Med. & Health Care 331, 336 (1990) (describing the ADA as an entitlement program placed on the private sector); Peter M. Shane, Structure, Relationship, Ideology, or, How Would We Know a "New Public Law" If We Saw It?, 89 Mich. L. Rev. 837, 862 (1991) (describing the ADA as "social welfare legislation" and not simply an "antidiscrimination" law). . . .

[97] The ADA permits "underwriting risks, classifying risks, or administering such risks." 42 U.S.C. §12201(c)(2); . . . Bernard B., 528 F. Supp. at 132-133 (holding that an insurance company did not discriminate under §504 in choosing to exclude mental health benefits from a minimum coverage plan), *aff'd*, 679 F.2d 7 (2d Cir. 1982).

The restrictions must not be a subterfuge and, unless the plan is self-insured, must comport with state law. The exemption applies to any "organization covered" by the ADA which has a "bona fide benefit plan." This very likely includes publicly funded health plans which use underwriting calculations to predict risks and shape coverage. . . .

patients. . . . As a result, only the cost portion of cost-effectiveness analysis has clear statutory blessing, and even then only when it is part of an underwriting process. . . .

Until the courts rule on this issue, it is possible . . . that employers will be flatly prohibited from adopting health benefits plans that discriminate on the basis of disability for nonunderwriting reasons. . . . [To overcome this objection, employers and insurers will need to establish that] the use of effectiveness criteria is vital to the goal of maximizing health outcomes from fixed resources. . . .

■ THE OREGON HEALTH PLAN'S PRIORITIZED LIST OF HEALTH SERVICES
1995

THE FIVE TOP ITEMS

Line 1   *Diagnosis:* severe or moderate head injury, hematoma or edema with loss of consciousness.
        Treatment: medical and surgical treatment.

Line 2   *Diagnosis:* insulin-dependent diabetes mellitus.
        Treatment: medical therapy.

Line 3   *Diagnosis:* peritonitis.
        Treatment: medical and surgical treatment.

Line 4   *Diagnosis:* acute glomerulonephritis, with lesion of rapidly progressive glomerulonephritis.
        Treatment: medical therapy, including dialysis.

Line 5   *Diagnosis:* pneumothorax and hemothorax.
        Treatment: tube thoracostomy or thoracotomy, medical therapy.

THE FIVE BOTTOM ITEMS

Line 741   *Diagnosis:* mental disorders with no effective treatments.
        Treatment: evaluation.

Line 742   *Diagnosis:* tubal dysfunction and other causes of infertility.
        Treatment: in vitro fertilization, gamete intrafallopian transfer.

Line 743   *Diagnosis:* hepatorenal syndrome.
        Treatment: medical therapy.

Line 744   *Diagnosis:* spastic dysphonia.
        Treatment: medical therapy.

Line 745   *Diagnosis:* disorders of refraction and accommodation.
        Treatment: radial keratotomy.

SIX ITEMS NEAR THE 1997 CUTOFF LINE

Line 576   *Diagnosis:* internal derangement of the knee and ligamentous disruptions of the knee, grade III or IV.
        Treatment: repair, medical therapy.

Line 577   *Diagnosis:* keratoconjunctivitis sicca, not specified as Sjogren's
           syndrome.
           Treatment: punctal occlusion, tarsorrhaphy.
Line 578   *Diagnosis:* noncervical warts, including condyloma acuminatum and
           venereal warts.
           Treatment: medical therapy.
Line 579   *Diagnosis:* anal fistula.
           Treatment: fistulectomy.
Line 580   *Diagnosis:* relaxed anal sphincter.
           Treatment: medical and surgical treatment.
Line 581   *Diagnosis:*dental conditions (e.g., broken appliances).
           Treatment: repairs.

Notes: Rationing Insurance Benefits; Disability Discrimination; Cost-Effectiveness Studies

1. *The Scope of Disability Discrimination Laws.* The potential impact of disability discrimination law on many aspects of medical decisionmaking is only gradually coming to light. Elsewhere, these materials explore whether the ADA prevents physicians from refusing to treat patients infected with the AIDS virus, and whether hospitals can restrict the clinical privileges of HIV-infected physicians. See page 465. The main issues there are what constitutes a disability, and what is required by way of "reasonable accommodation." Here, the primary issue is what constitutes discrimination. You should take it for granted that many medical conditions qualify under the broad definition of "disability," not just stereotypical "handicaps." That being the case, it is difficult to arrive at an understanding of these statutes that would keep courts and agencies from micromanaging medical decisions and medical institutions. Observe how hard the *Choate* Court struggles simply to rule that a facially neutral restriction on coverage is not discriminatory. The *Choate* precedent has nothing to say, however, about coverage and treatment restrictions that target specific diseases and treatments. It is these restrictions whose legality is still very much in doubt. For instance, most commentators believe that the employer's restriction of AIDS treatment in the *McGann* case, page 227, would clearly violate the ADA and §504, and this is the interpretation that the EEOC has taken in a number of enforcement actions.

It is also important to realize how many activities and programs the discrimination laws cover. Section 504 covers government jobs, programs, and contractors. The ADA covers private entities. It is divided into several titles, each of which covers different realms of activity (employment, transportation, public accommodations). The most obvious application to private health insurance is through the employment title, since insurance is an employment benefit. It is also possible, however, to construe insurance as a public accommodation. The public accommodations title is usually thought of as requiring only physical access to places of business, but some courts initially interpreted this title to require businesses to design their products and services to accommodate disabilities.

Regarding insurance, this might mean that not only the refusal to sell insurance but also the terms of coverage would be subject to ADA scrutiny. Several circuit courts, however, have rejected this interpretation, holding instead that the public accommodations title was not intended to "require a seller to alter his product to make it equally valuable to the disabled." Doe v. Mutual of Omaha Insurance Co., 179 F.3d 557 (7th Cir. 1999). See also Parker v. Metropolitan Health, 121 F.3d 1006 (6th Cir. 1997) (en banc). As a consequence, courts have upheld caps of $10,000 on payment for AIDS treatment, when they are in insurance plans not purchased by employers (and therefore not subject to the employment discrimination portion of the ADA). See generally Sharona Hoffman, AIDS Caps, Contraceptive Coverage, and the Law, 23 Cardozo L. Rev. 1313 (2002); Jeffrey S. Manning, Are Insurance Companies Liable under the Americans with Disabilities Act?, 88 Cal. L. Rev. 607 (2000); Luke Sobota, Does Title III of the ADA Regulate Insurance?, 66 U. Chi. L. Rev. 243 (1999); Comment, 28 Am J.L. & Med. 107 (2002).

2. *Excluding Specific Diseases.* If disease-specific restrictions like those in McGann v. H & H Music, constitute disability discrimination under employer-based insurance, what about other more common, less objectionable restrictions? In *Choate* the Supreme Court cited approvingly a Second Circuit opinion holding that the limitation of mental health coverage does not violate §504. See also Modderno v. King, 82 F.3d 1059 (D.C. Cir. 1996) (disparity in coverage of mental health treatment is not disability discrimination; to rule otherwise would be "to invite challenges to virtually every exercise of the [insurer's or employer's] discretion with respect to the allocation of benefits amongst an encyclopedia of illnesses"). But what is the difference between AIDS restrictions and mental health restrictions? Could it be the fact that many mental health patients are not disabled, whereas all AIDS patients are? Then what about the exclusion of experimental cancer treatment? See Henderson v. Bodine Aluminum, 70 F.3d 958 (8th Cir. 1995) (denying expensive new therapy for breast cancer is potentially discrimination based on disability type where the plan covers this treatment for other cancers and there is evidence it works for breast cancer). But see Lenox v. Healthwise of Kentucky, 149 F.3d 453 (6th Cir. 1998) (no ADA violation in excluding coverage for heart transplants). See Jane Korn, Cancer and the ADA: Rethinking Disablity, 74 S. Cal. L. Rev. 339 (2001).

Are these distinctions made any easier by the Supreme Court's "meaningful access to benefits" test? Meaningful access to which benefits? To the particular item of treatment being sought or to insurance coverage generally? See Doe v. Chandler, 83 F.3d 1150 (9th Cir. 1996) (limiting welfare for disabled recipients but not for dependent children does not discriminate against the disabled because state may craft different benefits for different programs). Even if it is conceded that meaningful access exists at a threshold level, does this justify discrimination above the threshold? For an argument that these distinctions fail to adequately protect against disability discrimination through disparate impact, see D. Orentlicher, Destructuring Disability: Rationing of Health Care and Unfair Discrimination Against the Sick, 31 Harv. C.R.-C.L. L. Rev. 51 (1996). According to another law professor, "the ADA is an inadequate and even inept tool for resolving whether we should tolerate cost-conscious [insurance] policies" because its concepts are so poorly suited for articulating and understanding the underlying social policy debate. Mary A. Crossley, Medical Futility and Disability Discrimination, 81 Iowa L. Rev. 179 (1995). For additional discussion of ADA issues generally and in insurance coverage and medical care, see Alexander Abbe, "Meaningful Access" to Health Care and the Remedies Available to Medicaid Managed Care Recipients under the ADA and the Rehabilitation Act, 147 U. Pa. L. Rev. 1161 (1999); Mary Crossley, Medicaid Managed Care and Disability Discrimination Issues, 65 Tenn. L. Rev. 419 (1998); Mary Crossley, Becoming Visible: The ADA's Impact on Health Care for Persons with Disabilities, 52 Ala. L. Rev. 51 (2000); Mary Crossley, The Disability Kaleidoscope, 74 Notre Dame L. Rev. 521 (1999); Maxwell J. Mehlman et al., When Do Health Care Decisions Discriminate against People with Disabilities?, 22 J. Health Pol. Pol'y & L. (Dec. 1997).

3. *Medicaid Coverage.* Many of the decisions discussed below at pages 265-266 that require Medicaid to fund controversial procedures such as sex-change operations and liver transplants for former alcoholics are reasoned in terms of handicap discrimination, even though they are based on the Medicaid statute. They reason that the basic standard of rationality and nonarbitrariness required by the Medicaid statute prevents covering a medically beneficial treatment for some conditions but not for others. Therefore, Medicaid must either exclude the treatment altogether or selectively exclude it under generic criteria such as medically necessary or experimental. See, e.g., Salgado v. Kirschner, 878 P.2d 659 (Ariz. 1994) (unreasonable to cover liver transplant only for children; medically relevant factors, not age alone, should determine coverage).

Imagine that you are in charge of allocating limited government health care funds. Where, if anywhere, would you want to set limits? Would you fund a liver transplant for a patient whose recovery is only 50 percent certain? For a patient with only partial liver disfunction whose life is not at stake? For an alcoholic? Would you support lung transplants for cigarette smokers? Heart transplants for overeaters? If the legislature appropriated an additional $5 million to use at your discretion, would you choose (1) a large expansion in low-cost prenatal care, which would help decrease the high costs of caring for premature births, or (2) a few expensive organ transplants, or (3) some of both? Which of these decisions would handicap discrimination principles allow? On transplant funding issues generally, see Lisa Deutsch, Medicaid Payment for Organ Transplants: The Extent of Mandated Coverage, 30 Colum. J.L. & Soc. Probs. 185 (1997); Clark Havighurst & Nancy King, Liver Transplantation in Massachusetts: Public Policymaking as Morality Play, 19 Ind. L. Rev. 955 (1986); Schuck, Government Funding for Organ Transplants, 14 J. Health Pol., Pol'y & L. 169 (1989); Note, 79 Minn. L. Rev. 1232 (1995); Note, 89 Nw. U. L. Rev. 268 (1994).

4. *Actuarial Justification.* The analysis under the ADA is complicated by the specific exception in the Act for health insurance benefits. As Philip Peters indicates, however, this exclusion is limited to cost-based restrictions by insurers. (Ironically, Oregon dropped these legally defensible factors early on because of the political backlash from the public and from physicians.) Also, the protection of underwriting does not apply if a restriction is found to be a "subterfuge" for disability discrimination, for instance, if the purpose is to make the job unattractive for disabled workers. The EEOC's interpretive guidelines suggest that solid

actuarial justification is necessary to avoid a "subterfuge" characterization for disease-specific restrictions, and, moreover, that similarly costly conditions must be equally restricted. But see Leonard F. v. Israel Discount Bank, 199 F.3d 99 (2d Cir. 1999) (rejecting EEOC's interpretation of "subterfuge"). See generally Bonnie Tucker, Insurance and the ADA, 46 DePaul L. Rev. 915 (1997).

5. *"Fundamental Alteration."* Public and private insurers also have the potential defense, discussed in *Choate,* that removing particular coverage restrictions would be unreasonably costly or would fundamentally alter the nature of the product or program. This is the defense on which Philip Peters rests most of his justification for effectiveness analysis in the remainder of his article. (Additional excerpts can be found on the Web site for this book, www.health-law.org.) But this issue is also largely untested in the courts. In contrast with *Choate,* see Olmstead v. L.C., 527 U.S. 581 (1999) (finding a potential ADA violation where state Medicaid plan covered long-term hospitalization for mental illness but not less restrictive community placement options, and suggesting that it would not be a "fundamental alteration" to require the state to expand its coverage if doing so can be "reasonably accommodated" without straining the budget for other mental health services); Lovell v. Chandler, 303 F.3d 1039 (9th Cir. 2002) (finding an ADA violation where the state expanded eligibility for Medicaid up to three times the poverty level but excluded disabled participants from the increased eligibility parameters, even though the state said this was all it could afford). See Sara Rosenbaum, *Olmstead v. L.C.:* Implications for Medicaid and Other Publicly Funded Health Services, 12 Health Matrix 93 (2002).

6. *Race or Gender Discrimination.* Insurance restrictions can be challenged under other discrimination statutes besides disability. Suppose, for instance, that an excluded disease category has a disproportionate impact on blacks. Most commentators conclude that this alone is not sufficient without some indication of racial animus or subterfuge. More compelling, however, is the argument that a treatment exclusion has a categorical effect on only one gender. In Newport News Shipbuilding v. EEOC, 462 U.S. 669 (1993), the Court held that an employer violates Title VII's prohibition of sex discrimination by providing more generous pregnancy benefits to female employees than to the wives of male employees. See also Arizona Governing Comm. v. Norris, 463 U.S. 1073 (1983) (pension plans must be equal for men and women even though women's cost more because they live longer). Similarly, would the exclusion of fertility treatment such as in vitro fertilization constitute either gender or disability discrimination? Krauel v. Iowa Methodist Medical Center, 95 F.3d 674 (8th Cir. 1996) (no, because infertility is not always a disability, and plan excluded fertility treatment for both men and women). See Lisa Kerr, Can Money Buy Happiness? An Examination of the Coverage of Infertility Services under HMO Contracts, 49 Case W. Res. L. Rev. 559 (1999). D'Andra Millsap, Sex, Lies, and Health Insurance: Employer-Provided Health Insurance Coverage of Abortion and Infertility Services and the ADA, 22 Am. J.L. & Med. 51 (1996). For a related issue, see L. Dechery, Do Employer-Provided Insurance Plans Violate Title VII When They Exclude Treatment for Breast Cancer?, 80 Minn. L. Rev. 945 (1996); Christine Nardi, When Health Insurers Deny Coverage for Breast Reconstructive Surgery: Gender Meets Disablilty, 1997 Wis. L. Rev. 778.

Among the various controversies concerning what health insurance should cover, debates about contraception and sexual health have been especially lively, following the introduction of Viagra, the impotence pill for men. Viagra was easily covered by traditional health insurance because it addresses a physical dysfunction often caused by health problems such as heart disease or side effects from medication. However, Viagra is also prescribed in more discretionary situations to enhance sexual performance, especially among elderly men, for whom a decline in sexual vitality is an expected consequence of aging. Rather than drawing age-based lines or crafting sexual performance indicators that would be hard to defend or administer, insurers simply capped the number of Viagra pills permitted per month. (One wonders how they arrived at the cutoff.) See Alison Keith, The Economics of Viagra, 19(2) Health Aff. 147 (Mar. 2000). The coverage of Viagra highlights the inequities of not covering contraceptives for women, which are similarly important to sexual health. Because fertility is a normal condition, blocking fertility does not fit within the traditional insurance concepts of treatment for illness or disease. Nevertheless, many insurers have agreed to include contraceptive coverage, and some state legislatures have mandated the same. For a good overview of this debate, see Hazel Glenn Beh, Sex, Sexual Pleasure, and Reproduction: Health Insurers Don't Want You to Do Those Nasty Things, 13 Wis. Women's L.J. 119 (1998); David Chavking, Medicaid and Viagra: Restoring Potency to an Old Program?, 11 Health Matrix 189 (2000); Comment, 35 Tulsa L.J. 399 (2000). For an analysis from the perspective of sex discrimination law, see Sylvia Law, Sex Discrimination and Insurance for Contraception, 73 Wash. L. Rev. 363 (1998). For a constitutional analysis, see Note, 54 Vand. L. Rev. 451 (2001).

Civil rights discrimination statutes apply to government programs as well, under Title VI. These statutes have had less effect. A series of public interest lawsuits have attempted to block cities from closing public hospitals in low-income communities, finding that the disparate impact on minorities does not constitute prohibited discrimination. See, e.g., Bryan v. Koch, 627 F.2d 612 (2d Cir. 1980); NAACP v. Wilmington Medical Center, 657 F.2d 1322 (3d Cir. 1981). See generally Marianne Lado, Breaking the Barriers of Access to Health Care: A Discussion of the Role of Civil Rights Litigation, 60 Brook. L. Rev. 239 (1994); Sidney Watson, Reinvigorating Title VI: Defending Health Care Discrimination— It Shouldn't Be So Easy, 58 Ford. L. Rev. 939 (1990).

7. *Who Decides Medical Effectiveness?* Assuming fair and nondiscriminatory measures of medical effectiveness can be devised, who should apply them? Philip Peters' discussion of QALYs is purposefully somewhat abstract in this regard, because QALYs can be used by any number of decisionmakers to tailor medical decisions. Doctors can use them to trim costs incrementally at the bedside; employers, insurers, and the government can use them to limit the benefit packages they are willing to pay for; and courts can use them to resolve disputes over what those benefit packages actually promise. These notes are focused on the second set of decisionmakers. The two cases that follow focus on the courts. Physicians as decisionmakers are considered throughout these materials, including under informed consent, malpractice, and financial incentive payments. For a more overarching discussion of these themes, see Chapter 3.E.3.

8. *Medical Effectiveness Measures.* It is important to distinguish among ordinary medical effectiveness, cost-effectiveness analysis, and cost-benefit analysis. Ordinary effectiveness determines simply whether a medical procedure works at all or whether it works better than another for the same condition. Cost-effectiveness analysis asks how much it costs to achieve an increment in health improvement. QALYs were devised in order to have a common measure of health improvement other than simply number of lives or years of life saved. A generic unit of health improvement then allows comparisons between totally different treatments and disease conditions, such as determining whether prenatal care is a more cost-effective use of medical resources than are liver transplants. The comparative analysis can help determine the best use of limited funds, but it cannot tell us what total health expenditures should be, that is, whether to do *both* prenatal care and liver transplants, or *neither*, and instead spend the money on education or housing. If that decision is to be made quantitatively, it requires a cost-benefit analysis, which compares the cost of medical procedures with their benefit in terms of dollars. This is obviously much more controversial since it requires that a value be placed on human life and suffering. It is important to stress that none of the techniques surveyed by Philip Peters goes this far. They only ask, comparatively, whether one benefit is greater than another, not whether the expenditure is worth it at all.

For example, it has been estimated that the cost of administering Pap smears, which detect cervical cancer, is $12,000 per additional year of life expectancy for testing every three years and $930,000 for annual testing. Does this tell you conclusively which should be funded? Which would you choose as a patient paying out-of-pocket? As a gynecologist? As a Medicare bureaucrat? See N.Y. Times, Jan. 7, 1988, at 10, col. 1 (gynecologists and oncologists compromise by recommending testing every three years after a series of negative one-year exams). Are these decisions made any easier by comparing these cost-effectiveness ratios with those for other treatments? "[An] analysis compar[ing] the costs and outcome of heart transplantation with those of conventional care for congestive heart failure yield[ed] a figure of $23,000 [to $33,700] per added year of life [for heart transplants].... By comparison, in 1984 dollars, coronary-artery bypass grafting cost about $10,000 per added year of life, [and] hemodialysis for [kidney failure] about $32,000.... Treatment of [AIDS] costs about $140,000 per case." Cassells, Heart Transplantation: Recent Policy Developments, 315 New Eng. J. Med. 1365, 1366 (1986). See generally L. Russell et al., The Role of Cost-Effectiveness Analysis in Health and Medicine, 276 JAMA 1172 (1996). For broader discussions of the use of cost-benefit analyses in legal and regulatory settings generally, see Matthew Adler & Eric Posner, Cost-Benefit Analysis: Legal, Economic, and Philosophical Perspectives (2001); Symposium, 29 J. Leg. Stud. 837 (2000).

CMS has issued a long-awaited rule on criteria for deciding what treatments are covered by Medicare. 65 Fed. Reg. 31,124 (May 11, 2000). The rule says that cost-effectiveness criteria will be used to exclude coverage if an equally effective but cheaper option is available.

9. *Rationing Criteria.* QALYs are objectionable on other moral grounds besides disability discrimination. As discussed most forcefully by David Hadorn and John Harris, cited by Peters, the mathematics of QALYs mean that it is equally as valuable to save ten years from one person's life as it is to save one year of life for

ten people. This utilitarian logic does not fit most people's intuitions. See John Taurek, Should the Numbers Count?, 6 Phil. & Pub. Aff. 293 (1977). On the other hand, if we are to avoid use of rationing criteria that contain any controversial value judgments, we would have to adopt completely arbitrary rationing criteria such as a simple lottery, or treating whoever asks first. Most people would view these "neutral" criteria as even more irrational and objectionable. Einer Elhauge, Allocating Health Care Morally, 82 Cal. L. Rev. 1449 (1994). Prof. Gregg Bloche argues that health care law and policy is in a "confused, even chaotic state" because it assumes that medical resources can be allocated in a "systematically rational manner," which is not feasible or even desirable considering differing values, limitations on human rationality, and inconsistent understandings about what rationality means or requires. Instead, he urges an "inelegant" approach that "defines our aims more modestly, consistent with a picture of rationality as limited by context, discontinuous across different settings, and changeable with time." Gregg Bloche, The Invention of Health Law, _____ 91 Cal. L. Rev. _____ 247 (2003).

10. *Social Values.* Those who advocate more explicit rationing of limited resources usually object to the fact that our society spends too much on heroic, high-tech rescue efforts for those who are visibly threatened with death or disability at the same time that we neglect inexpensive preventive measures that would keep the situation from arising in the first place. This is known as the paradox of "statistical versus identifiable lives," or as the "rescue ethic," and it exists not only in medicine but in other social arenas such as traffic safety and high-risk recreational activity. If the thrust of this argument is to spend more on prevention, few would disagree, but if the thrust is to spend less on heroic measures, the argument is met with the following response:

> I will risk my life on the roads to do nothing more than secure a bag of potato chips, not to mention take the risk of eating them simply for fleeting gustatory sensations. But should I come up short in the potato chips v. life lottery, and suffer either a car or a cardiovascular accident, I do not expect society to respond by saying, "Well, tough luck, but you made an open-eyed trade-off here." No, I expect EMTs to rush to the scene and pound on my chest and speed me to the hospital in reckless disregard of the laws set down to reduce the risk faced by other travelers in search of potato chips and other goods. This social response, I am suggesting, can be seen as a way of marking the fact that our lives are shot through with incommensurable values, and that we have to wind our way through them in a way that does its best to acknowledge their separate significance.

J. L. Nelson, Publicity and Pricelessness: Grassroots Decisionmaking and Justice in Rationing, 19 J. Med. & Phil. 333 (1994). In a similar vein, Calabresi and Bobbitt explain that rationing is more socially acceptable when the tragic choices are hidden from view, as they are when the harms are merely statistical, than when identifiable victims of rationing can clearly be seen. G. Calabresi & P. Bobbitt, Tragic Choices (1978). Does this suggest to you that we satisfy a social value when we spend much more on rescues than on prevention, or does it mean that social policy is wrong?

11. *Kidney Dialysis.* Health care rationing issues first came to the public's attention when kidney dialysis was developed in the late 1960s. Moved by the

plight of patients dying from kidney failure who could not afford this expensive treatment, Congress in 1973 expanded Medicare to cover virtually all costs for dialysis (and later for kidney transplants), for anyone afflicted with "end stage renal disease" (ESRD), i.e., kidney failure—regardless of whether they were elderly or disabled. This is the only time Congress has enacted a disease-specific insurance program, and may well be the last time. Congress drastically underestimated the costs of this program, which now runs several billion dollars a year and has spawned a huge industry in dialysis clinics. In contrast, British doctors, because of severe overall funding limits, generally do not order dialysis for older patients and those with other serious illnesses. See generally J. Iglehart, The End Stage Renal Disease Program, 328 New Eng. J. Med. 366 (1993); H.B. Southern, Medicare's End-Stage Renal Disease Program: Its Development and Implications of Health Care Policy, 26 Harv. J. Leg. 225 (1989); Note, 26 Harv. J. Leg. 225 (1989).

12. *Oregon's Rationing List.* It is fascinating to observe how Oregon's bold approach actually functioned when implemented in real-world settings. Subsequent evaluation reveals that the list has not generated substantial savings. Many of the items eliminated from funding are fairly "small ticket," are requested only rarely, or were not covered in the first place. In other instances, physicians have been able to obtain coverage by recharacterizing the patient's condition as being more serious. Also, many Oregon Medicaid patients are covered by HMOs in which physicians are paid a capitation payment rather than fee-for-service, so physicians often provide the service even when they are not required to if it is relatively inexpensive. Accordingly, Oregon's expansion of Medicaid eligibility has been financed mostly by increased taxation and legislative appropriations, not by savings from The List. The main impact of the list, according to the following reviews, is its use as a political tool to secure more funds from the legislature. Lawrence Jacobs et al., The Oregon Health Plan and the Political Paradox of Rationing: What Advocates and Critics Have Claimed and What Oregon Did, 24 J. Health Pol. Pol'y & L. 161 (1999); Howard M. Leichter, Oregon's Bold Experiment: Whatever Happened to Rationing?, 24 J. Health Pol. Pol'y & L. 151 (1999). Another study, however, found that more than 12 percent of Oregon Medicaid recipients have been denied a needed medical service due to the rationing list. Half of these people managed to get the service in any event, either by paying for it themselves or by receiving charity care. On balance, Oregon's Medicaid recipients were found to be as satisfied with their health care and to have better access to care than other low-income people who had private insurance. Janet B. Mitchell & Fred Bentley, Impact of Oregon's Priority List on Medicaid Beneficiaries, 57 Med. Care Res. & Rev. 216 (2000). For further discussion of the Oregon scheme and the legality of QALYs under the ADA, see Kevin P. Quinn, Viewing Health Care as a Common Good: Looking Beyond Political Liberalism, 73 S. Cal. L. Rev. 277 (2000); W. John Thomas, The Oregon Medicaid Proposal: Ethical Paralysis, Tragic Democracy, and the Fate of a Utilitarian Health Care Program, 72 Or. L. Rev. 47, 135-145 (1993); Note, 83 Geo. L.J. 2697 (1995); Comment, 31 Houston L. Rev. 265 (1994); Note, 93 Colum. L. Rev. 1985 (1993); Note, 106 Harv. L. Rev. 1296 (1993); Symposium, 1 Health Matrix 135 (1991).

13. *Additional Readings on Rationing.* It is impossible to overemphasize the importance of health care rationing as an aspect of health law and policy. Other aspects of this issue, perhaps the most perplexing of the health care policy issues of our time, are explored in Chapter 1.D.5. For further elaboration of moral and public policy objections to QALYs and other criteria for rationing, see Larry Churchill, Rationing Health Care in America (1987); Frances Kamm, Morality and Mortality (1993); John Kilner, Who Lives? Who Dies? (1990); Paul Menzel, Strong Medicine: The Ethical Rationing of Health Care (1990); Eric Rakowski, Taking and Saving Lives, 93 Colum. L. Rev. 1063 (1993).

Problem: Allocation Choices in a Public Program

You are CEO of a municipal hospital, funded by the county, looking at next year's budget. This forces you to make tough allocation decisions. Due to your brilliant administrative leadership, the hospital managed to treat all patients who requested service last year, and it still has a $5 million surplus left over. After receiving recommendations from a task force, you have to choose among these three options:

> (1) Return the money to the county to help them avoid an anticipated property tax increase.
> (2) Buy one Very Big Fancy Machine (VBFM), which, over the course of its five-year useful life, will treat 100 patients a year, with a 1 percent better chance of saving their life compared with existing technologies. In other words, the machine is expected to save five lives at a cost of $1 million/life. On average, each person saved will live for ten more years. (Imagine a machine that helps resuscitate patients in the emergency room.)
> (3) Buy 5,000 Really Simple Little Things (RSLTs), which have a 1 percent chance to extend life one year for each person who uses one. In other words, this will provide one additional year for 50 people, at a cost of $100,000 per person. (Imagine an expensive drug that does a better job of delaying but not avoiding death from cancer.)

Now, suppose you learn that patients treated with the VBFM will be left bed ridden and debilitated but fully conscious, whereas RSLT patients are left ambulatory but in pain and with diminished mental capacities. Unfettered by the ADA, (since it applies to public hospitals) what do you do? Does the ADA potentially force you to change your mind? What factors determine what effect the ADA might have?

2. Determining What Is Medically Appropriate

Once insurance language is written, disputes do not disappear. We still must decide which treatments are actually covered by insurance in effect. The main readings view these issues from a more substantive perspective, and the following notes take a more procedural look. The focus in the main readings is on private insurance; the notes include public programs as well. Regardless, the issues remain essentially the same throughout: who should decide what is medically appropriate, and according to what criteria?

■ MOUNT SINAI HOSPITAL v. ZOREK
271 N.Y.S.2d 1012 (N.Y. Civ. Ct. 1966)

GREENFIELD, Judge.

One of the most celebrated trials of our literature was the confrontation of Portia and Shylock as they struggled with the problem of the removal of a pound of flesh. Now, once again, the removal of a pound of flesh, or more properly several pounds, has created a weighty legal problem for resolution by the court.

The hopes, despairs, and conflicts of our time, and ultimately every crisis, custom and social neurosis find reflection in the matters brought before the courts, the great mirror of our society. While not of the same magnitude as wars, depressions or the disasters of nature, the problem of obesity has persistently troubled part of mankind, but even more of womankind, ever since man first eked out more than the marginal subsistence required for bare survival, accumulated the luxury of a surplus food supply, and began to live to eat instead of eating to live.

With the plump and fleshy females portrayed by Rubens no longer in vogue, having been supplanted by the ideal of the lithe and willowy high-cheekboned model, the plight of those women whose rotundity does not conform to the ideal has been accentuated. The plaintiff cry "O! that this too too solid flesh would melt Thaw and resolve itself into a dew" is re-echoed today by the plump and portly, and has evoked a burgeoning and varied response from Elizabeth Arden, reducing pills, milk farms, steam baths and slenderizers to No-Cal and the Drinking Man's Diet.

Grace, felicity and beauty are qualities ardently sought after—but aesthetic considerations aside, excess avoirdupois also creates problems of health, vigor, longevity, hygiene and a general state of well-being that call for the arts of the medical practitioner. Obesity is definitely a medical problem. The correlation between overweight and a shortened life-span has been amply demonstrated. What a challenge to a medical Michelangelo, to liberate from beneath mountains of flesh the slender, sylphlike creature yearning to be free!

Doctor John J. Bookman was one who rose to the challenge. Among his patients was Jane Zorek, the wife of the defendant and third-party plaintiff in this action. Mrs. Zorek was 5' 2", but could not exactly be described as petite, for she had weighed well over 200 pounds. The doctor had been treating her for a number of medical problems arising from her obesity—including abscesses, cysts, and skin grafts. In 1962, when this had caused sebaceous gland trouble, he had her hospitalized. In the hospital she was put on a rigid reducing diet restricted to 800 calories a day and lost 7 1/2 pounds. The third-party defendant, Associated Hospital Service of New York, with whom Mr. Zorek had a family Blue Cross contract, on that occasion paid the expenses of Mrs. Zorek's hospital stay without a murmur of protest.

Out of the hospital, Mrs. Zorek was unable to maintain her weight loss, and was plagued by recurring boils and cysts. Hence, in May of 1963, Doctor Bookman again concluded that hospitalization was required and had her admitted to the plaintiff Mount Sinai Hospital. This time she was put on what is known as the "Duncan Regime"—a rigid starvation diet, in which the patient receives no calories at all, only fluids, vitamins and minerals. During her three weeks stay in the hospital on this stringent program, Mrs. Zorek lost 17 1/2 pounds without adverse effects.

When pressed by the hospital for payment, Mr. Zorek looked to his Blue Cross policy with Associated Hospital Service of New York for reimbursement. AHS, however, this time refused payment, contending that obesity was not within the coverage of the contract, and that Mrs. Zorek's hospital confinement was not necessary for treatment of her condition. This lawsuit then followed.

[Although] AHS argued that obesity is neither a disease nor an injury, it is clear that Blue Cross coverage is not limited only to those calamities. Since the policy spells out the "condition, disease, ailment or accidental injury" which is *excluded* from coverage, it should be plain that there *is* coverage for hospitalization resulting from any condition, disease, injury or ailment which is not excluded. While it is debatable whether or not obesity is an illness or ailment, certainly it is a "condition," and the test of coverage must be determined on other grounds.

The policy provides:

> Such Hospital Service shall be available to a Subscriber, following his admission to a hospital and during the time he is confined herein as a registered bed patient and while he is under the treatment of a physician, *when such hospital confinement is necessary for his proper treatment.* . . . However, there shall be available only such items of Hospital Service as are necessary and consistent with the diagnosis and treatment of the Condition for which such hospitalization is required. (Italics supplied.)

Under Exclusions appear the following: "A. Hospital Service Shall Not Be Provided: . . . 5. For a hospital stay or that portion of a hospital stay which is primarily for custodial, convalescent or sanitarium type care or for a rest cure."

Associated Hospital Service, the third-party defendant, argues that hospital confinement was not necessary for proper treatment of Mrs. Zorek's obese condition, and that the care rendered to her during her stay in the hospital was convalescent or sanitarium type care which the contract excludes. . . .

The words *necessary for proper treatment* call into play the exercise of judgment. "Proper" in whose eyes? The patient's, the treating physician's, the hospital's, an AHS administrator's, or a court's looking back on the events sometime afterwards? Although no cases have been brought to the court's attention directly dealing with this problem, this court concludes that the applicable standards of judgment as to the treatment prescribed must be those of the treating physician.

Only the treating physician can determine what the appropriate treatment should be for any given condition. Any other standard would involve intolerable second-guessing, with every case calling for a crotchety Doctor Gillespie to peer over the shoulders of a supposedly unseasoned Doctor Kildare. The diagnosis and treatment of a patient are matters peculiarly within the competence of the treating physician. The diagnosis may be insightful and brilliant, or it may be wide of the mark, but right or wrong, the patient under his doctor's guidance proceeds upon his theories and sustains expenses therefor. Can a hospitalization insurer rightfully decline to pay for the expenses incurred on the theory that subsequent events may have proved the diagnosis or the recommended treatment to have been wrong?

Once the treating doctor has decided on the treatment, we may of course review his judgment as to whether or not hospital confinement was necessary for the particular treatment prescribed. The doctor who orders hospital confinement for the removal of a simple splinter or the lancing of a boil has almost certainly exceeded the bounds of proper medical judgment in providing for his patient. The doctor who orders hospitalization for major surgery clearly is correct in concluding that hospital confinement is necessary for that treatment, even though he may be in egregious error in deciding that major surgery is called for. Once the treating doctor has decided on a course of treatment for which hospitalization is necessary, his judgment cannot be retrospectively challenged.

A gall-bladder or a liver condition may be treated by a radical operation or by allowing a healthy regimen and the healing passage of time to work the miracle of regeneration. Who can say with certainty which course of treatment is correct? But if the operation is decided on, can there be a denial of Blue Cross coverage because alternative courses of treatment were available?

In this case doctors might differ as to what treatment should have been given to Mrs. Zorek for obesity and related disorders. The doctor who treated her concluded the appropriate treatment for the condition would be not further home dieting, or intensive exercise, or sanitarium care, but the Duncan regime. Other doctors might disagree as to prescribing the Duncan regime, but they were not treating Mrs. Zorek. . . .

The Duncan regime is a recognized medical treatment for obesity. While there is some controversy about it, and not all doctors would choose to resort to that treatment, many reputable doctors do. Doctor Bookman chose that treatment here. He having determined, within the scope of his medical competence, that the treatment was necessary, the sole question remaining is whether hospitalization was necessary for the treatment decided on.

AHS contends that what was done for Mrs. Zorek in the hospital demonstrates that hospitalization was not necessary. Apart from restricting her intake of food and administering vitamins, the patient was permitted to continue ambulatory and was weighed daily. All these things, AHS contends, were in the nature of custodial care and could have been done at home or in any sanitarium or rest home. Looking back, Mrs. Zorek's stay was indeed uneventful. However, we must measure the necessity for hospitalization by the prospective potentialities for danger inherent in a treatment, and not by fortuitous actuality.

Dr. Bookman testified that the Duncan regime was a dangerous course of treatment, and because of the dangers involved called for careful supervision at all times. The patient's blood pressure, temperature, and body fluids had to be continuously checked to be certain that proper chemical balance was maintained, and he insisted much more than mere custodial care would be required. Indeed, severe shock and even death are known to have ensued for persons following the Duncan regime even under carefully supervised conditions, since the changes which occur may be sudden and drastic. Even the medical expert who testified for Blue Cross stated that while he personally would not recommend the Duncan regime, the reason he would not do so is because of its inherent danger. In fact, he said, it would be foolishness to place someone on a Duncan diet outside of a hospital with facilities for 24 hour supervision and a well-trained medical staff.

Fortunately, there were no adverse developments or complications for Mrs. Zorek during her hospital stay. The possibilities were ever-present however, and in any sensible society penalties are not to be imposed where common-sense precautions are taken. The court concludes that not only was hospitalization necessary once the Duncan regime was decided upon, but that it would have been medically irresponsible to have had anything less. Certainly we must presume that a busy metropolitan hospital complex like Mount Sinai was not going to make one of its much sought-after beds available for three weeks for a person who merely was seeking a "rest cure," and the kind of enforced diet she could otherwise get on a milk farm. It was medical necessity and not cosmetic vanity which dictated the hospital stay....

It is the holding of this Court in construing the Blue Cross contract that when multiple courses of treatment are available, whether for the obese, the alcoholic, or the addicted, if the treating physician chooses that treatment for which hospitalization is required, and rejects those treatments which can be adequately administered in a rest home or sanitarium, then, absent a specific contractual exclusion, there is full coverage for the hospital stay....

The amount of the hospital bill in this case attributed to Mrs. Zorek's treatment for obesity came to $557.90, for which sum the plaintiff, Mount Sinai Hospital, is entitled to judgment....

■ BECHTOLD v. PHYSICIANS HEALTH PLAN OF NORTHERN INDIANA
19 F.3d 322 (7th Cir. 1994)

COFFEY, Circuit Judge.

BACKGROUND

...The parties have stipulated to the relevant facts in this case and legal issues only need be determined. Penny Jo Bechtold is a 40 year-old premenopausal adult female. She is employed by Magnavox Electronic Systems which maintains a health plan administered by the defendant Physicians Health Plan of Northern Indiana [PHP]. The plan is an "employee welfare benefit plan" as defined [by ERISA].

In October, 1991, the plaintiff was diagnosed as having breast cancer and underwent a modified radical mastectomy. The surgery disclosed heavy lymph node involvement with the breast cancer cells. After the removal of the tumor she was treated with standard chemotherapy and radiation. Her oncologist recommended that she receive heavy dose chemotherapy with an autologous bone marrow transplant (HDC/ABMT) and referred her to the Cleveland Clinic for this treatment.

HDC/ABMT is a two-step procedure. Physicians first extract ("harvest") the bone marrow cells from the patient's body and place them temporarily in frozen storage. Next, the patient undergoes a cycle of high-dose chemotherapy in hopes of killing the cancer cells. . . . [T]he patient's own ("autologous") stored marrow is [then] reinfused intravenously into the bloodstream to relieve the patient from the toxic effects of the chemotherapy. HDC/ABMT has proven effective in treating certain cancerous blood diseases such as leukemia and Hodgkin's disease but to date it has not been universally accepted treatment for solid-type tumors including breast cancer.

Before Bechtold proceeded with the treatment, PHP advised her that the HDC/ABMT treatment was not a covered service under the plan. . . . [T]he plaintiff . . . appeal[ed] the denial of benefits and received a hearing before a committee [composed of one PHP doctor, one PHP patient, and a representative of PHP management]. The committee recommended that even though the insurer had met its obligations to the plaintiff under the contract, that the insurer should change its policy and authorize payment for the procedure because the treatment was reasonable for a patient of Bechtold's age. PHP did not agree with the committee's recommendation, and refused to pay for the treatment stating that it had "lived up to its Contract obligations" under the "clear and unambiguous language in the Contract.". . .

DISCUSSION

We are aware that Mrs. Bechtold and her immediate family have undoubtedly endured a great deal of heartache, frustration and depression during her battle with cancer.[2] There is no doubt that the policy questions posed in cases like this are of grave concern to all of us, yet we, as a court of law, are called upon to make legal determinations.[3] The issue in this case is very straightforward: Does the PHP benefit plan authorize coverage of HDC/ABMT? This is a matter of contract interpretation that does not implicate the broader policy issues involved in whether insurers should cover medical procedures that are presently of unknown medical value and extremely costly.

---

[2] Fortunately for Mrs. Bechtold she has secondary insurance that paid for the treatment and thus this action will merely determine which of two insurers will pay for the treatment.

[3] In Harris v. Mutual of Omaha Cos., 1992 WL 421489, 1992 U.S.Dist. LEXIS 21393 (S.D. Ind. Aug. 26, 1992), aff'd, 992 F.2d 706 (7th Cir.1993), a similar case of a claimant seeking coverage for HDC/ABMT, U.S. District Judge Tinder succinctly summarized the problem facing courts in these difficult claims for medical coverage:

> Despite rumors to the contrary, those who wear judicial robes are human beings, and as persons, are inspired and motivated by compassion as anyone would be. Consequently, we often must remind ourselves that in our official capacities, we have authority only to issue rulings within the narrow parameters of the law and the facts before us. The temptation to go about, doing good where we see fit, and to make things less difficult for those who come before us, regardless of the law, is strong. But the law, without which judges are nothing, abjures such unlicensed formulation of unauthorized social policy by the judiciary. Plaintiff Judy Harris well deserves, and in a perfect world would be entitled to, all known medical treatments to control the horrid disease from which she suffers. In ruling as this court must, no personal satisfaction is taken, but that the law was followed. The court will have to live with the haunting thought that Ms. Harris, and perhaps others insured by the Mutual of Omaha Companies under similar plans, may not ultimately receive the treatment they need and deserve. Perhaps the question most importantly raised about this case, and similar cases, is who should pay for the hopeful treatments that are being developed in this rapidly developing area of medical science?

A claim for benefits under an ERISA-governed plan "is a matter of contract interpretation."... The parties have devoted considerable time arguing what the proper standard of review is in this case. In Firestone Tire & Rubber Co. v. Bruch, 489 U.S. 101 (1989), the United States Supreme Court ruled that the denial of benefits by an ERISA plan administrator must be reviewed under the de novo standard unless the benefit plan gives the administrator or fiduciary discretionary authority to determine eligibility for benefits or to construe the plan. "[I]f a benefit plan gives discretion to an administrator or fiduciary who is operating under a conflict of interest, that conflict must be weighed as a 'facto[r] in determining whether there is an abuse of discretion.'" (quoting Restatement (Second) of Trusts §187, Comment d (1959)). The plaintiff argues that because PHP was operating under a conflict of interest (i.e., PHP stood to gain a greater profit if the claim was denied) we should grant less deference to PHP's determination that HDC/ABMT is experimental. We need not decide what level of deference to give to the defendant's interpretation of the contract term because under the facts in this case, even applying de novo review, the clear and unambiguous language of the policy dictates that the defendant, Physicians Health Plan of Northern Indiana, properly denied coverage for the HDC/ABMT treatment.

DENIAL OF COVERAGE

In part, the Plan provides:

"Experimental or Unproven Procedures" means any procedures, devices, drugs or medicines or the use thereof which falls within any of the following categories: 1. Which is considered by any government agency or subdivision, including but not limited to the Food and Drug Administration, the Office of Health Technology Assessment, or HCFA Medicare Coverage Issues Manual to be: a. experimental or investigational; b. not considered reasonable and necessary; or c. any similar finding; 2. Which is not covered under Medicare reimbursement laws, regulations or interpretations; or 3. Which is not commonly and customarily recognized by the medical profession in the state of Indiana as appropriate for the condition being treated. PLAN reserves the right to change, from time to time, the procedures considered to be Experimental or Unproven. Contact PLAN to determine if a particular procedure, treatment, or device is considered to be Experimental or Unproven.

The HCFA Medicare Coverage Issues Manual (which is referenced in the PHP Plan) provides in §35-31:

C. Autologous Bone Marrow Transplantation (Effective for Services Performed on or After 04/28/89)....—Insufficient data exist to establish definite conclusions regarding the efficacy of autologous bone marrow transplantation for the following conditions:... Acute leukemia in relapse, Chronic granulocytic leukemia or Solid tumors [such as breast cancer] (other than neuroblastoma). In these cases, autologous bone marrow transplantation is not considered reasonable and necessary within the meaning of §1862(a)(1)(A) of the Act and is not covered under Medicare.

The plaintiff does not challenge the language of the HCFA Medicare Coverage Issues Manual but argues that the phrase in the Plan that PHP "reserves the right to change, from time to time, the procedures considered to be Experimental or Unproven" creates an obligation on the part of PHP to cover the contested treatment in light of recent medical research endorsing the procedure for solid tumors like breast cancer ... rather than to hide behind outdated or inapplicable guidelines and therefore if the treatment is no longer experimental—as the plaintiff argues—she is entitled to coverage....

The "right to change" the classification of procedures certainly does not obligate PHP to reclassify hourly, weekly, monthly or annually whether a treatment should be covered on the basis of competing views of medical experts (oncologists). Rather, PHP chose to link the experimental nature of a treatment to the neutral (third party) determination of the medical experts responsible for drafting the HCFA Medicare Coverage Issues Manual.[6] Clearly, PHP's intent was to avoid a case-by-case battle of the experts in which PHP would be required to reevaluate covered treatments each time a self-proclaimed "expert" publishes a new article.... [The contract] is ... clear and unambiguous. Heller v. Equitable Life Assur. Soc., 833 F.2d 1253, 1257 (7th Cir.1987) ("In the absence of a clear, unequivocal and specific contractual requirement [placing a duty on a party,] we refuse to order the same. To hold otherwise and to impose such a requirement would, in effect, enlarge the terms of the policy beyond those clearly defined in the policy agreed to by the parties.").[7] ...

ERISA ... does not dictate what a plan such as the PHP plan before us should cover. Hickey v. A.E. Staley Mfg., 995 F.2d 1385, at 1393 (7th Cir. 1993) ("Congress never intended ERISA to dictate the content of welfare benefit plans, much less for the federal courts to determine the content of such plans; ... the discretion to make decisions concerning the content of the Plan rests with the Plan administrator"). Therefore, we hold that the language of the PHP Plan excludes coverage for HDC/ABMT as a treatment for breast cancer.

FULL AND FAIR REVIEW

Bechtold's second argument is that she was denied full and fair review ... because PHP refused to accept the recommendation of its own complaints

---

[6] The HCFA Medicare Coverage Issues Manual is updated when new medical data becomes available and the updates are published quarterly in the Federal Register. The provision relating to autologous bone marrow transplants for solid tumors (breast cancer) was published in the Federal Register on June 11, 1992, and was in effect at all times relevant to this proceeding (Bechtold was denied coverage in October 1992).

[7] In Heller, ... [w]e [noted] that

[t]he insurance company seeking to [limit] coverage ... need only incorporate a specific requirement to that effect in the policy, and we would not hesitate to enforce the same. On the other hand, insurers who fail to include this express ... contractual requirement, and who refuse to cover an insured after entering into a binding and enforceable agreement after accepting substantial premiums, in circumstances such as those before us, cause problems not only for the insured, but for the insurance industry as well. Insurance companies, members of a service industry, ... must conduct themselves accordingly instead of attempting to rely on the courts to correct their own deficiencies in underwriting and/or careless policy drafting.

committee and instead denied the benefits based on the Plan Chief Operating Officer's disagreement with the committee's recommendation. We cannot agree with Bechtold's argument on this account because a review of the letter from PHP denying the benefits makes clear that the committee recognized that the HDC/ABMT treatment was not covered under the plan. The committee, however, recommended a change of policy by the insurer to allow coverage of the procedure because: (1) the procedure was not experimental and PHP has an express intent of providing reasonable care for patients of this type; (2) Medicare supporting claims for this type of noncovered condition, is not that of a patient of Ms. Bechtold's age; (3) supportive data suggests the proposed treatment as very appropriate....

The only authority vested in the committee was to recommend whether a specific claim for benefits had been properly denied based upon the language of the policy; it was not free to cast aside the agreed upon terms of the insurance contract....

CONCLUSION

As stated above, cases of this nature pose troubling social as well as ethical questions that go well beyond the legal issues. As a court of law we are empowered to decide legal issues presented by specific cases or controversies. The greater social questions must be decided by the political branches of government which can engage in legislative factfinding and benefit from public hearings and constituent expression of opinion.... Chesterfield Smith, the former president of the American Bar Association once stated in a Law Day address: "Courts are being asked today to solve problems for which they are not institutionally equipped.... The American public perceives the courts as a jack-of-all trades available to furnish the answer to whatever may trouble them." The question of what procedures insurance companies should cover is just the type of problem to which Mr. Smith was referring.

In order to resolve the question of whether health insurance providers should cover treatments like HDC/ABMT, the prudent course of action might be to establish some sort of regional cooperative committees comprised of oncologists, internists, surgeons, experts in medical ethics, medical school administrators, economists, representatives of the insurance industry, patient advocates and politicians. Through such a collective task force perhaps some consensus might be reached concerning the definition of experimental procedures, as well as agreement on the procedures, which are so cost prohibitive that requiring insurers to cover them might result in the collapse of the healthcare industry. While such a committee would in no way be a panacea for our skyrocketing health care costs, it may help to reduce the incidence of suits in which one "expert" testifies that a procedure is experimental and another equally qualified "expert" testifies to the opposite effect. This so called battle of the experts occurs all too frequently in federal court....

■ BROKEN BACK: A PATIENT'S REFLECTIONS
ON THE PROCESS OF MEDICAL NECESSITY
DETERMINATIONS
Margaret Gilhooley*
40 Vill. L. Rev. 153 (1995)

... On New Year's Day 1994, while I was ice skating, a young girl crossed suddenly in front of me. I fell to the ice in a sitting position and "broke my back." That accident, unreal at the time, became an encounter with modern medicine, its miracles and its efforts to control cost. Fortunately, I have emerged from my operation and rehabilitation able to walk and function with no significant impairment.

When my insurer determined that my continued hospitalization was "medically inappropriate," my reactions were initially those of all patients. Later, my experience as a patient led to some reflections both on the needs of patients who are suddenly hospitalized and on the general process of utilization review and medical necessity decisionmaking. ...

My spinal fracture and compressed disc, or "broken back," necessitated an operation to stabilize the spine. In the operation, rods were inserted to support the spine and allow the burst disc to decompress, fortunately without any impairment of the spinal cord. After the operation, it was necessary to wear a back brace. The brace, made of heavy plastic, was uncomfortable to wear all day and I required assistance to put it on and remove it. Moreover, it was very painful to sit while wearing the brace for more than a few minutes, and the brace pressed against the neck when seated. By the eleventh day after the operation, I began to walk in the brace without feeling faint, but I did so very cautiously, with a cane and with supervision. I was to receive instruction the next day on climbing stairs and on functioning with a brace, before I was discharged from the hospital.

My insurance plan was a fee-for-service plan that had adopted elements of managed care. Thus, for care provided in participating hospitals, there was full reimbursement, but my insurance required pre-admission review. The insurer approved admission and a hospital stay of ten days. Even if I had heard of this time period, I did not appreciate its significance. Late on the eleventh day after my admission, a member of the hospital's utilization review office brought me a copy of a fax from my insurer to my doctor notifying my doctor that my continued stay in the hospital was "medically inappropriate." Furthermore, the doctor's request for an additional stay had been denied. ... I was stunned by the notice that my benefits had already ended and that they had been labeled "medically inappropriate."

The utilization review officer suggested that I call my insurer to make an appeal. ... [On the phone,] I protested that I could not leave the hospital because of my difficulties with the brace and inability to walk up steps. I was told that the insurer was not saying that I did not need medical care, but only that I did not need medical care in an acute care facility. Because I was not receiving intravenous fluids, I no longer needed to be in a hospital and could be in a semi-skilled nursing

*Professor of Law, Seton Hall University.

facility [or a rehabilitation institute]....Thus, the call ended, my appeal for continued hospital benefits was denied, and I was uncertain and distressed. There was something about being termed "medically inappropriate" that seemed like a personal failing, some inability to measure up to accepted standards....

I decided I would stop fighting the insurance company's efforts to "evict" me from the hospital. Instead, I would initiate a request to go to a rehabilitation institute on an inpatient basis to receive additional care for dealing with my difficulties with the brace. My stay in the rehabilitation institute was key to my recovery. The institute changed my ill-fitting brace, enabling me to sit in a chair. Moreover, I had sufficient time and space to learn to walk and to climb stairs gaining confidence in my ability....

Insurers have a fiduciary responsibility to inform patients of their appeal rights and not to hinder appeals. The failure to provide a timely notice about the limitation of benefits can frustrate the patient's ability to make an appeal or a request for an extension....[T]here needs to be adequate safeguards to ensure that this obligation is observed....]

When a specific claim is denied, the payer should...provide an explanation of the denial that indicates the basis for the criteria used for the denial. The information may provide some reassurance to the patient that the denial has substantial support and is fair. The patient may be less inclined to pursue an appeal if the grounds are satisfactorily explained....

The contractual exclusion of medically unnecessary claims provides little guidance as to the test that will be used. The term by itself suggests to patients that the treating physician's judgment fails to meet minimally acceptable medical standards....

Notes: Insurance Coverage Disputes

1. *Medicare and Medicaid Coverage.* The coverage of public programs such as Medicare and Medicaid is defined in the same "medically necessary" and "experimental" terms as is commonly used in private insurance contracts. A related body of case law addresses whether novel or alternative treatments are covered under these public programs, reaching similarly mixed results. In favor of coverage, one court held that Medicaid must cover AZT treatment for both early and advanced stages of AIDS, even though FDA approval of the drug was limited to the latter. The court reasoned that "it would be improper...to interfere with a physician's judgment of medical necessity" based on FDA drug-labeling requirements because "FDA approved indications [are] not intended to limit or interfere with the practice of medicine;...the package insert is only informational." Weaver v. Reagan, 886 F.2d 194, 198 (8th Cir. 1989). In another case, the court found that a sex change operation is medically necessary and nonexperimental under Medicaid. Pinneke v. Preisser, 623 F.2d 546 (8th Cir. 1980). In a third, the court ordered Medicare to cover artificial lens implants for cataract correction despite the fact they were still under research investigation, explaining that

> manufacturers and physicians working to develop [lens implants] need to be assured that they will be reimbursed for their efforts during these investigational

periods. Withdrawing Medicare coverage...[will likely cause the lens] industry's remarkable level of invention [to] decrease dramatically....HCFA's stultifying regulatory strategy, with its preference for government rules over market-generated innovation, is reminiscent of the central planning apparatuses that other nations are now struggling to leave behind....If this type of thinking were to prevail, the status quo would be frozen and research and development would become a thing of the past. That is not the American way.

American Society of Cataract and Refractive Surgery v. Sullivan, 772 F. Supp. 666 (D.D.C. 1991). For decisions the other way, see Goodman v. Sullivan, 891 F.2d 449 (2d Cir. 1989) (Medicare regulation denying payment for MRI scans does not impermissibly supervise or control the practice of medicine); Rush v. Parham, 625 F.2d 1150, 1154 (5th Cir. 1980) ("a state may adopt a definition of medical necessity that places reasonable limits on a physician's discretion [to order sex change operation]"); Cowan v. Myers, 232 Cal. Rptr. 299, 303, 306 (Cal. Ct. App. 1986) ("plaintiffs are in error when they assert the physician is the sole arbiter of what constitutes medical necessity [under Medicaid]....Not only would such a rule result in inconsistent and unfair applications based on the variation between physicians, but the state's requirement of reimbursement would be limited only by the imagination of physicians.").

Especially controversial have been cases involving major organ transplants (liver, heart, lung, etc.) under Medicaid. In favor of coverage, see Pereira v. Kozlowski, 996 F.2d 723 (4th Cir. 1993); Allen v. Mansour, 681 F. Supp. 1232 (E.D. Mich. 1986) (Medicaid must cover liver transplant for former alcoholic); Salgado v. Kirschner, 878 P.2d 659 (Ariz. 1994). Allowing states to limit or refuse coverage, see Ellis v. Patterson, 859 F.2d 52 (8th Cir. 1988); Dexter v. Kirschner, 984 F.2d 979 (9th Cir. 1992). See generally Timothy Blanchard, "Medical Necessity" Denials as a Medicare Part B Cost-Containment Strategy, 34 St. Louis U. L.J. 939 (1990); Note, 89 Nw. U. L. Rev. 268 (1994); Note 79 Minn. L. Rev. 1232 (1995).

2. *Appeal Procedures.* In addition to the *substance* of coverage decisions, the proper *procedures* for challenging and reviewing these decisions have been controversial under both public and private insurance. Under Medicare and Medicaid, this topic is enormously complex, and so is addressed separately in materials below. You will find that the analysis varies along each of the following lines, and for each of these categories there are several points of view: There are constitutional, statutory, and regulatory dimensions. Not only do each of these dimensions differ between the two programs, but within Medicare the appeal procedures differ between Part A and Part B, and within Medicaid they vary state by state. Within each program, appeal procedures also differ between fee-for-service and HMO providers. And, appeal issues differ according to what is at stake: basic eligibility or particular covered services. The issues also differ according to whether a patient is challenging a fact-based ruling in an individual case, a general substantive rule or policy decision, or a procedural rule. And, there are various levels of decision, from initial review by "fiscal intermediaries" (insurers under contract with CMS), to administrative review within CMS, to judicial review. To top it all off, a whole different set of procedures and institutions govern appeals

by patients over eligibility for coverage than those that govern appeals by providers challenging how much they are paid when services are covered.

Under conventional *private* insurance, appeal procedures were once fairly straightforward—if you were unhappy, you hired a lawyer and sued—although ERISA preemption complicates which court to sue in and what the standard of review will be. These disputes were then resolved like any other contract dispute. But that is true only so far as judicial review is concerned. The decision process by the insurer at the initial stage of decision is increasingly attracting the attention of state regulators and legislators, for reasons illustrated by Margaret Gilhooley's experience. This is especially true under managed care because then the denial of coverage does not simply affect who will pay, it often affects whether treatment will be rendered at all. Therefore, it is not sufficient for patients eventually to have their day in court. They need a prompt and fair review process on the spot. Similar provisions are imposed on self-insured employers through rules issued by the Department of Labor, under the authority of ERISA. Most states have gone even further to create "external review" mechanisms that allow patients or providers to appeal medical necessity decisions promptly to independent physicians with relevant expertise. In Rush Prudential HMO v. Moran, 122 S. Ct. 2151 (2002), excerpted at page 207, the Court ruled that ERISA does not preempt these state laws because they do not conflict with ERISA's remedial scheme. The Court reasoned that external review is more akin to a second medical opinion than to arbitration or a judicial proceeding, and that external review does not enlarge the types of remedies that patients can recover. To this extent, private law is being influenced by administrative law and constitutional principles. Do you think the telephone call Gilhooley had with the insurer would constitute an adequate "hearing"? See generally Grijalva v. Shalala,152 F.2d 1115 (9th Cir. 1998), and the new federal regulations at 62 Fed. Reg. 23,368 (1997), which require Medicare HMOs to conduct internal review for urgent care within three days, and outside review within ten days, with services to be continued pending final decision. For in-depth commentary and analysis, with numerous suggestions for improvement, see Eleanor Kinney, Procedural Protections for Patients in Capitated Health Plans, 22 Am. J.L. & Med. 301 (1996); Susan Stayn, Securing Access to Care in Health Maintenance Organizations: Toward a Uniform Model of Grievance and Appeal Procedures, 94 Colum. L. Rev. 1674 (1994); Symposium, Consumer Protection in Managed Care, 26 Seton Hall L.J. 1007 (1996).

For extensive analysis of the full range of these procedural issues, see Eleanor D. Kinney, Protecting American Health Care Consumers (2002); Kathy L. Cerminara, Contextualizing ADR in Managed Care: A Proposal Aimed at Easing Tensions and Resolving Conflict, 33 Loy. U. Chi. L.J. 547 (2002); Karen A. Jordan, Coverage Denials in ERISA Plans: Assessing the Federal Legislative Solution, 65 Mo. L. Rev. 405 (2000); Aaron Kesselheim, What's the Appeal? Trying to Control Managed Care Medical Necessity Decisionmaking through a System of External Appeals, 149 U. Pa. L. Rev. 873 (2001); Naomi Karp & Eriza Wood, Health Plan Internal Consumer Dispute Resolution Practices, J. Health Care L. & Pol'y 283 (2002); Eleanor D. Kinney, Tapping and Resolving Consumer Concerns about Health Care, 26 Am. J.L. & Med. 335 (2000); Ann Nevers, Consumer Managed Care Appeals: Are the Available Procedural

Protections Fundamentally Fair?, 33 J. Health L. 287 (2000); Symposium, 5 J. Health Care L. & Pol'y 283 (2002).

3. *Block that Metaphor.* For another court moved to literary heights by an insurance coverage dispute, see Zuckerberg v. Blue Cross & Blue Shield, 464 N.Y.S.2d 678, 683 (1983) (requiring Blue Shield to pay for a course of nutritional cancer therapy of unproven benefit that the plaintiff obtained in Mexico), *rev'd on other grounds,* 490 N.E.2d 839 (N.Y. 1986), where the court recited:

> A possible path was opened, had it not been taken, what then? At least, it was tried. "For of all sad words of tongue or pen, The saddest are these: 'It might have been!'" (*Maud Muller,* by John Greenleaf Whittier, stanza 53).

For a more somber view, consider the following thoughts from Judge Gladys Kessler in Salazar v. District of Columbia, 1996 WL 768038 (D.D.C. 1996):

> This case is about people—children and adults who are sick, poor, and vulnerable—for whom life, in the memorable words of poet Langston Hughes, "ain't been no crystal stair." It is written in the dry and bloodless language of "the law"— statistics, acronyms of agencies and bureaucratic entities, Supreme Court case names and quotes, official governmental reports, periodicity tables, etc. But let there be no forgetting the real people to whom this dry and bloodless language gives voice: anxious, working parents who are too poor to obtain medications or heart catheter procedures or lead poisoning screens for their children, AIDS patients unable to get treatment, elderly persons suffering from chronic conditions like diabetes and heart disease who require constant monitoring and medical attention. Behind every "fact" found herein is a human face and the reality of being poor in the richest nation on earth.

And, a more balanced view:

> Coverage litigation has become one of the American health system's Crimeas, a designated battleground for opposing armies. On one side are arrayed individual patients with idiosyncratic needs, and the physicians and hospitals who stand ready to serve them. On the other side can be found employers, insurers and government—in each case claiming to represent the interest of beneficiaries or taxpayers as a whole by denying relief to one member or the group. This is, of course, the core challenge of managed care: creating an efficient system of population-based health management which nonetheless accounts equitably for the interests of individuals.

William Sage, Judicial Opinions Involving Health Insurance Coverage: Trompe L'Oeil or Window on the World?, 31 Ind. L. Rev. 49 (1998).

4. *The Doctor Knows Best.* In case there is any confusion on this point, realize that three weeks of hospitalization at Mount Sinai Hospital would no longer cost $557.90; now, this might not even buy *one day's* hospitalization. Should this fact change the outcome in *Zorek*? The *Zorek* court appears quite absolute in its statement that "only the treating physician can determine what the appropriate treatment should be for any given condition." What more prosaic phrase do we usually apply to allowing the one who is paid (or, here, a member of its medical

staff) to be the sole judge of the necessity of its services? Consider the contrasting literary viewpoint found in George Bernard Shaw's preface to his play *The Doctor's Dilemma*:

> That any sane nation...should...give a surgeon a pecuniary interest in cutting off your leg, is enough to make one despair of political humanity. But that is precisely what we have done. And the more appalling the mutilation, the more the mutilator is paid. Scandalized voices murmur that...operations are necessary. They may be. It may also be necessary to hang a man or pull down a house. But we take good care not to make the hangman and the house breaker the judges of that.

Shumake v. Travelers Insurance Co., 383 N.W.2d 259, 263 (Mich. 1985) (insurer must pay for laetrile (ground apricot pits) for cancer, even though not approved by the FDA; the terms *necessarily incurred* and *required* in an insurance contract are ambiguous, and a physician is generally better equipped than lawyers to determine what is medically necessary).

5. *In Search of the "Iron Clad" Insurance Contract.* *Bechtold* demonstrates that the legal landscape has changed considerably since *Zorek*. This is true in several respects. First, coverage decisions under private insurance are now typically decided prior to or during the course of treatment through requests for prior authorization, rather than in the ordinary process of claims review. Second, as the result of ERISA preemption, these cases are now decided in federal court under a potentially more lenient standard of review than that governing garden variety contract disputes. Third, insurers have rewritten contracts to make their decisions more enforceable. They declare that questions of interpretation are to be determined in the discretion of the insurer, whose decision is binding. And they more frequently exclude specific controversial treatments by name.

None of these changes has dramatically altered the favorable treatment that patients usually receive in court, however. The shift from retrospective to prospective or concurrent utilization review has introduced a different form of hardship. Now, rather than merely risking loss of money, patients risk not getting the treatment at all. See Wickline v. State, 239 Cal. Rptr. 810, 812 (Cal. Ct. App. 1986) ("A mistaken conclusion about medical necessity following retrospective review will result in the wrongful withholding of payment. An erroneous decision in a prospective review process, on the other hand, in practical consequences, results in the withholding of necessary care, potentially leading to a patient's permanent disability or death.").

Although ERISA allows a more lenient standard of review, as noted in *Bechtold* ERISA requires more exacting scrutiny when insurers are under a conflict of interest. The obvious conflict of interest is that insurers usually have already collected their premium and each medical payment comes out of their bottom line. Moreover, a more recent Supreme Court decision, Rush Prudential HMO v. Moran, 122 S. Ct. 2151 (2002), held that a deferential standard does not apply to administrative appeal procedures created by state law. Therefore, even under ERISA, courts still frequently construe ambiguous terms such as *experimental* and *medically necessary* in favor of patients. See, e.g., Kunin v. Benefit Trust Life Insurance Co., 910 F.2d 534 (9th Cir. 1990) (it is arbitrary and capricious to conclude that autism is excluded as a "mental illness"); Reilly v. Blue Cross & Blue Shield United, 846 F.2d 416, 426-427 (7th Cir.) (fact issue exists whether it is arbitrary and capricious to conclude that in vitro fertilization is experimental); Bradley v. Empire Blue Cross & Blue Shield, 562 N.Y.S.2d 908 (N.Y. Sup. Ct. 1990) (patient likely to prevail in showing that ABMT is not experimental treatment for AIDS, even though his doctor was the only one in the country who had ever used the procedure this way and the patient had signed an informed consent form acknowledging that he was participating in an "experiment"). As for the contract technique used in *Bechtold,* other courts have ruled that incorporation by reference does not give subscribers fair notice of what is excluded, and it is particularly unconscionable to govern young policyholders with rules written for the elderly under Medicare. See, e.g., Waldrip v. Connecticut National Life Insurance Co., 573 So. 2d 1172 (5th Cir. 1991); Hyde v. Humana Insurance Co., 598 So. 2d 876 (Ala. 1992).

The contractual change that has had the most impact is assigning to the insurer the authority to make binding interpretations of ambiguous phrases. Courts have ruled that, in effect, ERISA allows the contract to nullify the usual judicial presumption against the party that drafted the contract (*contra proferentum*). Winters v. Costco Wholesale Corp., 49 F.3d 550 (9th Cir. 1995). See generally M. Hall et al., Judicial Protection of Managed Care Consumers: An Empirical Study of Insurance Coverage Disputes, 26 Seton Hall L.J. 1055 (1996); Symposium, 31 Ind. L. Rev. 1 (1998).

6. *Conflicts of Interest.* As these cases and notes suggest, various conflicts of interest permeate the arena of insurance coverage determinations. The most obvious conflict is that of the insurer who has to pay. But is an insurer under a conflict of interest if it merely administers claims and does utilization review for a self-insured employer rather than bearing the risk of medical costs itself? In this situation, the insurer is paid a per-case or per-annum administrative fee and the financial risk is borne by the employer. Does this then put the employer under a conflict of interest, or is it accurate to say that the employer has in mind the interests of the employee group as a whole? One interesting case allowed an employer and its workers to sue under ERISA for wrongly *paying out* medical benefits from a self-funded plan under the theory that this depleted the plan's assets, which otherwise would have been available to pay more legitimate claims. IT Corp. v. General American Life Insurance Co., 107 F.3d 1415 (9th Cir. 1997). What about letting committees composed of employees decide these disputes? Are they conflict free, considering that they may trade off the interests of one patient to favor the interests of the rest of the group?

Various expressions of opinion on these issues can be found in the case law, but suffice it to say that judicial opinions are still inconsistent and evolving. See generally Brown v. Blue Cross & Blue Shield, 898 F.2d 1556 (11th Cir. 1990). One notable instance of a decision apparently affected by an insurer's conflict of interest occurred in an unreported California trial verdict that was later settled (Fox v. HealthNet). That case also involved HDCT/ABMT for breast cancer. There, an HMO refused coverage and the patient later died. The case was tried under state law because her insurance came from her government job, which ERISA does not cover. Therefore, her family was free to seek punitive damages. The jury returned a whopping $89 million verdict. According to press reports, the jury was influenced by two aggravating circumstances: that the HMO's medical director received a bonus determined in part by the amount of money he saved through coverage denials, and that the HMO had recently approved this same procedure for one of its own employees.

A different type of conflict surfaced in another notable case against HealthNet, one that illustrates an important trend. As discussed in section 3.E.3, HMOs sometimes shift the insurance risk to treating physicians by contracting with them on a fully capitated basis. This in effect tosses the hot potato of making coverage denials to the doctor, because it is the doctor who bears most of the costs. This also minimizes the potential for coverage disputes arising in the first place, since a patient is much less likely to be presented conflicting opinions between her doctor and her insurer if the doctor simply declines to order the treatment. This new dynamic was revealed when the same lawyer who represented Mrs. Fox in the prior case began to investigate a similar case involving Mrs. DeMeurs, also with breast cancer. He found that her doctor initially recommended her for HDCT/ABMT but he changed his mind after the HMO medical director called the doctor to question his initial judgment. This case was decided in arbitration, resulting in a $1 million award. In the arbitrators' opinion,

> the [HMO's] actions designed and intended to interfere with an existing doctor/ patient relationship constitute extreme and outrageous behavior exceeding all bounds usually tolerated in a civilized society. It is conduct undertaken with reckless disregard of the probability of causing severe emotional distress. This conduct clearly crosses the line of appropriate communication between insurer and doctor.

Do you agree?

7. For commentary generally supportive of the *Bechtold* point of view, see Mark Hall & Gerard Anderson, Health Insurers' Assessment of Medical Necessity, 140 U. Pa. L. Rev. 1637 (1992); Richard Saver, Reimbursing New Technologies: Why are the Courts Judging Experimental Medicine?, 44 Stan. L. Rev. 1095 (1992); Note, 1 Widener L. Symp. J. 389 (1996); Comment, 22 Capital U. L. Rev. 465 (1993). For contrasting commentary, supportive of *Zorek*, see David Frankford, Food Allergy and the Health Care Financing Administration: A Story of Rage, 1 Widener L. Symp. J. 159 (1996); Sara Rosenbaum et al., Who Should Determine When Health Care Is Medically Necessary?, 340 New Eng. J. Med. 229 (1999); Comment, 31 Duq. L. Rev. 777 (1993); Comment, 66 Wash. L. Rev. 809 (1991). See generally David Eddy, Benefit Language: Criteria that will Improve Quality While Reducing Costs, 275 JAMA 650 (1996); William Giese, Adjudication of Third Party Payment for HDC-ABMT in the Treatment of Breast Cancer, 1 DePaul J. Health Care L. 205 (1997); Sharona Hoffman, A Proposal for Federal Legislation to Address Health Insurance Coverage for Experimental and Investigational Treatments, 78 Or. L. Rev. 203 (1999); Peter Jacobson & Neena Patil, Managed Care Litigation: Legal Doctrine at the Boundary of Tort and Contract, 57 Med. Care Res. & Rev. 440 (2000); Shirley Sanematsu, Taking a Broader View of Treatment Disputes beyond Managed Care, 48 UCLA L. Rev. 1245 (2001); Symposium, 43 St. Louis L. Rev. 1 (1999); Note, 37 Harv. J. Legis. 237 (2000); Annot., 75 A.L.R.4th 763 (1990).

8. *Courts, Committees, or Congress?* Suppose we view this situation as one involving two, unavoidably competing conflicts of interest: that of the physician who is to be paid, and that of the insurer/employer who is to pay. Is there any "neutral" third party capable of resolving this conflict? Are the courts themselves neutral, given their tendency, noted by Judge Coffey, to "go about doing good where we see fit"? Is the proper, "unbiased" perspective that of the individual patient who is presently sick and has insurance, or instead that of the pool of subscribers at the point they are deciding how much insurance coverage they can afford? Which perspective are courts more likely to take? Legislatures? Employers? Panels of expert doctors? Panels like those suggested by Judge Coffey composed of various interest groups and expertise? Isn't the hearing committee that actually reviewed Ms. Bechtold's case potentially one such representative panel? See Barnett v. Kaiser Foundation Health Plan, 32 F.3d 413 (9th Cir. 1994) (advisory board composed of HMO's own doctors provides neutral, expert review). If so, why was Judge Coffey so reluctant to accept its recommendation? Which of these various processes do you have the most confidence in, considering the full range of medical conditions and expenditures that are potentially at stake? For a general analysis, see Mark A. Hall, Making Medical Spending Decisions, ch. 3 (1997); David Hsia, Benefits Determination under Health Care Reform: Who Should Decide Coverage Policy?, 15 J. Leg. Med. 533 (1994).

9. *Cookbook Medicine.* Why would insurers ever have adopted such broad terms as *medically necessary* and *experimental* in the first place? One could have predicted that it would be impossible to police physicians' decisions by using their own conceptual norms. One reason contracts might contain such open-ended terms is that health insurance originated from the medical establishment itself, in the form of Blue Cross/Blue Shield. But why has this not changed now that insurers are much more aggressively competitive? Courts frequently urge insurers to make their contracts more specific if they want to reliably exclude coverage. Indeed, it is possible to make coverage terms quite specific using the detailed practice guidelines that are being produced by the health services research community in great numbers. See Clark C. Havighurst, Practice Guidelines for Medical Care: The Policy Rationale, 34 St. Louis U. L.J. 777 (1990). But how realistic is this really? The most extensive effort to date is that in Oregon, described in section 3.D.1, which uses more than 600 treatment-condition pairings (e.g., surgery for appendicitis) to specify Medicaid coverage across the entire range of medical practice.

The difficulty with this approach is aptly captured in Aaron and Schwartz's criticism of the Oregon list as "meat-ax" rationing. All covered treatments are always covered, no matter how mild the condition or how effective the medical intervention, while excluded items are not covered at all no matter how severe the condition or how great the potential is for improvement. The Achilles Heel of Health Care Rationing, N.Y. Times, July 9, 1990, at A15. To achieve the desirable level of specificity would require rigorous scientific information on each of the almost 10,000 diagnostic entries in the *International Classification of Diseases* (9th ed.) (known as "ICD-9") and for each of the 10,000 medical interventions listed in the AMA's *Common Procedural Terminology* (known as "CPT" codes). Moreover, each complication and sequence of events for each of these items would have to be evaluated in all possible combinations. In other words, for two conditions, A and B, we would have to consider A alone, B alone, and AB, as well as A before B,

A after B, and A and B simultaneously. For even a single, modestly complex disease category (say, heart disease) with only 20 conditions, this analysis would produce some 10 billion different clinical scenarios. R. Dubois & R. Brook, Assessing Clinical Decision Making: Is the Ideal System Feasible?, 25 Inquiry 59 (1988).

The practical impossibility of adequately capturing the judgmental and nuanced aspects of medical decisionmaking in a detailed, prescriptive fashion has led legal scholars to refer to this as a problem in "relational contracting." Contracts that call for the exercise of professional judgment or that define complex, ongoing service relationships present unique problems as compared with classic contractual settings that simply specify the purchase of identified products. These relational contracts require inventive and flexible contracting tools in order to accomplish their purposes. In health insurance contracts, we see a persistent desire on the part of both subscribers and insurers to use contract terms that invoke broad medical norms rather than precise clinical details. If courts insist on in construing these terms against insurers, are they not forcing the parties to adopt suboptimal contracting techniques like the one used in *Bechtold* of simply cross-referencing Medicare rules designed for old people?

Perhaps there is a workable middle ground between hyper-specific contracts and the open-ended discretion conferred by "medically necessary"? Consider these thoughtful comments by Prof. Sage:

> The most important thing to appreciate about "medical necessity" is that it operates symbolically as well as substantively.... To many physicians, the term "not medically necessary" means "not clinically indicated," which increases their resistance when a seemingly nonprofessional party such as a health plan challenges their opinion. To many health plans, it means "not covered even though not expressly excluded from coverage," which gives them a degree of comfort issuing denials based on established insurance practice but outrages physicians who focus on the clinical implications of the decision. Consequently, decisions involving medical necessity are frequently characterized by inconsistent administration, poor communication, distrust, and, if disputes arise, relatively unprincipled, results-oriented judicial resolution....
>
> Medical necessity cannot do the heavy lifting of cost control, or of quality assurance, in health care.... [T]he financial "meat" of today's medical necessity language should be placed elsewhere in the design of insurance benefits, such as by reworking current categories of covered services, rethinking specific inclusions and exclusions, reevaluating the role of employers and other purchasing agents in promoting contractual fairness, and revisiting both consumer cost-sharing and the structure and compensation of provider networks....
>
> [However], health plans and policymakers have paid too much attention to standardized rules for coverage decisions and too little attention to therapeutic effect. Health care is both an outcome and a process, and all parts of the process, including ones involving insurers, need to be caring as well as efficient. Determinations regarding medical necessity should indeed be scientific and fair, but like good medicine, should also demonstrate compassion, offer hope, promote trust, and avoid abandonment.... In brief, I believe that the interaction among an insured individual, her physicians, and her health plan should be made to resemble, to the greatest extent possible, the classic doctor-patient relationship.

William M. Sage, Medical Necessity 3 (2002).

10. *Paying for Medical Research.* Another important public policy implication of these cases is who should pay for the necessary costs of medical experimentation? Manufacturers bear most of the costs for clinical trials that test new *drugs* and *devices* subject to FDA approval. Medical *procedures,* in contrast, are not required to be tested and are not owned by anyone. If new medical and surgical techniques are tested at all, the funding usually comes from the National Institutes of Health. Remarkably, its $25 *billion* budget is sufficient only to cover the *research* expenses of clinical trials (patient recruitment, data collection and analysis, etc.), not the *clinical* costs. Conventionally, the clinical costs have been paid by the patients' private and public insurance. Until recently, the "experimental" exclusions were used to refuse payment only for unscientific, "alternative" medicine. This is quickly changing, however, under pressure from private market forces and public program deficits. Insurers are now also refusing to pay for some treatments that are rendered in scientific research studies. Despite the explicitly "experimental" setting, insurers have not been uniformly successful. For instance, Medicare decided in 1994 to stop paying for experimental medical devices, but this action was enjoined, following which Medicare agreed to pay for the study of new medical devices that are variations of existing devices. 60 Fed. Reg. 48417 (1995). For additional discussion, see Angela Holder, Funding Innovative Medical Treatment, 57 Albany L. Rev. 795 (1994); Earl Steinberg et al., Insurance Coverage for Experimental Technologies, 14 Health Aff. 143 (Winter 1995).

11. *ERISA Preemption.* The seminal decision holding that ERISA preempts insurance contract disputes is Pilot Life Insurance Co. v. Dedeaux, 481 U.S. 41 (1987). Thereafter, most of these cases have shifted to the federal courts, where they are decided without a jury and without the possibility of personal injury or punitive damages. Also, as discussed in Chapter 3.F, ERISA allows recovery of only the monetary value of the treatment at issue. When ERISA does not apply, state court juries have sometimes awarded punitive damages in the range of $50 million to $100 million. See page 147. Most commentators believe that, although some of the punitive awards were excessive, it is unconscionable to disallow any recovery of basic compensatory damages for bodily injury when there is a clear breach of a contract for medical services.

Notes: Peer Review Organizations and Utilization Review

1. *Medicare Peer Review.* The very first section of the Medicare statute prohibits any federal "supervision or control over the practice of medicine." 42 U.S.C. §1395. Despite this guarantee of physician autonomy, someone obviously has to scrutinize the necessity of the medical services Medicare pays for. Medicare uses the mechanism of physician peer review, that is, doctors monitoring themselves, to reconcile the principle of noninterference with the need for judging medical necessity. How well this functions is illustrated by an anecdote in the popular press reporting one participant's view of how this worked:

> They'd get a group of doctors together and ask something like, "How long are you guys keeping patients in the hospital for gallbladders?"... If one doctor said 6 days, and another said 8, and a third said 12, they'd put down 12 as the standard.

> There was no attempt to be parsimonious, only catch the very small percentage who were pulling truly outrageous things.

Newsweek, Jan. 26, 1987, at 44, col. 3. In the view of the Congressional Budget Office, "Peer review may alter utilization by patients of physicians whose standards are substantially different from the norm, but such review is unlikely to effect major changes in the standards of physicians as a group."

See generally Timothy Jost, Administrative Law Issues Involving the Medicare Utilization and Quality Control PRO Program, 30 Ohio St. L.J. 1 (1989); Timothy Jost, Policing Cost Containment: The Medicare Peer Review Organization Program, 14 Puget Sound L. Rev. 483 (1991).

2. *UR: Friend or Foe?* In the private sector, reviewing insurance claims by a utilization review (UR) process is now pursued much more thoroughly and aggressively than in prior decades, leading to a growing backlash from physicians and patients. Prof. Gilhooley offers a description from the patient's point of view of how utilization review is conducted. Consider also the following:

> In the predawn hours of March 27, 1993, Esther Nesbitt was working the night shift at Kaiser's nurse hotline. She had been a nurse for 20 years, working in New York City emergency rooms early in her career.... On Nesbitt's desk was a *Manual of Pediatric Protocols,* including a three-page tip sheet entitled "Fever." The tip sheet was arranged much like a set of college notes, with a nine-line definition of fever at the top, an explanation of fever's causes, and only then a series of questions that parents should be asked. Down near the bottom of the first page, ninth in a list of 11 questions, was a question that many emergency-room doctors would pose right away: "Is [the] child having problems breathing?"
>
> From her perch at Kaiser's offices, Nesbitt decided after a few minutes that little James Adams wasn't in respiratory distress.... There would be no ambulance called, no authorization for the family to seek the closest hospital. Kaiser had given its instructions. It was up to Lamona Adams to stand in her driveway, holding her baby in the dark, and wait for her husband to come home. [The couple drove 40 miles through a severe rain storm to reach the hospital designated by Kaiser. At that point, their baby had stopped breathing. He turned out to have meningitis, a severe but easily treatable infection when caught in time. With aggressive treatment, the doctors saved his life, but they had to amputate all his hands and feet because of damage to his circulatory system.]

George Anders, Health Against Wealth: HMOs and the Breakdown of Medical Trust (1996).

> To call myself a vascular surgeon, I had to do well in college, then spend the next 12 years working grueling hours, depriving myself of most of the joys of young adulthood and immersing myself in other people's worst misery.... I now have an army of vindictive bureaucrats and largely untrained reviewers nipping at my heels, and must spend many hours a week defending myself against their overwhelmingly wrongheaded second-guessing of clinical decisions.

Stephen D. Leonard, M.D., Letter to the Editor, N.Y. Times, April, 28, 1992, at A16. For additional narrative accounts of the maddening logic and personal impact of medical necessity determinations, see Andrew Batavia, Of Wheelchairs and Managed Care, 18(6) Health Aff. 171 (Dec. 1999); Lisa Iezzoni, Boundaries 18(6) Health Aff. 171 (Dec. 1999); an excerpt of the Web site for this book, www.health-law.org.

Gerald Grumet, 31 New Eng. J. Med. 607 (1989) (railing against the "managerial-review process in which armies of claims clerks, administrators, auditors, form processors, peer reviewers, functionaries, and technocrats of every description insinuate themselves into a complex system that authorizes, pays for and delivers medical care"). For a more neutral and academic account of how health insurance medical directors go about their work, see Thomas Bodenheimer & Lawrence Casalino, Executives with White Coats—The Work and World View of Managed-Care Medical Directors, 341 New Eng. J. Med. 1945 (1999). For the view from an actual medical director, see S. D. Boren, I Had a Tough Day Today, Hillary, 330 New Eng. J. Med. 500 (1994).

3. *The Legality of Prior Authorization.* The fact that utilization review is now done more often on a prospective basis, prior to treatment, than as part of ordinary insurance claims review, means that decisions to deny coverage are likely to result in denial of treatment as well. Therefore, it can give rise to tort liability as well as contractual liability.

The legality of UR can also be challenged under regulatory and contract law. Because coverage denials affect treatment decisions, utilization review might be characterized as an illegal interference with medical judgment. This might occur, for instance, if the utilization reviewer making a medical necessity determination is not a licensed physician in the relevant state. The usual process is for nonmedical personnel to review coverage requests with screening criteria that flag certain requests for review by a nurse. The nurse then decides which cases to refer for physician review. Usually the request is not denied without physician review, but the physician may be in some central office out of state, and usually is not trained in the particular specialty involved, unless the insurer decides to refer the request for independent review. See Institute of Medicine, Controlling Costs and Changing Patient Care? The Role of Utilization Management (1989).

Courts generally have upheld this process when challenged based on licensure or on general principles of interference with medical judgment. They reason that utilization reviewers do not purport to make medical treatment decisions, only payment decisions. See Morris v. District of Columbia Board of Medicine, 701 A.2d 364 (D.C. 1997) (reviewing medical appropriateness for an insurance company does not constitute the practice of medicine); Association of American Physicians and Surgeons v. Weinberger, 395 F. Supp. 125 (N.D. Ill. 1975) (three-judge court), *aff'd mem.* 423 U.S. 975 (1975) (medical necessity review under Medicare does not unduly interfere with physicians' judgment). But see Murphy v. Board of Medical Examiners, 949 P.2d 530 (Ariz. Ct. App. 1997) (medical licensing board has jurisdiction over insurance company doctor who allegedly exercised bad medical judgment in denying claims); State Board of Registration for Healing Arts v. Fallon, 41 S.W.3d 474 (Mo. 2001) (same). Might a utilization review requirement that denies coverage unless the patient obtains advance approval be struck down as an illegal forfeiture or penalty clause under contract law? Consider a case where it is clear the request would have been approved if submitted but the insurer denies payment simply because the patient or doctor did not follow the proper channels. Nazay v. Miller, 949 F.2d 1323, 1335 (3d Cir. 1991) (upholding insurer under ERISA, but only where the failure to obtain advance permission cost the patient a 30 percent copayment, not complete denial of coverage). See generally Gail Agrawal, Resuscitating Professionalism: Self-Regulation in the Medical Marketplace, 66 U. Mo. L. Rev. 341 (2001); John Blum, An Analysis of Legal Liability in Health Care Utilization Review and Case Management, 26 Hous. L. Rev. 191 (1989); Mark Hall, Institutional Control of Physician Behavior, 137 U. Penn. L. Rev. 431 (1988); Edward P. Richards, The Police Power and the Regulation of Medical Practice: A Historical Review and Guide for Medical Licensing Board Regulation of Physicians in ERISA-Qualified Managed Care Organizations, 8 Ann. Health L. 201 (1999); David L. Treuman, The Liability of Medical Directors for Utilization Review Decisions, 35 J. Health L. 105 (2002); Note, 9 B.U. Pub. Int. L.J. 89 (1999).

Legal oversight of UR has resulted more through legislation than through judicial doctrine. Utilization review regulations now exist in most states. They require insurers and third-party UR firms to maintain proper licensure and expertise of personnel (including M.D.'s licensed in the state), to give a prompt response to coverage requests, and sometimes to disclose the screening criteria they use.

4. *The Success of UR.* Research shows that cost-savings from UR are modest. Utilization review successfully reduces hospitalization expenses, but savings overall are muted by the administrative expense of running these programs. See Uwe Reinhardt, Spending More Through Cost Control: Our Obsessive Quest to Gut the Hospital, 15 Health Aff. 145 (Summer 1996); M. Shapiro & N. Wenger, Rethinking Utilization Review, 333 New Eng. J. Med. 1353 (1995). This anemic performance, coupled with the public and professional backlash UR engenders, has caused health insurers to cut back on the amount of UR they do. Many insurers have greatly reduced the list of services that require prior authorization, and one prominent HMO (United) says that it has eliminated UR almost entirely. Instead of case-by-case utilization review, insurers intend to use physician profiling to monitor the patterns of utilization and expenditures each physician generates over a range of patients and to compare those patterns among peer physicians. What exactly they will do with this information remains to be seen.

Research Exercise: Medicare Covered Services

Your clients are a group of ophthalmologists (eye doctors). Their biggest revenue producer is radial keratotomy, a form of surgery that corrects for nearsightedness. They want to provide a new form of radial keratotomy using laser surgery. The target age group for this procedure is people 40 years of age and older. Most private insurance plans in your area do not pay for eye services that are elective surgery. The most lucrative market will surely be the Medicare population. Use one of the practitioner treatises such as the *CCH Medicare & Medicaid Guide* to determine whether this procedure is a Medicare-covered service?

■ HECKLER v. RINGER
466 U.S. 602 (1984)

Syllabus. . . . Judicial review of a claim under the Medicare Act is available only after the Secretary of Health and Human Services renders a "final decision" on the claim in the same manner as is provided in 42 U.S.C. §405(g). . . . [This is] the sole avenue for judicial review of all "claim[s] arising under" the Medicare Act. Pursuant to her rulemaking authority, the Secretary has provided that a "final decision" is rendered on a Medicare claim only after the claimant has pressed the claim through all designated levels of administrative review.

In January 1979, the Secretary issued an administrative instruction to all fiscal intermediaries [which are private insurance companies that work with Medicare to process claims. The Secretary instructed] that no payment is to be made for Medicare claims arising out of a surgical procedure known as bilateral carotid body resection (BCBR) when performed to relieve respiratory distress. [BCBR involves the surgical removal of the carotid bodies, structures the size of a rice grain that are located in the neck and that control the diameter of the bronchial tubes. Proponents of the procedure claim that it reduces the symptoms of pulmonary diseases such as asthma, bronchitis, and emphysema.] Until October 1980, Administrative Law Judges (ALJs), who were not bound by the instruction, consistently ruled in favor of claimants whose BCBR claims had been denied by the [fiscal] intermediaries. The Appeals Council also authorized payment for BCBR Part A expenses in a case involving numerous claimants. On October 28, 1980, the Secretary issued a formal administrative ruling, intended to have a binding effect on the ALJs and the Appeals Council, prohibiting them from ordering Medicare payments for BCBR operations occurring after that date, the Secretary having concluded that the BCBR procedure was not "reasonable and necessary" within the meaning of the Medicare Act.

Without having exhausted their administrative remedies, respondents brought an action in Federal District Court challenging the Secretary's instruction and ruling. . . . Respondents are four Medicare claimants for whom BCBR surgery was prescribed to relieve pulmonary problems. Three of the respondents (Holmes, Webster-Zieber, and Vescio) had the surgery before October 28, 1980, and filed claims for reimbursement with the fiscal intermediary, and the fourth respondent (Ringer) never had the surgery, claiming that he was unable to afford it. . . . The District Court dismissed the complaint for lack of jurisdiction, holding that . . . respondents must exhaust their administrative remedies pursuant to §405(g) before pursuing their action in federal court. The Court of Appeals reversed, holding that to the extent respondents were seeking to invalidate the Secretary's procedure for determining entitlement to benefits, those claims were cognizable under the federal-question and mandamus statutes, without the administrative exhaustion requirement of §405(g) since exhaustion would be futile and might not fully compensate respondents for their asserted injuries in view of the fact that they sought payment without the prejudice—and the necessity of appeal—resulting from the existence of the Secretary's instruction and ruling. . . .

Justice REHNQUIST delivered the opinion of the Court.

. . . [The first three] respondents clearly have an adequate remedy in §405(g) for challenging all aspects of the Secretary's denial of their claims for payment for the BCBR surgery, including any objections they have to the instructions or to the ruling if either ultimately should play a part in the Secretary's denial of their claims.... §405(g) is the only avenue for judicial review of respondents' Holmes', Vescio's, and Webster-Zieber's claims for benefits, and, when their complaint was filed in District Court, each had failed to satisfy the exhaustion requirement that is a prerequisite to jurisdiction under that provision. [Editor's note: Section 405(g) states: Any individual, after any final decision of the Commissioner of Social Security made after a hearing to which he was a party, ...may obtain a review of such decision by a civil action commenced within sixty days...." 42 U.S.C. §405(h) further states that "no...decision of the Secretary shall be reviewed by any person, tribunal, or governmental agency except as herein provided. The statute further states that "claims arising under" Medicare may not be brought under other statutes that normally provide for jurisidiction over federal controversies.]...

Respondents urge us to hold them excused from further exhaustion and to hold that the District Court could have properly exercised jurisdiction over their claims under §405(g). We have held that the Secretary herself may waive the exhaustion requirement when she deems further exhaustion futile. Mathews v. Eldridge, 424 U.S., at 328.... [But] it cannot be said that the Secretary has in any sense waived further exhaustion. In the face of the Secretary's vigorous disagreement, the Court of Appeals concluded that the Secretary's formal ruling denying payment for BCBR claims rendered further exhaustion by respondents futile. But as we have pointed out above, the administrative ruling is not even applicable to respondents' claims because they had their surgery before October 28, 1980.... Although respondents would clearly prefer an immediate appeal to the District Court rather than the often lengthy administrative review process, exhaustion of administrative remedies is in no sense futile for these respondents, and they, therefore, must adhere to the administrative procedure which Congress has established for adjudicating their Medicare claims....

Respondent Ringer is in a separate group from the other three respondents in this case...because he wishes to have the operation and [he] claims that the Secretary's refusal to allow payment for it precludes him from doing so. ...[Therefore], it can be argued that Ringer does not yet have a "claim" to present to the Secretary and thus that he does not have a "claim arising under" the Medicare Act so as to be subject to [the statute's] bar to [ordinary] federal-question jurisdiction....We find that argument superficially appealing but ultimately unavailing.

Although it is true that Ringer is not seeking the immediate payment of benefits, he is clearly seeking to establish a right to future payments should he ultimately decide to proceed with BCBR surgery. The claim for future benefits must be construed as a "claim arising under" the Medicare Act because any other construction would allow claimants substantially to undercut Congress' carefully crafted scheme for administering the Medicare Act.... If we allow claimants in Ringer's position to challenge in federal court the Secretary's determination, embodied in her rule, that BCBR surgery is not a covered service, we would be inviting them to bypass the exhaustion requirements of the Medicare Act by simply bringing declaratory judgment actions in federal court before they undergo the medical procedure in question. Congress clearly foreclosed the possibility of obtaining such advisory opinions from the Secretary herself, requiring instead that a claim could be filed for her scrutiny only after the medical service for which payment is sought has been furnished....

Because Ringer has not given the Secretary an opportunity to rule on a concrete claim for reimbursement, he has not satisfied the nonwaivable exhaustion requirement of §405(g). The District Court, therefore, had no jurisdiction as to respondent Ringer.... The judgment of the Court of Appeals is accordingly reversed.

Justice STEVENS, with whom Justice BRENNAN and Justice MARSHALL join, concurring in the judgment in part and dissenting in part.

The Medicare Act is designed to insure the elderly against the often crushing costs of medical care.... The complaint indicates that Ringer, "who is 68 years of age, suffers from severe, chronic obstructive airways disease, (i.e., severe emphysema), cor pulmonale and right heart strain," and that he is eligible for Medicare benefits and needs the operation but cannot afford it unless the Secretary agrees to pay for it.... Today, the majority holds that Ringer must have the operation that he cannot afford and cannot obtain because of the Secretary's ruling before he can challenge that ruling.... Of course, the reason he has not filed such a claim is that there is nothing to reimburse—he has incurred no expenses because he cannot afford to do so. Without anything to reimburse, the Secretary refuses to provide a hearing on what she and the Court believe to be a nonexistent "claim." Thus the only way Ringer can pursue his §405(g) remedy is by doing something that the Secretary will not let him do.

Thus, it would seem, Ringer both does and does not have a claim which arises under the Medicare Act. He cannot file a claim under the Medicare Act until after he has the operation; he cannot have the operation unless he can challenge the Secretary's ruling; and he cannot challenge that ruling except in an action seeking judicial review of the denial of a claim under the Medicare Act. This one-eyed procedural analysis frustrates the remedial intent of Congress as plainly as it frustrates this litigant's plea for a remedy. The cruel irony is that a statute designed to help the elderly in need of medical assistance is being construed to protect from administrative absolutism only those wealthy enough to be able to afford an operation and then seek reimbursement....

■ **DANIELS v. WADLEY**
926 F. Supp. 1305 (M.D. Tenn. 1996), vacated in part, 145 F.3d 1330
(6th Cir. 1998)

JOHN T. NIXON, Chief Judge.
... This case is the continuation of a class action started in 1979 regarding the provision of medical assistance under Tennessee's pre-1994 Medicaid program. Plaintiffs in the current action are Medicaid-eligible enrollees of the Tennessee Medicaid Demonstration Project ("TennCare"). Plaintiffs seek to modify the Second Consent Decree in this action,... in order to prevent the denial, delay, reduction, suspension or termination of medical assistance or other adverse action

to enrollees without due process and a timely fair hearing in accordance with ...the "Medicaid Act" [and] the United States Constitution.[1] ...

Under TennCare...Managed Care Organizations ("MCOs") have financial incentives to deny enrollees health care even when such health care is medically appropriate. These incentives arise out of significant changes to Tennessee's Medicaid Program, which took effect with the inception of TennCare. Based on these changes, the Court finds that it is appropriate to modify the Second Consent Decree.

The Tennessee Medicaid program in place at the time that the Second Consent Decree was negotiated permitted a recipient to choose his or her provider. The program required providers, for the most part, to directly bill the state for services rendered....If the Medicaid Bureau denied a provider's claim for payment, the provider could sometimes directly bill the recipient. A Medicaid recipient could be directly billed if the recipient was ineligible at the time that the service was provided, if the service was not covered, or if limits for a particular service had been exceeded. If payment was denied due to provider error, the provider was prohibited from seeking any payment from the recipient.

In many situations prior authorization for medical care was not required under the Tennessee Medicaid program. Where prior authorization was required, the Medicaid Act permitted the recipient to request a fair hearing...to appeal a denial of authorization....The Medicaid Act required that the coverage dispute be resolved within ninety days of the recipient's request for a hearing. In many circumstances, the Medicaid Act mandated that services to the recipient continue until the coverage dispute was resolved through a fair hearing....

Under TennCare enrollees are not free to choose their own providers. To obtain services from specialists, enrollees must obtain a referral from their primary care physician who is under contract with an MCO. TennCare forms contracts with MCOs to pay for enrollees' health care. MCOs receive a flat fee for each enrollee that the MCO covers. MCOs make a profit to the extent that their total income in flat fees exceeds the amount that the MCO pays to doctors and hospitals for treating sick enrollees. In order to prevent enrollees from receiving "too much" care, which would hurt an MCO's profit margin, MCOs screen enrollee care requests through primary care physicians with whom the MCOs have contracts....

Under TennCare if an enrollee wishes to appeal an adverse coverage decision, the enrollee does not have immediate access to an impartial decision maker. An enrollee's claim is not heard before an administrative [law] judge [ALJ] or hearing officer...until after the enrollee has waded through several stages of preliminary review.[2] The entire appeals process may take more than ninety

---

[1] ...Defendants argue that Plaintiffs do not have the capacity to bring this action. The Court rejects this argument....Plaintiffs allege that state officials have failed to comply with fair hearing requirements imposed under the Medicaid Act. The Medicaid Act contains no provisions designed to resolve disputes of the nature presented here, so there is no statute-based remedy to preempt Plaintiffs' claims....

[2] ...The point at which an ALJ or hearing officer becomes involved in an adjudication is significant because under Tennessee law such adjudicators must be objective and impartial. The impartiality necessary to fairly resolve coverage disputes under the TennCare program might not be possible where the adjudicator has a pecuniary or employment interest in a given case, as would be the case where an MCO employee presided over a TennCare coverage dispute....The Court notes that a

days. And services do not continue pending resolution of the coverage dispute by an impartial decision maker.

The Court finds that because of the pecuniary incentives that MCOs have for denying, suspending, or terminating care under the TennCare system... TennCare enrollees need strong due process protections to protect themselves from inappropriate denials of health care....

The appeals process currently in place is designed to address [two] categories of appeals: (1) appeals of adverse decisions regarding applications, premiums, and disenrollment;... (2) appeals of decisions to deny medically necessary services.

If an MCO issues an unfavorable decision regarding an enrollee's enrollment status,... the enrollee or prospective enrollee has thirty days to request administrative review by the TennCare [Medical] Review Unit [MRU].... If the enrollee disagrees with the decision, the enrollee may, within thirty days, request a hearing before the Commissioner of the Tennessee Department of Finance and Administration. If the matter involves an amount in controversy of less than $500, there will be an informal hearing. Otherwise there will be a formal hearing. Either variety of hearing will be presided over by an administrative judge or a hearing officer. [The adequacy of these procedures to challenge enrollment decisions was not questioned.]...

[Once enrolled,] if an MCO has denied an enrollee's request for care, the enrollee's physician may, with the enrollee's authorization, choose to request an expedited review of that decision. To obtain an expedited review, the enrollee's physician must notify the MCO that an expedited review is medically necessary. (Given that such physicians are effectively employed by the MCOs, the Court notes that they may receive pressure not to request expedited review.) The MCO must reconsider its decision within two working days of notification. If the MCO denies the request on review, the MCO must notify the physician in writing of the reason for the denial. Within two working days, the physician may request an expedited administrative review of the decision by the MRU. The MRU will request that the MCO, within five working days, provide any documents that the MCO wishes to submit in support of its decision. The MRU then must issue a written decision within two working days of receiving the documents from the MCO. If the decision is favorable to the enrollee, the decision is binding on the MCO. If it is not, the physician may request an expedited medical appeal, conducted by an ALJ or hearing officer, within two working days of receipt of the MRU's decision. Such a hearing will be held within ten working days, and a decision will be rendered within two working days....

The Court finds that the TennCare process for appealing disputed coverage decisions fails to meet Medicaid Act requirements. TennCare violates the Medicaid Act for two reasons: (1) TennCare fails to provide pre-deprivation hearings in situations in which the Medicaid Act would require such hearings; (2) TennCare fails to provide for sufficiently rapid resolution of disputed claims.

First, under the Medicaid Act benefits may rarely, if ever, be terminated prior to a hearing....

---

hearing [in court] would pose even less of a risk of partiality than a hearing before an ALJ or hearing officer, but given the speed with which disputes regarding health care coverage must be resolved in order to prevent harm to an enrollee, such hearings are not plausible.

Second, under TennCare, claim resolution takes too long. Under the Medicaid Act, the agency must take final administrative action within ninety days from the date that a hearing is requested. 42 C.F.R. §431.244(f). The current TennCare procedures appear to allow claims to languish longer than that before they are resolved.... [T]he TennCare appeals process [also] violates procedural due process requirements set forth under the Fourteenth Amendment.

In Goldberg v. Kelly, 397 U.S. 254, 90 S. Ct. 1011, 25 L. Ed. 2d 287 (1970), New York City residents receiving benefits through the federal program Aid to Families with Dependent Children or through New York State's Home Relief program brought suit challenging the adequacy of procedures for notice and hearing in connection with decisions to terminate aid. The Supreme Court held that procedural due process requires pretermination evidentiary hearings before public assistance payments to welfare recipients may be discontinued. The Court also held that due process requires that such hearings provide recipients with an opportunity to appeal personally with or without counsel before an impartial decision maker and orally present evidence and confront adverse witnesses. The *Goldberg* Court noted that welfare recipients are entitled to pre-deprivation process because of their extreme vulnerability in the face of wrongful benefit termination....

Like the plaintiffs in *Goldberg,* the Plaintiffs in the current action, Medicaid-eligible TennCare enrollees, have limited financial resources. Moreover, they have no means other than Defendants' fastidious adherence to Medicaid requirements to ensure that they are not wrongfully denied their property [and liberty] interest in continued coverage. If Plaintiffs' health care benefits are wrongfully denied, they will likely be forced to forgo the contested medical treatment and could suffer substantial physical harm as a result. Several Plaintiffs in this action, and undoubtedly others like them, suffered harm due to denial of coverage during the protracted process of resolving coverage disputes.[3] Given the importance of prompt medical treatment, and Plaintiffs' lack of other alternatives, this is unacceptable. The potential damage to Plaintiffs in this situation is much worse than the potential damage to the state if the state continues providing benefits pending the completion of a hearing by an impartial adjudicator and then subsequently recoups the benefits if it prevails. See Mathews v. Eldridge, 424 U.S. 319 (1976). The Court rejects the suggestion that Defendants should be allowed to terminate coverage pending resolution of a claim dispute with the stipulation that they reimburse an enrollee if the enrollee prevails at the hearing. Given that Medicaid-eligible enrollees lack financial resources, it is unrealistic to expect them to continue coverage on their own pending resolution of the coverage dispute....

[3] There are many examples of the harm that TennCare enrollees suffer when coverage is denied during a protracted dispute resolution process. For example, during the course of H.B.'s coverage dispute, her condition deteriorated so much that she may now require a liver transplant as well as a small bowel transplant. H.G. suffered a stroke while contesting her MCO's denial of coverage for specialist care to clear arteries in her neck. M.T. suffered serious pain as a result of being denied coverage for pediatric oral surgery to cap her badly decayed teeth. As a result of this decay M.T. has had to ingest large quantities of antibiotics. Such scenarios are capable of repetition among TennCare's other Medicaid-eligible enrollees under the current TennCare dispute resolution process.

Moreover, the Court finds that the hearing requirements, which must be met to comport with the Fourteenth Amendment, are not satisfied until an appeal is heard by an impartial adjudicator.... In the current action the MCOs have a direct and substantial pecuniary interest in denying or delaying costly services for which the MCOs must pay. [Therefore, they are not impartial.]...

For these reasons the Court finds that the current TennCare hearing process violates the procedural due process requirements of the Constitution.

PLAINTIFFS' RELIEF

The Court denies Plaintiffs' request for reimbursement of money that they have already paid to secure health care. The Court bases this decision on the principle of sovereign immunity. Edelman v. Jordan, 415 U.S. 651 (1974)....

The Court finds that the facts of this action meet the standard for issuing an injunction.... In the meantime, the Court enjoins Defendants from denying benefits to any Medicaid-eligible TennCare enrollee prior to a hearing conducted by an impartial adjudicator where the Medicaid Act would provide for such a hearing. The Court also enjoins Defendants from permitting coverage disputes to continue unresolved for over ninety days after an enrollee's request for review of an adverse decision....

Notes: Medicare and Medicaid Appeal Procedures

1. *Medicaid Judicial Review.* The Medicaid statute contains no special limitation of judicial review like that in the Medicare statute. Therefore, judicial review of Medicaid decisions is readily available under general federal question jurisdiction (via the §1983 civil rights statute) without the same need for thorough exhaustion of administrative remedies. Wilder v. Virginia Hospital Ass'n, 496 U.S. 498 (1990). Some doubt was raised on this score by Suter v. Artist M., 503 U.S. 347 (1992), which found that the public has no right to challenge whether child protection services meet statutory requirements. *Suter* appears inconsistent with *Wilder,* which led commentators to predict that new members of the Court would overturn *Wilder.* Others worried that these precedents allowed only providers to challenge Medicaid decisions but not patients. See generally Rand Rosenblatt, The Courts, Health Care Reform, and the Reconstruction of American Social Legislation, 18 J. Health Pol. Pol'y & L. 439 (1993). However, most courts continue to allow Medicaid appeals both by patients and by providers. See, e.g., Wood v. Tompkins, 33 F.3d 600 (1994). Even where judicial jurisdiction exists, though, the TennCare case indicates that judicial remedies against state government are sharply limited in federal court, to prospective injunctive relief rather than retrospective monetary awards. Therefore, litigants may sometimes find state court preferable. See Jeanne Finberg, Litigating Medicaid Class Actions, 26 Clearinghouse Rev. 1592 (1993); Ann Lever & Herbert Eastman, "Shake It Up in a Bag": Strategies for Representing Beneficiaries in Medicaid Litigation, 35 St. Louis U. L.J. 863 (1991).

2. *Medicare Judicial Review.* Under Medicare, judicial review is available only for claims above $1000, even if administrative remedies are exhausted as required

by *Ricker*. Litigants have sometimes found inventive ways to circumvent these jurisdictional limitations. See Mathews v. Diaz, 426 U.S. 67 (1976) (administrative exhaustion waived by agency); Bowen v. Michigan Academy of Family Physicians, 476 U.S. 667 (1986) (under prior version of statute, allowing judicial review of the method for determining reimbursement but not of reimbursement amounts (whatever that means)); City of New York v. Heckler, 476 U.S. 467 (1986) (failure to follow normal appeals route excused by the futility and irreparable injury of strict compliance); Mount Sinai Medical Center v. United States, 13 Ct. Cl. 561 (1987) (jurisdictional limitations do not apply to review by the Court of Claims); Bartlett v. Bowen, 816 F.2d 695 (D.C. Cir. 1987) (amount-in-controversy limits do not apply to constitutional claims); VNA v. Heckler, 711 F.2d 1020 (11th Cir. 1983) (All Writs Act may be invoked in cases of extreme hardship to obtain an injunction preserving the status quo pending full administrative appeals). However, the Supreme Court subsequently closed a number of these loopholes by ruling that the requirement of first pursuing administrative remedies prior to going to court is "nearly absolute." Shalala v. Illinois Council of Long Term Care, 529 U.S. 1 (2000). Moreover, even when judicial review is obtained, courts give heavy deference to federal and state agencies' interpretations of their governing statutes, so it is difficult to win on the merits. See Gray Panthers v. Schweiker, 453 U.S. 34 (1981); Atkins v. Rivera, 477 U.S. 154 (1986). See generally Eleanor Kinney, ed., Guide to Medicare Coverage Decision-Making and Appeals (2002); John Cogan & Rodney Johnson, Administrative Channeling under the Medicare Act Clarified, 9 Ann. Health L. 125 (2000); Eleanor Kinney, The Role of Judicial Review Regarding Medicare and Medicaid Program Policy, 35 St. Louis U. L.J. 761 (1991); Eleanor Kinney, The Medicare Appeals System for Coverage and Payment Disputes, 1 Admin. L.J. 1 (1987); J. M. Rogers, A Way Out of the Social Security Jurisdiction Tangle, 21 Ariz. L. Rev. 689 (1979); Note, 25 New Eng. L. Rev. 617 (1990); Annot., 43 A.L.R. Fed. 484 (1979).

3. *Administrative Appeals.* The TennCare case emphasizes that speedy, impartial administrative appeals may be more important than ultimate judicial review. The greatest threat to impartiality occurs in managed care settings where the insurer stands to profit from claims it denies. But, even in fee-for-service settings where insurers are paid merely to administer claims, not to render treatment, can it be said that a hearing office employed by the insurer is wholly impartial? See Schweiker v. McClure, 456 U.S. 188 (1982) (Medicare hearing officer appointed by insurer is not disqualified from reviewing insurer's own decisions). What else is required in a fair hearing besides an impartial decisionmaker? Would a simple telephone call suffice? Gray Panthers v. Schweiker, 652 F.2d 146 (D.C. Cir. 1980) (telephone hearings are permissible in most circumstances). "Hearings" can also consist of simply an exchange of paperwork. Is it realistic for non-law professors to be able to argue and defend their position in this fashion without assistance? Can HMO patients expect their doctors to help them, as might occur in a fee-for-service setting?

4. *Constitutional Requirements.* The constitutional arguments applied to Tennessee's Medicaid program do not have as strong a force under Medicare, because its recipients are not presumed to be financially needy. Therefore, formal hearings prior to denying benefits are not usually constitutionally required; it is sufficient to provide a hearing after the denial. See Mathews v. Eldridge, 424 U.S.

319 (1976) (no hearing required prior to terminating disability recipients); Himmler v. Califano, 611 F.2d 137 (6th Cir. 1979) (same for denial of Medicare benefits). Also, Goldberg v. Kelly concerned welfare recipients whose benefits were cut off entirely, not simply limited. Moreover, an applicant for a program does not have the same constitutional rights as one who is already receiving its services. Given these precedents and distinctions, how should we regard an existing Medicare or Medicaid recipient who is seeking a particular treatment?

Under Medicare, some courts have ruled that due process requirements are just as stringent as in Goldberg v. Kelly when the denial of benefits affects not just financial liability but also the opportunity to obtain services. This occurs when Medicare recipients are subject to prospective utilization review, that is, the denial of coverage prior to treatment. Kraemer v. Heckler, 737 F.2d 214 (2d Cir. 1984); Grijalva v. Shalala, 152 F.3d 1115 (9th Cir. 1998); cf. Gray Panthers v. Schweiker, 652 F.2d 146 (D.C. Cir. 1981). Heckler v. Ringer did not confront this issue because it was decided on jurisdictional grounds, but elsewhere the Supreme Court has held that due process does not require a fair hearing prior to transferring or discharging a Medicaid nursing home patient. In one case it reasoned that patients do not have a protected constitutional interest in being at a particular facility, only in receiving benefits generally, O'Bannon v. Town Court Nursing Center, 447 U.S. 773 (1980), and in another case it reasoned that a private facility's own transfer decision does not constitute state action. Blum v. Yaretsky, 457 U.S. 991 (1982). Despite these rulings, the court in Grijalva v. Shalala, 152 F.3d 1115 (9th Cir. 1998), vacated, 526 U.S. 1096 (1999), imposed hearing requirements on Medicare HMOs similar to those imposed in Daniels v. Wadley. It reasoned that HMOs are state actors when they contract with Medicare for the full range of program obligations and benefits, and that many medical services have life-saving or life-altering effects.

These rulings are cast into some doubt, however, by the Supreme Court's subsequent decision in a workers' compensation case. In American Manufacturers Mutual Insurance Co. v. Sullivan, 526 U.S. 40 (1999), the Court found no constitutional violation in a state allowing workers' comp insurers to withhold payment of medical benefits pending a utilization review for medical necessity. Rather than balancing the costs and benefits of requiring payment pending review, the Court preempted any due process analysis by holding: (1) private insurers are not state actors even though they provide their benefits under a state-administered and heavily regulated scheme; and (2) there is no protected property interest in receiving medical benefits until claimants establish their entitlement, so there can be no due process deprivation in refusing the benefits prior to resolving disputes over entitlement. It is unclear what impact this ruling will have on utilization review by Medicare HMOs. (The Supreme Court vacated the *Grijalva* decision noted above for reconsideration in light of its *American Manufacturers* opinion, and the state action aspect of the *Daniels* opinion was vacated as moot due to the parties' having settled the substance of the case.) Although Medicare HMOs are also private insurers, they are not merely regulated by the state; they contract with the government to provide benefits under a public insurance program, so the argument for state action is stronger. However, the second point might be used to undermine the argument that due process requires more procedural protections than those afforded by regulations, since it seems to accept the previously rejected argument that substantive entitlements can be conditioned on limited procedural protections. For a contrasting decision under state law, see Rudolph v. Pennsylvania Blue Shield, 717 A.2d 508 (1998) (UR entity created by statute for Blue Cross is subject to constitutional due process requirements, and a UR entity affiliated with Blue Cross is not an impartial panel).

5. *Statutory and Regulatory Appeal Rights.* Many of these administrative appeal issues have been resolved by statutes or regulations. For nursing home patients, Medicaid requires notice and a hearing for all patients, not just public patients, before discharging or transferring them, and many states impose similar requirements on nursing homes through their licensing laws. See M. Schuster et al., Nursing Home Transfer and Discharge Protections, Clearinghouse Rev., Oct. 1992, at 619. How these notice and hearing requirements apply to Medicaid HMOs, however, is still being decided. The denial of some medical services has as much or more impact as transfer from a nursing home, but not so for all medical services. Is it feasible to provide an advance hearing before each contested medical decision?

Under Medicare, decisions to discharge a patient from the hospital can be challenged by an immediate appeal to the local Quality Improvement Organization (formerly called "Peer Review Organization"). Hospitalized Medicare patients must be given written notice of discharge decisions, and a several-day grace period in which to pursue their appeal, during which time they can remain in the hospital with full coverage.

Outside the hospital, Medicare and Medicaid regulations are sensitive to the retroactive effect of billing patients after the fact for services they thought were covered but ultimately learn are not. For instance, Medicare contains "liability protection" provisions that prevent physicians from billing for Part B services that Medicare refuses to cover as unnecessary or unreasonable. In order to bill for noncovered services, physicians must have their patients sign a waiver prior to treatment that discloses the treatment may not be covered by Medicare. 42 U.S.C. §1395u(*l*). This is not allowed under Medicaid.

As a result of these "hold harmless" protections, often times providers have much more at stake in these administrative and judicial appeals than do patients. Providers ultimately receive most or all of the reimbursement, and the patient may not be financially liable at all. Indeed, one court held that Medicaid patients have so little financial stake in coverage denials that they have no appeal rights at all! Banks v. Secretary, Indiana Family and Social Services Admin., 997 F.2d 231 (7th Cir. 1993). Accordingly, providers often attempt to invoke these appeal procedures designed for patients. In some cases, they are allowed to do so in their own right, in other cases they are allowed to assist patients by representing them, but in a few situations they may not participate at all. You'll be relieved to know that we won't go into the details here.

6. *The Components of Administrative Appeals.* Observe that the administrative appeal procedures under Medicare are similar to the four or five steps outlined in Dennis v. Wadley. However, the precise steps and the institutional names vary between Part A and Part B, and between fee-for-service and HMOs. Under Part B, "fiscal intermediaries" are known as "carriers." For hospitalization, most issues are determined by "Quality Improvement Organizations" (QIOs, formerly

called "Peer Review Organizations"). The multiple steps required in pursuing full administrative appeal and judicial review can easily consume many years.

The TennCare case illustrates that patients' appeal rights must be given even more attention in an HMO setting, due to their doctors' inherent conflict of interest and the greater likelihood that patients will never learn there is a medical difference of opinion. In addition to Medicaid regulations, state HMO licensing regulations also impose requirements for grievance and appeal procedures that cover private patients as well, but licensing regulations do not impose the same extensive protections as mandated by Dennis v. Wadley. For another decision that amasses a thorough catalogue of the defects in HMO review procedures, this time under Medicare, see Grijalva v. Shalala, 946 F. Supp. 747 (D. Ariz. 1996), aff'd, 152 F.3d 1115 (9th Cir. 1996), vacated, 526 U.S. 1096 (1999). That court required internal review for urgent care within three days, and outside review within ten days, with services to be continued pending final decision. Most acute care services are considered "urgent." *Grijalva* was vacated because new federal regulations under Medicare usurped the decision by requiring many of the elements sought by the plaintiffs, such as requiring that Medicare HMOs ordinarily resolve initial appeals within 72 hours rather than the 60 days previously allowed. 62 Fed. Reg. 23,368 (1997). Administrative appeal procedures have also been included in the set of provisions known as Medicare + Choice that seek to implement a managed competition system for Medicare. See 42 U.S.C. §1395ff; Jennifer E. Gladieux, Medicare + Choice Appeal Procedures: Reconciling Due Process Rights and Cost Containment, 25 Am. J.L. & Med. 61 (1999). See generally Jennifer L. Wright, Unconstitutional or Impossible: The Irreconcilable Gap Between Managed Care and Due Process in Medicaid and Medicare, 17 J. Contemp. Health L. & Pol'y 135-180 (2000); Gordon Bonnyman & Michele Johnson, Unseen Peril: Inadequate Enrollee Grievance Protections in Public Managed Care Programs, 65 Tenn. L. Rev. 359 (1998); Gail Edson, Medicare and Managed Care, 44 U. Kan. L. Rev. 793 (bibliography).

7. *Informal Rules.* Patients often find it frustrating to pursue full exhaustion of administrative remedies because insurance carriers, hearing officers, and administrative law judges consider themselves bound by agency rules and policy statements like those issued in *Ricker.* As in *Bechtold* above, these administrative reviewers cannot alter coverage policy, only interpret and apply it. Moreover, the Medicare statute limits substantive relief even in court. For "national coverage determinations" (general rulings like the one at issue in *Ricker*), the statute declares that the determination does not have to comply with full rulemaking procedures, and it limits the remedy for an improper ruling to simply a remand to HCFA for reconsideration. 42 U.S.C. §1395ff(b)(3). Moreover, many of the rulings that intermediaries, carriers, HMOs, and ALJs feel bound by are not adopted as official determinations and therefore cannot be clearly challenged as such. Instead, they are maintained as "secret" criteria for conducting utilization review screens, or they are adopted informally simply as program instructions such as those in the Medicare Coverage Issues Manual referred to in *Bechtold*, supra. These informal pronouncements have caused considerable legal difficulty in determining whether they must be issued through formal rulemaking procedures. See generally Erringer v. Thompson, _____ F.3d _____, 2004 WL 1276840 (9th Cir. 2004); Eleanor Kinney, Rule and Policy Making Under the Medicaid Program:

A Challenge to Federalism, 51 Ohio St. L.J. 855 (1991); Eleanor Kinney, National Coverage Policy Under the Medicare Program, 32 St. Louis U. L.J. 869 (1988).

Problem: Appealing Adverse Coverage Decisions by HMOs

This problem is adapted from a real case history developed by the Center for Health Care Rights in California. What procedural remedies does the patient likely have under private insurance and under Medicare or Medicaid? Are they adequate?

Mr. H. was a diabetic and had severe ulcers on his feet. He was a member of an HMO, and his primary care physician had prescribed a treatment regimen that was proving ineffective. In response, the primary care physician offered Mr. H. an amputation below the knee as his only option. Mr. H. went out of plan to a local wound care center that specialized in diabetic wound treatment where he was advised that vein by-pass surgery would likely take care of his problem. The HMO denied such surgery because Mr. H. referred himself to the specialist without permission. The HMO advised Mr. H.'s family that its utilization review department was reviewing the case, but that it would take at least a month to review. Subsequently, the HMO agreed to approve such surgery, but only if done by Mr. H.'s current medical group, which did not have any physician who had ever performed vein by-pass surgery. Mr. H.'s family asked for him to be transferred to a primary care physician at the medical group that staffs the wound care center. The HMO responded that although they sometimes approve such requests, they would not do so in Mr. H.'s case and that they had already granted enough of his requests. They gave as their reason a provision in the plan documents that prevent referrals outside the plan's network when the network's physicians have the capability to perform the required procedure.

Problem: Choosing Health Insurance

From what you have learned so far, which of the following insurance plans do you personally prefer, assuming each one costs the same? Defend your choice (both your selection and rejections) with reasons drawn from these readings:

- Plan A: Covers the full range of medical care, subject to standard medical necessity or experimental exclusions, without any deductibles or copayments, but you must receive all care at an HMO clinic where doctors are paid a bonus for saving money.
- Plan B: Excludes mental health and preventative care, and the rest is subject to a $200 deductible and 20 percent copayment up to a maximum of $1,500 per year. Your choice of doctor, but all expensive treatments must be submitted for prior approval by the insurer to determine medical appropriateness.

- Plan C: Covers the full range of medical care, with no major exclusions and your choice of doctor, and no prior authorization requirement, but subject to a $3,000 deductible.
- Plan D: Coverage is defined in an approach similar to the Oregon plan, only using 5,000 specific categories of inclusion and exclusion taken from the latest practice guidelines based on medical research, as selected by a national panel of politically appointed experts. No other restrictions or financial limitations.

E. PROVIDER REIMBURSEMENT

We now shift from patients to providers. Providers are affected by health insurance not only in who and what it covers, but also in how they are paid for services that are covered. The following materials reveal that various methods of provider reimbursement are important in all three arenas of legal practice: litigation, business planning, and public policy.

■ REIMBURSING PHYSICIANS AND HOSPITALS*
Thomas Bodenheimer & Kevin Grumbach**
272 JAMA 971 (1994)

During the course of a typical day, many physicians experience four or five distinct types of reimbursement. In this article, we describe the different ways by which physicians and hospitals are paid. Although reimbursement has many facets, from determinations of prices to processing of claims, we focus our discussion on one of its most basic elements: establishing the unit of payment. This unit-of-payment taxonomy is essential for understanding such concepts as managed care and physician-borne "risk," concepts that feature prominently in many health system reform proposals.

Units of Payment in Order of Least to Most Aggregated

Payee	Procedure	Day	Episode of Illness	Patient	Time
Physician	Fee for service	Not applicable	Surgical or obstetric fee or physician diagnosis related group	Capitation	Salary
Hospital	Fee for service	Per diem	Hospital diagnosis related group	Capitation	Global budget

**The authors are physicians in the Department of Family and Community Medicine at the University of California-San Francisco.

Methods of payment lie along a continuum that extends from the least to the most aggregated unit. Under fee-for-service reimbursement, the unit of payment is the visit or procedure. All other reimbursement modes aggregate or bundle together several services into one unit of payment. Reimbursement by episode of illness pays physicians or hospitals one sum for all services delivered during one illness, for example, global surgical fees to physicians and DRGs for hospitals. Per diem payments to hospitals bundle all services delivered to a patient during one day. A further bundling of services is accomplished by capitation payment, in which one payment is made for each patient's treatment during a month or year. Capitation payment is generally associated with managed care. Payment based on all services delivered to all patients within a certain period includes global budget reimbursement of hospitals and salaried payment of physicians. . . .

1. Cost-Based Reimbursement

■ HEALTH PLAN*
Alain Enthoven**
1980

Most people think of the need for medical care as an insurable event, very similar to insured hurricane or automobile collision damage. You are either sick or well. If you are sick, you go to the doctor. The doctor diagnoses your illness, applies the standard treatment, and sends the bill for his or her "usual, customary, and reasonable fee," all or most of which is paid by your insurance company. Our entire Blue Cross-Blue Shield and commercial insurance system was built on that view of the problem. Medicare and Medicaid, the public insurance systems for the elderly and poor, were built on the same model. The consequence is a financial disaster. Our society has accepted the casualty insurance model for health care financing, only to find that it contributes to excessive and excessively costly care. . . .

Many people seem to think that medical care is like mechanical engineering—that for each medical condition there is a "best treatment," a "professional standard." It is up to the doctor to know that treatment and use it. People do not fully understand the great uncertainties that pervade medical care and the variety of acceptable treatments. They think of medical care as mostly treatment for acute life-threatening conditions, as if it were accurately represented by the television dramas about the emergency room. Based on these misconceptions, we have applied to medical care a financing system that was developed for casualty (fire and collision) insurance.

The ideal case for casualty insurance is one in which the damage is caused by an act of God and the cost of repair can be determined objectively. In such a case the financial incentives inherent in insurance do not play a significant role in either the incidence of damage or the cost of repair. Insurance of houses against

*Alain Enthoven is an economist on the faculty of the Graduate School of Business, Stanford University.
**Copyright © 1980. Addison-Wesley Publishing Co., Inc., Reading, Massachusetts. Reprinted by permission.

hurricane damage or fires caused by lightning does not bring on more storms. Collision insurance for automobiles fits the model tolerably, but much less well. Most people do not drive less carefully just because they have insurance. But those who do have insurance are likely to demand more and better repairs than those who do not—because someone else is paying the bill. Still, ordinarily, having your collision-damaged car repaired is not an open-ended task.

Medical insurance hardly fits the model at all. The element of judgment and choice in the decision to seek care and in the amount of care provided is too great. Caring for a patient can be open-ended, especially if he or she has a chronic disease. Uncertainty pervades medical diagnosis and treatment. In most cases there is not one correct or standard treatment. There may be several accepted therapies. Most medical care is not a matter of life and death, but rather of darker or lighter shades of grey concerning the quality of life....

When thinking about medical care, then, we should think in terms of a variety of legitimate treatments for each condition, with their relative merits in a particular case depending on the unique circumstances and values of the people involved. We should remember that there is pervasive uncertainty and that medicine is more an art based on judgment than a science based on calculation. Medical care deals more with the quality of life than with the quantity (length) of life. The "product" does not come in standard units. Medical care is a matter of subtle and complex judgments about more versus less, and more may often not be better....

In view of this, it should not be surprising that the institutional arrangements for providing care, including the financial incentives facing the doctor, are very important. The casualty insurance model does not fit medical care at all well, because making more care free to the patient and remunerative to the doctor leads to more, and more costly, care being demanded and provided....

To observe that financial incentives play an important role in the use of medical services is not to imply that they are the only, or even the most important, factor. Physicians are concerned primarily with curing their sick patients, regardless of the cost. That ethic has been instilled in them through years of arduous training. Many take a failure to cure a sick patient as a personal defeat. When we are sick, we want our doctors to be concerned with curing us and nothing else. Physicians and other health professionals are also motivated by a desire to achieve professional excellence and the esteem of their peers and the public. But their use of resources is inevitably shaped by financial incentives. Physicians who survive and prosper must ultimately do what brings in money and curtail those activities that lose money....

■ MEMORIAL HOSPITAL/ADAIR COUNTY HEALTH CENTER v. BOWEN
829 F.2d 111 (D.C. Cir. 1987)

BUCKLEY, Circuit Judge.

The Secretary of Health and Human Services issued two decisions denying a rural hospital in Oklahoma full reimbursement for pharmacy services rendered to Medicare patients in 1979 and 1980. The Secretary's decisions are based on findings of Medicare's Provider Reimbursement Review Board which found Memorial's pharmacy costs to be unreasonable. The hospital, Memorial Hospital/Adair County Medical Center, disagreed with the board's conclusions and filed complaints challenging the two decisions....

I. BACKGROUND

In 1983 Congress changed the method of reimbursing hospitals for costs incurred in caring for Medicare patients.... Under the new system the Department of Health and Human Services ("HHS" or "Department") reimburses Medicare health care providers, including hospitals like Memorial, according to standard national rates for particular therapies.

This case arises under the Medicare reimbursement scheme previously in effect. In Part A of the Social Security Act, 42 U.S.C. §§1395c-1395i (1982) (the "Act"), Congress permitted the Secretary of HHS to consider cost audits before approving hospital applications for Medicare reimbursement. Section 1395f(b) of the Act states: "The amount paid to any provider of services...[shall be] the reasonable cost of such services."... The regulation further defines "reasonable cost" in a broad fashion:

> The costs of providers' services vary from one provider to another and the variations generally reflect differences in scope of services and intensity of care. The provision in title XVIII of the Act for payment of reasonable cost of services is intended to meet the actual costs, however widely they may vary from one institution to another. This is subject to a limitation where a particular institution's costs are found to be substantially out of line with other institutions in the same area which are similar in size, scope of services, utilization, and other relevant factors.

42 C.F.R. §405.451(c)(2) (1985). In addition to this regulation, §2103 of the Secretary's Provider Reimbursement Manual...states that "[t]he prudent and cost-conscious buyer not only refuses to pay more than the going price for an item or service, he also seeks to economize by minimizing cost."...

Two weeks before it was ready to open in 1977, Memorial's administrator requested Oklahoma State Health Department personnel, then under contract with the Secretary, to "'survey' [Memorial's] facilities to determine whether ...Medicare standards are satisfied. This team found [Memorial's] pharmacy to be very deficient in pharmacy services." When Memorial's administrator asked how that deficiency could be corrected, "[t]he surveyor told him to come to Oklahoma City (Doctors Hospital of Oklahoma) to observe an acceptable pharmacy operation. He observed a contract pharmacy, HPI [Hospital Pharmacies, Inc.], for the first time. He requested HPI to...provide a proposal for operating [his] pharmacy."

HPI's proposal offered Memorial's patients the most advanced of three commonly used methods for administering medications. Some hospitals keep a stock of drugs in each ward or floor, permitting nurses to retrieve and administer supplies without supervision by a pharmacist. According to Memorial, that system "poses a threat to patient safety...[and] can result in decreased care to patients and financial loss to hospitals employing this procedure." Other hospitals use a second method. They store drugs in a pharmacy where a pharmacist places each patient's medications in prescription containers and distributes them to nurses for dispensation. These may contain large quantities of medication for use over several days. In [the third method, called an "intravenous admixture" program], an HPI pharmacist would prepare each single dose for each patient and, whenever prescribed, mix drugs in intravenous solutions for particular patients under sterile conditions ("intravenous" or "IV admixture"). In exchange Memorial would compensate HPI an amount equal to 45 percent of the gross inpatient billings of the pharmacy department, less 5 percent of said billings to cover bad debts....

Memorial did not advertise or request competitive bidding. Memorial nevertheless accepted HPI's [third] proposal.

At the end of fiscal year 1979, Memorial requested reimbursement for that portion of HPI's charges relating to pharmacy services for Medicare patients. The Act entrusts the initial determination of the reimbursement a hospital may receive to an intermediary agency or organization appointed by the Secretary. See 42 U.S.C. §1395h (1982). The Secretary appointed Blue Cross of Oklahoma ("Blue Cross"), a private insurer, as intermediary to audit Memorial's Medicare reimbursement claim for 1979. Using a cost-per-patient-per-day ("per diem") method of accounting, Blue Cross compared Memorial's total pharmacy costs and those of "peer" hospitals. All the hospitals in this peer group had between 46 and 60 patient beds, were located in Oklahoma, and used drug-dispensation methods different from those HPI furnished Memorial's patients. For instance, not one of the peer hospitals operated an intravenous admixture program similar to Memorial's.

The intermediary found Memorial's 1979 pharmacy costs "substantially out-of-line with the hospitals in the peer group." It then decided to reduce Memorial's claimed cost figures to the highest per diem cost figures of any hospital in the peer group, and adjusted the result by an inflation factor. This calculation resulted in an approved reimbursement that was $30,000 short of Memorial's 1979 claim.... Blue Cross had calculated that the total costs of pharmacy services per diem were $18.03 at Memorial and approximately $12.42 at the costliest peer group hospital, Tahlequah. None of the hospitals in the peer group, however, employed a pharmacist to prepare intravenous drug solutions. Instead they all relied on nurses to perform that task....

On cross motions for summary judgment, the district court presented the issue as "whether a hospital whose total costs are unexceptional is thereby entitled to reimbursement under the Medicare Act ... for the extraordinary expenses of a single costly state-of-the-art service it elects to operate." Rejecting all arguments Memorial presented to the board, the district court concluded that the board's decisions were not "irrational," in part because

> subsidizing a hospital's elevated aspirations for one of its services by way of disproportionate reimbursements (possibly to the neglect of other services in the same hospital, and the disappointment of other hospital competing for the same limited government funds) is at variance with the statutory purpose. The Medicare Act vests broad power in the Secretary to control costs of medical care subject to reimbursement which health care providers should not be allowed to circumvent by artful accounting at reimbursement time....

II. DISCUSSION

It should be self-evident that one objective of §405.451(c)(2) is to ensure that apples are compared with apples, and that the apples to be compared are the services provided by a particular institution....

The board denied Memorial reimbursement of actual per diem pharmacy costs that were in excess of the highest per diem pharmacy costs in the 1979 and 1980 peer hospital groups, even though none of the comparison hospitals used a pharmacist-supervised intravenous admixture program that accounted for most of Memorial's purportedly excessive costs. The board thus interpreted the phrase "similar...size, scope of services, utilization, and other relevant factors" to permit it to limit its comparison to the category of "pharmacy services." The board did not consider intravenous admixture, a part of pharmacy services, a relevant category of comparison.

We reject this approach. Under the regulations at issue, intermediaries must arrive at truly comparable bases for comparison in determining whether the actual costs of a particular provider are out of line. It was incumbent on Blue Cross in this case to come up with an appropriate basis for determining whether the costs allocated to pharmacist-supervised intravenous admixture were reasonable in light of the costs incurred by other providers offering that service. This Blue Cross failed to do.... Section 405.451(c)(2) clearly requires that the costs to be compared be truly comparable; that is to say, that they be comprised of the same basic elements.... Thus, on remand, the intermediary should be required to [compare] Memorial's pharmacy costs...with those incurred by peer groups offering comparable IV and other pharmacy services.

■ "REASONABLE COST" REIMBURSEMENT FOR INPATIENT HOSPITAL SERVICES UNDER MEDICARE AND MEDICAID*
Stephen M. Weiner**
3 Am. J.L. & Med. 1 (1977)

[The annual rate of increase in both charges and costs for hospital rooms doubled in the five years following 1965, compared to the rate of increase in prior years.] This rapid escalation in the costs of and charges for hospital services is related in significant part to the creation in 1965 of the Medicare and Medicaid programs (Titles XVIII and XIV of the Social Security Act)....Both programs, through legislative action and subsequent administrative implementation, required reimbursement for inpatient hospital services on the basis of "reasonable cost."

"Reasonable cost" reimbursement, or reimbursement based on a provider's cost, means simply that the payment made to a hospital for services rendered to Medicare or Medicaid patients is calculated to reimburse the hospital for its

*Reprinted with permission. Copyright © American Society of Law, Medicine, and Ethics.
**Chairman, Massachusetts Rate Setting Commission.

expenses, or costs, incurred in providing such services. As will be described below, the definition of "cost" is a critical element in the use of such a methodology. Suffice it to say here that because the approach, as originally employed, contained a guarantee that costs incurred by a hospital would be recouped, hospitals had a clear incentive to expand services and increase costs to meet anticipated new demand, and had no incentives under the reimbursement methodology to control costs. The methodology itself was inherently inflationary in its impact on the payment obligations of the Medicare and Medicaid programs. It substantially increased the pressure to increase costs that was a function of the expanded entitlement to health care created by the programs themselves.

The decision to base Medicare and Medicaid reimbursement on "reasonable cost" reflected congressional concern that hospitals would be unwilling to participate voluntarily in those programs unless adequate reimbursement were assured. The approach did succeed in attracting the voluntary participation of most American hospitals. But the introduction of the Medicare and Medicaid programs stands as an example of the fiscal dangers inherent in a program that rapidly measures entitlement to services without, at the same time, taking strong measures to contain the cost impact of that expansion. . . .

The initial HEW regulations defining "reasonable cost" under §1861(v) chose not to emphasize the *reasonableness* of costs but rather the determination of whether the costs fell into defined *allowable* categories. The regulations provided, in effect, for full reimbursement of all costs falling within these defined categories. . . . The only limit on the magnitude of a cost item appears to be an exclusion from allowability if "a particular institution's costs are found to be *substantially out of line* with other institutions in the same area which are similar in size, scope of services, utilization, and other relevant factors." However, no adequate criteria were adopted further defining "substantially" for these purposes or providing a method for determining what might constitute a "similar" institution.

In adopting such provisions, then, HEW effectively abdicated all responsibility for evaluating—or assisting the hospitals in determining for themselves—the necessity of efficiency of costs incurred by hospitals. The regulations stood as a promise to hospitals that if they accepted patients under these public programs they would receive all costs *they* chose to incur in providing that care. . . . The benefits to hospitals from the approach to "reasonableness" taken in the regulations were buttressed by the liberality of the definition of "cost." Indeed, in operation the Medicare regulations provided for a "cost-plus" formula, with the most prominent "plus" factors being the rather generous depreciation provisions and an "allowance in lieu of specific recognition of other costs."

One must question, of course, why there should be a need for "plus" factors in an industry dominated by nonprofit institutions. The answer, in the author's opinion, is that hospitals could use the additional revenues generated by the "plus" factors to generate capital funds. . . . The concept is at variance with the more traditional notion of depreciation as a cost attendant in the use of an asset, intended to reimburse for the wearing away in value of the asset. . . . Depreciation was allowed on assets originally financed with federal or other public funds, despite the fact that the hospital incurred no cost in acquiring the asset. Finally, depreciation was allowed on assets in use at the time the hospital entered the program, even though the assets may have been fully depreciated on the hospital's books or fully depreciated with respect to other third party payors.

The other major "plus" factor reflecting the hospitals' efforts to generate capital funds through "cost" reimbursement appears in the "allowance in lieu of specific recognition of other costs in providing and improving services." The regulations, as promulgated, provided for an allowance, in addition to all other categories of reimbursable cost, equal to 2 percent of allowable costs (excepting interest and the instant allowance itself). This allowance [for a "return on equity capital"] was wholly unanticipated by Congress, was not contemplated in the actuarial projections underlying the original cost estimates of the programs, and generally had little basis to justify itself.[1] It had the effect of providing hospitals with a reserve, a "profit" as it were, which was directly correlated with the level of *spending*, not efficiency, of the facility. Therefore, not only were the Medicare reimbursement principles unconducive to hospital efficiency, but the 2 percent allowance presented a positive incentive to increased inefficiency. The more the hospital spent, the greater the "plus" it received.

In summary, the formula for reasonable hospital cost reimbursement developed for Medicare represented a guarantee to hospitals not only that their "actual" patient-related costs would be reimbursed in full but that they would receive significant payments even above actual cost, in the form of accelerated depreciation amounts and the 2 percent allowance. As a result, following the inception of Medicare, the net income of hospitals rose substantially. As indicated earlier, especially with the nonprofit hospitals, this excess revenue would find its way back into operations, generally through capital expenditures, and thereby generate a constantly escalating cost in a hospital's operations.

Notes: Cost-Based and UCR Reimbursement

1. *Open-Ended Reimbursement: Down But Not Out.* As *Memorial Hospital* observes, Medicare no longer reimburses most hospitals on a reasonable cost basis. However, this is still the basis for paying specialized hospitals, and some nonhospital facilities. It is also the way that Blue Cross and Medicaid historically paid hospitals and in some instances still do. Other private insurers still pay hospitals a negotiated discount from charges. Similarly, as Alain Enthoven notes, doctors traditionally were paid their "usual, customary, and reasonable" (UCR) rates—both by Medicare and Medicaid and by private insurers, although now both types of insurers pay physicians using fee schedules they determine or negotiate. Commenting on the incentive effects of this older, "blank-check" form of payment, one surgeon in Manhattan confessed:

> When I finished my [medical] training some years ago, the surgeon who directed my department was routinely allowed $800 from Medicare for a commonly performed surgical procedure. This was considered top dollar for such a procedure

[1] See generally Eleanor Kinney, Medicare Payment to Hospitals for a Return on Capital, 11 J. Contemp. L. 453 (1985); Comment, The Role of Medicare Reimbursement in Contemporary Hospital Finance, 11 Am. J.L. & Med. 501 (1986).—EDS.

but was entirely commensurate with his skill and reputation. Acting upon the advice of my predecessors, ... I began to bill $1,000 in order to "up" my profile for the same procedure—and, to my surprise, I began receiving higher fees than my former chief despite my nearly novice status. Neither I nor the American Medical Association complained about these arrangements.

Sislowitz, Doctors' Faustian Deal, N.Y. Times, Jan. 7, 1988, p.23. Although Medicare has replaced these open-ended forms of reimbursement with various forms of "prospective payment," it is still important to understand traditional payment methods. They are the basis for reimbursement under much private insurance, and their incentive effects are what newer payment methods are meant to counteract.

2. *Per Diem Limits*. Sacred Heart Hospital v. United States, 616 F.2d 477 (Ct. Cl. 1980) is a case similar to *Memorial Hospital*. There, the court upheld a hospital's claim for respiratory therapy services that were ten times costlier than neighboring hospitals, reasoning that the costs were justified since the quality and quantity of its services were so superior to peer hospitals. For a number of years, these limits were struck down by some courts as inconsistent with the overriding statutory requirement of reimbursing all reasonable costs. The Supreme Court held in a closely divided vote, however, that CMS has statutory authority to set binding cost limits. Good Samaritan Hospital v. Shalala, 508 U.S. 402 (1993). Why do you think per diem cost limits failed to successfully constrain total hospital reimbursement?

Even if CMS could control the amount spent *per service*, limiting the *number* of services proved even more problematic. The facts of *Sacred Heart* provide a good illustration of the effects of cost-based reimbursement on the intensity of service: "Prior to 1963, ... the [respiratory therapy] department, as such, consisted of a noncertified therapist and a technician who were trained to administer oxygen.... [Since then], the department has grown to eight full time, board certified anesthesiologists, nine trained technicians, two therapists and two registered therapists." 616 F.2d at 479.

3. *Corporate Structure*. Cost accounting rules have tremendous influence not only on financial and operational management, but also on basic corporate structure. For instance, a cost-reimbursed facility might find that it is more profitable or efficient to vertically integrate by acquiring or affiliating with one or more of its suppliers. That way, the facility captures the profit that the supplier was making off of sales to the facility. When this happens, however, Medicare has no assurance that future purchases from the wholly owned or sibling subsidiary are at arms-length prices. Rather than auditing these prices between related organizations, Medicare rules state that it will pay only the costs incurred *by the supplier*, that is, it will no longer reimburse the buyer facility for any costs attributable to profits earned by a related supplier. These "related party" rules are sweeping enough that it is possible for a facility to enter into various alignments and affiliations that unexpectedly penalize it for "profits" it is not in fact capturing and that unexpectedly subject nonmedical enterprises to intrusive Medicare audits. For instance, in one case Medicare refused to reimburse the interest expense a hospital incurred in borrowing substantial funds from the university it was affiliated with. Regents of the University of California v. Shalala, 82 F.3d 291 (9th Cir. 1996). These examples are only a glimpse at the many corporate planning problems created by

cost-reimbursement rules. See, e.g., Lodi Community Hospital v. Shalala, 94 F.3d 1251 (9th Cir. 1996) (Medicare pays for interest costs of asset purchases but not stock purchases; multi-step transaction involving the creation of new subsidiaries, the transfer of assets, and the sale of stock did not qualify as an asset purchase).

4. *Nickeling and Diming.*

With upward pressures on health care costs continuing to mount, managed care plans have sought innovative steps to control costs through automated claims processing. Such efforts, though, may well have impacts on the legal landscape for health care plans. That is made clear, for example, by several [class action] lawsuits brought against CIGNA Corp. by its network physicians, . . . alleg[ing], among other things, breach of contract by CIGNA. The physician plaintiffs contend that the claims processing software leads to arbitrary and irrational denials of claims submitted for services rendered to the plan's insureds. . . . For example, a network CIGNA gynecologist will see a plan member in the office who complains about heavy irregular bleeding. The physician conducts an examination, and asks the patient a series of questions regarding her health. A biopsy is then taken to check for cancer. The physician then sends to CIGNA a bill of $250, for the exam and the biopsy, using separate five-digit codes. CIGNA remits to the network provider only $175, after CIGNA unilaterally subtracted $75 from the claim. The explanation given for that decision is that the software construed the biopsy charge as [being] includ[ed] in the office visit.

The[se] lawsuits against CIGNA are examples of the general discord between . . . network providers [and] health plans over the use of automated claims processing which . . . uses standardized codes (CPT Codes) [to] bundle, or down code, [claims that physicians submit]. . . . CIGNA, and other health plans, have stated that the software used is good practice to cut back on fraudulent billings and reduce health care costs.

HMO Practice Group Leadership of the American Health Lawyers Ass'n, Suits by Network Providers Challenge Claims Processing (e-mail dated Aug. 8, 2002). These practices have also attracted the attention of legislators and regulators. A large number of states have enacted laws requiring insurers to use "fair business practices" in paying providers, including paying claims promptly, and regulators in several states have issued large fines for violation of these laws.

5. *Contingent Fees for Doctors.* Prof. Hyman and Prof. Silver propose, as an alternative to traditional fee-for-service payment, that providers be paid based on the success of treatment—either a bonus for doing better or avoiding complications, or no payment at all if the procedure fails at a defined level. David Hyman & Charles Silver, You Get What You Pay for: Result-Based Compensation for Health Care, 58 Wash. & Lee L. Rev. 1427 (2001). Such contingent fee arrangements are currently seen only on a very limited basis, for some fertility and vision correction services. An AMA ethical opinion (number 6.01, amended 1994) prohibits fee arrangements that are contingent on the success of treatment. Hyman and Silver argue this is misguided and that contingent fees would make physicians better agents and reward higher quality. For commentary focusing on the practical difficulties with this proposal, see Haavi Morreim, Result-Based Compensation in Health Care: A Good, but Limited Idea, 29 J.L. Med. Ethics 174 (2001).

2. Prospective Payment

Open-ended cost-based reimbursement still exists, but both public and private insurance are rapidly moving toward various forms of prospective payment. Prospective payment systems (PPS) reverse the incentives created by retrospective reimbursement by setting a fixed rate in advance that does not vary as much according to the nature or extent of treatment given. In this regard, prospective payment mimics the incentives created by a competitive market in which, in theory, firms are "price takers," meaning that they are forced to sell at the market rate and cannot unilaterally determine their price. Therefore, providers have a profit/loss-based incentive to cut costs and attract more business. Depending on the form of payment, however, they also have an incentive to manipulate the payment system in socially unproductive ways.

There are huge differences in the degree of prospectivity and the types of manipulation created by different forms of prospective payment. These various forms are defined by the unit of payment and by the methods used to adjust the fixed rate among different patients and providers. The first form we look at is the "DRG" system under Medicare, so named because payment rates are fixed according to "diagnosis-related groups." Although the focus is on Medicare, this payment method, and other types of prospective payment, are in wide use among private insurers and other government programs. Thus, both the details and the general structure of Medicare DRGs have pervasive importance across the landscape of health care financing.

▪ THE COMPLEXITY OF MEDICARE'S HOSPITAL REIMBURSEMENT SYSTEM: PARADOXES OF AVERAGING*
David M. Frankford**
78 Iowa L. Rev. 517 (1993)

...Medicare's spending for the health care furnished by hospitals is an irritating burr stuck in the soft underfoot of the American federal budget. Over time the program has spent ever increasing amounts on hospital care, and these dollars are by far the largest portion of total spending....

As a nation we are now debating the manner in which we insure against the costs of illness. Because health care insurance and reimbursement practices go hand and hand, and because the hospital is the most important component of all health care expenditures, the structure of hospital reimbursement is of enormous significance....

In this article, ... I study the structure of Medicare's inpatient hospital reimbursement system from its inception in fiscal year 1967 to the present. I argue that this system is a mass of contradictions and that, as a result, it has been growing increasingly complex. I further argue that these contradictions are wrapped up

---

*Reprinted with permission. A portion of this excerpt is taken from Prof. Frankford's other article on Medicare payment, excerpted at page 304.

**Professor of Law, Rutgers University School of Law, Camden.

with . . . our extremely individualistic culture. A dominant belief in this culture is that each individual should be responsible for her selection of health care providers and her decision to purchase health care insurance and health care goods and services. This belief, however, collides with a fact of social life and dependence: Insurance, by definition, rests on the averaging of costs and benefits among individuals. Caught between the myth of individualism and the fact of social dependence, our Medicare hospital reimbursement system steers in two directions at once. It unites Medicare beneficiaries within a single institution of social insurance, yet it simultaneously expends enormous effort to assign costs to individual beneficiaries' episodes of care. No other western nation engages in a similar effort. Indeed, while our trading partners exercise sovereign power to unite all citizens into a common insurance fund, our sovereign exercises power to divide us into many quarrelling camps. Our Medicare reimbursement system thoroughly revels in encouraging a peculiar form of competition, one in which the name of the game is to shift as much cost as possible to others. We excel in this competition and the concomitant accounting because we try to have it both ways—to have our individualism and to maintain some semblance of social insurance. . . .

When Medicare was enacted in 1965, . . . [t]he statute contained no detailed list of the diagnostic and treatment modalities to be furnished to beneficiaries; nor did it delegate to an administrative agency the authority to construct such a list. Rather, discretion remained where Congress found it in 1965: in the hands of the physician, the "captain of the ship." . . .

The task of the Department of Health, Education, and Welfare was not to oversee the exercise of medical discretion; rather, the role of the agency was to obtain claims-processing services through contracts with the insurance carriers that historically had been processing the insurance claims arising from physicians' decisions. In sum, Medicare neither relegated nor delegated authority over health care decisions; Medicare simply provided a mechanism for beneficiaries to pool their claims. . . .

During the mid-1970s and the early 1980s the costs of hospital inpatient care continued to rise at a double-digit rate of inflation. These increases sparked a revolutionary change in the basic structure of hospital reimbursement, a transformation which began with the Tax Equity and Fiscal Responsibility Act of 1982 ("TEFRA"). . . . Shortly thereafter, the Department announced that it intended to switch hospital reimbursement to a prospective plan revolving around "diagnosis-related groups," or DRGs.[193] The revolution was at hand. . . . Medicare officials would no longer just process the insurance claims generated by the exercise of physicians' discretion. Instead, to a much greater extent, Medicare administrators both "pay the piper and call the tune." . . .

The DRGs are a scheme for classifying hospital inpatients around such characteristics as primary and secondary diagnoses, primary and secondary procedures performed, age, discharge status, and complications and comorbidities. . . . The DRG system was initially developed by experts in industrial management as a

---

[193] . . . Bruce C. Vladeck, Medicare's Prospective Payment System at Age Eight: Mature Success or Midlife Crisis?, 14 U. Puget Sound L. Rev. 453, 456 (1991); see David G. Smith, Paying for Medicare: The Politics of Reform at 28-35, 41-61, 105 (1992).

tool for internal cost accounting and quality assessment. Through a review of patients' medical records, those researchers collected historical data regarding patients' lengths of stay in the hospital, along with various potentially "explanatory" characteristics such as diagnoses, age, or procedures. They then used statistical methods to derive the tightest possible clusters of patients in which length of stay could be correlated with the best explanatory characteristics, with appropriate adjustments to make the clusters and explanatory criteria clinically coherent.... The patient classification scheme can thus be used as the basis for a reimbursement system by assigning an appropriate price to each product—to each DRG. Such a prospective payment system will supposedly enable government to protect its fiscal integrity through stabilizing hospital reimbursement around predictable, easily administrable and efficiency-enhancing payments per DRG....

Under Medicare's DRG-based reimbursement system, each patient is assigned to a DRG when the patient is discharged from the hospital.[209] Then, stated most generally, the amount that the hospital receives for this patient... is calculated by multiplying the value of the DRG—its "relative weight"—by an average cost for all discharges (across all DRGs) from all hospitals within a particular classification of hospitals—large urban, other urban, and rural.[210] The latter averages—the "standardized payment amounts" calculated each year by the Health Care Financing Administration for each of the three categories of hospitals—are constructed from the national averages for each classification of hospitals. They "can be thought of as the average cost of a medicare case in an average, nonteaching hospital."[211] ...

When one "thinks in DRGs," one thinks in averages.... Medicare could simply pay these average [standardized] amounts to every hospital for every case. Such a reimbursement system, however, would not be considered either fair or efficient. Stated generally, prospective payment attains (or perhaps aspires to attain) fairness and efficiency by holding hospitals accountable for factors they control, while Medicare, as a federal insurance system, is responsible for factors not under hospitals' control, such as those relating to patient demographics. These aspirations have been set rather high:

> Payment on the basis of a per-case rate for each DRG is intended to create specific financial incentives that encourage hospital management to adopt desirable methods of controlling the cost of care. It was hoped that hospital management, facing a separate payment rate per discharge for each DRG, would have strong incentives to: (1) improve productivity; (2) use less expensive inputs where possible; (3) influence physicians to reduce the length of stay, limit the volume of inpatient services, and use a less expensive mix of services to treat each patient; (4) specialize in treating types of cases the hospital can produce efficiently; and (5) adopt cost-reducing technologies, while avoiding cost-increasing technologies.[231]

---

[209] See 42 C.F.R. §412.60(c) (1992). See generally 1 Medicare & Medicaid Guide (CCH) ¶4204, at 1513 to 1513-3 (1990).

[210] Louise B. Russell, Medicare's New Hospital Payment System: Is It Working? 11 (1989); Karen Davis et al., Health Care Cost Containment 43 (1990).

[211] Russell, supra n.210, at 11.

[231] Prospective Payment Assessment Comm'n, Report and Recommendations to the Department of Health and Human Services 16 (Mar. 1, 1990).

The severity of illness of a case is supposedly a factor not within a hospital's control.... The DRGs provide the mechanism to adjust reimbursement for severity of illness, for, taken together, they are supposed to constitute a systematic measure of severity of illness, or, in other words, a case-mix index. Each DRG "represents" the average severity for the average of a type of case: an average coronary bypass with cardiac catheterization; an average coronary bypass without cardiac catheterization; an average fracture of the hip or pelvis; and so on. Each DRG is assigned a weight, "reflecting" the relative use of resources required to treat the average case of such severity: The average coronary bypass with cardiac catheterization might have an indexical value of 5.5415, while the average hip fracture has one of 0.9036. Payment for a case is then a product of the relevant standardized amount times the DRG weight for that type of case....

[T]he standardized payment amounts were to be freed, to a great degree, from actual cost experience. Although the standardized amounts were initially dependent upon that experience—they were calculated through cost data from individual hospitals in the "base-year period."...Thereafter, currency would be maintained and prospectivity imposed by "updating" the standardized amounts...by "forecasting" the legitimate rate of "inflation" for the upcoming year...which supposedly takes into account changes in technology, productivity, and case mix....Overall, there has been a clear downward trend, with hospitals receiving, on aggregate, year-by-year increases lower than historical rates of inflation....[O]n average the screw has slowly been turning downward....

Analogously, the DRGs would be adjusted periodically so that they would "reflect" changes in medical practices and technology over time.... Federal authorities initially seemed to imagine that they could set the averages in play and then revisit them once in a while in the form of an "update." Events have proved such expectations to be wrong, for administering hospitals has proven to be much more dynamic than anything that could be provided in a formula. Nonetheless, the heart of the system is an attempt to reduce the rhythm of hospital life to the variables of a regression....

However, it is not clear what is being "measured" and how the regression can help. The entire process looks like improvisation.... [E]ach year...the weights are "recalibrated." These steps are often described as involving "measurement," in which HCFA "refine[s] the DRG classifications and respond[s] to changing medical practice[s]" such that the weights continue to "reflect changing technology, medical practice patterns, and complexity of cases."...[But] HCFA has been very reluctant to allow particular technologies or practice patterns to drive the DRG classifications.... [In its view]:

> It is not the intent of the prospective payment system to meet the costs of care for every case in every hospital. Rather, the DRG weighting factors are based on the average resources consumed for procedures in a given DRG relative to the average case at the average hospital.... In dealing with a system of averages, there will always be some cases both above and below the mean. Hospitals are expected to use the excess payment on low cost cases to offset the excess costs of other cases.... [T]he fact that some hospitals will continue to receive payments below costs for some procedures is inevitable under a system that is based on averages....

[Even though the weights are not intended to be precisely accurate,] because the DRGs supposedly represent the distinct product lines of a multiproduct firm, their use in accounting and reimbursement would allow hospital costs to be assigned to particular products. Clinicians, hospital administrators, and regulators could thereby make appropriate comparisons within and among different hospitals in order to improve, first, the efficiency by which hospitals produce laundry, meals, laboratory tests and the like, and, second, the effectiveness of the practice patterns by which clinicians organize these inputs into clinical care....

To understate the matter, things have not gone quite so smoothly.... [I]t has become much more apparent in recent years that the health care system, Medicare, and the prospective payment system resemble balloons: Changes made in one reimbursement sector have mushroomed unintentionally into effects elsewhere. Given this dynamism, there have not been, and there are unlikely to be, long periods of equilibrium. Indeed, one could say that there has been a basic clash of goals. "Prospectivity" implies that rates, once set, remain fixed; accounting for developing fiscal considerations and the changing characteristics of the health care sector imply that fixed rates do not remain fixed. The collision of these two goals has spawned an enormous amount of work in the Congress, in the agencies and in the industry....

■ THE MEDICARE DRGS: EFFICIENCY AND ORGANIZATIONAL RATIONALITY*
David M. Frankford**
10 Yale J. Reg. 273 (1993)

[This article] assesses whether there is a relationship between DRG-based per-case payment and efficiency. My answer is that there appears to be none....

Hospitals impose unique problems for internal and external management.... Given both the individuality of each patient and the difficulty of measuring the outcome of care provided to each one, there are difficult problems in pricing (or rate regulating) and evaluating quality. As summarized by the developers of the DRGs, "unlike gallons of water or kilowatt hours of electricity, medical care is not delivered in standardized units of services, all uniform and measurable, the quality of which is easily assessable."[4]

The second managerial problem is the concomitant difficulty in defining the costs of each of the hospital's products. Much of the hospital's plant and labor is structured so that it can be used to care for patients with diverse needs. Some services, such as meals, are delivered in standardized form and are easily attributed to the care of particular patients. However, other plant and services, such as those

---

**Professor of Law, Rutgers University School of Law, Camden.
[4] Robert B. Fetter et al., A System for Cost and Reimbursement Control in Hospitals, 49 Yale J. Biology & Med. 123, 127 (1976)....

pertaining to an operating room, are used in the treatment of many patients and are not necessarily delivered in standardized units.[5] . . .

[I]n an environment composed of a multitude of payers, each acting for its own interests, . . . each payer reimburses the hospital just for the care provided its patients, and it must therefore know the costs attributable to them alone. Hence there is a pressing practical reason to define the "hospital product" much more narrowly, even toward the limit at which the care provided to a single patient is defined as a separate product. . . . In theory, a system of workable competition would solve these problems. . . . Therefore, at least in this conception, the problem for Medicare is that it must set its prices so as to mimic the results that would obtain in an open market. . . .

Medicare regulators believed that they could impose uniform national rates fine-tuned by adjustments to attain the behavioral effects they desired with only a tolerable degree of undesired subsidiary effects. Hospitals would be forced to become efficient in their production of intermediate products, and physicians would be forced to utilize effective processes of care in the packaging of those products. . . . Stated generally, the hospital, qua organism, was predicted to act like the "firm" modeled by neoclassical economics. Responding to the financial incentives embedded within PPS, it would rationally weigh margins of revenue against margins of cost for a case or a highly differentiated group of cases. . . .

For purposes of analysis, the predicted [behavior] can be organized around three categories: (1) the site of care; (2) the process of care; and (3) the financing of care. With regard to the site of care, . . . hospitals were expected to shift some entire episodes of care to outpatient facilities. These shifts were supposed to occur selectively, with hospital managers weighing the differences in costs and reimbursement between the alternative sites. Hospitals were also expected to unbundle some services from the inpatient stay and to provide them prior to admission. Second, hospitals were expected to release patients earlier and to discharge them home or to various types of nursing care facilities, home health care, or exempt facilities and distinct-part units. These decisions too were expected to be differentiated by DRG. . . .

[W]ith regard to the process of care, there were four linked groups of predictions, organized around the four major ways that hospitals can alter their costs. It was predicted that hospitals would alter (1) length of stay; (2) physicians' use of

---

[5] See, e.g., Keith E. Braganza, Cost Finding, in 1 Handbook of Health Care Accounting and Finance 197, 197 (William O. Cleverly ed., 1982). . . . William A. Glaser has summarized the difficulty as follows:

> Perhaps some simple and recurrent procedures in the hospital's industrial services can be costed plausibly; for example, the cost of each laboratory test, the cost of each X-ray, and the cost of laundering can be estimated just as the costs of each output of a business firm are estimated. But many other procedures—such as a thoracic operation or a physiotherapy session—are not so standardized and vary in their resource use each time. The inputs throughout a hospital appear more heterogeneous than the inputs throughout an industrial factory, and clustering them to estimate the costs of an output is more difficult than cost assignment in a factory.

William A. Glaser, Paying the Hospital: the Organization, Dynamics, and Effects of Differing Financial Arrangements 33 (1987).

diagnostic and treatment modalities during the stay; (3) the rate of technological innovation and diffusion; and (4) the labor and nonlabor inputs provided physicians and the mix of nonphysician and physician labor used in treatment.... These actions were to occur selectively in that a hospital would attempt to hit or better the norm embodied in the rate for a DRG, while weighing, first, the manner in which a deviation would affect its own unique financial picture and, second, the constraints imposed by such factors as malpractice, peer review, the ethical commitment to quality of care, and competition among hospitals with regard to reputation....

Finally, with regard to the financing of care, our last category of predicted [behavior], hospitals were expected to act as "reimbursement-maximizing" firms. There were three major predictions. First, because the system is built on payments for "cases," hospitals were expected to increase the number of "cases" by generating a greater number of admissions overall and by admitting, discharging and then readmitting some patients. They were also supposed to admit and to transfer selectively, cream-skimming the lucrative cases and turning away types of cases for which reimbursement was too low or the relationship between expected costs and reimbursement too uncertain. Second, hospitals were expected to take advantage of the discretion in the classification system by coding discharges into more lucrative categories where possible—the phenomenon known as "DRG creep." Third, hospitals were expected to take advantage of the facts that PPS is not an all-payer system and that substantial discretion remains in the accounting and charging practices used to allocate costs among different payers. Accordingly, hospitals were expected to shift as many costs as possible to payers without the market power or the will to defend themselves—most prominently the commercial insurance companies and to a lesser extent the Blues—or to charitable and other public sources of revenue....

Did the hospital organism make these rational choices?... [O]verwhelming evidence shows that across many DRGs, there occurred a sharp increase in both discharge planning and the use of home health care services.... In none of these areas concerning the reorganization of the medical division of labor between organizational types has there been a documented, discernible adverse effect on quality, at least from well-designed studies controlling for severity of illness, patient demographics or both.... Moreover, the evidence from the most well-designed study indicates that both the timing and destination of discharge were driven not by the net profit consequences of particular DRGs but by the overall pressure PPS exerted to reduce length of stay....

With regard to the rate of technological innovation and diffusion, there seems to have been no generalized effect.... Finally, there has been an immense surge in capital expenditures, but mainly in the construction of hospital outpatient departments and stand-alone ambulatory and exempt-care facilities....

In sum, while many believe that PPS, taken as a whole, has increased the productivity of the average inpatient stay,... continuing cost inflation in hospitals is attributable to the practice patterns of physicians, not the efficiency of the laundry service.... Therefore, it appears that "hospitals" are not generally "controlling" their physicians' packaging habits.... PPS perhaps has caused some generalized effects across all or most DRGs, such as reduced length of stay across the board. It is also possible that these generalized effects are attributable to the pressure imposed on a hospital by the sum total of its Medicare reimbursement and the fact that hospital administrators do react to such a broad bottom line if they can, with general exhortations pitched to the entire medical staff to reduce length of stay, to order fewer tests and services, and to substitute less expensive therapies for more expensive ones.... [T]here has been attention to particular procedures shifted to outpatient surgery; unbundling of preadmission tests; ... some substitution of the use of long-term hospitals and rehabilitation hospitals or distinct-part units for long-term inpatient rehabilitation; enhanced attention given to intensive-care units; one-time, panicked reductions in non-medical staff; attention to capital investments able to escape the net thrown by PPS; a selective focus on a few very expensive new technologies; a large commitment of resources to coding; and a commitment of resources by some hospitals to maximize opportunities for cost-shifting. Otherwise, no other inferences of DRG-based product-line rationality are possible from observed behavior....

Maximizing, organistic organizational rationality could exist only if the hospital were structured along the lines of Weber's rational-legal bureaucracy.[190] ... Our actual hospitals, however, do not resemble these models. They are extremely complex organizations, with a multitude of diverse actors, all of whom interact in complex and variable ways. To the extent that work is organized by a structure or process at all, that organization is certainly not hierarchical....

Perhaps it would be more fruitful for public policy if we ... instead utilize a regulatory structure built upon budgeting focused around each different institution.... Each hospital would remain subject to prospective reimbursement, but the basic unit of payment would be the hospital, not the case. Regulatory authority to make distributional decisions would be transferred from a national administrative agency, which now acts in conjunction with congressional log-rolling, to some form of local community institutional arrangements. Hospital budgets would then be set through institutions in which sovereign power would be conjoined with communal process....

[B]y abandoning the attempt to assign costs to individuals and their fragmented payers, this budgeting process would build upon and instill the value that a hospital serves a community of patients drawn from a community of citizens.[262] ... The averaging of costs among patients—in other words, the mutual sharing of the burdens of illness—would then be seen, not as a deficit to be overcome, but as a positive virtue. Moreover, the locus of mediating between individual and social interests would be changed.... State and local regulatory frameworks would serve as important mediating institutions, but more importantly, we would utilize local institutional arrangements for the provision of meaningful community input and as means to prevent the continuing erosion of non-medical belief systems and networks of social support. That might be the sort of evaluative framework we need....

---

[190] See generally Max Weber, Economy and Society 956-1005 (Guenther Ross & Claus Wittich eds., 1978).

[262] Cf. Ezekiel J. Emanuel, The Ends of Human Life: Medical Ethics in a Liberal Polity (1991) (describing local institutions founded on ideals of community).

Notes: DRGs; Relative Value Scales; Rate Regulation

1. *The Structure and Scope of DRGs.* Hopefully, the complexity of hospital rate regulation can be simplified with the following explanation. Every rate control system is composed of (1) a base rate, which is fixed; (2) an annual rate adjustment; and (3) a method to achieve equity and accuracy among different providers. Most of the complexities of DRGs are concerned with the third component. But most of what you need to understand about prospective payment in general, including most of the issues in *Multicare,* are concerned with the first two components.

Prospective payment methods have spread to most other Medicare facilities. A DRG-type system has been implemented for hospital outpatient services and ambulatory surgical centers, and nursing homes and home health agencies are now paid according to per diem rates fixed by formula rather than through cost-based reimbursement. See Max Reynolds, HCFA's New Restrictions on the Operation of Hospital Outpatient Facilities, J. Health & Hosp. L. 615 (2001). The only major types of facilities still paid cost-based reimbursement are psychiatric and other long-term care hospitals. For a comprehensive description, see Medicare Payment Advisory Commission (MedPac), Medicare Payment Policy (Mar. 2002).

2. *The Myth of Institutional Control.* The annual adjustment to the standardized hospital rate provides a convenient tool for continuously ratcheting down Medicare outlays, almost like a form of Chinese finger torture: The more economizing effort hospitals exert in response to the incentives of prospective payment, the more leeway Medicare will have each year to tighten up the standardized rate. DRGs thus have the prospect of not only halting future increases in spending (relative to inflation) but also gradually eliminating the system's built-up fat. But this is true only to the extent that hospital managers actually control the costs of treatment. As David Frankford observes, physicians control most clinical decisions that drive hospital costs, and they are notoriously independent from institutional control.

This physician independence is not just a matter of professional and institutional culture; it is supported by various legal constraints that protect physicians from outside control. Mark A. Hall, Institutional Control of Physician Behavior: Legal Barriers to Health Care Cost Containment, 137 U. Pa. L. Rev. 431 (1988). Based on the topics covered in Chapters 4.B.1, 4.C.1, and 4.E, imagine what legal objections could be raised if a hospital were to: (1) impose mandatory treatment protocols that physicians must follow (unlicensed, corporate practice or medicine); (2) pay physicians a reward for keeping their patients' costs within DRG limits ("fraud and abuse" fee splitting); or (3) kick off of the medical staff any physician who consistently loses money ("economic credentialing"). Responding to Hall's prediction, supra, that courts will systematically frustrate cost containment initiatives, Peter Jacobson argues this has not in fact occurred. Peter Jacobson, Strangers in the Night: Law and Medicine in the Managed Care Era (2002).

Hospitals have begun to assert more administrative control of patient care decisions by hiring hospital-based physicians called "hospitalists" to take over primary responsibility for case management of hospitalized patients rather than having patients being seen primarily by their regular physicians. So far, hospitalist programs are voluntary, in the sense that primary care physicians can use them at their discretion; but it is anticipated that hospitals may start to make this new system mandatory. For a general overview of ethical and public policy issues, see Farrin A. Manian, Whither Continuity of Care?, 340 New Eng. J. Med. 1362 (1999); Steven Pantilat et al., A New Doctor in the House: Ethical Issues in Hospitalist Systems, 282 JAMA 171 (1999).

3. *Adjustments to Hospital Rates.* Following the logic that hospitals should bear the brunt of only the costs they control, the Medicare DRG system has been forced to add numerous adjustments other than simply those related to patients' diagnoses. As David Frankford explains in his first article:

> [T]he reimbursement system contains a very complicated set of mechanisms to determine this question. The most important of these adjustments is for geographic variations among hospitals in their cost of labor.... [A]ll agree that labor constitutes the most important component of a hospital's operating costs. Accordingly, the statute clearly provides for some type of "wage adjustment." To make this adjustment, HCFA divides the country into numerous—and hotly contested—geographic wage areas, and each area is ranked vis-a-vis a national average wage, thereby creating a "wage index"—an indexical ranking of labor costs in different locations. Each hospital is placed into a particular area, and thus its reimbursement for any case is a product of its relevant category of standardized payment amount—rural, large urban, or other urban—weighted to take into account its local labor costs....
>
> There are then "additional payment amounts" made for other factors for which hospitals are not held accountable. Teaching activities in hospitals are thought to generate increased costs indirectly, due to the treatment of more severely ill patients through use of technology and utilization patterns which differ from those prevalent in nonteaching hospitals. Accordingly, payments to teaching hospitals are increased by percentages, called the "indirect medical education adjustment," which vary with the size of the hospital and its teaching program. Somewhat related, but not completely coextensive, is an adjustment made for hospitals which treat a "disproportionate share" of indigent patients. These patients too are thought to generate higher costs because they are more severely ill at admission than the average Medicare beneficiary. Furthermore, treatment of these patients imposes higher costs because post-discharge care is often harder to arrange and because there are generally higher costs associated with operating in areas accessible to the poor.... [H]ospitals which are the sole facilities in their respective communities... are eligible for designation as a "sole community hospital."... [B]oth sole community hospitals and Medicare-dependent, small rural hospitals are given... a lump sum payment that is calculated to cover their fixed costs and the costs of maintaining core staff and services.... Finally, all hospitals are paid a separate, additional amount for extraordinarily expensive cases—the so-called "outlier cases" which deviate greatly from the average case in a DRG.

78 Iowa L. Rev. at 579-584.

For the most part, these adjustments deal with factors that determine relative weights within a zero-sum game. Concerning the overall level of reimbursement, DRGs and other payment reforms appear to be achieving their goal of reducing overall costs. Hospitals, nursing homes, and home health agencies have complained bitterly that the Balanced Budget Act of 1997 reduced payment too drastically, resulting in the largest decrease in total payments in the history of the program, amounting to about $100 billion over five years. In the Balanced Budget Refinement Act of 1999, Congress reversed some of the funding cuts and scaled back numerous provisions in the 1997 Act, but the industry continues to press for additional relief.

4. *The Ethics of Considering Costs.* The thorniest dilemma that DRGs and other forms of prospective payment present is the ethical bind they impose on practicing physicians. Is it morally right for a doctor to be influenced by the inevitable resource constraints placed on hospitals or on society at large, if, as a result of third-party reimbursement, the doctor's patients are sheltered from these constraints? Consider the following hypothetical (but very real) problem:

> Lakeview Hospital's medical director, Jared Lapin, M.D., ... analyzed a lengthy computer report that matched, for each physician, the revenue the hospital received with the costs incurred for treating patients in each of the DRGs in one month. While studying the 15 DRGs under Major Diagnostic Category number 14 (Pregnancy, Childbirth, and the Puerperium), [he] noticed that, ... across all deliveries, the costs of treating Dr. Weiner's patients exceeded the revenue received from the DRG rates. But the total cost incurred in providing care to the other obstetricians' patients was considerably below revenue and hence the hospital was able to earn a "profit." ... The reason for Dr. Weiner's comparatively poor overall "financial performance" ... was that he performed many fewer cesarians than did his colleagues. ... Dr. Lapin countered that "it's in all our interests to look out for the financial health of the hospital. And since it is unclear which of the two approaches benefits the patient more, I urge you to reconsider the way you handle these cases."
>
> Was it ethical for Dr. Lapin to approach Dr. Weiner if there was no indication he was delivering poor quality care? How should financial considerations, both those related to the hospital and society at large, be weighed against physician judgment?

Wasserman, The Doctor, The Patient and the DRG, 13 Hastings Center Rep., Nov. 1983, at 23. See also the materials in section 3.E.3.

5. *Discharging Patients "Quicker and Sicker."* Critics of DRGs have documented that they caused hospitals to discharge patients "quicker and sicker." But is it necessarily wrong that a patient is not allowed to remain in the hospital for the full period of recuperation? Contrast these critics with Katherine Kahn et al., The Effects of the DRG-Based Prospective Payment System on Quality of Care for Hospitalized Medicare Patients, 264 JAMA 1953 (1990) (finding no systematic effects on quality of care).

> At least part of the [premature discharge] problem appears to stem from simple ignorance. When the DRGs and their respective weights were first published, the average LOS [length of stay] for each DRG was also published. Some hospital administrators have taken this average figure as a maximum. ... It is reported that in some instances when the average DRG days are up, patients have been told they must leave the hospital because "their Medicare coverage has run out." These are obviously abuses of the system, but they are not the result

of defects inherent to PPS/DRG itself.... The remedy is not to change the system; it is to better inform the system's participants about how it works.

J. Timothy Phillips, Don Wineberg & Adam Elfenbein, Meeting the Goals of Medicare Prospective Payments, 88 W. Va. L. Rev. 225, 236 (1985). CMS has attempted this remedy by requiring that all Medicare patients be given upon admission a written statement of their rights to protest a discharge decision. Patients have a grace period of several days after written notice of discharge to remain in the hospital and appeal the decision to the local Quality Improvement Organization (formerly called Peer Review Organization).

    6. *DRG Creep.*

> In New Jersey, a study found that 26.4 percent of the patients had been misclassified [to the wrong DRG].... One of the most publicized examples was the softball player who had injured his finger. He had to be hospitalized for two days so that the bone in his finger could be repaired with a metal pin. The DRG category assigned to this patient was "fracture with major surgery," usually reserved for serious cases such as total hip replacement. While the patient's actual charges would have been less than $1000, the DRG classification resulted in a bill for $5,000.

P. Feldstein, Health Care Economics 296 (2d ed. 1982). These and other manipulations such as unnecessary admissions are policed by Medicare's Quality Improvement Organization (formerly called Peer Review Organizations).

    7. *Physicians' Fee Schedules.* It is critical to observe that DRGs only cover inpatient hospital costs. What difficulties would be encountered in extending DRGs to physician services? Consider the following explanation by the former head of CMS:

> In view of the generally successful change in Medicare's hospital-payment system, many wonder why we cannot repeat the accomplishment with respect to Medicare payment of physicians. The answer is simple: Paying physicians is far more complicated. When developing a hospital-payment system for Medicare, one must handle 11 million admissions to 7,000 hospitals for 475 diagnosis-related groups. Those numbers pale in comparison to Medicare's 350 million claims from 500,000 physicians for 7,000 different procedure codes. Moreover, whereas hospitals can average their gains and losses under a prospective payment system across many cases, physicians' smaller caseloads and greater specialization make such averaging much more risky for them. These differences mean that improving the way Medicare pays physicians will be vastly more difficult, both analytically and administratively.

William Roper, Perspectives on Physician-Payment Reform, 319 New Eng. J. Med. 865 (1988).

    Instead of physician DRGs, the federal government adopted a modified form of fee-for-service reimbursement that employs a "resource-based relative value scale," which introduced yet another acronym: RB-RVS. A relative value scale attempts to achieve some degree of parity in the amount that physicians charge for various services by measuring the relative costs of each service according to the time, mental effort, and technical skill required, as well as differences in the costs of malpractice premiums and specialty training. The initial projection under Medicare's fee schedule, for instance, was that "the average family practitioner could receive 60 percent more revenue from Medicare, whereas the average ophthalmologist could lose 40 percent of current revenues." Roper, supra.

Commenting on this approach, Roper, supra contends:

> A fee schedule based on a relative-value scale, no matter how carefully constructed, cannot be expected to address the growth in the volume and intensity of services. Whatever their merits, fee-for-service systems do not provide physicians with incentives to control this growth. At best, a revamped fee schedule may send physicians "better" signals, rewarding those who provide cognitive services as opposed to those who perform procedures. In the long run, . . . this may improve the mix of services provided to Medicare beneficiaries, . . . reduce perceived inequities in payment and establish fairer relative prices—a goal I support. . . . [But], to be clear, a relative-value scale cannot do for physicians what diagnosis-related groups did for hospitals. The question facing . . . the Congress is one I asked at a hearing on physician payment:
>
> > Is it worth investing the lion's share of our analytic, administrative, and political resources to substitute one fee-for-service payment system for another, leaving Medicare's most important issue—increased volume and intensity—untouched?

In response to these concerns, Congress included certain complex measures in the RB-RVS system to control the volume of physician services. The "volume performance standard" adjusts future payment rates if physicians' fees exceed projections in the current year. For further discussion and debate on relative value scales, see Regulating Doctors' Fees (H. Frech ed., 1991); the annual reports of MedPac, the Medicare Payment Advisory Commission; symposium, 30 Inquiry 226 (1993); Symposium, 34 St. Louis U. L.J. 749 (1990).

The difficulty of capturing even routine medical services in an accurate, fair, and easily administrable prospective payment system is well illustrated by the roaring controversy over Medicare rules for physicians' "evaluation and management" (E & M) services. These rules govern physician payment for routine office visits. They attempt to distinguish among short, medium, and long visits, to prevent what was believed to be widespread upcoding (short visits seemed to be disappearing and long visits were becoming much more common). Various commentators, mostly physicians, opine that "the guidelines are a misguided attempt to capture clinical reasoning, they destroy the legitimate purposes of the medical record," they are "stupefyingly complicated, irrelevant to actual patient care, and adversarial in intent," and are "worse than useless." Allan S. Brett, New Guidelines for Coding Physicians' Services: A Step Backward, 339 New Eng. J. Med. 1705 (1999); Jerome P. Kassirer & Marcia Angell, Evaluation and Management Guidelines: Fatally Flawed, 339 New Eng. J. Med. 1697 (1999).

8. *Public Utility Regulation.* The approach that David Frankford advocates— community-based regulation of entire institutions based on their individual circumstances—is an example of the general conception that a hospital is a public utility, similar in both its economics and its social importance to the telephone and electric companies. William Corley, Hospitals as a Public Utility, 2 J. Health Pol. Pol'y & L. 304 (1978). Accordingly, during the 1970s, about a dozen states

instituted comprehensive regulation of hospital rates. The purpose was both to contain costs and to more equitably spread the burden of uncompensated care borne by different hospitals. The latter was accomplished by building into hospital rates an explicit component for the costs of treating indigent patients, which was then collected into a common fund and redistributed to hospitals based on the amount of charity care they actually performed. After a period of uncertainty, this and other aspects of state regulation of hospital rates were held to survive ERISA preemption. New York State Conf. of Blue Cross & Blue Shield Plans v. Travelers Insurance Co. (1995). Hospital rate regulation has also survived attacks on its constitutionality. See William Brewbaker, Health Care Price Controls and the Takings Clause, 21 Hastings Const. L.Q. 669 (1994). However, every one of these states except Maryland has since repealed its hospital rate regulation, believing that competitive market forces were sufficiently constraining hospital charges by the 1990s. J. McDonough, Tracking the Demise of State Hospital Rate Setting, 16 Health Aff. No. 1, at 13 (Jan. 1997).

The methods used by hospital rate regulators varied widely. Some reviewed entire hospital budgets under discretionary criteria. Others created complex formula similar to Medicare, although not necessarily using DRGs. More often, they regulated hospital per diem rates. These programs were modestly successful in holding down the rate of inflation for hospital costs, but less successful at holding down total health care spending. They also proved enormously complex to administer, and were a constant battleground between hospitals and state government.

9. *Hospital Appeals under Medicare.* There are few judicial challenges under Medicare to the basic DRG methodology because of provisions in the statute expressly precluding review of the DRG weights and severely limiting the opportunity to challenge individual hospital rates. See Skagit County Public Hospital District v. Shalala, 80 F.3d 379 (9th Cir. 1996). Query, then, whether the system has sacrificed accuracy and fairness in order to obtain deceptive legal simplicity? At the administrative level, however, administrative appeals have run so rampant that the Provider Reimbursed Review Board (PRRB) has a backlog of several years. The single matter of adjusting a hospital's rate to accurately reflect geographically determined factors (wages, rural status, etc.) became so burdensome for the PRRB that a separate review board was created for this sole purpose—the Medicare Geographic Classification Review Board. David W. Thomas, Review of Medicare Reimbursement Disputes under 42 U.S.C. Section 1395oo: Delineating a Unified Theory of the Provider Reimbursement Review Board's Jurisdiction and Scope of Review, 39 Duq. L. Rev. 287 (2001).

10. *Future Prospects.* DRGs and RB-RVS are not the government's final word. Dr. William L. Roper, former head of CMS, was quoted as follows:

> Over the long term, this administered price system is going to collapse of its own weight. I am angry over the terrible complexity of the system, . . . but I don't think the solution is further fine-tuning of a terribly flawed system. The answer is a new system, based on private health plan options.

New York Times, Nov. 23, 1987, at 10, col. 3. This new system would use vouchers to allow patients to select among competing HMOs, a system like that described at page 336.

Problem: Technology Innovation

What effects are DRGs and other forms of prospective payment likely to have on technology acquisition and medical innovation? The answer depends on the type of innovation. Consider: Those that involve greater cost versus lesser costs. Those that increase admissions by finding new things to treat versus those that shorten length of stay for existing diagnoses. And, those that improve diagnostic accuracy versus those that improve treatment. Here are several concrete examples. For each example, consider the technology from a perspective of when it was first introduced, that is, assuming that a specific DRG has not yet been created for it or that overall payment rates have not yet been adjusted to reflect the new technology.

1. A procedure known as P.T.C.A. (percutaneous transluminal coronary angioplasty) or "balloon angioplasty," is an alternative to bypass surgery that involves inserting a balloon into an artery and inflating it to clear blockage
2. A PET (positron emission tomographer) scanner, a multi-million-dollar machine that produces images of biochemical activity inside the body, in contrast with an MRI, which depicts soft tissues, or a CAT scan, which depicts bones and hard tissue.
3. Extracorporeal shock-wave lithotripter, a space-age machine that pulverizes kidney stones by concentrating blasts of focused shock (sound) waves delivered through a vat of water, as an alternative to either surgical removal or waiting for the stones to be excreted naturally.

3. Capitation Payment

■ REIMBURSING PHYSICIANS AND HOSPITALS
Thomas Bodenheimer & Kevin Grumbach*
272 JAMA 971 (1994)

...Traditionally, physicians and hospitals have been paid on a fee-for-service basis. During the 1980s, more and more Americans enrolled in managed care plans, which often change the methods by which hospitals and physicians are paid for the purposes of controlling costs. We will not explore managed care in detail in this article, but will describe only those aspects of managed care needed to understand physician and hospital reimbursement....

TWO-TIER STRUCTURES

Capitation payments to physicians in the United States are complicated, yet in the United Kingdom, they are relatively simple. Under the British NHS, people

---

*The authors are physicians in the Department of Family and Community Medicine at the University of California-San Francisco.

sign up with a general practitioner who becomes their primary care physician. For each person on the general practitioner's list, the physician receives a monthly fee called a capitation payment (i.e., a per capita payment or payment "by the head." The more patients on the list, the more money the physician earns. As part of the capitation arrangement, patients are required to route all their nonemergency medical needs through the general practitioner gatekeeper, who, when necessary, refers patients for specialist services or hospital care.... This simple capitation arrangement is referred to as a "two-tier" capitation structure; one tier is the health plan and the other tier the individual primary care physician or a small number of physicians in group practice. The British NHS has traditionally paid for referral services (e.g., specialist physician care, radiology, and laboratory tests) through a separate funding channel....

Approximately 20 percent of U.S. HMO plans involve two-tier structures, with HMOs paying capitation fees directly to primary care physicians. Unlike the British system, many U.S. HMOs subsume payments for referral services under the primary care capitation payment. Rather than the HMO plan paying for these services separately, the HMO shifts the financial risk to the primary care physician.

The nature of risk is quite different under these two types of capitation arrangements.... [A U.S. doctor] is at much greater financial risk.

> Stay Fit pays Dr. Kinderhoff's practice $30 per month for each patient...enrolled in the practice whether or not the patient visits Dr. Kinderhoff. John twists his knee playing basketball and is unable to bear weight on his leg. Dr. Kinderhoff examines John's knee and prescribes a knee immobilizer, ice, rest, and antiinflammatory medications. After two weeks, John's knee has not improved. Dr. Kinderhoff considers sending John to an orthopedist. She anticipates that four visits with the orthopedist will cost $400, and an MRI of the knee, an additional $900. She will have to pay these charges out of her Stay Fit capitation income.

In this example, Dr. Kinderhoff would receive $360 per year for John's care but wind up spending $1,300 for specialty care for John's knee injury. That is the real meaning of "at risk." This risk may be balanced by the fact that many enrolled patients rarely visit Dr Kinderhoff; for these patients, $360 per year in capitation payments may yield a generous profit for Dr. Kinderhoff's practice, but the potential remains for high cost patients to erode Dr. Kinderhoff's take-home earnings. Generally, a dollar limit [which is called "stop loss"] is placed on the physician's risk such that excessive costs for an extremely ill patient are covered by the HMO....

THREE-TIER STRUCTURES

... In this type of structure, physicians remain in their own private offices but join together into [practice groups]. With the addition of the [practice group] intermediary, physician payment takes on a three-tier structure....

Sorting out the flow of payments and nature of risk sharing becomes difficult in this type of three-tier capitation structure. In most three-tier HMOs, the financial risk for diagnostic and specialist services is borne by the overall [practice group] organization and spread among all the participating primary care physicians in the [practice group]. The spreading of risk among a larger group of physicians avoids some of the high-stakes risk that occurs when only one or a few primary care physicians accept a full-risk capitation contract.... [Practice groups] usually provide financial incentives to primary care physicians to limit the use of diagnostic and specialist services by returning to these physicians any surplus funds that remain at the end of the year. The lower the use of diagnostic and specialist services, the higher the year-end bonus for physician gatekeepers. Some people feel that this arrangement represents a conflict of interest for primary care physicians, because these physicians' personal income is increased by denying diagnostic and specialty services to their patients. Because year-end bonuses are usually based on the collective performance of primary care physicians, financial risk in a [practice group] setting presents less of a potential conflict-of-interest problem than financial incentives in a two-tier setting that are directly indexed to an individual physician's use of ancillary services....

Three-tier structures become even more confusing when the unit of reimbursement differs across tiers. In the [simpler] model, capitation is the basic payment method for both the [practice group] as a whole and the [practice group's] constituent physicians. In the [more complex] model, however, the [practice group] receives capitation payments from the health insurance plan but then reimburses its participating primary care physicians on a fee-for-service basis. Under this arrangement, the fees billed by the physicians may well exceed the amount of money the [practice group] has received from the insurance plan on a capitated basis to pay for physician and related outpatient services. To reduce this risk, many [practice groups] pay their physicians only a portion, for example 60 percent, of a predetermined fee schedule and withhold the other 40 percent. If money is left over at the end of the year, the physicians receive a portion of the withholding as a bonus. Under [this] system, the [practice group] is the main entity at risk because provision of more services can cause the [practice group] to lose money. Individual physicians also are partially at risk, because high expenditures by the [practice group] mean no bonus and thus lower individual physician income. The economic incentive for individual primary physicians is a mixed one. It is to the physician's financial advantage to schedule as many patient visits as possible, since the physician receives a fee for each visit. However, a large number of visits overall by [practice group] patients, as well as high use of laboratory and X-ray studies and specialist services, will deplete the [practice group's] budget, thereby reducing the possibility of a large bonus payment at the end of the year....

[When hospitals are paid] [u]nder the capitation method, hospitals are at risk for admissions, lengths of stay, and resources used, i.e., hospitals bear all the risk and the insurer—usually an HMO—bears no risk. (Some HMOs do accept a portion of the risk by agreeing to make extra payments to the hospital once charges to an individual patient exceed a specified limit in a given year.) Under capitation contracts, the HMO has no need to perform utilization review, but the hospital itself conducts strict utilization review to ensure that each admission and each hospital day is justified....

PAYMENT PER TIME: SALARY

... In contrast with traditional private physicians, physicians in the public sector—municipal, Veterans Affairs and military hospitals, state mental hospitals, and community clinics—are generally paid by salary. Salary aggregates payment for all services delivered during a month or year into one lump sum. There appears to be a trend toward salaried practice in the private sector, chiefly in private group practices, medical schools, and group-model and staff-model HMOs....

Health maintenance organization physicians paid purely by salary usually bear little, if any, financial risk. The entire HMO is at risk of financial loss if its expenses are too great. To manage its risk, administrators at group-model and staff-model HMOs may place constraints on their physician employees, for example, scheduling them for a high volume of patient visits or creating waiting times for X-rays, laboratory tests, and specialty referrals. Many HMOs also offer end-of-the-year bonuses to physicians if overall HMO expenses (or costs to the physician group practice) come in under budget. For physicians, the main risk concerns their time....

[RISK ADJUSTMENT]

As physicians and hospitals assume greater financial risk under more aggregated units of payment, providers begin to experience the basic dynamic of insurance underwriting: Patients with costly illnesses are a financial liability; patients in good health are a financial advantage. The intent of more aggregated payment units, such as capitation, is to encourage providers to make more efficient use of resources for a set bundle of services. However, just as insurance companies and HMOs have discovered an irresistible market logic in skimming off the healthiest subscribers, physicians . . . face a financial incentive to economize under more aggregated payment units by caring for healthier patients. Concern about this undesirable risk-skimming incentive has given rise to attempts to risk adjust reimbursement—that is, to pay at a higher rate for higher-risk patients.

Traditional fee-for-service payment has an intrinsic risk-adjustment factor. The sicker the patient, the more services provided. More services provided means greater reimbursement. In the episode-of-illness mode of payment, risk adjustment has been factored into such payment methods as the Medicare hospital DRG system.... Thus, DRG reimbursement is higher for a patient hospitalized for septic shock than for a patient admitted for elective cholecystectomy....

Risk adjustment has been a technically greater challenge in setting capitation payments. The ideal risk-adjustment method for capitation payments would characterize each individual's health status or need for health care services to attach a higher payment rate to the higher-risk patients. For example, [an HMO] could pay a higher capitation rate for . . . HIV patients than for . . . healthy ones. Unfortunately, accurately predicting individuals' need for care is difficult. Data routinely collected during insurance enrollment, such as age, offer only a crude estimate of an individual's likelihood of using services. More accurate predictions necessitate examining an individual's medical history or current level of health, a relatively expensive proposition that often still falls short of the desired precision at estimating an individual's future health care expenses.

Current systems of capitated reimbursement often come with safety valves for dealing with this problem. Health maintenance organization contracts typically have stop-loss clauses, whereby reimbursement reverts to a fee-for-service method once a patient generates costs above a certain threshold. Interest in improving the "science" of risk adjustment is increasing as payers in the United States increasingly turn to capitation and other aggregated units of reimbursement.[17] ...

■ PEGRAM v. HERDRICH
530 U.S. 211 (2000)

Justice SOUTER delivered the opinion of the Court.

The question in this case is whether treatment decisions made by a health maintenance organization, acting through its physician employees, are fiduciary acts within the meaning of the Employee Retirement Income Security Act of 1974 (ERISA). We hold that they are not.

Petitioners, Carle Clinic Association..., function as a health maintenance organization (HMO) organized for profit. Its owners are physicians providing prepaid medical services to participants whose employers contract with Carle to provide such coverage. Respondent, Cynthia Herdrich, was covered by Carle through her husband's employer, State Farm Insurance Company. The events in question began when a Carle physician, petitioner Lori Pegram, examined Herdrich, who was experiencing pain in the midline area of her groin. Six days later, Dr. Pegram discovered a six by eight centimeter inflamed mass in Herdrich's abdomen. Despite the noticeable inflammation, Dr. Pegram did not order an ultrasound diagnostic procedure at a local hospital, but decided that Herdrich would have to wait eight more days for an ultrasound, to be performed at a facility staffed by Carle more than 50 miles away. Before the eight days were over, Herdrich's appendix ruptured, causing peritonitis.

Herdrich sued Pegram and Carle in state court for medical malpractice, and...prevailed [against] both, receiving $35,000 in compensation for her injury.... [She also sued in federal court under ERISA, the federal statute discussed in Chapters 2.C. and 4.C that regulates pension plans and other fringe benefits. The ERISA suit alleged that Carle HMO's] rewarding its physician owners for limiting medical care entailed an inherent or anticipatory breach of an ERISA fiduciary duty, since these terms created an incentive to make decisions in the physicians' self-interest, rather than the exclusive interests of plan participants.... [This claim was dismissed by the district court but was reinstated by the Seventh Circuit.]

Whether Carle is a fiduciary when it acts through its physician owners as pleaded in the ERISA count depends on some background of fact and law about HMO organizations, medical benefit plans, fiduciary obligation, and the meaning of Herdrich's allegations....

In a fee-for-service system, a physician's financial incentive is to provide more care, not less, so long as payment is forthcoming. The check on this incentive is a physician's obligation to exercise reasonable medical skill and judgment in the patient's interest.... The defining feature of an HMO is... [that it] assumes the financial risk of providing the benefits promised.... Like other

---

[17] Hornbrook MC, Scheffler RM, Rossiter LF, eds. Risk-based Contributions to Private Health Insurance: Advances in Health Economics and Health Services Research, XII. Greenwich, Conn.: Jai Press; 1991.

risk-bearing organizations, HMOs take steps to control costs, [such as utilization review]. These cost-controlling measures are commonly complemented by specific financial incentives to physicians, rewarding them for decreasing utilization of health-care services, and penalizing them for what may be found to be excessive treatment. Hence, in an HMO system, a physician's financial interest lies in providing less care, not more. The check on this influence (like that on the converse, fee-for-service incentive) is the professional obligation to provide covered services with a reasonable degree of skill and judgment in the patient's interest.

The adequacy of professional obligation to counter financial self-interest has been challenged no matter what the form of medical organization. HMOs became popular because fee-for-service physicians were thought to be providing unnecessary or useless services; today, many doctors and other observers argue that HMOs often ignore the individual needs of a patient in order to improve the HMOs' bottom lines. In this case, for instance, one could argue that Pegram's decision to wait before getting an ultrasound for Herdrich, and her insistence that the ultrasound be done at a distant facility owned by Carle, reflected an interest in limiting the HMO's expenses, which blinded her to the need for immediate diagnosis and treatment.

Herdrich focuses on the Carle scheme's provision for a "year-end distribution" to the HMO's physician owners. She argues that this particular incentive device of annually paying physician owners the profit resulting from their own decisions rationing care can distinguish Carle's organization from HMOs generally, so that reviewing Carle's decisions under a fiduciary standard as pleaded in Herdrich's complaint would not open the door to like claims about other HMO structures. While the Court of Appeals agreed, we think otherwise, under the law as now written.

Although it is true that the relationship between sparing medical treatment and physician reward is not a subtle one under the Carle scheme, no HMO organization could survive without some incentive connecting physician reward with treatment rationing. The essence of an HMO is that salaries and profits are limited by the HMO's fixed membership fees. See Orentlicher, Paying Physicians More to Do Less: Financial Incentives to Limit Care, 30 U. Rich. L. Rev. 155, 174 (1996). This is not to suggest that the Carle provisions are as socially desirable as some other HMO organizational schemes; they may not be. But whatever the HMO, there must be rationing and inducement to ration.

Since inducement to ration care goes to the very point of any HMO scheme, and rationing necessarily raises some risks while reducing others (ruptured appendixes are more likely; unnecessary appendectomies are less so), any legal principle purporting to draw a line between good and bad HMOs would embody, in effect, a judgment about socially acceptable medical risk. A valid conclusion of this sort would, however, necessarily turn on facts to which courts would probably not have ready access: correlations between malpractice rates and various HMO models, similar correlations involving fee-for-service models, and so on. . . . [S]uch complicated factfinding and such a debatable social judgment are not wisely required of courts unless for some reason resort cannot be had to the legislative process, with its preferable forum for comprehensive investigations and judgments of social value, such as optimum treatment levels and health care expenditure. We think,

then, that courts are not in a position to derive a sound legal principle to differentiate an HMO like Carle from other HMOs. . . .

c

We turn now from the structure of HMOs to the requirements of ERISA. A
fiduciary within the meaning of ERISA must be someone acting in the capacity of
manager, administrator, or financial adviser to a "plan." . . . Rules governing collection of premiums, definition of benefits, submission of claims, and resolution of
disagreements over entitlement to services are the sorts of provisions that constitute a plan. Thus, when employers contract with an HMO to provide benefits to
employees subject to ERISA, the provisions of documents that set up the HMO are
not, as such, an ERISA plan, but the agreement between an HMO and an employer
who pays the premiums may, as here, provide elements of a plan by setting out
rules under which beneficiaries will be entitled to care.

As just noted, fiduciary obligations can apply to managing, advising, and
administering an ERISA plan. . . . In general terms, fiduciary responsibility
under ERISA is simply stated. The statute provides that fiduciaries shall discharge
their duties with respect to a plan "solely in the interest of the participants and
beneficiaries." . . . These responsibilities imposed by ERISA have the familiar ring
of their source in the common law of trusts: . . . "The most fundamental duty owed
by the trustee to the beneficiaries of the trust is the duty of loyalty. . . . It is the duty
of a trustee to administer the trust solely in the interest of the beneficiaries." 2A A.
Scott & W. Fratcher, Trusts §170, 311 (4th ed. 1987).

Beyond the threshold statement of responsibility, however, the analogy
between ERISA fiduciary and common law trustee becomes problematic. This is
so because the trustee at common law characteristically wears only his fiduciary hat
when he takes action to affect a beneficiary, whereas the trustee under ERISA may
wear different hats.

Speaking of the traditional trustee, Professor Scott's treatise admonishes that
the trustee "is not permitted to place himself in a position where it would be for his
own benefit to violate his duty to the beneficiaries." 2A Scott, §170, at 311. Under
ERISA, however, a fiduciary may have financial interests adverse to beneficiaries.
Employers, for example, can be ERISA fiduciaries and still take actions to the
disadvantage of employee beneficiaries, when they act as employers (e.g., firing
a beneficiary for reasons unrelated to the ERISA plan), or even as plan sponsors
(e.g., modifying the terms of a plan as allowed by ERISA to provide less generous
benefits). . . . ERISA does require, however, that the fiduciary with two hats wear
only one at a time, and wear the fiduciary hat when making fiduciary decisions. . . .

The pleadings must also be parsed very carefully to understand what acts by
physician owners acting on Carle's behalf are alleged to be fiduciary in nature.[8] It
will help to keep two sorts of arguably administrative acts in mind. Cf. Dukes v. U.S.

---

[8] . . . The fraud claims in Herdrich's initial complaint could be read to allege breach of a fiduciary
obligation to disclose physician incentives to limit care, whereas her amended complaint alleges an
obligation to avoid such incentives. . . . cf. Varity Corp. v. Howe, 516 U.S. 489, 505, (1996) (holding that
ERISA fiduciaries may have duties to disclose information about plan prospects that they have no duty,
or even power, to change). But failure to disclose is no longer the allegation of the amended
complaint. . . .

Healthcare, Inc., 57 F.3d 350, 361 (3rd Cir. 1995) (discussing dual medical/administrative roles of HMOs). What we will call pure "eligibility decisions" turn on the plan's coverage of a particular condition or medical procedure for its treatment. "Treatment decisions," by contrast, are choices about how to go about diagnosing and treating a patient's condition: given a patient's constellation of symptoms, what is the appropriate medical response?

These decisions are often practically inextricable from one another.... This is so not merely because, under a scheme like Carle's, treatment and eligibility decisions are made by the same person, the treating physician. It is so because a great many and possibly most coverage questions are not simple yes-or-no questions, like whether appendicitis is a covered condition (when there is no dispute that a patient has appendicitis), or whether acupuncture is a covered procedure for pain relief (when the claim of pain is unchallenged). The more common coverage question is a when-and-how question. Although coverage for many conditions will be clear and various treatment options will be indisputably compensable, physicians still must decide what to do in particular cases. The issue may be, say, whether one treatment option is so superior to another under the circumstances, and needed so promptly, that a decision to proceed with it would meet the medical necessity requirement that conditions the HMO's obligation to provide or pay for that particular procedure at that time in that case.... In practical terms, these eligibility decisions cannot be untangled from physicians' judgments about reasonable medical treatment, and in the case before us, Dr. Pegram's decision was one of that sort. She decided (wrongly, as it turned out) that Herdrich's condition did not warrant immediate action; the consequence of that medical determination was that Carle would not cover immediate care, whereas it would have done so if Dr. Pegram had made the proper diagnosis and judgment to treat. The eligibility decision and the treatment decision were inextricably mixed, as they are in countless medical administrative decisions every day....

Based on our understanding of the matters just discussed, we think Congress did not intend Carle or any other HMO to be treated as a fiduciary to the extent that it makes mixed eligibility decisions acting through its physicians. We begin with doubt that Congress would ever have thought of a mixed eligibility decision as fiduciary in nature. At common law, fiduciary duties characteristically attach to decisions about managing assets and distributing property to beneficiaries. Trustees buy, sell, and lease investment property, lend and borrow, and do other things to conserve and nurture assets. They pay out income, choose beneficiaries, and distribute remainders at termination. Thus, the common law trustee's most defining concern historically has been the payment of money in the interest of the beneficiary.

Mixed eligibility decisions by an HMO acting through its physicians have, however, only a limited resemblance to the usual business of traditional trustees.... [T]he physicians through whom HMOs act make just the sorts of decisions made by licensed medical practitioners millions of times every day, in every possible medical setting: HMOs, fee-for-service proprietorships, public and private hospitals, military field hospitals, and so on. The settings bear no more resemblance to trust departments than a decision to operate turns on the factors controlling the amount of a quarterly income distribution. Thus, it is at least questionable whether Congress would have had mixed eligibility decisions in mind when it provided that decisions administering a plan were fiduciary in nature. Indeed, when Congress took up the subject of fiduciary responsibility under ERISA, it concentrated on fiduciaries' financial decisions, focusing on pension plans, the difficulty many retirees faced in getting the payments they expected, and the financial mismanagement that had too often deprived employees of their benefits. Its focus was far from the subject of Herdrich's claim.

Our doubt that Congress intended the category of fiduciary administrative functions to encompass the mixed determinations at issue here hardens into conviction when we consider the consequences that would follow from Herdrich's contrary view.... Although Herdrich is vague about the mechanics of relief, the one point that seems clear is that she seeks the return of profit from the pockets of the Carle HMO's owners, with the money to be given to the plan for the benefit of the participants. Since the provision for profit is what makes the HMO a proprietary organization, her remedy in effect would be nothing less than elimination of the for-profit HMO. Her remedy ... might well portend the end of nonprofit HMOs as well, since those HMOs can set doctors' salaries. A claim against a nonprofit HMO could easily allege that salaries were excessively high because they were funded by limiting care, and some nonprofits actually use incentive schemes similar to that challenged here....

It is enough to recognize that the Judiciary has no warrant to precipitate the upheaval that would follow a refusal to dismiss Herdrich's ERISA claim. The fact is that for over 27 years the Congress of the United States has promoted the formation of HMO practices.... If Congress wishes to restrict its approval of HMO practice to certain preferred forms, it may choose to do so. But the Federal Judiciary would be acting contrary to the congressional policy of allowing HMO organizations if it were to entertain an ERISA fiduciary claim portending wholesale attacks on existing HMOs solely because of their structure, untethered to claims of concrete harm....

The fiduciary is, of course, obliged to act exclusively in the interest of the beneficiary, but this translates into no rule readily applicable to HMO decisions or those of any other variety of medical practice. While the incentive of the HMO physician is to give treatment sparingly, imposing a fiduciary obligation upon him would not lead to a simple default rule, say, that whenever it is reasonably possible to disagree about treatment options, the physician should treat aggressively. After all, HMOs came into being because some groups of physicians consistently provided more aggressive treatment than others in similar circumstances, with results not perceived as justified by the marginal expense and risk associated with intervention; excessive surgery is not in the patient's best interest, whether provided by fee-for-service surgeons or HMO surgeons subject to a default rule urging them to operate. Nor would it be possible to translate fiduciary duty into a standard that would allow recovery from an HMO whenever a mixed decision influenced by the HMO's financial incentive resulted in a bad outcome for the patient. It would be so easy to allege, and to find, an economic influence when sparing care did not lead to a well patient, that any such standard in practice would allow a factfinder to convert an HMO into a guarantor of recovery....

[T]he defense of any HMO would be that its physician did not act out of financial interest but for good medical reasons, the plausibility of which would require reference to standards of reasonable and customary medical practice in like circumstances. That, of course, is the traditional standard of the common law. Thus, for all practical purposes, every claim of fiduciary breach by an HMO physician making a mixed decision would boil down to a malpractice claim, and the fiduciary standard would be nothing but the malpractice standard traditionally applied in actions against physicians.

What would be the value to the plan participant of having this kind of ERISA fiduciary action? It would simply apply the law already available in state courts and federal diversity actions today, and the formulaic addition of an allegation of financial incentive would do nothing but bring the same claim into a federal court under federal-question jurisdiction. It is true that in States that do not allow malpractice actions against HMOs the fiduciary claim would offer a plaintiff a further defendant to be sued for direct liability, and in some cases the HMO might have a deeper pocket than the physician. But we have seen enough to know that ERISA was not enacted out of concern that physicians were too poor to be sued....

We hold that mixed eligibility decisions by HMO physicians are not fiduciary decisions under ERISA.

■ PAYMENTS TO INDUCE REDUCTION OR LIMITATION OF MEDICARE AND MEDICAID SERVICES
42 U.S.C. §1320a-7a(b)(1)

If a hospital . . . knowingly makes a payment, directly or indirectly, to a physician as an inducement to reduce or limit services provided with respect to [Medicare or Medicaid patients who] are under the direct care of the physician, the hospital . . . shall be subject . . . to a civil money penalty of not more than $2,000 for each such individual with respect to whom the payment is made. . . .

42 U.S.C. §1395mm(8)

(A) Each [Medicare] contract with an [HMO] shall provide that the [HMO] may not operate any physician incentive plan (as defined in subparagraph (B)) unless the following requirements are met:

(i) No specific payment is made directly or indirectly under the plan to a physician or physician group as an inducement to reduce or limit medically necessary services provided with respect to a specific individual enrolled with the organization.

(ii) If the plan places a physician or physician group at substantial financial risk (as determined by the Secretary) for services not provided by the physician or physician group, the [HMO]—

(I) provides stop-loss protection for the physician or group that is adequate and appropriate, based on standards developed by the Secretary that take into account the number of physicians placed at such substantial financial risk in the group or under the plan and the number of individuals enrolled with the organization who receive services from the physician or the physician group, and

(II) conducts periodic surveys of both individuals enrolled and individuals previously enrolled with the organization to determine the degree of access of such individuals to services provided by the organization and satisfaction with the quality of such services.

(B) In this paragraph, the term "physician incentive plan" means any compensation arrangement between an [HMO] and a physician or physician group that may directly or indirectly have the effect of reducing or limiting services provided with respect to individuals enrolled with the [HMO].

Notes: Capitation; Financial Conflicts of Interest; and Risk Adjustment

1. Capitation payments and other incentive plans common in HMOs raise a variety of legal and regulatory issues that are considered in other chapters (liability in Chapter 2.C and insurance regulation in Chapter 3.B). This section explores only the structure and accuracy of capitation arrangements, and the ethical conflict of interest they create. Additional, detailed descriptions of the various incentive plans in common use can be found in Boyd v. Albert Einstein Medical Center, excerpted at page 133; T. Bodenheimer & K. Grumbach, Capitation or Decapitation: Keeping Your Head in Changing Times, 276 JAMA 1025 (1996); and in Marsha Gold et al., Financial Risk Sharing with Providers in HMOs, 1999, 39 Inquiry 34 (2002). For further discussion of ethical and public policy issues, see Conflicts of Interest in Clinical Practice and Research (Roy Spece et al., eds. 1996); Peter A. Ubel, Pricing Life: Why It's Time for Health Care Rationing (2000); Gail Agrawal, Resuscitating Professionalism: Self-Regulation in the Medical Marketplace, 66 U. Mo. L. Rev. 341 (2001); Mark A. Hall, Rationing Health Care at the Bedside, 69 N.Y.U. L. Rev. 693 (1994); William M. Sage, Physicians as Advocates, 35 Hous. L. Rev. 1529 (1999).

2. *Global Capitation.* Early studies of HMOs, both private sector and under public programs, have found no major deterioration in the quality of care, but these studies have looked mainly at HMOs that paid doctors salaries or modified fee-for-service, not those that use full capitation. In California, where physicians sometimes undertake "global" capitation risk covering the full costs of hospitalization and medical treatment they order, hospitalization rates plummeted in the 1990s, even from their previously low level. Raising concerns about this new arrangement, see Steffie Woolhandler & David Himmelstein, Extreme Risk: The New Corporate Proposition for Physicians, 333 New Eng. J. Med. 1706 (1995).

3. *Risk Adjustment.* Do you see the nightmare of DRGs recurring in the guise of risk adjustment? Medicare has begun phasing in a new risk adjustment method for paying HMOs, one that pays more for patients with a history of designated chronic illnesses. The amount of extra payment is based on days of hospitalization and primary diagnoses in the prior year. Although this creates an incentive for HMOs to hospitalize their patients more in one year to increase payment in the next year, CMS claims there are sufficient checks in place to prevent this incentive for increasing costs. See Lisa Iezzoni et al., 339 New Eng. J. Med. 1933 (1999).

Discussing the general problem of risk-adjusting capitation payments, Robert Kuttner observes that "in building adequate risk-adjustment models, there are subtleties of Byzantine complexity.... Like so much else about the U.S. health system, [this] seems an astonishingly complex way to achieve some straightforward policy goals." He concludes that "the superior approach would be to cut the increasingly convoluted knot and move to a universal, unfragmented system of health insurance or a neutral form of payment for doctors, such as by salary." Robert Kuttner, The Risk-Adjustment Debate, 339 New Eng. J. Med. 1952 (1999). For general discussion of the methods, purpose, and performance see Fred Hellinger & Herbert Wong, Selection Bias in HMOs: A Review of the Evidence, 57 Med. Care Res. & Rev. 405 (2000); J.P. Newhouse, Patients at Risk: Health Reform and Risk Adjustment, Health Aff. (Spring 1994), at 132; Charles Tiefer & Heather Akehurst-Krause, Risky Business: Medicare's Vulnerability to Selection Games of Managed Care Providers, 28 U. Balt. L. Rev. 319 (1999); Symposium, 6(3) Healthcare Rev. Online 1 (June 2002); Symposium, Private Employers and Risk Adjustment, 38 Inquiry 242 (2001).

4. *Regulation of Physician Incentives Plans.* The two statutes that are excerpted are the first of a new generation of regulation directed at cost-minimizing incentives. Tracy E. Miller & William M. Sage, Disclosing Physician Financial Incentives, 281 JAMA 1424-1430 (1999). Contrast these statutes with those discussed in Chapter 4.E that regulate inflationary payment incentives. *Pegram* says that legislators and regulators are better able to oversee the proper structure of physician incentives, but this isn't an easy task for them either. To what extent should the structure and degree of physician incentives be left simply to market forces? Consider the following forceful commentary from a prominent economist:

> Physician payment mechanisms are inevitably subject to more public monitoring than compensation systems in other occupations, since we all care more about our doctor's immediate motivation than we do about our accountant's or plumber's.... The tendency to overregulate must be recognized, however. The complexity of clinical services, combined with the importance that we all ascribe to what happens between physicians and patients, is conducive to the most egregious manifestations of what legal theorists refer to as the inhospitality tradition. That which cannot be understood without effort is deemed ipso facto to be designed for fraud, monopolization, or some other antisocial purpose.... The contemporary moment in health policy is nothing short of a Dionysian rhapsody of regulation, the inhospitality tradition gone riot, the formal and final enshrinement of the doctrine that everything not mandatory is prohibited. The complexity of physician behavior, the emergence of payment methods that blend fee-for-service and capitation, the interdependence of price mechanisms with nonprice mechanisms, the salience of organization as a support for compensation systems, and the remarkable variety and continual change in all arenas suggest that public policymakers should adopt a stance of intellectual humility and a tone of cautious optimism. In physician payment, as in most other aspects of life, matters are never as good as we might hope but never as bad as we might fear.

James C. Robinson, Theory and Practice in the Design of Physician Payment Incentives, 79 Milbank Q. 149, 173-174 (2001).

Read these two statutes carefully to observe their qualifications and distinctions. Note, for instance, that the first (hospital) statute appears to prohibit only physician-specific payments and not incentives that are pooled across a group of physicians, whereas the second (HMO) statute addresses both. However, for most incentives, the HMO statute is merely regulatory, not prohibitory. Its only prohibition is for inducements to reduce *medically necessary* treatment of *individual* patients. In contrast, the prohibition contained in the hospital statute is not limited by these qualifiers.

Why should the prohibition of economizing incentives be much stricter in hospitals than in HMOs? If Congress did not want money to influence decisions about hospital treatment, why did it adopt the DRG prospective payment system? The first statute was enacted in 1986 in response to several for-profit hospitals in California that paid each doctor a percentage of the profits the hospital earned under DRGs from the doctor's Medicare patients. Initially, the statute was intended to cover HMOs as well, until Congress realized it would prohibit the way most of them already paid their doctors, so, after further study, Congress adopted a more regulatory approach for HMOs.

5. *Hospital Incentives.* For hospitals, the Inspector General of DHHS ruled in 1999 that so-called gainsharing arrangements violated this statute. These arrangements are incentive programs that reward physicians for initiatives that improve the efficiency of care, such as by identifying and eliminating wasteful practice patterns. Hospital lawyers believed these worthy purposes would avoid the statutory prohibition by focusing on practice patterns and professional standards rather than on discrete treatment decisions for particular patients, and by pooling the incentive payments and refusing to reward any initiatives that compromised medically necessary care. Regardless, the DHHS ruling broadly pronounced these efforts illegal because it would be problematic to say precisely which hospital incentive programs are and are not permissible. See Comment, 79 N.C. L. Rev. 157 (2000). These arrangements might also threaten tax exemption. Thomas Hyatt, One for You and Two for Me: Revenue Sharing Arrangements in Charitable Healthcare Organizations, 34 J. Health L. 541 (2001).

Following an outcry from hospitals and their lawyers, a subsequent ruling in 2001 indicated some flexibility; it approved a plan to pay cardiac surgeons a share of the savings from being more efficient in using operating room supplies, with various safeguards, limits, and oversight mechanisms to guard against abuses. Hospital lawyers now are beginning to look for other ways around this statute. What do you think about the legality of (1) rewarding physicians only for the portion of cost savings that comes from privately insured rather than Medicare/Medicaid patients, or (2) rewarding physicians with a flat fee for designing, implementing, and monitoring cost-saving initiatives rather than a percentage based on the amount of savings?

6. *HMO Incentives.* Read the HMO statute again and carefully map its several dimensions. Implementing regulations define the "substantial risk" threshold to be 25 percent of a physician's income from the HMO. 42 C.F.R. §417.479. In other words, HMOs can put physicians at risk for losing up to one quarter of their Medicare compensation without incurring any regulatory oversight; above that, reporting and monitoring requirements are imposed, as well as a "stop-loss" requirement that limits loss above the threshold to 10 percent of the physician's

HMO payment. These restrictions do not apply at all, however, to incentives that affect a physician's provision of his own services; they apply only to placing physicians at financial risk for services they order from others (for instance, the hospitalization and speciality referral expenses approved by a primary care "gatekeeping" physician). Do you see how the statute captures that distinction? Finally, the implementing regulations declare that incentives that are pooled across physician groups that treat more than 25,000 patients are not at "substantial risk," even if their entire payment is at risk, because spreading the risk over such a large pool dilutes the incentive sufficient to minimize a serious threat of abuse. Does the statute authorize this controversial position? For additional discussion of this complex set of rules, see M. Hall, Physician Rationing and Agency Cost Theory, *in* Spece, supra; Orentlicher, supra; Douglas Blair, The "PIP" Regulations in Perspective, 29 U. Mem. L. Rev. 137 (1998); Henry T. Greely, Direct Financial Incentives in Managed Care: Unanswered Questions, 6 Health Matrix 53 (1996); Stephen R. Latham, Regulation of Managed Care Incentive Payments to Physicians, 22 Am. J.L. & Med. 399 (1996).

7. *The Ethics of Bedside Rationing.* The two federal statutes express different poles of the ethical debate over whether physicians should ever consider costs in making medical decisions. The following two excerpts give a flavor for this debate. The first is from a prominent physician at Boston University:

> [P]hysicians are required to do everything that they believe may benefit each patient without regard to costs or other societal considerations. In caring for an individual patient, the doctor must act solely as that patient's advocate, against the apparent interests of society as a whole, if necessary. An analogy can be drawn with the role of a lawyer defending a client against a criminal charge. The attorney is obligated to use all ethical means to defend the client, regardless of the cost of prolonged legal proceedings or even of the possibility that a guilty person may be acquitted through skillful advocacy. Similarly, in the practice of medicine, physicians are obligated to do all that they can for their patients without regard to any costs to society.
>
> This [ethic] may become blurred if physicians are pressed to balance the needs of their patients with societal needs. The practitioner may make decisions for economic reasons but rationalize them as in the best interest of the individual patient.... It is society, not the individual practitioner, that must make the decision to limit the availability of effective but expensive types of medical care.... Society, through its elected officials, is entitled to decide that the resources required for [expensive treatment] are better used for other purposes. However, a physician who thinks that his or her patient may benefit from [the treatment] must make that patient aware of this opinion and assist the patient in obtaining the [treatment]....

Norman Levinsky, The Doctor's Master, 311 New Eng. J. Med. 1573 (1984). The contrasting viewpoint is from a well-known economist at M.I.T.:

> [From an economic perspective], physicians must stop treatments when marginal benefits are equal to marginal costs. But where lies the point at which marginal costs equal marginal benefits? And who is to make this ethical decision?... One answer is that third-party payers can write rules and regulations concerning what they will and will not pay for and can prohibit their clients from buying services that

are not allowed under the private or public insurance systems. . . . Such a procedure works, but it works clumsily, since no set of rules can be adjusted to the nuances of individual medical problems. It will be far better if American doctors begin to build up a social ethic and behavioral practices that help them decide when medicine is bad medicine—not simply because it has absolutely no payoff or because it hurts the patient—but also because the costs are not justified by the marginal benefits. . . .

The medical profession now has professional norms concerning what constitutes bad medical practice. Those norms have to be expanded to include cases in which high costs are not justified by minor expected benefits. If such norms are developed and then legally defended against malpractice suits, it just may be possible to build up a system of doctor-imposed cost controls that will be much more flexible than any system of cost controls imposed by third-party payers could be. But if the medical profession fails to do this, sooner or later the United States will move to a system of third-party controls. Something will have to be done.

Lester Thurow, Learning to Say "No," 311 New Eng. J. Med. 1569 (1984). Which position do you think is more convincing? For additional perspectives, see the readings and sources cited in note 1 and in Chapters 1.D.4 and 4.D.1.

Does it make you any more comfortable to know that according to empirical research, physicians under financial incentives tend to adjust their practice styles across the board, for both HMO and fee-for-service patients? In other words, incentives do affect how physicians behave, but a physician is likely to respond impartially to all his patients rather than to differentiate among them based on each patients particular source of payment. See Rajesh Balkrishnan et al., Capitation Payment, Length of Visit, and Preventive Services, 8 Am. J. Managed Care 332 (2002). Is this the ethical way to respond, or should patients with more generous insurance receive better service?

8. *Theories of Liability.* Are you convinced by *Pegram* that it is not a proper judicial function to adjudicate financial conflicts of interest under fiduciary principles? If this claim were brought under common law, should it still be dismissed? See note 9 below.

By restricting its holding to "mixed eligibility decisions" by treating physicians, *Pegram* leaves open the possible claim that it violates ERISA to financially reward non-clinicians whose only role is to conduct utilization review activities. If such a claim were entertained, which forms of payment would be permissible and impermissible for utilization reviewers? What about rewarding them for productivity goals, such as the number of claims reviewed per hour, or the reduction in the number of days spent in the hospital?

In one fascinating case, a court found that plaintiffs could go to trial on a claim that HMO incentives violated the Americans with Disabilities Act by causing physicians to delay or deny treatment for patients with disabilities. Zamora-Quezada v. HealthTexas Medical Group of San Antonio, 34 F. Supp. 2d 433 (W.D. Tex.1998).

9. *Disclosing Incentives.* What if the claim involves the failure to *disclose* physician incentives rather than the argument that the incentives *themselves* violate fiduciary duties? Notice in footnote 8 that even *Pegram* says that failing to disclose financial incentives might violate ERISA. Indeed, this is one of the allegations in the massive class action suits, discussed at page 149, that prominent plaintiffs'

lawyers have brought against the leading HMOs. See also Shea v. Esensten, 208 F.3d 712 (8th Cir. 2000) (suggesting in dictum that Minnesota would recognize an action against physicians for failing to disclose financial incentives). Prior to *Pegram*, this theory had received only mixed success so far in the federal courts under ERISA. See Comment, 106 Dick. L. Rev. 415 (2001).

Could this theory of liability be based simply on informed consent law? See Mark Hall, A Theory of Economic Informed Consent, 31 Ga. L. Rev. 31 (1997) (arguing no); Devon C. McGraw, Financial Incentives to Limit Services: Should Physicians Be Required to Disclose These to Patients?, 83 Geo. L.J. 1821 (1995) (arguing yes); E. Haavi Morreim, Diverse and Perverse Incentives of Managed Care: Bringing Patients into Alignment, 1 Widener L. Symp. J. 89, 123 (1996) (yes); Grant H. Morris, Dissing Disclosure: Just What the Doctor Ordered, 44 Ariz. L. Rev. 313 (2002) (yes); Susan M. Wolf, 35 Hous. L. Rev. 1631 (1999) (yes); Joan H. Krause, Reconceptualizing Informed Consent in an Era of Health Care Cost Containment, 85 Iowa L. Rev. 261 (1999) (maybe).

One important decision recently refused to allow such a suit under state law, citing *Pegram* for support. Neade v. Portes, 739 N.E.2d 496 (Ill. 2000). However, the court held that evidence of physician incentives could be relevant in assessing medical negligence. *Neade* also observed that Illinois, like many other states, has a statute requiring disclosure of incentives but imposes this duty only on the HMO, not on the physician. Therefore, like *Pegram*, the *Neade* court felt that the issue should not be dealt with through common law.

Under either tort law or regulatory law, what is the optimal timing for disclosing physician incentives: when someone is deciding which health insurance to choose, when the person is picking a physician, or when the person is considering a treatment option? How much detail should patients be given? How much is this information likely to really matter to people in making these decisions? See generally Mark A. Hall, The Theory and Practice of Disclosing HMO Physician Incentives, 65(4) Law & Contemp. Probs. 207 (2002).

Additional discussion of "gag clauses" can be found in Gordon Brand et al., The Two Faces of Gag Provisions: Patients and Physicians in a Bind, 17 Yale L. & Pol'y Rev. 249 (1998); Joan H. Krause, The Brief Life of the Gag Clause, 67 Tenn. L. Rev. 1 (1999). For a discussion of how fiduciary law principles apply to these issues generally, see Peter D. Jacobson & Michael T. Cahill, Applying Fiduciary Responsibilities in the Managed Care Context, 26 Am. J.L. & Med. 155 (2000); Marc A. Rodwin, Strains in the Fiduciary Metaphor: Divided Physician Loyalties and Obligations in a Changing Health Care System, 21 Am. J.L. & Med. 241 (1995).

10. Pegram's *Importance for Preemption.* Because *Pegram* broadly discusses the purpose and functioning of HMOs, it has importance in a number of other areas of litigation. For instance, consider what this decision has to say about the issue addressed in Chapter 2.C of whether ERISA preempts malpractice claims against HMOs, based on the Court's assumption that Pegram has tort remedies available under state law.

For general commentary on this case and the issues it raises, see Michael T. Cahill & Peter D. Jacobson, *Pegram's* Regress: A Missed Chance for Sensible Judicial Review of Managed Care Decisions, 27 Am. J.L. & Med. 421 (2001); Peter J. Hammer, On Peritonitis, Preemption, and the Elusive Goal of Managed

Care Accountability, 26 J. Health Pol. Pol'y & L. 767 (2001); Richard A. Ippolito, Freedom to Contract in Medical Care: HMOs, ERISA and Pegram v. Herdrich, 9 Sup. Ct. Econ. Rev. 1 (2001); Arnold J. Rosoff, Breach of Fiduciary Duty Lawsuits against MCOs, 22 J. Leg. Med. 55 (2001); William M. Sage, UR Here: The Supreme Court's Guide for Managed Care, 19(5) Health Aff. 219 (Sept. 2000); Jeffrey Stempel & Nadia Magdenko, Doctors, HMOs, ERISA and the Public Interest after Pegram v. Herdrich, 36 Tort & Ins. L.J. 687 (2001); Symposium, 1 Yale J. Health Care L. Ethics & Policy (2001).

F. HEALTH INSURANCE REFORM

1. *Reform Proposals and Foreign Models*

■ WHO SHALL PAY? POLITICS, MONEY, AND HEALTH CARE REFORM*
Lawrence D. Brown**
13 Health Affairs 175 (Spring II 1994)

Politics is how society manages conflicts about values and interests. . . . [N]o issues trigger battles over values and interests more quickly and acutely than do the source and use of money in health reform proposals. . . .

BILL CLINTON'S EXCELLENT ADVENTURE

The [comprehensive health care reform] proposed by the Clinton administration tackl[ed] three broad goals—universal coverage, delivery system reform, and cost containment—in one fine-grained legislative package. [The Clinton proposal sought to guarantee universal insurance coverage by expanding Medicaid to cover all those who are poor, and by requiring employers to purchase insurance for most workers. This prompted widespread debate in Congress and the media over the merits of different approaches to health care reform, and it is credited with precipitating the market restructuring that is still on going. But the entire process ultimately came to naught. The Clinton plan was defeated without it or its contenders ever coming to a floor vote, because it received insufficient support in even democratically controlled congressional committees.]

The sweep and integration of the [Clinton] plan no doubt partly reflect[ed] the thrill of the intellectual chase among its highly intelligent designers, but these features also reflect[ed] a quest to steer within tight political constraints by ensuring universal coverage without calling forth Big Government or major new taxing and spending measures. The plan would [have] use[d] delivery system reform to get the cost containment that yields the savings that fund the universal coverage.

**The author is a political scientist in the School of Public Health at Columbia University.

This approach is politically implausible for three main reasons. First, the times are hardly so ripe for reform that they admit simultaneous achievement, in one fell swoop, of three goals that have eluded the United States for decades....

[I]t is far from clear that what the public means by "fundamental change" bears much resemblance to the Clintons' vision. That 30-40 percent of the system's facilities and services could be in some sense wasteful and unnecessary does not mean that there is a constituency for eliminating concrete inefficiencies—which are tied to jobs, incomes, peace of mind, cherished community institutions, and more. And it is equally doubtful that consumers are ready to extend their embrace of managed care—the growth of which has so far centered mainly on such relatively toothless forms as preferred provider organizations (PPOs) and individual practice associations (IPAs)—to more aggressively managed group- and staff-model health maintenance organizations (HMOs) that might save significant sums of money. To date, managed care seems to be most acceptable when it declines to do what its aficionados insist upon: depart substantially from the norms of third-party payment and fee-for-service practice.

These non sequiturs and the fragile policy solutions built on them mean that the politics of financing reforms have so far been viewed through a glass darkly. Yet the political economy of the matter is as analytically straightforward as it is practically convoluted. There are two sources of money for reforms—public and private—and two ways to tap them—by raising new monies and by redistributing existing funds. The two dimensions combined yield four cells, each a site of politically painful choices. Cell one (new public money) means new taxes, anathema to new Democrats and their old Republican antagonists alike. Cell two (new private money) requires mandates or some other way of getting funds from private-sector purchasers (employers and families) that have not anted up before. Cell three (redistributed public money) entails cuts in Medicare and Medicaid, duly proposed by the Clinton plan to the tune of $238 billion. Cell four (redistributed private funds) looks to savings by means of managed care and reorganized markets.... If the critique of the Clinton plan sketched above is accurate, financing politics will probably be obliged to shift emphasis considerably from cells three and four onto the treacherous terrain of cells one and two. What, then, are the major options for doing so.

Individual mandate. One approach would require that all citizens buy health insurance for themselves and their families, with government subsidies for lower-income households that need help. This proposal has several appeals. It gets everyone covered, eliminates free riders, avoids the conflicts and possible economic dislocations of an employer mandate, severs the illogical link between employment and health insurance, and demands no heroic transformations of the delivery system. It also has several potential political liabilities. Designing subsidies that are equitable but not costly may be difficult.... [A]lthough proponents contend that the plan would have negligible effect on the willingness of employers to maintain existing coverage, others fear that new public subsidies might encourage employers to withdraw contributions to the coverage of many workers, especially in low-wage jobs. If so, government (meaning the taxpayer) would pay more....

Employer mandate. Some—including the Clinton administration—would require that all employers buy or contribute to the purchase of health insurance coverage for all of their workers. Prima facie, this approach is highly attractive. Most of the nonaged population now gets coverage in the workplace, so an employer mandate can wear the halo of incrementalism.... Moreover, most of the uninsured either work or are dependents of workers, so an employer mandate would meet the needs of the vast majority of that 15 percent or so of nonelderly Americans who now lack coverage.

On the other side of the political ledger, however, lies a potent triple threat: ideology, economics, and influence. Many business groups oppose an employer mandate on principle.... [M]any small employers swear that a mandate will drive them out of business, slash their precarious profits, force them to lay off workers, or inflict other adversities. These complaints register heavily with political leaders, few of whom expect that a steady parade of foreign automotive plants descending into their districts will assure prosperity. Most value small business, want to see it thrive and prosper, and resist policy measures that might depress it....

Facing these obstacles, policymakers...can consecrate small business as an economic class so vulnerable and valuable as to warrant special exemption from duties binding on other private purchasers and cover their workers with public funds. That strategy might buy peace with small business but could antagonize taxpayers, who hold the quaint conviction that all employers should contribute their fair share. Third, they could...insist on a universal employer mandate but sweeten it with subsidies and contribution caps that offset economic hardship for marginal firms. This may be the most politic approach, but to date it has not won over many opponents within the business community, and analysts deplore the generosity of subsidies to firms....Assuaging business antagonism seems to require a steady enlargement of the public monies the strategy was supposed to relieve.

Single-payer system. The United States could adopt a system that funds care mainly with public revenues and in which providers get paid by the government without the intermediation of insurance plans. Such an arrangement, often called the "Canadian system," offers several advantages. It plainly identifies the health care system as a democratic construct: How much it spends, how, and on what are decided by political leaders who answer directly to the electorate....

Eliminating private insurance ends difficulties in monitoring and regulating the behavior of an industry with no evident social rationale. All citizens can seek care from any provider they please simply by presenting their health care card....A single-payer model gets high marks for equity, simplicity, and accountability.

The American political setting, however, turns each of these virtues into a vice. Managed care enthusiasts (and investors) fear that a "retreat" to broad freedom of choice between patients and providers will spoil their efforts to control utilization and to discipline providers. There may be no convincing, normative reasons for retaining a private health insurance industry, but there are millions of potent political reasons—jobs—for sparing its sorry life. Providers have not warmed to the prospect of direct bilateral bargaining between themselves and government agencies over fee schedules and payment levels, nor would they relish participation in the budgetary competition among social arenas for scarce public dollars that sets the context for such bargaining. Consumers used to demanding and getting the most and the best medical care at readily accessible facilities may reject government "planning" and "rationing" to extract value for money. And looming above these points of contention is of course the issue of taxes, with which the system would largely be funded. A single-payer, Canadian-style system would shift the 7 percent or so of gross domestic product (GDP) now spent in the private sector on health to public budgets, and taxes would supplant private insurance premiums. This approach stands at the opposite strategic pole from the Clinton plan, which assures the electorate that universal coverage demands no new general taxes....

None of the three "pure" financing strategies reviewed here is likely to be politically acceptable as it stands. Each requires modification and meshing with others into some impure (and perhaps inefficient) package if funding sources are to be varied, and costs diffused, enough to sustain a coalition. But this will not be achieved easily. Health financing politics is tough because it demands contributions from people who are not convinced that they should make them, so massaging and mixing strategies that are individually unpalatable will not necessarily yield a higher political synthesis. The nation may be unwilling to make the financial commitment to sustain universal coverage after all.

■ HEALTH CARE FINANCING IN SELECTED INDUSTRIALIZED NATIONS: COMPARATIVE ANALYSIS AND COMMENT*
Deborah J. Chollet**

Many nations that are comparable to the United States in culture and economic development have centralized, universal health care financing—that pays for all of their people at a substantially lower cost than in the United States.... Per capita, health care spending in the United States average[s] 40 percent more than in Canada, [about] twice the average cost of health care in [Germany], and [almost three times the per capita spending in] the United Kingdom. These differences in coverage and cost have led to growing speculation about whether aspects of other countries' financing and delivery systems might be adapted to use in the United States....

CANADA

Structure and covered services. Canada's health care financing system consists of primary public insurance for most health care services and voluntary, supplemental private insurance for services not covered by the public program. Canada's public insurance system covers all residents; 90 percent of residents also have supplemental private insurance [usually from their employer].

*Excerpted from U.S. Department of Labor, Trends in Health Benefits (1993).
**Formerly, Associate Professor and Associate Director, Center for Risk Management and Insurance Research, Georgia State University.

Each of Canada's ten provinces and two territories separately administers the public insurance system, subject to federal requirements. . . . [U]nder federal law, private insurance plans may not cover services or items also covered by the public programs. Consequently, private insurance plans in Canada typically cover such services or items as private or semi-private hospital accommodations, prescription drugs, ambulance services, out-of-country expenditures and long-term care services not covered by the provincial plan.

Financing. Canada's public insurance program is financed jointly by the federal and provincial governments from general revenues. Three provinces supplement this financing with a mandatory payroll tax, and two provinces charge enrollees a nominal premium for coverage.

Provider relationships and cost management. As in the United States, Canadian hospitals may be publicly or privately owned; most of Canada's physicians are in private practice. Binding hospital per diem rates and physician fee schedules are periodically negotiated between the provincial governments and each province's hospital and medical associations. The medical associations are responsible for allocating fees between general practitioners and specialists in the province. In five provinces (including over 80 percent of Canada's population), the provincial governments set quarterly expenditure caps or targets. In these provinces, when individual providers exceed their quarterly target, the provincial government pays only 75 percent of subsequent charges. . . .

GERMANY

Structure. German's principal health insurance system is comprised of some 1,200 individually funded and administered sickness funds, each organized around a specific trade or professional group. Approximately 90 percent of the population is enrolled in these sickness funds. For about 75 percent of the population (including all hourly, salaried, or self-employed workers who earn less than a threshold amount; unemployment beneficiaries; disabled workers and pensioners), membership in a sickness fund is compulsory. While participation by other workers and their dependents is voluntary, once these individuals choose not to participate in a sickness fund they may not rejoin later. The sickness funds cover the full cost of nearly all medical goods and services, and emphasize primary care as well as some preventive care. . . .

[A]bout 9 percent of the population is enrolled in a private insurance plan as their primary source of coverage. . . . The service coverage offered by primary private insurance plans is generally comprehensive, similar to the coverage provided by the sickness funds. . . .

Financing. Germany's sickness funds are privately managed; each sets a participant contribution rate to cover annual expenses. These contribution rates are paid as taxes on payroll which are levied on both employers and employees.

To support participation by pensioners and their dependents, the national social security pension system and private retirement pensions both make special payments to the sickness funds. Since these payments are not calculated to cover the full cost of pensioners' health care, pensioners are subsidized by other participants in the sickness fund.

Provider relationships and cost management. Hospital per diem rates in Germany are negotiated between each sickness fund and their contracting hospitals, subject to approval by the State government. While most physicians in Germany are private practitioners, hospital-based physicians are salaried hospital employees. The sickness funds set physician fee schedules, establish expenditure targets, and reduce scheduled physician fees for physicians whose costs exceed 140 percent of the average cost profile. Physicians who treat privately insured patients are allowed to charge those patients as much as 2.3 times their scheduled fee....

GREAT BRITAIN

Structure. Great Britain's National Health Service (NHS) is arguably the most centralized delivery and financing system of any in Western Europe. Participation in the NHS is compulsory for all residents. Private insurance is relatively unusual.... The NHS is operated by approximately 200 District Health Authorities within 14 regional health authorities. While much health planning occurs at the regional level, the District Health Authorities oversee day-to-day health services delivery and administer NHS benefits. The NHS provides comprehensive coverage for most hospital and medical care, with nominal fees for auxiliary services.

Financing. The NHS is financed directly from general revenues. For some services (prescription drugs, dental care, and eye examinations and eyeglasses), the NHS requires patients to pay significant user fees, substantially supporting the cost of those services.

Provider relationships and cost control. The NHS owns and operates most hospitals in the United Kingdom. Physicians in general practice are paid a capitated (per patient) amount by the NHS; specialty physicians are salaried employees of the NHS hospital system.

Each District Health Authority's operating budget is based on the district's population demographics as a predictor of fiscal year costs. Capital budgets are allocated to the 14 regions based on a formula that is designed to equalize resources among regions relative to each region's estimated health care needs.

Together with central government budgeting, the centralized ownership of hospitals and the complete absence of fee-for-service payment of physicians in the NHS afford an exceptional degree of control over total health care spending. The NHS accounts for approximately 85 percent of all health care spending in the United Kingdom. However, more than a decade of government decisions to fund the NHS at levels insufficient to cover the growth of underlying production costs has constrained the amount of care provided within the NHS system, encouraging greater use of private insurance and fee-for-service payments for hospital and specialty care....

CONCLUSION

The relevance to the United States of other nations' experiences in financing health care is a matter of discussion among researchers and public policymakers. While the countries reviewed in this chapter have achieved more widespread access to health care at lower cost than the United States, the historical differences between the United States and other nations are considerable, both with respect to popular expectations about health care and popular acceptance of centralized solutions....

The U.S. system of health care financing—mostly private insurance with public financing only for selected poor and the elderly—is unlike that found in any other Western industrialized nation. While the U.S. system readily accommodates innovation and technological change relative to more centralized and regulated systems, we pay a high price for it. The U.S. system is rightly criticized as providing truly exceptional life-saving health care for many people, but denying basic care and preventive care to a significant and growing minority.

Various scholars have noted that the health care financing systems of developed nations may ultimately converge to a single general model.[1] While the more centralized systems in Western Europe—for example, the United Kingdom and the Netherlands—are experimenting with decentralizing decisionmaking to improve efficiency, the least centralized system—that in the United States—is increasingly looking to features of the European systems: specifically, negotiation and regulation of health care prices to control cost.... Reformers wishing to traverse the shortest distance between the current, "pluralistic" system of health care financing in the United States and a more coordinated system might look to the relatively decentralized German model.

■ MANAGED COMPETITION AND ITS POTENTIAL TO REDUCE HEALTH SPENDING
Congressional Budget Office
1993

Managed competition is one of several proposed strategies for fundamentally reforming health care. It emphasizes motivating consumers, insurers, and providers to be more cost-conscious, and it tries to imbue the health care system with the efficiency, flexibility, and innovation of competitive markets, without the undesirable outcomes of the present system.... To alter incentives for consumers, managed competition would ... make individual consumers use their own after-tax incomes to pay the additional costs of purchasing insurance plans other than the least expensive one within their region.

In th[is] way, managed competition would encourage consumers to be more price-conscious when making decisions about their health insurance. In turn, that would give insurers, and through them providers, motives to become more cost-conscious and efficient. Managed competition would shift the focus of competitive behavior in health care markets from amenities and perceived quality to differences in price for measured differences in quality....

Managed competition—an approach that has not been tried anywhere in the world—would require new kinds of institutions to be established, new information and analyses to be developed and used, and new patterns of behavior among

---

[1] Davis, Karen, Symposium: International Comparisons of Health Care Systems, Health Care Financing Review, Annual Supplement (December 1989), pp.104-107.

health care providers, insurers, and consumers. Its success or failure would hinge on the interaction of its many parts....

One key feature is to create regional organizations (for example, health insurance purchasing cooperatives, or HIPCs) that would oversee and operate the restructured insurance market and help consumers make better-informed choices of standardized plans. Among other things, each HIPC would determine which insurers could offer plans in its region, notify all potential purchasers about the various plans available and the quality of their care in previous years, enroll consumers in the plan of their choice, collect premiums, remit the premiums to insurers after adjusting them for differences among plans in the average health status of each plan's enrollees, and monitor whether insurers complied with their contractual obligations....

A second key feature is a requirement that employers contribute no more than a fixed dollar amount toward their employees' health benefits. The limit could not exceed the premium for the least expensive plan available through the HIPC. This feature would effectively limit the open-ended tax subsidy to employment-based health insurance and would require the additional cost of purchasing a more expensive plan to be paid out-of-pocket from the consumer's after-tax income....

Fifth, changes in the marketing of insurance would create open access to health insurance for all individuals on an essentially equal basis. Insurers would be required to offer open enrollment periods, base premiums on community rating (with only a small number of categories), eliminate restrictions on coverage for preexisting conditions, and guarantee renewal of coverage. Individual consumers could choose for themselves which of the plans offered through the HIPC they preferred, rather than having an employer select one plan for all employees. In addition to promoting access to insurance and thus to health care services, open enrollment would make it harder for insurers to enroll only the healthiest consumers and, in this way, would induce insurers to compete by organizing more cost-effective systems for delivering care.

Sixth, some mechanism would be required that assured insurance coverage for each individual. This mechanism would almost certainly have to include subsidies for those with low earnings or limited resources. Universal access would also help to contain costs because the strengthened appeal for consumers of basing their choice among insurers on price would apply to the entire population.

The seventh feature is an accurate method to adjust for differences among insurers in the health status of their enrollees. To the extent that it was accurate, the mechanism for adjusting risk would eliminate the incentive for insurers to pursue enrollees who are healthier than average, and it would protect insurers from the financial disadvantage that would otherwise accompany random, unfavorable risk selection....

Introducing managed competition in a form that might achieve its full potential for lower spending would change the health care system radically. The health insurance industry would be totally restructured. Policies would be standardized, experience rating would be eliminated, and payments to insurers would be adjusted for the average health status of their enrollees. The focus of competition would then shift from the selective enrollment of the healthiest people to cost-effective delivery of high-quality care for covered medical needs. In response, insurers would probably develop networks of affiliated providers whose styles of practice were cost-effective, and the number of insurers could fall greatly.

Notes: Comprehensive Financing Reform

1. *Socialized Medicine*. An important dimension cutting across all proposals for health care reform is the extent to which the financing and delivery system is in the private market or is run by the government. The spectrum of private/public options ranges from a wholly owned and operated government system ("socialized medicine"), like the British National Health Service and like the Veteran's Administration and the Indian Health Service in our country, to a wholly privatized system that relies on individual or employer purchase of private insurance. Two hybrids are (1) a "single payer" ("socialized insurance") system like Medicare and Canada, where public insurance pays private health care providers, and (2) a voucher system where public funds subsidize the purchase of private insurance. Medicare, which primarily is a single-payer public system, also has an option for private HMOs. This demonstrates that the source of funding does not necessarily dictate the public-private mix.

Consider these thoughts on the role of government generally in health care financing and delivery:

> We must apply some modest degree of scrutiny to the proposition that health care is special: surely it is important, but so is food, clothing, shelter, education, entertainment, and all the other goods and services that are necessary to sustain life and to make the life sustained worth living. Importance, however, is not an argument for government subsidy or support, for if it were then socialism would apply to things where it matters most, and lead to the most ruinous of consequences. Instead the importance, so to speak, of importance is simple: It is important to get the right set of solutions, be it private or public, to the problem at hand. Importance does not create a presumption in favor of government, or for that matter against it. It only raises the stakes for making a correct decision in the matter at hand.

Richard A. Epstein, Why Is Health Care Special?, 40 Kan. L. Rev. 307 (1992). See also Richard Epstein, Mortal Peril: Regulating Health Care in America (1997), which contains an extensive argument against entitlements and positive rights to health care. For a collection of articles commenting on Prof. Richard Epstein's libertarian critique of positive rights, along with his response, see Symposium: Is America's Health Care System in Mortal Peril?, 1998 U. Ill. L. Rev. 683.

Contrary to conventional wisdom, one study reports that having health insurance does not contribute to better health overall; rather, better health is linked to higher socioeconomic status, independent of insurance status. Catherine Ross & John Mirowsky, Does Medical Insurance Contribute to Socioeconomic Differentials in Health?, 78(2) Milbank Q. 263 (2000). See also James Auerbach & Barbara Krimgold, Income, Socioeconomic Status, and Health: Exploring the Relationships (2001). Does this suggest that the poor would be better off with more money rather than free insurance?

2. *Single-Payer Reform.* There are obviously strong equity arguments for a Canadian-style single-payer system that treats everyone alike (horizonal equity) and that imposes financing (tax) burdens progressively on higher income citizens (vertical equity). There is an equally strong efficiency argument, based on administrative costs. Only 70 to 80 percent of health insurance premiums in the private sector end up paying for medical care because the rest is eaten up in the overhead costs of selling and administering the insurance, as well as by profits. In contrast, over 95 percent of funding for public programs ends up paying for treatment because the overhead and administration costs are much lower. This potential savings of 15 to 25 percent is alone sufficient to fund everyone who presently has no insurance. In response, critics reply that some of these administrative costs are necessary because they serve useful purposes. Some go simply to paying taxes; others are for utilization management, without which total medical costs would be higher. Costs attributable to competition among profitmaking insurers are argued to be necessary in order to preserve consumer choice. For arguments pro and con, see Patricia Danzon, Hidden Overhead Costs: Is Canada's System Really Less Expensive?, 11 Health Aff. 21 (Spring 1992); Steffie Woolhandler & David Himmelstein, The Deteriorating Administrative Efficiency of the U.S. Health Care System, 324 New Eng. J. Med. 1253 (1991).

Even if administrative costs could be virtually eliminated, this still does not grapple with the problem, noted at page 353, that the main obstacle to affording universal access is not so much the present cost of health care but its rapid rate of inflation. Eliminating administrative costs, like eliminating unnecessary care, would result in only a one-time savings that would soon be overtaken by the relentless pace of inflation for the costs of the remaining necessary services. It is for this reason that proposals for universal coverage are so closely tied to proposals for cost control. For the most part, cost controls are embedded in the manner in which doctors and hospitals are paid. Deborah Chollet's survey of foreign health care systems gives a very brief overview of different options. These are explored in more detail in section E of this chapter, which discusses provider reimbursement methods under Medicare and Medicaid.

3. *Foreign Health Care Systems.* The Canadian and British systems have been held up as examples of not only what is right about universal health insurance, but also what is wrong about government-run systems:

> [R]ationing is an inevitable result of government decisions to allocate fixed annual sums for health care....A striking example [from England] is access to kidney machines which is rationed by putting a "use-value" on people's lives. If you are over 55 or have diabetes or a bad heart, or no dependents, or are not well known, it is likely that you will score a low "use-value" and be allowed to die.

D. Green, Challenge to the NHS (1986).

> Waiting lists for admission to British hospitals are long. One-third of all admitted patients were on waiting lists for three months or more, 6 percent for one year or more....Nearly all the people on these lists were waiting for surgery, much of it elective in that delay does not threaten the patient's life....[W]aiting times for specific treatments such as orthopedic surgery [e.g., hip replacement or knee ligament repair] are very long, stretching into years in some regions.

Henry Aaron & William. Schwartz, The Painful Prescription: Rationing Hospital Care (1984).

> [H]ow do England and other countries achieve their savings? By...limiting the availability of high-tech diagnostic equipment. Britain, for example, has 80 percent fewer CAT scanners per capita than the U.S. Yet Britain is far better off than Alberta, Canada, where two suffice for 2.5 million people.

Carl Weber, In Health Care, U.S. Is Best, N.Y. Times, May 30, 1990.

For additional readings on foreign health care systems generally, see Robert J. Blendon et al., Physicians' Perspectives on Caring for Patients in the United States, Canada, and West Germany, 328 New Eng. J. Med. 1011 (1993); Timothy Jost, Private or Public Approaches to Insuring the Uninsured: Lessons from International Experience with Private Insurance, 76 N.Y.U. L. Rev. 419 (2001); Robert Rich, Health Policy, Health Insurance, and the Social Contract, 21 Comp. Lab. L.J. 397 (2000); Richard B. Saltman & Joseph Figueras, Analyzing the Evidence on European Health Care Reforms, 17(2) Health Aff. 85 (Mar. 1998); Symposium, 21(3) Health Aff.—(May 2002); Symposium, 18(3) Health Aff. 1 (May 1999); Symposium, 17 J. Health Pol. Pol'y & L. 613 (1992); Symposium, 17 J. Health Pol. Pol'y & L. 613 (1992); Symposium, 10 Health Aff. (Fall 1999). For the latest developments in the British NHS, see Rudolf Klein, What's Happening to Britain's National Health Service?, 345 New Eng. J. Med. 305 (2001); Rudolf Klein, Why Britain Is Reorganizing Its National Health Service—Yet Again, 17(4) Health Aff., 111 (July 1998); Symposium, 19(3) Health Aff. 1 (May 2000). On Canada, see R. Evans et al., Controlling Health Expenditures—The Canadian Reality, 320 New Eng. J. Med. 571 (1989); John K. Iglehart, Revisiting the Canadian Health Care System, 342 New Eng. J. Med. 2007 (2000). On Germany, see John K. Iglehart, Germany's Health Care System, 324 New Eng. J. Med. 503 (1991).

4. *Designing Fair and Affordable Subsidies.* Perhaps the greatest design difficulty in patching together universal insurance coverage based on the existing fragmented system in the United States is creating a smooth border between public and private insurance. Neither an individual mandate nor an employer mandate is feasible without substantial subsidies for those whom the costs are beyond reach, even at average community rates. Comprehensive health insurance typically costs more than $5,000 per year for a family. The federal poverty guideline is roughly $15,000 for a family. Therefore, even with community rating and tax breaks, insurance is obviously not affordable for many families above the poverty line. Most universal coverage proposals call for sliding scale subsidies that pay for 100 percent of insurance at or below the poverty level and then phase out to zero for people at two to three times poverty, which approaches the median family income. This is obviously expensive; almost half of all families would receive some subsidy. But more troubling, it creates a strong disincentive for low-income workers to earn more money. Depending on how rapidly the subsidies are phased out, each extra dollar earned might cost a family 20 to 35 cents in additional insurance premiums. This is on top of ordinary federal and state income and payroll taxes that have to be paid for each extra dollar of earnings. The net effect could be a marginal "tax" rate of 70 percent; coupled with the possible loss of other

public benefits, the effective marginal tax might approach a confiscatory (100 percent) level; in other words, low-income workers would get to keep virtually none of any increased earnings. The only way to mitigate this effect is to stretch out the sliding scale subsidies so they reach into even higher income ranges.

The same problems apply to subsidies directed to employers, plus the fact that it is more difficult to accurately target employer subsidies. Most employer-based proposals call for subsidizing only small employers, but size of employment is only a rough proxy for economic vulnerability. A better proxy would be average wages, but this would expand the pool of subsidized firms into much larger work-forces that presently are purchasing insurance without the subsidy. Is doesn't seem fair to subsidize only employers that, so far, have gotten away with not providing insurance, yet it is too expensive to subsidize those who presently are providing insurance but might be equally deserving of subsidy.

A related difficulty in attempting to fill the gaps of a mixed public-private system is that expanding public programs to cover those who fall between the cracks can also induce people who currently have private coverage to opt for free or subsidized coverage. If this happens, some or most of the additional spending is "wasted" on people who are already covered elsewhere. This general phenomenon is known as "crowd-out"—i.e., expanding public programs crowds out private coverage. For discussion and analysis, see John V. Jacobi, Medicaid Expansion, Crowd-out, and Limits of Incremental Reform, 45 St. Louis U. L.J. 79 (2001).

5. *Managed Competition's Appeal.* Voucher systems for the purchase of health insurance are now more commonly referred to as "managed competition." This concept was first devised in 1977 by Alain Enthoven, a Stanford economist, and has since been expanded by the "Jackson Hole group," an ad hoc committee of business and insurance leaders that meets periodically at the home of one of its members in Wyoming. Alain Enthoven, Consumer Choice Health Plan: A National Health Insurance Proposal Based on Regulated Competition in the Private Sector, 298 New Eng. J. Med. 650, 709 (1978); Jackson Hole Group, Managed Competition II: A proposal, 46 Wash. U. J. Urb. & Contemp. L. 33 (1994). The essence of managed competition is to concentrate buying power through purchasing cooperatives and, at the same time, increase individual choice and price competition by allowing each subscriber to decide which insurance plan to buy and how much to pay. The poor and the elderly can participate in the managed competition purchasing cooperative if they are given publicly funded vouchers. Employees can participate if employers pay for a portion of the premiums. Individuals can also purchase from cooperatives on their own. So the idea is widely adaptable. Indeed, managed competition now exists for most very large workforces such as giant corporations and government workers, where the employer itself functions as a purchasing cooperative and deducts different amounts from employees' paychecks according to which insurance they select. This differs from conventional practice where employers choose a single insurance plan and pay most or all of the premium. A number of states (notably, California and Florida) have created purchasing cooperatives that are voluntary for employers. Some state Medicaid programs function as managed competition systems (notably, Arizona and Tennessee). Medicare now contains a new Part C called Medicare + Choice or Medicare Advantage, which creates a managed competition

framework for its enrollees. See generally Paul Starr, The Logic of Health-Care Reform (1992); Walter Zelman, The Changing Health Care Marketplace (1996); Alain Enthoven, The History and Principles of Managed Competition, 12 Health Aff. 24 (Supp. 1993)

6. *Managed Competition's Flaws.* Managed competition faces two fundamental structural difficulties. First, it is feasible only in areas of the country with sufficient population to support several competing networks of managed care providers. Managed competition will not necessarily require managed care networks, but it is believed (and intended) that, once individuals have a direct financial stake in the cost of their insurance, they will tend to choose HMOs and other managed care plans much more often. That's the primary way managed competition is expected to save money. According to one calculation, a competitive managed care market requires a base population of from 180,000 to 1.2 million, which would restrict the reach of managed competition to anywhere from 42 to 71 percent of the population—depending on the number of separate networks desired. R. Kronick et al., The Demographic Limitations of Managed Competition, 328 New Eng. J. Med. 148 (1993).

The second problem, as mentioned in the CBO report, is that, in order for competitive pressures to focus on efficient delivery of quality care, competing plans must be paid proportionately to each subscriber's actuarial risk. Otherwise, insurers will have a strong incentive to compete based more on their ability to select healthier subscribers. At the same time, it would be unfair to sick or elderly subscribers to force them to pay much higher premiums simply because of their health status, yet government and employers cannot hand subscribers a blank check without defeating the primary purpose of the entire scheme. Some method must be devised, then, for subsidizing and redistributing premiums in a fashion that solves each of these problems without aggravating the other. This challenge is being analyzed in terms of "risk adjustment," namely, how to adjust voucher amounts or community-rated premiums to accurately reflect each subscriber's health risk. So far, we are a long way from doing a good job of this; the various rating restrictions and risk adjustment techniques that have been attempted are either ineffective or highly inaccurate. Workable risk adjustment is thus the Achilles heel of managed competition. See John Newhouse, Patients at Risk: Health Reform and Risk Adjustment, 13 Health Aff. 132 (Spring 1994); Symposium, Private Employers and Risk Adjustment, 38 Inquiry 242 (2001).

For a trenchant critique of the theory and implementation of managed competition, see Donald W. Light, From Managed Competition to Managed Cooperation: Theory and Lessons from the British Experience, 75 Milbank Q. 297 (1997). Documenting and discussing the failure of managed competition to take hold in private, employment-based insurance because of employers' reluctance to increase workers' choice of insurance, see M. Susan Marquis & Stephen H. Long, Trends in Managed Care and Managed Competition, 1993-1997, 18(6) Health Aff. 75 (Dec. 1999). Additional discussion of managed competition from a variety of perspectives can be found in Competitive Managed Care: The Emerging Health Care System (John Wilkerson et al. eds., 1997).

7. *The Clinton Plan.* The most heated objections to the Clinton reform plan were against the government-run purchasing cooperatives, which would have put a large number of private insurers out of business, and the strict price controls,

which would have limited future increases in insurance premiums to the consumer price index (general inflation). Almost no one strongly favored the proposal. Those to the left would have preferred a simpler Canadian-style plan that expanded Medicare to cover everyone and that controlled costs by regulating payments to providers. For descriptions, critiques, and postmortems of the Clinton reform debate, see Jacob S. Hacker, The Road to Nowhere (1997); Theda Skocpol, Boomerang: Health Care Reform and the Turn against Government (1999); Marie Gottschalk, The Missing Millions: Organized Labor, Business, and the Defeat of Clinton's Health Security Act, 24 J. Health Pol. Pol'y & L. 489 (1999); Symposium, 21 J. Health Pol. Pol'y & L. 1 (1996); Symposium, 14 Health Aff. (Spring 1995); Symposium, 46 Wash. U. J. Urb. & Contemp. L. 33 (1994); Symposium, 31 Inquiry 129 (1994).

8. *The AMA's Opposition.* As noted in several of the readings in the prior section, the AMA has steadfastly opposed national health insurance throughout this century, attacking it as "socialized medicine." Is this label accurate? During the Clinton reform debate, the AMA ultimately endorsed a conservative Republican proposal (which also did not pass) that contained mainly incremental reforms but that gave the AMA many of the special protections from malpractice and antitrust laws that it had lobbied for. Other medical groups, however, such as the American College of Surgeons, supported comprehensive reforms even more liberal than President Clinton's. See, e.g., S. Himmelstein et al., A National Health Program for the United States: A Physicians' Proposal, 320 New Eng. J. Med. 102 (1989). Why doesn't the AMA see it in its interest to expand insurance so that everyone can pay for medical services? If you were a doctor, would you prefer the restrictions as well as the protections of a government-run system over the ravages of the un-regulated managed care marketplace? See George Lundberg, Severed Trust: Why American Medicine Hasn't Been Fixed (2000); Robert Berenson, Do Physicians Recognize Their Own Best Interests?, 13 Health Aff. 185 (Spring II 1994) (cri-tiquing as inconsistent and shortsighted the AMA's historical antipathy to government regulation). Realize that the unregulated market was much more attractive in the 1950s when organized medicine controlled health insurance through Blue Cross, when there was little antitrust scrutiny of physician collusion, and when the corporate practice of medicine doctrine more actively preserved physicians' independence from medical institutions—topics that are discussed in Chapter 4. For additional discussions of the failure of national health insurance generally, see Vincente Navarro, Dangerous to Your Health: Capitalism in Health Care (1993); Paul Starr, The Social Transformation of American Medicine (1982); Carol S. Weissert & William. G. Weissert, Governing Health: The Politics of Health Policy (1996); S. Steinmo & J. Watts, It's the Institutions, Stupid! Why Comprehensive National Health Insurance Always Fails in America, 20 J. Health Pol. Pol'y & L. 329 (1995).

9. *State Health Care Reform.* Due to the continuing failure to achieve universal health insurance at the national level, some individual states have contemplated comprehensive reforms over the past decade, but they too have not achieved great success. See Symposium, 22 J. Health Pol. Pol'y & L. 687 (1997); Symposium, 12 Health Aff. No. 2 (Summer 1993). The first and only state to accomplish near universal coverage is Hawaii, which has an employer mandate. This mandate was initially struck down in court as a violation of ERISA, which, as discussed in

section C, preempts state laws affecting employee benefits. Standard Oil v. Agsalud, 633 F.2d 760 (9th Cir. 1980), aff'd mem., 454 U.S. 801 (1981). Congress later enacted an exception, but one that covers only Hawaii. Subsequently, other states (notably, California, Massachusetts, and Washington) have attempted to avoid the barrier of ERISA preemption through a technique known as "play or pay." Under this scheme, employers are not forced to purchase insurance; they are given the option of either purchasing ("playing") or of paying an additional payroll tax that will be used to provide insurance to their workers. It is thought this play or pay law evades ERISA preemption since ERISA does not prohibit general payroll taxes, but this proposition is still untested in the courts. It may be a moot point in any event since most of the states that enacted this idea have since abandoned it, due to resistance from the employer community and the difficulty of funding the subsidies required to make it feasible for small employers. ERISA does not preempt more incremental state reforms, such as those that make it easier to purchase insurance or that create compensation pools for uncompensated hospital care. See New York State Conf. of Blue Cross & Blue Shield Plans v. Travelers Insurance Co., 514 U.S. 645 (1995); NYS Health Maintenance Organization Conference v. Curiale, 64 F.3d 794 (2d Cir. 1995). See generally Mary Anne Bobinski, Unhealthy Federalism: Barriers to Increasing Health Care Access for the Uninsured, 24 U.C. Davis L. Rev. 255 (1990); Jeselyn Alicia Brown, ERISA and State Health Care Reform: Roadblock or Scapegoat?, 13 Yale L. & Pol'y Rev. 339 (1995); Pamela Paul-Shaheen, The States and Health Care Reform: The Road Traveled and Lessons Learned from Seven That Took the Lead, 23 J. Health Pol. Pol'y & L. 319 (1998).

Problem: Universal Access to Health Care

Be prepared to either defend or attack each of the following propositions, using analysis and facts from the readings in this chapter.

1. A two-tier health care system—one that tolerates different standards of access and care according to wealth and social position—is morally unjustified because health care is a basic human right of fundamental importance.
2. A system of socialized medicine like that in Canada is distinctly un-American and will lead to massive rationing of services.
3. In order to have a coherent health care financing system, it is essential to sever the link between employment and insurance.
4. The best feasible way to guarantee everyone access to a decent minimum level of health care is to fund a comprehensive network of public hospitals and outpatient clinics as a safety net for those without health insurance.

Exercise: Negotiating Health Care Reform

Assume you represent the interests of one of the following groups: physicians, low-income public, upper- and middle-income public, large insurance companies and HMOs, small employers, or large employers. Now, develop your legislative lobbying position with respect to each of the following reform ideas:

1. A Canadian type system
2. A British type system
3. Filling the cracks in our present fragmented system by expanding Medicaid to cover all of the poor, requiring all employers to provide coverage for their workers, and requiring all self-employed individuals to buy their own private insurance
4. An entirely privatized system that gives each person a voucher, funded by the government, sufficient to pay for 60 to 100 percent (depending on income) of the cost of the lowest-priced insurance policy in the market, and then leaving it entirely to individual choice whether and what to buy

Meet with representatives from the other interest groups and attempt to negotiate comprehensive health care reform.

2. Economic and Regulatory Theory

As an interlude between this and the next chapter, this section addresses economic and regulatory theory in more depth, as it applies to health care public policy. In Chapter 1, we learned that American medicine is thought to be in a crisis, both because of the growing number of people without either public or private health insurance coverage and because of steeply escalating medical costs. This chapter has helped us to understand why this crisis arose and some of the public policy responses; the next chapter considers additional responses to the crisis in spending. These responses are sometimes focused on activating market forces and at other times on regulatory controls; often, reforms contain a mix of these objectives.

It is obvious, then, that a full understanding of these issues requires some appreciation of economic and regulatory theory. Economic theory also helps us to better understand the root of the problems that cost containment measures are designed to correct, so we can better assess how well they are likely to work. Specifically, we must be able to intelligently discuss the extent to which health care delivery should be left to market forces, whether government regulation should displace market mechanisms because of the unique attributes of medicine, or whether government should try to make the market work better. Do not expect to be able to resolve these issues. Instead, as you read these selections, focus your thoughts on the legal and public policy positions you have seen so far and ask yourself which are supported or undermined by each of the points the authors make.

■ HEALTH PLAN
Alain Enthoven
1980

[Read the excerpt at page 70.]

■ HEALTH CARE INTO THE NEXT CENTURY
Mark A. Peterson
22 J. Health Pol. Pol'y & L. 291 (1997)*

What are we to make of the market transformation of health care in the
United States, the core legacy of the current decade? Should we favor the dynamics
of markets, standing alone, as a vehicle for reform? What are the limitations? What
has motivated the restructuring of the private insurance system? What happens
when the market transformation extends from private insurance to the publicly
financed programs for the elderly and poor? . . . Before launching into that analysis, it is imperative to . . . [ask] what do we mean when we speak of markets in the
health care setting? . . . [R]elatively few people, beyond some libertarian and right-
wing politicians, believe that all matters pertaining to the delivery of medical care
services should be left to the marketplace, however conceived. Some individuals
may believe that health care is no different from toothpaste, but that view is shared
by few analysts and citizens.

Most market advocates, such as health economists Alain Enthoven and Mark
Pauly, support major interventions by the government to subsidize insurance coverage and promote improved rules of the game for an otherwise inefficient
market. Analysts across the spectrum of opinion reject the simplistic dichotomies
of government versus the market, or regulation versus competition. More pertinent are questions about where, when, in what form, and under what conditions
both markets and government have a role.

In the health care setting, the market is more typically a reference to a set of
market-like instruments or arrangements. These include privately owned or managed institutions, which can range from stockholder-owned insurance companies
to nonprofit sickness funds in the German tradition. They often refer to the use of
incentives embedded within institutions of whatever sort (private or public) that
are designed to promote more efficient individual-level behavior. Fully capitated
payments to physicians by corporate HMOs, which shift risk to the doctor
and reward the utilization of fewer services, would certainly be included. But
one would also have to consider the hospital payment methodology of diagnosis-
related groupings (DRGs) used by a public program like Medicare. The market
frequently is taken to refer to a process of decision making; for example, using
competition among substitutable entities to identify and select the best choice
according to some measure of utility. That competition, however, can be among
private firms, nonprofit institutions, or even public agencies or employees. It can
occur within an unregulated marketplace or within the bowels of the public sector.
The same can be said of another market-like arrangement: contracting between
relevant parties.

■ CALIFORNIA DENTAL ASS'N v. FEDERAL TRADE COMMISSION
526 U.S. 756 (1999)

SOUTER, J.

[The issue in this case is] whether a "quick look" sufficed to justify finding that certain advertising restrictions adopted by the California Dental Association violated the antitrust laws. . . . The CDA is a voluntary nonprofit association of local dental societies to which some 19,000 dentists belong, including about three-quarters of those practicing in the State. . . . [These dentists] agree to abide by a Code of Ethics (Code) including the following:

> Although any dentist may advertise, no dentist shall advertise or solicit patients in any form of communication in a manner that is false or misleading in any material respect. In order to properly serve the public, dentists should represent themselves in a manner that contributes to the esteem of the public. . . .

The CDA has issued a number of advisory opinions interpreting this section, and through separate advertising guidelines intended to help members comply with the Code and with state law the CDA has advised its dentists of disclosures they must make under state law when engaging in discount advertising. . . .

The FTC brought a complaint against the CDA, alleging that . . . the CDA had unreasonably restricted two types of advertising: price advertising, particularly discounted fees, and advertising relating to the quality of dental services. An Administrative Law Judge (ALJ) . . . found a violation of §5 of the FTC Act, [which prohibits "unfair competition and deceptive acts or practices." 15 U.S.C. §45(a)(1). We reverse and remand.] . . .

The restrictions on both discount and nondiscount advertising are, at least on their face, designed to avoid false or deceptive advertising in a market characterized by striking disparities between the information available to the professional and the patient.[10] In a market for professional services, in which advertising is relatively rare and the comparability of service packages not easily established, the difficulty for customers or potential competitors to get and verify information about the price and availability of services magnifies the dangers to competition associated with misleading advertising. What is more, the quality of professional services tends to resist either calibration or monitoring by individual patients or clients, partly because of the specialized knowledge required to evaluate the services, and partly because of the difficulty in determining whether, and the degree to which, an outcome is attributable to the quality of services (like a poor job of tooth filling) or to something else (like a very tough walnut). Patients' attachments

---

[10] "The fact that a restraint operates upon a profession as distinguished from a business is, of course, relevant in determining whether that particular restraint violates the [antitrust laws]. It would be unrealistic to view the practice of professions as interchangeable with other business activities, and automatically to apply to the professions antitrust concepts which originated in other areas. The public service aspect, and other features of the professions, may require that a particular practice, which could properly be viewed as a violation of [antitrust laws] in another context, be treated differently." Goldfarb v. Virginia State Bar, 421 U.S. 773, 788-789, n. 17, 95 S. Ct. 2004, 44 L. Ed. 2d 572 (1975).

to particular professionals, the rationality of which is difficult to assess, complicate the picture even further. The existence of such significant challenges to informed decisionmaking by the customer for professional services immediately suggests that advertising restrictions arguably protecting patients from misleading or irrelevant advertising call for more than cursory treatment as obviously comparable to classic horizontal agreements to limit output or price competition.

■ WHERE YOU STAND DEPENDS ON WHERE YOU SIT: MUSINGS ON THE REGULATION/COMPETITION DIALOGUE*
Donald R. Cohodes**
7 J. Health Pol. Pol'y & L. 54 (1982)

An analysis of alternative approaches to containing medical care costs—especially an analysis oriented toward market approaches—must be firmly based on an understanding of the medical care market: why medical care is different from other products; why the nature of medical care leads to institutional factors that do not exist in other markets; why institutional arrangements that do exist and work well in other markets cause problems in the market for medical care; why governmental attempts to deal with the medical care market often have perverse or inflationary effects; and why the interaction of all these factors tends to undermine the means and the incentives for an efficient, cost-effective market for medical care.

Medical care has a number of characteristics that distinguish it from most other products in important ways:

1. *Demand for health.* Medical care services are not purchased from any desire for such services in themselves. The demand for medical care services is derived from the "demand" for good health.
2. *Medical care and health.* Medical care is only one determinant of health status, and for most people at most times it is not even a very important determinant. Environment, exercise, nutrition, and personal habits also are important factors affecting health status.
3. *Risk.* The need for medical care is unpredictable, requiring expenditures that are irregular and of uncertain magnitude.
4. *Immediacy.* The need for medical care is often immediate, allowing little time for shopping around and seeking advice or alternatives.
5. *Lack of information.* Consumers are usually ignorant of their medical care needs. They cannot possibly obtain the knowledge and training to diagnose their own medical care needs and "demand" the required services.

6. *Uncertainty.* Physicians, though highly trained and better able to diagnose needs and prescribed treatment, also are often uncertain about the appropriate services to provide.

These factors clearly hamper the operation of a normal market. . . .

Certain institutional developments and responses to the unique characteristics of medical care have further aggravated the problem. These include:

1. *Physician as agent.* Because of the consumer's uncertainty about the medical services he needs, the physician serves a dual role. Once the consumer has decided to seek care and select a physician, the physician diagnoses problems and decides on the course and place of treatment. The physician thus acts as agent for the consumer. But the physician provides more than advice; he also provides medical services. Unlike most producers, the physician may control the demand for his services. The more services he prescribes, the more fees he collects. It is this factor that makes fee-for-service pricing of physician services a concern to those who would like to see a more competitive medical care market. The problem is compounded by the uncertainty of medical science. The physician may not know exactly what the patient needs. The lack of accepted standards of medical practice, and the consequent fear of malpractice claims, leads to "[defensive] medicine"—the provision of services that may be neither warranted nor efficient. When the physician makes decisions for the consumer, there is little incentive for efficient use of resources.

2. *Third-party payment.* Due to the risk and uncertainty of incurring medical expenses, consumers purchase insurance to regularize their expenses. The predominant form of insurance purchased today is characterized by direct third-party payments of some or all medical expenses. The consequent reduction or absence of direct consumer payment for services has been found to be a significant factor affecting consumer and provider decision-making. The insulation of the consumer from direct payment for care has been shown to undermine incentives for cost-conscious consumer behavior. When a consumer pays little or nothing out-of-pocket for the services he is receiving, economic theory and empirical evidence indicate that more service will be demanded than if out-of-pocket expenses reflect the full cost of care.

3. *Retrospective cost reimbursement.* Not only are payments made by a third party, but payments are generally based on incurred costs. This rewards physicians and hospitals with more revenues for generating more costs. In contrast to the competitive theory of economic efficiency, where producers are rewarded for lowering costs, providers of medical services are rewarded for raising costs.

Together, these factors undercut virtually all normal incentives for market efficiency. Consumers trust providers to make consumption decisions; and since they often pay little or nothing *directly* for medical services, consumers have little incentive to economize. Providers are generally paid by a third party; and since they are reimbursed for their fees and incurred costs, providers have little incentive to economize. Insurers spread the costs among all subscribers, who in the end

Table 1.
The Market for Medical Care

Assumptions Underlying a Perfectly Competitive Market	Match with Market for Medical Care	Specific Differences
Market Structure		
Large number of buyers and sellers	Mixed	Many consumers and physicians; few hospitals
Complete information (absence of uncertainty)	No	Consumer ignorance of the product risk and uncertainty of need
Firms operate independently (no one seller can influence price)	No	Price fixing (physician fee schedules); Cost reimbursement for hospitals
Free entry and exit of all producers	No	Barriers to entry (personnel licensure, hospital accreditation, certificate-of-need programs, a limited number of medical schools)
The product is homogeneous	No	Multiple, undefined products; varied quality
The consumer is the key decision-maker	No	Physicians act as agents on behalf of consumers
Market Conduct		
Firms are price-takers	No	Hospitals and physicians are price setters
Firms maximize their profits	No	In general, hospitals are nonprofit organizations which seek to maximize other objectives (growth, prestige) Similarly, physicians may have noneconomic motives, such as intellectual curiosity, esteem of peers

pay for this inefficiency in the *indirect* costs of their premiums. No one in this triangular flow of dollars has sufficient incentives to make economizing choices; indeed, the predominant incentives are for more and more spending.

Other institutional and attitudinal factors compound the cost-inflating incentives described above:

1. *Medical ethic.* Physicians are generally unconcerned with, and unaccountable for, the costs of services recommended and rendered. This is especially true of hospital costs. Physician training emphasizes thoroughness and the use of all available resources to help the patient, rather than

the management of health care resources and the trade-off of cost and effectiveness. While difficult to change, this attitude has serious efficiency implications in a system where resources are allocated by physicians.

2. *Medical mystique.* Physicians are among the most respected members of society, and in the medical marketplace few consumers question the wisdom of physician recommendations. Moreover, the idea that "money is no object" in medical care decisions is widespread among consumers as well as physicians. Few consumers even ask about the prices of medical care. Again, these attitudes have serious implications in a system where individual consumers do not bear much of the direct costs of resource consumption.

3. *Nonprofit institutions.* In a society where health has no price, institutions are not expected to profit from illness. Large segments of the medical care industry are nonprofit, and the response to financial incentives differs from that of a profit-making industry. While profit-making firms strive to maximize earnings and thus to minimize cost per unit of output, nonprofit hospitals place more emphasis on maximizing quality of service or capital investment. The growth-with-quality imperative creates incentives for greater costs. This must be a concern in a financing system based on cost reimbursement.

These societal and institutional attitudes—that cost should not be a factor in medical decisions, that health has no price, that quality is of paramount concern—are unique to the medical care market. They create strong pressures for spending. The institutional and financing arrangements in the market offer little resistance to cost increases and little incentive for efficient resource allocation.

Some government policies also contribute to the incentives for cost-increasing behavior in the medical care sector. This happens at both the federal and state levels through direct and indirect subsidies, health care financing programs, and extensive regulation:

1. *Tax subsidies.* By exempting from taxation employer contributions to health care plans, the federal income and payroll tax structures provide an enormous ($[60] billion) subsidy for private insurance coverage. This, in effect, allows employees to purchase insurance with pre-tax dollars rather than after-tax dollars, an average subsidy of 30 percent of the employer's contribution. This subsidy distorts the employee's incentive for efficient health care expenditures by encouraging the purchase of more expensive, first-dollar coverage.

2. *Hidden premium costs.* The tax incentive to pay for medical insurance through employers results in substantial consumer ignorance of full premium costs. Approximately 80 percent of health insurance premiums are paid through employment-related group insurance plans. Under these group plans, on average, the employer pays two-thirds of the total premium. . . . These institutional and consumer responses to the government subsidy provide further incentives for consumers to seek more comprehensive, cost-inflating coverage than if the premium costs were paid directly.

3. *Medicare and Medicaid.* These two health care financing programs rely almost entirely on third-party, fee-for-service, and cost-reimbursement financing. They pay more on behalf of people who choose more costly systems of care, and they pay more to providers that cost more.

4. *Regulatory barriers to efficiency.* Federal and state legislatures and regulatory agencies, often with the advice of medical associations, have adopted regulations that in many respects serve as barriers to cost-reducing innovation. The use of supervised para-professionals and physician extenders for routine services, for example, has been severely restricted by regulation. Restrictive laws and practices have also inhibited the growth of alternative, more efficient health delivery systems. Even the Health Maintenance Organization Act, which was intended to spur the growth of HMOs, encumbered developing HMOs with enough restrictive "quality controls" to raise the cost of their operation and make them less competitive than they could be.

While some government policies have attempted to contain medical costs through direct economic regulation, other policies have exacerbated the inflationary pressures within the market.

A brief sketch of the medical care market cannot provide a definitive background for understanding the regulation/competition debate. However, it is essential to begin an assessment of the debate with an examination of intrinsic market characteristics. Only by distinguishing those elements that are intrinsic and cannot be changed (e.g., risk, uncertainty) from those elements that are institutional responses and may be changed (e.g., third-party cost reimbursement), and by distinguishing both from the symptoms (e.g., excess bed capacity), can the true sources of the problem be identified and effective policy alternatives be developed.

■ THE INEVITABLE FAILURE OF CURRENT COST-CONTAINMENT STRATEGIES: WHY THEY CAN PROVIDE ONLY TEMPORARY RELIEF*
William Schwartz
257 JAMA 220 (1987)

The problem of hospital costs is not simply that they are high, but that they have been rising rapidly and consuming an ever larger fraction of gross national product (GNP). If the fraction of GNP spent on hospital care were relatively constant, the current level might still be criticized but with little sense that a crisis is impending. This distinction between the level of current expenditures and the upward trend in expenditures is critical, but it has not figured in the discussion of policy options.... In principle, the attempt to control rising costs can have either of two quite distinct effects. One of these is to lower current baseline expenditures. The other is to restrict the rate at which expenditures are growing, without cutting current outlays. It is possible, of course, that a particular intervention will have both effects, but the more interesting and important possibility is that one of these outcomes will be mistaken for the other. In the long run, only measures that reduce the growth in costs can solve the fundamental problem of a cost spiral....

Three variables appear to account for most of the current increase in hospital costs: population growth, rising real input prices ("hospital market basket"), and increased intensity of services, caused almost entirely by technologic innovation and diffusion....Only one element remains readily susceptible to control: the introduction and diffusion of new technology. How much this factor contributes to the growth of hospital costs must be determined by subtracting the contribution of other factors: population growth, rising input prices, and changes in the number of adjusted patient days per capita. The difference—an average of 3.5 percentage points annually from 1977 through 1983—reflects increased intensity of services, resulting mainly from technologic change....

There is good reason to believe that the future rate of technologic change will be at least as great as in the past 10 or 15 years. We can thus anticipate serious problems in controlling costs unless we are willing to forgo, at least in part, introduction and diffusion of innovative diagnostic and therapeutic measures. A host of expensive new technologies is now being deployed and an equally promising group is currently being developed. Consider, for example, expensive diagnostic methods such as magnetic resonance imaging (MRI) and spectroscopic examinations of tissues by MRI, positron emission tomography, and laser holography. Therapeutic advances promise to have an even larger impact. Transplantation of organs, the artificial heart, monoclinal antibodies, interventional cardiology, implantable defibrillators, genetic engineering, cochlear implants, and treatments for metastatic tumors (such as interleukin 2) are simply examples of technologies that are likely to add billions to costs if all the benefits they offer are to be exploited.

Although there is hope that future research will lead to the development of technologies that will check the rise in costs, the near or midrange prospects for such an outcome appear to be small. One major reason is the ongoing development of noninvasive diagnostic technologies. Such new devices may provide a unit of service more cheaply than their predecessors, but they can be used on many more patients because the level of risk and pain is negligible. They can thus be employed even when the likelihood of obtaining useful information is small....

Some observers have suggested that eliminating unnecessary laboratory tests and X-ray examinations could make a major contribution to cost-containment efforts. Indeed, within the last year, it has been stated that such ancillary activities "are the most rapidly swelling component of health-care costs." This statement appears to be without foundation. From 1950 to the early 1970s, the use of "little ticket" tests (X-ray examinations, chemical laboratory tests, immunologic studies, etc.) did rise dramatically, but since then standard laboratory tests and diagnostic procedures have not been used with increased frequency and have therefore not contributed to rising costs for a given episode of illness. Rather, new procedures and high-technology care have been the major culprits....

Long-term control of the rate of increase in expenditures thus requires that we curb the development and diffusion of clinically useful technology. Moreover, for the attenuation achieved in year 1 to be maintained in subsequent years, additional rationing of equal magnitude must be imposed in each successive year....

The mechanisms used for rationing might range from diagnosis related groups and budget caps to the evolution of powerful competitive forces. Whatever the cost-containment strategy, it appears that painful choices lie ahead once we have exhausted the easy savings that can be achieved by eliminating unnecessary hospital care.

■ HEALTH CARE CHOICES: PRIVATE CONTRACTS AS INSTRUMENTS OF HEALTH REFORM
Clark C. Havighurst*
1995

The nature of the challenge posed by health care costs can be appreciated best by seeing the graphic demonstration in figure 4-1....

The "benefits" curve in figure 4-1 shows heuristically the probable relationships between the benefits of health care (measured in dollars on the vertical axis) and the inputs needed to obtain them. It is assumed that "inputs" are all uniform and that they will be added in a sequence dictated by their ability to yield benefits.

FIGURE 4-1 Targets in the War on Health Care Costs

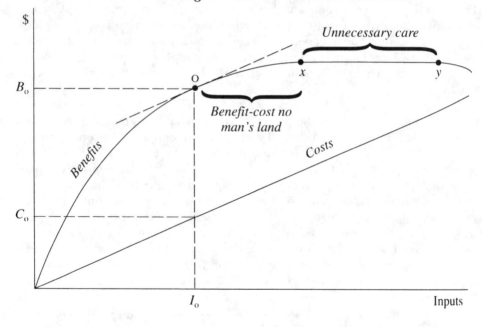

Source: Adapted from Clark C. Havighurst and James F. Blumstein, "Coping with Quality/Cost Trade-offs in Medical Care: The Role of PSROs," Northwestern University Law Review, vol. 70 (1975), p.6 at 17.

*Professor of Law, Duke University. See also Clark Havighurst, How the Health Care Revolution Fell Short, 65(4) Law & Contemp. Prob. 55, 82-86 (Autumn 2002).

Thus, at low input levels, the benefits curve rises steeply, reflecting the true miracles of modern medical science. The curve rises more and more gradually, however, as the inputs being added yield either cures at increasingly higher cost or benefits of increasingly equivocal kinds. The curve is flat after point x, as added inputs yield no benefit, illustrating the notion of unnecessary care. (The curve actually falls after point y, showing that some medical care is positively harmful.)

The benefits curve alone cannot reveal where society or any given purchaser should stop adding inputs. Although no care should be purchased beyond point x, cost-containment efforts that stop there would not ensure an efficient level of consumption. Efficiency demands that costs be taken into account. The diagram therefore introduces a cost curve, a straight line illustrating the cumulative dollar cost of adding uniform inputs. The critical feature of this line for present purposes is its slope (rate of increase), which is reflected in the dotted parallel line having a point of tangency with the benefits curve at point o. At that point, the benefits curve is rising at exactly the same rate as the cost line. Up to that point, the inputs added yield benefits that exceed the costs incurred. Beyond point o, however, the benefits obtainable by adding additional inputs are no longer as great as the cost of those inputs. In other words, marginal costs exceed marginal benefits. Io then represents ... the optimal (efficient) level of inputs, and Co represents the (provisionally) optimal level of spending.

The first crucial point in this demonstration is that even though adding inputs and expenditures beyond point o would improve aggregate health, that fact does not justify such additional spending; employing the same resources in other ways, dedicating them to nonhealth purpose, would increase welfare even more. This conclusion, while theoretically correct, may be hard to accept because of doubts about valuing the health benefits of individuals in dollars and trading them off against other things beneficial to other individuals. It is not proposed, however, to operationalize this calculus in making social decisions or in rationing care. Instead, the analysis here is offered simply to make the point that it is almost certainly socially wrong—in the sense that it reduces aggregate welfare—to pay for every health service that yields some benefit. This point, however, is the beginning, not the end, of the discussion.

An equally important implication of the foregoing demonstration is the obvious practical difficulty of deciding what specific services to omit and of preventing them from being rendered in particular cases. This difficulty will be encountered at whatever level the requisite actions must be taken, whether by society as a whole acting through government, by financing intermediaries, by providers of care, or by individual patients. To highlight this aspect of the problem we are setting for ourselves, the diagram labels the portion of the benefits curve between point o and point x as the benefit-cost no man's land. In this area, health care, being beneficial, will seem desirable as long as the decisionmaker—public or private, as the case may be—does not consider the true cost of providing it. The potential for conflict is clear. Precisely because anyone venturing to fight the battle for cost containment in this range is likely to draw criticism of the most intense kind, including lawsuits, the no-man's-land metaphor seems apt. Again and again in the discussion ahead, there will be occasions to ask whether the cost-containment weapons being used are capable of fighting the battle in the bene-fit-cost no man's land. We will discover that virtually all of the cost-containment measures in use today seek to eliminate only flat-of-the-curve care and not to take on the more dangerous challenge.

■ HEALTH CARE, MARKETS, AND DEMOCRATIC VALUES*
Rand E. Rosenblatt**
34 Vand. L. Rev. 1067 (1981)

Proposals to restructure the health care industry by increasing market competition currently have much political and academic momentum. Whether such proposals will work necessarily depends in part upon the criteria for success that are applied. Viewed from the market perspective, the question is whether procompetitive reforms will achieve their stated goals of containing costs, increasing efficiency, and enhancing consumer sovereignty over health care decisions. From a broader perspective, other questions are also of concern: whether increased competition in health care will actually improve people's health, and whether the operations and effects of health care competition are consistent with important values such as individual dignity, democracy, and equality. These questions need to be seriously addressed, if not finally answered, before the federal and state governments embark on a policy of widespread market reform....

Market advocates attempt to structure the patient's relationship to health care as an economic transaction, namely, as an exchange of a commodity for money in a competitive market setting. A primary justification for increasing market competition in health care is to promote efficiency in the use and delivery of services. Some proponents argue that market competition also has value in its own right as a uniquely legitimate method of defining and promoting efficiency. It is argued that collective social decisions, however made, are inherently coercive and inevitably inefficient. Market mechanisms are said to promote only the value of individual liberty, which enables consumers to express their own preferences by their economic "votes"; otherwise, these mechanisms are considered to be value-neutral.

Despite its considerable superficial appeal, this position is misguided. The distribution of health services through competitive markets promotes at least three major and related nonneutral values. First, in a competitive market individuals are encouraged to make decisions about health care primarily from an economic perspective, as opposed to a broader, more realistic view. Second, individuals also are encouraged to perceive health care choices and health itself as an individual matter, rather than as a matter based upon a close interrelationship between individual decisions and social patterns concerning nutrition, work, environmental quality, economic opportunity, and many other factors. Last, in a competitive market, individuals in their role as citizens or government officials are encouraged to believe that the proper goal of most government policy is to encourage voluntary market transactions. As a result, issues of equality become confined to the special and limited sphere of redistribution purchasing power, the purpose of which is to permit deserving low income persons to participate in the free market. These three values may be defensible, but they certainly are not neutral, at least not in the sense of simply allowing individuals to express their own preferences. On the contrary, they are designed to exert influence over what those preferences might be, as well as to limit the kinds of social settings in which preferences can be expressed and satisfied. . . .

Health can be understood rather simply as the absence of disease and death, and health care as a "curative defense" against both. Health care, . . . however, also must be understood as a caring rather than purely a curative activity, the goal of which is to reduce pain and anxiety and increase the patient's sense of self-determination and quality of life. . . . From this perspective, a central need of health care reform is not more refined quantitative cost-benefit analyses, but rather a restructuring of the patient-provider relationship that ideally could increase the sense of self-determination and satisfaction for both.

The market advocates recognize that much of modern health care has both a caring and a curing function. While conceding that caring services are of "undeniable value," the market advocates also argue that this value is very difficult to measure in quantitative or statistical terms. Because of our inability to measure the benefit generated by caring services, Enthoven argues that "we cannot give a clear answer to the question of whether or not we are getting much health improvement for [the] large increases in [health] spending." In other words, although the market advocates in theory recognize the importance and value of caring services, as a practical matter these benefits are excluded from the cost-benefit analysis. The rationale for this de facto exclusion is that since the benefits of many types of health care are not clear in curative or statistical terms, they are best treated as matters of individual consumption to be paid for out of patients' own current assets, instead of from collective funds such as government programs or insurance. . . .

Enthoven uses the example of the terminal patient who may not desire life-prolonging treatment as a case in support of his thesis. Under current financing arrangements, most insurance policies would cover the expenses of such care, assuming these costs did not exceed some stated dollar or service limit. In these circumstances, the decision whether to prolong life would be made on quality of life grounds, without consideration of monetary cost to the patient. A market approach presumably would add the factor of economic cost in some form to the decision. Havighurst, for example, advocates the marketing of cheaper insurance policies that would exclude one or another form of costly care for catastrophic illnesses. As Enthoven suggests, the consumer would be permitted in such a market to opt for greater financial risk in return for more cash to expend on immediate consumption. It is more likely, however, that the vast majority of patients faced with the decision whether to incur a $25,000 liability for continued treatment, for example, would not feel that their capacity for self-determination had been expanded, nor would they be consoled by the knowledge that they had exercised their self-determination in the prior choice of premium. . . .

A question of great importance about the market approach to health care delivery is how it will affect people with low incomes. By their very nature, markets respond to those consumer preferences that are expressed with money, and people with the least money, therefore, tend to have their preferences given the least attention. Market advocates are aware that some number of low income people could not afford to pay for services or insurance in a competitive health care market. Consequently, they usually propose the simple solution of income transfers—typically effected through a voucher for medical care—that would be sufficient to purchase "basic or necessary" services....

Despite this apparently benign intention of the market advocates, there are strong reasons to believe that poor and low income persons will suffer grievously. A society that embraces a market approach to most of its daily economic life, including the socially sensitive area of health care, is unlikely to redistribute adequate purchasing power to people in economic need. Whether it is theoretically possible for a market society to be strongly egalitarian as well need not be definitively resolved; it is sufficient to note the major reasons why the market perspective is often inconsistent with egalitarian redistribution. First, such a society, or the dominant groups within it, are likely to have a strong belief that the income distribution produced by the market is just. Moreover, they are likely to see unequal economic rewards as necessary incentives for socially desirable qualities such as hard work, risk taking, and enterpreneurial initiative. Income redistribution—even in the form of in-kind vouchers for medical care—probably will be viewed as threatening work incentives and efficient allocation of resources.

4

Regulation of Health Care Facilities and Transactions

Little more than a generation ago, practically the only legal representation hospitals and doctors required, aside from malpractice defense, was occasional tax advice. It was common for even large hospitals to rely solely on sporadic pro bono counsel. These idyllic days are now long past. Today, virtually every major law firm and most medium-sized ones have an identified health law practice, and hospitals and HMOs employ in-house lawyers. Health law has been one of the most rapidly growing areas of legal specialization for two decades. Despite its focus on a single industry, health law calls on a broad array of legal talents and requires sophistication in subjects as diverse as antitrust, corporate and tax law, administrative law, and securities regulation.

This transformation in the legal climate has resulted from the strong winds of economic and organizational change that are buffeting the health care delivery system. What was once a tranquil service industry dominated by religious orders is now a dynamic sector of the economy driven by a new-found entrepreneurial fervor. "Vertical integration," "diversification," "joint venturing," and "strategic planning" are the buzzwords that fill today's health care trade press and board-rooms. The days of solo physician practice, freestanding hospitals, and bright-line divisions among doctors, hospitals, and insurers are giving way to various forms of joint ventures, diversifications, complex corporate structures, and integrated alternative delivery systems.[1]

The driving force behind this massive restructuring is the fear that unless individual providers are affiliated with larger institutions, alliances, or ventures,

---

[1] A particularly telling sign of how the industry is being fundamentally reshaped is the fact that *Hospitals* magazine, which has been published by the American Hospital Association under this name for more than 50 years, in 1993 changed its name to *Hospitals and Health Networks*.

their business will dwindle under intensified competition or they may be forced out of business entirely. Because no single physician, small physician group, or individual hospital is capable of delivering the full array of services required to meet marketplace demands, hospitals and doctors must collaborate among themselves and perhaps with insurers to be included in the new financing and delivery systems that are emerging. Forming various kinds of networks or affiliations is increasingly perceived as necessary in order to have the full continuum of care that is required to offer "one-stop" shopping to potential buyers.[2] The stakes are high, and the time is now. Few providers have failed to act.

The Structure of Integrated Delivery Systems

These different affiliations among hospitals, doctors, and insurers have spawned a multitude of new terms and acronyms, some of which will be described shortly, but the most general label is "integrated delivery systems" (IDSs). These new types of affiliations cover a much broader range of services than earlier types of joint ventures did. An integrated delivery system includes, at a minimum, a full array of hospital and physician services in both inpatient and outpatient settings. It may also include long-term-care facilities and specialized services such as mental health or physical therapy. Most important, they incorporate insurance risk, either by selling insurance directly, or contracting with insurers or employers on a capitated basis.

The frenzy of networking that is now occurring reflects not only a fear of being left out or being bested by one's immediate competitors but also a power struggle among the three fundamental components of the market: doctors, hospitals, and insurers. As more fully described below, a successful network includes each component, either by way of ownership, investment, or contract. The critical issue is which component will be in control.

Network formation requires sizeable amounts of capital to meet regulators' requirements for insurance reserves and to acquire hospitals and doctors. Hospitals and insurers have large amounts of capital, but physicians generally do not. Nevertheless, these networks are critically dependent on their physicians, particularly primary care physicians (general practitioners, obstetricians, and pediatricians). Under managed care arrangements common in HMOs, the primary care physician base determines the size of the network because these are the physicians whom patients first see and who act as "gatekeepers" to hospitalization and specialist referral. Also, the number of primary care physicians determines the number of enrollees, which controls the amount of payment. Insurers, on the other hand, bring to the table the critical expertise necessary to market insurance to employers and individuals, such as the ability to calculate actuarial risk and to manage a claims system.

---

[2] See generally James C. Robinson, The Corporate Practice of Medicine (1999); W. Richard Scott et al., Institutional Change and Healthcare Organizations: From Professional Dominance to Managed Care (2000); Stephen M. Shortell et al., Remaking Health Care in America: Building Organized Delivery Systems (1996); Symposium, Physician-System Alignment, 39(7) Med. Care 782 (Supp. July 2001); Symposium, 15(2) Health Aff. 1 (Spring 1996).

Whether hospitals, physicians, or insurers end up dominating a local market depends heavily on which is the first to "get its act together." If a critical source of physicians bands together, it could dictate the terms under which it will join a network. A chain of hospitals that contracts directly with employers can preempt insurers entirely. But an insurer or employer with a large number of employees that signs up one set of hospitals can end up excluding another altogether.

It is easy enough to draw in broad outline the forces that are restructuring health care financing and delivery. It is much more difficult to classify all of the variety of forms in which these restructurings can take shape. This difficulty arises in part from the lack of a settled vocabulary of consistent usage, in part from the still developmental nature of the market, and in part from the vast complexity that is inherent in the field. To begin, however, it might be helpful to describe how each of the three essential components of the market affiliate at a horizontal level, and then to discuss the continuum of integration techniques used to create a vertical network among them.[3]

As just explained, the three critical components of the market are insurance, hospitals, and physicians. We use "insurance" loosely here to describe a variety of management functions such as marketing, financial accounting, claims processing, utilization review, and data functions such as monitoring and rating individual physicians' performances. An insurance/management operation that focuses solely on claims processing and utilization review, but does not sell policies or deliver care, is known as a "third-party administrator" (TPA firm). One that only manages the finances and personnel for physician practices or facilities, but bears no financial risk and delivers no care directly, is referred to as a "management services organization" (MSO). Otherwise, these insurance/management entities are referred to by the type of insurance the parties have chosen: HMO, preferred provider organization (PPO), point-of-service plan (POS), etc.

The hospital component of the market refers broadly to all institutional facilities. Successful networks usually require more than one hospital in order to achieve sufficient geographic coverage and to provide both primary and tertiary care cost-effectively. Also, networks may include nursing homes and a variety of outpatient facilities such as ambulatory surgery and freestanding emergency centers. These institutions might be under single or joint ownership, either by way of merger and acquisition or by way of direct construction. Alternatively, they might be independently owned facilities that affiliate by contract. Or, intermediately, they might be joint venturers whose relationship is better described as a partnership.

Physicians may associate as members of a single, integrated group practice, but these rarely encompass enough primary care physicians and specialists to supply an entire network. Therefore, it is usually necessary for groups to align themselves by way of contract or partnership, or, more typically, for an insuring or hospital entity to acquire a number of physician practices. A large number of disparately located physicians aligning themselves by contract has come to be

---

[3] The following discussion is drawn from Jeffrey A. Alexander et al., Organizational Approaches to Integrated Health Care Delivery: A Taxonomic Analysis of Physician-Organization Arrangements, 53 Med. Care Res. & Rev. 71 (1996); Carl H. Hitchner et al., Integrated Delivery Systems: A Survey of Organizational Models, 29 Wake Forest L. Rev. 273 (1994); James F. Owens et al., Integrated Delivery Systems: The Second Generation, 16 Whittier L. Rev. 951 (1995).

known as a "clinic without walls"—physicians who claim to be part of the same practice group, but who are not really so. They may share the same name, and certain management services such as billing and collections, but they are not actually a single economic entity with significant shared business risk. Instead, they resemble the looser contractual network among individual practicing physicians known as an "IPA" (for independent practice association).

A hospital or insurer "acquiring" a physician practice has a number of still unsettled meanings. Aside from actually employing physicians, networks can contract with them or make them equity partners (i.e., investors). One common arrangement, referred to above as the MSO, is for the network to acquire the tangible assets of a physician practice—the office building, files, medical records, etc.—for a lump sum price but for the physicians themselves to remain independent contractors. They agree to treat network patients under a predetermined compensation arrangement, and the network agrees to manage their office practice (staffing, billing, etc.).

Once it is understood how each of these component parts is integrated to some degree along a horizontal dimension (that is, physicians with physicians, hospitals with hospitals), then one can focus on how each layer is integrated vertically using a spectrum of integration techniques that have already been suggested. At the most tightly integrated end is an institution that has top-down ownership or control of all components of a fully integrated delivery system. In the simplest manifestation, this would be an ordinary staff-model HMO that owns its own hospitals, employs its own physicians, and markets its own insurance. This is roughly typified by Kaiser-Permanente, an early HMO from California. Other examples are the Mayo and Cleveland Clinics, which were formed by doctors but then acquired their own hospitals and are beginning to market their own insurance.

A contrasting model is one in which each of these components remains in a separately governed entity but is affiliated with the others by some commonality of ownership or contract. A holding company might tie the three together, or one of the three components—usually the insurer or the hospital—might be the dominant party. A structure in which the insuring entity is the dominant party is a group- or network-model HMO. A structure in which a nonprofit hospital or its nonprofit parent is the dominant party has come to be known as the "Foundation model."[4]

A third category of integration techniques lies at the other end of the spectrum. Hospitals, physicians, and insurers can be linked in a loose, contractual network with no common ownership. This typifies a PPO, in which an insurer enters into nonexclusive contracts with a number of hospitals and many doctors to accept patients on a discounted fee-for-service basis. Another version of this contracting category is one in which the hospitals and physicians stand on approximately equal footing, commensurate with a partnership arrangement. Such structures are sometimes known as "physician-hospital organizations" (PHOs).

---

[4] This terminology arose in California, the first state to be swept by integrated networks, so as to take advantage of a provision in the California statutes that exempts so-called foundations from a certain legal restriction that otherwise precludes the employment of physicians. Although a "foundation" is not actually any certain type of legal entity, here it is interpreted to mean a nonprofit corporation.

This description should not be taken as a fixed categorization, much less a "how-to" guide. The variety of organizational techniques are far too numerous, and the field of activity is far too fluid, for any such codification. Many of the structures in use are fairly conventional forms of HMOs and hospital holding companies. Others are hybrids whose names seem to change every six months or so, and many of the terms just defined are used by others in different and inconsistent ways.

Moreover, the nature and volume of health care transactions are continually in flux. At the turn of the century, the pace of mergers and acquisitions involving hospitals had slackened a good deal, due to the dwindling opportunities for these deals, but also due to negative experiences from the transactions earlier in the 1990s. Many hospitals found they were not able to recoup the expenses of acquiring, or even operating, physician practices or other hospitals. This has resulted in a smaller wave of divestitures, which raise their own unique legal issues. Also, many hospital-based HMOs found they lacked the scale to be competitive with more established insurers and so closed or folded into larger insurers. At the moment, one hot spot of activity is among physicians, who are forming more focused single-specialty groups in order to gain market power over insurers in particular medical specialties. To counter this, insurers are changing how they contract with providers to create "tiered" networks rather than a single network, according to how deep a discount each provider agrees to. What happens next is anyone's guess. The only thing that is certain about the future is that things will not stay the same.

The Scope of This Chapter

The result of this cauldron of activity, aside from a never-ending stream of new acronyms and buzz phrases, is a tremendous surge in legal work. Each of these innovative ventures must be examined against the backdrop of both traditional legal doctrine and new bodies of health care regulation. This chapter covers a range of issues that modern health care attorneys must contend with at the cutting edge of their practice field. This is necessarily a grab bag of legal issues. Because we cannot hope to convey the universe of law relevant to the multitude of organizational and operational activities of health care business, we will set aside the areas of doctrine that have more general applicability — such as contract law and securities regulation — and focus instead on the doctrinal areas of unique importance to health care. Those who desire greater detail or depth might consult one of the following multivolume treatises: Aspen's Hospital Law Manual and Managed Care Law Manual; Thomas C. Fox et al., Health Care Financial Transactions Manual; Mark A. Hall & William S. Brewbaker III, Health Care Corporate Law; Michael G. MacDonald et al., Treatise on Health Care Law; National Health Law Ass'n, Health Law Practice Guide. Those who wish a much shorter but still comprehensive overview should read William Sage, "Health Law 2000": The Legal System and the Changing Health Care Market, 15(3) Health Aff. 9 (Fall 1996); Symposium, 29 Wake Forest L. Rev. 1 (1994).

This chapter progresses through the layers of complexity in the health care industry as follows. The chapter begins with the regulation, corporate structure, and taxation of hospitals and other facilities as discrete, freestanding institutions.

It then explores how these institutions relate with physicians. Then the chapter addresses the application of antitrust law to a range of key activities and organizations. The chapter concludes with the topic of greatest complexity: the regulation of financial relationships among all components of the health care financing and delivery system. Throughout, there are two central questions: What are the motivating concerns and concepts of each discrete body of law? Are they still relevant in the rapidly changing environment in which health care institutions currently find themselves? This inquiry is not simply whether courts correctly discern the technical aspects of each separate body of law; it is whether health care law more generally suffers from a "pathology" (to quote Prof. Elhauge at page 59) of viewing each topic too parochially and dissecting problems too narrowly. The risk is that courts will fail to see the overall, interactive effects of the many strands of legal doctrine that determine how medical institutions are formed and operated and that have a major impact on our nation's health care public policy.

Problem: The History of Marcus Welby Hospital and How It Grew*

This hypothetical serves as the basis for several of the problems in the readings that follow. It illustrates the profound transformations that have occurred in the health care sector over the last half-century.

Marcus Welby Hospital (MWH) is a private, nonprofit 400-bed facility employing more than 2,000 workers, with more than $100 million in annual revenues. It is located on the outskirts of a metropolitan area of one million people that contains three other major tertiary care hospitals of 300 beds or more and four smaller, community hospitals of 100 to 150 beds. Currently, 38 percent of MWH's gross revenues are from Medicare, 12 percent are from Medicaid, 40 percent from private insurance or out-of-pocket payments. The remaining 10 percent is bad debt or charity care partially subsidized by a major Protestant denomination with which it has long been affiliated.

Marcus Welby Hospital was born in the 1950s as a small community hospital. It began as an effort by persons from the local church and medical communities joining forces with local business leaders to provide convenient hospital care in the growing suburbs. When the federal Hill-Burton program created a reservoir of construction loan money in the 1950s, the group of town boosters chose to apply for a construction loan to build a 100-bed facility. Its affiliation with the religious denomination has never been formalized through ownership. Nevertheless, the charitable role of the hospital is taken seriously by the board of directors, which always includes one or two members of the denomination.

In the latter 1960s, increased revenues through the Medicare program enabled the hospital to obtain further construction loans, and the hospital expanded to add 100 more beds and more sophisticated inpatient services. Another wave of change swept through the health care industry in the 1980s, in

---

* This fact scenario and many of the problems in this chapter that grow from it are based on ones originally developed by Prof. Phyllis Bernard at Oklahoma City University School of Law. The editors appreciate her permission to adapt them for use in this book.

response to a fundamental alteration in the way Medicare pays hospitals. Some hospitals consolidated, whereas Marcus Welby sought to diversify operations and increase its patient base by providing a wider range of services and much larger bed capacity. Using a bond issue financed through the state, the hospital doubled in size to 400 beds. In addition, the hospital reorganized as the Marcus Welby Healthcare Corporation in order to expand into nursing home, home health, and other related ventures.

In the 1990s the city had grown to reach Marcus Welby Hospital's doorstep. MWH was no longer merely a suburban hospital. It became a major tertiary hospital serving the metroplex. However, revenues were beginning to dip due to the advent of managed care systems. Its average occupancy rate dropped from 85 to 70 percent.

In response, the hospital merged in 1990 with two other hospitals on the same side of town and formed the Marcus Welby Network. The objective was to curb the loss of patients to other managed care networks by signing up a number of physicians, mainly in primary care but also in common specialities, and then marketing this network directly to employers and also to large insurance companies who then offer the network to their customers. This effort was partially a bust, but in other ways was a great success. The idea of marketing directly to employers did not work because the network does not cover a broad enough geographic area to appeal to the largest employers, and smaller employers prefer a network that includes most of the physicians in town so they don't have to force their employees to switch doctors. The network was a great advantage, however, in contracting with insurers. Because of employers' demands for broad networks, and regulators' requirements that managed care insurers provide adequate network capacity, insurers feel they have to include Marcus Welby's facilities and physicians in their networks if they want to sell insurance in the region. Therefore, over the past few years, Marcus Welby has been able to insist on double-digit increases in the payment rates from managed care plans.

Recently, however, insurers have countered by making these hospital prices much more visible to patients. They are threatening to place Marcus Welby in the highest of their tiered networks, which will force patients to decide whether to pay much higher co-payments and deductibles in order to receive care locally, or instead to travel to distant parts of the city to receive care from lower-cost providers. Marcus Welby is now considering what its next moves should be.

A. FACILITY REGULATION

1. Licensure and Accreditation

■ PATIENT POWER: SOLVING AMERICA'S HEALTH CARE CRISIS
John C. Goodman & Gerald L. Musgrave
(1992)

In terms of rules, restrictions, and bureaucratic requirements, the health care sector is one of the most regulated industries in our economy. Consider Scripps Memorial Hospital, a medium-sized (250-bed) acute care facility in San Diego,

California. As [the following] table shows, Scripps must answer to 39 governmental bodies and 7 nongovernmental bodies, and must periodically file 65 different reports, about one report for every four beds.[1] ... Regulatory requirements intrude in a highly visible way on the activities of the medical staff and affect virtually every aspect of medical practice. Another California hospital, Sequoia Hospital in the San Francisco Bay area, has attempted to calculate how many additional employees are required as a result of government regulations. Sequoia's [administrative and nursing] staff increased by 163.6 percent [from 450 to 736] between 1966 and 1990, even though the average number of patients per day (250) did not change. . . .

Regulatory Agencies Over Scripps Memorial Hospital, 1989

Agency

Government
   Occupational Safety and Health Administration
   San Diego County Health Department
   State Board of Equalization (hazardous waste tax return)
   Internal Revenue Service
   Franchise Tax Board
   Secretary of State
   Medicare
   State Board of Equalization (sales tax return)
   California Hospital Facilities Commission
   State Board of Health
   Environmental Protection Agency
   Department of Transportation
   Department of Health Services
   Air Resources Board
   Office of Emergency Services
   Health and Welfare Agency
   Air Pollution Control/Air Quality Management District
   Regional Water Quality Control Board
   Local Sewering Agencies
   San Diego Department of Health Services
   State Licensing Board
   Board of Registered Nursing
   Licensed Vocational Nursing Board
   U.S. Department of Labor
   Industrial Welfare Commission

[1] The hospital association in New York once claimed that its members were subject to 174 regulatory bodies, and another survey found that hospitals have to submit themselves to over 50 different inspections and reports each year, often requiring into similar matters. B. Gray, The Profit Motive and Patient Care 112 (1991). The American Hospital Association claims that, for every hour of patient care, hospitals engage in 30 to 60 minutes of paperwork. Patients or Paperwork? The Regulatory Burden Facing America's Hospitals (2001). — EDS.]

    Fair Employment Practice Commission
    National Labor Relations Board
    Immigration and Naturalization Service
    Employment Development Department
    Social Security Administration
    Employee Retirement Income Security Requirements
    State Board of Pharmacy
    Drug Enforcement Agency
    Food and Drug Administration
    Bureau of Narcotic Enforcement
    California Department of Health, Radiologic Health Branch

Nongovernment
    Joint Commission on Accreditation of Hospitals
    American Hospital Association
    American Conference of Governmental Industrial Hygienists
    California Medical Association
    Radiation Safety Organization (Syncor, Inc.)
    National Association of Social Workers
    American College of Surgeons
    San Diego and Imperial Counties Organization for Cancer Control

Note: Facility Licensing, Accreditation, and Certification

Three terms are commonly used to describe the multi-level process for inspecting and approving health care facilities by state, federal, and private agencies: licensure, accreditation, and certification. Each of these terms has a specific meaning, and each represents a different level of significance for operation within the health care community. The requirements for licensure, accreditation, and certification exert a strong regulatory force on the organization and operation of health care facilities.

Licensure is the mandatory governmental process whereby a health care facility receives the right to operate. In the United States, licensure operates on a state-by-state basis. A health care facility (as that term is defined in the statute) cannot open its doors lawfully without a license from the appropriate state agency. Licensed health care facilities include hospitals, nursing homes, ambulatory surgery centers, freestanding emergency centers, pharmacies, and, in some instances, diagnostic centers. State licensing schemes also exist for various financing systems, both for ordinary health insurance and for innovative delivery systems such as HMOs, preferred provider organizations, and utilization review systems.

Accreditation is a private voluntary approval process through which a health care organization is evaluated and can receive a designation of competence and quality. Most private accreditation for health care organizations today is done under the auspices of the Joint Commission for the Accreditation of Healthcare Organizations (called "JCAHO," "Jayco," or "Joint Commission," formerly known as the Joint Commission for the Accreditation of Hospitals). The Joint

Commission is governed by the major trade associations, primarily the American Medical Association, the American Hospital Association, the American College of Surgeons and the American College of Physicians, and its accreditation programs serve all sorts of health care organizations, although its primary participants are hospitals. Although the Joint Commission is private and purely voluntary, historically it has wielded enormous power and influence because virtually no hospital of respectable size risks the business consequences of jeopardizing its accreditation status. However, the Joint Commission's dominance of facility accreditation is starting to wane somewhat in the face of increasing competition from other accrediting bodies for nonhospital facilities.

Certification is a voluntary procedure for health care organizations to meet the qualifications for participation in government funding programs, specifically Medicare and Medicaid. Although certification is voluntary, more often than not Medicare and Medicaid certification are necessary to the economic survival of a health care organization.

The three functions of licensure, accreditation, and certification are intertwined to a considerable extent. Joint Commission accreditation, for example, frequently satisfies the requirements for both state licensing and Medicare/Medicaid certification. Where this is not the case, Medicare/Medicaid certification surveys are often performed by the same agency and personnel that conduct state licensing surveys. Not only are the three functions intertwined, but there is also a high level of congruence among the various standards and processes employed in each function. Therefore, these materials will examine all three systems interchangeably.

■ ESTATE OF SMITH v. HECKLER
747 F.2d 583 (10th Cir. 1984)

McKay, Circuit Judge.

Plaintiffs . . . brought this class action on behalf of medicaid recipients residing in nursing homes in Colorado. They alleged that the Secretary of Health and Human Services (Secretary) has a statutory duty . . . to develop and implement a system of nursing home review and enforcement designed to ensure that Medicaid recipients residing in medicaid certified nursing homes actually receive the optimal medical and psychosocial care that they are entitled to under the Act. The plaintiffs contended that the enforcement system developed by the Secretary is "facility oriented," not "patient oriented," and thereby fails to meet the statutory mandate. . . .

[P]laintiffs instituted the lawsuit in an effort to improve the deplorable conditions at many nursing homes. They presented evidence of the lack of adequate medical care and of the widespread knowledge that care is inadequate. Indeed, the district court concluded that care and life in some nursing homes is so bad that the homes "could be characterized as orphanages for the aged." . . . [Nevertheless] [t]he trial court denied relief. This appeal is from that judgment. . . .

An understanding of the Medicaid Act (the Act) is essential to understand plaintiffs' contentions. The purpose of the Act is to enable the federal government to assist states in providing medical assistance to "aged, blind or disabled individuals, whose income and resources are insufficient to meet the costs of necessary medical services, and . . . rehabilitation and other services to help such . . . individuals to attain or retain capabilities for independence or self care." To receive funding, a state must submit to the Secretary and have approved by the Secretary a plan for medical assistance which meets the requirements of 42 U.S.C. §1396a(a). . . . The plan must include descriptions of the standards and methods the state will use to assure that medical or remedial care services provided to the recipients "are of high quality." . . . The appropriate state agency must determine on an ongoing basis whether participating institutions meet the requirements for continued participation in the Medicaid program. . . . In conducting the review, however, the states must use federal standards, forms, methods and procedures. . . .

Among other things, the regulations provide for the frequency and general content of patients' attending physician evaluations, nursing services with policies "designed to ensure that each patient receives treatments, medications, . . . diet as prescribed . . . rehabilitative nursing care as needed, . . . is kept comfortable, clean, well-groomed, [is] protected from accident, injury, an infection, and [is] encouraged, assisted, and trained in self-care and group activities." The rehabilitative nursing care is to be directed toward each patient achieving an optimal level of self-care and independence. The regulations require a written patient care plan to be developed and maintained for each patient. . . . Finally, the regulations provide for treatment of the social and emotional needs of recipients.

The Secretary has established a procedure for determining whether state plans comply with the standards set out in the regulations. This enforcement mechanism is known as the "survey/certification" inspection system. Under this system, the states conduct reviews of nursing homes. . . . The Secretary then determines, on the basis of the survey results, whether the nursing home surveyed is eligible for certification and, thus, eligible for Medicaid funds. . . .

The plaintiffs do not challenge the substantive medical standards, or "conditions of participation," which have been adopted by the Secretary and which states must satisfy to have their plans approved. Rather, plaintiffs challenge the enforcement mechanism the Secretary has established. The plaintiffs contend that the federal forms . . . which states are required to use, evaluate only the physical facilities and theoretical capability to render quality care. They claim that . . . out of the 541 questions contained in the Secretary's form which must be answered by state survey and certification inspection teams, only 30 are "even marginally related to patient care or might require any patient observation. . . ." Plaintiffs contend that the enforcement mechanism's focus on the facility, rather than on the care actually provided in the facility, results only in "paper compliance" with the substantive standards of the Act. Thus, plaintiffs contend, the Secretary has violated her statutory duty to assure that federal Medicaid monies are paid only to facilities which meet the substantive standards of the Act — facilities which actually provide high quality medical, rehabilitative and psychosocial care to resident Medicaid recipients. . . .

Congress intended the Secretary to be responsible for assuring that federal Medicaid money is given only to those institutions that actually comply with Medicaid requirements. The Act's requirements include providing high quality medical care. . . . Being charged with this function, we must conclude that a failure to promulgate regulations that allow the Secretary to remain informed, on a continuing basis, as to whether facilities receiving federal money are meeting the requirements of the Act, is an abdication of the Secretary's duty. . . .

■ COSPITO v. HECKLER
742 F.2d 72 (3d Cir. 1984)

GARTH, Circuit Judge.

Appellants Douglas Cospito, et al., ("the Patients") are or have been patients at the Trenton Psychiatric Hospital (TPH). In 1975, TPH lost its accreditation from codefendant Joint Commission on Accreditation of Hospitals (JCAH). As a result, codefendant Secretary of the Department of Health, Education, and Welfare (now the Department of Health and Human Services) terminated various federal benefits which were conditioned upon the beneficiaries being treated at a qualified psychiatric hospital. . . . The Patients brought this action in district court challenging the loss of their federal benefits on several constitutional grounds. . . .

Beginning in 1973, TPH was surveyed under the standards for "psychiatric facilities" recently promulgated under the auspices of JCAH. Following the 1973 survey, major deficiencies were disclosed in several areas, including patient treatment, staffing, environment, and fire safety. TPH was accredited for only one year, and was notified that these deficiencies must be corrected to maintain accreditation. In 1974, however, many of the same deficiencies were found again. A preliminary decision was made by JCAH not to accredit. At TPH's request, a resurvey was conducted in May, 1975, which again resulted in a preliminary decision not to accredit. TPH did not appeal from that decision, and the deaccreditation became final. . . .

JCAH is an Illinois not-for-profit corporation formed in 1951 for the purpose of creating and maintaining professional standards for evaluating hospital performance. The body is governed by a 22-member Board of Commissioners. Its constituent members consist of the American College of Physicians, the American College of Surgeons, the American Dental Association, the American Hospital Association, and the American Medical Association. . . .

The survey itself consists of an on-site visit conducted by a team of surveyors designated by JCAH. The surveyors evaluate the quality of the facility's environment and review its administrative records to determine whether they conform to applicable standards. . . .

JCAH accreditation, however, must be distinguished from certification by the Secretary for eligibility in federal assistance programs. While JCAH accreditation may, depending on the circumstances, be a component of certification, the two are not necessarily coextensive, and at least as a matter of terminology, we will refer to the two separately. . . .

The Patients at TPH had, before decertification by the Secretary, been the beneficiaries of three types of federally funded benefits: (1) Medicare, (2) Medicaid, and (3) Supplemental Social Security Income. . . . When TPH was decertified in 1975, all of the benefits described above were terminated, since TPH was no longer an institution eligible under Medicare and Medicaid. . . . The Patients brought suit in district court alleging that deprivation of their

Medicare, Medicaid, and Social Security benefits was unconstitutional. They alleged lack of procedural due process, lack of substantive due process, lack of equal protection, and unconstitutional delegation of authority to JCAH. . . .

Our analysis of the procedural due process aspects of this case is guided by the Supreme Court's decision in O'Bannon v. Town Court Nursing Center, 447 U.S. 773 (1980), which involved facts comparable to those presented here. In *Town Court*, residents of a nursing home claimed a violation of due process when they lost federal benefits as a result of the decertification of their facility. Like the Patients here, they claimed a right to a pretermination hearing.

The Supreme Court found as a threshold matter, however, that the residents of the nursing home had not been deprived of any protectable property interest, and thus, absent this foundation, no due process right was triggered. Writing for the Court, Justice Stevens found that patients did not have a settled interest in receiving benefits at any [particular] facility, including a decertified one, and therefore there had been no deprivation of "property." . . .

[T]he only factor which even arguably distinguishes this case from *Town Court* is the fact that the Patients are unable to transfer out of TPH [because they were involuntarily committed under state mental health law]; [therefore], they are barred from receiving federal benefits at another qualified institution. Thus, they contend that there has been an actual "deprivation" of a protectable interest. Even accepting that contention, however, . . . [b]ecause any loss of benefits to the Patients was only "indirectly" caused by the Secretary's decision to decertify TPH, whatever deprivation which was suffered [by virtue of the state-law psychiatric commitment] was not the result of any [federal] governmental action. The Patients are therefore not in a position to claim any Fifth Amendment due process protection, even if they alleged a "deprivation."[17] . . .

Finally, we turn to the Patients' argument that the Medicare (and thus Medicaid) provisions improperly delegate authority to JCAH, in derogation of Congress' ultimate responsibility to establish federal policy. . . . We need not reach the question of whether delegation of such authority to a private entity breaches the constitutional barrier, since our reading of the Medicare statute, which in turn is applicable to the Medic[aid] and Social Security programs, convinces us that the Secretary retains ultimate authority over decertification decisions, through the ability to engage in a "distinct part" survey. . . .

While JCAH accreditation may, under certain circumstances, independently satisfy the statutory requirements for participation in Medicare, the Secretary is free to prescribe standards which are higher than those of the Commission, in which case JCAH accreditation would not be effective. Moreover, if the Secretary determines that, despite JCAH accreditation, a particular hospital nevertheless has serious deficiencies, he may, after appropriate notice, decertify the institution. On the other hand, if the Secretary chose to promulgate a standard lower than that of JCAH, a general hospital could presumably be certified by meeting only that lesser standard, even if it did not meet the requirements imposed by the Commission.

---

[17] The district court granted summary judgment on the procedural due process claim for the reason that, in its opinion, the procedures used adequately safeguarded the Patients' interests, [a]pplying the tests of Mathews v. Eldridge, 424 U.S. 319 (1976). . . . Without disagreeing with the district court's reasoning, we note that our analysis makes it unnecessary to reach the issues addressed by the court below. . . .

The Patients argue, however, that in the case of psychiatric hospitals, the statute places JCAH accreditation in a position of ascendancy over approval by the Secretary, thus leading to the question of unconstitutional delegation to a private group. Our reading of the statute leads us to disagree. While Congress did choose to give special attention to JCAH accreditation in the context of psychiatric hospitals,[27] it still provided the "distinct part" survey as a mechanism whereby the Secretary could independently determine whether a particular institution was qualified for participation. Through consecutive or simultaneous distinct part surveys, therefore, it is possible to obtain a de novo evaluation by the Secretary on the adequacy of a hospital's facilities. . . .

Since, in effect, all actions of JCAH are subject to full review by a public official who is responsible and responsive to the political process, we find that there has been no real delegation of authority to JCAH.[29] . . .

BECKER, Circuit Judge, dissented.

Notes: Facility Regulation and Accreditation

1. *Which Facilities Are Covered?* The first question under any licensing scheme is its jurisdiction. Jurisdictional issues arise with increasing frequency as the result of innovative service delivery and ownership arrangements in the medical industry. One common issue is whether a license for a central facility such as a hospital covers satellite facilities such as urgent care centers, or whether they must be separately licensed. Another issue is whether a speciality clinic, say for abortions or for expensive diagnostic scans, can be treated as simply a physician's office, which does not require a facility license. See RIH Medical Foundation v. Nolan, 723 A.2d 1123 (R.I. 1999) (physician-owned corporation that operates physician offices is exempt from health facility licensing). A third issue is whether an existing license covers the buyer or lessor of a health facility, and whether turning the facility's operation over to a management company requires applying for a formal transfer of the license. Often, the same questions apply generally to accreditation and certification. Usually, the only way to know the answer is to simply ask the governing authorities, since statutes and regulations frequently fail to flesh out these details. The consequences for wrongly interpreting licensing jurisdiction can be severe. In one case, the court refused to enforce any of the contracts entered into by an unlicensed nursing agency. U.S. Nursing Corp. v. St. Joseph Medical Center, 39 F.3d 790 (7th Cir. 1994). See also section 4.B.3 discussing the corporate practice of medicine doctrine.

2. *"Doc-in-a-Box."* Sometimes, these jurisdictional issues are resolved by statute. One contemporary instance relates to ambulatory care centers, colloquially known as "Doc-in-a-Box." These store-front medical clinics cater to no-wait, no-appointment medical needs of an urgent nature, short of life-or-limb threatening

---

[27] The legislative history reveals that Congress intended "to support the efforts of the various professional accrediting organizations sponsored by the medical and hospital associations. . . ."

[29] Our resolution of this issue renders somewhat academic the Patients' contention that it was improper for JCAH to "subdelegate" the responsibility for evaluating psychiatric hospitals to the various accreditation councils. Since we have found that no real authority was actually vested in JCAH, it follows that there could be no improper "subdelegation" of authority to divisions of the Commission. . . .

conditions. They provide a more convenient and sometimes less expensive alternative to hospital emergency rooms for conditions such as broken legs, bad cuts, and sudden illnesses. There is an argument that ambulatory centers are nothing more than glorified doctors' offices and therefore require no facility license apart from the physicians' medical licenses. However, states are beginning to amend their statutes to cover these facilities, especially when they specialize in surgery. Note, 11 Health L. 1 (1999); Note, 36 U. Fla. L. Rev. 465 (1984); Comment, 11 Am. J.L. & Med. 105 (1985).

3. *Measuring Quality Through Structure or Outcomes.* The next question under any of these regulatory or quasi-regulatory schemes is their content. A detailed understanding is beyond the scope of this book. However, it is possible to convey the gist of this content in terms of Donabedian's famous distinction among structural, process, and outcomes measures of quality. State licensing authorities, like the Medicaid nursing home requirements in *Estate of Smith*, do not inquire into the actual outcomes of patient treatment. Instead, facility licensure provisions typically read like a gigantic building code for the industry, specifying a host of architectural, safety, and sanitation minutia. Similarly, the Joint Commission accreditation standards traditionally have addressed only the organizational and structural aspects of each hospital department—issues such as whether bylaws are properly drafted, whether proper committees are established, and whether administrative structures contain proper monitoring and documentation—rather than attempting any direct assessment of the actual outcomes of medical care in the hospital. This point was articulated in an Internet discussion group by someone who worked as a hospital therapist and department manager for 13 years:

> We never worried about JCAHO until the three months prior and the two days of the inspection. In the three months prior we backdated all the documentation that we needed to get through the inspection, and in the two days they were there we spent telling them how focused we were on quality, etc. As long as the paperwork is in order, people can be dying in the halls and there could be guppies in the IV fluids; the JCAHO wouldn't notice.

For an extensive critique of the traditional structural and process measures of institutional quality and an argument for adopting outcomes measures, see Troyen Brennan & Donald Berwick, New Rules: Regulation, Markets and the Quality of American Health Care (1996), which also contains an excellent overview and historical account of licensure and accreditation.

4. *Process and Outcomes Measures.* The *Smith* case presaged a move away from purely structural measures of quality. That decision resulted in a statutory amendment (known as OBRA '87) and an extensive set of regulations that govern in considerable detail the treatment plans, living environment, legal rights and human dignity of nursing home patients. 42 C.F.R. §§483 et seq. These regulations are focused primarily on the process of care. See generally David Bohm, Striving for Quality Care in America's Nursing Homes, 4 DePaul J. Health Care L. 317 (2001); Jennifer Brady, Long-Term Care under Fire: A Case for Rational Enforcement, 18 J. Contemp. Health L. & Pol'y 1 (2001); Comment, 73 U. Colo. L. Rev. 1013 (2002).

Recently, there has been a considerable push to move even further toward evaluating institutions based on the outcomes of treatment. For instance, CMS has proposed fundamentally revising the standards for hospital participation in Medicare and Medicaid to focus much more extensively on outcomes of care and systems for continuous quality improvement. For instance, the proposed standards would require each patient to receive a comprehensive assessment of care needs and a coordinated plan of care within 24 hours of admission, and would require hospitals to have systems that continuously monitor and improve care through data-driven methods of quality assessment that focus on patient outcomes and satisfaction. 62 Fed. Reg. 66,726 (1997). So far, however, the only provisions that have been adopted are those resembling the nursing home standards that focus on informing patients of their rights and protecting them from excessive use of restraints. 64 Fed. Reg. 36,070 (1999).

Another prominent initiative has been taken by the Joint Commission, which intends to streamline accreditation standards and focus more on patient safety issues. One key feature is a self-assessment and a "sentinel event" policy that requires hospitals to take the following actions whenever there is an unexpected death or serious injury resulting from treatment: inform the patient or family, conduct a "root cause" analysis, and institute a corrective action plan. However, hospitals do not have to report these events to the Joint Commission, since doing so might compromise the hospital's ability to protect the information from discovery in lawsuits. Symposium, 35 J. Health L. 179 (2002). As a result, this outcomes initiative has become simply another process measure, one that requires institutions to assess internally their bad outcomes rather than enforcing mandatory outcomes standards.

Outcomes measures of quality may find their purest expression in the accreditation of HMOs and other types of integrated delivery systems. The National Committee for Quality Assurance (NCQA) is the leading accreditation organization for these new comprehensive financing and delivery systems. From the start, this organization has spearheaded a focus on outcomes measures in the form of the quality report cards discussed at page 30. These report cards adopt a standard reporting format about matters such as patient satisfaction, childhood immunization rates, and other broad indicators of health status (not just medical treatment) in the covered population. The aim is to provide this information as a basis on which subscribers and employers can comparison shop based on both price and quality, thereby substituting more market-based forces for regulatory oversight.

5. *Challenging Adverse Decisions.* The third major area of concern under licensure, accreditation, and certification programs are the processes for determining compliance and challenging adverse decisions. Space limitations preclude us from covering these important aspects of public oversight and legal practice. In brief summary, substantial procedural protections are usually built into these regulatory schemes, so challenges for denial of due process usually fail. The most intense disputes arise when licensing inspectors find such glaring safety concerns that the facility is shut down immediately without a chance for correction or rebuttal. These shutdowns have been challenged as unconstitutional, but usually without success considering the patient protection concerns at stake and the ample procedural rights following a temporary shutdown.

Constitutional challenges depend on the presence of state action, which usually does not exist for private accreditation. McKeesport v. Accreditation Council for Graduate Medical Education, 24 F.3d 519 (3d Cir. 1994). Contra St. Agnes Hospital v. Riddick, 668 F. Supp. 478 (D. Md. 1987) (state action exists where private accreditation affects state licensure). Therefore, suit against accreditation organizations depends on somewhat obscure common law theories of fairness in business dealings. There are only a few such cases, the leading ones arising in connection with physician accreditation and membership in professional societies. They reason, similar to Greisman v. Newcomb Hospital, page 452, that when membership organizations control important economic and public interests, they must provide rational reasons and a fair process for their exclusion decisions. See Pinsker v. Pacific Coast Society of Orthodontists, 526 P.2d 253 (Cal. 1974); Falcone v. Middlesex County Medical Society, 170 A.2d 791 (N.J. 1961). See generally Robert Trefney, Judicial Intervention in Admissions Decisions of Private Professional Associations, 49 U. Chi. L. Rev. 840 (1992).

6. *The Public Role of Private Accreditation. Cospito* raises the important public policy question of whether public regulatory authorities cede too much control to private accreditation organizations that are controlled by the regulated industry. State licensure of health care facilities, like federal certification, sometimes defers to the Joint Commission, either by using its accreditation as a proxy for licensure or by incorporating many of its standards. Even if this passes constitutional muster, it still deserves critique for whether this essentially self-regulatory approach is good public policy. See generally Symposium, Private Accreditation in the Regulatory State, 57 Law & Contemp. Probs. No. 4 (1994) (exploring this and a number of other important legal and public policy issues concerning accreditation). It is worth observing that, although the Joint Commission arose from the hospital industry, it is now sufficiently independent that it is receiving harsh criticism from hospitals for the expense and intrusiveness of its inspections. At the same time, consumer groups such as Public Citizen are lashing out against the Joint Commission for its "dangerously cozy relationship" with the hospital industry and its "clear conflict of interest" as both industry regulator and industry advocate. Modern Healthcare, July 15, 1996, at 6.

7. *Competing Accreditors.* Another important public policy issue is the potentially anticompetitive effect of private accreditation. Because accreditation arises as a cooperative effort among competing firms in the affected industry, it creates a setting rife with opportunities for antitrust violation. However, accreditation also has procompetitive benefits because it provides useful information to consumers that helps them make more informed choices. See generally C. Havighurst, Accrediting and the Sherman Act, 57 Law & Contemp. Probs. 199 (Autumn 1994). Professor Clark Havighurst argues that a partial solution to some of the anticompetitive concerns is to encourage competition among accreditation organizations. This appears to be happening in the health care industry. As the focal institution shifts from in-patient hospitals to out-patient facilities and fully integrated financing and delivery systems, there has been a proliferation of competing accrediting organizations. For instance, Medicare and Medicaid now recognize accreditation by the Community Health Accreditation Program (CHAP) as an alternative for certifying homecare health programs. Several organizations have vied for accreditation of managed care programs and organizations, with NCQA

eventually prevailing. Do you think this kind of competition among accreditors is helpful to consumers? Is it sustainable or too confusing to have alternative accreditation regimes, on top of overlapping licensing and certification systems?

8. *Occupational Hazards and Medical Wastes.* These are not the only regulatory authorities affecting health care facilities. Because of the size, complexity, and public importance of hospitals, they are subject to numerous specialized regulatory laws and generalized laws that have special importance in the hospital setting. Two prime examples are the laws governing workers' exposure to infectious diseases and the disposal of medical waste, which this note briefly summarizes. The federal Occupational Safety and Health Administration (OSHA) is quite involved in regulating health care facilities to ensure that health care workers are protected from occupational hazards. Some of the hazards confronted by health care workers are identical to those found in other job settings: dangerous machinery, exposure to chemicals, and so forth. See generally Mark Rothstein, Occupational Safety and Law (4th ed. 1998). The health care environment also creates unique risks, particularly through potential exposure to communicable diseases. In 1991, the OSHA enacted regulations designed to reduce the risk of workplace exposure to disease, particularly to HIV and hepatitis. Under the "Bloodborne Pathogen" rule, employers must develop an exposure control plan, which means that they must identify workers whose jobs create a "reasonably anticipated" exposure to infectious body fluids and they must develop a training and protection program to reduce the risk of exposure. 29 C.F.R. §1910.1030. Health care facilities must also provide employees with protective equipment, establish safe workplace practices, and employ "engineering controls" (such as use of puncture resistant containers for used needles). Employers are required to monitor exposures and to keep records of incidents. Each of these requirements imposes significant costs and administrative burdens on health care facilities. See, e.g., American Dental Ass'n v. Martin, 984 F.2d 823 (7th Cir. 1993). See also Paula E. Berg, When the Hazard Is Human: Irrationality, Inequity, and Unintended Consequences in Federal Regulation of Contagion, 75 Wash. U. L.Q. 1367 (1998). Health facilities in violation of OSHA standards can face significant fines. Most people do not think of health care facilities as producing hazardous waste. Yet the point can be driven home — literally — when medical waste, including used needles and bloody refuse, washes up on our nation's beaches. In 1990, the EPA estimated that hospitals, medical offices, and other facilities produced about a half million tons of medical waste that " 'contains pathogens with sufficient virulences and quantity so that exposure to the waste by a susceptible host could result in an infectious disease.' " Laura Carlan Battle, Regulation of Medical Waste in the United States, 11 Pace Envtl. L. Rev. 517, 518, 524 (1994). States have been the primary regulators of the disposal of medical waste produced by health care facilities. States regulate the ways in which the waste is transported, stored, and decontaminated or destroyed. See, e.g., Battle, supra, at 564-570; Shumaker, Infectious Waste: A Guide to State Regulation and a Cry for Federal Intervention, 66 Notre Dame L. Rev. 555 (1990). See also William B. Johnson, Annot., Validity, Construction, and Application of State Hazardous Waste Regulations, 86 A.L.R. 4th 401 (1991).

The federal government briefly entered the regulatory arena with the Medical Waste Tracking Act of 1988, 42 U.S.C. §§6992-92k, which established a demonstration project. The EPA has not specifically regulated medical waste.

Lisa A. Jensen, Medical Waste Regulation in the United States, 9 Nat. Resources & Env't 21, 21 (Fall 1994). Attempts to assert more federal control over medical waste under the various environmental statutes have been largely unsuccessful. See Battle, supra, at 552-563. See also Comment, 13 Pace Envtl. L. Rev. 1063 (1996) (discussing problems with applying the federal Clean Water Act to medical waste dumping). In addition, improper waste disposal can result in tort liability to those exposed to hazardous substances. See, e.g., DeMilio v. Schrager, 666 A.2d 627 (N.J. L. Div. 1995) (negligence action based on dentist's improper disposal of dental instrument, which injured sanitation worker); Alan Bavley, Funeral Home Faces Lawsuit from State; Babies' Remains Disposed as Medical Waste, Kansas City Star, Aug. 27, 1996.

Research Exercise: Medicare/Medicaid Certification*

Your client is a hospital that has recently undergone a series of layoffs. A disgruntled former employee, a nurse, has complained to the state health department that the quality of patient care has suffered significantly. The hospital has had reason to be concerned about high rates of nosocomial infections (infections acquired in a hospital). There is also concern about bedsores and soiled linen. One patient's open wound was infected by maggots. The nurse's call to the state health department triggered a surprise inspection by the unit charged with overseeing certification for participation in the Medicare and Medicaid programs. It appears likely that the state Department of Health will seek summarily to terminate the hospital's status under these programs as a "participating provider" (also known as the "provider agreement"). Consult the Code of Federal Regulations or one or more of the relevant practitioner treatises (e.g., the CCH Medicare and Medicaid Guide or the Aspen Hospital Law Manual) to determine what this means and what can be done about it.

2. Certificate of Need Regulation

Certificate of need (CON) laws are another important type of facility regulation, one that operates essentially like a building permit for hospitals and other medical facilities, but with a focus on costs rather than on quality. Medical facilities must show that a need exists in the community, and that they satisfy financial feasibility and other criteria, before undertaking any of several enumerated new activities. These typically include substantial new construction, the purchase of major new equipment, the initiation of important new services, or a change in ownership. Hospitals, nursing homes, and outpatient clinics are all usually covered by this legislation, but physician offices are frequently excluded.

These laws are an outgrowth of community health planning efforts that began in the 1940s, when the country first recognized a shortage and maldistribution of

---

*The editors are grateful to Prof. Phyllis Bernard for permission to use this problem, which she devised.

hospitals. At that time, planning efforts were attached to federal grants and loans for hospital construction under the Hill-Burton Act of 1946 to make sure new hospitals were placed where they were most needed. In 1964, New York state adopted the first state CON law. It made health planning mandatory for all facilities and it was concerned with both hospital excess capacity as well as hospital shortages. The American Hospital Association quickly embraced this mandatory planning philosophy and began lobbying other states to follow suit.

CON laws became widespread after the federal government enacted the National Health Planning and Resources Development Act (NHPRDA) of 1974, 42 U.S.C. §§300k-300t-14 (repealed). NHPRDA required states to follow a model CON process in order to continue receiving certain federal funding for public health activities, and to continue participating in Medicaid. By 1980, all states had enacted some version of CON legislation. This federal initiative quickly came to an end when President Reagan signed the Omnibus Health Package of 1986 repealing NHPRDA. About a dozen states thereafter replaced their CON laws, but most states still retain this regulation. The old federal law thus remains influential on the interpretation of the state laws because it served as the model enacted by most states.

The following materials examine how this regulatory scheme functions in the three dozen states in which it is still active. As you read the next case, consider whether the rationale for this regulation was sound when it was first enacted, and whether it remains sound today.

■ STATEWIDE HEALTH COORDINATING COUNCIL v. GENERAL HOSPITALS OF HUMANA, INC.
660 S.W.2d 906 (Ark. 1983)

GEORGE ROSE SMITH, Justice.

The principal appellee, General Hospitals of Humana, which we will refer to as Humana, is a subsidiary corporation of a parent company that owns about 90 hospitals, nearly all of them in the United States. In 1982 Humana applied to the Arkansas Health Planning & Development Agency, which we will refer to as the State Agency, for a certificate of need that would authorize Humana to construct and operate a 150-bed community hospital at Sherwood, in Pulaski County. The application was opposed by the Baptist Medical System, St. Vincent Infirmary, and Arkansas Blue Cross & Blue Shield. After a hearing the director of the State Agency, acting for the Agency, granted the application.

The three protestants asked for a review by an independent agency, as permitted by the State Agency's rules. The governor appointed the Arkansas Social Services as the independent reviewing agency. A Social Services attorney conducted a hearing and upheld the award of the certificate of need. That decision was affirmed by the circuit court. The protestants present several arguments for reversal, but we need consider only one: The State Agency was not authorized to grant a certificate of need that was inconsistent with the State Health Plan. On the record that argument must be sustained, which disposes of the case.

First, a preliminary procedural matter. Humana has filed a motion to dismiss the appeal as moot, asserting that it was compelled . . . to enter into a construction contract (and it actually began construction) within one year after the certificate of need was awarded on August 5, 1982, else the certificate would have expired. [The court rejected this motion because it found Humana could have requested an extension to keep the certificate in effect. As a result of the holding that follows, therefore, Humana was forced to abandon a partially complete hospital in which it had invested $7 million.] . . .

Turning to the merits, we must emphasize at the outset that there is in progress a national effort to limit the construction of new hospitals. . . . The policy of restricting hospital construction stems from Congress's belief that competition among hospitals, unlike competition in the market place, does not reduce the cost of in-patient hospital services to the consuming public. To the contrary, the testimony in the case at bar shows that such competition actually increases hospital charges. Fixed hospital costs are so great that an empty bed costs about half as much to maintain as an occupied bed. Hospitals compete not for patients but for doctors, who usually select the patient's hospital. Hospitals vie with one another in acquiring expensive equipment, with unnecessary and costly duplication of facilities. Hospital charges are apt to be paid without question by public and private health insurers. The hard fact is, as one witness stated bluntly: "The cost of hospital care is just outrageous to the consumer." . . .

The federal law, in its endeavor to control the proliferation of hospital beds throughout the nation, contemplates that each state will be divided by its governor, subject to revision by the Secretary, into health service areas so that the distribution of health care units can be conformed to local conditions. Arkansas has been divided into four such areas [each with] its own Health Systems Agency and Health Systems Plan. There is also a detailed State Health Plan, which must be and was adopted by the Statewide Health Coordinating Council. . . .

Various different figures were given in the testimony about the number of hospital beds in the Central Arkansas area, because the witnesses did not count the beds in the same way. There is no question, however, but that the area, like most of the nation, is overbedded in that its licensed hospital beds already exceed the federal and state maximum of 4 beds per 1,000 persons. Humana did submit figures purporting to show that in 1986 there would be no overage even with its 150 added beds, but when this isolated testimony is weighed along with the other proof it cannot be considered substantial evidence. . . .

The State Health Plan is not inflexible. Both the federal and state law permit the maximum bed limit to be exceeded locally to meet exceptional conditions, which are specified as being (1) an unusually high proportion of persons over 65 years old, (2) seasonal population fluctuations, (3) rural areas in which, for example, a majority of the residents would otherwise be more than 30 minutes travel time from a hospital, (4) urban areas having a large number of beds compensated by fewer beds in the same metropolitan area, and (5) areas having referral hospitals attracting nonresident patients. There has been no finding that any such exceptional condition exists. . . . Thus it is established without substantial dispute that Humana's application for a 150-bed hospital in an area already overbedded is contrary to the Central Arkansas Health Systems Plan and to the State Health Plan. . . .

Counsel for Humana do not and could not seriously argue that the proof supports the State Agency's determination. Instead, it is contended that the federal and state laws are mere guidelines which the director of the State Agency is free to disregard if he chooses to do so. If that were true, the entire federal and state effort to confine the number of hospital beds to the target limitation would be futile, for every agency director would be free to ignore the limitation whenever he saw fit to do so. . . .

Reversed.

PURTLE, Justice, dissenting.

. . . It is obvious that we are dealing with a case of overregulation here. Governments are not authorized to act except within the confines of the power granted to them by the people. I do not believe the people intended to grant the government the power to regulate every facet of their affairs. A less narrow construction of these statutes and regulations would allow the state agency to depart from strict compliance, as it did in this case. . . . In the interest of public policy I would apply a very broad interpretation of these restrictive regulations. After all, the health, safety and welfare of the residents of north Pulaski County will be affected by this decision. . . .

It seems to me that competition will drive the cost of hospitalization down, not up as argued by respondents. Furthermore, the cost of hospitalization is not the only consideration involved here. Human lives may well be at stake in this instance; acutely ill persons who reside in northern Pulaski County may not survive the longer trip to other area hospitals. No value can be placed upon a human life but it seems to me the life of a north Pulaski County resident should be valued the same as one south of the river. . . .

Notes: Certificate of Need Regulation

1. *The Failure of CON Regulation.* "Certificate-of-need laws establish entry controls which are similar in intent and impact to the certificate-of-public-convenience-and-necessity device widely employed in public utility and common carrier regulation." Clark Havighurst, Regulation of Health Facilities and Services by "Certificate of Need," 59 Va. L. Rev. 1143, 1153 (1973). As such, they appear to be an aggressive regulatory approach to containing health care costs. Yet, after years of operation, CON laws have had essentially no impact on hospital costs. See M. Morrisey & R. Ohsfeldt, Endogenous Hospital Regulation and its Effects on Hospital and Non-hospital Expenditures, 3 J. Reg. Econ. 137 (1991). One reason for the failure of CON regulation is the law's limited scope. CON laws address primarily capital investment, not operating expenses. Thus, CON programs may slow the increase in numbers of beds, but the funds saved are simply moved to new services and equipment. Moreover, CON laws constrain only what hospitals spend, not what they charge. In the latter respect, certificate of need programs constitute incomplete public utility regulation. Most such regulation imposes price controls in addition to entry controls. Indeed, price control would seem essential since restricting entry tends to create monopoly power. One court relied on this effect of conferring state sanctioned monopolies without controlling for monopolistic abuse to support its holding that the original North Carolina CON statute was unconstitutional. In re Certificate of Need for Ashton Park Hospital, 193 S.E.2d 729 (N.C. 1973). All other courts to consider the issue, though, have upheld the constitutionality of CON regulation.

2. *Needs vs. Wants.* When CON laws were first adopted, the CAT scanner was one of the primary examples cited of a technology much in need of centralized planning. Ironically, the capital expenditure threshold for CON review of equipment purchases has risen to the extent that CAT scanners usually require no approval. A greater irony is that the CON laws have proven inadequate for controlling even far more expensive technological devices. See Hospitals, April 20, 1987, at 124 ("Mount Sinai's diagnostic imaging department sounds like the '12 Days of Christmas': five nuclear medicine cameras, four MRIs, three mammography machines, two regular [CAT] scanners, and PET."). How has this happened? Consider the following explanation:

> Need is a medical concept, largely defined by professionals. It is subjective, rather than objective, and consequently is not a limiting, but an expansive concept. Unlike economic "demand" for goods and services, which reflects both consumers' wants and their resource limitations, medical need reflects what professionals deem desirable, rather than what patients can afford. Professionals decide what is needed according to their concept of what constitutes good care, which tends to be established according to the state of the art—what is medically possible at a given time. Virtually any medical benefit is seen as a need; medical professionals are generally guided by a more-is-better philosophy, which has been characterized as a "technological" or a "quality imperative." . . . The most obvious way to judge future need is to extrapolate from past patterns of growth for the institution or area under consideration. Historically, such projections have been the major quantitative tool of health planners. Simply applied, such methods perpetuate past patterns—including presumably inappropriate growth. . . . [T]he appropriateness of current utilization is not challenged. . . .

Randall Bovbjerg, Problems and Prospects for Health Planning: The Importance of Incentives, Standards, and Procedures in Certificate of Need, 1978 Utah L. Rev. 83. See also H. Aaron & William Schwartz, The Painful Prescription (1984) ("the prevention of all duplication would achieve only modest, one-time savings, which would not affect the subsequent rate of increases in cost."). Consider, for example, whether, after the development of X-rays, CAT scans, and now MRIs, there will be a "need" for PETs: positive emission tomographers. "They are remarkable medical detectives that reveal all sorts of information about chemical activity, show what parts of the brain you use when you move an arm or leg or think, and diagnose certain kinds of heart and brain disease and cancer. But PETs have expensive taste. They need to be near a cyclotron. The combined cost of the PET and the cyclotron approaches $5 million; cyclotrons cost at least $1,000 per hour to run." J. Califano, America's Health Care Revolution 103 (1986).

For additional discussions of the history and theory behind CON regulation, see Cost, Quality and Access in Health Care: New Roles for Health Planning in a Competitive Environment (F. Sloan et al. eds., 1988); Robert Hackney, New Wine in Old Bottles: Certificate of Need Enters the 1990s, 18 J. Health Pol'y & L. 926 (1993); Sallyanne Payton & Rhoda Powsner, Regulation Through the Looking Glass: Hospitals, Blue Cross, and Certificate-of-Need, 79 Mich. L. Rev. 203 (1980).

3. *The Binding Effect of Bed Need Criteria.* Courts are split on whether quantitative bed need criteria can be rigidly applied, to the exclusion of more "qualitative" criteria. In agreement with the *Humana* case, see Appeal of New Hampshire

Catholic Charities, 546 A.2d 1085 (N.H. 1988) (error to approve application for 85 nursing home beds based on factors of marginal importance when predetermined bed need was for only 82 beds); Yankton v. South Dakota Department of Health, 432 N.W.2d 68 (S.D. 1988) (enforcing agency's bed need formula despite contrary evidence of waiting lists and high occupancy rates). Other courts, however, reason that quantitative standards are merely one factor to consider and they can be rebutted by more direct evidence that existing facilities are unsatisfactory, too far away, or overcrowded. See generally Annot., 61 A.L.R.3d 278 (1994).

For additional discussion of the methods for determining need and of other aspects of CON criteria, see E. Flash et al., Certificate of Need Regulation, *in* Health Care Corporate Law: Formation and Regulation (1993); Lauretta Wolfson, State Regulation of Health Facility Planning: The Economic Theory and Political Realities of Certificates of Need, 4 DePaul J. Health Care L. 261 (2001).

4. *Hospital Competition, Pro and Con.* CON regulation has been criticized for being anticompetitive. Like other public utility regulation of natural monopolies, the intent of CON is to replace competition with comprehensive state planning. Moreover, existing competitors are naturally favored because they are in a better position to propose the least expensive project and the one in which regulators have the most confidence. "Thus, an existing provider, which can offer to replace old facilities even at a different location, has almost a license in perpetuity." Havighurst supra, 59 Va. L. Rev. at 1187. See also C. Havighurst, Deregulating and Health Care Industry (1982) (proposing reforms to CON laws to make them a better vehicle for enhancing competition). Do you agree with the dissent in the *Humana* case that market forces are capable of restraining excess capital investment in health care facilities? One student author believes this is now the case, even if it was not so before, due to the increasing competition among HMOs and other managed care systems that aggressively bargain over what they will pay facilities. P. McGinley, Beyond Health Care Reform: Reconsidering Certificate of Need Laws in a "Managed Competition" System, 23 Fla. St. U. L. Rev. 141 (1995).

Nevertheless, because the existing CON laws were meant to displace competition, there has been extensive discussion of the extent to which these state laws preempt or impliedly repeal federal antitrust law. See National Gerimedical Hospital v. Blue Cross, 452 U.S. 378 (1981) (no blanket preemption, but there may be limited preemption with respect to specific planning activities); Hospital Building Co. v. Trustees of Rex Hospital, 691 F.2d 678 (4th Cir. 1982) (partial preemption, to extent planning activities are in good faith). The repeal of the model federal CON law alters the terminology of this debate somewhat by focusing on whether the remaining state laws meet the federal requirements for "state action immunity."

■ IRVINGTON GENERAL HOSPITAL v. DEPARTMENT OF HEALTH
374 A.2d 49 (N.J. Super. Ct. 1977)

Irvington General Hospital submitted an application for a certificate of need in November 1973. It sought permission to construct an addition to the hospital and to add . . . 19 medical/surgical beds. After several delays attributable both to the Department [of Health] and the applicant, hearings were held in September and October 1975. The hearing officer recommended that the application be approved. . . .

Between the time of the hearing and the time when the Health Care Administration Board considered the hearing officer's recommendation, the Board reclassified 150 long-term care beds at Clara Maas Hospital as medical/surgical beds, thereby creating an excess of medical/surgical beds in Essex County, the county in which Irvington General Hospital is located. . . . [O]n May 6, 1976 the Board remanded this application to the hearing officer, instructing him to make additional findings of fact "particularly pertinent to the current effect of the reclassification of the beds in the area."

The remand hearing was held, and thereafter the hearing officer recommended that the application be denied solely on the ground that Department of Health statistics now showed an excess of medical/surgical beds in the county. . . .

We agree with plaintiff's contention that the Board erred in giving conclusive weight to the[se] Department of Health statistics. . . . [T]he Legislature has required the Health Care Administration Board to take into account several factors:

. . . (a) the availability of facilities or services which may serve as alternatives or substitutes, (b) the need for special equipment and services in the area, (c) the possible economies and improvement in services to be anticipated from the operation of joint central services, (d) the adequacy of financial resources and sources of present and future revenues, (e) the availability of sufficient manpower in the several professional disciplines, and (f) such other factors as may be established by regulation.

It is clear, therefore, that in light of those established considerations and the general policy of providing the highest quality health care, it is not sufficient for the Board to consider only the number of beds available in the area, particularly where the area designated by the Department as the "area to be served" may not, in fact, coincide with the area for which the services will, in fact, be provided. Total reliance upon bed statistics would permit the Board to make its decision solely on the basis of the first factor noted in N.J.S.A. 26:2H-8: "the availability of facilities or services which may serve as alternatives or substitutes." It would permit the Board to ignore the remaining factors, notably, in this case, the second one: "the need for special . . . services in the area."

The extensive record compels the conclusion that Irvington General Hospital primarily serves the population of the Town of Irvington. That town has the largest density of citizens over 65 of any municipality in this State. Testimony of various experts establishes that the elderly patients who make up the largest portion of the Hospital's population have a greater need than other patients for the support of relatives and friends during their illnesses, and that the knowledge that they and their families are secure is a significant factor in their successful medical treatment.

The testimony also shows that public transportation to other hospitals in Essex County is poor and that many elderly patients are at least reluctant to go to those hospitals because they are located in high crime area. Moreover, their elderly spouses and friends are unable to visit them at other locations because of the lack of transportation and threats to their safety. . . .

[W]e believe that the Board, in deciding whether to grant a certificate of need, may not, as it did here, rely solely on bed need statistics. Unquestionably, it must also take into account all of the factors set out in N.J.S.A. 26:2H-8 and must, if appropriate, recognize and accept a need for special services in any local area smaller than the larger health care area established by the Department.

Because the Board failed to make those considerations a remand is required. On remand we direct that the Board take into account an additional factor: At the time of the original hearing the Department statistics showed that Essex County needed 73 more medical/surgical beds. By the time of the remand hearing 150 beds at Clara Maas Hospital had been reclassified to medical/surgical. That fact created an excess of beds in the county. The reclassification had been made upon application by Clara Maas suggested by the Department. We cannot tell from the record when the Clara Maas application was made. If, in fact, it was made after the application by Irvington General, we direct that the Irvington General application be considered first, since it was submitted first. In other words, on remand the Irvington General application should be considered as if the Clara Maas application had not yet been determined. . . .

■ CERTIFICATE OF NEED FOR HEALTH CARE FACILITIES: A TIME FOR REEXAMINATION
Roberta M. Ross
7 Pace Law Review 491 (1987)[2]

[A. THE SCOPE OF CON LAWS]

[The model federal act, the National Health Planning and Resources Development Act (NHPRDA) of 1974,] required . . . CON review prior to:

1) acquisition of major medical equipment costing in excess of $400,000;
2) other obligations of capital expenditures in excess of $600,000, indexed for inflation;
3) capital expenditures resulting in a substantial change in bed capacity;
4) capital expenditures resulting in a substantial change in health services provided by a health care facility; and
5) offer[ing] of a new health service or reinstatement of a discontinued health service.

Institutional health care providers, such as hospitals or nursing homes, were subject to CON review [but doctors' offices were not]. Federal regulations defined "health care facilities" as hospitals, skilled nursing facilities, kidney disease treatment centers, intermediate care facilities, rehabilitation facilities, and ambulatory facilities. Health maintenance organizations (HMO's) were largely exempt from CON review.

NHPRDA's focus on institutional health care providers created a loophole that permitted private physicians to purchase equipment for their offices without

---

[2] Reprinted with permission.

CON review, while hospitals could purchase the same equipment only after going through CON review. . . . In response to this concern, an amendment. . . . broadened NHPRDA's scope to include noninstitutional health care providers, such as individual physicians or groups of physicians, to the extent that they acquired expensive equipment located outside of a hospital but used to service inpatients of a hospital. Another provision of the 1979 amendment brought within the scope of CON acquisitions made "on behalf of a health care facility" as well as acquisitions made "by" the health care facility itself. . . .

B. Burdens Encountered in Complying With Requirements

Once a health care facility decides to make an application for a Certificate of Need, there are many potential sources of delay. The actual application can take months to prepare and, regardless of how lengthy it is, additional information is frequently requested. For example, the CON application filed by a group of Connecticut hospitals for a magnetic resonance imaging (MRI) center was over 1400 pages, and the required supplement exceeded 1700 pages. From conception until final approval, Greenwith Hospital's noncontroversial and unopposed request for a CON to replace its telephone system took one year, and that period was "brief" only because the hospital agreed to waive its right to a hearing.

Review of an application may also be delayed by "batching," which requires applications for similar facilities or services to be evaluated contemporaneously and measured against each other. . . . Further delays may be caused by declarations of moratoria on review of CON applications.

The cost of applying for a CON can be considerable, exceeding $100,000 for major projects. If litigation is required, the cost may reach $350,000. . . .

C. Circumventing the Requirements

The burdens imposed by CON review have prompted health care facilities to seek ways of avoiding the requirement. Among the approaches they have taken are: piecemeal acquisition of major equipment where the components are below the monetary threshold for CON review; use of parent corporations and their subsidiaries to provide benefits to health care facilities; and arrangements between health care facilities and private physicians whereby the private physicians obtain major medical equipment, the benefits of which are made available to the health care facility. . . .

The first of the circumvention devices, piecemeal acquisition, is illegal in most instances. . . .

There is a paucity of cases involving the use of parent corporations to avoid review. This method, however, is not uncommon, and is openly employed. In a typical situation, a hospital seeks to construct a parking garage for the convenience of its patients and staff. Because the hospital is a health care facility, and because the garage may involve a capital expenditure in excess of the threshold, the hospital must apply for a CON. To avoid this, the hospital creates a parent corporate entity with two subsidiary corporations, one of which is the hospital. The second subsidiary is not a health care provider and, arguably, not subject to the CON statute. It builds and operates the garage with the result that the hospital has the parking facilities it requires, without subjecting the project to CON review.

. . . The use of creative corporate structuring devices to avoid review depends upon whether the state statute includes a CON requirement for acquisitions "on behalf of" a health care facility and, where it does have this requirement, how the phrase on behalf of is interpreted. For example, a Washington, D.C., court read this language to include the benefit to a hospital of a parking garage developed by a subsidiary of the hospital's corporate parent. An injunction was granted, halting the construction of a four and a half million dollar garage. . . . District of Columbia v. Washington Hosp. Center Health Sys., No. 6970-83 (D.C. Super. Ct. Jul. 25, 1983). . . . A Nebraska court, on the other hand, has interpreted "on behalf of" more narrowly, holding that a separate tax entity that constructs a physicians' office building adjacent to a hospital is not subject to CON, because on behalf of does not necessarily mean for the benefit of. State v. Coleman, No. 354-194 (Lancaster County Dist. Ct. Sept. 24, 1982). . . .

The third device, arrangements between health care facilities and private physicians, has been possible in states that failed to extend their CON statutes to physicians' offices in accordance with the federal amendment. Challenges to such arrangements have occurred in New York and New Jersey. . . . Using private funds, Clifton Springs Sanitarium purchased a trailer which it installed on its grounds eight feet from its hospital building. A walkway and electrical lines connected the trailer to the hospital building. The trailer was leased to a staff radiologist who leased, and later purchased, a CAT scanner. The radiologist performed CAT scans on inpatients of Clifton Springs Sanitarium, inpatients of other hospitals, and outpatients in the area. No CON was obtained. . . . The Administrative Law Judge concluded that the hospital had violated the law, and the state then ordered the doctor to discontinue performing CAT scans on patients of Clifton Springs Sanitarium. The Appellate Division annulled the determination, holding that a CON was not required because the CAT scan services were provided by a private physician and not by the hospital. Clifton Springs Sanitarium Co. v. Axelrod, 115 A.D.2d 949, 497 N.Y.S.2d 525 (4th Dep't 1985). The court took note that the trailer was purchased with private money and was not part of the hospital or constructed according to the hospital building code; that the scanner was the property of the doctor; that the doctor was not required to perform scans on the hospital's patients; and that the radiologist paid the staff and billed the patients directly. . . .

Conversely, a New Jersey court, deciding Radiological Society of New Jersey v. New Jersey State Department of Health, Hospital Rate Setting Commission, 208 N.J. Super. 548, 506 A.2d 755 (1986), read that state's CON statute as being applicable to private physicians who provide services to inpatients of a hospital. Despite the New Jersey statute's private physician exclusion, the *Radiological* court held that a physician who acquires a CAT scanner and magnetic resonance imaging (MRI) equipment must first obtain a CON. . . .

Whether it is desirable to close the loopholes that permit circumvention of the CON process is a policy decision that should be made only after an evaluation of the efficacy of the process. If the process does not make a significant contribution toward cost containment and equitable distribution of health care resources and if it provides, as some critics suggest, an obstacle to improved health care, it may be that the CON requirement should be abandoned.

[D. The Impact of CON Laws]

Viewed in terms of equitable distribution of health care resources, the effect of the CON process has been limited. There is little evidence that HSA's have initiated programs for underserved areas. . . . Success of the CON process in cost containment is similarly questionable. . . . [E]ven with CON, health care costs are growing at a substantially greater rate than the rest of the economy. The extent to which CON has kept health care costs from growing at an even faster rate remains to be established.

The enormous expenditure of time and money by both administrative agencies and health care providers in complying with the CON process substantially reduces any savings that might be attributable to it. For all its promise, CON review has resulted in the elimination of few projects. Of over 20,000 CON applications reviewed throughout the country between 1979 and 1981, only ten percent were ultimately disapproved.[3] Such statistics prompt understandable concern as to the wisdom of continuing to invest significant amounts of time, money, and effort on the CON process.

It has been suggested that the CON process actually increases the cost of providing health care. . . . The substitution of expensive labor for capital invest-ment in an already labor intensive industry increases total health care costs. By discouraging the entry of new providers, giving, in effect, a franchise to existing providers, CON eliminates competition and the restraining effect that competi-tion can have on prices. P. Joskow, Controlling Hospital Costs (1981). . . .

The lack of convincing evidence that CON programs make a significant contribution to health care cost containment, or to a more equitable distribution of health care resources, suggests that states should develop and implement alter-native approaches to solving these problems. Should a state determine, however, that CON programs have value and merit a role in the state's health planning scheme, the state must make a judgment regarding the scope of the program — the activities and providers that should be included. . . . Failure of legislatures to engage in this re-examination will result in continued circumvention of the law on the one hand, and overreaching by administrative agencies on the other. More importantly, failure to engage in a probing re-examination of the problems of rising health care costs and inequitable distribution of health care resources will create an even greater distance between those problems and their solutions.

Notes: Certificate of Need Review Criteria and Process

1. *Competing Criteria.* How is an agency to "take into account all of the factors set out in [the CON statute]" as required by *Irvington* when those factors are as diverse and opposed as quality, cost, and access?

---

[3] Office of the Assistant Secretary for Planning and Evaluation, Dep't of Health and Human Services, Report to Congress, Hospital Capital Expenses: A Medicare Payment Strategy for the Future 48-50 (1986). This figure, however, represents only the percent of filed applications that were rejected and not the percent of dollar expenditures rejected. This figure may be tempered by the fact that the prospect of CON review may dissuade hospital administrators from developing plans for projects they anticipate will be rejected. The result, however, may not be entirely salutary because among the abandoned projects may be ones of great value to the quality of health care.

Most CON programs . . . have one stated goal: the promotion of equal access to quality health care at reasonable cost. The problem is that this single, seemingly unimpeachable goal is in reality three goals that compete and are often mutually irreconcilable: quality, accessibility, and cost control. How these three goals are interpreted and implemented varies directly with who is doing the interpreting and for what purpose. Health care providers, for example, tend to perceive need from the quality side of the spectrum. . . . Consumers, while also oriented to issues of quality, tend to view accessibility as a major goal of CON. . . . As for the regulators, there can be little doubt that CON has one essential purpose: to keep costs down.

Medicine in the Public Interest, Certificate of Need: An Expanding Regulatory Concept (1978).

2. "Perhaps the chief source of discouragement about health planning is the complexity of the task. Among the factors relevant in the planning effort are [the nature of existing facilities and their service areas, population size and characteristics, and current use patterns.] Even this list fails to convey the difficulty of projecting changes in population, technology, . . . and patterns of utilization. . . . The complexity is such that the agencies themselves lack confidence in their ability to make hard-and-fast judgments, and the result is a lack of firm standards for decision making. In such circumstances, the pressures of politics necessarily become dominant." Havighurst, supra, 59 Va. L. Rev. 1202-1204. See D. Altman, R. Greene & H. Sapolsky, Health Planning and Regulation: The Decision-Making Process (1981).

3. *The Scope of CON Laws.* States have departed from the federal model in several ways. About a dozen states have entirely repealed their CON laws. Many others have modified their laws to narrow the range of health care facilities and projects subject to review. For instance, many states have raised the dollar thresholds to double or more the original federal levels. A few states have reinvigorated this regulation by adopting an entirely different approach to defining the scope of their CON laws. These states cover specified new health services regardless of their capital or operating cost and regardless of whether a "health care facility" undertakes the expenditure. This approach is typical for organ transplant and heart surgery programs and for expensive diagnostic machinery.

4. *Circumvention Techniques.* The doctor's office exemption has proven to be quite a large loophole. For instance, the exemption has been used frequently to purchase magnetic resonance imagers (MRIs) without CON approval. Boulware v. State Dep't of Human Resources, 737 P.2d 502 (Nev. 1987). MRIs are highly sophisticated diagnostic scanning devices that cost up to $3 million installed. Although they originally were found only in major medical centers, the majority of MRIs are now located outside the hospital setting, largely because of the CON laws. See Earl Steinberg et al., X-Ray CT and Magnetic Resonance Imagers: Diffusion Patterns and Policy Issues, 313 New Eng. J. Med. 859 (1985). As Ross summarizes, a number of states have attempted to close this loophole by extending CON laws to outpatient facilities intended primarily to treat inpatients, while others apply CON review to specified equipment and services regardless of institutional sponsorship.

Health care facilities have found various other inventive techniques for circumventing the CON laws. One is suggested by *Irvington*'s willingness to "recognize and accept a need . . . in [a] local area smaller than the larger health care area established by the Department." For instance, a hospital applicant in an over-bedded metropolitan area may try to carve out an unserved area in the affluent, growing suburbs. Whether this technique is successful turns on whether the suburbs are considered to be within the service area of the existing "downtown" hospitals. States vary in their methodologies for defining service areas. Without entering into the full complexities of service area gerrymandering, consider what the policy impli-cations are of: (a) refusing local hospital facilities to newly emerging communities; (b) locating new construction in affluent white suburbs to the detriment of patient census in older, city-center hospitals.

Another technique for circumventing numerical bed-need limitations is for an existing hospital to construct a new facility that "replaces" older beds, some-times in an entirely different location. This technique of trading in old beds for new ones has created a lively market in the sale of older hospitals. In some cases, the replaced capacity consists of only "paper beds," i.e., licensed bed capacity that has long since been taken out of operation to make room for other uses and services.

5. *Review Procedures. Irvington* required the earlier CON application to be considered first. But what if both applications were filed at approximately the same time? In such circumstances, courts require the applications to be considered in a comparative hearing, which seeks to determine not only whether there is a need for the service or facility, but, if so, who among many hospitals will best serve that need. Bio-Medical Applications v. Dep't of Health and Rehab. Services, 370 So. 2d 19 (Fla. App. 1979). Comparative hearings can turn into surprisingly complex affairs that last for weeks. Once one application is filed, it is usually followed by several other competing ones that are batched together in the same review cycle. In the experience of one of your authors, these contests quickly degenerate into disputes over trivia such as who has the superior parking lot design or who is cutting down the most trees. See, e.g., In re Health Care and Retirement Corp., 364 S.E.2d 150 (N.C. App. 1988).

Among the controversial procedural disputes that arise in CON litigation are:

a. whether states are authorized to impose a moratorium on CONs for certain types of services — United Hospital Center v. Richardson, 328 S.E.2d 195 (W. Va. 1985) (moratorium invalid);

b. whether expiration of the statutory period for the agency to review an application results in the application being "deemed approved" automat-ically — Platte County Medical Center v. Missouri Health Facilities Review Comm'n, 734 S.W.2d 608 (Mo. App. 1987) (deemed approved); Myers v. State, 503 N.E.2d 451 (Ind. App. 1987) (same); Benedictine Sisters Benevolent Ass'n v. Petterson, 299 N.W.2d 738 (Minn. 1980) (contra);

c. whether competing hospitals have standing to challenge the grant of an application — Community Care Centers v. Missouri Health Facilities Review Comm'n, 735 S.W.2d 13 (Mo. App. 1987) (no standing); St. Joseph Hospital v. Dep't of Health, 87 P.2d 891 (Wash. 1995) (stand-ing); Andrew Dolan, Who Has Standing to Appeal Certificate-of-Need Decisions?, 1978 Utah L. Rev. 155; and

d. whether an approved project can be altered without further approval. Appeal of Rehabilitation Associates of New England, 556 A.2d 1183 (N.H. 1989) (yes).

See generally J. Simpson & T. Bogue, Guide to Health Planning Law: Topical Digest of Case Law (1985); E. Flash et al., supra; Annot., 61 A.L.R.3d 278 (1994).

B. CORPORATE FORM

1. Nonprofit and Public Entities

Regulatory constraints on medical institutions are not always imposed from external sources. Some derive from their own internal organization. For instance, because most hospitals and some HMOs are organized as nonprofit corporations, they are subject to a special set of corporate governance and tax rules, which the next case introduces. Public hospitals are subject to similar restrictions. These ancient rules, derived from the law of charitable trusts, are becoming increasingly relevant as various health care facilities contemplate expanding their range of activities or converting to a more commercialized corporate form.

■ QUEEN OF ANGELS HOSPITAL v. YOUNGER
136 Cal. Rptr. 36 (Cal. 1977)

KAUS, Presiding Justice.

[Queen of Angels Hospital (Queen) was founded in 1927 in connection with the Catholic church. The Franciscan Sisters of the Sacred Heart, known as "the Motherhouse," is a large religious order that, for 30 years, has staffed an outpatient clinic in the hospital.] . . . In April 1971 — the details will be supplied in the discussion — Queen's board of directors approved a lease to be effective May 1, 1971, between Queen as lessor and W.D.C. Services, Inc., hospital entrepreneurs, as lessee. Queen leased the hospital, excepting the outpatient clinic and a convent house, to W.D.C. for 25 years with two options for ten additional years each. The minimum annual rental guaranteed Queen was $800,000 for the first two years and one million dollars a year thereafter.

Queen intends to use a substantial portion of the lease proceeds to establish and operate additional medical clinics in East and South Central Los Angeles, which clinics will dispense free medical care, aid and advice to the poor and needy. It is not disputed that an outpatient clinic is not functionally equivalent to a hospital.

In June 1971, the Motherhouse submitted a claim for 16 million dollars for the value of the Sisters' past services to Queen's board of directors. . . . [A]n agreement was executed between Queen and the Motherhouse, effective May 1971, settling and compromising the claim for the Sisters' past services by agreeing that Queen should pay to the Motherhouse $200 per month for each Sister in the Order over the age of 70 years, . . . whether or not the particular Sister performed services at Queen of Angels Hospital. The initial annual cost of the agreement would be $309,600 — in July 1971, there were 129 Sisters over the age of 70. . . .

[Queen and Motherhouse] filed a declaratory relief action against the Attorney General to determine the validity of [the] lease agreement . . . and the . . . retirement pay. . . .

1. THE HOSPITAL [LEASE]

The Attorney General contends that under its articles of incorporation, Queen held its assets in trust primarily for the purpose of operating a hospital, and the use of those assets exclusively for outpatient clinics would constitute an abandonment of Queen's primary charitable purpose and a diversion of charitable trust assets. . . .

The rules governing the use of the assets of a nonprofit charitable organization are well established: "(A)ll the assets of a corporation organized solely for charitable purposes must be deemed to be impressed with a charitable trust by virtue of the express declaration of the corporation's purposes. . . . It follows that . . . (a nonprofit corporation cannot) legally divert its assets to any purpose other than charitable purposes. . . ." Pacific Home v. County of Los Angeles, 41 Cal. 2d 844, 852, 264 P.2d 539, 543. "Since there is usually no one willing to assume the burdens of a legal action, or who could properly represent the interest of the trust or the public, the Attorney General has been empowered to oversee charities as the representative of the public." Holt v. College of Osteopathic Physicians & Surgeons, 61 Cal. 2d 750, 754, 40 Cal. Rptr. 244, 247, 394 P.2d 932, 935. . . .

With this apparent agreement in principle we turn to an examination of the articles of incorporation and the relevant undisputed facts. The articles of incorporation, as amended in 1941, provides in relevant part as follows:

> . . . the purposes for which said corporation is formed are:
>
> (1) To establish, . . . own, . . . maintain, . . . and operate a hospital in the City of Los Angeles, . . . to furnish, . . . hospital care, . . . and medical and surgical treatment of every kind and character, and to receive, treat and care for patients, invalids, the aged and infirm, and generally to conduct and carry on, and to do all things necessary or advisable in conducting and carrying on a hospital;
>
> (2) To perform and to foster and support acts of Christian charity particularly among the sick and ailing; to practice, foster and encourage religious beliefs and activities, particularly those of the Holy Roman Catholic Church; to house and care for unprotected and indigent sick, aged and infirm persons regardless of race, creed, sex or age;
>
> (3) To educate, . . . nurses and medical students, and to provide facilities for the same;
>
> (4) That it is a corporation which is not formed for pecuniary gain . . . and any revenue received . . . from the operation and carrying on of said hospital shall be used in improving the same . . . or shall be used in enlarging

and improving said hospital and in enlarging the field and scope of its charitable, religious and educational activities;

    (5) To lease or purchase any real estate, . . . which may be necessary, proper or useful in carrying out the purposes or for the benefit of the hospital, or as may be deemed to be conducive to the welfare of this corporation; . . .[2]

    [W]hat is most apparent in the articles of incorporation is that . . . the framework of those multiple purposes is the operation of a hospital. Clinics are not even mentioned. . . . [A]lthough Queen did operate a clinic from 1932 to the present time, that clinic was physically housed within the hospital and drew on hospital resources. . . .

    Queen also represented to the public that it was a hospital. In its statement to the Franchise Tax Board, it stated that it was in the "business of running a hospital." Similar statements were made to the Internal Revenue Service and Los Angeles county tax authorities. Funds were solicited from the public for the hospital or hospital purposes. Such acts further bind Queen to its primary purpose of operating a hospital. In brief, whatever else Queen of Angels Hospital Corporation may do under its articles of incorporation, it was intended to and did operate a hospital and cannot, consistent with the trust imposed upon it, abandon the operation of the hospital business in favor of clinics.

    Queen's argument in response does not meet the issue. Plaintiffs point out, as we have noted, that the corporation has multiple "purposes"; that the purpose "to furnish, . . . medical and surgical treatment" is broad enough to authorize the operation of a clinic or clinics and that acts of "Christian charity" encompass all forms of medical aid, care, and advice to the poor and needy. None of the foregoing is disputed. The question is not whether Queen can use some of its assets or the proceeds from the operation of the hospital for purposes other than running a hospital; it certainly can and has. The question is whether it can cease to perform the primary purpose for which it was organized. That, we believe, it cannot do.

    Moreover, the issue is not, as plaintiffs contend, whether the operation of clinics serving the poor in the areas in which they live is as worthy a use of charitable funds. . . . This corporation is bound by its articles of incorporation. Queen may maintain a hospital and retain control over its assets or it may abandon the operation of a hospital and lose those assets to the successor distributees, but it cannot do both. . . .

2. THE RETIREMENT PLAN

The trial court made the following relevant findings: . . . The property of Queen does not belong to either the Motherhouse or the Roman Catholic Church. From the inception of the hospital through 1971, services . . . provided Queen by the [M]otherhouse . . . were considered donated to Queen by both

---

[2] The articles also contain a "parity clause" which provides that the corporation may generally "do all acts and things which may be necessary, proper, useful or advantageous to the full carrying out of the purposes of this corporation." . . .

parties. Neither the Motherhouse nor the Sisters expected any further or future compensation for those services. Although the claim for compensation for past services was made in good faith and was not a dishonest claim, "there was no basis for such claim and neither the Motherhouse nor Queens had a reasonable basis for believing in the validity of the claim." The compromise of the claim — e.g., the retirement plan — "was not a proper exercise of sound business judgment or of the fiduciary duties of Queens' Board." The court concluded that . . . the retirement plan was invalid and that, if implemented, it would constitute a diversion of charitable assets.

First, although plaintiffs make much of the relationship between Queen and the Motherhouse and attempt to present this relationship in terms of Roman Catholic Canon Law, the trial court properly rejected this approach. Plaintiffs' assertion that such evidence is material reflects an attempt to bootstrap a First Amendment argument by citing . . . moral and ecclesiastic duties of Queen and the Motherhouse, and then arguing that whether the retirement plan accords with church doctrine is an internal ecclesiastic matter. Throughout, plaintiffs have sought the benefits of and conformed to the general requirements of civil law; they cannot now decline to be ruled by the principles which Queen has itself invited.

Applying neutral principles, . . . there was no reasonable basis for compromising the 16 million-dollar claim submitted by the Motherhouse for past services. Although plaintiffs attempt to analogize the pension plan to a — sometimes — enforceable promise to pay for past services, as the Attorney General points out, the compromise "bore no relationship whatsoever to a traditional retirement plan as it provided payments to all of the Sisters of the Order over the age of 70 wherever situated, regardless of whether they had ever served at Queen of Angels, or if so, how long, or when, and regardless of any other provisions being made for such Sisters through retirement plans at any of the other ten hospitals established by the Franciscan Sisters." . . .

3. [Legal and Business] Fees

[The lease was negotiated by an attorney, John Brandlin, who was also a member of Queen's board of directors.] The Attorney General contends that Queen's agreement to pay [Brandlin and his business partners] 3 percent of the annual rentals for the first five years of the lease and 2 percent of the annual rentals for each year thereafter as fees for negotiating the lease is, in fact, an agreement to pay real estate brokers' fees and, since none of the recipients is licensed, the agreement is invalid. . . .

The underlying facts are as follows: During the time in which this lease was negotiated, prepared and executed, Brandlin was Queen's attorney and also a member of Queen's board of directors. The hospital was in financial difficulties and Brandlin was authorized to find out what could be done about leasing the hospital, an idea he had proposed informally. Another of Brandlin's clients was John L. Donovan, a stockbroker, through whom Brandlin met Glenn Thomason, "a kind of hospital entrepreneur" who "deals in hospitals." None of the three was licensed as a real estate broker. In late 1969, Brandlin, Donovan and Thomason had contemplated the formation of a corporation — "American Hospital

Administrators"—to acquire or lease hospitals and go "public" with them, but the project never got off the ground.

In July 1970, after preliminary discussions, Brandlin was told by Sister Timothy Marie that Queen was interested in pursuing the possibility of a lease. . . . After further discussions with W.D.C. and with the Order's headquarters in Illinois, Brandlin began preparing the documents. Brandlin did all of the legal work.

The agreement presented to the Board covering the services of Thomason, Donovan and Brandlin states that the three "are entitled to reasonable compensation" for their "services." . . . Brandlin was employed on a retainer basis by Queen until about April 1971, and thereafter he billed his legal services—other than the fee in dispute—based upon an hourly rate. . . .

That Brandlin's involvement in three capacities—lawyer, trustee and frustrated entrepreneur—was legal and professional dynamite is obvious. Nevertheless, professional protocol—such as disclosure [and] disqualification as trustee when called for—appears to have been scrupulously observed. . . .

In essence, this is what happened: Brandlin rendered legal services to Queen's. These were undoubtedly of such a nature that a layman would have been required to be a licensed real estate broker. Brandlin, however, was an attorney and, as such, came within [an] exception. . . . The Attorney General claims that Queen could not obligate itself to pay Donovan and Thomason anything because they were more than mere finders [and thus were seeking a sales commission without a real estate license]. To be brief and blunt, we disagree on the facts. . . .

The judgment is reversed.

■ COLUMBIA/HCA AND THE RESURGENCE OF THE FOR-PROFIT HOSPITAL BUSINESS*
Robert Kuttner**
335 New Eng. J. Med. 362 (1996)

This two-part article addresses the medical, ethical, and public-policy issues posed by the resurgence of for-profit chains and their acquisition of nonprofit community hospitals. The prime case in point is Columbia/HCA Healthcare Corporation, the largest and most aggressive of the for-profit chains, the product of three large and several smaller mergers. With 340 hospitals, 135 outpatient-surgery offices, and 200 home health care agencies in 38 states, Columbia/HCA now controls nearly half the for-profit beds, and 7 percent of all hospital beds, in the United States. The company's gross earnings exceed 20 percent of revenues, and its 1995 profits were just under $1 billion, with $20 billion in assets. . . .

Columbia's founder, Richard Scott, bought his first two hospitals in El Paso, Texas, from Healthtrust in 1988. From a base of 12 hospitals in 1991, Columbia acquired Basic American Medical (1992, 8 hospitals), Galen (1993, 71 hospitals), HCA (1994, 97 hospitals), Medical Care America (1994, 96 ambulatory surgical

* Excerpted with permission of the publisher. Copyright © 1992, Massachusetts Medical Society.
** The author is a respected journalist and social critic.

centers), and the rest of Healthtrust (1995, 117 hospitals) after a bidding war with NME. . . . In 1995 alone, Columbia/HCA acquired or negotiated joint ventures with 32 nonprofit hospitals. . . .

The company has targeted and achieved a formidable corporate goal of a 20 percent gross return on revenues. I was told by a Columbia/HCA executive that chief executives of company hospitals who fall short of this goal are regularly called to corporate headquarters in Nashville to explain and are ordered to redouble their efforts. Further economies at the local hospital usually follow. . . .

Columbia/HCA's most audacious recent foray [is] in Ohio. . . . In March, Blue Cross and Blue Shield of Ohio, the state's largest insurer, with annual revenues of some $2 billion, agreed to sell 85 percent ownership to Columbia for $299.5 million through a complex venture called BlueCo, legally crafted to avoid the form of a conversion, thus eliminating a payout obligation to policyholders or a charitable foundation. Because $223 million of Blue Cross and Blue Shield reserves would go to the new venture, Columbia/HCA would be buying Blue Cross and Blue Shield largely with the latter's own assets. . . . Under the proposed acquisition, Columbia/HCA will pay three top executives of Ohio Blue Cross and Blue Shield over $15 million in severance payments characterized as consulting fees and agreements not to compete, with millions more going as a consulting fee to the Blues' outside lawyer. . . .

[T]he big nonprofits are now in many ways defensively emulating Columbia/ HCA and other for-profits. . . . A market culture and market idiom are becoming pervasive, even among nonprofits. Within living memory, service areas were not called markets; heads of hospitals were administrators, not chief executive officers; hospitals did not advertise for patients; and few hospital administrators spoke of market share, let alone EBITDA (earnings before interest, taxes, depreciation, and amortization). All this has changed, perhaps irrevocably. . . .

[A year after this was written, Richard Scott was ousted by Columbia/HCA's board of directors, in part because the company's image had become so tarnished by his management style. This occurred amid a sweeping federal probe of billing practices at several of Columbia's hospitals, and was followed by criminal fraud indictments against several of Columbia's managers. The company has since dropped Columbia from its name and returned to HCA, for Hospital Corporation of America. It is still the largest hospital chain in the country. See Symposium, 17(2) Health Aff. 1 (Mar./Apr. 1998).]

Notes: Charitable Trust Law; Public and Religious Hospitals; For-Profit Conversions

1. *Queen of Angels* succinctly applies three distinct doctrines of nonprofit and charitable trust law: (1) *ultra vires* or charitable purpose; (2) duty of care or the business judgment rule; and (3) duty of loyalty and conflict of interest. These notes will explore each in turn. The leading authority on this area of law is Michael W. Peregrine. See his series of articles in the Journal of Health Law (formerly, Health and Hospital Law), and his treatise with James R. Schwartz, The Application of Nonprofit Corporation Law to Healthcare Organizations (2002). See also

Evelyn Brody, The Limits of Charity Fiduciary Law, 57 Md. L. Rev. 1401 (1998); Scott M. Himes, The Collision of Healthcare and Corpoate Law in a Hospital Closure Case, 34 J. Health L. 335 (2001); Naomi Ono, Boards of Directors under Fire: An Examination of Nonprofit Board Duties in the Health Care Environment, 7 Ann. Health L. 107 (1998); Dana Reiser, Decision-Makers Without Duties: Defining the Duties of Parent Corporations Acting as Sole Corporate Members in Nonprofit Health Care Systems, 55 Rutgers L. Rev. 979 (2001); Developments, Nonprofit Corporations, 105 Harv. L. Rev. 1578 (1992).

2. *Ultra vires* ("beyond its powers") is the term sometimes used to describe the court's first holding. How would you revise the articles of incorporation to avoid this holding? Where bylaws are worded differently, courts are usually not nearly such sticklers about modifying corporate purposes, as long as the new purpose still pursues the same general charitable aims. See, e.g., Attorney General v. Hahnemann Hospital, 494 N.E.2d 1011 (Mass. 1986) (allowing hospital to devote proceeds of its sale to other health care institutions but not to "any activity that promotes the health of the general public" such as research or education). Restrictions can be even more stringent than in *Queen of Angels*, however, if the hospital has received gifts with specific strings attached. Especially troubling are gifts limited to a particular facility's location or ownership, not just to the facility type. One commentator explains:

> Unrestricted gifts received by a charitable corporation must be used for a purpose for which the charitable corporation exists generally; gifts which have certain terms or conditions attached must be used in accordance with such specifications. These restrictions can be extraordinarily burdensome to the sale or lease of an entire facility, particularly since the facility might be constructed with gifts from thousands of individual donors. As an example, Professor Bloche [infra] recounts the difficulty faced by Creighton University when it sold its primary teaching hospital to American Medical International. . . . The University had to consider whether the sale of the hospital was consistent with [a] single [restricted] gift, even though it constituted only a tiny fraction of the hospital's original construction costs.

Jeffrey Heidt, Conversion of Status and Facility Closure, in Health Care Corporate Law: Facilities and Transactions (M. Hall & W. Brewbaker eds., 1996).

3. *Public and Religious Hospitals.* Public hospitals, those owned by government and chartered by statute, are subject to similar limitations on their powers, depending on how their corporate purposes are stated in the governing statutes. See, e.g., New York City Council v. Giuliani, 93 N.Y.2d 60 (1999) (public hospital not authorized to enter long-term sublease agreement); Baird v. Charleston County, 511 S.E.2d 69 (S.C. 1999) (finding a variety of charitable trust and municipal law problems in a proposal for a county to issue tax-exempt bonds to assist a state medical school in acquiring a nonprofit hospital). But see In re University Hospitals Authority, 953 S.W.2d 314 (Okla. 1997) (approving a state university hospital's long-term lease and management agreement with an HCA subsidiary); Taylor v. Richland Memorial Hospital, 495 S.E.2d 431 (S.C. 1998) (approving a virtual merger between a public hospital and a nonprofit hospital). See generally Phyllis E. Bernard, Privatization of Rural Public Hospitals: Implications for Access and Indigent Care, 47 Mercer L. Rev. 991 (1996).

Queen of Angels Hospital also highlights another source of restriction for corporate transactions — religious law — which is particularly important for Catholic hospitals because of the formality of Canon law. Although the court found that Canon law does not *supersede* secular law, it does *supplement* secular law in practical effect. Before undertaking a major corporate transaction, a Catholic institution must receive approval from the Holy See that it satisfies the Ethical and Religious Directives for Catholic Health Facilities. This requirement stopped another effort by the Queen of Angels board to sell its hospital. The archbishop of Los Angeles refused approval, and the state attorney general ruled that the hospital's bylaws make this decision binding on the corporation. 7 BNA Health L. Rep. 322 (1998). But see Kansas East Conference of the United Methodist Church v. Bethany Medical Center, 969 P.2d 859 (Kan. 1998) (Methodist church is not entitled to the proceeds from the sale of a hospital it helped to found). See generally Kathleen Boozang, Deciding the Fate of Religious Hospitals in the Emerging Health Care Market, 31 Hous. L. Rev. 1429 (1995); Lisa C. Ikemoto, When a Hospital Becomes Catholic, 47 Mercer L. Rev. 1087 (1996); Lawrence Singer, Realigning Catholic Health Care: Bridging Legal and Church Control in a Consolidating Market, 72 Tulane L. Rev. 159 (1997); Comment, 17 St. Louis Univ. Pub. L. Rev. 157 (1999).

4. Cy Pres. As the court briefly notes, the *ultra vires* doctrine does not require a nonprofit board to continue running a money-losing hospital until it goes bankrupt. The board is permitted to wind up operations and transfer ownership entirely to a new corporation. In such an event, another trust law doctrine, *cy pres* ("as near as possible"), determines what alternative use to make of the proceeds from the sale. *Cy pres* precedents allow considerably more flexibility in selecting alternate charitable purposes of the same general type when the original purpose is no longer possible or practical. Should a long-term lease be treated so differently than a complete sale, especially when the lease was approved by the same religious order that founded the hospital? Should courts give nonprofit hospitals greater managerial leeway today as a result of the greatly increased competition caused by the rapid infiltration of managed care? One commentator has opined in the context of teaching hospitals that "courts should give considerable weight to the argument that intensified competitive pressures in the hospital industry are 'circumstances not . . . foreseen' by a donor and [thus a gift to a medical school would be rendered] more effective in advancing teaching and research if applied to some activity other than hospital operations." M. Gregg Bloche, Corporate Takeover of Teaching Hospitals, 65 S. Cal. L. Rev. 1035 (1992).

Where circumstances justify invoking the *cy pres* doctrine, then the alternative uses for the proceeds are usually quite broad. As Heidt, supra, explains:

> Nonprofit hospitals that sell or lease their facilities will usually attempt to comply with these restrictions in one of three ways. First, they might use the proceeds to operate a different type of health care facility such as an outpatient clinic or long-term care facility. Second, the nonprofit can consider converting to a funding agency that supports other health care facilities or activities. For instance, the proceeds from the sale or lease of a teaching hospital might be used to fund medical research. Third, the proceeds might be used to support charitable activities at the very facility being sold or leased. Such activities include not only medical education

and research, but also charity care. In structuring this latter arrangement, however, care must be taken to avoid the characterization that the nonprofit is paying a rebate to the for-profit buyer by helping the buyer to reduce its bad debt.

5. *Conversions to For-Profit.* As Kuttner explains, nonprofit health care entities, including hospitals and HMOs, are increasingly converting to for-profit status by selling out to investor-owned corporations — not so much because they are losing money but because they can make more if they have better access to capital. In one of the most notable instances, Blue Cross of California created a for-profit HMO subsidiary called WellPoint Health Networks. WellPoint was a big success, and its stock became very valuable along with the early 1990s runup in stock value for other for-profit HMOs. In 1993, California Blue Cross proposed to fold itself into WellPoint, thereby giving up its nonprofit status. California regulators declared that Blue Cross had to leave $3 billion of assets behind in a nonprofit foundation to support medical research and care for the poor.

In such cases, the difficult legal issue is not only what alternative uses to make of the charitable proceeds, but also whether the buyer is paying sufficient value for the business and its assets so that the past support from donors and from tax exemption is not dissipated. The bargained-for price is often not reliable because the purchasing corporation is often not at arm's length, especially when it is simply part of an internal corporate reorganization, as in the Blue Cross example. These concerns have prompted state attorneys general to assert jurisdiction over these transactions by invoking their authority under either common law or under newly enacted statutes in many states designed to regulate (or perhaps discourage) these transactions. Also, consumer advocates have sued to enforce charitable trust principles. In some cases, converting hospitals and insurers have been required to turn over to a foundation only a relatively modest sum ($50 million to 150 million), based on the net asset value of the company. In other instances, however, such as the California Blue Cross conversion, the foundation has been given full stock ownership of the new company, which avoids the need to agree to a valuation. When the foundation divests the stock, it is usually worth many times more than the company's asset value. Which measure of value is more appropriate: the historical asset value while the company was still a nonprofit, or the new equity value created by the conversion to for-profit status? See In re Manhattan Eye, Ear & Throat Hospital, 715 N.Y.S.2d 575 (Sup. Ct. 1999) (blocking a transaction similar to that in *Queen of Angels* because the sales price failed to account for the goodwill value of the hospital's name and its value as an ongoing business).

For detailed analysis, see Bernard, supra; Bloche, supra; David Cutler, ed., The Changing Hospital Industry (2000); Joy M. Grossman & Bradley C. Strunk, Blue Plans: Playing the Blues No More, *in* Understanding Health System Change: Local Markets and National Trend 156 (Paul B. Ginsburg & Cara S. Lesse eds., 2001); John Colombo, A Proposal for an Exit Tax on Nonprofit Conversion Transactions, 23 J. Corp. L. 779 (1998); Joel Ferber & Jo Anna King, A Cure for the Blues: Resolving Nonprofit Blue Cross Conversions, 32 J. Health L. 74 (1999); David Hyman, Hospital Conversions: Fact, Fantasy, and Regulatory Follies, 23 J. Corp. L. 741 (1998); Mark Krause, "First, Do No Harm": An Analysis of the Nonprofit Hospital Sale Acts, 45 UCLA L. Rev. 503 (1997); Jill Marsteller et al., Nonprofit Conversion: Theory, Evidence and State Policy Options, 33 Health Serv.

Res. 1495 (1998); Theresa McMahon, Fair Value? The Conversion of Nonpofit
HMOs, 30 U.S.F. L. Rev. 335 (1996); Terri R. Reicher, Assuring Competent
Oversight of Hospital Conversion Transactions, 52 Baylor L. Rev. 83 (2000);
Lawrence Singer, The Conversion Conundrum: The State and Federal Response to Hospitals' Changes in Charitable Status, 23 Am. J.L. & Med. 221
(1997); Eric Tower, Directors' Duty to Obtain a Fair Price in the Conversion of
Nonprofit Hospitals, 6 Ann. Health L. 157 (1997); Note, 16 N. Ky. L. Rev. 361
(1988); Symposium, 74 Bull. N.Y. Acad. Med. Winter 175 (1997) (focusing on
Empire Blue Cross); Symposium, 16(2) Health Aff. 2 (Spring 1997) (especially
thorough coverage of the issues). Should these conversions concern us? Perhaps
the incentive that insurers and HMOs have to compromise care is much more
tolerable if we know that denying care to one patient is likely to help another
patient who is more needy. Norman Daniels, Why Saying No to Patients in the
United States Is So Hard: Cost Containment, Justice, and Provider Autonomy, 314
New Eng. J. Med. 1380 (1986). Could the nonprofit form offer this assurance?
Nonprofit insurers may not distribute earnings to owners; there is thus a greater
chance their earnings will be devoted to patient care. One indication this is true is
that the "medical loss ratio" (the amount of premium dollars devoted to medical
care rather than to overhead) is generally higher for nonprofit HMOs than for for-
profits (85 to 90 percent versus 75 to 80 percent). Also, some research studies have
found that nonprofit HMOs perform notably better than for-profits on a number of
measures of quality of care. David Himmelstein et al., Quality of Care in Investor-
Owned vs. Not-for-Profit HMOs, 282 Jama 159 (1999); Ha T. Tu & James D.
Reschovsky, Assessments of Medical Care by Enrollees in For-Profit and
Nonprofit Health Maintenance Organizations, 346 New Eng. J. Med. 1288
(2002). For-profit HMOs have also received bad press lately because of "obscene"
CEO compensation amounting to millions a year. Should these profits and com-
pensation be limited by regulation? Should they be disclosed to consumers? Based
on these concerns, Minnesota requires all HMOs to be nonprofit. For a debate on
this issue, see M. Hasan, Let's End the Nonprofit Charade, 334 New Eng. J. Med.
1055 (1996); P. Nudelman & L. Andrews, The "Value Added" of Not-for-Profit
Health Plans, 334 New Eng. J. Med. 1057 (1996). See also Robert Kuttner, Must
Good HMOs Go Bad? The Commercializations of Prepaid Group Health Care, 338
New Eng. J. Med. 1558 (1998); Steffie Woolhandler & David Himmelstein,
Extreme Risk: The New Corporate Proposition for Physicians, 325 New Eng. J.
Med. 1706 (1995).

6. *Business Judgment.* The Motherhouse pension plan was struck down as an
improper "exercise of sound business judgment," which the board members are
required to exercise as part of their fiduciary duty of care. Again, this appears to be
an especially strict application of fiduciary rules. In contrast, the business judgment rule that applies to for-profit directors is considerably more forgiving. Other
courts have rejected the stricter charitable trust scrutiny and ruled that the same
leniency should be given to nonprofit as to for-profit directors, considering that
they often serve for free and they increasingly are functioning in a more commercial business climate that requires broader business discretion. The leading case
to this effect was decided in relation to another hospital, one whose board members were sued for investing its funds in low-interest accounts at banks affiliated
with board members. Stern v. Lucy Webb Hayes National Training School for

Deaconesses & Missionaries, 381 F. Supp. 1003 (D.D.C. 1974) (holding, despite the more lenient scrutiny, that fiduciary duties were violated by the conflict of interest). This liberalized business judgment rule is adopted by the Revised Model Nonprofit Corporation Act §8.30. See generally Michael Peregrine, Doing "Big Deals" and the Board's Duty of Care, 28 J. Health & Hosp. L. 327 (1995); Peregrine, supra, at 29 J. Health & Hosp. L. 211 (1996); Michael Peregrine & James Schwartz, The Business Judgment Rule and Other Protections for the Conduct of Not-for-Profit Directors, 33 J. Health L. 455 (2000); Mary O'Byrne, Directors' Duty of Care to Monitor Information Systems in HMOs: Some Lessons from the Oxford Health Plan, 14 J.L. & Health 45 (2000).

7. *Conflicts of Interest.* Brandlin, the Queen of Angels lawyer, ran a serious risk of violating his duty of loyalty because of the conflict of interest between his board position and his own law practice and entrepreneurship. He was saved by full disclosure and because his terms were reasonable. But for that, the transaction might have been declared void and Brandlin held liable for damages to the corporation. In Boston Children's Heart Foundation v. Nadal-Ginard, 73 F.3d 429 (1st Cir. 1996), the court upheld a $6.5 million award against a physician board member and employee who failed to disclose he was being paid to work for a competing hospital and research center at the same time. A California jury awarded over $12 million against two physicians who developed various health care ventures directly across the street from the hospital on whose board they sat. 23 Health L. Dig., No. 11, at 67 (1995).

Is it appropriate for existing board members and top management to participate in the profits realized by a conversion to for-profit status? This might occur if they take an ownership position in the new for-profit corporation, or if they are given stock as part of a severance bonus. Although the initial ownership share or severance bonus might be valued only modestly, when the for-profit decides to "go public" (sell shares in the stock market), the initial directors and managers might find themselves suddenly wealthy, as happened with Blue Cross of California and with many other recent hospital and HMO conversions like those described by Kuttner. See also McMahon, supra. The usual remedy for a conflict of interest is disclosure and ratification by the board, but this does not work where most or all of the board is subject to the same conflict. As a result, a state court may be asked to evaluate the fairness of the transaction to the nonprofit entity under common law principles of fiduciary responsibility. Also, these transactions raise dangerous red flags of "private inurement" under principles of tax exemption discussed below. See Stephen J. Weiser, Sale of a Tax Exempt Hospital to a For-Profit Corporation: Federal Tax Issues, 25 J. Health & Hosp. L. 129 (1992).

Problem: For-Profit Joint Venture

To seek shelter from the competitive storm, Marcus Welby Hospital (MWH) is considering forming a joint venture with an existing for-profit HMO. MWH would be given 30 percent ownership of the privately held HMO, and each of its five board of trustee members would be given 1 percent ownership, in exchange for MWH contributing $10 million in capital funds, which is 35 percent of the HMO's appraised net worth. Since the HMO already owns its own nursing home,

MWH will raise the capital by selling its nursing home. MWH will receive 30 percent of whatever profit distributions the HMO board chooses to make from time to time and the trustees will receive their 1 percent shares. MWH also hopes to increase its patient base for hospital admissions and to secure a better bargaining position for reimbursements from the HMO, but the HMO is making no promises about where its subscribers will be sent for hospital care, nor how it will pay MWH for hospital services to its subscribers.

Assume that MWH has articles of incorporation similar to Queen of Angels', only covering nursing home as well as hospital services, and that it has received only general, unrestricted gifts from donors. Also, assume there is no other management or personal connection between MWH and the HMO. What issues would you want to alert the hospital board to concerning whether this is a permissible venture and how the HMO can use its capital funds? Would these parties be advised to have the HMO pledge some portion of its revenues to pay for charity care services at MWH?

2. Charitable Tax Exemption

This section explores the fundamental justification for classifying various medical institutions as charitable for purposes of tax exemption. The question you should ask yourself is how nonprofit hospitals differ from their for-profit counterparts, and whether those characteristics also allow others in the health care sector to qualify for exemption. These readings then explain the detailed organizational and operational constraints that must be met in order to maintain charitable status.

■ EASTERN KENTUCKY WELFARE RIGHTS ORGANIZATION v. SIMON
506 F.2d 1278 (D.C. Cir. 1974)

JAMESON, Senior District Judge:

. . . Sections 501(a) and (c)(3) of the Internal Revenue Code of 1954 exempt from federal income tax: "(3) Corporations, and any community chest, fund, religious, or foundation, organized and operated exclusively for charitable . . . purposes, . . . no part of the net earnings of which inures to the benefit of any private shareholder or individual." . . . Other related sections of the Code provide that contributions to such tax exempt charitable organizations are deductible for purposes of computing federal income tax and estate and gift taxes.

Hospitals and other health organizations have never been expressly categorized as tax exempt organizations and have achieved that status only by qualifying as "charitable" organizations under the Code. Long established Internal Revenue Service (I.R.S.) policy held that hospitals qualified as charitable organizations under §501(c)(3) only if they provided free or below cost service to those unable to pay. This policy was articulated in Revenue Ruling 56-185, which held that a hospital could qualify for tax exempt status only if it was "operated to the extent of its financial ability for those not able to pay for the services rendered and not exclusively for those who are able and expected to pay."[2]

The I.R.S. modified this position in 1969 with the issuance of Revenue Ruling 69-545. The new ruling broadly defines "charitable" in terms of community benefit and holds that the promotion of health constitutes a "charitable purpose" in the "generally accepted legal sense of that term" and within the meaning of §501(c)(3) of the Code. According to the ruling, "The promotion of health . . . is one of the purposes in the general law of charity that is deemed beneficial to the community as a whole even though the class of beneficiaries eligible to receive a direct benefit from its activities does not include all members of the community, such as indigent members of the community." . . .

Based on this community benefit concept, a nonprofit hospital can qualify as a charitable organization under §501(c)(3) "by operating an emergency room open to all persons and by providing hospital care for all those persons in the community able to pay the cost thereof either directly or through third party reimbursement . . ." (e.g. private health insurance, Medicare, or Medicaid). Thus, for a hospital to qualify as a tax exempt organization, the provision of free or below cost service to those unable to pay is no longer essential.

Alleging harm from this new ruling, the plaintiffs-appellees, a group of health and welfare organizations and indigent persons, brought this action seeking to declare Revenue Ruling 69-545 invalid and to enjoin its implementation. They submitted affidavits recounting incidents in various parts of the country involving the denial of hospital services to indigents by institutions enjoying tax exempt status as "charitable" organizations. . . .

We conclude that Revenue Ruling 69-545 is not inconsistent with 26 U.S.C. §501(c)(3) and that the modification of the prior ruling was authorized. The definition of the term *charitable* has never been static and has been broadened in recent years. . . . In promulgating Revenue Ruling 69-545, the Commissioner [relied] on an analogy to the law of charitable trusts. [T]he Commissioner cited both the Restatement (Second) of Trusts, §368 and §372,[16] and IV Scott on Trusts (3rd ed. 1967) §368 and §372 in holding that the promotion of health is a charitable purpose within the meaning of §501(c)(3).

The term *charitable* is thus capable of a definition far broader than merely the relief of the poor. The law of charitable trusts supports the broader concept. . . . While it is true that in the past Congress and the federal courts have conditioned a hospital's charitable status on the level of free or below cost care that it provided for indigents, there is no authority for the conclusion that the determination of "charitable" status was always to be so limited. Such an inflexible

---

[2] Other pertinent parts of Revenue Ruling 56-185 state: "It is normal for hospitals to charge those able to pay for services rendered in order to meet the operating expenses of the institution without denying medical care or treatment to others unable to pay. . . . It may furnish services at reduced rates which are below cost, and thereby render charity in that manner. . . . It must not, however, refuse to accept patients in need of hospital care who cannot pay for such services."

[16] The Restatement (Second) of Trusts §368 (1959) states: "Charitable purposes include: (a) the relief of poverty; (b) the advancement of education; (c) the advancement of religion; (d) the promotion of health; (e) governmental or municipal purposes; (f) other purposes the accomplishment of which is beneficial to the community."

construction fails to recognize the changing economic, social and technological precepts and values of contemporary society.

In the field of health care, the changes have been dramatic. Hospitals in the early part of this nation's history were almshouses supported by philanthropy and serving almost exclusively the sick poor. Today, hospitals are the primary community health facility for both rich and poor. Philanthropy accounts for only a minute percentage of the hospital's total operating costs. Those costs have soared in recent years as constant modernization of equipment and facilities is necessitated by the advances in medical science and technology. The institution of Medicare and Medicaid in the last decade combined with the rapid growth of medical and hospital insurance has greatly reduced the number of poor people requiring free or below cost hospital services. Much of that decrease has been realized since the promulgation of Revenue Ruling 56-185. Moreover, increasingly counties and other political subdivisions are providing nonemergency hospitalization and medical care for those unable to pay. Thus, it appears that the rationale upon which the limited definition of "charitable" was predicated has largely disappeared. To continue to base the "charitable" status of a hospital strictly on the relief it provides for the poor fails to account for these major changes in the area of health care. . . .

It is important to note also that Revenue Ruling 69-545 . . . entails the operation of an emergency room open to all regardless of their ability to pay and providing hospital services to those able to pay the cost either directly or through third party reimbursement. Thus, to qualify as a tax exempt charitable organization, a hospital must still provide services to indigents.

The required provision of emergency room services is of great import to the indigent. Emergency room service is often the only means of access that the poor have to medical care. Furthermore, the fact that hospitals seeking to qualify as charities pursuant to Revenue Ruling 69-545 must accept Medicare and Medicaid patients is also significant. A large percentage of the indigent populace of the nation is now covered by either Medicare or Medicaid. In the final analysis, Revenue Ruling 69-545 may be of greater benefit to the poor than its predecessor Ruling 56-185. . . .

[On appeal, the Supreme Court dismissed this case for lack of standing under the reasoning that, even if the plaintiffs won, they may not be any better off since nonprofit hospitals would be free to relinquish their charitable status rather than agreeing to treat more indigent patients. Eastern Kentucky Welfare Rights Organization v. Simon, 426 U.S. 26 (1976).]

▪ UTAH COUNTY v. INTERMOUNTAIN HEALTH CARE, INC.
709 P.2d 265 (Utah 1985)

DURHAM, Justice.

[This case arose when the the Utah County Board of Equalization revoked the property tax exemption for several hospitals owned or operated by Intermountain Health Care (IHC).] IHC's policy with respect to all of its hospitals is to make charges to patients for hospital services whenever it is possible to do so. Hospital charges are paid either by patients, by private insurance companies such as Blue Cross and Blue Shield, or by governmental programs such as Medicare and Medicaid. IHC and its individual hospitals also are the recipients of private bequests, endowments, and contributions in amounts not established in the record.

. . . [T]he charitable exemption granted by article XIII, §2 of the Utah Constitution (1895, amended 1982), . . . provides in pertinent part: "[P]roperty . . . used exclusively for either religious worship or charitable purposes, . . . shall be exempt from taxation. . . ." These exemptions confer an indirect subsidy and are usually justified . . . not only because charitable entities relieve government of a burden, but also because their activities enhance beneficial community values or goals. Under this theory, the benefits received by the community are believed to offset the revenue lost by reason of the exemption. . . . Essential to this definition is the element of gift to the community. . . . A gift to the community can be identified either by a substantial imbalance in the exchange between the charity and the recipient of its services or in the lessening of a government burden through the charity's operation. . . .

Because the "care of the sick" has traditionally been an activity regarded as charitable in American law, and because the dissenting opinions rely upon decisions from other jurisdictions that in turn incorporate unexamined assumptions about the fundamental nature of hospital-based medical care, we deem it important to scrutinize the contemporary social and economic context of such care. We are convinced that traditional assumptions bear little relationship to the economics of the medical-industrial complex of the 1980s. Nonprofit hospitals were traditionally treated as tax-exempt charitable institutions because, until late in the nineteenth century, they were true charities providing custodial care for those who were both sick and poor. The hospitals' income was derived largely or entirely from voluntary charitable donations, not government subsidies, taxes, or patient fees.[7] The function and status of hospitals began to change in the late nineteenth century; the transformation was substantially completed by the 1920s. "From charities, dependent on voluntary gifts, [hospitals] developed into market institutions financed increasingly out of payments from patients." The transformation was multidimensional: Hospitals were redefined from social welfare to medical treatment institutions; their charitable foundation was replaced by a business basis; and their orientation shifted to "professionals, and their patients," away from "patrons and the poor." . . .

Also of considerable significance to our review is the increasing irrelevance of the distinction between nonprofit and for-profit hospitals for purposes of discovering the element of charity in their operations. The literature indicates that two models, described below, appear to describe a large number of nonprofit hospitals as they function today. (1) The "physicians' cooperative" model describes nonprofit hospitals that operate primarily for the benefit of the participating physicians.

---

[7] Paul Starr, The Social Transformation of American Medicine at 150 (1982). "Voluntary" hospitals, like public hospitals (which evolved from almshouses for the dependent poor), performed a "welfare" function rather than a medical or curing function: The poor were housed in large wards, largely cared for themselves, and often were not expected to recover. See id. at 145, 149, 160. Early voluntary hospitals had paternalistic, communal social structures in which patients entered at the sufferance of their benefactors, "had the moral status of children," and received more moralistic and religious help than medical treatment. Id. at 149, 158.

Physicians, pursuant to this model, enjoy power and high income through their direct or indirect control over the nonprofit hospitals to which they bring their patients. The nonprofit form is believed to facilitate the control by physicians better than the for-profit form. Pauly & Redisch, The Not-For-Profit Hospital as a Physicians' Co-operative, 63 Am. Econ. Rev. 87, 88-89 (1973). This model has also been called the "exploitation hypothesis" because the physician "income maximizing" system is hidden behind the nonprofit facade of the hospital. Clark, Does the Nonprofit Form Fit the Hospital Industry?, 93 Harv. L. Rev. 1416, 1436-1437 (1980). . . . (2) The "polycorporate enterprise" model describes the increasing number of nonprofit hospital chains. Here, power is largely in the hands of administrators, not physicians. Through the creation of holding companies, nonprofit hospitals have grown into large groups of medical enterprises, containing both for-profit and nonprofit corporate entities. Nonprofit corporations can own for-profit corporations without losing their federal nonprofit tax status as long as the profits of the for-profit corporations are used to further the nonprofit purposes of the parent organization. . . . The emergence of hospital organizations with both for-profit and nonprofit components has increasingly destroyed the charitable pretentions of nonprofit organizations: "The extension of the voluntary hospital into profit-making businesses and the penetration of other corporations into the hospital signal the breakdown of the traditional boundaries of voluntarism. Increasingly, the polycorporate hospitals are likely to become multihospital systems and competitors with profit-making chains, HMO's and other health care corporations." Starr, supra note 7, at 438.

The foregoing discussion of the economic environment in which modern hospitals function is critical to our analysis in this case because it is an analysis which is generally not present in any of the cases relied upon by the dissenting opinions. Those cases, in our view, do not take into account the revolution in health care that has transformed a "healing profession" into an enormous and complex industry, employing millions of people and accounting for a substantial proportion of our gross national product. . . .

[W]e now examine the record respecting the two hospitals ("the defendants") whose eligibility has been challenged by Utah County. . . . [The hospitals provided only negligible free care and that their charges were no lower than comparable hospitals. They also received relatively few donations. The hospitals had a policy of billing all patients and collecting from those who are reasonably able to pay, but they claimed to have a policy of never refusing care solely based on lack of funds. On the other hand, they did not advertise the availability of free care out of fear of a "deluge of people" trying to take advantage of it. Instead, every effort was made to recover payment for services rendered, and there were two documented instances of turning patients away from the emergency room who were unable to pay.]

The defendants argue that the great expense of modern hospital care and the universal availability of insurance and government health care subsidies make the idea of a hospital solely supported by philanthropy an anachronism. We believe this argument itself exposes the weakness in the defendants' position. It is precisely because such a vast system of third-party payers has developed to meet the expense of modern hospital care that the historical distinction between for-profit and nonprofit hospitals has eroded. . . .

The dissent of Justice Stewart suggests that the fact that "ability to pay" is not a criterion for admission to IHC's facilities is dispositive of the question of "charitable purpose," regardless of the actual amount of free care provided therein. This argument overlooks the fact that for-profit institutions may well implement similar policies, either for public relations reasons or by virtue of regulations mandated by their receipt of federal- or state-funded payments. . . .

Because the vast majority of their services are paid for, the nonprofit hospitals in this case accumulate capital as do their profit-seeking counterparts. . . . A large portion of the profits of most for-profit entities is used for capital improvements and new, updated equipment, and the defendant hospitals here similarly expend their revenues in excess of operational expenses. There can be no doubt, in reviewing the references in the record by members of IHC's administrative staff, that the IHC system, as well as the two hospitals in question, has consistently generated sufficient funds in excess of operating costs to contribute to rapid and extensive growth, building, competitive employee and professional salaries and benefits, and a very sophisticated management structure. While it is true that no financial benefits or profits are available to private interests in the form of stockholder distributions or ownership advantages, the user entity in this case clearly generates substantial "profits" in the sense of income that exceeds expenses. This observation is not intended to imply that an institution must consume its assets in order to be eligible for tax exemption — the requirement of charitable giving may obviously be met before that point is reached. However, there is a serious question regarding the constitutional propriety of subsidies from Utah County taxpayers being used to give certain entities a substantial competitive edge in what is essentially a commercial marketplace. . . .

In summary, after reviewing the facts in this case in light of the factors we have identified, we believe that the defendants in this case confuse the element of gift to the community, which an entity must demonstrate in order to qualify as a charity under our Constitution, with the concept of community benefit, which any of countless private enterprises might provide. We have no quarrel with the assertion that [IHC] meet[s] great and important needs of persons within their communities for medical care. Yet this meeting of a public need by a provision of services cannot be the sole distinguishing characteristic that leads to an automatic property tax exemption. . . . Such a "usefulness" rule would have to be equally applied to for-profit hospitals and privately owned health care entities, which also provide medical services to their patients. . . . [C]onsequently we hold that the defendants have not demonstrated that their property is being used exclusively for charitable purposes under the Utah Constitution. . . .

Hall, C.J., and David Sam, District Judge, concur.

STEWART, Justice (dissenting). . . .

The court's holding is without precedent either in Utah or elsewhere in the United States. . . . The Supreme Court of Nebraska in Evangelical Lutheran Good Samaritan Society v. Gage County, 181 Neb. 831, 151 N.W.2d 446, 449 (1967), stated that hospitals operated as nonprofit institutions "are universally classed as charitable institutions." The cases which support that proposition are legion. . . .

The legal concept of charity does not require, as the majority apparently requires, that a hospital incur a deficit to qualify as a charitable institution. Charitable hospitals need not be self-liquidating. . . . More importantly, there is in fact a very substantial imbalance between the total cost of the hospital care given and the revenues of the hospital in this case, which is so apparent from the record as to be undeniable.

The basic facts are not disputed. Both hospitals render wholly free patient services in substantial amounts. In addition, they subsidize the cost of hospital services to the poor, the elderly, and workers whose hospital bills are paid only in part by worker's compensation. During the years 1978-80, [IHC] rendered wholly free services to indigents in the amount of [$240,000], and in each of those years the amount increased substantially over the preceding year. During the same period, the hospital[s] subsidized services rendered to Medicare, Medicaid, and worker's compensation patients in the amount of [$3,500,000]. . . . The majority argues that for-profit hospitals also have bad debts. That is, of course, true, but it completely evades the central point. Unlike for-profit hospitals, [IHC] has a policy against turning away indigent patients. . . .

Notes: The Basis for Health Care Tax Exemption

1. *The Benefits of Charitable Exemption.* "The voluntary [i.e., charitable nonprofit] hospital, like the government hospital, generally enjoys exemption from the federal income tax and from state and local property taxes. This has been true historically and it is true today. Any general repeal of the exemptions is most unlikely in the near future, despite the criticism of some respected authorities who see the exemptions as 'mindless subsidies' of the industry which could be carried out much more effectively in other ways. The complexities of current tax law are such, however, that even in a basically exempt industry the law impinges on many aspects of hospital operations and can be manipulated one way or another with resulting impact in hospital developments. It thus constitutes a de facto type of public regulation." A. Somers, Hospital Regulation: The Dilemma of Public Policy 38 (1969).

The requirements for maintaining tax exemption have such a strong influence because the financial stakes are so high—more than $10 billion a year according to one estimate. Hospitals own considerable real property that is subject to local property tax, and they generate a very high volume of revenues potentially subject to sales tax. Even a "nonprofit" hospital is likely to earn millions of dollars a year, which is subject to state and federal corporate income tax. Equally important, tax-exempt hospitals are eligible to use tax-exempt bond financing, which significantly lowers their capital costs. Perhaps the most obvious benefit of tax exemption—eligibility to receive tax-deductible gifts—is the least important since hospitals no longer rely substantially on donations. See Mark Hall & John Colombo, The Charitable Status of Nonprofit Hospitals: Toward a Donative Theory of Tax Exemption, 66 Wash. L. Rev. 307 (1991).

2. *The Erosion of Charity Care.* What do you think about the argument that, even if hospitals no long provide significant charity care, it should be sufficient if they simply maintain an "open door" policy by which they accept anyone who seeks care, regardless of ability to pay? Consider the role physicians play in determining whether a patient is admitted to a hospital. Suppose a hospital does not require its physicians to accept charity cases.

The *Utah County* holding continues to reflect a distinctly minority view. It has since been rejected in Medical Center Hospital v. City of Burlington, 566 A.2d 1352 (Vt. 1987) (exemption upheld despite only 1 percent free care because hospital had an "open door" policy), but partially accepted in Pennsylvania, School District v. Hamot Medical Center, 602 A.2d 407 (Pa. Commw. Ct. 1992) (hospital had become too entrepreneurial to be classified as a charity).

The IRS further liberalized its free care policy in 1983, ruling that even free emergency services are unnecessary if an emergency room isn't needed in the community or if the hospital is a specialized one that offers limited treatment (e.g., eye hospitals or cancer hospitals). Rev. Rul. 83-187.

3. *Exemption of Nonhospital Facilities.* Both the federal government and the states are more demanding of *non*hospital health care enterprises. Clinics and nursing homes are regularly denied exemption based on a low volume of free care. See, e.g., Rev. Rul. 72-124 (forbidding tax-exempt nursing homes from discharging patients whose funds run out); Highland Park Hospital v. State, 507 N.E.2d 1331 (Ill. App. Ct. 1987) (immediate care center and laboratory denied exemption); Share v. Commissioner, 363 N.W. 2d 47 (Minn. 1985) (HMO denied exemption); Sioux Valley Hospital Ass'n v. South Dakota State Board of Equalization, 513 N.W.2d 562 (S.D. 1994) (hospital-sponsored fitness center that sells memberships is not exempt); Grand Prairie Hospital Authority v. Dallas County Appraisal District, 730 S.W.2d 849 (Tex. Ct. App. 1987) (medical office building denied exemption). Similarly, the IRS refused to give charitable status to a nonprofit pharmacy, claiming that the sale of prescriptions is too "inherently commercial" to qualify under the "promotion of health" standard. Federal Pharmacy Service v. Commissioner, 625 F.2d 804 (8th Cir. 1980). Is there any reason to distinguish between the charitable status of inpatient versus outpatient health care services, hospital versus other institutional services, or surgery versus medication?

Both states and the federal government are also distinctly hostile toward extending the charitable exemption to physician groups. Under the modern rationale for hospital exemption, is there any justification for this distinction either? See John Colombo, Are Associations of Doctors Tax Exempt? Analyzing Inconsistencies in the Tax Exemption of Health Care Providers, 9 Va. Tax Rev. 469 (1990); Kenneth Levine, Obtaining 501(c)(3) Status for Professional Medical Corporations, 2 DePaul J. Health Care L. 231 (1998). The IRS's position is that physicians would personally benefit too much if their professional corporations were exempt, in violation of the private inurement and private benefit prohibitions discussed in the following readings. Reluctantly, the IRS is willing, however, to exempt medical school faculty groups and very large and prestigious physician groups such as the Mayo Clinic that run a hospital, conduct medical research, and set physician salaries through a somewhat independent governance process. See D. Bromberg, The Tax-Exempt Clinic, 8 Exempt Org. Tax Rev. 557 (1993).

4. *Unrelated Business Income.* A related concern is whether various activities of hospitals generate "unrelated business income." This is income from activities that are not connected with the hospital's exempt functions. The consequence of earning such income is not nearly so severe as finding private inurement. Usually, this merely results in an "unrelated business income tax" (UBIT) imposed only on that designated portion of income. IRC §§511-513. However, if unrelated income

constitutes a "substantial portion" of the hospital's total operations, it can threaten the entire exemption. See, e.g., GCM 39684 (Sept. 28, 1984) (hospital subsidiary that provided purchasing and data processing services to nonexempt hospitals lost exemption because of "substantial, nonexempt commercial purpose").

The major decision applying the unrelated business income tax to hospital operations is Carle Foundation v. United States, 611 F.2d 1192 (7th Cir. 1980). It sets forth the general rule that income from nonhospital patients is unrelated to the institution's exempt function. Thus, for instance, a nonprofit hospital's pharmacy sales to outpatients are taxable, even if sold to patients of physicians on the medical staff with offices in the hospital's own building, because these are not hospital patients. The service exempts pharmacy and laboratory sales to nonpatients only in "unique circumstances" where the hospital is the only available source for the service to nonhospital patients. Rev. Rul. 85-110. See also Hi-Plains Hospital v. United States, 670 F.2d 528 (5th Cir. 1982) (laboratory services for physicians' private patients produce related income if the services are necessary to attract doctors to underserved rural area). Why is it necessary to define the hospital's exempt function so narrowly? Why not conceive of the hospital's purpose as providing health care services generally to the community at large? This seems to be another example of the IRS's antagonism toward physicians benefiting from the exemption.

5. *Gift Shop and Parking Receipts.* The statute (IRC §513(a)) excludes from its definition of "unrelated trade or business" that which is "carried on . . . by the organization primarily for the convenience of its . . . members, patients, or employees." Thus, for instance, it might be argued that sales by hospital gift shops and cafeterias, and receipts by the hospital parking garage, are not taxable because of their convenience function. The IRS peculiarly has refrained from this straightforward reasoning and instead has held such receipts not taxable under a much more strained rationale: They are directly related to the hospital's exempt function (and therefore need not fall within the convenience exception) because gift shop and cafeteria sales encourage doctors to remain on the premises during their breaks so that they are more available for emergency calls, and parking lots serve the therapeutic function of encouraging visitors. Rev. Ruls. 69-463 (revenue from medical office building); 69-267 (gift shops); 69-268 (cafeteria); 69-269 (parking lot).

Could the exception for "conveniece to members" be used to undermine the holding of *Carle Foundation* by arguing that pharmacy sales to outpatients is for the convenience of the "members" of the hospital's medical staff? St. Luke's Hospital v. United States, 494 F. Supp. 85, 92-93) (W.D. Mo. 1980) (yes). The Service has refused to accept this view, however, reasoning that in the context of nonprofit institutions, "members" has a different meaning. Rev. Rul. 85-109.

For further discussion of these issues, see Comment, 19, Loy. U. L.J. 1318 (1988).

6. *Bibliography.* For analysis and critique of the federal position on hospital tax exemption, see N. Crimm, Evolutionary Forces: Changes in For-profit and Not-for-profit Health Care Delivery Structures, 37 B.C. L. Rev. 1 (1995); Hall & Colombo, supra; David Hyman, The Conundrum of Charitability: Reassessing Tax Exemption for Hospitals, 16 Am. J.L. & Med. 327 (1988); Alice Noble et al., Charitable Hospital Accountability: A Review and Analysis of Legal and Policy

Initiatives, 26 J.L. Med. Ethics 116 (1998). See generally Bromberg, The Charitable Hospital, 20 Catholic U. L. Rev. 237 (1970); Comment, 49 Vand. L. Rev. 161 (1995). The following books cover health care tax exemption generally under both federal and state law: T. Hyatt & B. Hopkins, The Law of Tax-Exempt Healthcare Organizations (1995); Douglas Mancino, Taxation of Hospitals and Health Care Organizations (2000). Federal tax law is further discussed in the sources cited throughout these notes. A very good general treatise is F. Hill & D. Mancino, Taxation of Exempt Organizations (2002). The best practitioner journal is the *Exempt Organization Tax Review.*

7. *Measuring Charity Care.* A few states have enacted laws requiring tax-exempt hospitals to document that the value of their charity care and other community benefits exceed either some set percent of operations or exceed the value of their tax exemption. E.g., Texas Health & Safety Code §411.045 (hospital must give back to community the value of its exemption or 4 to 5 percent of revenues). Federal bills that would do the same have not advanced in Congress.

Professor Bloche argues that a charity care requirement is "deeply problematic" because it requires hospitals to fund the care for some patients by increasing charges to others. This "cost shifting" can be seen as an implicit form of "internal" taxation that is highly objectionable compared with a broad-based income tax: It is essentially a hidden tax on the sick that does a poor job of targeting resources to where they are most needed—preventive and primary care. M. Gregg Bloche, Health Policy below the Waterline: Medical Care and the Charitable Exemption, 80 Minn. L. Rev. 299 (1995). True enough, tax exemption is not a good substitute for national health insurance, but do these imperfections justify excusing hospitals from any concrete obligation in exchange for the exemption?

Where states impose a charity care standard, they must next decide how to measure the amount and value of unreimbursed services. Hospitals attempt to measure this value in terms of their listed charges rather than actual costs, but these list prices are rarely charged in full to insurance companies. Sometimes, hospitals even try to count as free care these voluntary "contractual adjustments" with paying customers. See St. Margaret Seneca Pl. v. Board of Property Assessment, 640 A.2d 380 (Pa. 1994) (accepting this argument with respect to Medicaid payments to nursing home, but only to extent that payments were less than average costs). Should hospitals be allowed to count their "bad debts," i.e., uncollectable accounts? For-profit hospitals argue that writing off bad debts is an ordinary rational business decision based on the costs of attempting to collect them. In contrast, "pure" charity care is given to patients who the hospital accepts at the outset of treatment knowing that they cannot pay in full. See generally Nancy M. Kane & William Wubbenhorst, Alternative Funding Policies for the Uninsured: Exploring the Value of Hospital Tax Exemption, 78 Milbank Q. 185 (2000).

8. *The Nonprofit Ethos.* Hospitals argue that the "community benefit" justification for exemption captured in the 1969 revenue ruling is warranted because nonprofit hospitals are inherently superior to their for-profit counterparts. The debate between the two hospital sectors has raged for almost a generation, ever since large corporate chains began to acquire significant numbers of for-profit hospitals in the late 1970s. The seminal article is A. Relman, The New Medical-Industrial Complex, 303 N. Eng. J. Med. 963 (1980). See also P. Starr, The Social Transformation of American Medicine ch. 5 (1982). Nonprofit advocates claim

that it is wrong to profit from people's medical misfortunes. Economists respond that the profit incentive is not inherently evil and may produce better service because it reacts more quickly and efficiently to consumer demands. Health policy researchers have produced an extensive body of empirical findings that fail to reveal any major differences in the cost or quality of care delivered by nonprofits and for-profits. J. Hollingsworth & E. Hollingsworth, Controversy About American Hospitals: Funding, Ownership and Performance (1987); Institute of Medicine, For-Profit Enterprise in Health Care (B. Gray ed., 1986); Jill Marsteller et al., Nonprofit Conversion: Theory, Evidence and State Policy Options, 33 Health Serv. Res. 1495 (1998). Others, however, point to notable instances where profit motivation has run amok, such as Columbia/HCA, described at page 394. The following exchange gives a glimpse of the highly charged nature of this debate:

> Nonprofit hospitals . . . receive billions of dollars annually in subsidies from the rest of us taxpayers through various tax exemptions. Our research showed that nonprofit hospital chains did not provide benefits to society that justified this multibillion dollar gift. When compared with for-profits, the nonprofit hospital chains had the same prices and the same level of access for patients with no or low levels of health insurance. Moreover, they had higher costs, more employees, less efficient use of beds, and much older capital than for-profits. The net result was that the nonprofits performed less and cost much more — billions of dollars more!

Regina Herzlinger, An Author Replies, 65 Harv. Bus. Rev., March-April 1987, at 135, replying in support of Regina Herzlinger & William Krasker, Who Profits from Nonprofits?, 65 Harv. Bus. Rev., Jan-Feb. 1987, at 93 (nonprofits "do more to maximize the welfare of the physicians who are their main consumers"). Uwe Reinhardt, a leading health economist, responds: "[T]his study is a truly shoddy statistical analysis. . . . The author's bias for privatization screams out from every page of the study. I'm concerned by the apparent attempt to propagate personal bias in the guise of science." N.Y. Times, Apr. 2, 1987, at 32, col. 3. Another round of this ongoing debate can be found in the Spring 1996 issue of *Frontiers of Health Services Management.*

Absent any evidence that a systemic, material difference exists between the two hospital sectors, this debate turns to intangibles such as whether nonprofits promote a superior institutional ethos because they are devoted primarily to healing, not to generating profits. See David Seay & Bruce Vladeck, Mission Matters, *in* In Sickness and in Health: The Mission of Voluntary Health Care Institutions (1988). The danger of accepting this justification on faith is that even defenders of the exemption concede that "self-satisfaction and self-righteousness . . . is perhaps an occupational hazard" among nonprofit hospital administrators, who tend to "have an almost reflexive belief in the inherent superiority of voluntary health care." Id. at 4-5. Skeptics observe that hospital administrators respond more to where the money comes from than to abstract mission statements in corporate documents. At one time, nonprofits received substantial funding from donations, but now they rely almost entirely on public and private insurance, as well as borrowed capital. Because the sources of financing for both types of hospitals are nearly identical, many observers conclude that their administrative style and institutional ideology are virtually indistinguishable. Defenders of the community benefit standard respond by pointing to counter-examples such as Columbia/HCA, discussed at page 394. They also encourage nonprofit hospitals to document their community responsiveness and social accountability by cataloguing their various public-spirited programs and activities, such as health education, free screenings, and other good works. Several states now require nonprofit hospitals to conduct these community benefit assessments and file annual reports. For-profits respond, however, that these are merely devices to create good will among potential customers, much like their own marketing activities. And so the debate continues.

9. *HMO Exemption.* Equally controversial is whether HMOs qualify for charitable tax exemption. The materials above cite state court opinions on either side of the question. Federal tax policy is somewhat confusing. The IRS requires tax-exempt HMOs to offer open enrollment and community rating, discounted fees for low-income subscribers, and support for research and education. For a time, it was thought that these attributes were sufficient for all HMOs, based on a Tax Court decision, Sound Health Ass'n v. Commissioner, 71 T.C. 158 (1978), but a subsequent court decision drew a different line. In Geisinger Health Plan v. Commissioner, 985 F.2d 1210 (3d Cir. 1993), the court found that these factors were not sufficient for an HMO that it incorrectly classified as an IPA. (It was actually a group or network model, one that resembles a staff model except that it contracts with full-time physicians rather than employs them.) The court's major concern was that contracting for, rather than directly providing, medical services is not a charitable purpose, even though the contracting parties were part of a hospital system each of whose other components is tax exempt.[4] Does this make sense to you? It is an apparent attempt to draw some distinction between HMOs that are more like hospitals, and those that are more like ordinary insurance. Nonprofit health insurers like Blue Cross lost their exemption by virtue of a 1986 statutory enactment, §501(m). To preserve some meaningful distinction between Blue Cross and HMOs, the HMO exemption appears limited to staff model HMOs like Kaiser, which employ physicians and own their own hospitals. This position was reiterated by the IRS, and affirmed by the Tax Court, in a case involving HMOs owned by the very same hospital company in the *Utah County* case, supra at page 403 (Intermountain Health Care). Even though the hospital retains its charitable status under federal law, the IRS revoked the exemption for its HMOs, following *Geisinger*, because the HMO it owns does not operate its own medical facilities. IHC Health Plans Inc. v. Commissioner, T.C. Memo 2001-246 (2001). Commenting on this decision, Prof. Colombo says: "What the heck is going on here? . . . The only answer I have been able to come up with is that sometime after issuing Rev. Rul. 69-545, folks at the Service realized that there were an awful lot of businesses that 'promote health' in this country by providing services or goods at a fee to anyone who can pay. . . . But instead of simply admitting that Rev. Rul. 69-545 was a well-meaning mistake and then revoking it (or limiting it to acute-care hospitals only), the Service embarked on what now is a 20-year struggle to find alternative means of limiting the scope of Rev. Rul. 69-545 while pretending that it still governs tax exemption for all health care providers. The Service's

---

[4] The court also reasoned that extending free services and discounted membership to subscribers was not the same as serving the community at large, even though membership was open to the community at large.

war on HMOs is one example of this struggle." John Colombo, The IHC Cases: A Catch-22 for Integral Part Doctrine, A Requiem for Rev. Rul. 69-545, 34 Exempt Org. Tax Rev. 401 (2001).

Are there any reasons that health policy and law might want to favor non-profit HMOs? Are the distinctions the IRS draws sensitive to these reasons? The loss of tax exemption is one reason given by many Blue Cross plans for converting to for-profit status in recent years. See page 398.

To complicate matters even further (if that's possible), HMOs can still qualify for a lesser form of charitable exemption under §501(c)(4). The major difference is that entities under this form of exemption are not eligible to receive tax-exempt donations or tax-exempt bond financing. However, nonprofit indemnity insurers like Blue Cross are not eligible for even this lesser status. Again, there is no easily discernible logic to this pattern. See generally, Loren Rosenzweig, *Geisinger*, HMO's and Health Care Reform, 72 Taxes 20 (1994); Mark Schlesinger, Bradford Gray, & Elizabeth Bradley, Charity and Community: The Role of Nonprofit Ownership in a Managed Health Care System, 21 J. Health Pol. Pol'y & L. 697 (1996); Symposium, 9 Exempt Org. Tax Rev. 271 (1994).

■ HARDING HOSPITAL, INC. v. UNITED STATES
505 F.2d 1068 (6th Cir. 1974)

PHILLIPS, Chief Judge.

The sole issue presented in this appeal is whether Harding Hospital, Inc. (the Hospital) qualified under 501(c)(3) of the Internal Revenue Code of 1954 as an organization exempt from federal income taxes. . . .

The Hospital, a nationally recognized psychiatric institution, treats mental and nervous diseases. It utilizes a method of treatment known as milieu therapy in which a patient's total environment is controlled on an around-the-clock basis and structured toward rehabilitation.

The Hospital was originally a corporation for profit. In December 1961, its articles of incorporation were amended to adopt its present name and to qualify under Ohio law as a corporation not for profit. . . . Before amending its articles of incorporation, the Hospital had a contract with a medical partnership composed of seven doctors. This medical partnership performed all the psychiatric treatment on 90 to 95 percent of the patients admitted to the Hospital. Immediately after the Hospital's change in status in 1962, the medical partnership was incorporated as the Harding-Evans Medical Associates, Inc. (the Associates).

Starting in 1962, and for the years in question, the Hospital entered into contracts with the Associates whereby the Associates provided medical supervision in the Hospital, teaching and supervision in the residency and other training programs, and medical service to the Hospital's indigent patients without a charge or at a reduced rate. For these services, the Hospital paid the Associates an annual amount of $25,000. This amount was raised to $35,000 as of July 1, 1968. Further, the agreement provided that the Associates were to pay the Hospital $1,000 per month as rental for facilities, equipment and business office services. This rental was increased to $35,000 per year as of January 1, 1965. It subsequently was lowered to $15,000 per year as of July 1, 1968, at the same time that the amount which the Hospital paid the Associates for medical supervision was increased from $25,000 to $35,000.

Since 1963, individuals not connected with the Associates have constituted a majority of the Board of Trustees of the Hospital. During the years in question, the Board consisted of nine members, only two of whom had any connection with the Associates of the Hospital prior to the 1961 reorganization.

The Harding-Evans Foundation (the Foundation) was set up in 1959 and is an entity separate from the Hospital and the Associates. The Foundation is a tax exempt organization, the principal activity of which is to provide a residency program in the field of psychiatry for the physicians. The Foundation collects charitable funds and expends them on the residency training program at the Hospital. . . .

Section 501(a) of the Code provides that the following organizations, which are listed in §501(c)(3), are exempt from federal income taxation:

> Corporations . . . organized and operated exclusively for religious, charitable, scientific, testing for public safety, literary, or educational purposes, or for the prevention of cruelty to children or animals, no part of the net earnings of which inures to the benefit of any private shareholder or individual, no substantial part of the activities of which is carrying on propaganda, or otherwise attempting, to influence legislation, and which does not participate in, or intervene in (including the publishing or distributing of statements), any political campaign on behalf of any candidate for public office.

In the context of the present case, this section essentially imposes three requirements for exemption: (1) the corporation must be organized and operated exclusively for charitable purposes; (2) no part of its net earnings may inure to the benefit of a private individual or shareholder; and (3) it cannot engage in certain lobbying and political activities. The government stipulated that the Hospital did not offend the third requirement for exemption. . . . [W]e proceed to determine if the district court was correct in holding that the Hospital "was operated almost exclusively for the benefit of the members of the . . . Associates and was not operated exclusively for charitable purposes." . . .

Based on the five factors set forth below, we hold that the Hospital was not entitled to tax exemption under §501(c)(3) during the years in question. We do not single out any one or combination of these factors as the consideration crucial to our holding. We conclude only that all these factors, as they occurred in the aggregate in this case, require denying the appellant Hospital the tax exemption for the years in question. . . .

(1) and (2) [The court observed that the hospital received virtually no charitable donations], and did not have a specific plan or policy for the treatment of charity patients during the years in question. . . . [P]ractically all patients presented themselves as paying patients and only when their funds were exhausted did the Hospital treat them on a charitable basis.

(3) Since the doctors who were members of the Associates treated between 90 and 95 percent of the patients admitted to the Hospital, they derived substantial benefit from the existence and operation of the Hospital. This was the primary source of the doctors' professional income. Although the Hospital did not pay over any of its net earnings to the Associates, except for the annual sum for supervision, this virtual monopoly by the Associates of the patients permitted benefits to inure

to the Associates within the intendment of the statute. Sonora Community Hospital, supra, 46 T.C. at 526.

(4) Associates also benefitted from the agreement with the Hospital whereby the Associates paid $35,000 annually as rental for office space, equipment, and business office services. See the fourth requirement of Rev. Rul. 56-185. The $35,000 amount was reduced to $15,000 as of July 1, 1968. . . .

The Hospital introduced the testimony of an appraiser who indicated, in sum, that the $35,000 figure was a fair rental for the office space. That essentially meant that the Associates were not adequately compensating the Hospital for the use of the equipment and business office services (including secretarial assistance). Further, when the annual rental was reduced to $15,000, the Associates were not adequately compensating the Hospital for office space alone.

(5) The Associates also received a private benefit from the agreement whereby the Hospital paid an annual sum of either $25,000 or $35,000 to the Associates for hospital supervision. . . .

On the basis of these five factors, the judgment of the district court is affirmed.

■ HOSPITAL-PHYSICIAN JOINT VENTURES
General Counsel Memorandum [GCM] 39862 (Dec. 2, 1991)

ISSUE

Whether a hospital, tax exempt because it is described in §501(c)(3), jeopardizes its exempt status by forming a joint venture with members of its medical staff and selling to the joint venture the gross or net revenue stream derived from operation of an existing hospital department or service for a defined period of time. . . .

FACTS

[The memorandum describes several hospital/physician joint ventures that all resemble the following example:] "Z-Hospital" proposed to establish a for-profit stock corporation for certain purposes that would be jointly owned in equal shares by the hospital and physicians on its medical staff. The new corporation would in turn establish and serve as the general partner in four limited partnerships (Z-LPs). The Z-LPs were to be formed to allow medical staff physician participation in the operation of four Z-Hospital outpatient departments. The four departments, Outpatient Surgery, Outpatient Diagnostic (CT Scan, Ultrasound, etc.), Ophthalmology, and Cardiac Nuclear Medicine, represented in the aggregate about 4 percent of Z-Hospital's gross revenues.

Z-Hospital stated that it would "in effect, lease the individual departments for a limited time period to the limited partnership[s]." Apparently, the Z-LPs would pay Z-Hospital an actuarially established price (discounted to present value) for the revenue stream of each of the subject departments. In addition, the Z-LPs would pay Z-Hospital a fee for managing the facilities and reimburse the hospital for all fixed and variable costs incurred in operating the departments. [In other words, the hospital would continue to own the equipment and deliver and bill for the services, but all the money would flow through the LPs. They would pay the hospital for its existing revenue stream and reimburse the hospital for actual expenses, but they would keep any remaining revenues.] Thus, according to the hospital, physician-investors would benefit only if utilization of the facilities increased because, in effect, they shared only in profits over and above the level the hospital already received.

Z-Hospital represented that it would retain, through its interest in the for-profit corporation, an interest in each Z-LP. Fifty percent of each Z-LP would be held by the corporation and 50 percent sold to medical staff physicians [for $5,000 each]. Z-Hospital also stated that it would retain actual control of the facilities through a management agreement, and that it alone would determine the rates charged patients for services in those facilities.

The stated reason for the proposed transactions was to maintain or increase utilization of Z-Hospital's various services, both inpatient and outpatient, so that it could provide the highest level of service at the lowest price to the public. Z-Hospital told the Service that, if it carried out the transactions, its utilization rate (then 65 percent) would be maintained or increased rather than experiencing a decline. At conference, Z-Hospital's chief financial officer predicted significant adverse effects if the hospital did nothing. The hospital was located in an over-bedded service area and faced competition from two nearby hospitals, one for-profit, the other nonprofit. It also faced potential competition from a private physician who was planning to develop free-standing outpatient facilities to be jointly owned with other doctors. Z-Hospital argued that failure to undertake the proposed transaction would raise a probability that it would be unable to continue providing the same high level of service to the community so, it reasoned, the transaction should be viewed as furthering its charitable purposes.

Z-Hospital maintained that the ventures would help it by creating incentives for medical staff physicians to increase inpatient admissions. The ventures would also create incentives for medical staff physicians to increase referrals to ancillary departments. These factors, combined with a feared loss of outpatient department business to competitors if the ventures were not undertaken, led the hospital to believe it would be better off by proceeding than by not doing so. . . .

ANALYSIS

The joint venture arrangements described above are just one variety of an increasingly common type of competitive behavior engaged in by hospitals in response to significant changes in their operating environment. Many medical and surgical procedures once requiring inpatient care, still the exclusive province of hospitals, now are performed on an outpatient basis, where every private physician is a potential competitor. The marked shift in governmental policy from regulatory cost controls to competition has fundamentally changed the way all hospitals, for-profit and not, do business.

A driving force behind the new hospital operating environment was the federal Medicare Program's 1983 shift from cost-based reimbursement for covered inpatient hospital services to fixed, per-case, prospective payments. This change to a diagnosis-related prospective payment system (PPS) dramatically altered hospital financial incentives. . . . Hospitals realized that, in addition to attracting more patients, they needed to control utilization of ancillary hospital services, discharge Medicare beneficiaries as quickly as is medically appropriate, and operate more efficiently. . . . Once hospital and physician economic incentives diverged, hospitals began seeking ways to stimulate loyalty among members of their medical staffs and to encourage or reward physician behaviors deemed desirable. . . . Since most medical staff physicians are not hospital employees, and typically do not provide services to or receive direct compensation from the hospitals at which they practice, managers have had to look for innovative ways to influence their behavior. . . .

Whenever a charitable organization engages in unusual financial transactions with private parties, the arrangements must be evaluated in light of applicable tax law and other legal standards. . . . We believe the transactions described above cannot withstand such scrutiny. . . . [T]hese transactions must be viewed as jeopardizing a hospital's tax exempt status for three reasons: they allow inurement of part of a charitable organization's net earnings to the benefit of private individuals; they confer more than incidental benefits on private interests; and they may well violate federal law [prohibiting referral fees. Only the first] of these reasons is discussed below. . . .

[Section 501(c)(3)] describes as charitable only an organization "no part of the net earnings of which inures to the benefit of any private shareholder or individual." . . . Violations of this prohibition are commonly referred to as private inurement, or simply, inurement.

Protecting charitable organizations against private inurement serves important purposes. A charitable organization is viewed under the common law and the Internal Revenue Code as a trust whose assets must irrevocably be dedicated to achieving charitable purposes. The inurement prohibition serves to prevent anyone in a position to do so from siphoning off any of a charity's income or assets for personal use.

The proscription against inurement generally applies to a distinct class of private interests — typically persons who, because of their particular relationship with an organization, have an opportunity to control or influence its activities. . . . While most physicians on the medical staffs of the subject hospitals presumably are not employees and do not provide any compensable services directly to the hospitals, they do have a close professional working relationship with the hospitals.[3] . . . Individually, and as a group, they largely control the flow of patients to and from the hospital and patients' utilization of hospital services while there. . . .

Even though medical staff physicians are subject to the inurement proscription, that does not mean there can be no economic dealings between them

---

[3] When considering hospital-physician relationships, the Service should be aware that many . . . "hospital based" physicians, notably radiologists, anesthesiologists, pathologists, medical residents, and some emergency room physicians typically are employees or contractors paid by the hospital. . . . Some states have laws . . . [that] restrict hospitals' ability to employ physicians to render professional services to patients. For federal employment tax purposes, however, physicians may be classified as hospital employees notwithstanding such laws.

and the hospitals. The inurement proscription does not prevent the payment of reasonable compensation for goods or services. It is aimed at preventing dividend-like distributions of charitable assets or expenditures to benefit a private interest. . . . Rev. Rul. 69-383, 1969-2 C.B. 113. In that ruling, the Service approved payment to a hospital-based radiologist of a percentage of the adjusted gross revenues from the radiology department in return for management and professional services. . . . Unlike the instant cases, the hospital in Rev. Rul. 69-383 was billing (presumably on a global charge basis) and collecting for the radiologist's professional services, as well as its own facility charge. Thus, the percentage compensation at issue represented an allocation of a portion of the global charge (referred to as the "professional component") to the physician to compensate him for his services. The hospital retained the remainder (the "technical" or "facility component") as compensation for use of its facilities and equipment. This type of arrangement was typical for pathology and radiology departments prior to the 1982 enactment of changes affecting Medicare reimbursement for hospital-based physicians. See Mancino, Nonexempt Uses of Tax-Exempt Hospital Bonds, 24 J. Health & Hospital Law 73, 79-80 (1991). Due to Medicare changes, the typical arrangement today provides for even hospital-based physicians to bill separately for their professional services, while the hospital bills separately for the technical component. Thus, while never revoked, Rev. Rul. 69-383 has little relevance to most hospital-physician relationships today, including the instant cases. In these cases, only hospital revenues derived from the technical or facility component are at issue.

Even while approving the specific arrangement in Rev. Rul. 69-383, the Service cautioned that the presence of a percentage compensation arrangement will destroy the organization's exemption where it transforms the principal activity of the organization into a joint venture between it and a group of physicians or is merely a device for distributing profits to persons in control. Also, it is equally clear that, if salaries or total compensation are not reasonable, they will result in inurement. . . . There is no de minimis exception to the inurement prohibition. . . . See also Lowry Hosp. Ass'n v. Commissioner, 66 T.C. 850 (1976) (use of hospital's funds to make substantial unsecured loans to nursing home owned by hospital's founding physician inured to his benefit). . . .

The proper starting point for our analysis of the net revenue stream arrangements is to ask what the hospital gets in return for the benefit conferred on the physician-investors. Put another way, we ask whether and how engaging in the transaction furthers the hospital's exempt purposes. Here, there appears to be little accomplished that directly furthers the hospitals' charitable purposes of promoting health. No expansion of health care resources results; no new provider is created. No improvement in treatment modalities or reduction in cost is foreseeable. We have to look very carefully for any reason why a hospital would want to engage in this sort of arrangement. . . .

Whether admitted or not, we believe the hospitals engaged in these ventures largely as a means to retain and reward members of their medical staffs; to attract their admissions and referrals; and to preempt the physicians from investing in or creating a competing provider. Even putting aside any legality issues [under Medicare fraud and abuse laws], . . . the structure of these transactions is problematic. Giving (or selling) medical staff physicians a proprietary interest in the net profits of a hospital under these circumstances creates a result that is indistinguishable from paying dividends on stock. . . . We do not mean to suggest that a §501(c)(3) hospital cannot have an appropriately structured incentive compensation plan for employees in which profits are a factor in the compensation formula. . . .

Another key principle in the law of tax exempt organizations is that an entity is not organized and operated exclusively for exempt purposes unless it serves a public rather than a private interest. Thus, in order to be exempt, an organization must establish that it is not organized or operated for the benefit of private interests such as designated individuals, the creator or his family, shareholders of the organization, or persons controlled, directly or indirectly, by such private interests. However, this private benefit prohibition applies to all kinds of persons and groups, not just to those "insiders" subject to the more strict inurement proscription. . . . Any private benefit arising from a particular activity must be "incidental" in both a qualitative and quantitative sense to the overall public benefit achieved by the activity if the organization is to remain exempt. . . . Such benefits might also be characterized as indirect or unintentional. . . .

In our view, some private benefit is present in all typical hospital-physician relationships. Physicians generally use hospital facilities at no cost to themselves to provide services to private patients for which they earn a fee. The private benefit accruing to the physicians generally can be considered incidental to the overwhelming public benefit resulting from having the combined resources of the hospital and its professional staff available to serve the public. . . . In contrast, the private benefits conferred on the physician-investors by the instant revenue stream joint ventures are direct and substantial, not incidental. . . .

Similar issues and arguments were considered in GCM 37789. There, a tax exempt hospital proposed to lease to certain members of its medical staff land adjacent to the hospital upon which the physicians would construct a medical office building. The agreement called for below market rent (99 years at one dollar per year), and the hospital also proposed to lend the physicians a portion of the construction costs on fair market terms. This Office determined that a more than incidental private benefit would flow to the physicians from the below market rental and that the hospital should lose its exemption if it entered into the transaction. . . .

Thus far, our discussion has focussed principally on the sales of the revenue streams involved in the instant arrangements. We also need to address the joint venture aspect. This area of the law has undergone significant change over the last decade. In Plumstead Theatre Soc'y, Inc. v. Commissioner, 74 T.C. 1324 (1980), aff'd, 675 F.2d 244 (9th Cir. 1982), the Tax Court disagreed with the Service's earlier stand [that opposed] charitable organization participation as a general partner in a limited partnership. . . . The Service no longer contends that participation as a general partner in a partnership is per se inconsistent with exemption. . . . However, close scrutiny is necessary to ensure that the obligations of the exempt organization as general partner do not conflict with its ability to pursue exclusively charitable goals. Thus, in all partnership cases, the initial focus should be on whether the joint venture organization furthers a charitable purpose. . . . This requires a finding that the benefits received by the limited partners are incidental to the public purposes served by the partnership. Hospital participation in a joint venture is inconsistent with exemption, then, if it does not further a charitable purpose or if there is inadequate protection against financial loss by the hospital or improper financial gain by the physician-investors. See [GCM 39005 (Dec. 17, 1982)]; GCM 39444 (July 18, 1985); GCM 39546 (Aug. 14, 1986). . . .

GCM 39732 considered three cases in which hospitals or affiliated exempt organizations participated as general partners in joint ventures with medical staff physicians to establish (1) a free-standing physical therapy center, (2) a free-standing ambulatory surgery center, and (3) a magnetic resonance imaging facility. . . . [W]e concluded that participation in the partnerships (and activities) in question furthered their exempt purposes. In each case, a new health care provider or resource was made available to the community. Also, the joint venture entity itself actually became the property owner or service provider, subject to all the attendant risks, responsibilities, and potential rewards.

In the instant cases, we have moved from joint venture ownership of property and operation of an activity typically viewed as promoting the health of the community to a shell type of arrangement where the hospital continues to own and operate the facilities in question and the joint venture invests only in a profits interest. These arrangements, despite the joint venture cloak, are merely an arrangement between an exempt hospital and its medical staff physicians through which the hospital shares its net profits from designated activities with the physicians. The partnership's only true function is to purchase, receive, and distribute the net revenue stream from the activity. A hospital's participation in this type of partnership does not clearly further any exempt purpose.

In each of the cases at issue, the hospital has stated that its reasons for participating in the joint venture were to maintain or enhance utilization of its facilities. . . . In our view, there are a fixed number of individuals in a community legitimately needing hospital services at any one time. Paying doctors to steer patients to one particular hospital merely to improve its efficiency seems distant from a mission of providing needed care. We question whether the Service should ever recognize enhancing a hospital's market share vis-à-vis other providers, in and of itself, as furthering a charitable purpose. In many cases, doing so might hamper another charitable hospital's ability to promote the health of the same community. . . .

In addition . . . the instant arrangements are distinguishable from the medical office building fact pattern in Rev. Rul. 69-464, 1969-2 C.B. 132. In that ruling, the Service recognized that leasing of office space adjacent to a hospital to members of the medical staff under the circumstances described furthers the hospital's exempt purposes by (1) increasing its efficiency, (2) encouraging fuller utilization of its facilities, and (3) improving the overall quality of its patient care. The hospital established that having members of the medical staff practicing next door would result in greater use being made of its diagnostic facilities, implying that attracting business may have been one reason for the arrangement. . . . Of course, the analysis would be completely different if, as in GCM 37789, the physicians paid below fair market rent. In the instant cases, the arrangements do not appear to result in improved patient convenience, greater accessibility of physicians, or any other direct benefit to the community. . . .

[In conclusion,] . . . participation in the subject net revenue stream purchase joint ventures is inconsistent with a hospital's continued exemption as a charitable organization. . . . Depending on the facts, revocation of the hospital's exemption might well be appropriate in such cases.

Notes: Private Inurement and Joint Ventures

1. *The Consequence of Private Inurement.* Finding private inurement can be fatal to tax exemption. Not only is the specific venture taxable, but the hospital's entire exemption can be revoked retroactive to the initiation of the venture. In the past, the "nuclear bomb" of complete revocation was the only enforcement measure the IRS could employ. The IRS is now authorized, however, to impose "intermediate sanctions" such as a fine proportionate to the size of the venture or the degree of inurement. As a consequence, IRS enforcement of compensation, joint ventures, and conflicts of interest has greatly intensified. It now issues a virtual code of conduct that nonprofit entities must comply with or pay a series of graduated penalties. See IRC §4958; Hill & Kirschten, Federal and State Taxation of Exempt Organizations ¶2.03[3][f].

2. *Private Benefit.* Observe the differences noted in the General Counsel Memoradum (GCM) between the private inurement prohibition and the requirement that charities not operate for the private benefit of any individual. The private benefit proscription does not require monetary payment, it is not limited to "insiders," but it does have a de minimis exception. *Harding Hospital* gives one prime example of private benefit: a hospital that does not open its medical staff to all physicians in the community. The other examples — below-market office space rental, and excess compensation for administrative services — might be classified as either private inurement or private benefit.

3. *Physician Recruitment.* If it is impermissible for hospitals to secure the loyalty of their *existing* medical staff members, can they devise various incentives to attract *new* staff members? Generally, the answer to that is also no, unless the hospital is in an underserved area (such as an inner city or a remote rural setting) where it is difficult to recruit physicians. Then, if the hospital can show a need for the particular physician, the IRS has approved a list of limited recruitment incentives to assist with the transitional costs of moving and setting up a new practice. Examples include income guarantees, office support, subsidized malpractice insurance, and loan guarantees. Hermann Hospital Closing Agreement, *reprinted in* 3 BNA Health L. Rep. 1519 (1994); Rev. Rul. 97-21 (1997).

4. *Whole Hospital vs. Ancillary Joint Ventures.* The gist of the GCM appears to be that joint ventures that create new facilities may be permissible, but not those that merely reallocate revenue streams from existing operations. What if a hospital were to shift its entire operation over to a for-profit entity? At first glance, it would seem to be a foregone conclusion that this is impermissible. However, careful lawyering can do wonders in this arena. Using a vehicle known as a "whole hospital" joint venture, some for-profit hospital companies like Hospital Corporation of America (HCA, which was formerly Columbia) have been able to acquire management of nonprofit hospitals without sacrificing their tax exemption. The nonprofit entity contributes all its operating assets, including the hospital, to

the joint venture, which it jointly owns, in exchange for a lump sum of money from the for-profit company. The joint venture then hires a management firm to run the hospital. In Rev. Rul. 98-15, the IRS ruled that the original nonprofit entity will retain its tax exemption if (1) it has majority control of the joint venture, (2) the agreement imposes specific operational requirements necessary to ensure that the hospital will continue meeting the community benefits test for charitable purpose, and (3) the management contract is with a firm that is unrelated to the for-profit party.

Although this ruling is permissive with respect to whole hospital joint ventures, the ruling raised concerns among hospital lawyers that some or all of its requirements will affect other, more traditional, joint ventures such as constructing a medical office building, or opening a satellite clinic. See Gerald Griffith, Revenue Ruling 98-15: Dimming the Future of All Nonprofit Joint Ventures?, 31 J. Health Hosp. L. 71 (1998). For instance, in Redlands Surgical Services v. Commissioner, 113 T.C. No. 3 (July 17, 1999), aff'd per curiam, 242 F.3d 904 (9th Cir. 2001), the Tax Court applied this ruling to deny exemption to a nonprofit entity formed by an exempt hospital to purchase an outpatient surgery center. The center was purchased through a joint venture between the exempt hospital and an unrelated for-profit company that owns surgical centers across the country. The Tax Court found the absence of a charitable purpose, and an unallowable level of private benefit, because the joint venture agreement gave complete operational control to the for-profit chain, and the surgery center provided no free care to indigents and had only a minuscule amount of Medicaid business. (The lengthy full opinion in this case is well worth reading for the detail it gives about the corporate and contractual documents and entities used to form joint ventures of this sort.)

In analyzing these situations, it is important to clarify what the main issue is. Usually, the issue is *not* whether the venture *itself* is exempt, since usually it clearly is not. Rather, it is whether the nonprofit's participation in a for-profit venture jeopardizes the nonprofit's exemption. *Redlands Surgical* is an unusual case that attempts to, but fails to, obtain exemption for the joint venture. No one suggested the joint venture might threaten the hospital parent's core exemption. As long as the joint venture is ancillary to a hospital's main activity, lawyers assume that the IRS will continue to allow an exempt hospital to put a portion of its assets at risk for legitimate purposes, even if the hospital does not retain full control of the venture's operations. See generally John D. Colombo, A Framework for Analyzing Exemption and UBIT Effects of Joint Ventures, 34 Exempt Org. Tax Rev. 187 (2001).

Notes: Hospital Reorganization and Integrated Delivery Systems

1. *Holding Companies.*

For most of this century, the legal structure of the hospital was uncomplicated. Most hospitals were operated as single nonprofit organizations or, perhaps, as public corporations. As health care delivery has become more complex, however, so have the corporate structures of health care institutions. . . .

The holding company structure is usually the result of a reorganization of a single hospital corporation into a group of affiliated corporations. The resulting corporations typically include a parent holding company, a hospital subsidiary and additional subsidiaries from which other components of the reorganized health care "system" are operated — components such as outpatient facilities, or real estate holdings. . . .

Complex hospital corporate structures are a relatively recent phenomenon. Hospital reorganizations began in the 1970s and were widespread by the early 1980s. The typical restructuring involved a freestanding hospital operated through a single, usually nonprofit, corporation. The reorganization resulted in the replacement of this simple corporate structure with a "parent holding company" controlling one or more operating subsidiaries, including a hospital subsidiary. As a result of this reorganization movement, few hospitals currently operate as stand-alone corporations without the benefit of a corporate parent, a so-called sister affiliate or a subsidiary.

The earliest hospital reorganizations were motivated primarily by Medicare reimbursement incentives. Prior to the adoption of the prospective payment system (PPS). . . . [r]eorganizing the hospital along the lines of the "parent holding company" model provided a number of different reimbursement advantages. . . . As part of a corporate reorganization, departments with low Medicare usage could be placed into separate corporations, leaving the bulk of hospital overhead costs to be allocated only among the Medicare-intensive departments that remained within the primary hospital corporation. Putting the low-usage activities in legally separate entities was thought to make it more difficult for the Medicare program to succeed in challenging overhead allocations. Separate incorporation of different components of hospital operations could also be used to avoid interest income offsets, to avoid provider cost limits, or, possibly, to obtain charge-based (as opposed to cost-based) reimbursement for certain services.[4]

Because most hospitals are no longer reimbursed on a cost basis, these reasons are now largely obsolete. Nevertheless, market incentives and regulatory rules still create significant additional reasons for hospitals to consider the holding company structure advantageous. . . . For example, in some states a hospital might be required to obtain a certificate of need to build a parking garage or a medical office building, whereas a separate corporation created for these specific purposes might be able to initiate the same project without CON review. . . . [Also], nonprofit health care systems may find it advantageous to put operations that generate unrelated business income into separate taxable subsidiaries in order to avoid jeopardizing tax-exempt status.[5] . . . [Finally], [s]eparating diverse functions into distinct entities can also create more precise accountability

[4] See generally David Frankford, The Complexity of Medicare's Hospital Reimbursement System: Paradoxes of Averaging, 78 Iowa L. Rev. 517 (1993).
    [5] . . . [However,] health care delivery systems may become so obsessed with diversification that corporations are created that have nothing to do with the initial and overall mission of the system. For example, Hamot Medical Center in Erie, Pennsylvania was publicly scrutinized when an affiliate was discovered to have purchased a marina for $375,000. In a fight to maintain its tax-exempt status, the hospital argued that the affiliate was furthering the hospital's purposes "by promoting urban redevelopment." A court reviewing the tax-exempt status of the Medical Center concluded that the hospital's primary business was no longer health promotion, but funding of affiliates that competed with local businessmen. School District of City of Erie v. Hamot Medical Center, 144 Pa. Commw. Ct. 668, 602 A.2d 407 (1992). . . .

and awareness of corporate performance. Thus, the goal of hospital reorganization is often to use separate corporations to reflect separate lines of business. . . .

Reorganization may also create competitive advantages for the health care system by providing greater flexibility for participation in the creation and operation of health care networks and other innovative transactions. . . . [T]he recent development of integrated delivery systems has made the creation of a parent corporation even more important than in the past.

Stephen Bernstein, Complex Corporate Structures, in Health Care Corporate Law: Facilities and Transactions (M. Hall & W. Brewbaker eds., 1996).

2. *Shared Services.* These reorganizations have led to a number of rulings concerning the extent to which hospital holding companies and other complex corporate structures comply with the requirements for charitable tax exemption under specialized doctrines known as the "integral part test" and the "shared service organization" rule. Hospitals sometimes find it efficient to operate certain internal functions such as laundry services on a shared, cooperative basis with other hospitals. Undue attention has been devoted to whether such supporting enterprises are themselves tax exempt. Ordinarily, the answer would be no because, while laundry services within a hospital clearly are related to the hospital's function, standing alone they do not constitute a charitable enterprise. However, section 501(e) provides a special exemption for "cooperative hospital service organizations" that perform the following services for tax-exempt hospitals: "data processing, purchasing, warehousing, billing and collection, food, clinical, industrial engineering, laboratory, printing, communications, record center, and personnel." Owing to effective lobbying from commercial laundries, laundry services are notably absent from this list, though. HCSC-Laundry v. United States, 450 U.S. 1 (1981). Construing this precedent, the IRS has ruled that a cooperative service organization loses its entire exemption if any of its activities are not on the list enumerated in the statute. Tech. Advice Mem. 9542002 (July 18, 1995) (shared security, parking, and housekeeping services are impermissible).

One way around this restrictive statute is to characterize a supporting institution as an "integral part" of an exempt organization. Scattered precedents allow subsidiaries to qualify as an integral part of a charitable whole even if, standing alone, they do not perform charitable activities, so long as the activity would be "related" if it were performed internally by the charitable parent. This doctrine was given a restrictive interpretation, however, in a court decision concerning an HMO run by a hospital. Based on some obscure reasoning, the court essentially ruled that an HMO is too different from a hospital to qualify for exemption under the integral part test. Geisinger Health Plan v. Commissioner, 30 F.3d 494 (3d Cir. 1994).

3. *Hospital Reorganization and Integration.* There are two basic tax exemption issues in complex corporate structures: (1) which subsidiaries will lose exemption if their functions are examined separately from the hospital's; and (2) will the parent company qualify for exemption even though it is a "shell" corporation that offers no charitable service directly, and even though a number of its subsidiaries are run as for-profit ventures? The answer to the former is explored above in terms of each of a number of different health care ventures (HMO, nursing home, physician group practice, etc.). The answer to the latter is generally yes, following the "integral part" thinking described above. The leading ruling is Northwestern Medical

Corp., described in Tax Notes, Sept. 9, 1993, in which the IRS approved the exemption of a "superparent" for a regional hospital network composed of several hospital systems, each with its own exempt parent. In Wilson Area School District v. Easton Hospital, 747 A.2d 877 (Pa. 2000), the court upheld the charitable status of a non-profit hospital that owned a number of for-profit subsidiaries because the subsidiaries helped to further the hospital's general health care purposes. See generally Melvin Horowitz, Corporate Reorganization: The Last Gasp or Last Clear Chance for the Tax-Exempt, Nonprofit Hospital?, 13 Am. J.L. & Med. 527 (1988); Mary Squires, Corporate Restructuring of Tax-Exempt Hospitals: The Bastardization of the Tax-Exempt Concept, 14 Law, Med. & Health Care 66 (1986); General Counsel Memorandum 39508 (May 28, 1986); General Counsel Memorandum 39598 (Dec. 8, 1986).

4. *Integrated Delivery Systems.* The most important application of these corporate restructuring rulings is to so-called vertically integrated networks or integrated delivery systems (IDSs), those that contain not only hospitals but also nursing homes, home health agencies, physician groups, and an HMO. Because of the IRS's varying standards for different types of health care services and its traditional hostility toward exempting physician groups, its first IDS ruling was awaited with considerable anticipation. In 1993, Los Angeles lawyer Peter Grant obtained a favorable ruling on behalf of Friendly Hills HealthCare Network. 7 Exempt Org. Tax Rev. 490 (1993). This ruling approved exempt status for the network parent that controlled the system as a whole, and not necessarily for its component members. Important to the decision were the facts that the network included a prominent teaching and research hospital, Loma Linda University Medical Center, and that the network clinics would accept indigent patients in immediate need of care. Of equal importance was the fact that the governing board was drawn from the general community, with no more than 20 percent membership from participating physicians. In subsequent rulings, the teaching hospital component has not proven essential, but free emergency care and the 20 percent limit on physician governance have become de facto requirements.

The 20 percent limit on physician board membership has proven to be the most troublesome tax exemption requirement for IDS formation. Is it consistent with the corporate practice of medicine doctrine to insist that physicians have a minimal role in the governance of health care ventures? Hospital-based networks need to include physicians in order to offer the "one-stop shopping" that managed care purchasers are seeking in the present marketplace, but hospitals find it difficult to form tight affiliations with physician groups without giving them greater governance authority. The 20 percent rule is stated as a safe harbor, based on obscure precedents dealing with tax-exempt bond financing. After sustained criticism, the IRS relaxed this limit to 49 percent as long as physician board members are insulated from decisions about physician compensation and other conflict of interest protections are in place.

For general discussion of the vertical network rulings, see John Colombo, Health Care Reform and Federal Tax Exemption: Rethinking the Issues, 29 Wake Forest L. Rev. 215 (1994).

5. *Are Hospital-Run Systems Optimal?* Although the IRS may be relaxing somewhat its opposition to physician governance, it still appears essential that the network be hospital-run. Otherwise, it would be difficult to invoke the generous

"promotion of health" precedents that apply to hospitals and difficult to meet the free emergency service requirements. On the other hand, hospital control may not prove to be the optimal, or even a viable, organizational structure for the emerging integrated systems. Ironically, the Friendly Hills system that received the first and now famous ruling abandoned its exempt status less than two years later and split up into several for-profit components owned by the physicians. Since then, many other provider-owned networks have failed or been bought out by larger insurers. A prominent health management consultant gives several, highly opinionated reasons this may have occurred:

> [T]here are a lot of Walter Mitty-like fantasies of power being realized in the creation of integrated systems. Some executives believe that management is finally about to triumph over physicians. . . . My experience . . . taught me early on that physicians crave order but despise authority. . . . While many physicians fall prey to an illusion of omnicompetence and believe that their medical training endowed them with superior management judgment, most are incapable of submitting to the authority of anyone, even a fellow physician. . . . As a consequence, many lack the interpersonal skills or civility to function as part of a larger enterprise. When physicians are unhappy, they whine — deafeningly. They passively resist initiatives that they cannot overtly oppose, often doing so with dazzling flair and elegance. They will agree in public meetings and subvert privately. They wait for temporary weakness in administrative personnel and savage them. . . . In short, . . . a sizeable fraction of the current generation of private practitioners or medical school faculties are poor candidates for participating in any integrated health care enterprise. . . . One thing becomes clear. . . . The hospital is not the appropriate nucleus of an integrated health care system. . . . Rather, the hospital is a high-maintenance core asset whose use must be rigorously limited by managed care incentives. Outside the integrated enterprise, the hospital is merely a vulnerable vendor of a surplus commodity. Owning a lot of hospital beds in the emerging managed care world will be as advantageous as owning a lot of rubles in post-Soviet Russia.

Jeff Goldsmith, Hospital/Physician Relationships: A Constraint to Health Reform, 12(3) Health Aff. 161 (Fall 1993).

Problem: Choosing a Corporate Form

Marcus Welby Hospital has decided to form an HMO in which it wants to give physicians a major stake, in order to foster allegiance and encourage cost-effective treatment. You are consulted as a legal and management expert to advise the hospital on the consequences of forming the HMO as a nonprofit versus a for-profit entity. What are the relevant considerations with respect to tax exemption, the ability to raise capital, the role of physicians, and operational constraints?

3. The Corporate Practice of Medicine

This section explores an old body of law known as the corporate practice of medicine doctrine, which now may appear archaic, but which has profound influence on the entire structure of the health care delivery system.

BARTRON v. CODINGTON COUNTY

2 N.W.2d 337 (S.D. 1942)

SMITH, Judge.

... The central question of law to be determined is whether certain exhibited bargains between Codington County and the Bartron Clinic, a corporation for profit, pursuant to which such corporation furnished medical and surgical services, and medicines to the county indigent, are illegal and unenforceable.

The "Bartron Clinic" was incorporated in February of 1929, "to conduct and operate a general medical and surgical hospital and clinic and employ duly licensed physicians, surgeons, nurses, students, and other persons to carry on the business of said corporation." Its 750 shares of capital stock were originally issued and held by duly licensed physicians and surgeons, and by nurses and other employees of the corporation. . . . Except for some minor services of an intern, all of the professional services involved herein were performed by duly licensed physicians and surgeons employed at fixed salaries by the corporation, and all charges therefor accrued to and were made by the corporation. The corporation owned all equipment used by the doctors and maintained the supply of drugs furnished patients. The corporation did not hold a license to practice medicine and surgery, nor to operate a pharmacy.

On January 3, 1933, the county and the corporation executed and delivered two contracts in writing wherein the corporation agreed to furnish hospitalization, medical and surgical services and medicine to the county for its poor persons. . . .

The court [below] found that there was not in connection with the organization of the Bartron Clinic, or at any time thereafter, any purpose or intent whatsoever on the part of Dr. Bartron or anybody else connected with said corporation to place the actual control of the practice of medicine with any person other than duly licensed physicians; that there was not at any time throughout the existence of said corporation any control, or effort to exercise control, as to the actual practice of medicine on the part of anybody other than a licensed physician and no interference, or attempted interference, by anybody other than a licensed physician, with the actual practice of medicine; that the actual purpose and intent of Dr. Bartron in promoting the organization of said corporation was to establish what amounted to a system of profit sharing, whereby the prominent and leading employees of said hospital and clinic business would have some actual interest in the success thereof.

[This case] originated as a claim before the county commissioners in aggregate amount of $3,649.63 for medicine supplied the county indigent between January 1, 1938 and September 1, 1938. . . . [T]he court found that the professional services were actually rendered by duly licensed physicians, except for a small item for intern's services, and that the medicines were prescribed by such physicians in treatment of the county poor, and that all of this was done pursuant to directions and orders of the county commissioners.

The court concluded as a matter of law . . . that it is unlawful and contrary to public policy for a corporation to practice medicine or surgery and to operate a pharmacy or sell medicine without a license as required by the statutes of South Dakota. These conclusions are challenged here by appropriate assignments of error. . . .

When conduct opposed to the public interest is made the subject of a bargain the courts ordinarily refuse to accord a party thereto a remedy predicated thereon. . . . While decision has rarely turned on the naked issue of public policy, the expressions of the courts indicate a current of opinion, to which there are but few dissentients, that such practice contravenes the public interest and is contrary to public policy.

The leading case is that of In re Cooperative Law Co., 198 N.Y. 479, 92 N.E. 15. The court said:

> The practice of law is not a business open to all, but a personal right, limited to a few persons of good moral character, with special qualifications ascertained and certified after a long course of study, both general and professional, and a thorough examination by a state board appointed for the purpose. . . . The relation of attorney and client is that of master and servant in a limited and dignified sense, and it involves the highest trust and confidence. It cannot be delegated without consent, and it cannot exist between an attorney employed by a corporation to practice law for it, and a client of the corporation, for he would be subject to the directions of the corporation, and not to the directions of the client. There would be neither contract nor privity between him and the client, and he would not owe even the duty of counsel to the actual litigant. The corporation would control the litigation, the money earned would belong to the corporation, and the attorney would be responsible to the corporation only. His master would not be the client but the corporation, conducted it may be wholly by laymen, organized simply to make money and not to aid in the administration of justice which is the highest function of an attorney and counsellor at law. The corporation might not have a lawyer among its stockholders, directors, or officers. Its members might be without character, learning or standing. There would be . . . no stimulus to good conduct from the traditions of an ancient and honorable profession, and no guide except the sordid purpose to earn money for stockholders. The bar, which is an institution of the highest usefulness and standing, would be degraded if even its humblest member became subject to the orders of a money-making corporation engaged not in conducting litigation for itself, but in the business of conducting litigation for others. *The degradation of the bar is an injury to the state.* . . .

Debasement of the learned professions is in fact inimical to the public welfare. The public is the ultimate beneficiary of its professional social organisms, and of the private, as well as of the unselfish public, exercise of the skills and talents of its professional practitioners. Although the members of the legal profession in their individual capacities as officers of the courts of justice sustain a relationship to the public without parallel in the medical professions, in all other respects the services of the two professions are of equal importance to the public, and debasement of the one, in our opinion, would constitute no less a public evil than would the degradation of the other.

These professions, as they exist in our social structure, rest upon a foundation of sturdy, sterling human character which, in turn, has been and is being shaped and moulded by the impact of traditional ideals and points of view. The licensing statutes with their emphasis on character and professional conduct evidence a fixed public desire and will not only to foster, but to develop and reinforce, these basic attributes of its professional servants. . . . We are therefore persuaded that that which tends to debase the learned professions is at war with the public interest and is therefore contrary to public policy.

Does practice of the learned professions by a profit corporation functioning through duly licensed practitioners tend to debase the professions? We pause to emphasize the word *tend* because the learned trial court has found that the Bartron Clinic was innocent of any unethical intention or practice, and that its licensed officers and employees controlled its professional activities. Our present concern is with the tendency of the challenged conduct. Though the exhibited instance of that conduct has accomplished no evil, if its inherent tendency be at war with public interest, it is contrary to public policy.

Because of the rights with which the law invests a stockholder in a corporation for profit, recognition of such a means of conducting a professional business involves yielding the right of participation in control of its policies and in its earnings to lay persons. . . . The object of such a company would be to produce an earning on its fixed capital. Its trade commodity would be the professional services of its employees. Constant pressure would be exerted by the investor to promote such a volume of sales of that commodity as would produce an ever increasing return on his investment. To promote such sales it is to be presumed that the layman would apply the methods and practices in which he had been schooled in the market place. The end result seems inevitable to us, viz., undue emphasis on mere money making, and commercial exploitation of professional services. To universalize the use of this method of organizing the professions, or to permit such a use to become general, would ultimately wipe out or blight those characteristics which distinguish the business practices of the professions from those of the market place. Such an ethical, trustworthy and unselfish professionalism as the community needs and wants cannot survive in a purely commercial atmosphere. . . .

That such is the tendency of the profit corporation when used to conduct a professional practice is not a matter of mere fancy or conjecture. It is a matter of common knowledge that this form of organization has been tried in the field of dentistry and resulted in such unethical and commercial practices as induced the legislature of this and many other states to pass statutes expressly prohibiting its use.

Being convinced that the practice of the learned professions by a profit corporation tends to the commercialization and debasement of those professions, we are of the opinion that such a mode of conducting the practice is in contravention of the public interest and is against public policy. It follows that we are of the view that insofar as the bargains of the Bartron Clinic and Codington County dealt with medical and surgical services, they were illegal. [As a result, the court refused to order the county to pay for medical services it had received, but the court did allow the clinic to keep funds previously paid.]

■ RIGHT OF CORPORATION TO PRACTICE MEDICINE
Note, 48 Yale L.J. 346 (1938)

Efforts to obtain adequate medical care at reasonable cost have stimulated extensive experimentation with methods of medical organization. The result has been widespread development of such diversified types as private group clinics, employee health associations, county physician bureaus, health insurance plans, and medical cooperatives. Many of the sponsors of these systems have attempted to take advantage of the corporate form in order to achieve limited liability and continuity of existence. Groups of physicians have incorporated to operate their own clinic; laymen have formed corporations, hiring physicians to treat patients for profit; and aggregations of prospective patients have organized nonprofit cooperative corporations. Yet the legal existence of these corporate types has been jeopardized at one time or another by attempted application of the principle that corporations may not practice the learned professions. . . .

While numerous state statutes directly forbid the corporate practice of law, express prohibition of the corporate practice of medicine is rare. Instead, denial of the right of some corporations to practice medicine has been based upon those statutes in every state which outlaws performance of the healing art by unlicensed persons. The obvious inability of a corporate entity to meet the educational and character requirements prerequisite to a license is said to inhibit a corporation from practicing medicine. To bolster this interpretation of the statutes, courts have commonly resorted to arguments of public policy. Since the judiciary do not possess an intrinsic power to regulate the medical profession as they do the legal, the validity of this viewpoint is necessarily dependent upon the soundness of the courts' inference that state licensing statutes automatically forbid utilization of the corporate power.

Courts which profess to deny all corporations the right to have any connection with medical activities have apparently misconstrued the purpose of the state licensing statutes. These statutes are designed to preserve the public health by excluding from practice persons with inadequate ability, morality, and training. Since the diagnosis and treatment of disease are obviously purely personal functions, a corporation can perform them only through the medium of doctors. But the mere fact that a corporation employs physicians, or is operated by physicians, provides no valid basis for requiring the corporation itself to be licensed. As long as the doctors are properly licensed and their professional activities are not interfered with by unlicensed persons, the purpose of the statutes is fully effected, for no one without proper qualifications is then directly or indirectly administering to the public. This is true even though laymen may be entrusted with considerable control over administrative details. Only when lay officers or directors exercise substantial supervision over the professional activities of the physicians employed is there ground for arguing that the corporation is enabling unlicensed persons to practice medicine. Thus the real issue is not whether corporations generally are unlicensed to practice medicine, but whether in each individual case physicians are *actually* controlled in their purely professional functions by unlicensed persons in such a manner as to nullify the purpose of the licensing statutes. . . .

Even in states following [this doctrine], numerous corporations engage unchallenged in activities which have all the indicia of corporate practice of medicine as defined by the same courts. It is common knowledge that private hospitals, sanitariums, fraternal organizations, educational institutions, and industrial concerns all administer medical services to their constituents through staffs of physicians hired and paid on a full or part time basis. Similarly, salaried physicians undertake part time contract practice on behalf of various companies, particularly railroads, to treat passengers and employees. The explanation for such discrimination may be that the social utility of these types of corporate medical service has long been tacitly recognized; nevertheless, the fact remains that some corporate forms have been permitted in the face of the same state licensing statutes which are so rigorously invoked against others.

Since the legal construction of state licensing statutes is by no means inexorable, their varying application to certain corporate forms is probably attributable to the judges' evaluation of social policy arguments against corporate medical practice. Impairment of the intimate doctor-patient relationship and commercialization of the medical profession are the two general social policy objections most commonly cited by the courts. The first evil will result, it is feared, from possible restrictions upon the patient's freedom of choice of physician and from a division of the physician's loyalty between patient and corporate employer. If the old-fashioned family doctor is used as the norm, this objection might assume serious proportions. But when the challenged corporate forms are compared with the many types of corporate medical service already accepted, any distinguishing basis must be fanciful indeed. Furthermore, consistency would require that the same charge be levelled against noncorporate forms such as county, municipal, and private partnership clinics. And even if the choice of doctors should be unusually restricted within a particular corporate scheme, many patients might prefer that scheme to other types of private group medical services or to receiving inadequate or no medical treatment whatsoever. . . . Moreover, insulation of the doctor from administrative and economic cares and elimination of the patient's concern over cost may actually enhance the relationship between patient and physician.

More plausible is the second social objection to the corporate furnishing of medical service. It is feared that the profession may be commercially exploited by laymen who, not being amenable to ethical standards, are free to engage in high pressure solicitation of patients and sharp competitive advertising. But the fact that this fear may at times be well-grounded should not justify resort to the drastic measure of barring corporate medical service entirely. A more sensible solution is for the state to combine its recognized regulatory powers over corporations and professions in order to curb objectionable professional activity. And even without special regulation, the state can undoubtedly hold contract physicians to the same standard of ethics as private practitioners. Moreover, the opposition of the American Medical Association to this type of corporate medical practice assures a zealous and vigilant supervision by a body dutybound to report to the state injurious professional activity.

. . . Some courts persist in trying to solve such cases by repeating generalizations which are meaningless in the abstract. A more realistic judicial approach would disregard the corporate form as such and inquire instead whether the actual setup is so provocative of abuses that the only solution is to deny the corporation existence altogether. However, the public interest in furthering experiments in medical care may suffer much by trusting to haphazard decisions by tribunals ill-fitted to investigate intricate specific cases. The surer method of achieving the benefits of corporate medical organization without possible attendant evils would be by enactment of legislation specifically authorizing the corporate form but carefully regulating its activities so as to insure the highest response to professional ethics by the corporation as an entity and by its physicians.

■ BERLIN v. SARAH BUSH LINCOLN HEALTH CENTER
688 N.E.2d 106 (Ill. 1997)

NICKLES, J.

... The [Sarah Bush Lincoln] Health Center is a nonprofit corporation duly licensed under the Hospital Licensing Act to operate a hospital. In December 1992, Dr. Berlin and the Health Center entered into a written agreement whereby the Health Center employed Dr. Berlin to practice medicine for the hospital for five years. The agreement ... contained a restrictive covenant which prohibited Dr. Berlin from competing with the hospital by providing health services within a 50-mile radius of the Health Center for two years after the end of the employment agreement. On February 4, 1994, Dr. Berlin informed the Health Center by letter that he was resigning effective February 7, 1994 and accepting employment with the Carle Clinic ... located approximately one mile from the Health Center. Shortly thereafter, the Health Center sought a preliminary injunction to prohibit Dr. Berlin from practicing at the Carle Clinic. ... The circuit court, finding the entire employment agreement unenforceable, granted Dr. Berlin's motion for summary judgment. ... [T]he circuit court determined that the Health Center, by hiring Dr. Berlin to practice medicine as its employee, violated the prohibition against corporations practicing medicine.[1] ...

... The corporate practice of medicine doctrine prohibits corporations from providing professional medical services. Although a few states have codified the doctrine, the prohibition is primarily inferred from state medical licensure acts, which regulate the profession of medicine and forbid its practice by unlicensed individuals. See A. Rosoff, The Business of Medicine: Problems with the Corporate Practice Doctrine, 17 Cumb. L. Rev. 485, 490 (1987). The rationale behind the doctrine is that a corporation cannot be licensed to practice medicine because only a human being can sustain the education, training, and character-screening which are prerequisites to receiving a professional license. Since a corporation cannot receive a medical license, it follows that a corporation cannot legally practice the profession. The rationale of the doctrine concludes that the employment of physicians by corporations is illegal because the acts of the physicians are attributable to the corporate employer, which cannot obtain a medical license. See M. Hall, Institutional Control of Physician Behavior: Legal Barriers to Health Care Cost Containment, 137 U. Pa. L. Rev. 431, 509-510 (1988). The prohibition on the corporate employment of physicians is invariably supported by several public policy arguments which espouse the dangers of lay control over professional judgment, the division of the physician's loyalty between his patient and his profitmaking employer, and the commercialization of the profession. See A. Willcox, Hospitals and the Corporate Practice of Medicine, 45 Cornell L.Q. 432, 442-443 (1960).

This court first [applied] the corporate practice doctrine [to strike down a restrictive covenant] in Dr. Allison, Dentist, Inc. v. Allison, 360 Ill. 638 (1935),

---

[1 This case challenges the legality of the employment relationship as a whole. The legality of restrictive covenants in particular has also been challenged, as discussed in the notes at page 448.— EDS.]

[whose facts were essentially the same as here, except that Dr. Allison was a dentist working for a dental office, not a physician at a hospital.] . . . Soon after the *Allison* decision, this court . . . addressed the corporate practice doctrine as it pertained to [physicians working in a clinic, in a ruling essentially the same as in Bartron v. Codington County, supra.] People ex rel. Kerner v. United Medical Service, Inc., 362 Ill. 442 (1936). . . . Prior to the instant action, apparently no Illinois court has . . . specifically addressed the issue of whether licensed hospitals are prohibited from employing physicians. We therefore look to other jurisdictions with reference to the application of the corporate practice of medicine doctrine to hospitals.

. . . [N]umerous jurisdictions have recognized either judicial or statutory exceptions to the corporate practice of medicine doctrine which allow hospitals to employ physicians and other health care professionals. . . . First, some states . . . determined that a hospital corporation which employs a physician is not practicing medicine, but rather is merely making medical treatment available. See, e.g., State ex rel. Sager v. Lewin, 128 Mo. App. 149, 155, 106 S.W. 581, 583 (1907); State Electro-Medical Institute v. Platner, 74 Neb. 23, 29, 103 N.W. 1079, 1081 (1905). Under the second approach, the courts of some jurisdictions determined that the corporate practice doctrine is inapplicable to nonprofit hospitals and health associations. These courts reasoned that the public policy arguments supporting the corporate practice doctrine do not apply to physicians employed by charitable institutions. See, e.g., Group Health Ass'n v. Moor, 24 F. Supp. 445, 446 (D.D.C. 1938); People ex rel. State Board of Medical Examiners v. Pacific Health Corp., 12 Cal. 2d 156, 159-161, 82 P.2d 429, 431 (1938). In the third approach, the courts of several states have determined that the corporate practice doctrine is not applicable to hospitals which employ physicians because hospitals are authorized by other laws to provide medical treatment to patients. See, e.g., Rush v. City of St. Petersburg, 205 So. 2d 11 (Fla. App. 1967); St. Francis Regional Medical Center, Inc. v. Weiss, 254 Kan. 728, 869 P.2d 606 (1994).

We find the [third] rationale . . . persuasive. . . . The Medical Practice Act contains no express prohibition on the corporate employment of physicians.[1] Rather, the corporate practice of medicine doctrine was inferred from the general policies behind the Medical Practice Act. . . . The [hospital licensing] statutes clearly authorize, and at times mandate, licensed hospital corporations to provide medical services. . . .

In addition, we find the public policy concerns which support the corporate practice doctrine inapplicable to a licensed hospital in the modern health care industry. The concern for lay control over professional judgment is alleviated in a licensed hospital, where generally a separate professional medical staff is responsible for the quality of medical services rendered in the facility.[2] Furthermore, we believe that extensive changes in the health care industry since [1936], including the emergence of corporate health maintenance organizations, have greatly

---

[1] In contrast, the Dental Practice Act, applied by this court in *Allison*, expressly prohibited a corporation from furnishing dentists and owning and operating a dental office.

[2] Moreover, in the instant case, the employment agreement expressly provided that the Health Center had no control or direction over Dr. Berlin's medical judgment and practice, other than that control exercised by the professional medical staff. Dr. Berlin has never contended that the Health Center's lay management attempted to control his practice of medicine.

altered the concern over the commercialization of health care. In addition, such concerns are relieved when a licensed hospital is the physician's employer. Hospitals have an independent duty to provide for the patient's health and welfare. See Darling v. Charleston Community Mem. Hosp., 33 Ill. 2d 326 (1965) (recognizing hospital's duty to assume responsibility for the care of its patients).

We find particularly appropriate the statement of the Kansas Supreme Court that "[i]t would be incongruous to conclude that the legislature intended a hospital to accomplish what it is licensed to do without utilizing physicians as independent contractors or employees. . . . To conclude that a hospital must do so without employing physicians is not only illogical but ignores reality." *Weiss*, 869 P.2d at 618. Accordingly, we conclude that a duly-licensed hospital possesses legislative authority to practice medicine by means of its staff of licensed physicians and is excepted from the operation of the corporate practice of medicine doctrine. Consequently, the employment agreement between the Health Center and Dr. Berlin is not unenforceable merely because the Health Center is a corporate entity. . . .

HARRISON, J. and MILLER, J., dissenting:
. . . [N]one of the statutes invoked by my colleagues supports their position. The most that can be said of those statutes is that they authorize hospitals to operate facilities for the diagnosis and care of patients and to make emergency service available regardless of ability to pay. . . . None of those endeavors, however, requires that hospitals have the power to employ physicians directly or to charge patients for the physicians' services. All may be accomplished by granting staff privileges to duly licensed private physicians, and the Hospital Licensing Act presumes that hospitals will staff their facilities in precisely that way. . . . [T]he General Assembly has expressly authorized the employment of physicians by Health Maintenance Organizations (HMOs) under the Health Maintenance Organization Act. If the General Assembly had intended to grant the same authority to hospitals, I believe that it would have been similarly straightforward and unambiguous in doing so. In addition to creating special rules for HMOs, the General Assembly has also decided to allow physicians to employ various forms of business organizations in practicing their profession. Physicians may incorporate in accordance with the Professional Service Corporation Act, they may form corporations to provide medical services under the Medical Corporation Act, they have the right to practice in a professional association organized pursuant to the Professional Association Act, and they can organize and operate limited liability companies to practice medicine under the recently amended Limited Liability Company Act. Again, however, none of these provisions pertains to hospitals, and no inference can be drawn from any of them that the General Assembly intended to alter the prohibition against the corporate practice of medicine by hospitals. . . .

Notes: Corporate Practice of Medicine and Choice of Entity

1. *The Fundamental Structure of American Medical Institutions.* This body of law may appear obscure and antiquated, but it continues to have fundamental

importance for the structure of institutional and economic relationships in American medicine. Observe, for instance, that the prohibition of institutions charging for medical services explains why doctors are paid separately from hospitals and why there used to be a distinction between Blue Cross and Blue Shield and still is between Medicare Part A and Part B. This doctrine also explains why, only in North America, hospital medical staffs are independent and self-governing. Elsewhere in the world, hospital physicians are uniformly employed or compensated by the hospital.

2. *Legal Landmines.* Following the 1930s and 1940s, the corporate practice of medicine doctrine entered a period of relative quiescence in the courts. It still continued to thrive, though, in state attorneys general opinions during the 1950s, in response to the growing technological sophistication of medical care and hospitals' resulting relationships with radiologists, pathologists, and other hospital-based specialists. Activity at even that level has slackened noticeably over the past three decades, leading one to consider whether the doctrine hasn't been quietly defused. However, in Professor Rosoff's apt metaphor, corporate practice prohibitions survive as "legal landmines, remnants of an old and nearly forgotten war, half-buried on a field fast being built up with new forms of health care organizations. Occasionally, usually at the instigation of those who resist the change not taking place, one is detonated, with distressing results." A. Rosoff, The Business of Medicine: Problems with the Corporate Practice Doctrine, 17 Cumb. L. Rev. 485 (1987). Instances of modern application in addition to those discussed in *Berlin* include Conrad v. Medical Board of California, 55 Cal. Rptr. 2d 801 (Ct. App. 1996) (hospital district may not employ physicians); and Morelli v. Ehsan, 737 P.2d 1030 (Wash. Ct. App. 1987) (corporate practice doctrine bars enforcement of medical clinic partnership agreement by a lay partner/business manager).

3. *Doctrinal Foundations.* The corporate practice doctrine is founded on two distinct bases: the Medical Practice Act and common law public policy. The courts rarely draw this distinction, however. *Bartron* is one court that did. In another portion of the opinion, the court, influenced by the Yale Note, rejected the literal terms of the Medical Practice Act as a basis for a corporate practice challenge. In doing so, it stands almost alone.

4. *Statutory Arguments.* The *Allison* decision, discussed in *Berlin*, provides an example of the typical reasoning of the statutory basis for the corporate practice prohibition: "The qualifications [to practice a profession] include personal characteristics such as honesty, guided by an upright conscience and a sense of loyalty to clients or patients. . . . These requirements are spoken of generically as that good moral character which is a prerequisite to the licensing of any professional man. No corporation can qualify. It can have neither honesty nor conscience. . . ." 196 N.E. 799, 800 (1935). Does this line of reasoning differ in form or in substance from the following?

- The actions of drivers hired by a corporation are attributed to the corporation
- An eyesight examination is required for a driver's license
- Corporations cannot take an eye exam
- Therefore, a corporation that hires drivers is guilty of driving without a license

See Sloan v. Metropolitan Health Council, 516 N.E.2d 1104, 1107 (Ind. Ct. App. 1987) (rejecting the doctrine on this basis).

5. *Public Policy Arguments.* Addressing corporate practice from a common law public policy perspective, how far should the courts go in striking down private contractual arrangements? Many of the original and leading cases address situations of apparent quackery in the peripheral medical professions (dentistry, optometry, etc.). See Laufer, Ethical and Legal Restrictions on Contract and Corporate Practice of Medicine, 6 Law & Contemp. Probs. 521, 526 (1939). *Bartron*, however, applies a strict rule despite the completely upright behavior of the individual doctors. Are there any countervailing harms to banning corporate practice, or should the courts lean as far as possible in the direction of a pristine practice setting? In 1979, the Federal Trade Commission permanently enjoined the AMA from enforcing *ethical* prohibitions against corporate practice because of the anticompetitive effects of the AMA controlling the economic and organizational aspects of medical practice. American Medical Ass'n, 94 F.T.C. 980, 1015 (1979), aff'd by equally divided court, 455 U.S. 676 (1982).

How great of a concern is the threat of divided loyalty, that is, the responsibility an employed physician owes to her employer as well as to her patient? Is the loyalty any greater than that owed by one physician *partner* to another? Than that owed by a physician to other patients? Is it not possible to serve two masters so long as they do not impose inconsistent duties?

And what of the commercialization concern, that is, that introduction of a profit motive will tend to debase the profession? Clearly a profit motive exists in medical practice regardless of the organizational form of practice. Doctors are the highest paid profession in the country.[2] What additional concerns are introduced by *incorporating* a profitable practice? Consider whether there isn't a form of hypocrisy or self-interest in keeping only nonphysicians from sharing in medicine's rich rewards. See Note, The Corporate Practice of Medicine Doctrine: An Anachronism in the Modern Health Care Industry, 40 Vand. L. Rev. 445 (1987).

6. *Implicit Exceptions.* The holding in *Berlin* would appear to exempt from the corporate practice prohibition all hospitals, nursing homes, and licensed outpatient clinics, but only to the extent covered by their licenses. Could a hospital operate a chain of physician offices under this rationale? In a subsequent decision, the Illinois Supreme Court refused to apply *Berlin* to a nonprofit corporation that ran physician offices as a joint venture between a hospital and a physician group because the particular corporation used did not hold a hospital license. Carter-Shields v. Alton Health Institute, 777 N.E.2d 948 (Ill. 2002). The court also refused to find an exception based on the hospital's or the corporate entity's

---

[2] "Lore holds that physicians are frequently more noble, altruistic and charitable than the patients they treat. If ever that belief was true, it no longer is. At the last annual meeting of the American Heart Association in Dallas, Robert Swank, an economist from the Johns Hopkins Medical School, released a study showing that when a physician's income drops, his blood pressure zooms and stays elevated for five years. Swank . . . found that for each 1% drop in income, the number of doctors with elevated blood pressure rose 2.5% the next year. In short, physicians are as vulnerable economically and reactive physically as the rest of us." Parade, Feb. 15, 1987.

nonprofit status, holding that "nonprofit status is unrelated to . . . safeguarding the physician's professional judgment from lay interference or protecting the public's general health and welfare."

What other exceptions to the doctrine are mentioned in *Berlin*? See Willcox, supra (some courts do not apply the doctrine to independent contractors). Not all courts agree with these exceptions, however. See, e.g., Conrad v. Medical Board of California, 55 Cal. Rptr. 2d 801 (Ct. App. 1996) (hospital district may retain physicians only as independent contractors, not as employees).

7. *PCs and LLCs*. The dissent in *Berlin* observes that exceptions to the corporate practice prohibition are sometimes explicit in licensing statutes. The most prominent example is a professional corporation. Practice groups organized like the one that was invalidated in *Bartron*, that are entirely owned by member physicians, are now permitted by professional corporation (PC) laws widely adopted during the 1960s. A PC essentially allows physicians and other licensed professionals (lawyers included) to enjoy the liability protections of corporate organization while enjoying the tax benefits of practicing as a partnership. (Note, though, that tax reform legislation in the 1980s substantially restricted PC pension and retirement benefits, the major tax advantage.) See J. Philipps, J. McNider & D. Riley, Origins of Tax Law: The History of the Personal Service Corporation, 40 Wash. & Lee L. Rev. 433 (1983). Do these laws change the public policy recognized in *Bartron*? Cf. Sloan v. Metropolitan Health Council, 516 N.E. 2d 1104, 1107 (Ind. Ct. App. 1987) (dictum) ("We believe that the Professional Corporation Act . . . totally abolished [the] public policy [prohibiting a corporation to practice medicine], if, indeed, it ever existed.").

A novel innovation to the PC format that gained widespread popularity in the 1990s is known as a professional limited liability corporation (PLLC). State laws authorizing limited liability corporations have proliferated in the past few years in response to an IRS ruling that makes it easier to avoid corporate taxation. Classically, corporations, which are taxed as entities, were distinguished from partnerships in which there is no entity-level tax, only the ordinary income tax paid by individual members. This distinction was based on certain classic attributes of corporations, such as limited liability, centralized management, and freely transferrable investment interests, which the IRS ruled could not be fully replicated by contract without incurring corporate tax. See United States v. Kintner, 216 F.2d 418 (9th Cir. 1954). It is this ruling the IRS relaxed, opening the way to a whole new species of business organizations. The new "check-the-box" regulations allow closely-held entities to choose either partnership or corporate tax treatment, regardless of their form. 26 C.F.R. §301 (1997).

This flexible taxation approach is now available to closely held business entities, regardless of the kind of entity in question. For a time, however, it was available only by virtue of special state laws that created a new breed of business entity known as "limited liability corporations" (LLCs). These are hybrids of partnerships and corporations in that they limit members' liability to the extent of their investment, like corporations, but they avoid an entity-level tax, like partnerships. LLCs also offer advantages over other hybrids such as limited partnerships and subchapter S corporations. Where authorized by statute, professional LLCs mimic professional corporations by making this new organizational form available to licensed professionals. However, these PLLC statutes usually contain some of the same provisions on governance authority and liability exposure that are in the PC statutes. For instance, membership and management may be limited to a single, designated category of licensed professionals (MDs, lawyers, dentists, etc.), and each member may be required to remain liable for the professional negligence of each of the others.

LLCs are now all the rage for physician practices, as well as for law firms. However, the restrictions hamper their use for larger, multi-specialty practice groups or for vertically integrated delivery systems. Therefore, more complex arrangements are being experimented with, such as a limited partnership composed of LLCs. See generally Robert W. Hamilton, Business Organizations: Essential Terms and Concepts (1996); Ribstein & Keatinge on Limited Liability; R. Keatinge et al., The Limited Liability Company: A Study of the Emerging Entity, 47 Bus. Law 378 (1992); Symposium, The Revolution of the Limited Liability Entity, 32 Wake Forest L. Rev. 1 (1997).

8. *HMO Exemptions.* The corporate practice prohibition is recognized as one of the major stumbling blocks in HMO development. Developments, The Role of Prepaid Group Practice in Relieving the Medical Care Crisis, 84 Harv. L. Rev. 887, 960-961 (1971). State HMO enabling statutes frequently provide protection from this doctrine, but it is nevertheless puzzling that the federal HMO Act initially did not include this body of state law in its preemption provision when enacted in 1973. However, 1988 amendments to the federal Act significantly broadened its preemptive provision to strike all state laws that "impose requirements that would inhibit" HMOs. 42 U.S.C. §300e-10(a)(1)(E). Does it make sense to limit this preemption to only federally qualified HMOs, to the exclusion of other innovative forms of health care financing and delivery?

9. *The Future.* The conflict between the corporate practice prohibition and the need for organizational experimentation, a dominant theme in the 1938 Yale Note, has an eerie resonance with present day circumstances. Do you agree with *Berlin* that the doctrine's public policy foundations no longer apply? Most commentators argue that the doctrine should yield to modern developments. See Sabra Engelbrecht, The Importance of Clarifying North Carolina's Corporate Practice of Medicine Doctrine, 33 Wake Forest L. Rev. 1093 (1998); Adam Freiman, The Abandonment of the Antiquated Corporate Practice of Medicine Doctrine: Injecting a Dose of Efficiency into the Modern Health Care Environment, 47 Emory L.J. 697 (1998); M. Hall, Institutional Control of Physician Behavior: Legal Barriers to Health Care Cost Containment, 137 U. Pa. L. Rev. 431, 510 (1988); E. Haavi Morreim, Playing Doctor: Corporate Medical Practice and Medical Malpractice, 32 U. Mich. J.L. Ref. 939 (1999); A. Rosoff, supra; Note, 7 Health Matrix 241 (1997); Note, 40 Vand. L. Rev. 445, supra. Others, however, argue that the doctrine should be revived in order to restrict the practice of medicine over the Internet — see, e.g., Brian Monnich, Bringing Order to Cybermedicine: Applying the Corporate Practice of Medicine Doctrine to Tame the Wild Wild Web, 42 B.C. L. Rev. 455 (2001) — or to protect physicians against excessive forms of managed care — see Andre Hampton, Resurrection of the Prohibition on the Corporate Practice of Medicine: Teaching Old Dogma New Tricks, 66 U. Cin. L. Rev. 489 (1998).

Problem: Hospital and Physician Contracting

Marcus Welby Hospital (MWH) realizes that, in order to survive in the current marketplace, it must promote greater loyalty and corporate identification with its physicians. It would also like to capture some of the money physicians are making from treating hospital patients. MWH could simply hire all or a portion or its medical staff, but it is concerned about the legality of doing this. Which of the following approaches would you suggest to minimize that concern, without sacrificing the business objectives?

1. Form a nonprofit subsidiary that hires as many physicians as it wants because it falls within an exception to the corporate practice prohibition. Then it can bill for all medical and hospital services, pay the physicians a salary, and keep the profits (or absorb the losses).
2. Encourage the physicians to form a for-profit entity of their own, and then contract with that entity. The billing and financial arrangements would be the same as just described.
3. Contract with each physician separately, but not to deliver medical services, only to manage their office practice, so that MWH would provide office space and clerical support, and would do the billing for these physicians, but it would forward these revenues to the physicians, less a 15 percent management fee.

C. MEDICAL STAFF STRUCTURE

This part of the chapter explores the structure of the relationship between physicians and health care facilities. It begins with the classic organization of the hospital medical staff, which is both central to and unique to the medical system in the United States. Later cases explore in more detail the fierce disputes that can arise over medical staff membership, and how these bodies of hospital law apply to membership in managed care networks.

■ DOCTORS, PATIENTS, AND HEALTH INSURANCE: THE ORGANIZATION AND FINANCING OF MEDICAL CARE
Herman Miles Somers & Anne Ramsay Somers
1961

[Read the excerpt at page 13.]

1. Medical Staff Bylaws

Physicians' rights and status with hospitals are defined by medical staff bylaws. Virtually unique from any other kind of organization, hospitals typically have two sets of bylaws, one for the medical staff and another for the hospital administration as a whole. The next two cases explore the relationship between these two governance structures, and whether it is possible to restructure the hospital medical staff.

■ ST. JOHN'S HOSPITAL MEDICAL STAFF v. ST. JOHN REGIONAL MEDICAL CENTER
245 N.W.2d 472 (S.D. 1976)

St. John's Hospital Medical Staff is an unincorporated association whose members . . . hold medical staff privileges at . . . the St. John Regional Medical Center [in] Huron, South Dakota. . . . In October 1947, as construction of the [hospital] neared completion, the Sisters of the Franciscan Order proposed certain medical staff bylaws to regulate the affairs of the physicians wanting to use the hospital. . . . The interpretation and effect of these articles formulate the main issues of this action. The "Amendment Article" provides: "These by-laws may be amended after notice given at any regular meeting of the staff. Such [amendments] . . . shall require a two-thirds majority of those present for adoption. Amendments so made shall be effective when approved by the governing body." . . .

In 1972, the [hospital] wished to make certain changes in the bylaws.[2] The attempted changes were unacceptable to the medical staff and an impasse developed, . . . [so] the board of directors of the [hospital] unilaterally adopted new medical staff bylaws which were not approved by the medical staff. The [hospital] now insists that the medical staff is bound by the bylaws so adopted. . . . The [hospital] argues that . . . the power to amend the articles must be lodged in the directors in order to avoid . . . the possibility of independent hospital liability in some future case of malpractice. After a review of the record, we find these arguments to be without merit. . . .

As a general rule, the bylaws of a corporation . . . constitute a binding contract between the corporation and its shareholders. . . . In the present case, we hold that the 1947 medical staff bylaws do constitute a contract which is, by its express terms, subject to amendment when the amendment is agreed to by both the medical staff and the [hospital]. The principles which govern the construction of contracts also govern the construction and interpretation of corporate bylaws. . . . Therefore, both the medical staff and the [hospital] are bound by them until they are amended in accordance with the procedure set out [above]. . . .

South Dakota statutes recognize the power in a corporation to delegate a voice in the adoption of new bylaws to another entity. Such is the case here. The original articles of incorporation and [hospital] bylaws authorize the medical staff to promulgate medical staff bylaws. These medical staff bylaws call for a specific amendment procedure which must be followed. The [hospital] by ignoring

---

[2] E.g., one change would allow the Chief Executive Officer of the [hospital] to temporarily suspend the clinical privileges of a staff physician upon a determination that the action must be taken immediately in the best interests of the patient care in the [hospital]. Another change would require [hospital] approval of all officers of the medical staff.

th[is] procedure and by not including the medical staff in the attempted bylaws amendment has breached this contractual relationship with the medical staff.

■ MAHAN v. AVERA ST. LUKES
621 N.W.2d 150 (S.D. 2001)

Orthopedic Surgery Specialists (OSS) . . . commenced this action against Avera St. Lukes (ASL) alleging breach of contract. . . . ASL is part of a regional health care system sponsored by the Sisters of the Presentation of the Blessed Virgin Mary of Aberdeen, South Dakota. [It is the only facility in a 90-mile radius.] Since 1901, the Presentation Sisters have been fulfilling their mission statement "to respond to God's calling for a healing ministry . . . by providing quality health services" to the Aberdeen community. . . .

In mid-1996, ASL's neurosurgeon left Aberdeen. . . . During the process [of recruiting his replacement], ASL learned that most neurosurgeon applicants would not be interested in coming to Aberdeen if there was already an orthopedic spine surgeon practicing in the area. This was due to the small size of the community and the probable need for the neurosurgeon to supplement his or her practice by performing back and spine surgeries. . . . ASL was successful in recruiting a neurosurgeon who arrived in December, 1996. Around this time, ASL learned that OSS, a group of Aberdeen orthopedic surgeons, had decided to build a day surgery center that would directly compete with ASL. During the first seven months that OSS' surgery center was open, ASL suffered a 1000 hour loss of operating room usage.

In response, . . . [ASL's Board] closed ASL's medical staff with respect to physicians requesting privileges for [spine surgery] . . . [and] closed ASL's medical staff to applicants for orthopedic surgery privileges. . . . The effect of "closing" the staff was to preclude any new physicians from applying for privileges to use hospital facilities for the named procedures. The Board's decision did not affect those physicians that had already been granted hospital privileges, including the physician-members of OSS. . . .

In the summer of 1998, OSS recruited Dr. Mahan, a spine-fellowship trained orthopedic surgeon engaged in the practice of orthopedic surgery. . . . Mahan officially requested an application for staff privileges with ASL [but] these requests were denied due to the Board's decision. . . . Mahan and OSS commenced this action against ASL, challenging the Board's decision to close the staff. The circuit court determined that ASL had breached the Staff Bylaws by closing the staff . . . without first consulting the staff. . . . The circuit court reasoned that because [the Board had delegated power regarding medical staff issues], the Board no longer had the power to initiate actions that affected the privileges of the medical staff. . . .

It is well settled in South Dakota that "a hospital's bylaws constitute a binding contract between the hospital and the hospital staff members." St. John's, 245 N.W.2d at 474. . . . [However,] under South Dakota law, "[t]he affairs of a [nonprofit] corporation *shall* be managed by a board of directors." . . . Pursuant to its authority, the Board of ASL has delegated certain powers associated with the appointment and review of medical personnel to its medical staff. These designated powers are manifested in the Staff Bylaws. Plaintiffs now claim that the Staff Bylaws trump the decision-making ability of the Board as to all decisions relating in any way to, or incidentally affecting, medical personnel issues. We do not agree.

The circuit court failed to give sufficient weight to the fact that the Staff Bylaws are derived from the Corporate Bylaws. . . . Their legal relationship is similar to that between statutes and a constitution. They are not separate and equal sovereigns. . . . The Corporate Bylaws state that "[t]he business and the property of the Corporation shall be managed and controlled . . . by a Board of Trustees. . . ." In addition, the Corporate Bylaws provide that . . . "the Members of the Board of Trustees shall have and exercise the authority . . . to delegate to the Medical Staff the authority to *evaluate the professional competence* of staff Members and applicants for staff privileges and to hold the Medical Staff responsible for *making recommendations* to the Members of the Board of Trustees concerning initial staff appointments, reappointments and the assignment or curtailment of privileges, *all subject to the final approval of the Members of the Board of Trustees*" (emphasis added). . . .

Clearly, under these explicit powers, the Board has the authority to make business decisions without first consulting the medical staff. . . . Plaintiffs rely on the Staff Bylaws as their source of authority to assume the Board's power. Yet, even within the Staff Bylaws, there is no explicit provision granting the medical staff control over personnel issues. Instead, the circuit court found that the actions of the Board violated "the spirit of the bylaws taken as a whole." Such reliance on the "spirit of the [Staff] bylaws" turns the corporate structure of ASL upside down. . . . ASL cannot continue to offer unprofitable, yet essential services including the maternity ward, emergency room, pediatrics and critical care units, without the offsetting financial benefit of more profitable areas such as neurosurgery. The Board . . . surely has the power to attempt to insure ASL's economic survival. . . .

[T]he circuit court determined that this was not an administrative decision by the Board. Instead it held this was a decision regarding the "granting or withholding [of] staff privileges," and that the action fell "within the provisions of the medical staff bylaws." . . . According to the circuit court, in matters of personnel, the Board has only "secondary approval authority . . . ; no actions originate with the Board itself." The circuit court further concluded that the Board is only allowed to give its "seal of approval" at the final stages of staff actions. As support for this view, the circuit court cited the Staff Bylaws . . . as follows: "Initial appointments and reappointments to the Medical staff shall be made by the Governing Body. The Governing Body shall act on appointments, reappointment, or revocation of appointment only after there has been recommendation from the Medical Staff as provided in these Bylaws." The circuit court also cited a provision in the Credentialing Manual to support its claim that the Board has essentially only rubber stamp authority. That provision states that "[t]he Board shall either accept or reject the recommendation of the Credentials and Executive Committee. . . ." Finally, the circuit court found that the procedure for hearings and appellate review [by the Board] was further evidence that the Board was not allowed to originate any actions relating to the medical staff, it was only allowed to hear appeals.

These provisions have been misconstrued by the circuit court. . . . The purpose of this limited delegation of authority was to obtain input from the staff on areas of its expertise. Decisions relating to the competence, training, qualifications and ethics of a particular physician are matters for which the medical staff is uniquely qualified, while the Board admittedly has limited expertise in those areas. Under the Corporate Bylaws, it is *only* in those confined areas of expertise that the staff has any authority at all. . . . [T]he medical staff gives recommendations to the Board on issues relating to appointment and privileges. However, this case is not about appointments or the assignment or curtailment of privileges. It is about an administrative decision to close ASL's staff for certain procedures; therefore, the medical staff has no part in the decision and the Staff Bylaws do not apply. . . . The procedure for hearings and review only applies if a decision by the Board "will adversely affect [the practitioner's] appointment to or status as a member of the Medical Staff or his exercise of clinical privileges. . . ." The disputed action by the Board did not affect any physician's appointment or status as a member of the staff. . . .

Within its broad powers of management, some of the business decisions made by the Board will undoubtedly impinge upon matters that relate to or affect the medical staff of the hospital. This fact is unavoidable. However, merely because a decision of the Board affects the staff does not give the staff authority to overrule a valid business decision made by the Board. Allowing the staff this amount of administrative authority would effectively cripple the governing Board of ASL. . . .

In its decision, the circuit court attempted to distinguish between this present situation and the situation wherein a hospital enters into an exclusive contract. We find this attempt to be unpersuasive. An exclusive contract arises when the hospital contracts with an outside physician or group of physicians, whereby the hospital agrees that the physician or group of physicians shall be the only personnel allowed to use certain facilities in the hospital, such as radiology units or emergency room units. Such exclusive contracts are common practice for most hospitals today, and have been almost universally found valid and enforceable, even if not explicitly provided for in corporate bylaws. In the past, ASL has closed several areas of its facility to physicians not part of an exclusive contract. Such areas include anesthesiology, radiology, emergency room care, pathology, EKG interpretation, pulmonary function interpretation and cardiac cathe[te]rization. Plaintiffs do not allege that the prior exclusive contracts entered into by ASL are invalid. . . . Yet there is no logical reason why ASL could close certain areas of its facility to all but a few physicians (via an exclusive contract), yet not be allowed to close its facilities to any new orthopedic surgeons performing certain, named procedures. . . .

The circuit court also concluded that ASL must accept an application from any doctor wishing to have privileges at ASL . . . if the staff is satisfied [that the doctor is qualified.] . . . Such a construction of the Staff Bylaws reaches a result that is contrary to the Corporate Bylaws and common sense. Are we to force ASL to grant privileges to every qualified physician that may stand at its doorstep and announce that he or she will henceforth be using the hospital's facilities, simply because the staff said they could? . . . The result reached by the circuit court . . . is impractical in a corporate business environment. Imagine the confusion and lack of clear lines of management authority that would ensue at the hospital if the Board had only the minimal amount of control over its medical staff that the circuit court would give it. . . .

Hospitals have legally defined responsibilities and duties. . . . [T]he negligent act of a doctor can impute liability to a hospital under a theory of *respondeat superior* . . . [Also], separate liability for negligence attaches to a hospital when it has breached its own standards, or those available in the same or similar community or hospitals generally, such as allowing a known incompetent doctor to remain on staff. . . . It would be completely illogical to first impose a duty of reasonable care upon a hospital, and then later strip the hospital of the ability and power to implement the policies and programs required to fulfill that duty. . . . Therefore, the circuit court's judgment is reversed.

Notes: Hospital and Medical Staff Bylaws; Exclusive Contracts; Economic Credentialing

1. *The "Two-Headed Monster."* Notice how the medical staff credentialing process was caricatured in *Mahan.* The court ridiculed the idea that the hospital has to "grant privileges to every qualified physician that may stand at its doorstep and announce that he or she will henceforth be using the hospital's facilities, simply because the staff said they could? . . . [This] is impractical in a corporate business environment. Imagine the confusion and lack of clear lines of management authority that would ensue at the hospital if the Board had only th[is] minimal amount of control over its medical staff. . . ." "Allowing the staff this amount of administrative authority would effectively cripple the governing Board." Yet many hospital administrators would say that this is precisely how hospitals have traditionally functioned, because hospitals are essentially required to maintain "open" medical staffs, and hospital boards are expected to, and do, simply "rubber stamp" medical staff recommendations. In the view of one experienced lawyer, "The internal organization of hospitals has remained essentially uniform and unchanged for the past seventy years.[1] Today, as in the past, the hospital is composed of three independent lines of authority: the medical staff, the management, and the board of directors.[2] . . . The self-governing medical staff is a feature of hospitals found only in the United States and Canada.[3] . . . The thesis of this article is that the self-governing medical staff model is an anachronistic mode of hospital organization that generally impedes the delivery of high-quality, cost-effective care. As other commentators have suggested, the law has imposed an organizational structure on hospitals that conflicts with the current regulatory agenda of promoting such care.[4] . . . Consequently, federal and state

---

[1] Harris, Regulation and Internal Control in Hospitals, 55 Bull. N.Y. Acad. Med. 88, 90-92 (1979).

[2] See Hall, Institutional Control of Physician Behavior: Legal Barriers to Health Care Cost Containment, 137 Pa. L. Rev. 431, 505-506 (1988).

[3] The Report of the Joint Task Force on Hospital-Medical Staff Relationships of the AMA and the AHA 10 (1985).

[4] See generally, Havighurst, Doctors and Hospitals: An Antitrust Perspective on Traditional Relationships, 1984 Duke L.J. 1071, 1087-1092; Hall, supra n.2, at 528-532.

laws should be amended or repealed to allow hospitals to organize themselves according to their own managerial vision of hospital organization." Thaddeus J. Nodzenski, A Critical Analysis of the Self-governing Medical Staff, 43 Okla. L. Rev. 591, 592 (1990). The unique structure of American hospitals has been described as "attractive as a two-headed monster" and as "stable as a three-legged stool." See H. L. Smith, Two Lines of Authority Are One Too Many, 84 Modern Hosp., March 1955, at 59. For general discussion of the nature, status, and powers of the hospital medical staff, see William Brewbaker, Antitrust Conspiracy Doctrine and the Hospital Enterprise, 74 B.U. L. Rev. 67 (1994); John Horty & Daniel Mulholland, The Legal Status of the Hospital Medical Staff, 22 St. Louis U. L.J. 485 (1978).

2. *Is the Paradigm Shifting?* Many commentators have noticed a possible paradigm shift in progress. They see in decisions like *Mahan* the potential demise of the independent medical staff, to be replaced by an ordinary employment contract model that gives the hospital much greater control over medical as well as managerial policy. See Nodzenski, supra. This development is also mirrored in financing structures like HMOs and other integrated delivery systems that combine hospital and physician services under a single capitation payment. Observe, though, that Nodzenski, who applauds the new-found authority of medical institutions, works for the hospital industry. Are his views sound nevertheless? The subordination of physicians is vehemently opposed by organized medicine, for reasons articulated in the discussion of the corporate practice of medicine doctrine in Chapter 4.B.3.

Consider what weapons physicians have in their legal arsenal to oppose fundamental structuring of the hospital medical staff. Realize that this organizational structure emerged as the result of accreditation standards set by the Joint Commission, which require separate medical staff bylaws that are under the control of member physicians. This structure is also embedded in law to the extent that many hospital licensing statutes incorporate the Joint Commission standards by reference. Other legal sources explored throughout this chapter support this structure less visibly. Consider, for instance, the impact of the charitable tax exemption, or the corporate practice of medicine doctrine, on how doctors relate to hospitals. Note also that this dual line of authority is mirrored in the structure of insurance, which pays hospitals separately from physicians, and which results in Blue Cross vs. Blue Shield, and Medicare Part A vs. Part B.

Assuming that the traditional medical staff structure remains intact at least on paper, how far can a hospital feasibly go in circumventing this structure? Could a hospital use exclusive contracts for the entire array of medical services? It is not possible to consider this question fully until other bodies of law are explored, such as tax exemption and referral fee prohibitions that are discussed in Chapter 4.B.2 and 4.E, and even then the answer is far from clear. The issue may be joined, however, by the growing use of physicians known as "hospitalists" — hospital-based primary care physicians who replace patients' regular physicians in managing care when the patients are hospitalized, as is the practice in European hospitals. Hospitals view this hospitalist system as an effective way to impose greater managerial discipline on patient care decisions, in order to improve scheduling, reduce costs, and increase quality. Primary care physicians like the convenience of being able to concentrate their attention on their office-based practice, especially under HMO payment structures that do not reward them, or may even penalize them, for hospital care. However, many physicians view this as an invasion of their established patient relationships, and specialists see this as a threat to their source of referrals and income. So far, hospitalist programs are voluntary, in the sense that primary care physicians can use them at their discretion, but it is anticipated that hospitals may begin to make this new system mandatory. For a general overview of ethical and public policy issues, see Farrin A. Manian, Whither Continuity of Care?, 340 New Eng. J. Med. 1362 (1999); Steven Pantilat et al., A New Doctor in the House: Ethical Issues in Hospitalist Systems, 282 JAMA 171 (1999); David Meltzer, Hospitalists and the Doctor-patient Relationship, 30 J. Leg. Stud. 589 (2001); R. M. Wachter & L. Goldman, The Emerging Role of "Hospitalists" in the American Health Care System, 335 New Eng. J. Med. 514 (1996).

3. *Bylaws Are Binding.* Are *St. John's* and *Mahan* in conflict? If not, how are they reconciled? If so, which has the better argument? Can you possibly justify *Mahan*'s statement that "this case is not about appointments or the assignment or curtailment of [clinical] privileges. It is about an administrative decision. . . . The disputed action by the Board did not affect any physician's appointment or status as a member of the staff."? What if this action were taken right after the orthopedic physician group had just hired a new physician who was in the process of applying for staff privileges? Is *Mahan* limited to a circumstance of dire economic or medical necessity? Does it turn on the wording of the particular bylaws used by that hospital?

Many other courts have agreed with *St. John's* that medical staff bylaws constitute a contract and cannot be amended or ignored unilaterally by the hospital board. But see Tredrea v. Anesthesia & Analgesia P.C., 584 N.W.2d 276 (Iowa 1998). Yet, most courts also agree with *Mahan* that hospitals are free to enter unilaterally into exclusive contracts or stop admitting new members to a portion or all of the medical staff. E.g., Garibaldi v. Applebaum, 742 N.E.2d 279 (Ill. 2000) (awarding an exclusive contract is an administrative decision and so does not require a medical staff hearing for excluded physicians because the decision is not necessarily based on physician competence); Dutta v. St. Francis Reg. Medical Center, 867 P.2d 1057 (Kan. 1994) (bylaws requirement of a hearing does not apply to "hospital's managerial decision based on business considerations," in contrast with decision based on individual physician's competence). Courts reconcile these two lines of authority in two ways: (1) They distinguish, as *Mahan* did, between administrative decisions reserved to the hospital board versus medical decisions made by the medical staff. When the reasons for action are economic, they fall in the board's realm to act unilaterally. How well does this square with *St John's*? (2) Courts also distinguish between the possession of clinical privileges and the right to exercise those privileges, reasoning that medical staff bylaws protect only the former, not the latter. This distinction arises in exclusive contract cases, where the hospital picks a certain set of physicians to staff a portion of the hospital, such as the emergency room or the room where anesthesia is administered. The result is that not only new doctors but also existing doctors lose the ability to practice in those areas of the hospital. Courts uphold this nonetheless by reasoning that, technically, the non-contracting doctors still retain their status as members of the medical staff and are entitled to practice in other areas of the hospital. One court said that "such reasoning simply defies logic.

Hospital privileges are not, in reality, some amorphous grant [of status]. . . . They are instead quite specific descriptions of very particular acts a doctor is permitted to do in that facility. Precluding a doctor from performing those acts is, as Plaintiffs here assert, very much a denial or termination of hospital privileges." Aluko v. Charlotte-Mecklenburg Hospital Authority, 959 F. Supp. 729 (W.D.N.C. 1997). However, this court also "recognize[d] the very real needs that hospitals . . . have to respond in a rapidly changing health care market with its unique blend of savage competition and heavy-handed governmental regulation." The court reconciled these competing considerations by reasoning that it is not the form of restriction that matters (denial of staff privileges versus limiting use of the facilities); rather, it is the reason given for the restriction: quality of care versus an economic reason. Where the physicians' "professional reputations are intact, . . . there is no foreclosure of opportunity to practice their profession nor bar to seeking privileges in other institutions." Is this reasoning convincing? In today's marketplace, might not a reputation for being a high-cost or inefficient physician potentially be just as damaging as having a reputation for poor quality? For a thorough analysis of these and other cases, see Bryan A. Liang, An Overview and Analysis of Challenges to Medical Staff Exclusive Contracts, 18 J. Leg. Med. 1 (1997). See generally Annot., 74 A.L.R.3d 1268 (1974).

4. *Economic Credentialing.* The focus in these cases on hospitals' motivation for closing departments or using exclusive contracts points to a broader issue of immense importance to health care law and public policy—whether hospitals can explicitly consider economic factors in choosing physicians in addition to, or instead of, quality-of-care factors. In the trade, this is known as "economic credentialing." The decisions discussed in the next section express the traditional attitude that only quality factors are relevant, but they arose before cost concerns became so paramount. Now that public policy embodies cost concerns as well, can they be included in the balance of considerations? Indeed, it appears from some cases that financially motivated exclusions are *easier* to justify than those motivated by quality concerns, because only the latter must be pursued through the medical staff hearing process and justified under the bylaws. If one is concerned about patient care, shouldn't this distinction cut in exactly the opposite direction?

This issue remains largely unsettled, however. In those jurisdictions that require economically based exclusions to be pursued through the bylaws process, two obstacles remain: (1) the need to amend traditional quality-based medical staff bylaws to make sure economic concerns are allowable criteria for reviewing physicians; (2) the legal uncertainty over whether economic concerns can *trump* quality concerns. Physicians who are excluded from contracts and medical staff membership because their treatment patterns are too expensive will likely complain that the hospital is sacrificing high quality for low costs. So far, hospitals have been able to avoid this charge by arguing that cost savings do not in fact compromise quality (e.g., swapping one good high-cost doctor for another good low-cost doctor), or by arguing that lower cost treatment produces higher quality (e.g., reducing the risks of unnecessary surgery or medication). See, e.g., Knapp v. Palos Community Hospital, 465 N.E.2d 554 (Ill. App. Ct. 1984) (physician whose costs were 31 percent higher than others also had serious quality problems from overutilization of tests and medication). The courts have not yet squarely faced a credentialing case with an overt trade-off of quality for cost. The same issues also exist for

HMOs, as discussed below. For additional analysis, see John Blum, Economic Credentialing: A New Twist in Hospital Appraisal Processes, 12 J. Leg. Med. 427 (1991); Hall, 137 U. Pa. L. Rev. at 518 supra.

5. *"Clean Sweep" Clauses.* Separate from the question of what rights physicians have who are not included in exclusive contracts, there is the question of what rights physicians have who do have such a contract. Exclusive contracts usually require contracting physicians to waive their hearing rights and to be subject to ordinary contract termination provisions. These contracts also usually contain "clean sweep" provisions that require contracting physicians to give up their medical staff membership and clinical privileges if the contract is terminated, without going through the normal hearing processes. Courts generally hold these provisions enforceable, even if they are not also in the bylaws, ruling that the contract prevails because physicians can waive their rights under the bylaws. Abrams v. Saint John's Hospital, 30 Cal. Rptr. 2d 603 (Ct. App. 1994); Hrehorovich v. Harbor Hospital Center, 614 A.2d 1021 (Md. Ct. App. 1992). When these contracts provide for "no cause" termination at will, however, they raise issues of public policy explored below in section 4.C.3 that result in some courts examining the actual reasons for termination.

Notes: Physician Employment; Labor Law

1. *Covenants Not to Compete.* As illustrated by Berlin v. Sarah Bush Lincoln Health Center, page 432, physician contracts, both with hospitals and with medical clinics and groups, also usually contain restrictive covenants that prevent them from practicing with competitors in the vicinity for a defined period of time. Physicians have been somewhat more successful in attacking these contract provisions. Covenants not to compete, in this and other employment contexts, are viewed with suspicion by the courts because they tend to contravene public policies in favor of free trade and the right to work. Nevertheless, these covenants are upheld if they are reasonable as to duration, geographic scope, and the range of activities covered, and if they are not otherwise contrary to the public interest. See generally P. Berg, Judicial Enforcement of Covenants not to Compete Between Physicians: Protecting Doctors' Interests at Patients' Expense, 45 Rutgers L. Rev. 1 (1992); Arthur S. Di Dio, The Legal Implications of Noncompetition Agreements in Physician Contracts, 20 J. Leg. Med. 457 (2000); Annot., 62 A.L.R.3d 970, 1014 (1975).

The issue of greatest relevance in the medical context is whether it violates public policy to restrain the practice of a physician whose specialized services are much needed in the community. For example, in Dick v. Geist, 693 P.2d 1133 (Idaho Ct. App. 1985), the court refused to enforce a restrictive covenant that would have excluded the two doctors who rendered 90 percent of the neonatal care in the community. See also Irdell Digestive Disease Clinic v. Petrozza, 373 S.E.2d 449 (N.C. Ct. App. 1988) (refusing to enforce covenant that would leave only one gastroenterologist in the local area). One court refused to enforce a restriction against a general practitioner who left an HMO and took 167 of his patients with him, even though there was no local shortage of physicians. The court was particularly disturbed by a penalty clause that assessed $700 for each patient the doctor took with him. The court reasoned that this "financial wedge . . . needlessly hindered the continuation of existing and successful doctor/ patient relationships . . . vital to the provision of health care." Humana v. Jacobson, 614 So. 2d 520 (Fla. Dist. Ct. App. 1992). However, another line of cases has reasoned that the public interest is equally well served if a doctor is allowed to treat different patients in another part of the state. Canfield v. Spear, 254 N.E.2d 433 (Ill. 1969) ("the health of persons elsewhere is just as important"); Concord Orthapaedics v. Forbes, 702 A.2d 1273 (N.H. 1997) (public policy not violated where convenant restricts physician from seeing only new, not existing, patients).

2. *Labor Laws.* In addition to the *private* law rights of *individual* doctors, the law is also concerned with the *public* law rights of *groups* of health care employees. By convention, the former set of issues is labeled "employment law" and the latter "labor law." Other employment law issues relating to "at will" employment, wrongful discharge, and various employment discrimination laws are explored below at pages 464 and 471. The remainder of these notes survey labor law.

The National Labor Relations Act (NLRA), 29 U.S.C. §§151 et seq., establishes a comprehensive regulatory scheme, administered by the National Labor Relations Board (NLRB), to protect employees' rights to form a union, to require their employer to bargain with the union in good faith and honor collective bargaining agreements, and to strike if they are dissatisfied with the terms or conditions of their employment. Employed physicians' efforts to unionize must clear a critical hurdle. The Supreme Court has interpreted the NLRA as excluding from its protections "managerial employees," those who assist management in setting and implementing policy. NLRB v. Bell Aerospace, 416 U.S. 267 (1974). In NLRB v. Yeshiva University, 444 U.S. 672 (1980), the Court determined in a 5-4 vote that this exclusion applies to professional employees — in that case, university professors — who serve on important committees and heavily influence hiring decisions. In Delphic dictum, however, the Court cautioned that not all employed professionals are ipso facto managers: "[E]mployees whose decision-making is limited to the routine discharge of professional duties in projects to which they have been assigned cannot be excluded from coverage. . . . Only if an employee's activities fall outside the scope of the duties routinely performed by similarly situated professionals will he be found aligned with management." 444 U.S. at 690.

The meaning of this distinction for employed doctors remains a matter of considerable dispute. In FHP and Union of American Physicians and Dentists, 274 N.L.R.B. 1141 (1985), the NLRB determined that all 70 doctors employed by an HMO were "managerial" and therefore not able to unionize because they served on numerous peer review and patient care committees that formulate and effectuate clinical policy. Even though these are the same committees typically found in a hospital, a prior decision ruled that the employed physicians at a teaching hospital (ironically, at Yeshiva University's medical school) were not managerial because clinical policy there was merely advisory, and department chairs exercised most of the managerial power. Montefiore Hospital, 261 NLRB 569 (1982). The NLRB has since applied the *Montefiore* precedent to HMOs, finding physicians are not managerial. E.g., New York University Medical Center, 324 NLRB 887 (1997). See generally Marina Angel, Professionals and Unionization,

66 Minn L. Rev. 383 (1982); David Wanger, Unionization by Salaried Physicians and the Managerial-Employee Exclusion: The Need for a Modified Approach, 15 L. Med. & Health Care 144, 149 (1987).

3. *Physician Unions*. Although the disturbing specter of a physician strike is uncommon, labor union activity in the health care sector is rapidly increasing. Most of this activity involves nonphysicians such as nurses and technicians, but even among physicians there is an increased interest in unionizing as a way to counteract loss of clinical and economic autonomy. In 1999, the AMA's House of Delegates took the unprecedented step of calling for the AMA to form a national bargaining unit under federal law to represent employed physicians and residents. The politically conservative leadership of the AMA has long opposed the formation of a union, but the AMA membership insisted on this move to give physicians a stronger voice against HMOs and hospitals, and to preempt efforts by other labor organization that are eager to take the lead in forming physician unions. It is important to realize, though, that the NLRA covers only employees. This limitation would seem to exclude independent physicians on hospital or HMO medical staffs from the NLRA's protections. 329 NLRB No. 55 (1999); Charles Craver, The Application of Labor and Antitrust Laws to Physician Unions, 27 Hastings L.J. 55 (1975). Despite this limitation, physician unionizing is still of pressing importance due to the great increase in physician employment projected in the near future, both within HMOs and within hospitals. For instance, the NLRB ruled that hospital residents and interns are eligible to form a union, reversing a 20-year precedent that had declared them to be only students, not employees. Boston Medical Center Corp., 330 NLRB No. 20 (1999). For commentary and discussion of the potentially dramatic implications for running large medical centers, see Symposium, 342 New Eng. J. Med. 429 (2000).

One advantage physicians seek by unionizing is protection from the antitrust laws, by virtue of the antitrust exemption for labor activities. 15 U.S.C. §17. (Otherwise, every employee strike over wages would constitute per se price fixing.) Subsequent sections of these materials describe the antitrust difficulties physicians face when they organize into groups to negotiate with insurance companies, HMOs and PPOs over reimbursement rates. See Chapter 4.D.2. As a result, doctors have begun to label their negotiating groups "unions." The flaw in this tactic is that doctors traditionally have not been employees of insurance plans; they are, at best, independent contractors. Therefore, their collective actions could result in huge damages or even criminal sentences. See AMA v. United States, 317 U.S. 519 (1943) (rejecting labor exemption claim made by physicians who boycotted an HMO). To avoid this, physicians are seeking legislative authority to engage in collective bargaining with HMOs (but not strikes or boycotts), in order to offset HMO market power. The physicians' first victory was in Texas in 1999; but so far, similar legislative proposals have not been adopted at the national level. Although state law cannot give physician unions the same status they have under federal labor law, it can achieve the same objective of conferring an exemption from antitrust laws using the "state-action immunity" doctrine discussed on page 515.

4. *Nurse Managers*. The "managerial employee" exclusion from the NLRA's protections has surprisingly proven troublesome for nurses as well. Nurse employees in hospitals and nursing homes historically had no problem qualifying unless they held explicitly supervisory positions. In 1994, the Supreme Court ruled, however, that nurses employed in a nursing home exercised sufficient de facto

supervision over nurses' aides to meet the managerial exclusion because they controlled work assignments. Health Care & Retirement Corp. of America v. NLRB, 511 U.S. 571 (1994). The NLRB, however, has resisted following this precedent, for instance, by finding that hospital "charge nurses" do not have managerial status. In NLRB v. Kentucky River Community Care, 532 U.S. 706 (2001), the Court reversed the NLRB again, holding that it read the Act too narrowly in ruling that supervising nurses at a mental health facility are not managers.

5. *Disruption of Patient Care; Definition of Bargaining Units.* Until 1974, nonprofit hospitals, which constitute the bulk of the industry, were not covered by the NLRA. In that year, however, Congress amended the act with provisions directed specifically to the health care industry. 29 U.S.C. §§152, 158, 169, 183. In doing so, Congress expressed a concern that union activity not disrupt patient care. Specifically, both the Senate and the House stated that "due consideration should be given by the Board to preventing proliferation of bargaining units in the health care industry" because too many unions within a single institution would pose an excessive risk of crippling, repetitive strikes. 1974 U.S. Code Cong. & Admin. News 3950. This "nonproliferation" directive has been a constant thorn in the side of the NLRB's numerous attempts to determine the appropriate scope of hospital bargaining units for nurses and other nonphysician employees. See, e.g., NLRB v. HMO International, 678 F.2d 806 (9th Cir. 1982) (improper to exclude vocational nurses from RN's union) (noting the "nearly perfect record of reversals of the NLRB by the court of appeals in review of health care bargaining units").

In response to a series of court reversals, the NLRB, which is notorious for deciding all policy issues in adjudication, took the extraordinary step of initiating a rulemaking proceeding to define the proper approach to health care unit determinations. Its final regulations allow up to eight, but only eight, separate bargaining units in any hospital, regardless of local circumstances: RNs, physicians, other professionals, technicians, clerical, maintenance, security guards, and others. 29 C.F.R. §103.30. These rules generated intense opposition from health care management, which perceives that carving units into this many divisions greatly increases the ease of unionizing. The rule was upheld by the Supreme Court, however. American Hospital Association v. NLRB, 499 U.S. 606 (1991).

6. *Additional Readings.* For general discussions of labor law issues in the health care industry, see Grace Budrys, When Doctors Join Unions (Cornell Univ. Press 1997); Wm. Brewbaker, Physician Unions and the Future of Competition in the Health Care Sector, 33 U.C. Davis L. Rev. 545-600 (2000); M. LeRoy et al., The Law and Economics of Collective Bargaining for Hospitals, 9 Yale J. on Reg. 1 (1992); Mark A. Rothstein, Labor and Employment Law Issues in Hospital Closures and Downsizing, 28 J. Health & Hosp. L. 336 (1995); Comment, 36 Hous. L. Rev. 951 (1999); Comment, 19 Cardozo L. Rev. 1125 (1997); Note, 34 Colum. J.L. & Soc. Probs. 1-48 (2000); Note, 42 Ariz. L. Rev. 803-833 (2000); Note, 52 Vand. L. Rev. 1051 (1999).

Problem: Economic Credentialing

You are the lawyer for Marcus Welby Community Hospital. The administrator approaches you about how best to amend the bylaws so that the hospital can get rid of doctors who are costing the hospital too much money under Medicare and

HMO insurance. The administrator is concerned about which removal actions can be defended in court and which bylaw amendments are politically feasible with physicians. Advise the administrator on each of these options:

- Amend the Hospital Bylaws to give the hospital board authority to remove doctors from the medical staff for any reason, regardless of the medical staff's own recommendations, as long as the medical staff is first consulted.
- Amend the Medical Staff Bylaws to declare that an additional criterion for medical staff membership is to practice an efficient style of medicine that avoids wasting medical resources or providing unnecessary care.
- Amend the Medical Staff Bylaws to declare that any physician who consistently loses money for the hospital will be removed from the medical staff.
- Forget about amending any bylaws. Instead, go after physicians who are economic losers based on their general medical competence and their unwillingness to be cooperative.
- Keep but supplant the entire medical staff structure by limiting who can practice in each department through one-year renewable contracts with the 200 best doctors out of the present 300.

2. Medical Staff Disputes

Access to a hospital is essential for most physicians to carry on a practice. Hospitals, on the other hand, are coming under increasing legal and economic pressure to monitor who joins the medical staff. From the intersection of these two competing interests springs a powerful flow of litigation, in the health care field, second only to malpractice. These materials explore which legal theories are available to physicians wanting to challenge their exclusion, and how much scrutiny courts impose on these decisions. We begin with common law doctrine, first as applied to hospitals and then to HMOs. Following that is antitrust law. As you read the first two cases, try to identify what species of common law is being used to review staffing decisions by private hospitals, and attempt to articulate what hospitals have to show to justify their decisions.

■ GREISMAN v. NEWCOMB HOSPITAL
192 A.2d 817 (N.J. 1963)

Jacobs, Judge.

In 1958, the plaintiff graduated from the Philadelphia College of Osteopathy with the degree of doctor of osteopathy. [See nn.3 and 4 in Weiss v. York Hospital below at page 481 for a definition of osteopathy.] He served an internship, took the full medical boards in New York, and was given an unqualified license to practice medicine and surgery in that state. Thereafter, he was admitted to practice in Michigan, Florida and New Jersey. His New Jersey admission by the State Board of Medical Examiners constituted an unrestricted license to practice medicine and surgery within the borders of our State. See Falcone v. Middlesex Co. Medical Soc., 34 N.J. 582, 170 A.2d 791 (1961). In July 1959, he began the general practice of medicine in the City of Vineland and, in November 1959, he opened an office in Newfield which is in the Vineland metropolitan area. Until January 1962 he also engaged in the practice of medicine from his home in Vineland. He is the only licensed physician in Newfield, is the plant physician for a Newfield company engaged in heavy industrial work and for an additional company engaged in the making of glassware, and is the school physician for Newfield's public school as well as for a Catholic school in the same community. He states that he is the only osteopathic physician fully licensed to practice general medicine and surgery in the metropolitan Vineland area which is said to have a population approximating 100,000; the defendants state that there is another osteopathic physician practicing in Vineland but the suggested variance is of no real significance here.

In 1961, the plaintiff sought to file an application for admission to the courtesy staff of the Newcomb Hospital which is located in Vineland about a mile from his home. The hospital was incorporated in 1921, is operated as a general hospital, and is the only hospital in the Vineland metropolitan area. Its certificate of incorporation sets forth the purposes for which it was formed including . . . the care of sick and injured persons residing in the vicinity of Vineland. . . . The hospital is a nonprofit corporation and its governing body is a Board of Trustees consisting of not less than 15 members. It solicits and receives funds annually in the form of charitable contributions and has received funds from the Ford Foundation. Several years ago it constructed a new building, the cost being borne almost entirely by public subscription. It receives funds from the City of Vineland for the treatment of indigent patients from within the city, and funds from the County of Cumberland for the treatment of indigent patients from other areas in the county. It receives tax exemptions available to nonprofit corporations operated for charitable and like purposes. It is eligible for federal funds under the Hill-Burton Act.

Despite suitable requests, the Newcomb Hospital refused to permit the plaintiff to file any application for admission to its courtesy staff. In taking that course it did not question his personal or professional qualifications nor did it purport to exercise a discretion in the process of administrative screening and selection. It rested entirely on a provision in the hospital bylaws which sets forth that an applicant for membership on the courtesy staff must be a graduate of a medical school approved by the American Medical Association and must be a member of the County Medical Society. The American Medical Association has long rejected schools of osteopathy, though the original supporting reasons have been largely dissipated. See Report of the Committee for the Study of Relations Between Osteopathy and Medicine, 158 JAMA 736 (1955). Admittedly, the plaintiff is not a graduate of a medical school approved by the American Medical Association and, because of his schooling, his application to the County Medical Society was never acted upon. The school he graduated from is an accredited school of osteopathy, has been approved as in good standing by the New Jersey State Board of Medical Examiners, and has long given the full traditional medical course as well as osteopathic teaching. . . .

The Law Division found that the Newcomb Hospital did not confine itself to any specialized branch of medicine and had assumed the position and status of the only general hospital open to the public within the convenient accessibility of the inhabitants of the metropolitan area of Vineland, including Newfield; that the plaintiff had suffered economic and other harm because he was not permitted to admit his patients to the hospital or to serve them professionally once they were admitted, or to use the emergency room services of the hospital; that his patients suffered restriction in their choice of physicians or hospital facilities because of the plaintiff's inability to attend them professionally at the hospital, and that this was not minimized by the fact that the plaintiff was permitted to visit them at the hospital without, however, any opportunity to read their charts or prescribe for them. . . .

The defendants contend that the Newcomb Hospital is a private rather than a public hospital, that it may in its discretion exclude physicians from its medical staff, and that no legal ground exists for judicial interference with its refusal to consider the plaintiff's application for membership. . . . Broad judicial expressions may, of course, be found to the effect that hospitals such as Newcomb are private in nature and that their staff admission policies are entirely discretionary. They are private in the sense that they are nongovernmental but they are hardly private in other senses. Newcomb is a nonprofit organization dedicated by its certificate of incorporation to the vital public use of serving the sick and injured, its funds are in good measure received from public sources and through public solicitation, and its tax benefits are received because of its nonprofit and nonprivate aspects. It constitutes a virtual monopoly in the area in which it functions and it is in no position to claim immunity from public supervision and control because of its allegedly private nature. Indeed, in the development of the law, activities much less public than the hospital activities of Newcomb, have commonly been subjected to judicial (as well as legislative) supervision and control to the extent necessary to satisfy the felt needs of the times. See Munn v. Illinois, 94 U.S. 113 (1877); German Alliance Ins. Co. v. Lewis, 233 U.S. 389 (1914); Nebbia v. New York, 291 U.S. 502 (1934).

During the course of history, judges have often applied the common law so as to regulate private businesses and professions for the common good; perhaps the most notable illustration is the duty of serving all comers on reasonable terms which was imposed by the common law on innkeepers, carriers, farriers and the like. See Falcone v. Middlesex Co. Medical Soc., supra, 34 N.J., at p. 594; Messenger et al. v. Pennsylvania R.R. Co., 36 N.J.L. 407 (Sup. Ct. 1873). In the *Messenger* case Chief Justice Beasley, speaking for the former Supreme Court, noted that a railroad, though a private corporation, is engaged in a "public employment," that it "owes a duty to the community" and that under considerations of public policy it must be held under obligation to serve without discrimination. On appeal, Justice Bedle, speaking for the Court of Errors and Appeals, expressed the view that although railroad corporations are private, they hold their property "as a quasi-public trust," and that as trustees they must conduct their operations in such manner so as to insure to every member of the community the equal enjoyment of the means of transportation.

Implemented by specific legislation, the supervision of private businesses and professions for the public good has gone far beyond the early common law fields. In Munn v. Illinois, supra, a state's imposition of maximum charges for the storage of grain in warehouses was sustained in an opinion which stressed that the private property was devoted "to a public use" and was therefore subject to public regulation; in German Alliance Ins. Co. v. Lewis, supra, a state's fixing of fire insurance rates was upheld on the ground that the business of insurance was "so far affected with a public interest" as to justify its regulation; and in Nebbia v. New York, supra, a state's extensive regulation of its milk industry was upheld in an opinion by Justice Roberts which frankly recognized that there is no closed class or category of businesses affected with a public interest, that the phrase means no more than that an industry, for adequate reason, is subject to control for the public good, and that "upon proper occasion and by appropriate measures the state may regulate a business in any of its aspects." . . .

It is evident that . . . similar policy considerations apply with equal strength and call for a declaration that . . . Dr. Greisman is entitled to have his application evaluated on its own individual merits without regard to the bylaw requirement rejected by the Law Division. His personal and professional qualifications are not in dispute here; he lives in Vineland, has an office in Newfield in the Vineland metropolitan area, has an unrestricted license to practice medicine and surgery, and is engaged in the general practice of medicine. All he seeks, at this juncture, is simply permission to file his application for membership on the courtesy staff of the Newcomb Hospital and have it considered to the end that, if he is passed on favorably in accordance with the hospital's valid bylaws, he and his patients, as such, will have hospital facilities when needed.

The Newcomb Hospital is the only hospital in the Vineland metropolitan area and it is publicly dedicated, primarily to the care of the sick and injured of Vineland and its vicinity and, thereafter to the care of such other persons as may be accommodated. Doctors need hospital facilities and a physician practicing in the metropolitan Vineland area will understandably seek them at the Newcomb Hospital. Furthermore, every patient of his will want the Newcomb Hospital facilities to be readily available. It hardly suffices to say that the patient could enter the hospital under the care of a member of the existing staff, for his personal physician would have no opportunity of participating in his treatment; nor does it suffice to say that there are other hospitals outside the metropolitan Vineland area, for they may be too distant or unsuitable to his needs and desires. All this indicates very pointedly that, while the managing officials may have discretionary powers in the selection of the medical staff, those powers are deeply imbedded in public aspects, and are rightly viewed . . . as fiduciary powers to be exercised reasonably and for the public good.

It must be borne in mind that we are not asked to pass on a discretionary exercise of judgment but only on the validity of the bylaw requirement. Therefore, we need not concern ourselves with any of the larger issues relating to discretionary limits or the general lengths to which a hospital may go in conditioning staff admissions on the approval of outside bodies. Viewed realistically, our proper concern here is whether the hospital had the right to exclude consideration of the plaintiff, solely because he was a doctor of osteopathy and had not been admitted, because of his osteopathic schooling, to his County Medical Society. . . . In this day there should be no hesitancy in rejecting as arbitrary, the stand that a doctor of osteopathy, though fully licensed by state authority and reputably engaged in the general practice of medicine and as the local school and plant physician, is nonetheless automatically, and without individual evaluation, to be considered unfit for staff membership at the only available hospital in the rather populous metropolitan area where he resides and practices. The public interest and considerations of fairness and justness point unerringly away from the hospital's position and we agree fully with the Law Division's judgment rejecting it.

Hospital officials are properly vested with large measures of managing discretion and to the extent that they exert their efforts toward the elevation of hospital standards and higher medical care, they will receive broad judicial support. But they must never lose sight of the fact that the hospitals are operated not for private ends but for the benefit of the public, and that their existence is for the purpose of faithfully furnishing facilities to the members of the medical profession in aid of their service to the public. They must recognize that their powers, particularly those relating to the selection of staff members, are powers in trust which are always to be dealt with as such. While reasonable and constructive exercises of judgment should be honored, courts would indeed be remiss if they declined to intervene where, as here, the powers were invoked at the threshold to preclude an application for staff membership, not because of any lack of individual merit, but for a reason unrelated to sound hospital standards and not in furtherance of the common good.

Affirmed.

■ NANAVATI v. BURDETTE TOMLIN MEMORIAL HOSPITAL
526 A.2d 697 (N.J. 1987)

POLLOCK, J.

This appeal arises out of the revocation of the staff privileges of Suketu H. Nanavati (Dr. Nanavati) as a cardiologist at Burdette Tomlin Memorial Hospital (the hospital). . . .

The background of this case is a dispute between Dr. Nanavati and Dr. Robert Sorensen, who at the time was the chief of cardiology, chairman of the Department of Medicine, and a member of the Board of Governors at the hospital. The dispute originated over the allocation of the reading of electrocardiograms (ECGs or EKGs), which, at $5 per reading, produced an annual income of approximately $75,000. Burdette Tomlin is the only hospital in Cape May County, and when he was granted staff privileges, Dr. Nanavati was the only board-certified cardiologist in the county. Before the arrival of Dr. Nanavati in 1979, Dr. Sorensen, an internist, enjoyed a virtual monopoly on reading ECGs. Dr. Nanavati was allowed to read ECGs one day each week, but when he requested an additional day, Dr. Sorensen rejected his request. The rejection stimulated Dr. Nanavati into criticizing Dr. Sorensen, who retaliated. As the discord between the two doctors escalated, Dr. Nanavati allegedly committed a series of violations of the hospital's bylaws. On August 2, 1982, the medical staff executive committee "voted unanimously to act toward the revocation of Dr. Nanavati's medical staff privileges." That action marked the beginning of lengthy proceedings before the hospital authorities and before federal and state courts in this state.

Pursuant to the hospital bylaws, the chairman of the medical staff executive committee requested the hospital executive committee to take corrective action.

The executive committee forwarded the request to the chief of the Department of Medicine, who appointed an ad hoc committee to investigate the matter. The charges against Dr. Nanavati were captioned as "Acts of Disruptive Behavior" and "Failure to Cooperate with Hospital Personnel Regarding the Use of Facilities Especially During the Summer Months and the Emergent Admissions Procedures."

Underlying these charges is the contention that Dr. Nanavati caused disruption in violation of a bylaw provision requiring a staff doctor to

> be of a temperament and disposition that will enable him to work in harmony with his colleagues on the Medical Staff; with the professional, technical, and other personnel in the hospital, and with the administration, accepting criticism without resentment and offering it in a spirit and manner that is constructive and devoid of offense and malice. . . .

The further allegation is that Dr. Nanavati violated a bylaw provision that a staff member "must enjoy the reputation of being an ethical and conscientious practitioner and must strictly abide by the Code of Ethics. . . ." At no time has the hospital questioned Dr. Nanavati's technical competence.

On August 23, 1982, the ad hoc committee "found against Dr. Nanavati on all charges and specifications" and recommended as the only appropriate punishment "his discharge from the Medical Staff of Burdette Tomlin Memorial Hospital, together with the permanent deprivation of Burdette Memorial Hospital privileges." The executive committee of the medical staff affirmed that finding, and Dr. Nanavati appealed to an ad hoc committee of the medical staff, which unanimously found against him and recommended that he be dismissed from the staff of the hospital. In November, the hospital administrator advised Dr. Nanavati of the revocation of his staff privileges.

Dr. Nanavati immediately filed an action in the Chancery Division, which found that the proceedings had not been conducted in accordance with the hospital's bylaws, enjoined the revocation of Dr. Nanavati's privileges, and remanded the matter for further proceedings to be conducted in accordance with the hospital's bylaws. The Board of Governors thereupon appointed a hearing committee, which recommended on April 15, 1983, "that the action of the medical staff in dismissing Dr. Nanavati be affirmed." Two weeks later, on April 29, the board affirmed the hearing committee's recommendation. . . .

[On appeal] the Chancery Division independently reviewed the record by a preponderance-of-the-evidence standard. The court determined that Dr. Nanavati's staff privileges should not be revoked on the ground of disharmony, absent a showing of actual interference with patient care, and concluded that the record did not support any such showing. Consequently, the court issued a permanent injunction against revocation of his privileges.

Although the Appellate Division affirmed the trial court's finding that the hospital proceedings were invalid, it disagreed with other portions of the trial court's opinion and held that the trial court, in reviewing the revocation of hospital staff privileges, should not have made independent findings of fact, but should have determined whether the hospital's decision was supported by sufficient credible evidence. In addition, the Appellate Division ruled that mere disharmony, although an insufficient ground by itself, is a relevant consideration in revocation proceedings. . . .

We granted Dr. Nanavati's petition for certification to determine the appropriate standard of review of the decision by a hospital to terminate a physician's staff privileges and to determine further whether actual interference with patient care is required in order to terminate those privileges. . . .

Twenty-five years ago we rejected the notion that decisions of private hospitals concerning staff privileges were beyond judicial review. Greisman v. Newcomb Hosp., 192 A.2d 817. By analogy to private businesses affected by the public interest, we ruled that courts should intervene when a hospital denied staff membership "for a reason unrelated to sound hospital standards and in furtherance of the common good." In reaching that conclusion, we also declared that "reasonable and constructive exercises of judgment should be honored. . . ." Thus, courts should sustain a hospital's standard for granting staff privileges if that standard is rationally related to the delivery of health care. A decision is so related if it advances the interests of the public, particularly patients; the hospital; or those who are essential to the hospital's operations, such as doctors and nurses.

Although not quite so deferential when reviewing individual decisions denying staff privileges, courts still apply a relaxed standard of review to those decisions. The test for judicial review of such a decision is whether it is supported by "sufficient reliable evidence, even though of a hearsay nature, to justify the result."

We have previously explained the difference between the two tests by analogy to judicial review of administrative actions. Setting a standard for admission to staff privileges is roughly analogous to the kind of policy decision reflected in administrative rulemaking. Carrying forward the analogy, a hospital's use of that standard to decide a particular case is like quasi- judicial agency action. . . .

Underlying the more relaxed standard is our growing awareness that courts should allow hospitals, as long as they proceed fairly, to run their own business. That sense is tempered by the recognition that doctors need staff privileges to serve their patients, and that the public interest requires that hospitals treat doctors fairly in making decisions about those privileges. . . .

In prior cases, we have considered the denial of privileges to new applicants. . . . Although we have not previously decided a case involving the *revocation* of privileges, . . . [n]onetheless, the standard of judicial review should remain the same. . . .

[I]f a hospital is to care for its patients, the staff, particularly doctors and nurses, must work together. As important as cooperation is to other corporations, it is even more critical in a modern hospital, where no single doctor cares for all the needs of any one patient. Hospital doctors depend on their colleagues, nurses, technicians, and other employees for total patient care. . . . Consequently, a hospital may adopt a bylaw providing that the inability of a doctor to work with nurses and other doctors is a ground for denying or terminating staff privileges. . . .

Doctors, like other people, have quirks, and some doctors are more disagreeable than others. The mere fact that a doctor is irascible, however, does not constitute good cause for termination of his or her hospital privileges. McElhinney v. William Booth Memorial Hosp., 544 S.W.2d 216, 218 (Ky. 1977). Nor should allegations of "disharmony" ever be used as a ruse to deny or terminate staff privileges because of a doctor's race, religion, color, or gender. Likewise, a doctor should not be cut off from staff membership merely because he or she has criticized hospital practices and other doctors. . . . A hospital need not wait for a disruptive doctor to harm a patient before terminating his or her privileges. Nonetheless, more should be required than general complaints of a physician's inability to cooperate with others. To constitute disruptive behavior meriting termination of staff privileges, hospital authorities should present concrete evidence of specific instances of misbehavior, such as unjustified altercations with other doctors or nurses, violations of hospital routines or rules, breaches of professional standards, or the commission of some other act that will adversely affect health care delivery. . . .

The judgment of the Appellate Division is affirmed as modified, and the cause is remanded to the hospital.

Notes: Judicial Review of Medical Staff Disputes

1. *Overview.* Why might a hospital want to exclude a doctor? More doctors, after all, mean more patients. If it is in a hospital's economic interest to exclude only bad doctors, why should we bother to scrutinize the hospital's decision at all?

In addressing these questions, the principal focus of these notes will be the common law fairness theory announced in *Greisman.* The notes explore first whether any judicial review is available, and then the scope of review. As *Nanavati* indicates, it is helpful to divide the scope of judicial review into two components — procedural and substantive — and, further, to divide substantive review into (a) the rationale for the general membership criteria contained in the bylaws and (b) the evidence supporting the application of the bylaws to an individual physician. The primary focus of these notes is on the next-to-last issue: the substantive validity of general criteria.

2. *Other Legal Causes of Action.* There are many other causes of action potentially available to excluded physicians besides common law fairness. Pursued below in section 4.D.1 are challenges under the federal antitrust laws. State antitrust statutes and common law unfair competition theories are another hook for the same hat. Under tort law, excluded physicians can allege defamation, e.g., Purgess v. Sharrock, 33 F.3d 134 (2d Cir. 1994) ($5.1 million damages), civil conspiracy, Nashville Memorial Hospital v. Brinkley, 534 S.W.2d 318 (Tenn. 1976), or tortious interference with contract. The prior section discusses the use of contract law to require hospitals to adhere to their bylaws when reviewing the credentials of existing medical staff members. Several states create statutory causes of action. See, e.g., N.Y. Pub. Health Law §2901-c(1) (McKinney 1985). Doctors excluded from public hospitals can bring constitutional claims. Caine v. Hardy, 905 F.2d 858 (5th Cir. 1990). Finally, as noted below, claims can be brought under the civil rights statutes that protect against discrimination based on suspect classifications such as race or disability, even though physicians, technically speaking, are not employees of the hospital.

Observe that each of these alternative legal theories is limited by elements of the cause of action that do not restrain the common law fairness theory.

3. *Constitutional Issues.* Care must be taken to distinguish the *common law* fairness theory articulated in *Greisman* from *constitutional* due process and equal protection. While the content of the doctrines may (or may not) be the same, their origins are distinctly different. Only public hospitals, that is, those *owned* by state or municipal authorities, are subject to the Constitution; it is well settled that the extensive involvement of private hospitals with public funding and regulation is not sufficient to constitute state action. Blum v. Yaretsky, 457 U.S. 991 (1982).

A constitutional theory that has not succeeded, even at public hospitals, is the *substantive* due process argument that "all licensed physicians have a constitutional right to practice their profession. It is not incumbent on the state to maintain a hospital for the private practice of medicine." Hayman v. City of Galveston, 273 U.S. 414, 417 (1926).

4. *Judicial Review, Pro and Con.* The *Greisman* public-facility theory has not won uniform acceptance. Consider the validity of the following objection to the quasi-public facility theory:

> It is far from clear today why hospitals are under any greater obligation than typical employers to account to the courts for the fairness with which they screen applicants for professional positions or why health care professionals deserve any special legal help in surmounting marketplace barriers to their pursuit of a livelihood. The due process requirements that common-law courts have required private hospitals to observe in allocating staff privileges are in fact anomalous and find weak support in the common-law ground in which they are rooted.

Clark Havighurst, Doctors and Hospitals: An Antitrust Perspective on Traditional Relationships, 1984 Duke L.J. 1071, 1099-1100.

The following are a sampling of cases pro and con: *Pro judicial review* — Silver v. Castle Memorial Hospital, 497 P.2d 564 (Haw. 1972); Barrows v. Northwestern Memorial Hospital, 525 N.E.2d 50 (Ill. 1988); Mahmoodian v. United Hospital Center, 404 S.E.2d 750 (W. Va. 1991). *Contra judicial review* — Pepple v. Parkview Memorial Hospital, 536 N.E.2d 274 (Ind. 1989); Lakeside Community Hospital v. Levenson, 710 P.2d 727, 728 (Nev. 1985); Medical Center Hospitals v. Terzis, 367 S.E.2d 728 (Va. 1988). Canada, which is virtually the only other country with a medical staff structure similar to ours, follows the New Jersey approach. The leading case is Abouna v. Foothills Provincial General Hospital, [1978] 2 W.W.R. 130. See F. Rozovsky, Canadian Hospital Law. See generally Craig W. Dallon, Understanding Judicial Review of Hospitals' Physician Credentialing and Peer Review Decisions, 73 Temp. L. Rev. 507 (2000).

5. *Monopoly Status.* In examining how faithful this body of law is to the common carrier/innkeeper precedent on which it is based, consider whether excluded physicians should be able to demand judicial review of the fairness of a private hospital's decision even if they (and their patients) have the choice of several other hospitals in town, or should the public-facility theory apply only where hospitals exercise monopoly power in their local markets? *Barrows*, supra, 525 N.E.2d 50 (Ill. 1988) (the former); Kelly v. St. Vincent Hospital, 692 P.2d 1350 (N.M. Ct. App. 1984) (the latter). Given that the vast majority of all municipalities in the United States with an acute care hospital have only one or two, usually with

similar medical staff membership, is it appropriate to overlook this technicality in those locations where there is effective competition?

6. *Physician Access vs. Patient Access.* Note that the common law public service duties of common carriers were owed to their *customers*, not to their employees. As *Greisman* recognizes, then, excluded doctors have cause to complain only by virtue of their control over patient admissions to hospitals. Consequently, should the public-facility doctrine apply to doctors such as anesthesiologists and consulting specialists who do not admit patients? No one appears to have considered this issue.

7. *Extensions of the Quasi-Public Theory.* It is fascinating to speculate what other applications might exist for a doctrine as novel as this. One case has extended the quasi-public facility theory to physician (as opposed to hospital) services, holding that a patient refused service by the only practice group in town after lodging a complaint against one of the doctors in the group may maintain an action alleging an arbitrary refusal to serve. Leach v. Drummond Medical Group, 192 Cal. Rptr. 650 (Ct. App. 1983). Consider, also, whether private hospitals owe common law fairness duties to their *employed* physicians. Ezekial v. Winkley, 572 P.2d 32 (Cal. 1977) (yes for existing employees but not for applicants).

And what about possible duties extending directly to *patients*? Chapter 2.A explains that the quasi-public characterization has been used by a few courts to prevent hospitals from refusing patients for arbitrary or invidious reasons. But can a hospital set limits on which services or accommodations it offers? For instance, could this doctrine be used by a woman in labor to demand that her husband be allowed to attend the birth? Hulit v. St. Vincent's Hospital, 520 P.2d 99 (Mont. 1974) (holding no, but only after finding that the hospital rule was "reasonable" and "fair"). Finally, if ancient common law precedents are to be given full force in this context, note that common carriers were subject to strict liability for accidents and to judicial scrutiny for the reasonableness of their rates!

8. *Valid and Invalid Criteria.* Among the numerous possible criteria for medical staff membership, those that are usually upheld include possessing a license to practice medicine, having board certification, or having satisfactory references. Criteria that are usually struck down: include being a member in the local medical society and having a recommendation from one or more current members of the medical staff. See American Health Lawyers Ass'n, Peer Review Guidebook (1995); Annot., 37 A.L.R.3d 645 (1971).

9. *Deference to Medical Judgment.* Is *Nanavati* consistent with the following frequently quoted standard of review?

> No court should substitute its evaluation of such matters for that of the Hospital Board. . . . Human lives are at stake, and the governing board must be given discretion in its selection so that it can have confidence in the competence and moral commitment to its staff. The evaluation of professional proficiency of doctors is best left to the specialized expertise of their peers, subject only to limited judicial surveillance. . . . In short, so long as staff selections are administered with fairness, geared by a rationale compatible with hospital responsbility, and unencumbered with irrelevant considerations, a court should not interfere.

Sosa v. Board of Managers, 437 F.2d 173 (5th Cir. 1971). See also Laje v. R.E. Thomason General Hospital, 564 F.2d 1159 (5th Cir. 1977) ("to discount the [hospital's] evidence against [the doctor] because of statistical flaws in the nonrandom selection of cases and the small sample size is improper. The hospital, and not the courts, must set the level of competence to be required of staff members."); Branch v. Hempstead County Memorial Hospital, 539 F. Supp. 908 (W.D. Ark. 1982) ("this court does not intend . . . to become a super hospital governing board").

10. *The Hard Cases.* In *Greisman*, the hospital did not attempt to defend its exclusion of osteopaths on the basis of a quality-of-care rationale. If it had, what justification would suffice? Is it necessary to establish *poor* quality of care, or only a relative *difference* in the quality of care? Which of the following exclusionary policies do you think are valid?

- A hospital limits staff membership to licensed physicians (M.D.'s or D.O.'s), which necessarily excludes other licensed health professionals such as clinical psychologists, podiatrists, nurse midwives, and chiropractors. Shaw v. Hospital Authority, 614 F.2d 946 (5th Cir. 1985) (constitutionally permissible to exclude podiatrists).
- A tertiary care hospital limits staff membership to specialists who are board eligible or board certified, which necessarily excludes osteopaths and other general practitioners. Silverstein v. Gwinnett Hospital Authority, 861 F.2d 1560 (11th Cir. 1988) (valid); Armstrong v. Board of Directors, 553 S.W.2d 77 (Tenn. 1977) (invalid).
- A Christian Science hospital excludes physicians who do not practice according to its religious beliefs. Cf. Watkins v. Mercy Medical Center, 520 F.2d 894 (9th Cir. 1975) (Catholic hospital may refuse to have abortions performed on premises, but may not exclude abortionists from staff).
- A hospital excludes osteopaths because they are trained under a different medical philosophy. Hayman v. City of Galveston, 273 U.S. 414, 417 (1926) (sufficient to pass constitutional muster); Stern v. Tarrant County Hospital District, 778 F.2d 1052 (5th Cir. 1985) (en banc) (same); Petrocco v. Dover General Hospital, 642 A.2d 1016 (N.J. Super. 1994) (permissible under *Greisman* for hospital to exclude chiropractors where it gave the issue careful thought and rational justification).

It may assist you in answering these questions to employ an equal protection type of analysis by asking what level of scrutiny do physician exclusion decisions warrant — minimum "rational basis," strict "compelling interest," or intermediate "substantial basis" scrutiny? Do you see any indication that courts heighten their level of scrutiny in response to suspicions about the genuineness of the asserted reasons for physician exclusion? Professor Havighurst, supra, argues that medical staff decisions should be presumed valid when they appear to be made independently by the hospital motivated by its own business concerns, but should be scrutinized when it appears that physicians controlled or influenced the decision for competitive or personal reasons. Does this appear consistent with what the courts are doing?

11. *Economic Credentialing.* The debate in physician exclusion cases usually turns on whether the decision was motivated by the public interest in quality of care or by the existing doctors' interest in limiting competition. But what about the *hospital's* interest? Is it ever allowed to exclude a physician to advance its private

economic interest, so long as that interest does not conflict with the public interest? In one limited context, courts have allowed explicitly self-interested hospital motives. They have held that a hospital has a "right to take reasonable measures to protect itself" against exposure to joint and several liability with a doctor by requiring all medical staff members to carry a certain level of insurance. Holmes v. Hoemako Hospital, 573 P.2d 477 (Ariz. 1977). See Annot., 7 A.L.R.4th 1238 (1977).

With the mounting pressure for improved efficiency in medical treatment, it is widely predicted that this question will take on much broader significance. Hospitals are contemplating using economic criteria in the credentialing process to screen out wasteful doctors. The notes at page 447 explore whether a body of law premised on excluding physicians for poor quality will accommodate physician exclusion for *excessive* quality. Assuming this is generally permissible, what evidence will be necessary in the particular case that a physician's treatment patterns are excessively costly: that the doctor's patients are more expensive than average, the most expensive of all, much more expensive than anyone else's? Will courts entertain objections by the doctor that his patients are especially difficult cases and therefore costly because (a) he is such a terrific doctor he gets all the hard cases; (b) he's been in practice longer and so naturally his patients are older and therefore sicker on average; (c) random luck of the draw? See Sokol v. Akron General Medical Center, 173 F.3d 1026 (6th Cir. 1999) (split decision on whether objections like these undermine statistics showing that a surgeon's patients died more frequently than those of other surgeons).

12. *Procedural Protections.* Much of the case law on medical staff disputes concerns only whether the excluded doctor received procedural due process. See, e.g., Kiester v. Humana Hospital Alaska, 843 P.2d 1219 (Alaska 1992); Silver v. Castle Memorial Hospital, 497 P.2d 564 (Haw. 1972); American Health Lawyers Ass'n, Peer Review Guidebook (1995). Physician credentialing usually proceeds through several stages: investigation by a departmental or hospital-wide credentialing committee; vote by the medical staff as a whole and/or its executive committee; consideration of the medical staff recommendation by the hospital board; and an evidentiary review hearing if the board's decision is negative. Courts require that an excluded physician, whether an applicant or an existing staff member, be given notice of the charges, an opportunity to present evidence, and the right to confront and cross-examine opposing witnesses. The decisionmakers in this quasi-adjudicatory hearing may not be exposed to ex parte communication and must not have prejudged the merits. Much of this law is codified in the Health Care Quality Improvement Act of 1986, discussed at page 507, which imposes fair procedure requirements as a condition for conferring an immunity on those who participate in the hospital peer review process. The major respects in which this act differs from the case law are (1) it allows the challenged physician representation by counsel and (2) it disqualifies from the hearing panel anyone who is in "direct economic competition" with the physician. 42 U.S.C. §11112(b). Observe, though, that this Act's procedural steps are not mandatory or exclusive; they only create a safe harbor that establishes one manner in which a hospital can qualify for immunity. Cf. Owens v. New Britain General Hospital, 643 A.2d 233 (Conn. 1994) (only substantial, not strict, compliance with bylaw procedures is required). Nevertheless, the procedures specified in the Act have quickly become the industry standard in practice.

What problems do these requirements present for a small rural hospital? See Applebaum v. Board of Directors, 163 Cal. Rptr. 831 (Ct. App. 1980) (procedures unfair where five physicians served on both the initial review committee and the hearing committee); A. Southwick, The Law of Hospital and Health Care Administration 618 (2d ed. 1988) ("in hospitals having a relatively small medical staff the risk of bias and partiality increases. A hearing panel composed of persons from outside the hospital may then be necessary.").

Notes: Civil Rights and Disability Discrimination Laws

1. *Civil Rights Violations.* Another basis for scrutinizing hospitals' and HMOs' rejection of physicians are federal and state antidiscrimination laws. For instance, a number of medical staff dispute cases have been litigated under Title VII of the Civil Rights Act of 1964, as discrimination based on race, gender, or national origin. In general, courts hold that medical staff membership is sufficiently analogous to employment to fall within the ambit of this statute. Doe v. St. Joseph's Hospital, 788 F.2d 411 (7th Cir. 1986); Pardazi v. Cullman Medical Center, 838 F.2d 1155 (11th Cir. 1988). But see Diggs v. Harris Hospital, 847 F.2d 270 (5th Cir. 1988) (no Title VII action exists where physician is independent contractor); Alexander v. Rush Medical Center, 101 F.3d 487 (7th Cir. 1996) (same). See generally Michael R. Lowe, Stirring Muddled Waters: Are Physicians with Hospital Medical Staff Privileges Considered Employees under Title VII or the ADA Act When Alleging an Employment Discrimination Claim?, 1 DePaul J. Health Care L. 19 (1996).

Title VII cases brought by nonphysician employees sometimes raise issues unique to the health care setting. In Backus v. Baptist Medical Center, 510 F. Supp. 1191 (E.D. Ark. 1981), the court found that business necessity justifies a hospital in restricting male nurses from labor and delivery work. Similarly, the court found in Carswell v. Peachford Hospital, 27 F.E.P. 698 (1981) that the potential for patient disturbance allowed a psychiatric hospital to terminate a nurse who insisted on wearing "Bo Derek" beads in her hair. See generally D. K. Martin, Discrimination in the Health Care Profession, 7 Med. Law 133 (1988); Barry Hartstein, EEO Issues in the Health-Care Field: A Roundup of Recent Developments, 12 Emp. Rel. L.J. 241 (1986).

Also of interest under Title VII is the 1978 amendment that includes pregnancy as an aspect of prohibited gender considerations. If a woman's pregnancy poses safety risks to customers or other third parties, employers may take pregnancy into account in workplace decisions. International Union, UAW v. Johnson Controls, Inc., 499 U.S. 187, 200-203 (1991). However, employers may not discriminate against female employees out of concern for fetal health. Thus, a company cannot deny jobs to fertile women on the ground that chemicals in the workplace are hazardous to fetal development. Id. at 204-207 (holding that a battery-making company could not refuse employment to fertile women despite the exposure to lead in the workplace).

2. *Disability Discrimination.* Disability discrimination is a new source of concern for hospitals and HMOs, both in their employment relationships and in their contractual and membership relations with independent physicians. As with Title VII, several courts have subjected medical staff decisions to scrutiny under the

Americans with Disabilities Act (ADA) even though they do not, strictly speaking, involve employment relationships. E.g., Scoles v. Mercy Health Corp., 887 F. Supp. 765, 771-772 (E.D. Pa. 1994); Altman v. New York City Health and Hospitals Corp., 903 F. Supp. 503 (S.D.N.Y. 1995), aff'd, 100 F.3d 1054 (2d Cir. 1996). In Ambrosino v. Metropolitan Life Insurance Co., 899 F. Supp. 438 (N.D. Cal. 1995), the court found that a state equivalent of the ADA applied to a physician's membership in a PPO. *Ambrosino* also held that past drug dependency constitutes a disability, even though present drug use and addiction does not. See also Wallace v. Veterans Administration, 683 F. Supp. 758 (D. Kan. 1988) (hospital unable to refuse employment to nurse who was a recovering drug abuser). But see Elbrecht v. HCA Health Services, 1994 U.S. Dist LEXIS 18877 (N.D. Fla.), aff'd, 91 F.3d 161 (11th Cir. 1996) (ADA does not apply since the physician was not employed by the hospital); *Altman,* supra (hospital entitled to demote chief of internal medicine on grounds that the physician had not demonstrated that his alcoholism was under control). Consider also whether physician membership decisions could be scrutinized under the public accommodations title of the ADA.

Several cases alleging discrimination on the basis of disability have arisen when HIV-infected health care workers have been dismissed or reassigned on account of their HIV infection. Although such persons are considered disabled for purposes of the ADA, they often receive little protection under the statute. For example, in Doe v. University of Maryland Medical System Corp., 50 F.3d 1261 (4th Cir. 1995), the court upheld a medical center's decision to permanently suspend a neurosurgical resident from surgical practice and offer him an alternative residency in a nonsurgical field. See also Bradley v. University of Texas M.D. Anderson Cancer Center, 3 F.3d 922 (5th Cir. 1993) (upholding a hospital's reassignment of an HIV-infected surgical assistant to the purchasing department); Leckelt v. Board of Commissioners, 909 F.2d 820 (5th Cir. 1990) (upholding hospital's dismissal of a nurse for failing to disclose his HIV test results); Estate of Behringer v. Medical Center, 592 A.2d 1251 (N.J. Super. Law Div. 1991) (upholding a hospital's revocation of surgical privileges of an HIV-infected physician under state discrimination statute).

3. Membership in Managed Care Networks

HMOs are also being drawn into disputes arising from staff selection decisions. When they exclude physicians from their networks, the stakes from the physicians' point of view can be just as high, but the reasons may differ, as may the available legal theories for judicial review. Think carefully about whether the legal theory announced in the following case produces a different standard of review than under the prior cases, and which exclusion decisions and reasons are valid or invalid as a result.

■ POTVIN v. METROPOLITAN LIFE INSURANCE CO.
997 P.2d 1153 (Cal. 2000)

KENNARD, Judge.

After removal from defendant insurance company's "preferred provider" lists, plaintiff physician brought this action. Citing the common law right to fair procedure, which forbids arbitrary expulsions from private organizations under certain circumstances, plaintiff alleged he should have been given reasonable notice and an opportunity to be heard before his removal.

We first applied the common law doctrine of fair procedure in the late 19th century. . . . Some 50 years later, relying on the general principles underlying this doctrine, we held that a union could not arbitrarily deny full membership privileges to African-American workers. Thereafter, in the 1960's and 1970's, we extended the doctrine in a trio of decisions . . . involv[ing] the exclusion of a dentist from professional organizations [and] a hospital's expulsion of a surgical resident. The general principles this court enunciated in the[se] decisions apply in this case as well.

On September 10, 1990, Metropolitan Life Insurance (MetLife) entered into an agreement with Dr. Louis E. Potvin, an obstetrician and gynecologist, to include him as one of 16,000 participants on two of its preferred provider lists. Potvin had practiced medicine for more than 35 years; he was a past president of the Orange County Medical Association; and he held full staff privileges at Mission Regional Hospital, where he had served as Chairman of the Obstetrics and Gynecology Department for nine years. . . . The agreement . . . provided for termination by either party "at any time, with or without cause, by giving thirty (30) days prior written notice to the other party."

On July 22, 1992, MetLife notified Potvin in writing that effective August 31, 1992, it was terminating his preferred provider status . . . without cause. MetLife then stated that even though it did not have to give a reason, Potvin's "delistment from the provider network was related to the fact that [he] did not meet [MetLife's] current selection and retention standard for malpractice history." At the time, MetLife would not include or retain on its preferred provider lists any physician who had more than two malpractice lawsuits, or who had paid an aggregate sum of $50,000 in judgment or settlement of such actions. Potvin's patients had sued him for malpractice on four separate occasions, all predating his 1990 agreement with MetLife. In three of these actions, the plaintiffs had abandoned their claims, while the fourth case had settled for $713,000.

After MetLife failed to respond to Potvin's request for a hearing, Potvin filed this lawsuit. . . . Potvin alleged that MetLife's termination of his preferred provider status devastated his practice, reducing it to "a small fraction" of his former patients. He asserted that he was required to reveal his termination to other insurers and managed care entities, which then removed him from their preferred provider lists, and that he suffered rejection by "physician groups . . . dependent upon credentialling by MetLife" and by current MetLife preferred provider physicians, who ceased referring patients to him. The trial court granted MetLife's motion for summary judgment. . . .

II

The purpose of the common law right to fair procedure is to protect, in certain situations, against arbitrary decisions by private organizations. As this court has held, this means that, when the right to fair procedure applies, the decisionmaking "must be both substantively rational and procedurally fair." . . . In James v. Marinship Corp., 25 Cal.2d 721, 155 P.2d 329 (1944), . . . we upheld an injunction restraining the labor union and the employer, a Marin County shipbuilder, from "discharging or causing the discharge of . . . Negro employees because they are not members of a labor union with which their employer has a closed shop agreement, but which will not grant Negroes full membership privileges." . . . We explained: "It was well established at common law that innkeepers and common carriers were under a duty to furnish accommodations to all persons, in absence of some reasonable ground. . . . Where, as here, a labor union has attained a monopoly of the labor supply through closed shop agreements, such a union, like a public service business, may not unreasonably discriminate against Negro workers for the sole reason [of their race]." . . . Thereafter, . . . we went on to say: "one may not be expelled from membership in a private association without charges, notice and hearing. This common law protection against arbitrary expulsion, judicially declared, is of broader application and has been extended not only to labor unions [citations] and professional and trade organizations [citations], but to mutual benefit societies [citations] and other fraternal and social groups [citations]. The underlying theme of these decisions, variously stated, is that membership in an association, with its associated privileges, once attained, is a valuable interest which cannot be arbitrarily withdrawn. Thus, they comport with the broader principle that one on whom an important benefit or privilege has already been conferred may enjoy legal protections not available to an initial applicant for the same benefit." Exekial v. Winkley, 752 P.2d 32 (Cal. 1977). . . .

Plaintiff here points out that when an insurance company with fiduciary obligations to its insureds maintains a list of preferred provider physicians to render medical services to the insureds, a significant public interest is affected. One practical effect of the health care revolution, which has made quality care more widely available and affordable through health maintenance organizations and other managed care entities, is that patients are less free to choose their own doctors for they must obtain medical services from providers approved by their health plan. . . .

Our conclusion that the relationship between insurers and their preferred provider physicians significantly affects the public interest does not necessarily mean that every insurer wishing to remove a doctor from one of its preferred provider lists must comply with the common law right to fair procedure. The obligation to do so arises only when the insurer possesses power so substantial that the removal significantly impairs the ability of an ordinary, competent physician to practice medicine or a medical specialty in a particular geographic area, thereby affecting an important, substantial economic interest. . . . Here, plaintiff's amici curiae, the American Medical Association and the California Medical Association, . . . predict that in the near future no more than a handful of health care entities will dominate the managed care industry. If participation in managed care arrangements is a practical necessity for physicians generally and if only a handful of health care entities have a virtual monopoly on managed care, removing individual physicians from preferred provider networks controlled by these entities could significantly impair those physicians' practice of medicine.

Here, Potvin alleged that among the adverse effects of removal from MetLife's preferred provider lists were rejection by "physician groups which were dependent upon credentialling by MetLife" and devastation of his practice, which was reduced to "a small fraction" of his former patients. Proof of these allegations might establish that, in terminating a physician's preferred provider status, MetLife wields power so substantial as to significantly impair an ordinary, competent physician's ability to practice medicine or a medical specialty in a particular geographic area, thereby affecting an important, substantial economic interest. . . . We therefore agree with Potvin that the "without cause" termination clause is unenforceable to the extent it purports to limit an otherwise existing right to fair procedure under the common law.

BROWN, J., dissenting.

With its decision today, the majority, in effect, declares that it is the public policy of this state that physicians are entitled to a minimum income. . . . What is the majority's authority for declaring this public policy, for singling out physicians for such special treatment? . . . Historically, the common law duty to serve arose in response to the fact that in the 15th century those engaged in certain public callings, for example, innkeepers and carriers, exercised virtual monopolies. "When the weary traveller reaches the wayside inn in the gathering dusk, if the host turn him away what shall he do? Go on to the next inn? It is miles away, and the roads are infested with robbers. The traveller would be at the mercy of the innkeeper, who might practice upon him any extortion, for the guest would submit to anything almost, rather than be put out into the night." (Wyman, The Law of the Public Callings as a Solution to the Trust Problem (1904) 17 Harv. L. Rev. 156, 159.) . . . Under the standard announced by the majority today, an insurer need not exercise monopoly power before the burdens of the common law right of fair procedure are imposed on it. Rather, . . . it is sufficient if the insurer has any significant share of a regional market. . . .

History has confirmed this court's judgment that the racial discrimination practiced by the union in *Marinship* was "an act against which the law has definitely set its face." However, it trivializes *Marinship* to suggest that anything like the same degree of public policy consensus has developed with regard to the question at bar. According to Dr. Potvin, the average physician who practices his specialty, obstetrics/gynecology, has been sued for malpractice 2.3 times. Metropolitan Life Insurance Company (MetLife) wishes to restrict its preferred provider lists to physicians with a slightly better than average malpractice history, to those who have not been sued more than twice. Potvin, by contrast, has been sued 4 times — nearly twice the average. Now the majority's public policy antennae may be more sensitive than mine, but I suspect the jury is still out on the question of whether an insurer should be able to control its costs by restricting its preferred provider lists to physicians with slightly better than average malpractice histories. That, surely, is a business judgment, and if the insurer makes the wrong judgment by depriving itself of doctors that patients insist upon, then the market will punish the insurer and force it to retreat from the impracticable standard. . . .

[T]his court has made doctors a protected class. Until the economy turned around recently, one could hardly open a newspaper without reading of yet another company that had laid off thousands of its employees. However, no one suggested that textile workers or bank employees, for example, had a right to a hearing before losing their jobs. The layoffs certainly affected "important, substantial economic interest[s]" of theirs. Indeed, they may well have exhausted their savings and lost their homes. And yet textile workers and bank employees must fend for themselves, while doctors are treated by the majority as if they are entitled to a minimum income. . . .

The majority insists that, "[o]ur decision here does not apply to employer-employee contractual relations. Rather, it applies only to an insurer's decision to remove individual physicians from its preferred providers lists." However, employers will not be comforted, for why wouldn't the majority's opinion apply to employer-employee contractual relations? . . . For that matter, why wouldn't the majority's opinion apply to the admission to, as well as the removal of physicians from, an insurer's preferred provider lists? . . .

The out-of-state case upon which the majority relies [Harper v. Healthsource New Hampshire, 674 A.2d 962 (N.H. 1996)] . . . provides little support for the majority's refusal to enforce the "without cause" termination clause of Potvin's contract with MetLife. . . . [U]nder the *Harper* rule, a physician terminated pursuant to a "without cause" provision is entitled to review only if "the physician believes that the decision to terminate was, in truth, made in bad faith or based upon some factor that would render the decision contrary to public policy." Indeed, under the *Harper* rule, the "without cause" termination provision of MetLife's contract with Dr. Potvin should be enforced because there is no showing that MetLife's decision was "made in bad faith or based upon some other factor that would render the decision contrary to public policy." Certainly it is not contrary to public policy for a business enterprise to seek to minimize its costs. Any successful business must do so, and in this era of spiraling health care costs, health care providers have a special societal responsibility to do so. . . . Therefore, to be competitive, a medical insurer would be wise to restrict its preferred provider lists to physicians with better than average malpractice histories, and, by his own admission, Dr. Potvin's malpractice history was considerably worse than average.

In conclusion, the judgment of the trial court granting MetLife's motion for summary judgment should have been affirmed.

[The decision was 4-3.]

Notes: Managed Care Contracting; Employment at Will; Interference with Doctor/Patient Relationship

1. *Medical Staff Deja Vu?* Managed care contracts between physicians and HMOs or PPOs usually contain some of the same due process hearing protections as do medical staff bylaws. This is also increasingly being required by state insurance regulations and by industry accreditation standards adopted by the National Committee for Quality Assurance. Managed care physician networks, therefore, have taken on many of the same structural attributes of hospital medical staffs. John Blum, The Evolution of Physician Credentialing into Managed Care Selective Contracting, 22 Am. J.L. & Med. 173 (1996). There are two key differences, however. First, insurers retain the option in managed care contracts to use either for-cause or no-cause termination, and only the former invokes due process protections. Second, these due process protections apply, for the most part, only to physicians once they join the network. HMOs and PPOs are still free to reject

physician applicants at the outset without judicial review of their reasons or process. Observe, though, tort law and state insurance regulation require managed care networks to review physicians' credentials before enrolling them. See sections 2.C and 4.B. If this initial credentialing is commonplace, can due process requirements be far behind?

Despite physicians' concerns over no-cause terminations, physicians themselves often insist on putting these provisions in their managed care contracts. Can you imagine why? Suppose you were a doctor about to be terminated for good cause. What would you prefer? Realize that HMOs with formal peer review processes who seek immunity under the Health Care Quality Improvement Act must report to the National Practitioner Data Bank any adverse actions "based on competence or professional conduct." Lawyers also insist on no-cause provisions in part to comply with the referral fee laws that, for complex reasons, make it difficult to enter into short-term renewable contracts with doctors (the fear being that contract renewal will be used as an inducement to refer more business). An indefinite contract with no cause termination therefore may be the only feasible way to maintain flexibility for both parties.

2. *"Deselection."* The unfortunate term that has emerged for terminating physicians from managed care networks is "deselection." Did the California Supreme Court disagree with the *substantive* reason for deselecting Dr. Potvin, or only the lack of procedural protections? As the dissent notes, other courts have allowed physicians to object only when they allege that the reason for termination violates public policy, as would be the case with an allegation of racial discrimination. More common are allegations that insurers retaliate against physicians for challenging insurers' limitations on coverage:

> Several California doctors have told the [California Medical Association (CMA)] that when they protested denials of treatment or UR policy with IPAs, PPOs, large group practices or integrated delivery systems, the organizations retaliated by exercising their right to terminate the physician without cause. One doctor reported denial of a necessary MRI scan. Repeated appeals by the doctor eventually overturned the UR decision, but the physician was terminated from the plan two weeks later. Another physician reported challenging a managed care plan's program that required his ill patients to travel long distances for second opinions. After listening to his criticisms, the plan terminated the doctor's contract. . . .
>
> HMO interests paint a different scenario. They say physicians challenge UR denials as a defensive medicine tactic, motivated by self-interest, to the detriment of cost-containment strategies and quality assurance initiatives. . . . But physician advocates still see the issue as part of an ominous trend that could be replayed across the country. . . . CMA pressed for state legislation that . . . provides legal recourse for doctors who can prove that they were fired from a managed care organization because they challenged a denial of necessary treatment or otherwise advocated on behalf of their patients. . . . "The legislators agreed with us that it was imperative to preserve the physician's role as the patient's advocate," said CMA General Counsel.

Brian McCormick, What Price Patient Advocacy?, Am. Med. News, Mar. 28, 1994. The California statute, Cal. Bus. & Prof. Code §2056, has been adopted in a number of other states. In what was hailed as a landmark verdict, a California pediatrician, Thomas W. Self, won a $1.75 million judgment under this statute against his medical group for wrongful termination, after he was fired in response to an HMO's complaint that he was ordering too many tests. 7 BNA Health L. Rep. 628 (1998). Under the common law fairness theory, is it permissible to terminate a physician for being excessively costly, or for simply not being among the lowest-cost providers?

> Anecdotal evidence of physician deselection has received considerable publicity over the past year or two. . . . Reports range from one insurer's decision to drop more than 100 physicians from its network to another . . . [that] dropped 600 specialists from its HMO network, including most of its African American physicians. . . . One plan's approach, which has received substantial publicity, may typify what others are doing. The Blue Cross Blue Shield plan based in Washington, D.C., uses a profiling system called Pro/File that compares resource consumption by each practice with that of other doctors in the same specialty and the same region. Pro/File considers a broad array of utilization measures (e.g., numbers of laboratory tests and office visits and what they call long-range utilization), but not patient outcomes. An adjustment for case mix is implemented by comparing groups of patients with similar diseases, ages, and treatments. Critics claim that small sample size is a significant problem and that Pro/File judges only resource consumption and not quality of care. . . .

Physician Payment Review Commission, Annual Report to Congress 226 (1995). Minority physicians are especially hard hit by deselection in some instances, it appears, because HMOs perceive that their patients are less profitable or because HMOs don't wish to market themselves in certain locations. See Note, The Impact of Managed Care on Doctors Who Serve Poor and Minority Patients, 108 Harv. L. Rev. 1625 (1995).

3. *Other States, Other Cases, and Other Theories.* Cases like *Potvin* are still few and far between. When they do arise, courts more commonly adopt the legal theory mentioned in the dissent, which allows physicians to challenge no-cause terminations only if they can show the true reason violates public policy. This is an extension of the "whistleblower" suits that arise under employment law, where courts have recognized a public policy exception to the "employment at will" doctrine.

Under either theory of action, should courts exert as much scrutiny as they do over hospital staffing decisions? Does the level of scrutiny depend on the theory of review? Is *Potvin* saying that HMOs are "quasi-public" facilities, relying on the same factors invoked in *Greisman*? If not, what level of scrutiny is justified by the public policy limitation proposed by the dissent? One way to think about this is to consider, under each of these theories, who bears the burden of proof to show exactly what? For instance, under the dissent's public policy theory, should HMOs be allowed to exclude osteopaths from their networks? Does the dissent's theory require the HMO to provide any due process procedures?

Is the dissent correct that the majority's theory might also apply to physicians who are refused initial admission into managed care networks? Under the majority's approach, are there any substantive grounds that would not require due process procedures? In another California case, the court held that it was illegal to summarily remove a physician from a network even though he had been disciplined by the state licensing board for prior substance abuse, improperly prescribing demerol, and treating patients under the influence of drugs. The court reasoned that the insurer failed to show that the physician was presently impaired or a threat to patients. Ambrosino v. Metropolitan Life Insurance Co., 899 F. Supp. 438 (N.D. Cal. 1995). For analysis of the full range of issues, see Peter Jurgeleit, Physician Employment under Managed Care: Toward a Retaliatory Discharge Cause of Action for HMO-Affiliated Physicians, 73 Ind. L.J. 255 (1997); Mark A. Kadzielski, Provider Deselection and Decapitation in a Changing Healthcare Environment, 41 St. Louis U. L.J. 891 (1997); Brian A. Liang, Deselection under Harper v. Healthsource: A Blow for Maintaining Patient-Physician Relationships in the Era of Managed Care?, 72 Notre Dame L. Rev. 799 (1997); William M. Sage, Physicians as Advocates, 35 Hous. L. Rev. 1529 (1999); Bethany J. Spielman, Managed Care Regulation and the Physician-Advocate, 47 Drake L. Rev. 713 (1999); Note, 49 Rutgers L. Rev. 1397 (1997).

4. *Interference with the Doctor/Patient Relationship.* In this body of law, to what extent should courts be concerned with patients' interests in addition to physicians'? If a patient's physician is excluded from the patient's HMO, what option does the patient have? Does the HMO have a "monopoly" over the patient's business? In one case, the court ruled that patients do not have a right to challenge the termination of their physician, because they can be treated by other physicians in the network. Maltz v. Aetna Health Plans of New York, 114 F.3d 9 (2d Cir. 1997). However, in Harper v. Healthsource New Hampshire, 674 A.2d 962 (N.H. 1996), the court noted that "the termination of [Dr. Harper's] relationship with [the HMO] affects more than just his own interest. Several relationships in our society stand on a different footing from the rest. The most visible are those between wife and husband, lawyer and client, pastor and penitent, and physician and patient. In these relationships, society values truthfulness in communication above other competing interests, such as evidence in the search for truth in legal actions. Evidentiary privileges protect communication within these relationships from being revealed in litigation because society has determined that the relationship 'ought to be sedulously fostered.' "

This viewpoint points to another possible theory of action. Tort law recognizes an action for tortious interference with advantageous relationships. Doctors whose clinical privileges are limited by a hospital often argue that the hospital interfered with their economic relationships with patients. Viewed as a business tort, this often fails because hospitals are pursing their own appropriate business interests and therefore lack the requisite bad motive. If the restriction of privileges is seen as interfering with something more sacred, however, these claims may have a greater chance of success. See Hammonds v. Aetna Casualty & Surety Co., 237 F. Supp. 96 (N.D. Ohio 1965) (doctor/patient relationship "is deserving of more attention from the law than a businessman's expectation of profit from a purely commercial transaction"). See generally Mark A. Hall, Institutional Control of Physicians Behavior, 137 U. Pa. L. Rev. 431, 467-473 (1988); Annot., 87 A.L.R.4th 845 (1991).

5. *Immunity Laws.* There has been little litigation yet over whether the federal Health Care Quality Improvement Act discussed below creates an immunity from

damages for formal peer review decisions by HMOs. It appears that immunity does not apply to no-cause contract terminations or to decisions based on economic grounds, but does apply to formal peer review actions based on quality concerns. Cf. Alexander v. Memphis IPA, 870 S.W.2d 278 (Tenn. 1993) (state immunity statute applies to peer review by IPA). Also, there is an unresolved possibility that these suits are preempted by ERISA, the federal law discussed in Chapter 3.C that overrides certain state laws affecting employer-provided health insurance. Compare Zuniga v. Blue Cross and Blue Shield of Michigan, 52 F.3d 1395 (6th Cir. 1995) (ERISA preempts breach of contract and due process claims by physician removed from an PPO), with Napoletano v. CIGNA Healthcare of Connecticut, 680 A.2d 127 (Conn. 1996) (ERISA does not preempt a similar action).

6. *Wrongful Discharge*. The public policy limitation on at-will employment and for-cause termination applies to nonphysicians as well. For some reason, these wrongful discharge cases seem to crop up with surprising frequency in the hospital industry. For instance, in Wagenseller v. Scottsdale Memorial Hospital, 710 P.2d 1025 (1985), a nurse alleged she was fired in retaliation for refusing to engage in lewd antics during a rafting trip with other hospital employees (including "a parody of the song 'Moon River,' which allegedly concluded with members of the group 'mooning' the audience"). The court held that firing for this reason is contrary to public policy since it penalizes conduct that arguably contravenes statutes concerning public indecency. More common are "whistleblower" cases, those where an employee is fired in retaliation for reporting, for example, workplace safety problems to the proper authorities. See, e.g., Jones v. Lake Park Care Center, 569 N.W.2d 369 (Iowa 1997) (refusing to produce false information for state auditor). Also, observe that public hospitals are subject to constitutional as well as contractual restrictions in their employment decisions. Waters v. Churchill, 511 U.S. 661 (1994); Vinyard v. King, 728 F.2d 428 (10th Cir. 1984). See generally Mark Rothstein et al., Employment Law (1994).

7. *Conscientious Objection*. Consider whether public policy should limit the ability to discipline medical employees for exercising conscientious objection to assisting in particular medical procedures, such as abortions or termination of life support. The leading case, Pierce v. Ortho Pharmaceutical Corp., 417 A.2d 505 (N.J. 1980), held that such discipline is permissible since the employee's objection is a purely private one that has no basis in public policy, as long as the medical procedure is consistent with the law. However, legislatures have been somewhat more sympathetic. Most states have "conscience clause" statutes that expressly prohibit discharge for refusal to perform abortions, and a federal statute known as the "Church Amendment" enforces a similar prohibition against institutions that receive certain forms of federal health care funding. See generally Anne Dellinger & Ann Vickery, When Staff Object to Participating in Care, 28 J. Health & Hosp. L. 269 (1995).

8. *Negotiating Managed Care Contracts*. Most physicians belong to several, sometimes many different and overlapping, managed care networks. This is especially true for specialists. One radiology group in the D.C. area had 97 different contracts with insurers and HMOs. Robert A. Berenson, Beyond Competition, 16(2) Health Aff. 171, 175 (1997). Once these networks are formed, insurers then market them to employers and to other insurers, thereby binding physicians

to payment and coverage terms that may vary from one purchaser to the next. In deciding whether to sign these contracts, physicians must grapple with many crucial issues in addition to no-cause termination clauses. Other issues include their basic service obligation and payment rights, whether they can limit the number of patients they accept, whether they must indemnify the HMO for liability arising from patient care, and how disputes are resolved. The following exercise provides an opportunity to sample some of these issues.

Exercise: Negotiating a Managed Care Contract*

Marcus Welby Hospital (MWH) is described above at page 364. One of its competitors established a successful IPA-model HMO two years ago. Fearing loss of patients, MWH is forming the Marcus Welby Managed Care Network (the Network). The objective is to sign up a number of physicians, mainly in primary care but also in common specialities, and then to market this network to these two sources: (1) large employers who provide health insurance to their workers on a self-insured basis; and (2) large regional or national insurance companies (such as Blue Cross) who then offer the network to their customers.

The Network is approaching each physician group individually and asking them to sign up nonexclusively, leaving them free to sign up with other networks or HMOs. The contract excerpts below contain some common sticking points in these negotiations. Read each pairing of contract options and determine what is at stake. Then, assume the position of lawyer/negotiator for either (a) the Network or (b) a physician group who wants to sign up but is concerned about the details. Meet with a representative from the other side and see if you can hammer out a deal, either adopting one version or the other, or making any changes you want.

Compensation

A. In exchange for providing Covered Services, Physician shall receive usual, customary, and reasonable rates that similarly situated physicians charge for like services, less a discount of 15 percent; provided, however, that Physician agrees that the Network shall receive his or her "most favored" discount, such that, if Physician gives a greater discount to another network, insurer, employer, or health plan, Physician shall extend the same discount to the Marcus Welby Network.
B. In exchange for providing Covered Services, Physician shall receive the same compensation the Network pays other similarly situated physicians for like services, which will be according to a proprietary fee schedule maintained by the Network and which the Network shall be free to modify from time to time as it deems fit, so long as it applies the fee schedule consistently to all physicians in the Network who are similarly situated.

Indemnification

A. Physician agrees to indemnify and hold harmless the Network against any negligent act or claim made with respect to items or services provided by

*This exercise is adapted form one developed by Jan Yarborough, a lawyer in Raleigh, N.C.

Physician under this Agreement. The Network agrees to indemnify and hold harmless Physician against any negligent act or claim made with respect to items or services provided under this Agreement to the extent that the Network is solely responsible for the negligent act or claim.

B. [No indemnification clause at all. Each party is left to bear its own liability.]

Availability of Physician's Services

A. Physician agrees to provide or arrange all Covered Services sought by Members in return for the compensation stated above. Physician shall provide such services on a twenty-four per day, seven day per week basis. During the term of this Agreement, Physician must have and maintain full and unrestricted medical staff privileges at a hospital which is under contract with Network.

B. Physician shall provide Covered Services sought by Members in the same manner provided to persons who are not Members in return for the compensation stated above. During the term of this Agreement, Physician must have and maintain medical staff privileges at a hospital in the geographic area covered by the Network. [*Note*: In case it matters, "Covered Services" is defined as "those health care services which the Network may be obligated to provide any employer or individual under a health insurance or health benefits plan sold by or on behalf of the network."]

Term and Termination

A. This Agreement may not be terminated as to any Physician prior to its expiration unless said Physician loses his or her license to practice medicine. Provided, however, the Physician shall have the option to terminate this Agreement in the event of the failure of the MCO to make payments when due.

B. This Agreement may be terminated by either party at any time without cause by written notice given at least one-hundred-twenty (120) days in advance of the effective date of termination without the need for prior consent of, or notice to any Member, Participating Provider, or other third party.

D. ANTITRUST LAW

Note: Introduction to Antitrust Law

Until the 1980s, the health care industry was remarkably complacent about the antitrust laws. Physicians openly threatened boycotts to enforce their interests; hospitals had few qualms about dividing markets with each other; and the AMA ruled supreme over the economics and organization of medical practice. No one thought to challenge this conduct because it was considered that the learned professions did not engage in the type of trade that is subject to antitrust scrutiny, that health care is an inherently local enterprise not subject to federal jurisdiction, and that lofty considerations of ethical practice and quality of care removed health care decisionmaking from base concerns of economic efficiency.

However, Supreme Court decisions over the past generation have systematically upset each of these assumptions. In Goldfarb v. Virginia State Bar, 421 U.S. 773, 787 (1975), the Court held that there was no antitrust exemption for professionals: "The nature of an occupation, standing alone, does not provide sanctuary from the Sherman Act." In Hospital Building Company v. Trustees of Rex Hospital, 425 U.S. 738 (1976), the Court held that hospital activities can meet the interstate commerce prerequisite to antitrust jurisdiction. And in American Medical Association v. FTC, 455 U.S. 676 (1982), the Supreme Court upheld without opinion an FTC injunction against the AMA using its code of professional ethics to ban physician advertising and certain physician contractual arrangements.

The result of suddenly exposing an entire industry that was once exempt from antitrust law has been an explosion of litigation and counseling. Health care antitrust cases are popping up all over the health care landscape faster than dandelions after a spring rain. Law firms are creating new health care practice groups and old antitrust litigators have found an area of revival in an otherwise sluggish specialty. Antitrust liability is a frightening prospect to physicians, hospitals, and insurers. Violations can be privately enforced in civil damage actions brought by injured plaintiffs, defendants face the possibility of treble damages, and losing defendants must pay the plaintiff's attorney fees. To top it off, professional liability insurance rarely covers antitrust exposure. Enforcement authority is also lodged in the Federal Trade Commission, which is empowered to bring civil injunction actions, and in the Department of Justice, which, in addition, may prosecute criminal violations. Both agencies also issue advisory rulings and general interpretative guidelines.

It is not possible in the course of this survey text to cover the entirety of a field as complex as health care antitrust.[1] Materials in this chapter and elsewhere explore some basic principles governing the more prominent areas of litigation. This section examines group boycott law in the context of the exclusion of practitioners from hospital medical staffs and managed care networks. The next section contains a discussion of the price-fixing ramifications of structuring Preferred Provider Organizations and other insurance innovations, and the following section explores antitrust merger doctrine as applied to various health care ventures. The following is a summary of antitrust law as it relates primarily to the first category of disputes, but it also explains principles that apply generally to all types of antitrust theories.

Physicians frequently challenge medical staff membership and network formation decisions under federal antitrust laws, contending that exclusion from the hospital or from a managed care network constitutes a concerted refusal to deal, which is pejoratively known as a group boycott. Health care boycott cases are emerging with such force and prominence that antitrust analysis can no longer be reserved to the litigation specialist. Health care lawyers must have a working understanding of this area of the law in order to advise their clients effectively on how to plan their activities in advance to minimize antitrust exposure. See

---

[1] For a more comprehensive overview, see William M. Sage & Peter J. Hammer, A Copernican View of Health Care Antitrust, 65 Law and Contemp. Probs. 241 (Autumn 2002); Symposium, Antitrust Policy and Health Care Reform, 1995 Utah L. Rev. 365; Symposium, Antitrust and Health Care, 51(2) Law & Contemp. Probs. (Spring 1988); Symposium, Antitrust Issues in Health Care, 14(2) & 14(3) Am. J.L. & Med. 245 (1988).

generally Francis Miller, Teaching Antitrust to Health Law Students: Peer Review as a Case Study, 38 J. Leg. Educ. 545 (1988).

The primary basis for these suits is §1 of the Sherman Act, 15 U.S.C. §1:

> Every contract, combination . . . or conspiracy in restraint of trade or commerce among the several states, or with foreign nations, is declared to be illegal.

The three elements of a §1 action, evident from the face of the statute, are (1) concerted, as opposed to unilateral, action; (2) an unreasonable restraint of trade; and (3) interstate commerce. A general overview of these three elements may be helpful to the uninitiated reader prior to tackling the principal cases.

1. *Conspiracy.* No Sherman Act §1 violation exists if the challenged activity is unilateral in nature, that is, if it is the action of a single entity. The theory underlying §1 is that competitive harm exists only where two or more economic actors collude to subvert the forces of competition. When a single hospital or HMO excludes a physician, concerted action is not readily apparent, even though many individual doctors and administrators within the hospital or HMO participate in the exclusion decision. The Supreme Court has clearly held that "[t]he officers of a single firm are not separate economic actors pursuing separate economic interests, so agreements among them do not suddenly bring together economic power that was previously pursing divergent goals. Coordination within a firm is as likely to result from an effort to compete as from an effort to stifle competition." Copperweld Corp. v. Independence Tube Corp., 467 U.S. 752, 769 (1984). This reasoning is referred to as the "intra-enterprise conspiracy rule": No conspiracy ordinarily can exist within a single business enterprise.

There is an exception to this intra-enterprise conspiracy rule, however. A combination or conspiracy may exist within a single enterprise if one or more of its members is motivated by an outside economic interest that is separate from the firm's. In such a situation, it is no longer the case that the various corporate actors are pursuing a single economic purpose, and, therefore, the potential for harmful collusion exists even within a single firm. For instance, suppose a malpractice insurance company owned and operated by obstetricians were to deny coverage to a doctor because he worked with midwives. There would be no conspiracy if the company simply thought the doctor posed an excessive insurance risk, but a conspiracy would exist if the corporate actors were motivated by an outside interest unrelated to the concerns of insurance, namely to suppress competition from midwives.[2] Likewise, the threshold issue in hospital or HMO exclusion cases is whether the economic interest that medical staff members have in competition with excluded practitioners (and with each other) results in the concerted behavior required to invoke Sherman Act §1. If not, a claim must be stated under Sherman Act §2 concerning monopolization. Its elements are more restrictive and are covered only briefly in these materials.

2. *Unreasonable Restraint of Trade.* If concerted action is present, then the core substantive question becomes whether the challenged conduct results in an

---

[2] These facts are suggested by Nurse Midwifery Associates v. Hibbett, 918 F.2d 605 (6th Cir. 1990), which found allegations similar to these to be sufficient to go to trial.

unreasonable restraint of trade. This is a complex and difficult inquiry, one that is not capable of completely accurate summation. Nevertheless, some preliminary analysis is useful before encountering the case law. First, observe that the language of the Sherman Act provides no useful guidance; it prohibits "*every* contract . . . in restraint of trade," which, taken literally, is an impossibility since *every* contract in fact restrains trade at least to some small extent by precluding the contracting parties from dealing with someone else for the subject matter of the contract. To make sense of the statute, courts have found it necessary to add a judicial gloss so that it prohibits only *unreasonable* restraints of trade. This generates what is known as the "rule of reason" test of illegality: A restraint is illegal only if its anticompetitive harms outweigh its procompetitive benefits. Such a finding often requires a complex, lengthy, and expensive inquiry. To avoid engaging in this burdensome undertaking in every case, the courts have crafted what is known as the "per se rule" of illegality: Certain restraints are automatically illegal if it is clear from their general nature that they are anticompetitive in the vast majority of situations. The primary example of per se illegality is horizontal price fixing, that is, price fixing among competitors.

In general, the *horizontal/vertical distinction* is crucial to characterizing and analyzing particular arrangements subject to antitrust challenge. A vertical arrangement is aligned up and down the chain of distribution for the good or service in question. A horizontal arrangement is one that exists among competitors at one level of this chain. For manufactured goods, the vertical chain is usually manufacturer-wholesaler-retailer. For medical services, the vertical alignment, generally speaking, is insurer-hospital-doctor. Practices or restraints that are only in a vertical alignment are, for the most part, much less of a concern for antitrust law because they are usually imposed by a single actor and they do not obviously restrain competition in the various affected horizontal levels. For instance, a manufacturer who restricts its dealers to certain cities or states so they don't compete with each other over its products imposes a vertical market division that enhances its ability to compete with other manufacturers. Therefore, it is judged under the rule of reason, whereas the same arrangement agreed to among the dealers themselves and imposed on the manufacturer would be a per se illegal horizontal market division.

In the context of medical staff disputes, plaintiffs attempt to invoke the rule of per se illegality for medical staff or network exclusion decisions by characterizing these decisions as both a horizontal and a vertical *group boycott* among the hospital and members of the medical staff, all of whom agree not to deal with the plaintiff. Unfortunately for litigants and for students of health care antitrust, "there is more confusion about the scope and operation of the per se rule against group boycotts than in reference to any other aspect of the per se doctrine." L. Sullivan, Law of Antitrust 229-230 (1977). Despite several Supreme Court precedents declaring boycotts per se illegal, "exactly what types of activity fall within the forbidden category is . . . far from certain." Northwest Wholesale Stationers Inc. v. Pacific Stationary and Printing Co., 472 U.S. 284, 294 (1985). In this case, the Court explained that "the mere allegation of a concerted refusal to deal does not suffice because not all concerted refusals to deal are predominantly anticompetitive." Therefore, "a plaintiff seeking application of the per se rule must present a threshold case that the challenged activity falls into a category likely to have predominantly anticompetitive effects." Id. at 297. This intermediate stance between per se illegality and rule of reason balancing is sometimes known as the "quick look" approach, in that it requires the court to make an initial assessment of a practice's likely competitive impact before deciding which way to characterize it.[3] How this general directive might apply to medical staff disputes is the second principal issue explored in the following section.

When restraints are judged under the rule of reason, two key issues emerge in medical cases. The first is what role *quality of patient care* plays in proper antitrust analysis. There are several possibilities explored below. Enhanced quality of care could be a relevant competitive benefit to be weighed in the balance of competitive effects pro and con. Quality of care could also be viewed as a noneconomic benefit that outweighs the competitive harms from the restraint. Or, medical markets might be thought to be so infused with noneconomic quality concerns that they deserve a sweeping exemption or extraordinarily lenient scrutiny under antitrust laws. You will see from the readings below that considerable confusion still reigns over these central questions.

A related point of confusion is whether the competitive impact of a restraint is to be judged more by the parties' *subjective motivation and purpose*, or instead by the likely *effects* of their actions. Black-letter law states that actual probable effects, not intent, should control the analysis, such that a good intent will not save a bad act nor will a bad intent impugn a harmless act. Nevertheless, courts still frequently place great weight on subjective intent, either in predicting the restraint's likely effects or in deciding how to characterize the nature of the restraint (e.g., as vertical vs. horizontal, or as price fixing vs. refusal to deal). Often, motive comes strongly into play in distinguishing *"ancillary"* from *"naked"* restraints. An ancillary restraint is one that occurs as a side effect of pursuing a primarily procompetitive purpose, whereas a naked restraint occurs where the core purpose of the activity is anticompetitive. For instance, a hospital or HMO that excludes chiropractors from the medical staff might be viewed as engaging in either a naked or an ancillary restraint depending on how one conceives of its primary purpose: making it more difficult for alternative providers to compete with M.D.s, or protecting its

---

[3] In a major 5-4 decision, California Dental Ass'n v. FTC, 526 U.S. 756 (1999), excerpted at page 347, the Supreme Court created considerable confusion about the appropriate standard of review in health care antitrust cases and in Sherman Act §1 cases generally. The FTC and the 9th Circuit had ruled that it was illegal for the California Dental Association to ban most forms of price and quality information in advertising by dentists. (For instance, dentists could not claim in general terms that they offer discounted prices or are especially good with children.) This ban was struck down using both the per se rule and a "quick look" version of the rule of reason, finding no plausible pro-competitive justifications asserted for conduct that otherwise appeared to be a restraint of trade. The Supreme Court reversed and remanded for further consideration, holding that neither the per se rule, the full-blown rule of reason, nor the particular version of the "quick look" standard of review used in this case were appropriate in this particular case. Instead, the Court wanted to see a "less quick look" than had been given, explaining that each case requires "an enquiry meet for the case, looking to a restraint's circumstances, details, and logic." The Court appears to be saying that the standard of review and the burden of proof in §1 cases do not fall into discrete categories but must be viewed as a continuum in which the standard and burden are adjusted to the particulars of each case, at least for categories of cases that have not yet received clear Supreme Court pronouncements. Needless to say, this makes it even more difficult to predict how particular arrangements and activities will be evaluated by the courts or the antitrust enforcement agencies in the future. See Marina Lao, The Rule of Reason and Horizontal Restraints Involving Professionals, 68 Antitrust L.J. 499 (2000).

own reputation by not associating with nonphysicians. Naked restraints are obviously much harder to defend.

Yet another generic analytical issue that is critical in health care antitrust is *market power*. A given arrangement creates greater or lesser anticompetitive concerns according to the power that the parties have to raise prices, restrict output, or lower quality. If they lack this power, competitive forces will discipline any adverse consequences because the offenders will lose business to other firms — either those presently in the market or those that might enter in order to exploit the competitive opportunity created by the restraint. Therefore, market power — measured in terms of market share and barriers to market entry — is critical to assessing the likely effects of a restraint of trade. Courts increasingly are ruling that, under the rule of reason, defendants need not offer any justification for their behavior whatsoever unless the plaintiff makes a threshold showing of market power.

The easiest way to gauge market power is to measure the actor's market share. Market power tends to increase the smaller or more compact the market is. Therefore, a given restraint is worse when the market within which it occurs is smaller because it has a larger proportionate impact. *Defining the relevant market* is therefore critical to deciding many antitrust cases. Markets are defined in two dimensions: the relevant product (or service) and the relevant geography. Medical markets tend to be small and highly concentrated because service delivery is inherently local and because hospitals are large dominant institutions. Thus, it is easy to imagine a market for hospital services with only a single hospital. Simply put, this is a monopoly and so, by definition, anything the hospital does has serious competitive consequences because it enjoys extreme market power. Therefore, defendants in many health care antitrust cases struggle to characterize the market in terms that enlarge its *geographic or product scope*. They also attempt to show that, despite large market share, their market power is diminished by unique attributes of medical markets.

3. *Interstate Commerce.* Because antitrust litigation is usually long, complex, expensive, high stakes, and of an uncertain outcome, defendants are eager to find defects in the plaintiff's case that avoid trial or even discovery. The elements of the action just summarized rarely result in dismissing a claim at the pleadings stage. Therefore, a more forceful defense is to claim absence of federal jurisdiction. In order for federal antitrust jurisdiction to attach, a restraint must have a substantial effect on interstate commerce. Initially, this requirement too was controversial in this body of law because health care delivery, like other types of personal service, appears inherently local in nature, in contrast with the manufacture and distribution of products. The Supreme Court resolved, however, that a competitive impact on even small local medical markets has interstate effects because reimbursement, equipment and supplies frequently cross state lines, even if patients do not. Summit Health v. Pinhas, 500 U.S. 322 (1991). Also, even if federal jurisdiction were lacking, most states have antitrust statutes similar to the federal laws, and some state attorneys general are notably active in enforcing these laws.

Still, courts often have a strong instinct that a single doctor should not be able to make a federal case out of a staffing decision at a single hospital or HMO. This instinct can express itself in some of the standard defenses outlined above or in other, somewhat more obscure, defenses summarized in the notes following these cases.

1. Medical Staff Boycotts

◼ WEISS v. YORK HOSPITAL
745 F.2d 786 (3d Cir. 1984)

BECKER, Circuit Judge.

This antitrust case arises from the refusal to grant hospital staff privileges to a physician. The plaintiff, Malcolm Weiss, is an osteopath[2] who was denied staff privileges at York (Pennsylvania) Hospital. Dr. Weiss brought this suit, both individually and as representative of the class of all osteopathic physicians in the York Medical Service Area (York MSA), against York Hospital (York), the York Medical and Dental Staff, and ten individual physicians who served on the York Medical Staff Executive Committee and the York Judicial Review Committee. York is controlled by, and, at the time Dr. Weiss applied for staff privileges, was exclusively staffed by doctors who graduated from allopathic medical schools.[3]

The gravamen of Weiss' lawsuit is that, although allopaths (hereinafter referred to as medical doctors or M.D.s) and osteopaths (D.O.s) are equally trained and qualified to practice medicine,[4] his application for staff privileges at York hospital was turned down solely because of his status as an osteopath. . . . In Weiss' submission, this scheme to exclude D.O.s from York Hospital was motivated by a desire to restrict the ability of D.O.s to compete with M.D.s, thereby increasing the profits of the M.D.s. [The jury found that the medical staff, but not the hospital, violated §1 of the Sherman Act.] . . .

II. THE FACTS

A. HOSPITAL SERVICES IN THE YORK MSA

There are two providers of in-patient hospital services in the York MSA: York, which is run by M.D.s, and Memorial Hospital (Memorial), which is run by D.O.s. York is by far the larger of the two, with approximately 450 beds

---

[2] Dorland's Illustrated Medical Dictionary defines Osteopathy as

> a system of therapy . . . based on the theory that the body is capable of making its own remedies against disease. . . . It utilizes generally accepted physical, medicinal and surgical methods of diagnosis while placing chief emphasis on the importance of normal body mechanics and manipulative methods of detecting and correcting faulty structure.

Osteopathic physicians signify their degree as D.O. [See Joel Howell, The Paradox of Osteopathy, 341 New Eng. J. Med. 1465 (1999).]

[3] Allopathy is defined as a system of remedial treatment in which it is sought to cure a disease by producing, through medicines, a condition incompatible with the disease. See Funk & Wagnalls New Standard Dictionary of the English Language (1942). Allopathy constitutes the common or "regular" system of medical practice. Allopathic doctors, signify their degree as M.D.

[4] At trial Dr. Merle S. Bacastow, an M.D. and the Vice-President of Medical Affairs at York, testified that at least since the mid-1960s there has been no difference in terms of medical training and ability to provide medical care between graduates of osteopathic medical schools and graduates of allopathic medical schools. This observation is born out by the fact that osteopaths and allopaths are equally qualified for state licensure to practice medicine and surgery within the Commonwealth of Pennsylvania. . . . See also Blackstone, The A.M.A. and The Osteopaths: A Study of the Power of Organized Medicine, 22 Antitrust Bulletin 405, 408-414 (1977). Professor Blackstone concludes that

and 2,500 employees. Memorial has 160 beds. The testimony at trial established that York had a market share of 80 percent of the patient-days of hospitalization in the York MSA.

In addition to York's overall market dominance, testimony at trial established that certain complex, highly technical "tertiary care" services and facilities are, for a number of reasons, only available at York. Included among the services offered only at York are therapeutic radiology, open heart surgery, cardiac catheterization, renal dialysis, neo-natal intensive care, short-term acute psychiatric care, monitored stroke treatment, audiology, burn care, cardiopulmonary laboratory, cardiopulmonary rehabilitation, electroencephalography, genetic counseling, prosthetic service, speech therapy, computerized axial tomography (CAT scan), and infusion aspirator. . . .

[I]n early 1976, Weiss and another osteopath named Dr. Michael Zittle, both of whom were engaged in family practice in the York MSA, applied for staff privileges at York. Dr. Weiss informed representatives of the York medical staff that if York excluded him because of his osteopathic training he would institute legal action.

The York medical staff considered the applications and Weiss' threat of legal action, and in November of 1976 amended its bylaws to permit admission of osteopaths at York. Dr. Weiss contends that the amendment of the bylaws was purely cosmetic, and that since 1976 the York medical staff has engaged in a deliberate covert policy of discrimination against osteopaths. . . .

D. DOCTOR WEISS' APPLICATION FOR STAFF PRIVILEGES

In 1976 Doctors Weiss and Zittle applied for staff privileges in York's Family Practice Department. In accordance with the procedures outlined above, the Family Practice Department Credentials Committee and the chairman of the Family Practice Department considered the applications. On January 17, 1977, the department recommended that they be accepted. The Medical Staff Credentials Committee then reviewed the applications and also recommended acceptance. The Medical Staff Executive Committee, however, did not approve either application. Instead, it took the unusual step of deciding to conduct a further investigation. The Committee made extensive oral and written inquiries concerning the professional competence and moral character of both Weiss and Zittle. No such survey had ever before been conducted by the hospital before. Ultimately the investigation turned up some questions about Dr. Weiss' personality.

---

in general D.O.s receive somewhat shorter, less expensive, and less specialized training than today's highly specialized M.D.s. He states that this difference may justify limitations on the privileges of osteopaths that are similar to limitations imposed upon general practice M.D.s and family practitioners, but that it would not seem to justify the total exclusion of osteopaths. See id. at 411; Kissam, Webber, Bigers, and Holzgraefe, Antitrust and Hospital Privileges: Testing the Conventional Wisdom, 70 Calif. L. Rev. 595, 641 n.218 (1982) [hereinafter cited as Antitrust and Hospital Privileges]; Dolan & Ralston, Hospital Admitting Privileges and the Sherman Act, 18 Houston L. Rev. 707, 728 (1981) ("Osteopaths undergo training regimens quite similar to that of M.D. practitioners, except that greater emphasis is placed on family practice and on some manipulative practices. Regardless of the situation 30 years ago, it is highly unlikely that any significant qualitative difference between the two groups exists today."). [See also Enders, Federal Antitrust Issues Involved in the Denial of Medical Staff Privileges, 17 Loyola U. Chi. L.J. 331 (1986).—EDS.]

The investigation also raised some glimmer of a question about Dr. Weiss' medical competence, but the sole "evidence" that was adduced was hearsay, often second or third level hearsay. Nevertheless, the Medical Staff Executive Committee, apparently based on this "new evidence," decided not to recommend Weiss for staff privileges.

On June 30, 1977, the hospital Board of Directors considered the recommendations of the various committees which had considered Weiss' and Zittle's applications. The board voted to approve Zittle's application and deny Weiss' application. . . . The Credentials Committee's written report is revealing in both its assessment of the "evidence" against Weiss, and in its frank recognition of the "controversy" at York over the admission of D.O.s to staff privileges:

> The Committee invited Dr. Weiss to discuss the reactivation of his application and to direct certain questions to him. He was told of the developments in the past and precisely how his application has been handled and of the problems that had arisen. He was specifically told that almost everybody with whom we spoke acknowledged him to be an intelligent, competent, conscientious physician whose care of his patients in the Hospital was quite competent. He was told that the Chairman of his Department suggested that he probably was the best general practitioner. However, almost everyone to whom we spoke acknowledged that he has had personality problems in the past which have caused him to have difficult interpersonal relations with other members of the staff. He was told that because of this personality problem, his application was rejected. It was further explained to him that because of the controversy that accompanied the application of osteopaths to the York Hospital, it was felt that acceptance of his application would jeopardize that endeavor. We explained to Dr. Weiss that his admission to the staff would be met in some instances with outright hostility and in others with indifference and it was a matter of real concern to the Committee how he would react to this sort of reception. . . .

IV. THE SHERMAN ACT CLAIMS

We now turn to the substantive-law questions presented by this appeal. . . .

A. SECTION 1 OF THE SHERMAN ACT

In order to establish a violation of §1 of the Sherman Act, 15 U.S.C. §1 (1982), a plaintiff must establish three elements: (1) a contract, combination, or conspiracy; (2) restraint of trade; and (3) an effect on interstate commerce. Each of these three elements has been the subject of extensive analysis by the courts, and we now turn to a discussion of that case law and its application to the facts of this case, taking the elements up in turn.

1. Proof of An Agreement: Is There A Sufficient Number of Conspirators?

In order to establish a violation of §1, a plaintiff must prove that two or more distinct entities agreed to take action against the plaintiff. Before the district court, Weiss contended that the hospital and its medical staff were legally distinct entities and therefore capable of conspiring in violation of §1. He also asserted that the doctors who joined together to form the medical staff were separate economic entities who competed against each other so that, as a matter of law, the medical staff was a "combination" of doctors within the meaning of §1. Finally, Weiss argued that even if the individual doctors who made up York's medical staff were deemed by the court to be the equivalent of "officers or employees" of the hospital and therefore ordinarily not capable of conspiring with the hospital, nevertheless the doctors were acting for their own benefit in discriminating against osteopaths, and therefore fell within an exception to the ordinary rule that "officers or employees of the same firm do not provide the plurality of actors imperative for a §1 conspiracy." Copperweld Corp. v. Independence Tube Corp., 467 U.S. 752 (1984).

The district court concluded, and instructed the jury, that the medical staff was an "unincorporated division" of the hospital, and as such the two were legally a "single entity" incapable of conspiring. . . . However, . . . the district court held the defendant medical staff liable to the plaintiff class under §1. On the question who conspired with the medical staff, the court stated only:

> The York Hospital Medical and Dental Staff conspired with another person or entity to deny or impede reasonable, fair, equal, and full access to staff privileges at York Hospital by osteopathic physicians other than Plaintiff Weiss.

We agree with the plaintiffs that, as a matter of law, the medical staff is a combination of individual doctors and therefore that any action taken by the medical staff satisfies the "contract, combination, or conspiracy" requirement of §1. . . .

Antitrust policy requires the courts to seek the economic substance of an arrangement, not merely its form. The "substance" of an arrangement often depends on the economic incentive of the parties. The York medical staff is a group of doctors, all of whom practice medicine in their individual capacities, and each of whom is an independent economic entity in competition with other doctors in the York medical community. Each staff member, therefore, has an economic interest separate from and in many cases in competition with the interests of other medical staff members. Under these circumstances, the medical staff cannot be considered a single economic entity for purposes of antitrust analysis. . . . In substance, the medical staff is a group of individual doctors in competition with each other and with other physicians in the York MSA, who have organized to regulate the provision of medical care at York hospital. Where such associations exist, their actions are subject to scrutiny under §1 of the Sherman Act in order to insure that their members do not abuse otherwise legitimate organizations to secure an unfair advantage over their competitors. . . .

Finally, we deal with the plaintiff's assertion that the district court erred in charging the jury that the hospital could not conspire with its medical staff. The district court found that the medical staff was an unincorporated division of the hospital, and as such the court determined that the two could not conspire. Although we do not necessarily agree with the district court's characterization of the medical staff as an unincorporated division of the hospital, we agree with its basic conclusion that, with respect to the issues in this case, the hospital could not, as a matter of law, conspire with the medical staff. The medical staff was empowered to make staff privilege decisions on behalf of the hospital. As such, with regard to these decisions, the medical staff operated as an officer of a corporation would in relation to the corporation. Although the members of the medical staff had independent economic interests in competition with each other, the staff as an entity had no interest in competition with the hospital. Accordingly, we conclude that the district court correctly charged the jury that there could not be a conspiracy between the hospital and the medical staff.[29]

2. Proof of Restraint of Trade

a. Introduction

Read literally, §1 prohibits every agreement "in restraint of trade." In United States v. Joint Traffic Ass'n, 171 U.S. 505, 19 S. Ct. 25, 43 L. Ed. 259 (1898), the Supreme Court recognized that Congress could not have intended a literal interpretation of the word *every*, and since Standard Oil Co. of New Jersey v. United States, 221 U.S. 1, 31 S. Ct. 502, 55 L. Ed. 619 (1911), courts have analyzed most restraints under the so-called rule of reason. As its name suggests, the rule of reason requires the factfinder to decide whether, under all the circumstances of the case, the restrictive practice imposes an unreasonable restraint on competition.[52]

The courts have also, however, applied a rule of per se illegality to certain types of business practices. The development of per se rules has resulted from a recognition that the case-by-case approach inherent in the rule of reason has significant costs, and that certain types of business practices almost always have anticompetitive effects without offsetting pro-competitive effects. In applying the per se rules, a court eschews the ordinary evaluation of the effect of the challenged practice, and concentrates instead on the question whether the practice falls within one of the categories of practices condemned by the per se rule. In this case, the plaintiffs argued that the actions of the defendants were the equivalent of a boycott, or as it is sometimes called, a concerted refusal to deal, and thus illegal per se. We now turn to that inquiry.

b. Is Defendants' Exclusionary Conduct the Equivalent of a Concerted Refusal to Deal ("Boycott")?

The jury found that the defendants had engaged in a policy of discrimination against Dr. Weiss and the other D.O.s in the York MSA by applying unfair, unequal, and unreasonable procedures in reviewing their applications. In addition, the district court concluded that this unfair, unreasonable, and unequal treatment "could reasonably be anticipated [by the defendants] to cause osteopathic physicians to refrain from applying for staff privileges at the York

---

[29] [Excerpted from earlier in the opinion.] We note however that exoneration of York Hospital on the §1 claims does not necessarily result in the dismissal of the action as to York. The medical staff . . . does not exist independent of the hospital, and therefore the hospital may be liable to pay any award of money damages in favor of the plaintiffs and against the staff . . . on a respondeat superior theory of liability. We leave this question to another day.

[52] Justice Brandeis provided the classic statement of the rule of reason in Board of Trade of City of Chicago v. United States, 246 U.S. 231, 238, 38 S. Ct. 242, 244, 62 L. Ed. 683 (1918):

> The true test of legality is whether the restraint imposed is such as merely regulates and perhaps thereby promotes competition or whether it is such as may suppress or even destroy competition. To determine that question the court must ordinarily consider the facts peculiar to the business to which the restraint was imposed; its condition before and after the restraint and its effect; the nature of the restraint and its effect, actual or probable. The history of the restraint, the evil believed to exist, the reason for adopting the particular remedy, the purpose or end sought to be attained, are all relevant facts.

Hospital." The question before us is whether these actions should properly be characterized as a "group boycott" or "concerted refusal to deal," in which case they are illegal per se under §1. If the defendants' actions cannot be so characterized, the rule of reason analysis would apply and the outcome of the case could be different. We conclude that the defendants' actions, as found in the district court, are the equivalent of a concerted refusal to deal.

The classic example of a concerted refusal to deal is the situation in which businesses at one level of production or distribution, e.g., retailers, use the threat of a boycott to induce businesses at another level, e.g., manufacturers, not to deal with competitors of the retailers. As Professor Sullivan has observed, "The boycotting group members, in effect, say to their suppliers or to their customers, 'If you don't stop dealing with non-group members, we will stop dealing with you.' If continued trade with group members is more important to a supplier or customer than is trading with non-group members, this threat will be effective." L. Sullivan, Handbook of the Law of Antitrust §83, at 230 (1977).

In this case York is a provider of hospital services; for the purpose of our analysis, the equivalent of the manufacturer in the example of a classical boycott. Similarly, the M.D.s are the equivalent of the retailers in the example, in the sense that physicians require access to a hospital in order to effectively treat patients. The difficulty with this analogy, at first blush, is that there is no evidence that the M.D.s have used coercion for the purpose of inducing York to exclude their competitors, the D.O.s. . . . In this case, however, because of the M.D.s' control over York's admission decisions, no coercion is necessary. . . .

[At this point, the court's opinion becomes somewhat confused. The following explanation may help to clarify the issues: The paradigm boycott case involves a "secondary boycott" (i.e., a boycott aimed at one party in order to exclude or discipline a third party) because competitors usually lack any ready means to boycott the target firm directly. A classic secondary boycott would have occurred here if the medical staff had threatened to leave the hospital if Dr. Weiss were admitted. An ordinary medical staff exclusion case differs from this paradigm only because doctors don't need to use this indirect threat if they possess the ability to keep out the unwanted practitioner themselves, that is, to engage in primary rather than a secondary boycott. — EDS.]

We recognize that the facts of this case do not precisely fit into the mold of the classical refusal to deal. The refusal to deal is less than total insofar as York admitted Dr. Zittle and a number of other osteopaths. Arguably then, what is at issue is not a boycott but mere discrimination, which sounds less like a per se antitrust violation. However, given the evidence of the different standards applied to osteopaths and M.D.s and the second class citizenship afforded D.O.s upon admission to staff privileges at York, and in view of the adverse impact of these factors upon D.O. applications for York staff privileges, we are satisfied that the restrictive policy is, in purpose and effect, sufficiently close to the traditional boycott, that the characterization is appropriate.

The Medical Staff is, however, entitled to exclude individual doctors, including osteopaths, on the basis of their lack of professional competence or unprofessional conduct. If York's policy toward D.O.s could be viewed as a form of industry self-regulation of this type, the rule of reason, rather than a per se rule, would be applicable. See generally L. Sullivan, Handbook of the Law of Antitrust

§§86-88 (1977). We recognize, therefore, that in many cases involving exclusion from staff privilege, courts will, more or less openly, have to utilize a rule of reason balancing approach. This case is different, however, because York has not contended that osteopaths as a group are less qualified than M.D.s. See supra n.4. In the absence of such a contention, or another legitimate explanation for the discrimination, we conclude that a per se rule should be applied, since the effect of the practice is identical to that of the traditional boycott, and plainly anticompetitive.

Congruent with the foregoing discussion, the Supreme Court has adopted an exception to application of the per se rule of illegality where the case involves a learned profession and where the restriction is justified on "public service or ethical norm" grounds. Thus unlike most cases where characterization of some activity as a classical boycott ends the inquiry, here, because the medical profession is involved, the rule of reason analysis may still control, as a "built-in" exception. We now turn to a discussion of this potential "escape hatch" to see if it can extricate the defendants from the "cut" of the per se rule.

c. The "Learned Profession" Exception

In Goldfarb v. Virginia State Bar, 421 U.S. 773, 788 n.17, 95 S. Ct. 2004, 2013 n.17, 44 L. Ed. 2d 572 (1975), in which the Supreme Court made clear that the medical profession is not exempt from the antitrust laws, the Court stated that the "public service aspect, and other features of the professions, may require that a particular practice, which could properly be viewed as a violation of the Sherman Act in another context, be treated differently." In Arizona v. Maricopa County Medical Society, 457 U.S. 332, 348-349 (1982), the Court partially explained this exception by stating that conduct which is normally subject to per se condemnation under §1 will instead be subject to rule of reason analysis where the challenged conduct is "premised on public service or ethical norms." In Maricopa, because the defendants did not attempt to justify their price fixing arrangements on either of these grounds, but instead attempted to argue that the maximum price levels were pro-competitive, the Court held that the per se rule controlled and consequently found that the defendants' conduct violated §1.

In this case the defendants have offered no "public service or ethical norm" rationale for their discriminatory treatment of D.O.s. Indeed, their defense at trial was that they did not discriminate against D.O.s. Since the jury believed otherwise, we conclude that the per se rule governs this case. . . .[61]

V. Conclusion

In summary, we reach the following conclusions. First, we find that the district court's decision that the medical staff violated Sherman Act §1 as to the plaintiff class is supported by sufficient evidence, and we therefore will affirm the district court on this point. . . . [W]e also agree that the issuance of an injunction by the district court in this case was proper.

---

[61] Several circuit court opinions have held the rule of reason analysis, not the per se rule of illegality, controls in boycott cases involving the learned professions. We believe these cases are readily distinguishable from the instant case. In Wilk v. American Medical Ass'n, 719 F.2d 207 (7th Cir. 1983), a case involving the refusal of M.D.s to deal with chiropractors, the Seventh Circuit stated: "boycotts are

■ HASSAN v. INDEPENDENT PRACTICE ASSOCIATES
698 F. Supp. 679 (E.D. Mich. 1988)

NEWBLATT, District Judge.

Before the court are defendants' Motion for Summary Judgment. . . . Plaintiffs Shawky Hassan and Fikria Hassan are allergists who practice through the Allergy & Asthma Center, P.C., a professional corporation wholly owned by the Drs. Hassan. Defendant Independent Practice Associates, P.C., (IPA) is an organization of physicians and osteopaths who provide medical care to subscribers of Genesee Health Care, Inc., doing business as Health Plus of Michigan (Health Plus), a state licensed, federally qualified health maintenance organization (HMO). . . . Plaintiffs allege . . . that IPA's participation in plaintiffs' separation from IPA and the group's subsequent refusal to readmit the doctors, constitute an illegal group boycott. . . .

IPA is the corporation through which the group of doctors that treat patients who subscribe to Health Plus practice. It is owned by the physicians who comprise the group. Health Plus, the HMO insurance contractor here, was formed by the Genesee County Medical Society in 1979. Its Board of Directors is made up of subscribers, the public and physicians. Health Plus is funded by subscribers who pay a fixed premium per month. With this money, Health Plus pays service providers, such as IPA, on a computed basis and also a fixed amount per member per month. IPA members are paid primarily on a fee-for-services basis, which the IPA determines according to a set maximum fee schedule. . . .

Defendants concede that IPA exists only to serve Health Plus patients. . . . Health Plus has experienced substantial growth since 1979 and its patient market share is 20 percent of the population in the area of Genesee-Lapeer-Shiawassee counties. . . . There is no evidence that IPA physicians cannot also belong to other such organizations.

---

illegal per se only if used to enforce agreements that are themselves illegal per se—for example price fixing agreements." Id. at 221 (quoting Marrese v. American Academy of Orthopaedic Surgeons, 706 F.2d 1488, 1495 (7th Cir. 1983)). Since the court could find no per se illegal purpose for the A.M.A.'s medical ethics principle 3, which in essence provided that M.D.'s should not associate with chiropractors, it concluded that the rule of reason analysis governed in that case. We believe that the Seventh Circuit was correct in utilizing a rule of reasons analysis in the *Wilk* case because the defendants were plainly asserting a "public service or ethical norm" justification for their concerted refusal to deal with chiropractors. In Virginia Academy of Clinical Psychologists v. Blue Shield of Va., 624 F.2d 476, 484-485 (4th Cir. 1980), the Fourth Circuit stated: "Because of the special considerations involved in the delivery of health services, we are not prepared to apply a per se rule of illegality to medical plans which refuse or condition payments to competing or potentially competing providers." . . . [A] "medical necessity" justification was apparently raised by the defendants, and in our view that would have been sufficient to bring the defendants within the purview of Maricopa's exception for conduct based on "public service or ethical norms." Finally, in Kreuzer v. American Academy of Periodontology, 735 F.2d 1479 (D.C. Cir. 1984), the D.C. Circuit Court held that the rule of reason analysis governed a §1 challenge to a rule promulgated by the American Academy of Periodontology (AAP) that limited membership in the AAP to licensed dentists who practice periodontics exclusively, and who do not practice other forms of dentistry. The court labeled the effect of the AAP's rule a "group boycott" but concluded that "[w]hen a conspiracy of this sort is alleged in the context of one of the learned professions, the nature and extent of its anticompetitive effect are often too uncertain to be amendable to per se treatment." . . . [See also Betkerur v. Aultman Hospital Ass'n, 78 F.3d 1079 (6th Cir. 1996) (no per se horizontal boycott existed where independent obstetricians agreed to designate one neonatologist for most of their referrals; the relationship between the two kinds of doctors was vertical, not horizontal, and no economic motives were apparent).]

Defendants contend that they face a competitive market. For example, they contend that the largest portion of Health Plus's membership is represented by General Motors (GM) employees. In order to obtain the GM business, defendants must compete on an annual basis by obtaining both GM and UAW approval as an authorized insurer and then, further, convince the employees to choose the Health Plus program. Thus, GM, the union, and the workers must be satisfied as to both price charged and benefits offered. . . . This has resulted in actions [to cut costs such as] denying physicians' applications for membership and terminations or resignations of physicians. . . .

Plaintiffs joined IPA in 1979, and until October of 1981, they were the only allergy specialists to provide such service to Health Plus subscribers. In 1980, a review of billing records revealed a high incidence of lab tests performed by plaintiffs and prompted the IPA's Care, Quality and Cost Committee to request justification for those tests from plaintiff Shawky Hassan. Moreover, the Committee began setting guidelines for allergy testing which prohibited routine testing. Further, in October of 1981, an IPA survey of allergy testing procedures indicated that plaintiffs performed far more tests than two other specialists, and a review of patient charts failed to satisfy the IPA that the Hassans' level of testing was justified. . . .

Health Plus sent out a notice that subscribers could no longer see the Drs. Hassan. . . . In August of 1983, the Hassans applied to IPA on behalf of their newly established Urgent Care Family Clinic to provide emergency care to IPA members. . . . On January 6, 1984, all of plaintiffs' applications were denied without explanation. The Hassan Clinic lost money and, in 1985, it was closed. . . .

1. WAS THERE A CONSPIRACY?

. . . [E]ach physician in IPA has a practice or other profession independent of IPA or Health Plus. The inferences from the undisputed facts lead the court to the conclusion that there is at least a question of fact as to whether there was a conspiracy to exclude plaintiffs from IPA. First, Health Plus was created by physicians, the Genesee County Medical Society, who are members of IPA. Moreover, although IPA members may not dominate the Health Plus Board of Directors, one third of its members belong to IPA. . . . [T]here is at least an inference which must be viewed in a light most favorable to plaintiffs, that IPA members have effective control. . . .

2. IS THERE A PER SE VIOLATION?

Defendants next argue that Northwest Wholesale Stationers, Inc. v. Pacific Stationary Printing Co., 472 U.S. 284 (1985) precludes treatment of this case under the per se illegal group boycott rule. . . . In *Northwest Wholesale Stationers*, . . . a cooperative buying agency expelled a member without procedural means for challenging the expulsion.[40] . . . The Court [refused to apply the per se

---

[40] Northwest was a purchasing cooperative of approximately 100 office supply retailers which acted as a primary wholesaler for the retailers. In 1978, members of Northwest voted to expel Pacific, offering no explanation at the time nor giving Pacific notice, a hearing, or any other opportunity to challenge the decision. Pacific contended that the explusion was a group boycott and a per se violation of §1.

categorization, explaining: "A plaintiff seeking application of the per se rule must present a threshold case that the challenged activity falls into a category likely to have predominantly anticompetitive effects. The mere allegation of a concerted refusal to deal does not suffice because not all concerted refusals to deal are predominantly anticompetitive."] . . . Thus, the court in *Northwest Wholesalers* required that, [before invoking the per se rule], those plaintiffs . . . make a threshold showing (1) whether that practice is [not] justified by plausible arguments that it is intended to enhance overall efficiency and make markets more competitive; and (2) a showing that defendant possesses—(a) market power, and (b) exclusive access to an element essential to effective competition. . . .

The court agrees with defendants that the acts of expulsion and the refusal to readmit plaintiffs are justified by enhancing efficiency and making the market more competitive. First, despite plaintiffs' counsel's contentions at the hearing, the record shows that plaintiffs do not dispute the fact that IPA adopted its allergy testing policy to prevent excessive use of costly tests and that plaintiffs disagreed with this policy. It is also undisputed that cost containment objectives are procompetitive. . . .

Although plaintiffs contend that defendants' decisions or policies as to allergy testing were incorrect, that is irrelevant. The issue is not whether the decisions were correct but "whether there are plausible arguments that they were intended to enhance overall efficiency and make markets more competitive." Northwest, 472 U.S. 284 at 294. . . . Finally, plaintiffs contend that the decision to deny membership to plaintiffs was made by primary care physicians who were interested in providing allergy care themselves. Not only is there no evidence of this, but allegations that defendants' motives were manifestly anticompetitive are more properly considered under a rule of reason analysis. . . .

[As for market power,] 20 percent market share is not sufficient market power in light of the competition from other providers in the relevant market. However, market share does not always indicate whether a firm really has market power. Therefore, other factors must also be examined and these support defendants' position.

First, there are no significant barriers to entry into this market—that is, the market for health care finance.[47] In Ball Memorial Hosp., Inc. v. Mutual Hosp. Ins., 784 F.2d 1325, 1335 (6th Cir. 1986), the Seventh Circuit stated that:

> The insurance industry is not like the steel industry, in which a firm must take years to build a costly plant before having anything to sell. The "productive asset" of the insurance business is money, which may be supplied on a moment's notice, plus the ability to spread risk, which many firms possess and which has no geographic boundary. In this case, defendants' expert has stated in his affidavit that any health care insurer in Michigan may serve patients in this market. Plaintiffs have not identified any barriers to entry and, in fact, Greater Flint HMO and PPO, Trust, have recently entered the market.

---

[47] Although plaintiffs contend that the relevant market is the "prepaid market share," which includes only HMOs, the relevant market "consists of the . . . services with which defendants' product competes." In this case, Health Plus must compete with the other sources of health care financing. . . .

... Plaintiffs, however, argue that defendants have market power through the percentage of physicians (75 percent) in this market who are members of IPA. ... The authority they cite does not apply because it is concerned with a different problem — that of deterring the establishment of new HMOs. Those concerns would only come into play if IPA was able to affiliate with physicians on an exclusive basis. There is simply nothing in the record to indicate that IPA physicians are not free to affiliate with other providers.[50] ... Accordingly, plaintiffs are not entitled to a finding of per se illegality.

3. RULE OF REASON

Defendants next contend that there is no unreasonable restraint of trade as no significant anticompetitive effect has resulted from the plaintiffs' expulsion or resignation, and subsequent rejection for readmittance, from IPA. The test under the rule of reason is whether competition in the overall market has been harmed, the antitrust laws not having been intended to protect merely individual competitors. ...

In this case, the undisputed facts indicate that there has been no anticompetitive impact on the overall market. First, as indicated above, IPA does not have significant market power. ... Even assuming that defendants did have the requisite market power, there is no evidence that the exclusion of plaintiffs had an impact on overall competition ... because the substitution of one company for another "does not limit competition in any substantial sense." ...

The plaintiffs' expulsion or departure from IPA was followed (or shortly preceded) by the admittance of two new allergists. ... Moreover, there is no indication that plaintiffs left the market, so the end result is that the public has just as many allergists from which to choose. Even if the plaintiffs were to leave the tri-county market, there is no reason to believe that they would not be easily replaced so that the market would be served by enough allergists. ... Finally, competition is not harmed because there are a sufficient number of allergists and primary care physicians who can provide allergy services in the tri-county area. ...

Next, plaintiffs claim that defendants' motives in excluding plaintiffs from IPA were anticompetitive.[56] Plaintiffs present no evidence of an anticompetitive motive other than that several doctors, primary care physicians who were involved in the decision stood to benefit from plaintiffs' exclusion. Not only does this ignore the fact that several allergists were admitted shortly before and after plaintiffs' expulsion, but it also ignores the rule of reason's requirement of injury to overall competition, not just to individual competitors. Thus, plaintiffs have failed to satisfy the requirements under the rule of reason. ...

---

[50] If there was exclusive affiliation, there would be a barrier to entry. [It can be seen from this discussion that antitrust law favors physicians contracting with networks on a non-mutually exclusive basis or under contracts of very short duration. However, another body of law regulating "referral fees" is hostile to these types of contracts. See page 534 for further discussion of exclusive dealing in managed care networks. — EDS.]

[56] Plaintiffs rely on FTC v. Indiana Federation of Dentists, 476 U.S. 447, 106 S. Ct. 2009, 90 L. Ed. 2d 445 (1986), for the proposition that "where clear anticompetitive motives are present and no clear competitive benefits exist, an extended market analysis is not required."

Having disposed of all plaintiffs' claims, judgment in this case shall hereby be entered for defendants.

Notes: Medical Staff Boycotts; Exclusive Dealing

1. *Medical Staff Conspiracies. Weiss* ruled that all physicians participating in a medical staff credentialing decision constitute a "walking conspiracy" as a matter of law. Granted that some physicians on the York Hospital medical staff have an independent interest in competition with Dr. Weiss, is this true of neurosurgeons, pathologists, or specialists who are not engaged in a general practice? Even for those doctors who potentially are in direct competition — in Dr. Weiss' case, say, general and family practitioners — should the court find a conspiracy as a matter of law? Individual doctors might in fact ignore their competitive interests in making a staffing decision. Following *Weiss*, several courts have held that no conspiracy exists unless special facts are shown. In one, the court held that pediatricians who voted to exclude nurse midwives were acting merely as agents of a single hospital because nurse midwives compete only with obstetricians, not pediatricians. As for the obstetricians, conspiracy would not be presumed; the midwives must show at least the possibility that they acted for other than legitimate reasons. Nurse Midwifery Association v. Hibbett, 918 F.2d 605 (6th Cir. 1990). See also Oksanen v. Page Memorial Hospital, 945 F.2d 696 (4th Cir. 1991) (en banc); Note, 75 Tex. L. Rev. 409 (1996).

In contrast with its holding as a matter of law that a conspiracy existed *within* the medical staff, *Weiss* held that the medical staff *as an entity* cannot, as a matter of law, conspire with the hospital because it is part of the hospital. But if members of the medical staff conspire with each other by virtue of their independent stake in the decision, why not with the hospital as well? Compare Bolt v. Halifax Hospital Medical Center, 891 F.2d 810 (11th Cir. 1990) ("we hold that a hospital and the members of its medical staff are all legally capable of conspiring with one another" because "a hospital and the members of its medical staff are legally separate entities").

Which of these approaches best captures the realities of the hospital/medical staff relationship, the typical reasons for peer review, and who controls the decisionmaking? For a detailed analysis of these issues, see William Brewbaker, Antitrust Conspiracy Doctrine and the Hospital Enterprise, 74 B.U. L. Rev. 67 (1994) ("given the typical economic and managerial independence of physicians from hospitals, . . . [concerted action exists unless] it can be demonstrated that the medical staff acted in a purely advisory role").

2. *Monopolies.* Where concerted action is not found and Sherman Act §1 is not implicated, an antitrust claim might still be stated under various §2 theories covering unilateral refusals to deal. Usually, unilateral refusals are beyond reproach, even if the hospital or HMO enjoys a monopoly, because the antitrust laws do not proscribe monopolies per se, nor do they proscribe the lawful exercise of monopoly power rightfully obtained. Antitrust law prohibits only obtaining monopoly power in certain unfair ways, or abusing that power in certain ways. Depending on the circumstances, a monopolist's unilateral refusal to deal might be considered abusive. However, understanding the qualifications embedded in the previous two

sentences is largely beyond the scope of these materials. The one §2 theory of particular note for hospital exclusions is the "essential facilities doctrine." This is based on a smattering of cases holding that, where access to a particular facility is essential for others to compete, the facility must be offered to all competitors on fair and reasonable terms. This doctrine applies, however, only where the hospital in question enjoys a monopoly position in the market. See generally Scott Makar, The Essential Facility Doctrine and the Health Care Industry, 21 Fla. St. U. L. Rev. 913 (1994).

3. *Different Levels of Scrutiny.* In order for the *Weiss* court to impose a rule of per se illegality, it first characterized the medical staff's decision as a class-based exclusion of all osteopaths not premised on any quality-of-care justification. How strong is the evidence for this characterization? Consider that the medical staff did amend its bylaws to allow in osteopaths and it in fact extended privileges to Dr. Zittle, a D.O. who applied at the same time as Dr. Weiss. Consider also the stated justification relating to Dr. Weiss' personality.

Where the exclusion is not class-based but is directed unambiguously to the professional competence of a single practitioner, plaintiffs have rarely succeeded. *Weiss* is unique in applying a per se rule because the jury found that the hospital's justification for an individual exclusion was a pretext, and the hospital did not offer any justification for a class-based exclusion of all osteopaths (which it believed it had not engaged in but the jury found it had). When exclusions *are* premised on quality of care, the *Weiss* court concedes that the rule of reason applies. Although rule of reason cases are usually long and complex, in hospital disputes courts usually find ways to dismiss the case quickly, on the pleadings or on motion for summary judgment, without going to trial. As one court explained:

> The cases involving staffing at a single hospital are legion. Hundreds, perhaps thousands of pages in West publications are devoted to the issues those circumstances present. Those cases invariably analyze those circumstances under the rule of reason — there is nothing obviously anticompetitive about a hospital choosing one staffing pattern over another or in restricting the staffing to some rather than many, or all. A hospital has an unquestioned right to exercise some control over the identity and number to whom it accords staff privileges. Malpractice concerns, quality of care, market perceptions, cost, and administrative considerations may all impact those decisions. Those hundreds or thousands of pages almost always come to the same conclusion: the staffing decision at a single hospital was not a violation of §1 of the Sherman Act. [Citations to 28 cases omitted.]
>
> The reasons advanced for that conclusion are varied. Insufficient nexus to interstate commerce, lack of standing, lack of antitrust injury, failure to show a detrimental effect on competition, the inability of a hospital to conspire with its staff, and insufficient market power in the relevant market are among the reasons relied upon for denying section 1 relief. Sometimes the conclusion follows a motion to dismiss; more often the decision is one of summary judgment, but often it appears that the record relied upon is the absence of facts indicating special circumstances raising antitrust concerns. . . .
>
> Before we enlist this court in the micromanagement of the staffing arrangements at [this hospital] under the aegis of the antitrust laws, we need better reasons than the plaintiffs have given us. . . . "If the law were otherwise, many a physician's workplace grievance with a hospital would be elevated to the status of an antitrust action. To keep the antitrust laws from becoming so trivialized, the reasonableness

of a restraint is evaluated based on its impact on competition as a whole within the relevant market." Oksanen v. Page Memorial Hospital, 945 F.2d 696, 708 (4th Cir. 1991).

BCB Anesthesia Care v. Passavant Memorial Area Hospital Ass'n, 36 F.3d 664 (7th Cir. 1994) (dismissing at the pleadings stage a complaint by three nurse anesthetists that the hospital conspired with a physician anesthetist to terminate their contract for anesthesiology services). This is consistent with a general trend in antitrust decisions toward making it easier for defendants to obtain summary judgment where the plaintiff's basic theory "simply makes no economic sense." Matsushita Elec. Indus. Co. v. Zenith Radio Corp., 475 U.S. 574 (1986).

A few courts since *Weiss* have found, however, that intensive review of hospitals' staffing decisions is justified under antitrust law. E.g., Brader v. Allegheny General Hospital, 64 F.3d 869 (3d Cir. 1995) (refusing to follow *BCB Anesthesia*). For example, one court reversed the grant of summary judgment to a hospital that excluded a doctor on quality grounds after he set up a competing clinic explaining:

> [Dr.] Miller contends that his hospital staff privileges were revoked and his applications for reinstatement denied because defendants wished to stifle his competition. He contends that . . . he was treated more severely than other physicians whose competence was in question but who presented no economic threat to the defendants. Defendants' argument that they revoked Miller's staff privileges because of his professional incompetence and unprofessional conduct is a defense they may present before the jury which, if convinced, will absolve them of any antitrust liability. It is inappropriate and unprecedented, however, to . . . defer to the manner in which defendants themselves, who are parties in interest, weighed the evidence and drew inferences.

Miller v. Indiana Hospital, 843 F.2d 139 (3d Cir. 1987). It appears from the remainder of the opinion that the court envisioned a de novo jury decision on the hospital's actual motives, not on the doctor's actual competence. Where the motives are more clearly appropriate, then courts are almost always deferential to the hospitals' assessment of competence. This pattern in the case law contrasts with frequent statements by the courts that legality is tested more by anticompetitive effects than by anticompetitive motives. See, e.g., Marrese v. American Academy of Orthopaedic Surgeons, 971 F.2d 585 (7th Cir. 1992). On remand, the district court in *Miller* granted summary judgment to the hospital based on a lack of market impact, even though this was the only hospital in the county. Miller v. Indiana Hospital, 814 F. Supp. 1254 (W.D. Pa. 1992), aff'd mem., 975 F.2d 1550 (3d Cir. 1992).

4. *Standing and Injury to Competition.* Courts at first expressed their hostility to hearing these antitrust disputes by finding no federal jurisdiction due to the lack of any impact on interstate commerce, but as summarized in the introduction, this route was closed off by the Supreme Court in 1991. Subsequently, courts have sometimes ruled based on lack of standing, holding that if there were any injury to competition, it would be suffered by patients or by hospitals, not by the excluded doctor. See Todorov v. DCH Healthcare Authority, 921 F.2d 1438 (10th Cir. 1991) (the reduced competition that theoretically might result from a hospital's exclusive

contract for CT scans would injure only consumers, not the excluded neurologist; his only injury is the inability to share in the allegedly illegal profits); Balaklaw v. Lovell, 14 F.3d 793 (2d Cir. 1994) (physician who lost exclusive contract has no standing to complain that he was replaced; remedy sought would not increase consumer choice); cf. Brunswick Corp. v. Pueblo Bowl-O-Mat, 429 U.S. 477 (1977) (competitor lacks standing to challenge merger of bowling alleys). More commonly, however, courts simply rule as in *Hassan* that no injury to competition exists and therefore no violation occurs if the doctors who remain possess no significant market power. A single competitor's loss of patients to another doctor or hospital does not harm the patients, nor does it necessarily threaten to raise prices or worsen quality. In a phrase, antitrust law, in contrast with tort law, is concerned with harm to competition, not harm to competitors.

The instinct that single-physician staffing decisions should not create a federal antitrust case is also captured in the Health Care Quality Improvement Act, discussed at page 507, which immunizes peer review of individual physicians based on quality concerns. This qualified immunity extends, however, only to damages actions, not to injunctive relief, and it does not cover exclusions (1) of nonphysicians, (2) of groups of physicians, or (3) based on economic or administrative concerns.

5. *Using Outside Reviewers.* For hospitals concerned that the antitrust exposure for aggressive peer review is still too intense, Professors Blumstein and Sloan offer an inviting solution:

> [H]ospitals concerned about antitrust exposure could avoid liability by . . . using outside professional consultants for quality assurance. . . . Peer Review Organizations (PRO's) might be authorized to perform such quality assurance services, and PROs enjoy their own independent statutory immunity from the antitrust laws. Even if non-PRO external reviewers are employed, however, the . . . lack of competitive status with staff physicians would remove such peer-review activities from coverage under §1 of the Sherman Act. No capacity to conspire would exist.

James Blumstein & Frank Sloan, Antitrust and Hospital Peer Review, 51 Law & Contemp. Probs. 7, 39-53 (1988). See also Mathews v. Lancaster General Hospital, 87 F.3d 624 (3d Cir. 1996) (no conspiracy as a matter of law despite possible economic motivation where hospital board acted independently and obtained outside review by independent consultant). Why do you suppose outside review is not more common, considering that it appears to create a nearly iron-clad defense against §1 antitrust claims? See Brewbaker, supra ("JCAHO standards may fairly be read to prohibit a governing body's unilateral decision to retain an external peer reviewer").

6. *Additional Reading.* For additional academic commentary on these lines of cases, proposing various degrees of scrutiny, standards of legality, and burdens of proof, see n.4 in *Weiss*; Blumstein & Sloan, supra (advocating that, for certain "cartal-behavior" decisions, courts should take "a precautionary prophylactic approach . . . requiring defendants to establish an overriding procompetitive justification . . . [that] is not just theoretical but factually demonstrable."); Clark Havighurst, Doctors and Hospitals: An Antitrust Perspective on Traditional

Relationships, 1984 Duke L.J. 1071, 1133-1134, 1157 ("To ensure that hospitals have reasonable freedom of action, . . . summary judgment or a directed verdict would be appropriate if documentary evidence and affidavits showed that the hospital's action reflected its [own] corporate concerns. . . . Under this test, a court would not concern itself . . . with whether the ostensible motives for the actions taken were the real motives or whether the adverse effect of the hospital action on competition among practitioners was outweighed by its actual contribution to fulfilling the hospital's objectives."). For an empirical analysis of this body of case law, see Peter J. Hammer & William M. Sage, Antitrust, Health Care Quality, and the Courts, 102 Colum. L. Rev. 545 (2002). See generally 89 A.L.R. Fed. 419 (1988).

7. *Exclusion from Managed Care Networks.* The paradigm boycott case consists of a hospital excluding practitioners for ostensibly quality of care reasons, but *Hassan* illustrates that this body of law also applies to exclusion by insurers and managed care networks, and exclusions based on economic grounds. Antitrust law is more familiar with these conventional commercial contexts and so, although these developments are somewhat novel in the industry, the legal analysis is in some ways easier. For a decision similar to *Hassan*, see Capital Imaging Associates v. Mohawk Valley Medical Associates, 996 F.2d 537 (2d Cir. 1993) (holding that member physicians of an IPA are capable of conspiring among themselves in deciding to award an exclusive radiology contract, but dismissing antitrust claim because of the IPA's small market share and consequent absence of any likely impact on prices or quality).

Levine v. Central Florida Medical Affiliates, 72 F.3d 1538 (11th Cir. 1996), presents perhaps the most startling set of facts. There, a general internist was able to earn $724,000 a year despite his exclusion from one of the area's largest PPOs. He complained that, had the exclusion not occurred, he would have been able to "score a [financial] touchdown." The court obviously found that the PPO lacked market power. The case is interesting for the way it treats a recent Supreme Court decision of importance for defining markets. Eastman Kodak v. Image Technical Services, 504 U.S. 451 (1992), held that a separate market could exist for the parts required to repair a Kodak brand photocopy machinery depending on whether Kodak parts are interchangeable with parts for other brands. If not interchangeable, once the Kodak machine is purchased the buyers are locked into that brand's repair parts. Similarly, Dr. Levine argued that the PPO has extreme power in a small market because subscribers to a managed care network are locked into an "aftermarket" of network providers. The court observed, however, that subscribers in a PPO can go outside the network, only at extra costs that providers such as Levine were free to make up through discounts, and that subscribers were generally able to change health insurance once a year. See generally Mark Glassman, Can HMOs Wield Market Power?, 46 Am. U. L. Rev. 91 (1996); James Ponsoldt, Refusals to Deal in "Locked-In" Health Care Markets, 1995 Utah L. Rev. 503; James Ponsoldt & Lance McMillan, The Judicial Legitimization of Horizontal Price-Fixing among Partially Integrated Health Care Providers: An Antitrust/Health Care Case Study, 50 Ala. L. Rev. 465 (1999). For additional discussion of market definition for managed care entities, see section 4.D.3.

So far, the only notable plaintiff's success by a provider excluded from a managed care network occurred in Reazin v. Blue Cross and Blue Shield of Kansas, 899 F.2d 951 (10th Cir. 1990), which sustained a $7.8 million verdict arising from a hospital's exclusion from a Blue Cross PPO. This case contained several unusual factors. First, the jury found that Blue Cross conspired with other member hospitals, thereby creating a horizonal conspiracy. Second, Blue Cross dominated the local insurance market. Third, the alleged motive for excluding the plaintiff hospital was its plans to create a competing PPO. This was seen as a signal to other hospitals that Blue Cross might also terminate them if the hospitals dealt with new managed care companies. For additional discussion of this line of cases, see Kathryn Fenton & Barry Harris, Vertrical Integration and Antitrust in Health Care Markets, 39 Antitrust Bull. 333 (1994); Thomas L. Greaney, Managed Competition, Integrated Delivery Systems and Antitrust, 79 Cornell L. Rev. 1507 (1994).

8. *Illegal "Tie-Ins."* The Supreme Court has, so far, spoken directly on physician exclusion issues in only one case, Jefferson Parish Hospital District v. Hyde, 466 U.S. 2 (1984), but it was decided on a more obscure antitrust theory relating to "tie-ins." In that case, a physician challenged an exclusive contract for anesthesiology services that kept him from practicing in the hospital. He argued that requiring surgery patients to use the services of only designated anesthesiologists constituted a per se illegal tie-in: Surgery patients were forced to use only designated anesthesiologists even if they might want someone else. Surprisingly, the Court seemed to agree that surgery and anesthesia are indeed separate services, but it rejected the tie-in claim nevertheless because the hospital lacked the requisite market power to force the packaged sale on the patient.

9. *Reimbursement Limits.* A related line of cases are those concerning health insurers' limitations on reimbursement for certain medical services. Chiropractors, for instance, would be severely affected if Blue Cross/Blue Shield refused to pay for their services. However, if Blue Cross/Blue Shield merely determines on its own the terms under which it is willing to do business and separately reaches an agreement with individual providers, there is no horizontal conspiracy — or is there? Law professor Sylvia Law, in her influential study Blue Cross: What Went Wrong? (2d ed. 1976), explains that providers historically have dominated the Blues and used them to enforce their economic interests. See Virginia Academy of Clinical Psychologists v. Blue Shield, 624 F.2d 476 (4th Cir. 1980), *cert. denied*, 450 U.S. 916 (1981) (§1 violation established by Blue Shield's refusal to reimburse psychiatrists directly); Hahn v. Oregon Physicians' Service, 868 F.2d 1022 (9th Cir. 1988) (physician-controlled HMO that excluded podiatrists can be challenged as group boycott). Where insurers are not controlled by physicians, however, most courts conclude that they are free to unilaterally pay or not pay for whatever medical services and in whatever amounts they want. Barry v. Blue Cross of California, 805 F.2d 866 (9th Cir. 1986). See generally Rebecca Berg, HMO Exclusion of Chiropractors, 66 S. Cal. L. Rev. 807 (1993); Clark Havighurst, Controlling Health Care Costs through Commercial Insurance Companies, 1978 Duke L.J. 728; Frances Miller, Vertical Restraints and Powerful Health Insurers: Exclusionary Conduct Masquerading as Managed Care? 51 Law & Contemp. Probs. 195 (1988). Price-fixing challenges to insurance payment policies are explored in section 4.D.2.

■ THE ROLE OF QUALITY OF HEALTH CARE CONSIDERATIONS IN ANTITRUST ANALYSIS

Thomas E. Kauper*

51 Law & Contemp. Probs. 273 (Spring 1988)

For decades, health care services markets have functioned, for better or worse, without the constraints imposed on markets by competitive market pressures. . . . Self-regulation has been the norm. Actors in these markets long assumed that the antitrust laws were of little or no relevance to their conduct. As a result, health care services markets have been characterized by a variety of structures and actions which in most other industries would raise serious antitrust questions. The introduction of antitrust policy into these markets has therefore resulted in direct challenges to a broad range of conduct within a short period of time. . . . In virtually every instance, the concern over quality of care is likely to be raised in justification for the conduct under antitrust attack.

A doctor is denied hospital staff privileges. Hospitals deny access to midwives or chiropractors, or enter into exclusive contracts with providers for the performance of specialized services. Groups of local hospitals, acting on their own or through regional planning groups, determine which hospitals will have emergency or burn treatment facilities. Doctors agree on, or communicate about, the amounts they will accept in reimbursement from insurers, or collaborate to resist other efforts by insurers to reduce costs. A hospital is denied accreditation by an accrediting group which relies in part on judgments by other hospitals. A physician is denied specialist certification by an organization made up of such specialists. A hospital (or group of hospitals) opposes the issuance of a certificate of need to a potential competitor. . . . Running through this broad range of cases is a single issue which is the central focus of this study. When, if ever, should an antitrust court weigh the impact of conduct on quality of care? . . .

II. QUALITY OF CARE: A FRAMEWORK FOR ANALYSIS

A quality-of-care "defense" can mean a number of quite different things. First, the [defendants] may seek recognition of a limited professional services exemption from the antitrust laws. Adverse competitive effects then would have no antitrust consequences. Second, the [defendants] may contend that even if the [action] in question has adverse price and output effects, those effects are offset in some way by the social and economic benefits of avoiding deaths and physical harm to [patients]. Such a justification proceeds on the premise that quality of care is a national goal to be achieved even at the cost of competition. . . . Third, the [defendants] may assert that . . . quality of care is a relevant competitive factor or that there are no adverse price and output effects because of the preservation of a high quality of care. . . . [This] is a quite different argument from either the first or second; it is consistent with the view that antitrust analysis is confined to an examination of price and output effects. Fourth, the [defendant] may contend that its [action] is saved by a good purpose. In cases where violation may depend on the

*Henry M. Butzel Professor of Law, University of Michigan.

presence of an anticompetitive intent, a good purpose may negate the presence of the bad. . . .

The quality-of-care "defense" is thus not a single contention, but a series of distinctly different arguments. . . . But courts confronted with quality-of-care claims have too often failed to understand these differences. The result has been analytical confusion, much of which can be attributed to the Supreme Court. . . .

This confusion began with the Supreme Court's decision in Goldfarb v. Virginia State Bar Association,[36] which found that the use of recommended fee schedules by the Fairfax County (Virginia) Bar Association violated §1 of the Sherman Act. The Court rejected the contention that the "learned professions" were not engaged in "trade or commerce" and were not therefore covered by the Sherman Act, noting that "the public service aspect of professional practice [is not] controlling in determining whether §1 includes professions." While *Goldfarb* dealt specifically with lawyers, it opened the door for the application of the antitrust laws to a wide variety of restraints involving health care markets. But in a now well-known footnote [17], inserted perhaps out of an abundance of caution, the Court sowed the seeds for the confusion about the relevance of quality-of-care concerns. [F]ootnote [17] states:

> The fact that a restraint operates upon a profession as distinguished from a business is, of course, relevant in determining whether that particular restraint violates the Sherman Act. It would be unrealistic to view the practice of professions as interchangeable with other business activities, and automatically apply to the professions antitrust concepts which originated in other areas. The public service aspect, and other features of the professions, may require that a particular practice, which could properly be viewed as a violation of the Sherman Act in another context, be treated differently. . . .

So the antitrust laws apply to the professions, but not quite. . . . *Goldfarb* was followed by the decision in National Society of Professional Engineers v. United States.[37] The canons of ethics of the Society prohibited competitive bidding. This, according to the government, was tantamount to price-fixing. In defense, the Society asserted that the prohibition was necessary because competitive bidding would result in "inferior work with consequent risk to public safety and health," a contention contrary to the repeated earlier assertions by the Court, noted above, that it is competition which assures quality. The Court's conclusion in *Professional Engineers* that the Society's ban on competitive bidding could not be justified on quality-of-service grounds is hardly surprising. . . . *Professional Engineers* makes clear that antitrust rules are directed solely to the *competitive* effects of the restraint. . . . But the Court went on:

> We adhere to the view expressed in *Goldfarb* that, by their nature, professional services may differ significantly from other business services, and, accordingly, the nature of the competition in such services may vary. Ethical norms may serve to regulate and promote this competition, and thus fall within the Rule of Reason.

[36] 421 U.S. 773 (1975).
[37] 435 U.S. 679 (1978).

While verbally adhering to the *Goldfarb* footnote, this reservation is more precise. Rather than public service, the touchstone is the nature of the competition. If professional services differ from others, the differences are in the markets themselves. Evaluation of competitive effects must take such differences into account. . . .

The Supreme Court's trilogy of health care antitrust cases following *Goldfarb*—Arizona v. Maricopa County Medical Society,[50] Jefferson Parish Hospital District No. 2 v. Hyde,[51] and FTC v. Indiana Federation of Dentists[52]—leaves little doubt about the general applicability of the antitrust laws to health care activities and considerable doubt about how they are to be applied. . . .

The final case in the trilogy is *Indiana Federation of Dentists*, where protection of the quality of dental care was the primary justification offered by defendants. At issue was a collective refusal by Indiana dentists, through the Indiana Federation, to supply X-rays along with claim forms to a number of dental care insurers. In order to contain dental care cost, insurers operated under policies limiting payments to the cost of the "least expensive yet adequate treatment," and often insisted that patient X-rays be submitted as part of the claims review process. . . . [T]he Federation attempted to justify its action on quality-of-care grounds, asserting that because X-rays alone do not furnish an adequate basis for evaluating dental problems, insurers who rely solely on X-rays would decline to pay for treatment which was in the best interest of the patient. . . . The Court declined to apply a per se rule, noting, inter alia, that "we have been slow to condemn rules adopted by professional associations as reasonable per se," but found that the [FTC's] findings of anticompetitive effects were sufficient . . . The decision gives little comfort to those urging that antitrust analysis in health care markets should take into account a variety of noneconomic factors.

Can the quality-of-care strands taken from *Goldfarb* through *Indiana Federation of Dentists* be woven into a coherent whole? The questions are being narrowed, and the nature of inquiry is now more sharply focused. A clear pattern is emerging. First, and most obvious, the Supreme Court has never found professional activity having adverse price and output effects justified by concerns over the quality of service provided. Second, justifications based on the view that competition will necessarily result in quality deterioration are unacceptable. . . . The Court's repeated assertions that professional conduct, and conduct in health care markets in particular, should be evaluated under standards that differ significantly from those more generally applied has created confusion. . . . These imprecise references to public service and ethical norms have allowed lower courts to treat quality-of-care issues in a variety of inconsistent ways, and in a manner reflecting biases more than consistent principles of antitrust analysis. . . .

Despite the confusion caused by the *Goldfarb* footnote and its progeny, the Court in its health care cases is generally moving in a direction in which quality of care is simply a factor in the analysis of adverse competitive effects. . . . Market structures and forces may be different in health care markets, and these differences

[50] 457 U.S. 332 (1981).
[51] 466 U.S. 2 (1984).
[52] 476 U.S. 447 (1986).

may be relevant in evaluating the price and output effects of particular conduct, but the antitrust principles applied remain the same. . . .

Firms compete not only on price, but also on quality of product or service. Both are integral factors in the consumer's decision to buy. . . . The most obvious example is a hospital's denial of staff privileges to a physician who is simply incompetent, or has a public reputation of incompetence. The hospital will contend that the effect of its action is to prevent debasement of the quality of care its patients receive. It is not, however, acting out of some purely altruistic, public service concern. The presence of such a physician on the staff will damage the hospital's reputation, and thus its ability to compete. It may also injure the reputation of other members of the staff through association, although this effect is less obvious. If these effects are strong enough, the hospital may lose patients not only through consumer choice but because other physicians, fearful for their own reputations, leave the staff, taking their patients with them. . . .

A court called upon to decide such a case need not consider these effects unless the denial of staff privileges is likely to have adverse price and output effects in the market served by the denied physician. In most cases, such effects are likely only when . . . the number of competing physicians with such privileges is small. Under these circumstances, the denial of entry may protect a cartel among those already established. Few denials of staff privileges to individual physicians (or other providers) are likely to have such adverse price and output effects.[131] But where they do, the reputational effects of granting privileges become relevant and should be treated in the same manner as [cost] efficiencies. The likelihood of these effects must be evaluated on the record. The problems of defining quality should not be an obstacle here. The focus is more on reputation than quality as such. It is not necessary to define quality in some absolute sense. . . .

Courts and commentators on occasion have suggested that with some types of conduct, a predicate to antitrust liability is a determination that the conduct was accompanied by a purpose to injure competition. . . . [But] [p]urpose is relevant only as a guide to a judgment about effects, both adverse and beneficial. Where those who know a market act for the avowed purpose of restraining it, their intention is some evidence that adverse effects will occur. Similarly, an unambiguous intention to promote efficiency is probative in determining whether conduct does so. . . . The role of purpose is evidentiary. Standing alone, it can neither justify nor condemn. . . .

Purpose is often relied upon in evaluating agreements among competitors to which rules involving boycotts might be applied. The reason apparently lies in those rules themselves. Traditionally, boycotts have been described as per se violations, illegal without consideration of effects. Until very recently the definition of boycott, for the purpose of this rule has been far too broad. . . . Virtually any professional association rule which is enforced through a denial of benefits, such as staff privileges or accreditation, can be described as a boycott. Emphasis on purpose in health care cases of this type has added flexibility and mitigated the harshness of the per se rule. With the Supreme Court's reformulations of boycott doctrine in Northwest Wholesale Stationers, Inc. v. Pacific Stationery & Printing

---

[131] Adverse effects are more likely where an entire class of competitors or potential competitors (e.g., podiatrists, nurse-midwives) are denied hospital access. . . .

Co.[154] and FTC v. Indiana Federation of Dentists, there is less need for such reliance on the parties' purposes. These decisions move in the direction of effects analysis.[156] . . .

III. Translating Theory into Reality: A Case Study

This section examines two decisions, Wilk v. American Medical Association[200] and Koefoot v. American College of Surgeons,[201] in which the boundaries of a quality-of-care, or patient care, defense, if any, are explored in depth. In both cases, the defendants placed primary reliance on the legitimacy of their efforts to guard the public in general, and their own patients in particular, against what, in their perception, was a significant threat to the quality of care provided. No other decisions discuss the issue as carefully or exhaustively. . . .

A. WILK

In *Wilk*, plaintiff chiropractors asserted that the American Medical Association and its members conspired among themselves and with other groups including the American Hospital Association, American College of Surgeons, American College of Physicians, American College of Radiology, American Academy of Orthopedic Surgeons, and the Joint Committee on Accreditation of Hospitals (JCAH) to conduct a nationwide boycott of chiropractic providers. While the facts are complex, the central feature of the alleged boycott was a 1966 AMA resolution stating: "It is the position of the medical profession that chiropractic is an unscientific cult whose practitioners lack the necessary training and background to diagnose and treat human disease." . . . The effect of the actions of the AMA and its co-conspirators was to discourage cooperation between chiropractors and physicians in the form of referrals, consultations, and the sharing of clinical and research results, and to deny chiropractors hospital facilities, including X-ray and laboratory facilities. . . .

Throughout the litigation, the defendants insisted that they had acted to protect the public health and safety from what they believed to be a form of quackery, a type of treatment without foundation in science. . . .

The court of appeals found the [trial court's] per se instructions erroneous. . . . Relying on *Goldfarb*'s reservations, the court noted that an ethical

---

[154] 472 U.S. 284 (1985).

[156] In *Northwest Wholesale Stationers*, the Court held that the per se rule did not apply to expulsion from a purchasing cooperative made up of plaintiff's competitors absent a showing that the cooperative "possesses market power or unique access to a business Element necessary for effective competition." 472 U.S. at 298 Without such a showing, a court could not find that the expulsion was per se illegal. The Court also noted that in prior cases in which it had applied a per se rule, the practices were not justified "by plausible arguments that were intended to enhance overall efficiency." . . . The boycott analysis in *Indiana Federation of Dentists* is similar, although qualified by the observation that "we have been slow to condemn rules of professional associations as unreasonable per se."

[200] 719 F.2d 207 (1983), *cert. denied*, 467 U.S. 1210 (1984). Following reversal by the court of appeals, the case was retried in a bench trial. Wilk v. American Medical Ass'n, 671 F. Supp. 1465 (N.D. Ill. 1987).

[201] 652 F. Supp. 882 (N.D. Ill. 1987). A prior decision on a partial summary judgment motion appears at 610 F. Supp. 1298 (N.D. Ill. 1985).

standard dealing with the role of scientific method presented sufficiently novel questions to avoid per se analysis. . . .

Had the appellate court stopped at this point, its analysis would have been fully consistent with conventional antitrust doctrine, . . . [b]ut the court then concluded that in accord with *Goldfarb*'s reservation it was free "to modify the rule of reason test in a case involving a certain kind of question of ethics for the medical profession." . . . In the court's words, "a value independent of the values attributed to unrestrained competition must enter the equation." If the defendants' dominant motive was a concern over scientific method in the care of patients, their conduct was reasonable even if competition was restricted. [The court constructed a four-part affirmative defense that tested the sincerity and objectivity of this motive and whether the defendants chose the least restrictive means of achieving their purpose. The trial court found in a bench trial that the least restrictive means test was not met because the defendants could have achieved their purpose through education. The court ordered sweeping injunctive relief requiring the trade associations to tell their members they are free to make individual decisions about whether to associate with chiropractors.] . . .

B. *KOEFOOT* [223]

Over half of all board certified surgeons in the country are members of the American College of Surgeons (ACS). . . . Board certification or status as an ACS fellow is required to hold staff privileges in hospitals accredited by JCAH. . . . The "itinerant surgery" rule of the ACS prohibits:

> [t]he performance of surgical operations (except on patients whose chances of recovery would be prejudiced by removal to another hospital) under circumstances in which the responsibility for diagnosis or care of the patient is delegated to another who is not fully qualified to undertake it.

The effect of the rule is that ACS surgeons may delegate responsibility for postoperative care only to other surgeons.

Dr. Koefoot is a general surgeon who performs surgery in three hospitals in Grand Island, Nebraska, and in several community hospitals some 20 minutes away. He gives postoperative care to his patients in Grand Island, but delegates responsibility for such care to nonsurgeon general practitioners in the community hospitals. After his expulsion from ACS for violating the itinerant surgery rule, he filed an antitrust suit against ACS, attacking the rule as a form of market allocation used by ACS members to block entry, as a boycott of non-surgeons, and as a tie-in between surgery and post-operative care. . . . ACS has defended the rule as a legitimate ethical canon adopted to enhance the quality of care provided surgical patients. . . .

[T]he trial court held that the itinerant surgery violation was not a per se violation and set an agenda for the trial under the rule of reason. A "facially legitimate ethical canon," defined as a rule of professional practice that establishes

---

[223] Koefoot v. American College of Surgeons, 610 F. Supp. 1298, 1301 (N.D. Ill. 1985).

standards of care "without reference to the economic interests of professionals," is not per se illegal. . . .

The trial court then dealt with the relevance of evidence offered by ACS to establish (1) that their motive was to safeguard the quality of patient care, and (2) that the practice of itinerant surgery was in fact harmful. As to the first, the court found *Wilk*'s patient care motive doctrine inapplicable. . . . [T]he later Supreme Court decisions in *Jefferson Parish* and *Indiana Federation of Dentists* . . . suggest that . . . [m]otive evidence is relevant and admissible, but only for the limited purpose of evaluating effect. Evidence that itinerant surgery was in fact harmful is relevant only to establish ACS's intent. . . . Because harm evidence is of limited relevance, and is a type of evidence that is likely to be prejudicial, the court concluded that its quality and quantity must be severely limited. . . .

Uncomfortable with the *Wilk* patient-care-motive justification, the court confined it to cases involving allegations of pure quackery. It is apparent that the court was determined not to make judgments about the medical consequences of itinerant surgery and feared that evidence about harm would distract the jury from its assignment to focus solely on competitive efforts. [After trial, the jury found that the rule had no anticompetitive effect.] . . .

C. [ANALYSIS]

. . . [The *Wilk* court was correct that] the AMA nonaffiliation rule and related actions cannot be . . . characterized as procompetitive . . . protection of reputation for quality. Physicians do have a legitimate competitive interest in reputation. And particular physicians could well decide that their competitive stance would be damaged by affiliation with chiropractors. But an *agreement* not to affiliate could be so justified only if a physician's ability to compete is impaired if *other* physicians affiliate with chiropractors. If such affiliation is harmful to reputation, however, affiliation by others would appear to enhance the competitive posture of those who reject it. . . .

[The *Wilk* court was wrong, however, to construct a special patient care affirmative defense.] Invariably, denial of access to these alternative providers is explained as a measure to protect the public from inferior care, [but this is] an explanation which in this broad sense is not cognizable in an antitrust case. . . . There is no single quality-of-care defense in health care antitrust cases. To the extent such a defense might be predicated on a balancing of social gains against adverse price and output effects, it is inconsistent with the focus on competitive effects which is central in antitrust analysis. Nor can such a defense be based on a dominant laudable purpose. Intent is relevant only as a predictor of effect. Where effect is established, intent is no longer of consequence.

Conduct that promotes efficiency, ameliorates the effects of market failures or imperfections, or increases quality rivalry among providers is, to this extent, procompetitive and may improve quality of care by enhancing the competitive process. Any further accommodation of quality-of-care concerns is a direct challenge to the central role of the market in the determination of quality, and therefore to the relevance of antitrust itself. It is for legislatures, not courts, to grant antitrust exemptions or otherwise displace the application of the antitrust laws.

■CALIFORNIA DENTAL ASS'N v. FTC
526 U.S. 756 (1999)

[Read the excerpt at page 347, and the footnote on pages 487-488.]

Notes: Quality of Care as a Defense; Allied Health Professionals; Professional Society Rules

1. On balance, does antitrust law or the common law fairness doctrine do a better job of subjecting hospitals and HMOs to the proper level of scrutiny for their staffing decisions? Does your answer differ with respect to matters of procedure and matters of substance?

2. *Other Readings.* For additional discussions of the role that quality of care plays in health care antitrust analysis, see Peter J. Hammer & William M. Sage, Antitrust, Health Care Quality, and the Courts, 102 Colum. L. Rev. 545 (2002); William M. Sage & Peter J. Hammer, A Copernican View of Health Care Antitrust, 65 Law & Contemp. Probs. 241 (Autumn 2002).

3. If only competitive effects are relevant to antitrust analysis, why is a Catholic hospital allowed to exclude abortionists? (Possibly because of overriding First Amendment concerns. Or, because such a policy does not advance the economic interests of member physicians, it does not constitute a conspiracy.)

Should Congress' 1986 enactment of an *explicit* qualified immunity in the Health Care Quality Improvement Act discussed below resolve any further debate about whether the courts should find an *implied* patient care affirmative defense?

4. *Recognition for Allied Health Professionals.* Both the *Weiss* case above and the *Wilk* case discussed by Prof. Kauper manifest the traditional medical establishment's longstanding hostility to competing schools of practitioners that are founded on less scientific theories of medicine. Chiropractors and osteopaths are only two among the several allied health professions that are engaged in active struggles to achieve professional recognition and hospital access. Similar challenges have been mounted by podiatrists, clinical psychologists, nurse anesthetists, and midwives, usually without success. See, e.g, Minnesota Ass'n of Nurse Anesthetists, 208 F.3d 2000 (8th Cir. 2000) (rejecting a boycott challenge to several hospitals' decisions to contract only with physician groups for anesthesia services); Oltz v. St. Peter's Community Hospital, 861 F.2d 1440 (9th Cir. 1988) (finding antitrust violation in hospital's termination of contract with nurse anesthetist's contract); Cooper v. Forsyth County Hospital Authority, 789 F.2d 278 (4th Cir. 1986) (refusing to entertain a suit by podiatrists).

An important indirect effect of this antitrust pressure has been to force a revision of the JCAHO accreditation standards. Prior to 1984, JCAHO standards were read as prohibiting hospitals from extending staff privileges to practitioners other than doctors and dentists. However, in that year, the JCAHO adopted an amendment that allowed hospitals to "include other licensed individuals permitted by law and by the hospital to provide patient care services independently." For a survey of these developments, see C. Dodd, Exclusion of Nonphysician Health Care Providers from Integrated Delivery Systems, 64 U. Cin. L. Rev. 983

(1996); Note, 19 Ind. L. Rev. 1219, 1232-1233 (1986); Note, 34 Vand. L. Rev. 1161 (1981).

In some states, allied health professionals have won their contest in the legislature by obtaining statutory enactments that require hospitals to grant them equal consideration in extending clinical privileges. Representative is D.C. Code Ann. §44-506, which requires individual, nondiscriminatory consideration of the credentials of podiatrists, psychologists, nurse anesthetists, nurse midwives, and nurse practitioners. See also Ohio Rev. Code Ann. §3701.35.1(B).

5. *Codes of Professional Ethics. California Dental Ass'n and the Koefoot* and *Indiana Federation of Dentists* cases discussed by Prof. Kauper are examples of the several challenges to various ethical restrictions in medical professional codes. The most prominent of these is American Medical Association v. FTC, 94 FTC 980, 1015 (1979), enforced 638 F.2d 443 (2d Cir. 1980), aff'd mem. by an equally divided Court, 455 U.S. 676 (1982), which invalidated ethical prohibitions against advertising and certain physician contractual arrangements. For additional commentary, see the articles cited in note 2, and Clark Havighurst & Nancy King, Private Credentialing of Health Care Personnel: An Antitrust Perspective, 9 Am. J.L. & Med. 131, 263 (1983).

Problem: Medical Staff Boycotts of Allied Health Professionals

Centerville Psychiatric (CP) is a for-profit psychiatric hospital in a large town with two other free-standing psychiatric hospitals and with four general hospitals that have smaller psychiatric units. CP attempts to distinguish itself from its competitors by claiming to offer better doctors and more state-of-the-art structured treatment programs that combine intensive counseling and drug therapy for acute espisodes of serious mental illness (so-called nervous breakdowns). This treatment approach contrasts with that in general hospitals, which is unstructured, much shorter in duration, and often administered by nonspecialists, and contrasts with other specialized psychiatric hospitals that offer long-term custodial treatment for more chronic conditions.

Consistent with its long-standing bylaws, CP's medical staff presently consists of only board certified psychiatrists, who are specially trained M.D.'s. Alfred Zock, Ph.D. is a psychologist of good reputation with an active counseling and therapy practice in Centerville. He has decided to break the mold by applying for medical staff privileges at CP. The major practical difference between psychiatrists and psychologists is that only the former can prescribe drugs; pyschologists are limited by state licensing laws to "couch therapy." In the past, psychologists have been allowed to see CP patients who were under their care before coming to CP, but only if a staff psychiatrist approved and supervised the psychologist. Dr. Zock would like to admit his own patients directly and treat them at CP without supervision or prior approval. He has admitting privileges at one of the general hospitals in town, but he finds their facilities unsatisfactory.

The existing psychiatrists oppose Dr. Zock's admission because they like things the way they are, for both clinical and financial reasons. The hospital administration is also not in favor, partly because it does not want to antagonize its medical staff in a competitive hospital market where they can take their patients elsewhere, and partly because reimbursement rates under managed care insurance are usually higher for drug therapy than for counseling. On the other hand, it is clear many patients would prefer their own psychologist to be their primary physician.

As lawyer for CP, advise it on the safest way to exclude Dr. Zock. Consider whether to use primarily quality or economic criteria, whether to act under the existing bylaws or to change them, and then consider Dr. Zock individually. Consider what procedures to follow in making these decisions.

After reading about all these lawsuits arising from medical staff disputes, both under the common law fairness doctrine and under antitrust law, it may surprise you to learn that a federal statute confers broad immunity on participants in hospital and HMO credentialing or peer review processes. As you read the following case, note the various qualifications and limitations imposed on this immunity by considering to what extent it would apply to each of the medical staff dispute cases you read in the previous three sections of this chapter.

■ BRYAN v. JAMES E. HOLMES REGIONAL MEDICAL CENTER
33 F.3d 1318 (11th Cir. 1994)

TJOFLAT, Chief Judge:
In this case, a Florida hospital, after completing a lengthy internal disciplinary process, terminated the clinical staff privileges of a staff physician. The physician sued the hospital, alleging various state and federal causes of action and seeking money damages. After an eleven-day trial, a federal jury concluded that the hospital had revoked the physician's staff privileges in violation of its bylaws and awarded the physician nearly $4.2 million in damages for breach of contract. The hospital appeals that judgment . . . contend[ing it] was immune from liability in money damages under the Health Care Quality Improvement Act of 1986 ("HCQIA") (1988 & Supp. IV 1992), and under Florida law, Fla. Stat. Ann. Sec. 395.0193(5) (West 1993). . . .

Congress enacted the Health Care Quality Improvement Act to encourage peer review activities, "to improve the quality of medical care by encouraging physicians to identify and discipline other physicians who are incompetent or who engage in unprofessional behavior." H.R. Rep. No. 903, 99th Cong., 2d Sess. . . . In furtherance of this goal, HCQIA grants limited immunity, in suits brought by disciplined physicians, from liability for money damages to those who participate in professional peer review activities. See also H.R. Rep. No. 903, at 3, reprinted in 1986 U.S.C.C.A.N. at 6385 (noting that "[e]ven though defendants may often win these lawsuits, that may not be sufficient to guarantee enthusiastic, or even minimally adequate, peer review" because "[d]octors who are sufficiently fearful of the threat of litigation will simply not do meaningful peer review"). . . .

HCQIA provides that, if a "professional review action" (as defined in the statute) meets certain due process and fairness requirements, then those participating in such a review process shall not be liable under any state or federal law for damages for the results. 42 U.S.C. Sec. 11111(a)(1). . . . (In another set of provisions, HCQIA requires health care entities to report certain specific disciplinary actions taken against a staff physician (or the acceptance of a resignation or suspension in return for not conducting investigations or disciplinary proceedings) to a national clearinghouse established to collect and disseminate information on health care providers. Then, prior to admitting a physician to its staff, a hospital must obtain that physician's records from the clearinghouse. These reporting requirements were designed to "restrict the ability of incompetent physicians to move from State to State without disclosure or discovery of the physician's previous damaging or incompetent performance." . . .)

The statute attempts to balance the chilling effect of litigation on peer review with concerns for protecting physicians improperly subjected to disciplinary action; accordingly, Congress granted immunity from monetary damages to participants in properly conducted peer review proceedings while preserving causes of action for injunctive or declaratory relief for aggrieved physicians. Section 11111(a)(1) expressly excludes from its coverage [civil rights] suits brought under 42 U.S.C. Sec. 1983 or Title VII of the Civil Rights Act of 1964, but it clearly does apply to antitrust claims. . . . Because the statutory scheme is somewhat convoluted, we discuss the immunity provisions in detail. . . .

The standards that professional review actions must satisfy to entitle the participants to such protection are enumerated in section 11112(a) as follows:

> For purposes of the protection set forth in section 11111(a) of this title, a professional review action must be taken—(1) in the reasonable belief that the action was in the furtherance of quality health care, (2) after a reasonable effort to obtain the facts of the matter, (3) after adequate notice and hearing procedures are afforded to the physician involved or after such other procedures as are fair to the physician under the circumstances, and (4) in the reasonable belief that the action was warranted by the facts known. . . .

Importantly, HCQIA also creates a rebuttable presumption of immunity: "A professional review action shall be presumed to have met the preceding standards . . . unless the presumption is rebutted by a preponderance of the evidence."

Section 11112(b) of HCQIA then enumerates the minimum, or "safe harbor" procedures that will, in every case, satisfy the adequate notice and hearing requirement of section 11112(a)(3). . . . We discuss this checklist in more detail infra. . . . Congress was careful to explain, however, that "[a] professional review body's failure to meet the conditions described in this subsection shall not, in itself, constitute failure to meet the standards of subsection (a)(3) of this section." The legislative history of section 11112(a) indicates that the statute's reasonableness requirements were intended to create an objective standard of performance, rather than a subjective good faith standard. . . .

A review of the facts of this case reveal that HCQIA's limitations on monetary liability dictate the outcome of this appeal. . . . [Dr. Bryan] is generally acknowledged to be an excellent surgeon, often undertaking long, detailed vascular procedures that other physicians in the field avoid. Bryan also has a reputation for being a volcanic-tempered perfectionist, a difficult man with whom to work, and a person who regularly viewed it as his obligation to criticize staff members at

Holmes [Hospital] for perceived incompetence or inefficiency. Hospital employees, however, often viewed Bryan's "constructive criticism" as verbal—or even physical—abuse. Because the Holmes board of directors found Bryan's behavior inappropriate and unprofessional, it terminated his medical staff privileges in November 1990. The means by which Holmes accomplished this termination is the subject of the dispute in this case. . . .

[P]rior to his termination, Bryan was the subject of more than fifty written incident reports involving unprofessional or disruptive behavior, usually complaints regarding Bryan's abusive treatment of nurses, technicians, and even fellow physicians. Some insight into the origins of this behavior came from Bryan himself during his testimony at trial. Shortly after completing his residency, Bryan obtained staff privileges at a Veterans Administration hospital in Miami. There, he explained, he soon learned that the hospital could not fire incompetent nurses and other technicians easily; the most effective way to avoid working with nurses he viewed as incompetent or inefficient, he discovered, was to insult them until they refused to participate in operations involving his patients. . . .

At first, the Hospital and the medical staff attempted to deal with Bryan's behavior informally. . . . The incidents continued unabated, however, over the next three years, and Hospital officials gradually began to take a more active approach in dealing with the problem. . . . On October 19, 1989 . . . the board advised Bryan by letter that his abusive behavior could no longer be tolerated and that any further incidents of unprofessional behavior would result in the permanent revocation of his staff privileges. . . .

Despite the board's warning, Bryan was involved in four additional incidents in the first five months of 1990; these four incidents led directly to the termination of Bryan's medical staff privileges. . . . After considering these latest incidents in light of Bryan's history of disruptive behavior and the hospital's varied attempts to correct such behavior . . . the executive committee recommended that Bryan's staff privileges be permanently revoked.

Once again, Bryan requested that a peer review hearing panel be appointed. Chaired by Dr. Joseph Chanda, the panel consisted of seven physicians, none of whom were vascular surgeons. . . . Bryan challenged the initial composition of the panel, alleging bias on the part of Dr. William Broussard, who advised Bryan to seek counseling for his interpersonal problems in 1982. Bryan also contended that the panel should be composed solely of surgeons. In response to Bryan's objections, [Dr.] Mills selected a new panel member to replace Broussard but did not remove the non-surgeons who had previously been named. . . .

The Chanda panel held four sessions of hearings; Bryan was represented by counsel at the proceedings, and he had both the opportunity to cross-examine the witnesses offered by the medical staff and to present witnesses and documentary evidence on his own behalf. A court reporter recorded the testimony at all of the hearing sessions. Two panel members were absent from at least part of the hearings, but Chanda testified at trial that the panel as a whole reviewed the testimony orally at the end of each session and during deliberations and that summarized what had transpired for the absent members. . . .

[T]he panel recommended that Bryan's clinical privileges be suspended for two years. After considering the Chanda panel's report, the executive committee stood by its recommendation that Bryan's staff privileges be revoked. Bryan appealed the executive committee's recommendation to the board of the directors; pursuant to the bylaws, the board appointed a board review panel, which also recommended revocation of Bryan's clinical privileges. The full board then considered the three recommendations . . . [and] unanimously voted to terminate Bryan's clinical privileges at Holmes. . . .

Bryan filed a complaint on behalf of himself and his professional association against the Hospital, the individual members of its board of directors, members of the medical staff executive committee, and two nurses. The complaint included federal and state antitrust claims as well as state law claims for defamation, negligent supervision of the peer review process (against only the individual members of the board of directors), and breach of contract for failing to follow the medical staff bylaws during the disciplinary process (against the Hospital). The complaint also included the following various ancillary claims: (1) constitutional and civil rights claims under 42 U.S.C. Sec. 1983 (1988); (2) federal contractual claims arising out of the Hospital's participation in the Medicare program; and (3) claims of "interference with prospective economic advantage" and intentional infliction of emotional distress. . . . The central allegation in the complaint was that the defendants, "individually and in concert, acted in bad faith and with intentional fraud, resulting in the destruction of Dr. Bryan's medical practice."

At trial, as before the Chanda panel, Bryan presented testimony from various expert witnesses explaining that Bryan's actions were proper and did not adversely affect patient care; nothing in the record, they testified, would justify the revocation of Bryan's clinical privileges. . . . Bryan also presented the testimony of witnesses who found fault with the Hospital's peer review procedures, particularly that a transcript of the Chanda panel hearings was not prepared for the Board's use and that the Chanda hearing officer had become too inquisitorial in his questioning. . . . At the close of Bryan's case, the district court . . . concluded . . . that the evidence supported Bryan's claims for breach of contract against the Hospital, and denied the Hospital's motion for a directed verdict because material issues of fact remained concerning the federal and state peer review immunity statutes. The court also found that the evidence supported Bryan's antitrust claims against the Hospital and accordingly submitted those claims to the jury. . . .

Congress clearly intended HCQIA to permit defendants in suits arising out of peer review disciplinary decisions to file motions to resolve the issues concerning immunity from monetary liability as early as possible in the litigation process. . . . Several courts have resolved the issue of HCQIA immunity from damages liability on summary judgment. See, e.g., Austin v. McNamara, 979 F.2d 728, 734-35 (9th Cir. 1991). . . . [I]f the standards of Rule 56 cannot be satisfied . . . the defense of qualified immunity should be decided by the court and should not be submitted for decision by the jury. . . .

If there are disputed subsidiary issues of fact concerning HCQIA immunity, such as whether the disciplined physician was given adequate notice of the charges and the appropriate opportunity to be heard, the court may ask the jury to resolve the subsidiary factual questions by responding to special interrogatories. Under no circumstances should the ultimate question of whether the defendant is immune from monetary liability under HCQIA be submitted to the jury. . . .

As the Ninth Circuit has explained, the rebuttable presumption of HCQIA . . . creates an unusual summary judgment standard that can best be expressed as follows: "Might a reasonable jury, viewing the facts in the best light for [the plaintiff], conclude that he has shown, by a preponderance of the evidence, that the defendants' actions are outside the scope of Sec. 11112(a)?" *Austin*, 979 F.2d at 734. If not, the court should grant the defendant's motion. In a sense, the presumption language in HCQIA means that the plaintiff bears the burden of proving that the peer review process was not reasonable. . . .

We must examine the record in this case to determine whether Bryan satisfied his burden of producing evidence that would allow a reasonable jury to conclude that the Hospital's peer review disciplinary process failed to meet the standards of HCQIA. . . .

The term "professional review action" is defined [as]:

> [A]n action or recommendation of a professional review body which is taken or made in the conduct of professional review activity, which is based on the competence or professional conduct of an individual physician (which conduct affects or could affect adversely the health or welfare of a patient or patients), and which affects (or may affect) adversely the clinical privileges . . . of the physician.

42 U.S.C. Sec. 11151(9). While its meaning is generally apparent, the statute does provide the following definition of "professional review activity":

> [A]n activity of a health care entity with respect to an individual physician — (A) to determine whether the physician may have clinical privileges with respect to, or membership in, the entity, (B) to determine the scope or conditions of such privileges or membership, or (C) to change or modify such privileges or membership.

42 U.S.C. Sec. 11151(10). . . .

. . . A "professional review body" is defined as "a health care entity and the governing body or any committee of a health care entity which conducts professional review activity, and includes any committee of the medical staff of such an entity when assisting the governing body in a professional review activity." Furthermore, the term "health care entity" includes "a hospital that is licensed to provide health care services by the State in which it is located," [as well as "a health maintenance organization, [a] group medical practice, . . . or a professional society (or committee thereof) of physicians or other licensed health care practitioners that follows a formal peer review process for the purpose of furthering quality health care (as determined under regulations of the Secretary)"]. The Holmes decisionmakers in Bryan's case fall within those categories. . . .

As stated above, a professional review action must satisfy the four standards of section 11112(a) in order to qualify for the immunity protections of section 11111(a). . . . First, a review of the record makes clear that the decision to terminate Bryan's clinical privileges at Holmes was taken "in the reasonable belief that the action was in the furtherance of quality health care." . . . At trial, Bryan asserted that the members of the board of directors and the executive committee were primarily motivated by personal animosity and not by concern for patient care. He introduced no evidence, however, that such hostility determined the outcome of the peer review process. Moreover, Bryan's "assertions of hostility do not support his position [that the Hospital is not entitled to the HCQIA's protections] because they are irrelevant to the reasonableness standards of Sec. 11112(a). The test is an objective one, so bad faith is immaterial. The real issue is the sufficiency of the basis for the [Hospital's] actions." *Austin*, 979 F.2d at 734. . . .

Second, a review of the record reveals that the Holmes board of directors took its action "after a reasonable effort to obtain the facts of the matter." . . .

Third, Bryan's staff privileges were revoked only "after adequate notice and hearing procedures [were] afforded to the physician involved or after such other procedures as [were] fair to the physician under the circumstances." As noted above, section 11112(b) sets forth the "safe harbor" conditions that a health care entity must meet regarding adequate notice and hearing. . . . As the summary of the facts of the case . . . reflects, each of these procedural requirements of section 11112(b) was satisfied. Documents introduced at trial indicate that the Hospital complied with the notice requirements and that the hearings were held in a timely fashion and in accordance with the Hospital's bylaws. Bryan was afforded full rights of representation, cross-examination, and confrontation.

Bryan's principal argument is that the board of directors did not have a transcript of the Chanda panel hearings when it rendered its decision. Yet HCQIA, like the Holmes bylaws, requires only that the Hospital ensure that a record of the proceedings be made; Bryan had the responsibility to request a complete transcript if he thought the board should have one, and he did not.

It should be noted that section 11112(b) specifically provides that the failure of a review body to meet the enumerated conditions does not, per se, constitute a failure to meet the standards of section 11112(a)(3). Indeed, "[i]f other procedures are followed, but are not precisely of the character spelled out in [section 11112(b)], the test of 'adequacy' may still be met under other prevailing law." H.R. Rep. No. 903, at 10. Moreover, Bryan made no contemporaneous objections to the manner in which the hearing procedures were conducted; section 11112(b) explicitly provides that compliance with its terms is not required if the physician voluntarily waives them. On the record of this case, we conclude that no reasonable jury could conclude that the Hospital had not afforded Bryan the adequate procedures.

Finally, there is no question that the board decided to terminate Bryan "in the reasonable belief that the action was warranted by the facts known." . . . Bryan concedes that the incidents that led to his termination actually occurred; his only argument is that they did not justify the severe sanction he received. HCQIA clearly grants broad discretion to hospital boards with regard to staff privileges decisions. Accordingly, as in all procedural due process cases, the role of federal courts "on review of such actions is not to substitute our judgment for that of the hospital's governing board or to reweigh the evidence regarding the renewal or termination of medical staff privileges." Shahawy v. Harrison, 875 F.2d 1529, 1533 (11th Cir. 1989). . . . "[T]he intent of [the HCQIA] was not to disturb, but to reinforce, the preexisting reluctance of courts to substitute their judgment on the merits for that of health care professionals and of the governing bodies of hospitals in an area within their expertise." Mahmoodian v. United Hosp. Ctr., Inc., 185 W. Va. 59, 404 S.E.2d 750, 756 (1991).

Given that all of the section 11112(a) standards were satisfied, we conclude that the Hospital was entitled to the immunity from damages liability granted by

HCQIA in Sec. 11111(a). . . . Bryan has not appealed the district court's refusal to grant injunctive relief. . . .

Notes: Peer Review and State Action Immunity

1. *Limitations of the Federal Statute.* Precisely which peer review actions does the federal immunity cover? A helpful guide is to check (carefully) how many of the preceding cases in this chapter it would preclude. Realize, for instance, that by virtue of the definition of professional review action, "actions against a class of physicians do not fall within the purview of this legislation." H.R. Rep. No. 99-903, p. 21. Observe also that the statute applies only to actions against physicians, not against other licensed medical professionals. Finally, observe that the statute applies only to peer review actions based on quality or competence factors, not to those based on economic or administrative concerns. The statute's application to non-hospital entities such as HMOs, PPOs, and IPAs is unresolved pending regulations that have not yet been issued. The statute indicates they are covered by the immunity but only if individual physicians are selected (or de-selected) following formalized criteria and processes based on quality/competence grounds.

How effective do you think the federal immunity is in encouraging vigorous peer review for those entities and decisions that it does cover, considering the showing that must be made to enjoy the immunity? Do the qualifications for immunity differ materially from the scrutiny imposed by common law judicial review? Are the immunity standards more exacting than common law? It appears that the statute's main effect is to shift the burden of proof and remove from the jury the merits of whether the hospital's decision was substantively and procedurally fair, allowing these issues to be decided at the summary judgment stage under a highly deferential standard of review. The Act also contains a fee shifting provision that allows the court to order the plaintiff to pay the defendants' costs of litigation. See Smith v. Ricks, 31 F.3d 1478 (9th Cir. 1994) (upholding award of over $300,000 in fees and costs).

Does summary judgment appear appropriate where there is a genuine issue of whether an ulterior, anticompetitive motive affected the decision? Should that kind of question be submitted to the jury? What if a hospital does not follow the elaborate hearing procedures or the careful insulation from conflict of interest that occurred here? See Brader v. Allegheny General Hospital, 64 F.3d 869 (3d Cir. 1995) (reversing dismissal of complaint on immunity grounds because full judicial review is especially important "now that the provision of health services is becoming increasingly concentrated and the opportunities for physicians more limited"); Islami v. Covenant Medical Center, 822 F. Supp. 1361 (N.D. Iowa 1992) (because the doctor's economic competitors were not excluded from the review process, "the jury [must] answer the question of whether the procedures . . . were fair given the entire factual circumstances; . . . the decision on immunity is hopelessly inter-twined with a decision on the merits of the contract claim"); Brown v. Presbyterian Healthcare Services, 101 F.3d 1324 (10th Cir. 1996) (jury was entitled to find lack of fair hearing where the hospital's inquiry focused too narrowly on only two patient records); Clark v. Columbia/HCA, 25 P.3d 315 (Nev. 2001) (reversing grant of summary judgment and finding no immunity as a matter of law because of evidence hospital was retaliating against physician for "whistleblowing"). Cf. Decker v. IHC Hospitals, 982 F.2d 433 (10th Cir. 1992) (denial of summary judgment is not immediately appealable because Act does not guarantee freedom from trial, only protection from damages). But see Brader v. Allegheny General Hospital, 167 F.3d 832 (3d. Cir. 1999) (awarding summary judgment on immunity claim despite minor flaws in the peer review proceedings and allegations of bad faith motivations); Parsons v. Sanchez, 46 F.3d 1143 (9th Cir. 1995) (allegations of personal bias and animosity do not rebut presumption of immunity); Alexander v. Memphis Individual Practice Ass'n, 870 S.W.2d 278 (Tenn. 1994) (same, under state immunity statute, for physician excluded from IPA); Cooper v. Delaware Valley Medical Center, 654 A.2d 547 (Pa. 1995) (vague allegations of malice not sufficient to avoid summary judgment under state immunity statute); Cardwell v. Rockford Memorial Hospital Ass'n, 555 N.E.2d 6 (Ill. 1990) (finding absolute immunity under state statute protecting hospital even if conduct was "willful and wanton"); Singh v. Blue Cross and Blue Shield, 182 F. Supp. 2d 164 (D. Mass. 2001) (awarding summary judgment to an HMO even though the evidence showed mixed economic and quality reasons for excluding physician). See generally Charity Scott, Medical Peer Review, Antitrust, and the Effect of Statutory Reform, 50 Md. L. Rev. 316 (1991) ("the Act appears to immunize only conduct that would not be actionable under the antitrust laws in the first place. . . . Remarkably, of the few . . . cases that courts have said were proper for jury resolution, only a handful could even in theory have qualified for immunity."); William Curran, Medical Peer Review of Physician Competence and Performance: Legal Immunity and the Antitrust Laws, 316 New Eng. J. Med. 597, 598 (1987) ("the shield for physicians now contains a plethora of gaping holes through which many a guided missile can reach its human target"); Clark Havighurst, Professional Peer Review and the Antitrust Laws, 36 Case West. L. Rev. 1117, 1161 (1986) ("the new act does more to complicate than to simplify litigation"): Jack Bierig & Robert Portman, The Health Care Quality Improvement Act of 1986, 32 St. Louis U. L.J. 977 (1989).

2. *State Confidentiality Statutes.* In addition to the federal immunity statute, virtually every state has a confidentiality statute that makes the proceedings of peer review committees inadmissible in certain legal actions. These peer review confidentiality statutes apply primarily to malpractice actions claiming negligence on the part of the reviewed physician and to malpractice actions against the hospital claiming negligent peer review. These statutes usually do not, however, apply to the physician's own action against the hospital, since the parties themselves usually want to introduce the records in order to litigate the propriety of what occurred in the proceedings. Possibly, a court might recognize an evidentiary privilege nevertheless to exclude such evidence in order to protect quality improvement activities. In one case, however, a federal court refused this invitation in a case in which the physician alleged racial discrimination motives, finding that the public policy in favor of ferreting out discrimination outweighs the competing policies in favor of hospitals protecting peer review committee deliberations. Virmani v. Novant Health Inc., 259 F.3d 284 (N.C. 2001). For critical commentary, see 80 N.C. L. Rev. 1860 (2002).

Several states have also passed immunity statutes similar to the federal HCQIA. See David Leonard, Codifying a Privilege for Self-Critical Analysis, 25

Harv. J. on Legis. 113, 119 (1988) (collecting citations). An empirical study concluded that these state confidentiality and immunity statutes have no effect on the number of adverse peer review actions taken by hospitals. Susan O. Scheutzow, State Medical Peer Review: High Cost But No Benefit—Is it Time for a Change?, 25 Am. J.L. & Med. 7 (1999).

3. *State Action Immunity.* Another potential defense in medical staff disputes, one that is applicable only under the federal antitrust laws, is known as "state action immunity." In Parker v. Brown, 317 U.S. 341 (1943), the Supreme Court held that the antitrust laws do not apply to activity engaged in or required by the states. For instance, it would be spurious to charge a state board of medical examiners with an antitrust violation for revoking a physician's license. For slightly different reasons, peer review and other activities (such as merger and acquisition) by public hospitals are also immune from antitrust suit. FTC v. Hospital Board of Directors of Lee County, 38 F.3d 1184 (11th Cir. 1994); Cohn v. Bond, 953 F.2d 154 (4th Cir. 1991); contra Lancaster Community Hospital v. Antelope Valley Hospital, 940 F.2d 397 (9th Cir. 1991) (state-conferred corporate power to engage in generic transactions or activities is not the same as legislative anticipation of specific anticompetitive consequences). See generally Dean Harris, State Action Immunity from Antitrust Law for Public Hospitals: The Hidden Time Bomb for Health Care Reform, 44 U. Kan. L. Rev. 459 (1996).

The state action defense potentially exists with respect to physician discipline even at private hospitals if state law mandates and "actively supervises" the private peer review process. This contention was the subject of Patrick v. Burget, 486 U.S. 94 (1988), which involved a doctor who was forced to resign from the staff of the only hospital in town in retaliation for refusing to join the group practice that composed a majority of the medical staff. The Ninth Circuit relied on the Parker v. Brown state action exemption in overturning a damage award of more than $2 million that had sent shock waves through the medical establishment. (It was this verdict that prompted Congress to enact the HCQIA immunity.) However, the Supreme Court reversed and reinstated the verdict, holding that private hospital credentialing decisions in Oregon are not sufficiently supervised by the state to bring them within the protection of this defense. The Court observed that Oregon so far has not recognized a common law right to judicial review of the substance of private hospitals' credentialing decisions.

Although *Patrick* was initially read as closing the door to state action exemption in medical staff disputes, it left open the slight possibility that this defense might be available in another state whose common law differs. However, it does not appear that even a *Greisman* common law theory of judicial review would meet the Court's objection that "[the courts do no] more than to make sure that some sort of reasonable procedure was afforded and that there was evidence from which it could be found that plaintiff's conduct posed a threat to patient care." So far, subsequent federal decisions have been in accord with this reading of *Patrick.* Pinhas v. Summit Health Ltd., 880 F.2d 1108 (9th Cir. 1989) (the "limited form of [judicial] review [in California] is similar to the standards applied by the Oregon courts that the Supreme Court found insufficient to constitute active supervision"), aff'd on other grounds, 500 U.S. 322 (1991); Shahawy v. Harrison, 875 F.2d 1529 (11th Cir. 1989) (same, for Florida). Courts are also unimpressed that a state licensing scheme might require peer review since a state agency does not review the merits of hospitals' decisions. Miller v. Indiana Hospitals, 930 F.2d 334 (3d Cir. 1991).

4. *Immunity via State Certification.* State action immunity from antitrust suits has been reinvigorated in a number of states that have created procedures intended specifically to meet the "active supervision" requirement missing in private peer review. These states have implemented a state governmental review process leading to a "certificate of public advantage" in which private parties submit certain risky ventures that they want blessed with antitrust immunity. This state review process is designed to meet the active supervision requirements set forth in FTC v. Ticor Title Insurance Co., 504 U.S. 621, 112 S. Ct. 2169 (1992). For the most part, however, these statutes do not apply to peer review decisions. Instead, they are directed to joint ventures and mergers, like those discussed in Section E in which hospitals and other providers seek to cooperate in order to achieve efficiencies and avoid costly duplication of facilities. See generally James Blumstein, Health Care Reform and Competing Visions of Medical Care: Antitrust and State Provider Cooperation Legislation, 79 Cornell L. Rev. 1459 (1994); Fred Hellinger, Antitrust Enforcement in the Healthcare Industry: The Expanding Scope of State Activity, 33 Health Serv. Res. 1477 (1998).

5. *Physician Unions.* Physicians are pushing harder to receive the exemption from antitrust scrutiny that unions enjoy, in order to engage in more forceful bargaining with insurers without achieving full integration. As discussed at page 450, the difficulty they face is that union status is available only to employees, not independent contractors. Nevertheless, in Texas, the AMA succeeded in its attempt to achieve the same result, only through antitrust exemption for "state action," discussed above. In 1999, Texas adopted legislation that allows up to 10 percent of physicians in a market to negotiate jointly with any HMO that has substantial market power, subject to the supervision of the state's attorney general. It remains to be seen whether this law contains sufficient "active supervision" to achieve full protection under federal antitrust law's state action exemption. See generally Fred Hellinger & Gary Young, An Analysis of Physician Antitrust Exemption Legislation: Adjusting the Balance of Power, 286 JAMA 83 (2001).

2. Price-Fixing Law

■ ARIZONA v. MARICOPA COUNTY MEDICAL SOCIETY
457 U.S. 332 (1982)

Justice STEVENS delivered the opinion of the Court.

The question presented is whether §1 of the Sherman Act, 26 Stat. 209, as amended, 15 U.S.C. §1, has been violated by agreements among competing physicians setting, by majority vote, the maximum fees that they may claim in full payment for health services provided to policyholders of specified insurance plans. The United States Court of Appeals for the Ninth Circuit held that the question could not be answered without evaluating the actual purpose and effect of the agreements at a full trial. Because the undisputed facts disclose a violation of the statute, we granted certiorari and now reverse.

I

In October 1978 the state of Arizona filed a civil complaint against two county medical societies and two "foundations for medical care" that the medical societies had organized. The complaint alleged that the defendants were engaged in illegal price-fixing conspiracies. . . .

The Maricopa Foundation for Medical Care is a nonprofit Arizona corporation composed of licensed doctors of medicine, osteopathy, and podiatry engaged in private practice. Approximately 1,750 doctors, representing about 70 percent of the practitioners in Maricopa County, are members. The Maricopa Foundation was organized in 1969 for the purpose of promoting fee-for-service medicine and to provide the community with a competitive alternative to existing health insurance plans. The foundation performs three primary activities. It establishes the schedule of maximum fees that participating doctors agree to accept as payment in full for services performed for patients insured under plans approved by the foundation. It reviews the medical necessity and appropriateness of treatment provided by its members to such insured persons. It is authorized to draw checks on insurance company accounts to pay doctors for services performed for covered patients. In performing these functions, the foundation is considered an "insurance administrator" by the Director of the Arizona Department of Insurance. Its participating doctors, however, have no financial interest in the operation of the foundation.

The Pima Foundation for Medical Care, which includes about 400 member doctors, performs similar functions. For the purposes of this litigation, the parties seem to regard the activities of the two foundations as essentially the same. No challenge is made to their peer review or claim administration functions. Nor do the foundations allege that these two activities make it necessary for them to engage in the practice of establishing maximum-fee schedules. . . .

The fee schedules limit the amount that the member doctors may recover for services performed for patients insured under plans approved by the foundations. To obtain this approval the insurers — including self-insured employers as well as insurance companies — agree to pay the doctors' charges up to the scheduled amounts, and in exchange the doctors agree to accept those amounts as payment in full for their services. The doctors are free to charge higher fees to uninsured patients, and they also may charge any patient less than the scheduled maxima. A patient who is insured by a foundation-endorsed plan is guaranteed complete coverage for the full amount of his medical bills only if he is treated by a foundation member. He is free to go to a nonmember physician and is still covered for charges that do not exceed the maximum-fee schedule, but he must pay any excess that the nonmember physician may charge.

The impact of the foundation fee schedules on medical fees and on insurance premiums is a matter of dispute. The state of Arizona contends that the periodic upward revisions of the maximum-fee schedules have the effect of stabilizing and enhancing the level of actual charges by physicians, and that the increasing level of their fees in turn increases insurance premiums. The foundations, on the other hand, argue that the schedules impose a meaningful limit on physicians' charges, and that the advance agreement by the doctors to accept the maxima enables the insurance carriers to limit and to calculate more efficiently the risks they underwrite and therefore serves as an effective cost-containment mechanism that has saved patients and insurers millions of dollars. Although the Attorneys General of 40 different states, as well as the Solicitor General of the United States and certain organizations representing consumers of medical services, have filed amicus curiae briefs supporting the state of Arizona's position on the merits, we must assume that the respondents' view of the genuine issues of fact is correct.

This assumption presents, but does not answer, the question whether the Sherman Act prohibits the competing doctors from adopting, revising, and agreeing to use a maximum-fee schedule in implementation of the insurance plans.

III

The respondents recognize that our decisions establish that price-fixing agreements are unlawful on their face. But they argue that the per se rule does not govern this case because the agreements at issue are horizontal and fix maximum prices, are among members of a profession, are in an industry with which the judiciary has little antitrust experience, and are alleged to have procompetitive justifications. Before we examine each of these arguments, we pause to consider the history and the meaning of the per se rule against price-fixing agreements.

Section 1 of the Sherman Act of 1890 literally prohibits *every* agreement "in restraint of trade." In United States v. Joint Traffic Assn., 171 U.S. 505 (1898), we recognized that Congress could not have intended a literal interpretation of the word *every*; since Standard Oil Co. of New Jersey v. United States, 221 U.S. 1 (1911), we have analyzed most restraints under the so-called rule of reason. As its name suggests, the rule of reason requires the factfinder to decide whether under all the circumstances of the case the restrictive practice imposes an unreasonable restraint on competition.

The elaborate inquiry into the reasonableness of a challenged business practice entails significant costs. Litigation of the effect or purpose of a practice often is extensive and complex. Judges often lack the expert understanding of industrial market structures and behavior to determine with any confidence a practice's effect on competition. And the result of the process in any given case may provide little certainty or guidance about the legality of a practice in another context.

The costs of judging business practices under the rule of reason, however, have been reduced by the recognition of per se rules. Once experience with a particular kind of restraint enables the Court to predict with confidence that the rule of reason will condemn it, it has applied a conclusive presumption that the restraint is unreasonable. As in every rule of general application, the match between the presumed and the actual is imperfect. For the sake of business certainty and litigation efficiency, we have tolerated the invalidation of some agreements that a fullblown inquiry might have proved to be reasonable. . . .

[P]rice-fixing agreements are unlawful per se under the Sherman Act and . . . "no showing of so-called competitive abuses or evils which those agreements were designed to eliminate or alleviate may be interposed as a defense." United States v. Socony-Vacuum Oil Co., 310 U.S. 150, 218 (1940). In that case a glut in the spot market for gasoline had prompted the major oil refiners to engage in a concerted effort to purchase and store surplus gasoline in order to maintain stable prices. Absent the agreement, the companies argued, competition was cutthroat and self-defeating. The argument did not carry the day:

> Any combination which tampers with price structures is engaged in an unlawful activity. . . . The Act places all such schemes beyond the pale and protects that vital part of our economy against any degree of interference. . . . Nor has the Act created or authorized the creation of any special exception in favor of the oil industry. Whatever may be its peculiar problems and characteristics, the Sherman Act, so far as price-fixing agreements are concerned, establishes one uniform rule applicable to all industries alike. . . . Under the Sherman Act a combination formed for the purpose and with the effect of raising, depressing, fixing, pegging, or stabilizing the price of a commodity in interstate or foreign commerce is illegal per se.

Over the objection that maximum-price-fixing agreements were not the "economic equivalent" of minimum-price-fixing agreements, [we held in] Albrecht v. Herald Co., 390 U.S. 145 (1968):

> Maximum and minimum price fixing may have different consequences in many situations. But schemes to fix maximum prices, by substituting the perhaps erroneous judgment of a seller for the forces of the competitive market, may severely intrude upon the ability of buyers to compete and survive in that market. Competition, even in a single product, is not cast in a single mold. Maximum prices may be fixed too low for the dealer to furnish services essential to the value which goods have for the consumer or to furnish services and conveniences which consumers desire and for which they are willing to pay. Maximum price fixing may channel distribution through a few large or specifically advantaged dealers who otherwise would be subject to significant nonprice competition. Moreover, if the actual price charged under a maximum price scheme is nearly always the fixed maximum price, which is increasingly likely as the maximum price approaches the actual cost of the dealer, the scheme tends to acquire all the attributes of an arrangement fixing minimum prices.

We have not wavered in our enforcement of the per se rule against price fixing. Indeed, in our most recent price-fixing case we summarily reversed the decision of another Ninth Circuit panel that a horizontal agreement among competitors to fix credit terms does not necessarily contravene the antitrust laws. Catalano, Inc. v. Target Sales, Inc., 446 U.S. 643 (1980). . . . The per se rule "is grounded on faith in price competition as a market force [and not] on a policy of low selling prices at the price of eliminating competition." Rahl, Price Competition and the Price Fixing Rule — Preface and Perspective, 57 Nw. U. L. Rev. 137, 142 (1962). In this case the rule is violated by a price restraint that tends to provide the same economic rewards to all practitioners regardless of their skill, their experience, their training, or their willingness to employ innovative and difficult procedures in individual cases. Such a restraint also may discourage entry into the market and may deter experimentation and new developments by individual entrepreneurs. It may be a masquerade for an agreement to fix uniform prices, or it may in the future take on that character.

Nor does the fact that doctors — rather than nonprofessionals — are the parties to the price-fixing agreements support the respondents' position. In Goldfarb v. Virginia State Bar, 421 U.S. 773, 788, n.17 (1975), we stated that the "public service aspect, and other features of the professions, may require that a particular practice, which could properly be viewed as a violation of the Sherman Act in another context, be treated differently." See National Society of Professional Engineers v. United States, 435 U.S. 679, 696 (1978). The price-fixing agreements in this case, however, are not premised on public service or ethical norms. The respondents do not argue, as did the defendants in *Goldfarb* and *Professional Engineers*, that the quality of the professional service that their members provide is enhanced by the price restraint. The respondents' claim for relief from the per se rule is simply that the doctors' agreement not to charge certain insureds more than a fixed price facilitates the successful marketing of an attractive insurance plan. But the claim that the price restraint will make it easier for customers to pay does not distinguish the medical profession from any other provider of goods or services. . . .

The respondents' principal argument is that the per se rule is inapplicable because their agreements are alleged to have procompetitive justifications. The argument indicates a misunderstanding of the per se concept. The anticompetitive potential inherent in all price-fixing agreements justifies their facial invalidation even if procompetitive justifications are offered for some. Those claims of enhanced competition are so unlikely to prove significant in any particular case that we adhere to the rule of law that is justified in its general application. Even when the respondents are given every benefit of the doubt, the limited record in this case is not inconsistent with the presumption that the respondents' agreements will not significantly enhance competition. . . .

It is true that a binding assurance of complete insurance coverage — as well as most of the respondents' potential for lower insurance premiums — can be obtained only if the insurer and the doctor agree in advance on the maximum fee that the doctor will accept as full payment for a particular service. Even if a fee schedule is therefore desirable, it is not necessary that the doctors do the price fixing.[26] The record indicates that the Arizona Comprehensive Medical/ Dental Program for Foster Children is administered by the Maricopa Foundation pursuant to a contract under which the maximum-fee schedule is prescribed by a state agency rather than by the doctors. This program and the Blue Shield plan challenged in Group Life & Health Insurance Co. v. Royal Drug Co., 440 U.S. 205 (1979), indicate that insurers are capable not only of fixing maximum reimbursable prices but also of obtaining binding agreements with providers guaranteeing the insured full reimbursement of a participating provider's fee. In light of these examples, it is not surprising that nothing in the record even arguably supports the conclusion that this type of insurance program could not function if the fee schedules were set in a different way.

The most that can be said for having doctors fix the maximum prices is that doctors may be able to do it more efficiently than insurers. The validity of that assumption is far from obvious, but in any event there is no reason to believe that any savings that might accrue from this arrangement would be sufficiently

---

[26] . . . [T]his case [does not] present the question whether an insurer may, consistent with the Sherman Act, fix the fee schedule and enter into bilateral contracts with individual doctors. . . . In an amicus curiae brief, the United States expressed its opinion that such an arrangement would be legal unless the plaintiffs could establish that a conspiracy among providers was at work. . . .

great to affect the competitiveness of these kinds of insurance plans. It is entirely possible that the potential or actual power of the foundations to dictate the terms of such insurance plans may more than offset the theoretical efficiencies upon which the respondents' defense ultimately rests. . . .

IV

Having declined the respondents' invitation to cut back on the per se rule against price fixing, we are left with the respondents' argument that their fee schedules involve price fixing in only a literal sense. For this argument, the respondents rely upon Broadcast Music, Inc. v. Columbia Broadcasting System, Inc., 441 U.S. 1 (1979).

In *Broadcast Music* we were confronted with an antitrust challenge to the marketing of the right to use copyrighted compositions derived from the entire membership of the American Society of Composers, Authors and Publishers (ASCAP). The so-called blanket license was entirely different from the product that any one composer was able to sell by himself. Although there was little competition among individual composers for their separate compositions, the blanket-license arrangement did not place any restraint on the right of any individual copyright owner to sell his own compositions separately to any buyer at any price. But a "necessary consequence" of the creation of the blanket license was that its price had to be established. We held that the delegation by the composers to ASCAP of the power to fix the price for the blanket license was not a species of the price-fixing agreements categorically forbidden by the Sherman Act. The record disclosed price fixing only in a "literal sense."

This case is fundamentally different. Each of the foundations is composed of individual practitioners who compete with one another for patients. Neither the foundations nor the doctors sell insurance, and they derive no profits from the sale of health insurance policies. The members of the foundations sell medical services. Their combination in the form of the foundation does not permit them to sell any different product. Their combination has merely permitted them to sell their services to certain customers at fixed prices and arguably to affect the prevailing market price of medical care.

The foundations are not analogous to partnerships or other joint arrangements in which persons who would otherwise be competitors pool their capital and share the risks of loss as well as the opportunities for profit. In such joint ventures, the partnership is regarded as a single firm competing with other sellers in the market. The agreement under attack is an agreement among hundreds of competing doctors concerning the price at which each will offer his own services to a substantial number of consumers. It is true that some are surgeons, some anesthesiologists, and some psychiatrists, but the doctors do not sell a package of three kinds of services. If a clinic offered complete medical coverage for a flat fee, the cooperating doctors would have the type of partnership arrangement in which a price-fixing agreement among the doctors would be perfectly proper. But the fee agreements disclosed by the record in this case are among independent competing entrepreneurs. They fit squarely into the horizontal price-fixing mold.

The judgment of the court of appeals is reversed.

Justices Blackmun and O'Connor took no part in this case [due to conflicts of interest].

Justice POWELL, with whom THE CHIEF JUSTICE and Justice REHNQUIST join, dissenting.

The medical care plan condemned by the Court today is a comparatively new method of providing insured medical services at predetermined maximum costs. It involves no coercion. Medical insurance companies, physicians, and patients alike are free to participate or not as they choose. On its face, the plan seems to be in the public interest. . . .

It is settled law that once an arrangement has been labeled as "price fixing" it is to be condemned per se. But it is equally well settled that this characterization is not to be applied as a talisman to every arrangement that involves a literal fixing of prices. Many lawful contracts, mergers, and partnerships fix prices. But our cases require a more discerning approach. . . . In Broadcast Music, Inc. v. Columbia Broadcasting System, Inc., supra, there was minimum price fixing in the most "literal sense." We nevertheless agreed, unanimously, that an arrangement by which copyright clearinghouses sold performance rights to their entire libraries on a blanket rather than individual basis did not warrant condemnation on a per se basis. Individual licensing would have allowed competition between copyright owners. But we reasoned that licensing on a blanket basis yielded substantial efficiencies that otherwise could not be realized. Indeed, the blanket license was itself "to some extent, a different product."

In sum, the fact that a foundation-sponsored health insurance plan literally involves the setting of ceiling prices among competing physicians does not, of itself, justify condemning the plan as per se illegal. Only if it is clear from the record that the agreement among physicians is "so plainly anticompetitive that no elaborate study of [its effects] is needed to establish [its] illegality" may a court properly make a per se judgment. National Society of Professional Engineers v. United States, supra, at 692. . . .

In a complex economy, complex economic arrangements are commonplace. It is unwise for the Court, in a case as novel and important as this one, to make a final judgment in the absence of a complete record and where mandatory inferences create critical issues of fact.

Notes: Price-Fixing Antitrust Liability; PPOs; Joint Ventures

1. *Foundation Plans.* Medical society "foundation plans," such as those considered in *Maricopa County*, arose in the 1970s as a way for the medical profession to resist the introduction of alternative financing and delivery systems such as HMOs. These arrangements illustrate the AMA's continuing "strategy of preemption and cooptation [through] professionally sponsored reforms." Clark Havighurst, Professional Restraints on Innovation in Health Care Financing, 1978 Duke L.J. 303. It is therefore not surprising that the Court found these plans to have anticompetitive potential, especially where they include most of the doctors in town. This ruling is borne out by subsequent developments in

Phoenix, where the number of PPOs and HMOs increased from 1 to 18 within three years of the *Maricopa County* decision.

2. *PPOs*. *Maricopa County*'s importance for health care markets extends far beyond the particular "foundation plans" the Court ruled on. Observe that these largely-defunct foundations plans were structurally identical to present-day preferred provider organizations (PPOs). This is a form of insurance that gives subscribers a discount if they seek care from doctors and hospitals within the preferred network, rather than allowing the completely free choice of provider that is traditional in conventional indemnity insurance. Providers agree to accept discounted payments in exchange for the prospect of a higher volume of business, and they agree to abide by certain utilization review protocols. PPOs are a popular alternative to HMOs from the subscriber perspective because patients are not locked into the network. From the provider's perspective, PPOs preserve fee-for-service reimbursement and practice autonomy. PPOs have experienced tremendous growth since they first emerged in the early 1980s, and they now are the dominant form of health insurance. Does *Maricopa County* remain convincing in the present-day climate where PPOs and provider networks are seen as *pro*competitive innovations? Note that, due to recusals, the majority opinion has the support of only four justices.

3. *Managed Care Provider Networks*. A similar structure exists for managed care provider networks that do not use the PPO label. When physicians and hospitals form networks to contract with HMOs or directly with employers, they perform many of the same market functions as do PPOs, except that patients may be required to rather than simply encouraged to seek care within the network.

The impetus for the formation of a PPO or other forms of provider networks can come from either purchasers or from providers. In a purchaser-based PPO, an employer or insurance company approaches doctors and hospitals individually and negotiates with each separately. More commonly, providers take the initiative by jointly agreeing to offer their services as a package to employers or insurers on a discounted fee-for-service basis, along with utilization and quality review. When they agree to accept different forms of payment such as capitation or withhold pools that create greater financial risk, they are usually no longer referred to as PPOs, but instead as Independent Practice Associations (IPAs), Physician-Hospital Organizations (PHOs), or Provider Service Networks (PSNs).

These provider-based networks raise the distinct aura of per se illegal price fixing, yet it may be necessary for groups of providers to cooperate in order for this potentially procompetitive activity to flourish. Thus, the primary legal concern for managed care provider networks is how to avoid price-fixing antitrust liability.

4. *Antitrust Enforcement Guidelines*. Both the Department of Justice and the Federal Trade Commission have enforcement authority over the antitrust laws. These agencies, in exercising their prosecutorial discretion, have taken a substantially more encouraging position against provider networks. In a joint set of "Statements of Antitrust Enforcement Policy in Health Care," called the "DOJ/FTC Antitrust Guidelines," 5 BNA Health L. Rep. 1295, the two agencies establish the following safety zones for physician (not hospital) networks:

> By developing and implementing mechanisms that encourage physicians to collaborate in practicing efficiently as part of the network, many physician network

joint ventures promise significant procompetitive benefits for consumers of health care services. . . . To qualify for [an] antitrust safety zone, the physicians participating in a physician network joint venture must share substantial financial risk. . . . Risk sharing provides incentive for the physicians to cooperate in controlling costs and improving quality by managing the provision of services by network physicians. The following are examples of situations in which participants in a physician network joint venture can share substantial financial risk:

(1) agreement by the venture to provide services to a health plan at a "capitated" rate; or . . .

(2) use by the venture of significant financial incentives for its physician participants, as a group, to achieve specified cost-containment goals . . . [such as] withholding from all physician participants a substantial amount of the compensation due to them, with distribution of that amount to the physician participants based on group performance in meeting the cost-containment goals. . . .

Physician network joint ventures that fall outside the antitrust safety zone . . . do not necessarily raise substantial antitrust concerns. . . . [They] will be analyzed under the rule of reason, and will not be viewed as per se illegal, if the physicians' integration through the network is likely to produce significant efficiencies that benefit consumers, and any price agreements . . . are reasonably necessary to realize those efficiencies. . . . Physician network joint ventures that do not involve the sharing of substantial financial risk may also involve sufficient integration to demonstrate that the venture is likely to produce sufficient efficiencies. Such integration can be evidenced by the network implementing an active and ongoing program to evaluate and modify practice patterns . . . and to create a high degree of interdependence and cooperation among the physician to control costs and ensure quality. . . .

In contrast to integrated physician network joint ventures, such as these, . . . there have been arrangements among physicians that have taken the form of networks, but which in purpose or effect were little more than efforts by their participants to prevent or impede competitive forces from operating in the market. . . . Determining that an arrangement is merely a vehicle to fix prices or engage in naked anticompetitive conduct is a factual inquiry that must be done on a case-by-case basis to determine the arrangement's true nature and likely competitive effects. . . . In assessing the competitive environment, the Agencies would consider such market factors as the number, types, and size of managed care plans operating in the area [and] the extent of physician participation in those plans. If in the relevant market there are many other networks or many physicians who would be available to form competing networks or to contract directly with health plans, it is unlikely that the joint venture would raise significant competitive concerns. . . . The Agencies will consider a broad range of possible cost savings, including improved cost controls, case management and quality assurance, economies of scale, and reduced administrative or transaction costs. . . .

Some networks that are not substantially integrated use a variety of "messenger model" arrangements to facilitate contracting between providers and payers and avoid price-fixing agreements among competing network providers. Arrangements that are designed simply to minimize the costs associated with the contracting process, and that do not result in collective determination by the competing network providers on prices or price-related terms, are not per se illegal price fixing. . . . For example, network providers may use an agent or third party to convey to purchasers information obtained individually from the providers about the prices or price-related terms that the providers are willing to accept. In some cases, the agent may convey to the providers all contract offers made by purchasers, and each provider then makes an independent, unilateral decision to accept or reject the contract offers. In others, the agent may have received from individual providers some authority to accept contract offers on their behalf. . . . The Agencies will examine whether the agent facilitates collective decision-making by network providers, rather than independent, unilateral, decisions.[65] . . .

Are the DOJ/FTC Antitrust Guidelines consistent with *Maricopa County*? See generally Scott Danzis, Revising the Revised Guidelines: Incentives, Clinically Integrated Physician Networks, and the Antitrust Laws, 87 Va. L. Rev. 531 (2001); Edward Hirshfeld, Interpreting the 1996 Federal Antitrust Guidelines for Physician Joint Venture Networks, 6 Ann. Health L. 1 (1997); Kim H. Roeder, The 1996 Antitrust Policy Statements: Balancing Flexibility and Certainty, 31 Ga. L. Rev. 649 (1997); Comment, 91 Nw. U. L. Rev. 1684 (1997).

Observe that these safe harbors do not apply to "multi-provider" networks, i.e., those that contain hospitals. Why might the antitrust risks be greater or different when hospitals are present?

5. *Joint Venture Techniques.* The *Maricopa County* decision and the enforcement guidelines suggest four possible avenues for organizing a provider network to avoid a per se price-fixing charge:

(a) *Financial or clinical integration.* No horizontal price fixing exists if doctors integrate into a single economic entity that bears substantial financial risk. This can occur through true corporate integration in which doctors invest capital and form a joint business enterprise. Or, it can occur through contractual joint venture arrangements. In the latter case, the focus is on the degree of financial risk sharing or clinical integration. The DOJ/FTC Guidelines give examples, but provide no quantification. A portion of Hassan v. Independent Practice Associates omitted from the excerpt at page 488 held that a "risk withhold" payment system that placed 12 to 25 percent of the physicians' payments at risk succeeded in classifying an IPA physician network as a "legitimate joint venture" under *Maricopa County*, thus escaping per se condemnation. This escape hatch raises a number of additional questions.

First, is it necessary for all doctors to share substantial risk for all of their services, or only for some or most? Payment schemes for specialists often differ substantially from those for primary care physicians. In two simultaneous consent orders (St. Joseph's and Danbury), the DOJ indicated that it is sufficient if the controlling physicians bear substantial risk; physicians who are paid by the network only as subcontractors may be reimbursed on a fee-for-service basis. 60 Fed. Reg. 51,809, 52,015 (1995).

---

[65] Use of an intermediary or "independent" third party to convey collectively determined price offers to purchasers or to negotiate agreements with purchasers, or giving to individual providers an opportunity to "opt" into, or out of, such agreements does not negate the existence of an agreement.

Second, are there other ways to establish integration besides financial risk sharing? After vehement argument from the AMA and others, the DOJ and FTC revised their initial guidelines to allow a showing of *clinical* integration to suffice, as quoted above. Observe how clinical integration is defined. Illustrations include utilization review, quality assurance, practice guidelines, and physician credentialing. Are these enough to demonstrate that physicians in different offices are practicing as a coordinated clinical enterprise, or are they merely "window dressing" as found in *Maricopa County*? In the first ruling to find clinical integration, the FTC ruled in February 2002 (letter regarding MidSouth, Inc.) that it would not constitute a per se violation for more than half the doctors in one part of Denver to jointly negotiate with insurers, as long as they did so on a nonexclusive basis (i.e., each doctor could opt out and negotiate independently). The FTC found clinical integration to exist because the doctors proposed to share medical information, develop practice guidelines, monitor performance, and reduce utilization. The FTC also "concluded that the joint contracting appears to be sufficiently related to, and reasonably necessary for, the achievement of the potential benefits [of clinical integration] to be regarded as ancillary to the operation of the venture." Does that sound plausible to you?

The third problem is that full-scale integration may not be the most attractive option for physicians, either from a business or from a legal antitrust perspective. From a business perspective, when provider groups assume substantial financial risk for medical treatment, they may as a result fall within the jurisdiction of state health insurance regulations that require them to maintain large capital reserves to protect consumers against their insolvency. See Chapter 3.B. From a legal perspective, consider what new antitrust problems would exist if 70 percent of the doctors in Phoenix had formed a joint venture. See the discussion of merger law that follows. On the other hand, what antitrust issues would exist if PPO physicians selectively limited membership to a smaller number of competitors? See the discussion of boycott law in Chapter 4.D.1; Reazin v. Blue Cross & Blue Shield of Kansas, 899 F.2d 951 (10th Cir. 1990) ($7.8 million verdict sustained in favor of hospital excluded by a PPO).

(b) *Creation of a new product.* A second way to avoid per se price fixing, based on the reasoning of the *Broadcast Music (BMI)* case discussed in *Maricopa County*, is for physicians to attempt to form a new product. In *BMI* the Court used the new product characterization to justify its holding that a "blanket license" for a library of music compositions did not constitute price fixing even though numerous music composers collectively agreed to market their compositions through a joint agency rather than dealing individually with each radio station and night club singer. See also NCAA v. Board of Regents, 468 U.S. 85 (1984) ("horizontal restraints on competition are essential if [an organized college football league] is to be available at all"). Why did the Court reject the Foundation plans' argument that the bulk sale of physician services to insurance companies and large employers, coupled with claims processing, quality assurance, and utilization review, constitutes a new health care product? What did the Court indicate would suffice to meet the new product test?

The DOJ/FTC Antitrust Guidelines do not speak in terms of a "new product," but instead analyze the *BMI* issue in terms of procompetitive efficiencies. The guidelines leave open the possibility that a network lacking financial integration may still be able to avoid per se condemnation if, after what some commentators call a "quick look" review, it appears not to be a "naked" restraint but instead is a "legitimate" joint venture. In such a case, the agencies will then weigh the pro-competitive benefits against the anticompetitive harms. The agencies remain skeptical, however, that a network will actually survive this scrutiny if it in fact lacks financial and clinical integration. Therefore, it still appears necessary to show that a network does something more than merely facilitate marketing of physician services.

(c) *The "messenger" model.* The easiest way to avoid per se condemnation is to show that no horizontal price agreement exists at all. This is so if physicians individually respond to unilateral price offers from potential buyers. See n.26 in the opinion; Barry v. Blue Cross of California, 805 F.2d 866 (9th Cir. 1986). The "messenger model" is an attempt to capitalize on this notion by using the physician network as merely a means to communicate and coordinate individual offers, counteroffers, and acceptances. The difficulty is that such coordinated price negotiations could easily be viewed as constituting an implicit horizontal agreement among the doctors, especially where most of them end up agreeing to the same prices. Consider, for instance, whether doctors could legally agree in advance to be bound by the best price a joint negotiator is capable of obtaining from each purchaser? The DOJ and FTC have taken a strict stance against versions of the messenger model that resemble this "black box" variation. In various rulings, they have looked with disfavor on price negotiations initiated by quotes from the providers rather than bids from the purchasers, and they have ruled against an arrangement where physicians are bound in advance to negotiators' best prices unless they opt out. This still leaves intact the possibility of an "opt-in" messenger arrangement, and at least one court has ruled that even an "opt-out" arrangement is legal where a nonphysician risk-bearing entity (e.g., an HMO) takes the initiative in formulating the fee schedule. Levine v. Central Florida Medical Affiliates, 72 F.3d 1538 (11th Cir. 1996).

(d) *Independent pricing.* The subsequent history in the *Maricopa County* case suggests yet a fourth escape hatch for provider networks. Following the Supreme Court decision, the Foundation revised its bylaws so that the maximum fee schedule is set by a committee composed of consumers and non-Foundation doctors. The Foundation's Board of Trustees selects the initial committee; successor committee members are then elected by subscriber groups from a slate chosen by the incumbent committee. Order of Declaratory Relief, No. Civ. 78-800 (D. Ariz. May 25, 1983) (approving revised bylaws). Is such a committee truly independent? If so, does this matter? Suppose a group of competing doctors agreed with each other to limit their price increases to the consumer price index. Should their lack of control over the CPI make a horizontal price-fixing characterization inapplicable? In Pennsylvania Dental Ass'n v. Medical Services Ass'n of Pennsylvania, 745 F.2d 248 (3d Cir. 1984), the court ruled that no per se price fixing exists where only two dentists sat on the 32-member board that had ultimate authority over pricing and payment decisions for dental services. There were other medical professional members on the board, but they constituted less than a majority.

6. *Criminal Violation or Leveling the Playing Field?* Price-fixing characterizations are not always so complex and debatable. The Department of Justice has initiated criminal grand jury investigations into alleged price fixing by doctors in several locations. In the one case to go to trial, the jury found and the appeals court sustained a criminal price-fixing violation against a dentist who recruited all the others in town to demand an increase in payment from several dental HMOs. United States v. Alston, 974 F.2d 1206 (9th Cir. 1991). However, the court sustained the trial judge's discretionary decision to order a new trial, and it offered the following assuaging observations:

> Many things that might occur at a meeting such as in Dr. Alston's office would escape the per se rule and might be perfectly legal under the rule of reason: dentists commiserating over the low fee schedules; or impugning the motivations or integrity of the Plans; even sabre-rattling about economic retribution at some indefinite time in the future if their grievances remain unaddressed. Some such activity, like clamoring for governmental protection of their economic interests vis-à-vis their antagonists or competitors, would even be constitutionally protected. . . .
>
> [H]ealth care providers who must deal with consumers indirectly through plans such as the one in this case face an unusual situation that may legitimate certain collective actions. Medical plans serve, effectively, as the bargaining agents for large groups of consumers; they use the clout of their consumer base to drive down health care service fees. Uniform fee schedules — anathema in a normal, competitive market — are standard operating procedure when medical plans are involved. In light of these departures from a normal competitive market, individual health care providers are entitled to take some joint action (short of price fixing or a group boycott) to level the bargaining imbalance created by the plans and provide meaningful input into the setting of the fee schedules. Thus health care providers might pool cost data in justifying a request for an increased fee schedule. Providers might also band together to negotiate various other aspects of their relationship with the plans such as payment procedures, the type of documentation they must provide, the method of referring patients and the mechanism for adjusting disputes. Such concerted actions, which would not implicate the per se rule, must be carefully distinguished from efforts to dictate terms by explicit or implicit threats of mass withdrawals from the plans. . . .

Dr. Alston eventually pled guilty to one count, and was given a fine and community service. The joint nonprice negotiations and exchanges of price and cost information discussed in *Alston* are also addressed by the DOJ/FTC Guidelines.

7. *Bibliography.* Law journals have hashed out in considerable detail the competitive benefits and antitrust risks of provider networks. Leading and influential analyses include Michael Classen, Provider-Based Preferred Provider Organizations: A Viable Alternative Under Present Federal Antitrust Policies?, 66 N.C. L. Rev. 254 (1988); T. Greaney & Jody Sindelar, Physician-Sponsored Joint Ventures: An Antitrust Analysis of Preferred Provider Organizations, 18 Rutgers L.J. 513 (1987); Clark Havighurst, Are the Antitrust Agencies Overregulating Physician Networks?, 8 Loy. Consumer L. Rep. 78 (1995); Charles Weller, "Free Choice" as a Restraint of Trade in American Health Care Delivery and Insurance, 69 Iowa L. Rev. 1351 (1984).

■ OCEAN STATE PHYSICIANS HEALTH PLAN, INC. v.
BLUE CROSS & BLUE SHIELD OF RHODE ISLAND
883 F.2d 1101 (1st Cir. 1989)

LEVIN H. CAMPBELL, Chief Judge.

. . . Defendant Blue Cross, a nonprofit corporation established in 1939, has long been the largest health insurer in Rhode Island. It purchases health services from physicians, hospitals, and other health care providers on behalf of its subscribers. . . . Plaintiff Ocean State is a for-profit health maintenance organization (HMO) that began operations in 1984. Like Blue Cross, Ocean State contracts with physicians to provide medical care to its subscribers, and then pays its contracted physicians on a fee-for-service basis. . . . Eighty percent of the shares of the Ocean State corporation are owned by its participating physicians. A physician may participate in more than one health insurance program. . . .

Apparently because Ocean State provided more coverage and charged lower premiums, many subscribers switched from Blue Cross to Ocean State. By the spring of 1986, Blue Cross had lost approximately 30,000 of its 543,015 enrollees, while Ocean State's enrollment had exceeded all expectations, growing to 70,000. . . . [T]o meet the challenge presented by Ocean State, Blue Cross instituted a three-pronged attack:

First, Blue Cross launched its own HMO "look-alike," dubbed HealthMate, which it marketed to employers who were offering the Ocean State plan to their employees. Like Ocean State, HealthMate provided 15 percent more coverage than the standard Blue Cross plan, including such added benefits as office visits, prescription drugs, and "good health" benefits. . . .

Second, Blue Cross instituted an "adverse selection" policy of pricing. "Adverse selection" refers to the tendency for younger and healthier people to opt for HMOs such as Ocean State when they are made available, leaving older and sicker people (on the average) in the standard Blue Cross pool. Because of such adverse selection, Blue Cross expected the health care costs for standard Blue Cross to be higher in those employer groups that offered an HMO option than in those employer groups that did not. . . . Blue Cross instituted a pricing plan that took account of this projected difference in health expenses. Under this policy, employers were offered three different rates for traditional Blue Cross coverage. The rate was lowest for an employer who offered only traditional Blue Cross, intermediate for an employer who also offered a competing HMO (usually Ocean State) and HealthMate, and highest for an employer who also offered a competing HMO but declined to offer HealthMate.

Third, Blue Cross initiated a policy, which it called "Prudent Buyer," of not paying a physician more for any service or procedure than that physician was accepting from any other health care cost provider (such as Ocean State). Blue Cross established this policy after it became apparent that Ocean State's contracting physicians were accepting about 20 percent less for their services from Ocean State than they were receiving from Blue Cross. . . . After the implementation of Prudent Buyer, about 350 of Ocean State's 1,200 physicians resigned, in many cases apparently in order to avoid a reduction in their Blue Cross fees. . . .

Ocean State alleged that Blue Cross's conduct violated, inter alia, §2 of the Sherman Act, which makes it unlawful to "monopolize . . . any part of the trade or commerce among the several States." Ocean State charged that Blue Cross launched HealthMate not because it was a viable long-term product, but in order to put Ocean State out of business. Through the adverse selection policy, Ocean State claimed, Blue Cross was able to raise its rates for standard Blue Cross for employer groups offering HealthMate — which, in turn, influenced employers not to make HealthMate available. Finally, Ocean State claimed that Blue Cross instituted the Prudent Buyer policy not in order to save money, but rather to induce physicians to resign from Ocean State. . . .

After a lengthy trial, the jury found Blue Cross "guilty" on the §2 claim, but it awarded no damages on this claim. . . . [T]he district court granted Blue Cross's motion for judgment notwithstanding the verdict. . . .

B. THE EFFECT OF THE MCCARRAN-FERGUSON ACT

The McCarran-Ferguson Act ("the Act"), 15 U.S.C. §§1012(b), 1013(b), exempts from the antitrust laws all conduct that is (1) part of the "business of insurance"; (2) "regulated by state law"; and (3) not in the form of "boycott, coercion, or intimidation." Blue Cross argued to the district court that both the introduction of HealthMate and the use of the adverse selection rate factors — but not the Prudent Buyer policy — were exempted from antitrust scrutiny by the Act. . . .

The Supreme Court has identified "three criteria relevant in determining whether a particular practice is part of the 'business of insurance' exempted from the antitrust laws": first, whether a particular practice has the effect of transferring or spreading a policyholder's risk; second, whether the practice is an integral part of the policy relationship between the insurer and the insured; and third, whether the practice is limited to entities within the insurance industry. Union Labor Life Insurance Co. v. Pireno, 458 U.S. 119 (1982). See also Group Life & Health Insurance Co. v. Royal Drug Co., 440 U.S. 205 (1979). . . .

Both HealthMate and the adverse selection policy qualify as the "business of insurance" under these criteria. HealthMate is an insurance policy which operates by spreading policyholders' risk; adverse selection is a pricing policy that inherently involves risk-spreading. Both HealthMate and adverse selection directly involve the relationship between the insurer (Blue Cross) and the insured (its policyholders). Such policies are, more or less by definition, limited to entities in the "insurance industry" as broadly construed. Accord Health Care Equalization Committee v. Iowa Medical Society, 851 F.2d 1020, 1029 (8th Cir. 1988).

Ocean State . . . bases [its] argument [against immunity] on a misreading of Royal Drug. In that case, the Supreme Court characterized Blue Shield's contacts with its health care providers as "merely arrangements for the purchase of goods and services by Blue Shield." But the Court took care to distinguish Blue Shield's provider contracts from its subscriber contracts. . . . This distinction was emphasized in Justice Brennan's dissenting opinion: "Neither the Court . . . nor the parties challenge the fact that the . . . policy offered by Blue Shield to its policyholders — as distinguished from the contract between Blue Shield and the [providers] — is the 'business of insurance.'" . . . [Based on this distinction], we conclude that the challenged actions of Blue Cross with respect to HealthMate and adverse selection are exempt from antitrust scrutiny under the McCarran-Ferguson Act.

C. THE PRUDENT BUYER POLICY

The Prudent Buyer policy involves Blue Cross's relationships not with its subscribers but with its provider physicians. Blue Cross makes no claim that this policy is protected by the McCarran-Ferguson exemption. We agree with the district court, however, that the Prudent Buyer policy . . . as a matter of law, [is] not violative of §2 of the Sherman Act.

Section 2 of the Sherman Act makes it unlawful to "monopolize . . . any part of the trade or commerce among the several states." 15 U.S.C. §2. The offense of monopolization has two elements: (1) the possession of monopoly power in the relevant market and (2) the willful acquisition or maintenance of that power as distinguished from growth or development as a consequence of a superior product, business acumen, or historic accident. United States v. Grinnell Corp., 384 U.S. 563 (1966). On this appeal, Blue Cross does not dispute its monopoly power in the market for health care insurance in Rhode Island. Ocean State, for its part, concedes that Blue Cross acquired its historical advantages legitimately. The issue in dispute is whether Blue Cross maintained its monopoly position through improper means.

Section 2 does not prohibit vigorous competition on the part of a monopoly. To the contrary, the primary purpose of the antitrust laws is to encourage competition. What §2 does prohibit is "exclusionary" conduct by a monopoly, often defined as "behavior that not only (1) tends to impair the opportunities of rivals, but also (2) either does not further competition on the merits or does so in an unnecessarily restrictive way." 3 P. Areeda & D. Turner, Antitrust Law ¶626b at 78. . . .

In the case at hand, the record amply supports Blue Cross's view that Prudent Buyer was a bona fide policy to ensure that Blue Cross would not pay more than any competitor paid for the same services. . . . Blue Cross estimated that it saved $1,900,000 through this policy. We agree with the district court that such a policy of insisting on a supplier's lowest price — assuming that the price is not "predatory" or below the supplier's incremental cost — tends to further competition on the merits and, as a matter of law, is not exclusionary. It is hard to disagree with the district court's view: "As a naked proposition, it would seem silly to argue that a policy to pay the same amount for the same service is anticompetitive, even on the part of one who has market power. This, it would seem, is what competition should be all about."

This conclusion is also compelled by this court's holding in Kartell v. Blue Shield of Massachusetts, 749 F.2d 922 (1st Cir. 1984), that a health insurer's unilateral decisions about the prices it will pay providers do not violate the Sherman Act — unless the prices are "predatory" or below incremental cost — even if the insurer is assumed to have monopoly power in the relevant market. *Kartell* concerned Blue Shield of Massachusetts's ban on balance billing, a price policy according to which Blue Shield paid participating physicians only if they agreed not to make any additional charges to the subscriber. We held that, for antitrust purposes, a health insurer like Blue Shield must be viewed "as itself the purchaser of the doctors' purchases." As such, the insurer—like any buyer of goods or services—is lawfully entitled to bargain with its providers for the best price it can get. "[E]ven if the buyer has monopoly power, an antitrust court . . . will not interfere with a buyer's (nonpredatory) determination of price." . . .

Ocean State argues that *Kartell* is a "vertical" case (involving the effects of Blue Shield's policy on its provider physicians), while the present case is "horizontal" (involving the effects of Blue Cross's policy on its competitor, Ocean State). But the distinction is of no consequence. In both cases the challenged activity is the price that the buyer offers to the seller. . . . Even a monopoly can engage in a competitive course of conduct, so long as it does so for valid business reasons (such as the desire to get the lowest possible price), rather than in order to smother competition. . . . .

[E]ven if we assume for argument's sake that Blue Cross selectively applied Prudent Buyer [only to Ocean State physicians], its conduct remains legitimate. It was primarily Ocean State physicians who were selling their services at a lower price to another provider (Ocean State) than to Blue Cross. Indeed, it was Ocean State's lower pricing policy—in particular, its 1986 decision not to return its participating physicians' withholds for 1985—that gave rise to Prudent Buyer. Therefore, it seems only logical—and not illegitimate—for Blue Cross to have focused its efforts in applying Prudent Buyer on Ocean State physicians. . . .

Finally, Ocean State points to evidence in the record that Blue Cross officials hoped that Prudent Buyer—together with HealthMate and adverse selection—would have the effect of destroying or weakening Ocean State. For example, there was testimony that Blue Cross's president had expressed—in none-too-polite terms—a desire to emasculate Ocean State. Another Blue Cross executive wrote in a handwritten note that "not one guy in the state isn't going to know the implication of signing with Ocean State." . . . The jury may reasonably have concluded, on the basis of this and other evidence, that Blue Cross's leadership desired to put Ocean State out of business. But the desire to crush a competitor, standing alone, is insufficient to make out a violation of the antitrust laws. . . . As long as Blue Cross's course of conduct was itself legitimate, the fact that some of its executives hoped to see Ocean State disappear is irrelevant. Under these circumstances Blue Cross is no more guilty of an antitrust violation than a boxer who delivers a perfectly legal punch—hoping that it will kill his opponent—is guilty of attempted murder. . . .

Notes: Vertical Restraints by Insurers

1. *Horizontal Conspiracy vs. Vertical Pricing.* The *Kartell* decision discussed in *Ocean State* was written by Justice Breyer when he sat on the First Circuit. Prior to that, he was an antitrust professor at Harvard. Justice Breyer offered the following important distinction elsewhere in his opinion:

There is no suggestion that Blue Shield's fee schedule reflects, for example, an effort by, say, one group of doctors to stop other doctors from competing with them. Cf. Virginia Academy of Clinical Psychologists v. Blue Shield of Virginia, 624 F.2d 476 (4th Cir. 1980) (Blue Shield found to be a combination, not of policyholders, but of physicians [with respect to decision not to cover services of psychologists]). . . . *Maricopa*, [therefore], is simply not on point. . . . [It] involved a horizontal agreement among competing doctors about what to charge.

Considering the origins of Blue Cross/Blue Shield, however, a few courts have agreed with *Virginia Academy* by finding that Blue Cross in particular constitutes a "walking horizontal conspiracy" among its controlling doctors. Glen Eden Hospital v. Blue Cross & Blue Shield of Michigan, 740 F.2d 423 (6th Cir. 1984) (possible conspiracy); Ratino v. Medical Service, 718 F.2d 1260 (4th Cir. 1983) (same). Also, it is always possible to find that, in a particular case, an insurer and providers have conspired even apart from the insurer's internal structure. See the discussion of Reazin v. Blue Cross & Blue Shield of Kansas at page 497. Nevertheless, in today's health care market structure, most courts agree with *Kartell* that insurers' vertical pricing decisions are beyond antitrust reproach. See SmileCare Dental Group v. Delta Dental Plan, 88 F.3d 780 (9th Cir. 1996) (insurer can prevent dentists from waiving copayments); Barry v. Blue Cross of California, 805 F.2d 866 (9th Cir. 1986) (insurer can exclude doctors from network); Comment, 34 St. Louis U. L.J. (1990).

The focus of these notes is on areas of special importance to health care where insurers' cost-containment initiatives might pose antitrust violations in a *vertical* dimension. Challenges might arise either under a §1 rule of reason analysis, or under the §2 monopolization theory outlined in *Ocean State*, depending on whether the action is wholly unilateral or involves a vertical agreement. Other types of vertical restraints and §2 theories relevant to health care markets — more to hospitals than to insurers — are discussed in the notes at pages 493 and 497 in terms of "unilateral refusals to deal," the "essential facilities" doctrine, and illegal "tie-ins." For general commentary see Thomas L. Greaney, Managed Competition, Integrated Delivery Systems and Antitrust, 79 Cornell L. Rev. 1507 (1994); Frances Miller, Vertical Restraints and Powerful Health Insurers: Exclusionary Conduct Masquerading as Managed Care? 51 Law & Contemp. Probs. 195 (1988); Mark Pauly, Managed Care, Market Power, and Monopsony, 33 Health Serv. Res. 1439 (1998).

2. *Most Favored Nation Clauses.* The "prudent buyer" policy at issue in *Ocean State* is more commonly known as a "most favored nation clause." Many antitrust experts consider this aspect of the decision to to be wrong, or at least overstated. See Arnold Celnicker, A Competitive Analysis of Most Favored Nations Clauses in Contracts Between Health Care Providers and Insurers, 69 N.C. L. Rev. 863 (1991). To understand why, consider the following scenario: A dominant insurer with market power attempts to ward off a new insurer by insisting that the dominant's participating physicians and hospitals contract exclusively with it, that is, they lose all of their existing business if they take any of the new business. This would clearly constitute a potential antitrust violation if there were no legitimate business reason for demanding exclusivity (such as that exclusive arrangements foster better quality service or lower prices). See Aspen Skiing Co. v. Aspen Highlands Skiing Corp., 472 U.S. 585 (1985) (sustaining jury finding that monopolist illegally excluded competitor by refusing to give the competitor's customers the same all-inclusive lift ticket discount package it gave its own customers). The main difference between this extreme scenario and *Ocean State* is that the most

favored nation provision made it very expensive, but not impossible, to do business with the new insurer: Physicians who accepted the insurer's terms in effect had to discount all their business by 20 percent. Most favored nation provisions obviously make it more difficult for a new insurer to stimulate downward pressure on prices for physicians' services and, ultimately, for its own insurance product. Thus, these vertical restraints potentially have horizontal effects. Accordingly, the DOJ and FTC take a dim view of these agreements. See also Reazin v. Blue Cross & Blue Shield of Kansas, 899 F.2d 951 (10th Cir. 1990). Is it possible to justify *Ocean State* nevertheless based on its unique facts, in which, with respect to HMO insurance in particular, Blue Cross was doing badly in the market and its only response was to meet Ocean State's price where they competed head to head? Doesn't this justification turn on an assessment of Blue Cross' motive and purpose, and are these not quintessential factual issues for the jury to resolve?

3. *Exclusive Physician Contracts.* For reasons explained in the preceding note, the DOJ and FTC also take a dim view of exclusivity agreements in managed care contracts, preferring that physicians participate nonexclusively in several networks. This can be seen in an additional portion of their health care antitrust enforcement guidelines:

> The Agencies will not challenge, absent extraordinary circumstances, an *exclusive* physician network joint venture comprising *20 percent or less* of the physicians in each physician specialty with active hospital staff privileges who practice in the relevant geographic market. . . . The Agencies will not challenge, absent extraordinary circumstances, a *nonexclusive* physician network joint venture comprising *30 percent or less* of the physicians in each physician specialty with active hospital staff privileges who practice in the relevant geographic market. In relevant markets with less than four [or five] physicians in a particular specialty, a . . . physician network joint venture otherwise qualifying for the antitrust safety zone may include one physician from that specialty [on a nonexclusive basis]. . . . The Agencies will determine whether a physician network joint venture is exclusive or nonexclusive by its physician participants' activities and not simply by the terms of the contractual relationship . . . [using] the following indicia of nonexclusivity, among others: . . . (2) that physicians in the network actually . . . contract with other networks or managed care plans. . . .

Statements of Antitrust Enforcement Policy in Health Care, 5 BNA Health L. Rep. 1295 (emphasis added). See also *Hassan*, excerpted at page 488.

Antitrust law favors nonexclusivity because this makes it much easier for new insurers to enter the market. Consider, though, whether nonexclusivity is good for competition in the *provider* market (in contrast with the insurance market). Eminent antitrust lawyer Charles Weller argues convincingly that the medical profession has long embraced the principle of "free choice of physician" with the purpose and effect that, if insurers must accept all providers, then they cannot force them to bid competitively against each other by choosing only some of them. Charles Weller, "Free Choice" as a Restraint of Trade in American Health Care Delivery and Insurance, 69 Iowa L. Rev. 1351 (1984). Managed care contracting breaks down the free choice principle and forces competition, even if it occurs on a nonexclusive basis; but, for the following reasons, forcing doctors to deal exclusively with only a single network would heighten competitive pressures among physicians:

> [T]o be effective in reducing the growth rate of spending on health care, a managed competition system would need to result in a relatively small number of insurance organizations that had substantially nonoverlapping networks of affiliated providers—or at least primary care physicians—and that competed on the basis of their efficiency in delivering care of high quality. Otherwise, the providers in any particular network would essentially be competing with themselves as they wore the different hats of other networks. Consequently, they would have few reasons for changing the way they practiced to be more cost-effective or to internalize the practice styles sought by insurers. . . .

Congressional Budget Office, Managed Competition and Its Potential to Reduce Health Spending (1993). Apparently, in the view of the antitrust enforcement agencies, these potential competitive benefits of exclusivity in the *physician* market are outweighed by the harms to competition in the *insurance* market, since an insurer with dominant market power could use exclusive contracts with most physicians to block entry by another insurer. According to standard antitrust doctrine, "antitrust effects in one market [cannot] be justified by procompetitive consequences in another." United States v. Philadelphia National Bank, 374 U.S. 321 (1963).

Where an insurer lacked market power, however, an exclusivity agreement in an HMO's contract with its physicians was approved by yet another First Circuit opinion. U.S. Healthcare v. Healthsource, 986 F.2d 589 (1st Cir. 1993). See also Blue Cross & Blue Shield United of Wisconsin v. Marshfield Clinic, 65 F.3d 1406 (7th Cir. 1995). It is also important to note, though, that in *U.S. Healthcare* the HMO allowed physicians to opt for nonexclusive status with 30 days' notice if they were willing to accept lower payments.

4. *Monopolization.* When vertical restraints are challenged under §2, it is necessary to establish the existence (or at least the "dangerous probability") of monopoly power. (Sometimes, the technical term *monopsony* is used to describe a *buyer* as opposed to *seller* monopoly.) Blue Cross has a very large market share in many states, especially in the Northeast. See, e.g., *Reazin*, supra (60 percent market share sufficient to support finding of monopolization); *Kartell*, supra (75 percent market share presumed to be a monopoly for sake of argument). Other courts, however, have found no monopoly power despite large market share because competing insurers elsewhere in the state or the nation face few inherent barriers to entering the same market or expanding their existing market share. The leading discussion is Ball Memorial Hospital v. Mutual Hospital Insurance Co., 784 F.2d 1325 (7th Cir. 1986) (no market power despite 50 to 80 percent market share). Is this a realistic assessment given the start-up capital costs of (1) complying with state insurance regulations concerning solvency and (2) assembling a managed care network of providers? The issue of market share and market power in managed care settings is considered further in the following section.

5. *The McCarran-Ferguson Exemption.* For additional discussion of the McCarran-Ferguson exemption of insurance from antitrust laws, see Jonathan Macey & Geoffrey Miller, The McCarran-Ferguson Act of 1945: Reconceiving the Federal Role in Insurance Regulation, 68 N.Y.U. L. Rev. (1993).

3. Antitrust Merger Law

■ FEDERAL TRADE COMMISSION v. TENET HEALTH CARE CORP.
186 F.3d 1045 (8th Cir. 1999)

BEAM, Circuit Judge.

Tenet Healthcare and Poplar Bluff Physicians Group, Inc., doing business as Doctors' Regional Medical Center (collectively, Tenet) appeal the district court's order enjoining the merger of two hospitals in Poplar Bluff, Missouri. . . . The district court found a substantial likelihood that the merger would substantially lessen competition between acute care hospitals in Poplar Bluff, Missouri, in violation of section 7 of the Clayton Act, 15 U.S.C. §15. We reverse.

Poplar Bluff is a city of 17,000 people in southeastern Missouri. It is located in Butler County, which has a population of 40,000. It is the largest city in several counties and has numerous major employers and manufacturing operations. Sikeston, Missouri, and Cape Girardeau, Missouri, both towns with populations of over 40,000 are forty and sixty miles away from Poplar Bluff. The population in the area surrounding Poplar Bluff is concentrated in Scott and Stoddard Counties, which lie between Poplar Bluff and Cape Girardeau. Poplar Bluff is within a few hours' drive of several large metropolitan centers including St. Louis, Missouri, Memphis, Tennessee, and Jonesboro, Arkansas.

Tenet Healthcare Corporation presently owns Lucy Lee Hospital in Poplar Bluff. Lucy Lee is a general acute care hospital that provides primary and secondary care services.[1] Lucy Lee has 201 licensed beds, 185 of which are staffed. It operates ten outpatient clinics in the surrounding counties. Its average daily census was 75 in 1994, 76 in 1995 and 104 in 1996. Doctors' Regional Medical Center in Poplar Bluff is presently owned by a group of physicians. It is also a general acute care hospital providing primary and secondary care services. It has 230 licensed beds, of which 187 are staffed. Its average census in 1994 was 106, in 1995 was 99, in 1996 was 95 and in 1997 was 77. It also operates several rural health clinics in the area. Though profitable, both hospitals are underutilized and have had problems attracting specialists to the area.

Tenet recently entered into an agreement to purchase Doctors' Regional for over forty million dollars. Tenet plans to operate Doctors' Regional as a long-term care facility and to consolidate inpatient services at Lucy Lee. It plans to employ more specialists at the merged facility and to offer higher quality care in a comprehensive, integrated delivery system that would include some tertiary care.[2] Pursuant to the Hart-Scott-Rodino Act, 15 U.S.C. §18a, the hospitals filed a

---

[1] Primary care involves relatively simple medical or surgical procedures. Secondary care is somewhat more complex, including procedures such as hernia repair or patient services related to a heart attack.

[2] A comprehensive, integrated healthcare delivery system is one that provides service along the spectrum of healthcare: inpatient clinics, home health, hospitalization, inpatient and outpatient surgery, and short- and long-term convalescent or rehabilitation care. Tertiary care is sophisticated, complex, or high-tech care that includes, for example, open heart surgery, oncology surgery, neurosurgery, high-risk obstetrics, neonatal intensive care and trauma services. Quaternary care is even more sophisticated and includes organ transplants.

premerger certification with the FTC. Shortly thereafter, the FTC filed a complaint alleging that the hospitals' merger would lessen competition for primary and secondary inpatient hospitalization services in the area. . . .

The evidence adduced at the hearing shows that Lucy Lee and Doctors' Regional are the only two hospitals in Poplar Bluff, other than a Veteran's Hospital. . . . There are several [larger, regional] hospitals in the surrounding area [that] offer the same or a greater range of services. . . . In addition, there are smaller rural hospitals located in nearby towns, . . . [which] have fewer than fifty beds and provide only primary care.

Lucy Lee's and Doctors' Regional's patient bases are composed primarily of patients who are covered by Medicare and Medicaid and thus remain largely insensitive to price differentials. Most of the remaining patient admissions at Lucy Lee and Doctors' Regional are covered by health insurance, under a plan administered by a managed care organization.[5] These organizations include health maintenance organizations (HMOs)[6] and preferred provider organizations (PPOs).[7] Hospitals are willing to discount their stated rates to managed care payers in order to entice the managed care entity to send its enrollees to that hospital. Managed care organizations have had a presence in Poplar Bluff for approximately fifteen years. Most employers in the Poplar Bluff area either subscribe to or administer a PPO. Both Lucy Lee and Doctors' Regional have entered into discount agreements with numerous managed care entities and employers.

The hospitals in Cape Girardeau, on the other hand, refused to negotiate with managed care plans until recently, when, at the insistence of area employers, Southeast Missouri Hospital entered into a discount arrangement with HealthLink, a managed care organization. Healthcare prices in Cape Girardeau have historically been significantly higher than prices in Poplar Bluff. However, there is also a perception of higher quality service at Cape Girardeau hospitals. Since the entry of managed care in the Cape Girardeau market, there has been some reduction in prices. . . . Cape Girardeau hospitals now [advertise] in Poplar Bluff.

Market participants, specifically, employers, healthplans and network providers testified that they had negotiated substantial discounts and favorable per diem rates with either or both Lucy Lee and Doctors' Regional as a result of "playing the two hospitals off each other." These managed care organizations and employers testified that if the merged entity were to raise its prices by ten percent, the health plans would have no choice but to simply pay the increased price. They testified that they perceive it is essential for the plans to include a

---

[5] Another form of healthcare coverage is traditional indemnity insurance. Traditional indemnity insurers cover a percentage of an insured's healthcare costs, with the remainder covered by the insured. Indemnity insurance is not implicated in this case, because it has become virtually nonexistent in the Poplar Bluff area. Historically, indemnity insurers have not attempted to gain discounts from providers.

[6] An HMO generally charges a set fee which covers all of an enrollee's healthcare needs, including hospitalizations. HMO enrollees are required to obtain care only from those physicians and hospitals who provide a discounted rate to the HMO. HMOs often have their own clinics and enrollees are obligated to go to those clinics for care. In addition, HMOs often consult with hospitals to insure that costs of hospitalization remain as low as possible.

[7] In a PPO, the PPO negotiates discounted rates with certain physicians or hospitals and then provides financial incentives, such as low deductibles or low co-payments, to its enrollees to use those providers.

Poplar Bluff hospital in their benefit packages because their enrollees would not travel to other towns for primary and secondary inpatient treatment. They stated that their employees and subscribers find it convenient to use a Poplar Bluff hospital; are loyal to their physicians in Poplar Bluff and would not be amenable to a health benefit plan that did not include a Poplar Bluff hospital.

The evidence shows that patient choice of hospitals is determined by many variables, including patient/physician loyalty, perceptions of quality, geographic proximity and, most importantly or determinatively, access to hospitals through an insurance plan. Managed care organizations have been able to influence or change patient behavior with financial incentives in other healthcare markets. This practice is known as "steering." Representatives of Poplar Bluff managed care entities testified, however, that they did not believe such efforts would be successful in the Poplar Bluff market, . . . in spite of the fact that such tactics had been successful in other markets. . . .

Lucy Lee and Doctors' Regional obtain ninety percent of their patients from zip codes within a fifty-mile radius of Poplar Bluff. In eleven of the top twelve zip codes, however, significant patient admissions—ranging from 22% to 70%—were to hospitals other than those in Poplar Bluff. There is no dispute that Poplar Bluff residents travel to St. Louis, Memphis, and Jonesboro for tertiary care. . . . [T]he FTC presented the testimony . . . based on an analysis of DRG data[9] that patients seeking care outside Poplar Bluff were seeking a more sophisticated level of service than that available in Poplar Bluff. . . . The evidence also shows, however, that significant numbers of patients in the Poplar Bluff service area travel to other towns for primary and secondary treatment that is also available in Poplar Bluff.

The evidence shows that the healthcare industry is rapidly changing. The emergence and growth of managed care—a system in which a third party monitors healthcare resources and expenditures—has had a large impact on healthcare. This monitoring has caused a corresponding decline in the number and length of inpatient admissions. Many procedures that formerly required a hospital stay are now performed on an outpatient basis. Another trend has been growth of outreach efforts such as rural clinics to extend the service area of a hospital. Patient loyalty to a certain doctor has diminished as patients' out-of-pocket expenditures have increased. . . .

Discussion

The determination of a relevant market is a necessary predicate to the finding of an antitrust violation. . . . A relevant market consists of two components: a product market and a geographic market. *See* Department of Justice, Federal Trade Commission, Antitrust Division, 1992 Horizontal Merger Guidelines, 57 Fed. Reg. 41552. The parties agree that the relevant product market at issue in

---

[9] A DRG is a numerical code that serves to classify patients into one of 503 clinically cohesive groups that demonstrate similar consumption of hospital resources and length of stay patterns. These classifications are used by the federal government in administering Medicare and Medicaid programs and by insurers to evaluate reimbursement, utilization of resources, treatment protocols, related conditions, and demographic distribution. Examples of DRGs would be "extracranial vascular procedures," "chronic obstructive pulmonary disease," and "specific cerebral vascular disorders."

this case is the delivery of primary and secondary inpatient hospital care services. They disagree, however, on the relevant geographic market.

A geographic market is the area in which consumers can practically turn for alternative sources of the product and in which the antitrust defendants face competition. . . . A properly defined geographic market includes potential suppliers who can readily offer consumers a suitable alternative to the defendant's services. Determination of the relevant geographic market is highly fact sensitive. . . . A monopolization claim often succeeds or fails strictly on the definition of the product or geographic market. . . .

The FTC proposes a relevant geographic market that essentially matches its service area: a fifty-mile radius from downtown Poplar Bluff. It is from this service area that the two hospitals obtain ninety percent of their patients. A service area, however, is not necessarily a merging firm's geographic market for purposes of antitrust analysis. The FTC's proposed geographic market includes four other hospitals: a Tenet-owned regional hospital in Kennett, Missouri, and three rural hospitals. The FTC contends that its evidence shows that the merged entity will have a post-merger market share of eighty-four percent of this geographic market.[10] Tenet, on the other hand, proposes a relevant geographic market that encompasses a sixty-five mile radius from downtown Poplar Bluff in addition to Barnes Hospital in St. Louis. The proposed area includes [20] hospitals. . . .

Because we conclude that the FTC produced insufficient evidence of a well-defined relevant geographic market, we find that it did not show that the merged entity will possess such market power. . . . The evidence in this case falls short of establishing a relevant geographic market that excludes the Sikeston or Cape Girardeau areas. The evidence shows that hospitals in either or both of these towns, as well as rural hospitals throughout the area, are practical alternatives for many Poplar Bluff consumers. In adopting the FTC's position, the district court improperly discounted the fact that over twenty-two percent of people in the most important zip codes already use hospitals outside the FTC's proposed market for treatment that is offered at Poplar Bluff hospitals. . . . If patients use hospitals outside the service area, those hospitals can act as a check on the exercise of market power by the hospitals within the service area. The FTC's contention that the merged hospitals would have eighty-four percent of the market for inpatient primary and secondary services within a contrived market area that stops just short of including a regional hospital (Missouri Delta in Sikeston) that is closer to many patients than the Poplar Bluff hospitals, strikes us as absurd. The proximity of many patients to hospitals in other towns, coupled with the compelling and essentially unrefuted evidence that the switch to another provider by a small percentage of patients would constrain a price increase, shows that the FTC's proposed market is too narrow. . . .

The district court rejected the Cape Girardeau hospitals as practicable alternatives because they were more costly. In so doing, it underestimated the impact of nonprice competitive factors, such as quality. The evidence shows that one reason for the significant amount of migration from the Poplar Bluff hospitals to either

---

[10] An inference of monopoly power can be drawn from an 84% market share. . . . Market shares of less than 60% are generally not sufficient to create an inference of monopoly power.

Sikeston, Cape Girardeau, or St. Louis is the actual or perceived difference in quality of care. . . . As the district court noted, healthcare decisions are based on factors other than price. It is for that reason that, although they are less expensive, HMOs are not always an employer's or individual's choice in healthcare services. See Blue Cross and Blue Shield United of Wisconsin v. Marshfield Clinic, 65 F.3d 1406, 1412, 1410 (7th Cir.1995) (Posner, J.) (noting "[g]enerally you must pay more for higher quality" and "the HMO's incentive is to keep you healthy if it can but if you get very sick, and are unlikely to recover to a healthy state involving few medical expenses, to let you die as quickly and cheaply as possible.") . . .

We further find that although Tenet's efficiencies defense may have been properly rejected by the district court, the district court should nonetheless have considered evidence of enhanced efficiency in the context of the competitive effects of the merger. The evidence shows that a hospital that is larger and more efficient than Lucy Lee or Doctors' Regional will provide better medical care than either of those hospitals could separately. The merged entity will be able to attract more highly qualified physicians and specialists and to offer integrated delivery and some tertiary care. . . . [Therefore,] the merged entity may well enhance competition in the greater Southeast Missouri area. . . .

The district court also relied on the seemingly outdated assumption of doctor-patient loyalty that is not supported by the record. The evidence shows, and the district court acknowledged, that the issue of access to a provider through an insurance plan is determinative of patient choice. Essentially, the evidence shows that patients will choose whatever doctors or hospitals are covered by their health plan. Undeniably, although many patients might prefer to be loyal to their doctors, it is, unfortunately, a luxury they can no longer afford. . . . As much as many patients long for the days of old-fashioned and local, if expensive and inefficient, healthcare, recent trends in healthcare management have made the old healthcare model obsolete.

The reality of the situation in our changing healthcare environment may be that Poplar Bluff cannot support two high-quality hospitals. Third-party payers have reaped the benefit of a price war in a small corner of the market for healthcare services in Southeastern Missouri, at the arguable cost of quality to their subscribers. . . . We are mindful that competition is the driving force behind our free enterprise system and that, unless barriers have been erected to constrain the normal operation of the market, a court ought to exercise extreme caution because judicial intervention in a competitive situation can itself upset the balance of market forces, bringing about the very ills the antitrust laws were meant to prevent. This appears to have even more force in an industry, such as healthcare, experiencing significant and profound changes.

Notes: Hospital and Physician Mergers; Managed Care Market Definition

1. *Merger Mania.* "The healthcare industry is buying into the benefits of bigness. Mergers and acquisitions hit a pace of 2.4 per day among all types of providers in the first half of 1996. Among hospitals alone, one deal every three days has occurred in the past $2\frac{1}{2}$ years. . . . All told, about one-fifth of community

hospitals changed hands in 1994 and 1995. . . . We all have heard the rationale: Mergers can end excess capacity. . . . Economies of scale can cut costs further. Meanwhile, organizing providers can facilitate better patient care. . . . Many people think that's bunk. Consolidation is a defensive strategy, they say. Companies hope market share equals leverage with the enemy, be it a hospital, drug company or HMO. . . . Consumer advocates are particularly vehement, attacking deals for making millionaires out of executives and stockholders. 'Efficiency for who? It's greed for the guys at the top,' said Ralph Nader." Lisa Scott, Will We Like Tomorrow's Giants?, Modern Healthcare, Aug. 5, 1996, at 79.

Commenting on these trends, Prof. Greaney has this to say:

> Segments of the judiciary are openly hostile toward applying traditional competition concepts to the health care sector . . . [and so] have dealt a number of important setbacks to government agencies and private plaintiffs litigating antitrust matters. A close examination of these cases reveals an admixture of factors ranging from plain judicial error, to subtle changes in legal doctrine, to a shifting jurisprudence that is increasingly deferential to professionalism in health market interactions. An undercurrent has been that a backlash against managed care has contributed to decisions that shield providers from the antitrust laws.
>
> The unfavorable reception to antitrust cases in court appears to have had a corresponding chilling effect upon federal enforcement efforts. The DOJ has filed only three health care antitrust cases in federal court since 1998 (one involving the manufacture of false teeth), and the FTC has redirected much of its enforcement agenda toward the pharmaceutical industry. Cases involving serious misconduct have resulted in mild civil sanctions rather than criminal prosecutions, and the overall level of investigatory and advisory activity appears to have declined. . . .
>
> The most pronounced change in the law has been in merger enforcement. . . . The box score for government enforcement is telling. Between 1984 and 1994 the FTC and DOJ won five of six cases challenging hospital mergers decided on the merits. Many others were settled by consent decree or abandoned after government inquiries spotlighted potential antitrust claims. Recently, however, the tide has turned: Since 1995 federal and state enforcers have lost all seven cases litigated in federal court. . . . [T]he government's failures in court have undoubtedly encouraged consolidation across the health care industry. Because they may supply precedent on issues such as market definition, the hospital merger decisions are likely to have a profound impact in other areas of antitrust concern such as physician consolidation, network formation, and restraints of trade. Experienced attorneys giving advice to physicians and hospitals see a judicial imprimatur for consolidation. As one practitioner put it, the cases "make almost any merger worth trying."

Thomas L. Greaney, Whither Antitrust? The Uncertain Future of Competition Law in Health Care, 21(2) Health Aff. 185 (Mar. 2002) (Copyright (c) 2000, Project HOPE, reprinted with permission).

2. *Enforcement Agencies.* As the *HCA* case illustrates, the Federal Trade Commission (FTC) has been a major force in extending antitrust scrutiny to the health care industry. The Department of Justice (DOJ), however, has scaled back its antitrust enforcement activities in health care.

3. *Joint Ventures and Other Transactions.* Merger analysis and related monopolization charges are not restricted to outright acquisitions. They are also relevant

to a variety of contractual networks and joint venture arrangements. Consider, for instance, the applicability of the *Tenet* analysis to a sole community hospital's formation of a joint venture with its medical staff to enter into managed care contracts with insurers and employers, or a joint venture between the only two hospitals in town to purchase and share the town's only MRI scanner. The DOJ/FTC Antitrust Enforcement Guidelines, quoted above at page 524, create safe harbors of either 20 or 30 percent market share for physician networks depending on whether the physician affiliations are exclusive or nonexclusive. The product market is defined in terms of the number of physicians practicing in the specialty. The Guidelines also observe that joint ventures between competitors to purchase expensive high tech equipment have never been challenged by the agencies and are not likely to be if efficiency justifications can be given for cost-sharing. In addition, a number of states have regulatory review processes designed to approve such joint ventures in a fashion that will likely invoke immunity from federal antitrust laws. James Blumstein, Health Care Reform and Competing Visions of Medical Care: Antitrust and State Provider Cooperative Legislation, 79 Cornell L. Rev. 1459 (1994). However, in one notable decision, the Eleventh Circuit held that a dominant hospital monopolized the market for "durable medical equipment" (wheelchairs, oxygen equipment, and other items used in patients' homes) by entering into a joint venture with one equipment supplier and then having the hospitals' nurses steer its patients to that supplier when they left the hospital. Key Enterprises v. Venice Hospital, 919 F.2d 1550 (11th Cir. 1990).

4. *Geographic Markets.* In contrast with *Tenet*'s treatment of the geographic market definition, Judge Posner had the following to say about a proposed merger of two of the three hospitals in Rockford, Illinois:

> It is always possible to take pot shots at a market definition (we have just taken one), and the defendants do so with vigor and panache. Their own proposal, however, is ridiculous — a ten-county area in which it is assumed (without any evidence and contrary to common sense) that Rockford residents, or third-party payors, will be searching out small, obscure hospitals in remote rural areas if the prices charged by the hospitals in Rockford rise above competitive levels. . . . For highly exotic or highly elective hospital treatment, patients will sometimes travel long distances, of course. But for the most part hospital services are local. People want to be hospitalized near their families and homes, in hospitals in which their own — local — doctors have hospital privileges.

United States v. Rockford Memorial Corp., 898 F.2d 1278 (7th Cir. 1990). See Mark Glassman, Can HMOs Wield Market Power?, 46 Am. U. L. Rev. 91 (1996); T. Greaney, Night Landings on an Aircraft Carrier: Hospital Mergers and Antitrust Law, 23 Am. J.L. & Med. 191 (1997); Jack Zwanziger et al., Hospitals and Antitrust: Defining Markets, Setting Standards, 10 J. Health Pol. Pol'y & L. 423 (1994).

5. *Product Market Definition.* The second aspect of market determination is defining the relevant product. Although *Tenet* did not contest the issue, how was the product market defined in that case and how might it have differed? Compare *Rockford Memorial*, supra:

> If you need a kidney transplant, or a mastectomy, or if you have a stroke or a heart attack or a gunshot wound, you will go (or be taken) to an acute-care hospital for

inpatient treatment. The fact that for other services you have a choice between inpatient care at such a hospital and outpatient care elsewhere places no check on the prices of the services we have listed. . . . If you need your hip replaced, you can't decide to have chemotherapy instead because it's available on an outpatient basis at a lower price. . . . Hospitals can and do distinguish between the patient who wants a coronary bypass and the patient who wants a wart removed from his foot; these services are not in the same product market merely because they have a common provider.

Consider also how physician markets should be defined: in terms of all physicians and alternative practitioners combined, or divided by specialities, and then which specialities? The DOJ/FTC Guidelines treat each practice specialty as a distinct market, but they fail to define what constitutes a specialty and how narrowly it might be drawn. Consider, for instance, Morgenstern v. Wilson, 29 F.3d 1291 (8th Cir. 1994), where the court overturned an order dissolving a physician practice group that the jury found had monopolized the adult cardiac surgery market in Lincoln, Nebraska. Surprisingly, the court did not object to the narrow *product* market definition, but instead found that the *geographic* market included Omaha 60 miles away. Although few Lincoln patients actually went there for heart surgery, the court saw no reason they should not be willing to if necessary. In HTI Health Services v. Quorum Health Group, 960 F. Supp. 1104 (S.D. Miss. 1997), the court lumped together GPs, family practitioners, and internal medicine physicians into a single market for primary care but recognized separate markets for pediatrics and obstetrics, among others. The court allowed the two largest physician groups in a smaller town to merge, despite the fact they controlled from 60 to 100 percent of these various market segments, reasoning that there were few barriers to entry by new physicians and that physicians should not be forced to work by themselves just because they live in a smaller town.

6. *Insurance Markets.* Consider how the issues might differ when antitrust cases involve insurers rather than providers. For instance, would HMOs constitute a market separate from indemnity insurance? See U.S. Healthcare v. Healthsource, 986 F.2d 589 (1st Cir. 1992) (no); Blue Cross & Blue Shield United of Wisconsin v. Marshfield Clinic, 65 F.3d 1406 (7th Cir. 1995) (no). Since indemnity insurers compete nationally and need no special contract with physicians to set up shop locally, does this mean that all managed care insurance markets are national in scope? According to some courts, market share is defined not only by *existing* competitors but also by *potential* competitors. See Ball Memorial Hospital v. Mutual Hospital Insurance Co., 784 F.2d 1325 (7th Cir. 1986). However, state insurance regulation might be viewed as a barrier to insurers easily crossing state lines.

7. *Natural Monopolies.* Observe that market share statistics are not the sole consideration. A merger even in a highly concentrated market is unlikely to lessen competition and, indeed, might help competition if one or both of the hospitals would not survive financially without the merger, or if a merged hospital would offer better service at lower cost. These arguments are known as the "failing firm" defense and the "efficiencies" defense. Although *Tenet* did not find that these arguments were sustained as affirmative defenses, the court did note that "the reality of the situation . . . may be that Poplar Bluff cannot support two high-quality hospitals."

This suggests the presence of "natural monopoly" conditions. In line with this thinking, the DOJ/FTC Antitrust Enforcement Guidelines establish a safe harbor for mergers between two hospitals, no matter how small the market, where one has fewer than 100 beds and 40 patients a day. Arguing for a much more extensive application to hospitals of the natural monopoly defense, see Dayna Matthew, Doing What Comes Naturally: Antitrust Law and Hospital Mergers, 31 Hous. L. Rev. 813 (1994). For a differing view, see Erwin Blackstone & Joseph Fuhr, Hospital Mergers and Antitrust: An Economic Analysis, 14 J. Health Pol. Pol'y & L. 383 (1989).

8. *Are Nonprofits Different?* For a time, it was disputed whether the FTC has jurisdiction over nonprofit entities, due to the wording of the FTC's governing statute. Although the Supreme Court rejected this argument as an absolute defense in *California Dental Ass'n*, supra, the substance of the argument sometimes surfaces when nonprofit hospitals argue they are not likely to abuse market power since they are not driven by a profit motive. See Comment, 52 Vand. L. Rev. 557 (1999). On this score, one district relied heavily on the difference in nonprofit governance in approving the merger of the two dominant hospitals in a medium-sized town (Grand Rapids). The court observed that having community and business leaders on the nonprofit hospital board dampens the incentive to raise prices, and it pointed to research that markets dominated by nonprofit hospitals have lower prices. The court concluded:

> In the real world, hospitals are in the business of saving lives, and managed care organizations are in the business of saving dollars. Managed care organizations' interest in maintaining a competitive edge cannot be allowed to trump either hospitals' conscientious endeavors to continue to provide comprehensive, high quality health care . . . or the consumer public's right to receive the same. Permitting defendant hospitals to achieve the efficiencies of scale that would clearly result from the proposed merger would enable the . . . combined entity to continue the quest for establishment of world-class health facilities in West Michigan, a course the Court finds clearly and unequivocally would ultimately be in the best interests of the consumer public as a whole.

FTC v. Butterworth Health Corp., 946 F. Supp. 1285 (W.D. Mich. 1996), *aff'd*, 121 F.3d 708 (6th Cir. 1997). However, in the *Rockford* case discussed above, the court reasoned to the contrary:

> [T]he defendants contend that they have no incentive to act anti-competitively because . . . monopoly profits garnered by a not-for-profit company cannot be distributed to anyone, let alone corporate decisionmakers. Instead, any excess of revenues over expense must be farmed back into the firm's operation. . . . The court rejects the defendants' narrow view as to the motivation behind anti-competitive action. . . . The not-for-profit decisionmaker may desire more money for a new piece of equipment or to hire a new specialist or for a better office, salary or title, or just to keep the firm afloat in particularly lean or dangerous times. . . . Simply put, decisionmakers need not be solely interested in the attainment of profit to act anti-competitively."

717 F. Supp. 1284.

9. *Is the FTC Right After All?* Do you agree with Prof. Greaney's criticism of the *Tenet* decision and other courts that have reversed the FTC? What do you think of the court's characterization of the impact of managed care on patient loyalty? Compare this with what the Supreme Court had to say in *California Dental Ass'n*, at page 347. See also William G. Kopit, Price Competition in Hospital Markets: The Significance of Managed Care, 35 J. Health L. 291, 319 (2002) ("The assertions [in *Tenet*] in support of the defendant's market definition are completely without factual support").

Notice the *Tenet* court's description of hospitals in the neighboring Cape Girardeau refusing to contract with managed care plans, at least for a time. There are increasing reports that this is happening around the country, even in metropolitan areas. Hospitals that control a significant share of the market have learned that when push comes to shove, insurers will often back down and give in to demands for higher rates. Insurers often feel they can't afford to have major gaps in their networks because employers, especially larger ones, look for insurers that cover most doctors and hospitals in the area. In recent rounds of negotiations, this has produced double-digit increases in hospital rates, which has fueled a resurgence in health care inflation. Barbara Martinez, With New Muscle, Hospitals Squeeze Insurers on Rates, Wall St. J., Mar. 12, 2002, at A1. See Kelly Devers et al., Hospitals' Negotiating Leverage with Health Plans: How and Why Has It Changed?, _____ Health Serv. Res. _____ (2003); Gregory Vistnes, Is Managed Care Leading to Consolidation in Health-Care Markets?, 37 Health Serv. Res. 595 (2002). In 2002, the FTC began to investigate the effects of selected mergers on hospital prices, including the merger in *Tenet*.

Coupled with increased market power is a regulatory requirement in most states that managed care plans maintain adequate hospital and physician networks (both primary care and specialists) in each county where they do business. At an extreme, having a major gap in the network may mean giving up a license to sell the product in certain counties. More commonly, however, regulators allow managed care plans to continue doing business but require them to pay non-network providers their full, non-discounted rates if the local network does not have adequate capacity for the number of people enrolled locally. Therefore, regulators constrain the ability of HMOs to send people long distances for care. Also, providers in some states realize that if insurers call their bluff and refuse to contract without deep discounts, the provider might be even better off financially.

Problem: Rural Hospital Merger*

Rural County has a population of 15,000, a small primary care hospital, and ten physicians, including seven general and family practitioners, an obstetrician, a pediatrician, and a general surgeon. All the physicians are solo practitioners. The nearest urban area is about 60 miles away in Big City, which has a population of 300,000, and three major hospitals to which patients from Rural County are referred or transferred for higher levels of hospital care. However, Big City is too far away for most residents of Rural County to use for services available in Rural County.

*This problem is excerpted directly from the DOJ/FTC antitrust guidelines.

Insurance Company, which operates throughout the state, is attempting to offer "managed care" programs in all areas of the state, and has asked the local physicians in Rural County to form an IPA to provide services under the program to covered persons living in the county. No other managed care plan has attempted to enter the county previously.

Initially, two of the general practitioners and two of the specialists express interest in forming a network, but Insurance Company says that it intends to market its plan to the larger local employers, who need broader geographic and specialty coverage for their employees. Consequently, Insurance Company needs more of the local general practitioners and the one remaining specialist in the IPA in order to provide adequate geographic, specialty, and backup coverage to subscribers in Rural County. Eventually, four of the seven general practitioners and the one remaining specialist join the IPA and agree to provide services to Insurance Company's subscribers under contracts providing for capitation. While the physicians' participation in the IPA is structured to be nonexclusive, no other managed care plan has yet entered the local market or approached any of the physicians about joining a different provider panel. In discussing the formation of the IPA with the Insurance Company, a number of the physicians have made clear their intention to continue to practice outside the IPA and have indicated they would be interested in contracting individually with other managed care plans when those plans expand into Rural County. Insurance Company requests your legal advice about whether this network formation is likely to be challenged by the federal government.

E. REFERRAL FEE LAWS

Many of the transactions and relationships surveyed in this chapter are affected by an entirely different set of laws that happen to be motivated by the same concerns about excess commercialization and distorting incentives: the collection of federal and state laws that prohibit or regulate referral fees. By referral fees, we mean explicit or implicit incentives to generate or refer medical business. These referral fee laws are unfortunately but unavoidably complex, and they have effects that permeate the medical enterprise. They are taken very seriously by lawyers, doctors, and institutions because their violation can result in denial of payment, inability to enforce contracts, or even criminal penalties. As you become acquainted with this highly specialized body of law, try first to focus on the gist of what it prohibits and why, and then begin to consider its less obvious applications and implications.

■ UNITED STATES v. GREBER
760 F.2d 68 (3d Cir. 1985)

Weis, Circuit Judge.

In this appeal, defendant argues that payments made to a physician for professional services in connection with tests performed by a laboratory cannot be the basis of Medicare fraud. We do not agree and hold that if one purpose of the payment was to induce future referrals, the Medicare statute has been violated. . . .

Defendant is an osteopathic physician who is board certified in cardiology. In addition to hospital staff and teaching positions, he was the president of Cardio-Med, Inc., an organization which he formed. The company provides physicians with diagnostic services, one of which uses a Holter-monitor. This device, worn for approximately 24 hours, records the patient's cardiac activity on a tape. A computer operated by a cardiac technician scans the tape, and the data is later correlated with an activity diary the patient maintains while wearing the monitor.

Cardio-Med billed Medicare for the monitor service and, when payment was received, forwarded a portion to the referring physician. The government charged that the referral fee was 40 percent of the Medicare payment, not to exceed $65 per patient.

Based on Cardio-Med's billing practices, counts 18-23 of the indictment charged defendant with having tendered remuneration or kickbacks to the referring physicians in violation of [the Medicare fraud statute]. . . . The proof as to the Medicare fraud counts was that defendant had paid a Dr. Avallone and other physicians "interpretation fees" for the doctors' initial consultation services, as well as for explaining the test results to the patients. There was evidence that physicians received "interpretation fees" even though defendant had actually evaluated the monitoring data. Moreover, the fixed percentage paid to the referring physician was more than Medicare allowed for such services.

The government also introduced testimony defendant had given in an earlier civil proceeding. In that case, he had testified that " . . . if the doctor didn't get his consulting fee, he wouldn't be using our service. So the doctor got a consulting fee." . . .

I. MEDICARE FRAUD

The Medicare fraud statute was amended [in] 1977. Congress, concerned with the growing problem of fraud and abuse in the system, wished to strengthen the penalties to enhance the deterrent effect of the statute. To achieve this purpose, the crime was upgraded from a misdemeanor to a felony. . . . A particular concern was the practice of giving "kickbacks" to encourage the referral of work. Testimony before the congressional committee was that "physicians often determine which laboratories would do the test work for their medicaid patients by the amount of the kickbacks and rebates offered by the laboratory. . . . Kickbacks take a number of forms including cash, long-term credit arrangements, gifts, supplies and equipment, and the furnishing of business machines."

To remedy the deficiencies in the statute and achieve more certainty, the present version of 42 U.S.C. §[1320a-7b(b), Social Security Act §1128B(b)(2)] was enacted. It provides:

> [W]hoever knowingly and willfully offers or pays any remuneration (including any kickback, bribe or rebate) directly or indirectly, overtly or covertly in cash or in kind to induce such person— . . . to purchase, lease, order, or arrange for or recommend purchasing . . . or ordering any . . . service or item for which payment may be made . . . under [Medicare or Medicaid] shall be guilty of a felony.

The district judge instructed the jury that the government was required to prove that Cardio-Med paid to Dr. Avallone some part of the amount received from Medicare; that defendant caused Cardio-Med to make the payment; and did so knowingly and willfully as well as with the intent to induce Dr. Avallone to use Cardio-Med's services for patients covered by Medicare. The judge further charged that even if the physician interpreting the test did so as a consultant to Cardio-Med, that fact was immaterial if a purpose of the fee was to induce the ordering of services from Cardio-Med.

Defendant contends that the charge was erroneous. He insists that absent a showing that the only purpose behind the fee was to improperly induce future services, compensating a physician for services actually rendered could not be a violation of the statute. The government argues that Congress intended to combat financial incentives to physicians for ordering particular services patients did not require.

The language and purpose of the statute support the government's view. Even if the physician performs some service for the money received, the potential for unnecessary drain on the Medicare system remains. The statute is aimed at the inducement factor.

The text refers to "any remuneration." That includes not only sums for which no actual service was performed but also those amounts for which some professional time was expended. "Remunerates" is defined as "to pay an equivalent for service." Webster Third New International Dictionary (1966). By including such items as kickbacks and bribes, the statute expands "remuneration" to cover situations where no service is performed. That a particular payment was a remuneration (which implies that a service was rendered) rather than a kickback, does not foreclose the possibility that a violation nevertheless could exist. . . .

We conclude that the more expansive reading is consistent with the impetus for the 1977 amendments and therefore hold that the district court correctly instructed the jury. If the payments were intended to induce the physician to use Cardio-Med's services, the statute was violated, even if the payments were also intended to compensate for professional services.

■ THE HANLESTER NETWORK v. SHALALA
51 F.3d 1390 (9th Cir. 1995)

TANNER, Senior District Judge.

[The Hanlester Network was formed in the 1987 by a doctor and several investors in order to create a number of limited partnerships to operate clinical laboratories in California. These limited partnerships were marketed as joint venture investments primarily to physicians who were in a position to refer business to the labs. Physicians could buy in for $1,500 each. The labs were staffed and managed under contract with Smithkline BioScience Laboratories, and most of the tests were performed at Smithkline's central facility. In other words, the joint ventures were not used to generate capital to construct or purchase new facilities but only to cover the operational costs of creating the limited partnership entities and contracting with Smithkline. For its services, Smithkline was paid 80 percent of the revenues from tests that it performed under the auspices of the joint ventures, so it bore the primary risk for any operational deficits. The physician investors were paid the remaining 20 percent of revenues regardless of whether there was any net profit. For most physician investors, this produced a return on their investment of at least 50 percent a year.]

... Hanlester was notified by the Inspector General of the Department of Health and Human Services (DHHS) in December 1989 that he had determined that the Hanlester respondents (hereafter referred to as appellants) had violated §1128B(b)(2) of the Social Security Act (the Act) by offering and paying remuneration to physician-investors to induce them to refer laboratory tests to the three Hanlester laboratories ... and that it would be proposed that all of the appellants be excluded from the Medicare and [Medicaid] programs ... for varying periods of time. ...

This is the first instance in which physician self-referral joint ventures have been challenged under the Act, and in which the Act has been applied to arrangements other than kickbacks, bribes, or rebates, as a basis for excluding persons from participation in Medicare/Medicaid programs. Nothing in the language of the statute itself prohibits joint venture arrangements. We must, therefore, look to the legislative history, the Act's purpose and context to determine whether such arrangements violate the statute. ... Both §1128B(b)(1), which prohibits solicitation or receipt of remuneration "in return for" the referral of program-related business, and (b)(2), which proscribes offers or payments of remuneration "to induce" referrals of program-related business, are implicated here. ...

Appellants claim that the statute does not give fair warning of the standards by which their conduct is to be judged. ... These factors militate against finding the anti-kickback statute void for vagueness. The statute regulates only economic conduct. It chills no constitutional rights. While the statute allows for criminal penalties, it requires "knowing and willful" conduct, a requirement which mitigates any vagueness in the statute. ...

The Secretary determined that the phrase "to induce" ... connotes "an intent to exercise influence over the reason or judgment of another in an effort to cause the referral of program-related business." We agree with this interpretation. We now look to the conduct of the parties to determine whether the statute was violated. ...

The Inspector General argued that appellants unlawfully induced referrals in the way in which they marketed the limited partnerships.[14] At the time appellants entered into the management agreements, these types of arrangements were fairly common. Health care joint ventures such as that entered into by appellants were not per se unlawful.[15] The evidence shows that Hanlester desired to comply with the law and structured its business operation in a manner which it believed to be lawful. There is ample evidence that appellants intended to encourage limited partners to refer business to the joint venture laboratories. The appellants offered physicians the opportunity to profit indirectly from referrals when they could not profit directly. Potential partners were told that the success of the limited partnerships depended on referrals from the limited partners. While substantial cash distributions were made to limited partners by the joint venture labs, dividends

---

[14] The marketing strategy was to enlist physician investors who were in a position to refer substantial quantities of tests to joint venture labs.

[15] [Joint ventures, structured as they are here, are now prohibited, however, by the 1993 statute that follows this case, which is known as the Stark Bill. — EDS.]

were paid to limited partners based on each individual's ownership share of profits, and not on the volume of their referrals. Payments were made to limited partners whether or not they referred business to the joint venture labs.

The fact that a large number of referrals resulted in the potential for a high return on investment, or that the practical effect of low referral rates was failure for the labs, is insufficient to prove that appellants offered or paid remuneration to induce referrals. The conduct of Patricia Hitchcock [vice president of marketing], however, is another matter.

Hanlester told prospective limited partners of the joint venture labs that the private placement memoranda issued for the limited partnerships were the only sales material which could be used in connection with the sale of shares. In spite of this, Ms. Hitchcock implied that eligibility to purchase shares depended on an agreement to refer program-related business; told prospective limited partners that the number of shares they would be permitted to purchase . . . would depend on the volume of business that they referred to the labs; and stated that partners who did not refer business would be pressured to leave the partnerships. Hitchcock also told potential investors that the partners' return on their investment would be virtually guaranteed. Hitchcock's representations to limited partners constitutes offers of payment to induce referrals of program-related business. . . .

In order to prove that appellants violated the anti-kickback statute, the government must also prove that appellants' conduct was knowing and willful. . . . [T]he Supreme Court has ruled that to establish willfulness, the government must prove that defendants knew their conduct was unlawful. Ratzlaf v. United States, 114 S. Ct. 655, 657 (1994). . . . We construe "knowingly and willfully" in §1128B(b)(2) of the anti-kickback statute as requiring appellants to (1) know that §1128B prohibits offering or paying remuneration to induce referrals, and (2) engage in prohibited conduct with the specific intent to disobey the law. . . .

Patricia Hitchcock's . . . actions reflect both knowledge that her conduct was unlawful, and a specific intent to disobey the law. Her conduct was knowing and willful. Because Hitchcock was acting as an agent for Hanlester and the joint venture labs, these corporate entities may be held vicariously liable for her actions. . . . We find that [the other individual] Appellants . . . did not knowingly and willfully violate subsection (b)(2) of the anti-kickback statute. There is no evidence that [they] either directed or approved of the unauthorized representations made by Patricia Hitchcock in any way. In fact, Ms. Hitchcock's actions were contrary to their directions.

The Inspector General did not prove that any of the individual appellants conditioned the purchase of shares on an agreement to order tests; or that they conditioned the number of shares sold on the amount of business that the physicians agreed to refer; or authorized the ouster of partners who failed to refer business. Therefore, these appellants are not personally liable for the unlawful conduct of Hanlester . . . which resulted from Ms. Hitchcock's unlawful acts. . . .

The Secretary characterized the joint venture labs as "sham" operations which served as mere conduits for the payment of monies to physicians in return for the referral of tests. . . . There is no question that appellants received substantial economic benefit from their relationship with [Smithkline]. In addition to a net profit, appellants received benefits in the form of (1) Smithkine's assumption of the operating risks and management responsibilities for the laboratories and appellants' corresponding relief from those duties, (2) Smithkline's payment of anticipated receipts in advance, and (3) the use of Smithkline's name and reputation as an enticement for enlisting potential limited partners.

The management services agreement between Smithkline and appellants reflects a relatively common practice in the clinical laboratory field. There is no evidence that appellants intended to conceal payments from Smithkline to physicians in return for referrals. The Hanlester appellants believed their conduct to be lawful. The evidence shows that . . . payments actually flowed . . . to Smithkline in the form of fees for its management services. . . . Therefore, the Secretary's finding that [these] appellants "knowingly and willfully" solicited and received remuneration in return for referrals is not supported by substantial evidence. . . .

Based on the foregoing, we affirm the Secretary's conclusion that appellant Hanlester . . . violated subsection (b)(2) of §1128B. We reverse the Secretary's conclusion that any [other] appellants violated [the Act].

■ LIMITATION ON CERTAIN PHYSICIAN REFERRALS
*42 U.S.C. §1395nn**

(a) Prohibition of certain referrals.

(1) In general. Except as provided in subsection (b) of this section, if a physician (or an immediate family member of such physician) has a financial relationship with an entity specified in paragraph (2), then the physician may not make a referral to the entity for the furnishing of designated health services [under Medicare or Medicaid and may not seek payment for such services]. . . .

(2) Financial relationship specified. A financial relationship of a physician (or an immediate family member of such physician) with an entity specified in this paragraph is —

(A) except as provided in subsections (c) and (d) of this section, an ownership or investment interest in the entity [through equity or debt], or

(B) except as provided in subsection (e) of this section, a compensation arrangement between the physician (or an immediate family member of such physician) and the entity. . . .

(b) General exceptions to both ownership and compensation arrangement prohibitions. Subsection (a)(1) of this section shall not apply in the following cases:

(1) Physicians' services. In the case of physicians' services provided personally by (or under the personal supervision of) another physician in the same group practice as the referring physician.

(2) In-office ancillary services. In the case of services . . . that are [billed by and] furnished personally by the referring physician, personally by a physician who is a member of the same group practice as the referring physician, or personally by individuals who are directly supervised by the physician or by another physician in the group practice. . . .

---

*This statute is known as the Stark Bill, after its sponsor, Rep. Pete Stark. It was enacted in 1993.

(c) General exception related only to ownership or investment prohibition for ownership in publicly traded securities and mutual funds. Ownership of the following shall not be considered to be an ownership or investment interest described in subsection (a)(2)(A) of this section: Ownership of investment securities which may be purchased on terms generally available to the public and which are [publicly traded on the stock exchanges] or [are] in a corporation that [has] . . . stockholder equity exceeding $75,000,000. . . .

(d) Additional exceptions related only to ownership or investment prohibition. The following, if not otherwise excepted under subsection (b) of this section, shall not be considered to be an ownership or investment interest described in subsection (a)(2)(A) of this section: . . .

(2) Rural provider. . . . [I]f substantially all of the designated health services furnished by such entity are furnished to individuals residing in [a] rural area.

(3) Hospital ownership. In the case of designated health services provided by a hospital if the referring physician is authorized to perform services at the hospital, and the ownership or investment interest is in the hospital itself (and not merely in a subdivision of the hospital).

(e) Exceptions relating to other compensation arrangements. The following shall not be considered to be a compensation arrangement described in subsection (a)(2)(B) of this section:

(1) Rental of office space; rental of equipment. Payments made by a lessee to a lessor for the use of premises [or equipment] if—

(i) the lease is set out in writing, signed by the parties, and specifies the premises covered by the lease,

(ii) the space [or equipment] rented or leased does not exceed that which is reasonable and necessary for the legitimate business purposes of the lease or rental and is used exclusively by the lessee when being used by the lessee, . . .

(iii) the lease provides for a term of rental or lease for at least one year,

(iv) the rental charges over the term of the lease are set in advance, are consistent with fair market value, and are not determined in a manner that takes into account the volume or value of any referrals or other business generated between the parties,

(v) the lease would be commercially reasonable even if no referrals were made between the parties, and

(vi) the lease meets such other requirements as the Secretary may impose by regulation as needed to protect against program or patient abuse.

(2) Bona fide employment relationships. Any amount paid by an employer to a physician (or an immediate family member of such physician) who has a bona fide employment relationship with the employer for the provision of services if—

(A) the employment is for identifiable services,

(B) the amount of the remuneration under the employment is consistent with the fair market value of the services and is not determined in a manner that takes into account (directly or indirectly) the volume or value of any referrals by the referring physician, [and]

(C) the remuneration is provided pursuant to an agreement which would be commercially reasonable even if no referrals were made to the employer. . . .

(3) Personal service arrangements. [This subsection covers independent contractors, and requires terms that reflect fair market and are unrelated to the volume of services, similar to the two exceptions above for leases and employment. The contract must cover at least 1 year, and must provide for fixed compensation set in advance.] . . .

(5) Physician recruitment. In the case of remuneration which is provided by a hospital to a physician to induce the physician to relocate to the geographic area served by the hospital in order to be a member of the medical staff of the hospital, if the physician is not required to refer patients to the hospital, and the amount of the remuneration under the arrangement is not determined in a manner that takes into account (directly or indirectly) the volume or value of any referrals by the referring physician. . . .

(g) Sanctions. [Medicare and Medicaid services delivered in arrangements that violate this section will not be paid for. Also, a knowing violation can result in the imposition of civil monetary penalties or exclusion from the Medicare and Medicaid programs.]

(h) Definitions and special rules. For purposes of this section: . . .

(1) The term "compensation arrangement" means any arrangement involving any remuneration between a physician . . . and an entity. . . . The term "remuneration" includes any remuneration, directly or indirectly, overtly or covertly, in cash or in kind. . . .

(3) The term "fair market value" means the value in arms length transactions . . . and, in the case of a lease of space, not adjusted to reflect the additional value the prospective lessee or lessor would attribute to the proximity or convenience to the lessor where the lessor is a potential source of patient referrals to the lessee. . . .

(5) . . . [T]he request by a physician for the item or service, . . . [or] the establishment of a plan of care by a physician which includes the provision of the designated health service, . . . constitutes a "referral" by the "referring physician." [The definition then clarifies that no referral occurs when certain specialists such as radiologists or pathologists order their own services or services rendered under their supervision.]

(6) Designated health services. The term "designated health services" means any of the following items or services: clinical laboratory services, physical therapy services, occupational therapy services, radiology services, . . . durable medical equipment and supplies, . . . home health services, . . . outpatient prescription drugs, and inpatient and outpatient hospital services. [Note that this list does not include basic physician services but only specified "ancillary" services. The inclusion of hospital services covers only the facility's services (nursing care, testing, use of operating room, etc.) and not services billed for by physicians.]

■ MAKING SENSE OF REFERRAL FEE STATUTES*
Mark A. Hall
13 J. Health Pol. Pol'y & L. 623 (1988)

Someone uninitiated to the intricacies of health care financing would find it startling to learn that it is potentially a felony punishable by five years imprisonment for a rural hospital to recruit a badly needed specialist to the community, for a doctor to discount his services by waiving insurance deductibles and coinsurance, or for a health care institution to pay its doctors a bonus as a reward for efficient practice. A case can be made that each of these activities falls within the literal terms of the broadly worded Medicare and Medicaid referral fee statute. Enticing a physician to join the medical staff necessarily involves implicit or explicit incentives to refer the physician's patients to that hospital. Price discounts can be characterized as payments to refer one's patients to one's self for treatment. And efficiency bonuses can induce doctors to admit patients to a particular hospital or encourage them to direct patients to a particular insurance plan.

Because these and other absurd applications of the referral fee concept are within a plausible reading of the federal referral fee statute, the statute has been a constant thorn in the side of the health care industry since the 1977 enactment of its current form. However, some relief is now in sight. The Department of Health and Human Services (DHHS) has issued a series of "safe harbor" regulations specifying payment practices that are deemed legal despite their potential referral incentive. 42 C.F.R. §1001.952. The difficulty with these safe harbors is that they identify only a limited list of uncontroversial transactions that are beyond any reproach and so, for the most part, were already considered legal. This generic transactional approach provides little guidance for novel, unanticipated business arrangements that fall outside the narrow safe harbors because it tends to resort to arbitrary distinctions and compromises that are not predictable based on any *a priori* principles. A preferred approach would be for DHHS to issue transaction-specific rulings to individual parties, but it refuses to do so claiming that it lacks statutory authority.[2] A third option, therefore, is to craft its regulations based on a definitional model — one that seeks to redefine the essence of prohibited referral fees in manner that provides some guidance beyond the limited safe harbors. Past interpretations of referral fee statutes suggest two definitional approaches: interpreting these statutes according to their purposes, and prohibiting only fees that are unearned.

Purposes of the referral fee prohibition. Health care attorneys have sometimes sought refuge in an analytical tool that the law customarily uses to shape the meaning of language: construing statutory text according to the purposes of the prohibition. Referral fee statutes are intended to prevent three abuses: ordering unnecessary services, increasing charges for needed services, and influencing with financial considerations the decision of where best to refer a patient. To illustrate

---

* Reprinted with permission. This article has been revised by its author to reflect changes subsequent to its publication. Nevertheless, it discusses only the statute involved in the first two cases above, and not the newer Stark law you just read. The issues covered are very similar, however.

[2] [This was remedied in a 1996 amendment that requires HHS to issue individual advisory rulings. — EDS.]

with the most common target of referral fee prosecutions, a clinical laboratory kickback to doctors who order tests might induce doctors to order unnecessary tests, increase a lab's billings for tests that are necessary, or persuade doctors to send tests to an inferior lab. A common mode of legal analysis is to reason that a particular practice does not violate referral fee statutes if the practice does not conflict with any of the three mentioned purposes, even though the practice falls within the literal language of these sweeping prohibitions.

For example, one might think that the waiver of insurance deductibles and copayments should not be prosecuted because this practice does not result in any increased costs to the government; indeed, it reduces costs for beneficiaries. Likewise, hospital efficiency incentive plans do not increase costs to the government because Medicare now pays hospitals a flat fee per patient that does not vary based on the ordering behavior of physicians. Indeed, such plans reduce costs in the long run by encouraging more efficient practice patterns.

Ultimately, this analysis is not likely to provide much relief. First, on the question of waiving copayments and deductibles, the safe harbor regulation protects only such price discounts by *hospitals and HMOs*, not by doctors. The DHHS reasoned that waiving deductibles and copayments for physician services might result in increased program costs by removing a deterrent to ordering unnecessary treatment.[3] . . . Almost by definition, any arrangement that possesses some referral incentive will have some tendency to increase utilization.

Moreover, "it should be noted that the law does not make increased cost to the government the sole criterion of corruption."[14] Any incentive plan that has a referral aspect in a literal sense will always conflict with at least one of the stated purposes—namely, the potential to influence *where* a patient is referred. Thus, other authorities have viewed as "irrelevant" the fact that the challenged activity "may not have involved an increase in cost."[16] . . .

---

[3] Another source of law relevant to the practice of waiving coinsurance and deductibles are insurance fraud statutes. To illustrate, a dentist who normally charges $100 for a procedure that is reimbursed at 80 percent by dental insurance may agree to waive the $20 copayment required of the patient. "Thus, the argument goes, the dental plan should only be responsible for 80 percent of $80, or $64, and the dentist by submitting a billing to the insurance carrier for $100 is 'overbilling' the carrier by misrepresenting the practitioner's true fee." Oregon Atty. Gen. Opin. No. 5415 (Jan. 18, 1983). See Parrish v. Lamm, 758 P.2d 1356 (Colo. 1988) (upholding constitutionality of statute that makes it a misdemeanor to "abuse health insurance" by routinely waiving deductibles and copayments); M. Lachs et al., The Forgiveness of Coinsurance: Charity or Cheating?, 322 New Eng. J. Med. 1599 (1990); Special Fraud Alert, 59 Fed. Reg. 65,372 (1994).

Insurers have attempted to play a similar game, only with their subscribers, by failing to pass along to subscribers the benefit of price discounts they obtain from providers. Using the example just given, if the nominal fee for a service is $100 but the doctor agrees with the insurer to accept only $80, the insurer would pay the provider only $64 but allow the doctor to bill the patient a full copayment of $20 (20 percent of the full $100). In short, the patient would end up paying a 25 percent copayment ($20 out of $80) without knowing it. Several courts and insurance regulators have declared this practice of secret discounts to be illegal, and insurers (mostly Blue Cross plans) have had to refund hundreds of millions of dollars. See Humana v. Forsyth, 525 U.S. 299 (1999) (holding that these secret discounts can form the basis for a violation of RICO, the federal white-collar crime statute).

[14] United States v. Ruttenberg, 625 F.2d 173, 177 n.9 (7th Cir. 1980).

[16] State v. Abortion Information Agency, Inc. 330 N.Y.S.2d 927, 929 (N.Y. App. Div. 1971), *aff'd* 334 N.Y.S.2d 174 (1972) (upholding an injunction against an abortion agency's negotiating discounts in hospital charges). See Mast v. [State Board of Optometry, 139 Cal. App. 2d 78, 91, 293 P.2d 148 (1956) ("an excessive charge is not an element of the offense").

Observing that any referral incentive entails some chance of increasing costs and influencing the choice of care is not to contend that all referral incentives should be banned. . . . My point is that inflationary and provider-selection incentives are so pervasive that it is impossible to fashion a limiting rule based on their absence.

Earned versus unearned fees. A superior definitional model can be found in state law interpretations of statutes prohibiting physicians from splitting their fees. A classic situation is the rental of hospital space and equipment to in-house pharmacies and radiologists in exchange for a percentage of their gross receipts. Since hospital pharmacies and radiologists obtain their patients from the hospital, these rental payments have the clear potential to induce referrals. California courts and attorney general opinions analyzing this situation under that state's felony statute have developed a penetrating distinction between earned and unearned referral fees:

> When called upon to apply or interpret [the referral fee prohibition], opinions of the [California attorney general] and of the courts concluded that only those arrangements were illegal wherein the consideration paid for the referral was not commensurate with the services rendered or expenses incurred by the receiver, but that no violation occurred where the fee paid reasonably approximated their true value.[17]

Thus, fees incidentally related to a referral are valid if they do not exceed the fair market value of legitimate nonreferral services bargained for at arm's length. Blank v. Palo Alto-Stanford Hospital Center[18] held that a radiologist paying a hospital two-thirds of his receipts does not constitute fee splitting because "the evidence sustains the conclusion that the portion of the fees received was commensurate with the expenses . . . incurred by the hospital in connection with furnishing the diagnostic facilities. . . . Under these circumstances there is no illegality."

Indeed, the analysis could hardly be otherwise. Referral incentives are fundamental to the financial foundation on which the superstructure of traditional medical practice has been erected. Inherent in a fee-for-service method of payment is an incentive to order more treatment — that is, to refer one's patient to oneself. Yet fee-for-service reimbursement, like earned fee splitting, survives a referral fee attack because the fees are (by definition) "for service," not for referral.

Potentially, the earned/unearned distinction neatly resolves the complication of secondary referral incentives incident to legitimate business practices. For instance, the safe harbor regulations allow hospitals to receive payments for space or equipment rental, or to make payments for management services, as long as they are at fair market value, the compensation is unrelated to the volume of referrals generated, and the contract itself is not a reward for referrals. These safe harbors do not cover financial arrangements with physicians for clinical services, however.

The reliability of the earned/unearned distinction outside these narrow safe harbors is cast in doubt by a number of imprecise interpretations of referral fee statutes that appear to treat as irrelevant the earned nature of the payment.

[17] 65 Cal. Atty. Gen. Op. 252, 254 (1982).
[18] 44 Cal. Rptr. 572, 580 (Cal. Dist. Ct. App. 1965).

Currently, the most widely discussed instance is Greber v. United States. . . . However, close attention to the facts of the *Greber* case suggest that the decision may not be as ominous as its reasoning portends. There are strong indications that the "interpretation services" were a bogus front to disguise what was in reality a true kickback scheme. Thus, there is good reason to suspect that the court would not have reached the same result if in fact the fee had been fully earned by legitimate services in a fully disclosed, arm's length relationship.

A helpful way to characterize the controversy is to consider whether an objective or a subjective test should be used to determine the referral nature of a fee. Decisions emphasizing the earned nature of the fee look to the value of and need for the services that generate the fee as an objective test of the claim that the fee is in consideration of only those services. Decisions that consider the earned aspect irrelevant tend to emphasize a state-of-mind test for detecting referral fees. They search for an "intent" to induce referrals and consider irrelevant the presence of nominally legitimate services. An objective test is preferable. Just as it would be inappropriate to determine tax liability based solely on whether a transaction was structured with an eye toward minimizing taxation, the subjective expectation of producing more health care business should not be determinative in referral fee cases.

Even if this distinction could be drawn, though, the earned/unearned distinction is still of limited utility. For this fair market value test to provide a meaningful differentiation from referral fees, surely it must be applied in situations where the service in question derives its value apart from any referrals. The difficulty this presents is that, for many of the most controversial transactions, the value the parties place on their relationship potentially reflects a referral dimension, and no referral-neutral reference point is available in the marketplace from which to assess a pure fair market value. Consider, for instance, a hospital that seeks to recruit badly needed new physicians. Although this may be good for the community, it is also good for the hospital's business. Any "market value" for new physicians surely must reflect, in part, the increased admissions that hospitals expect. Similarly, some hospitals have begun to charge hospital-based specialists such as radiologists and anesthesiologists a fee for the administrative services the hospital provides them in maintaining their practice there (billing, staffing, equipment use, etc.). It is impossible, however, to tell whether this practice management fee contains an implicit referral component that charges these specialists for access to the hospital's patients, since there is no referral-neutral arrangement between hospitals and physicians from which to derive an undistorted fair market value. Accordingly, the DHHS has warned that it considers these hospital access fees to be "reverse kickbacks" in violation of the statute.

At the moment, the most pressing example of the problems in assessing fair market value is the purchase of primary care physician practices by managed care networks. In order to form such networks, it is necessary to pay physicians for acquiring their practices, just as physicians can buy and sell each others' practices. However, such payments typically include not only the cash value of hard assets (equipment, accounts receivables), but also a softer valuation of the physician practice as an ongoing concern. This business valuation includes components such as good will, customer lists, patient records, and employee contracts that are very difficult to quantify objectively or, if valuation is possible, their value derives directly from the future referral of patients. In an informal ruling, the inspector general's office of DHHS opined that "traditional or common methods of economic valuation ... may be expressly barred by the anti-kickback statute. ... [I]t may be necessary to exclude from consideration any amounts which reflect ... the on-going flow of business to the practice. ... Thus, any amount paid in excess of the fair market value of the hard assets of a physician practice would be open to question."[19]

Subsequently, the same official indicated he had overstated his case, but the logic of his position is irrefutable. Under the statute as literally written, even the fair market value test does not resolve many of the most pressing questions of interpretation in a reasonable fashion. Ultimately, then, no one approach provides a workable interpretation of such a sweeping prohibition. A practicing lawyer must examine both the precedents that apply to his particular transaction and the transaction's objective business justification in view of the statute's purpose. Even with these guides, numerous legitimate and socially desirable arrangements will still be cast in doubt. Well-meaning health care lawyers and their clients therefore will continue to function under a threatening climate of illegality until Congress gives DHHS authority, like that under the tax and antitrust laws, to issues rulings on specific transactions undertaken by individual parties.[20] ...

Notes: Referral Fees

1. *Sources of Law.* There are four sources of referral fee prohibitions, two federal and two state. The most threatening is the federal statute discussed in the principal readings. It goes under several names, including the Medicare/Medicaid fraud and abuse statute or the anti-kickback statute. Also of importance is the self-referral legislation — the Stark Bill — which prohibits certain forms of physician investment and compensation. Many states also criminalize referral fees or prohibit physician investments. California's statute has received the most discussion: "[T]he ... receipt or acceptance, by any [physician] of any rebate, refund, commission ... or other consideration, whether in the form of money or otherwise, as compensation or inducement for referring patients ... to any person ... is unlawful ... and is punishable [as a felony]." Cal. Bus. & Prof. Code §650. Finally, state medical practice acts frequently enumerate fee splitting as one of the grounds for revocation or suspension of a physician's license to practice. A typical statute allows disciplinary action by the board of medical examiners for "division of fees ... received for professional services with any person for bringing or referring a patient." D.C. Code Ann. §2-1326(d)(8), (9).

In contrast with these prohibitions of referral incentives is the related prohibition of incentives to *reduce* Medicare or Medicaid services, which is quoted and discussed in Chapter 3.E.3. Also relevant is the False Claims Act, the general criminal statute used to prosecute fraud against the federal government, which is discussed briefly at page 175.

---

[19] Letter from D. McCarty Thornton, Associate Inspector General, to T.J. Sullivan, Associate Chief Counsel, IRS Employee Benefits and Exempt Organizations Division, dated Dec. 22, 1992, *reprinted in* BNA Health L. Rep., Feb. 23, 1993.

[20] [See n.2 supra. — EDS.]

2. *The Stark Bill.* The statute known as the Stark Bill applies to so-called self-referral arrangements in which physicians are rewarded for sending or keeping business in institutions they own, contract with, or are employed by. As a result, the specific arrangements addressed in *Hanlester* are now illegal. What changes in that investment deal would be necessary to comply with Stark?

Representative Stark introduced this law after increased attention to the abuses that result when physicians own or invest in the medical facilities where they practice or to which physicians refer business. This ownership interest in the facility means they profit not only from their own service fees but also from the earnings of the facility. This extra incentive to in essence refer business to themselves causes increased utilization of the facilities. Several studies have shown, for instance, that physicians who own or invest in clinical laboratories or expensive diagnostic equipment such as MRI scanners order from 40 to 100 percent more tests of this nature than do other doctors with similar patients. See Theodore McDowell, Physician Self-Referral Arrangements: Legitimate Business or Unethical "Entrepreneurialism," 15 Am. J.L. & Med. 61 (1989). Rep. Stark's first legislative response was to ban most physician investments in clinical labs. The statute quoted above (known as "Stark II") was expanded in 1993 to regulate all financial relationships between physicians and a host of medical institutions and services. Similar laws now exist in many states. See, e.g., Fla. Stat. Ann. §455.236.

Although the aim of the federal self-referral statute is essentially the same as the fraud and abuse statute, its structure is fundamentally different. First, it is primarily civil, not criminal; the main effect is to disallow payment for medical services in arrangements that violate the statute. Second, it imposes strict liability. Intent to induce referrals is not an element of the violation; all that matters is whether a defined financial relationship exists. Third, this statute does not have the large gray areas of legal uncertainty that plague the other legislation; under the self-referral statute, you are either on base or you are out. This statute replaces ambiguity with complexity, however. It begins by pulling within its scope virtually all financial relationships (including employment) between physicians and medical institutions, and then uses a series of intricate definitions and exceptions to protect those that are allowable.

3. *Separating the Wheat from the Chaff.* Is it possible in a health care system as complex as ours to intelligently regulate which potentially distorting incentives are allowable and which are not? See David Frankford, Creating and Dividing the Fruits of Collective Economic Activity: Referrals Among Health Care Providers, 89 Colum. L. Rev. 1861, 1937 (1989) ("laws like [this] are absolutely incapable of logically defining, much less policing against, inflated prices. [T]hey fail even to create a language for comprehensible debate. They simply obfuscate the issues."). Is any kind of physician payment incentive completely beyond reproach? Even straight salary has the perverse effect of inducing physicians to spend less time with patients or to make excessive referrals to other doctors. Consider the following from the prestigious Institute of Medicine's influential report on For-Profit Enterprise in Health Care 153 (B. Gray ed., 1986):

All compensation systems — from fee-for-service to capitation or salary — present some undesirable incentives for providing too many services, or too few. No system will work without some degree of integrity, decency, and ethical commitment on the part of professionals. Inevitably, we must presume some underlying professionalism that will constrain the operation of unadulterated self-interest.

Realizing this, could it be dangerous to single out individual incentives from the overall mix of counteracting incentives and regulate each one (or only some of them) in isolation? Even unadulterated referral fees might be beneficial if they are used to counteract the incentive that general practitioners have to not refer patients to specialists when needed. Mark Pauly, The Ethics and Economics of Kickbacks and Fee Splitting, 10 Bell J. Econ. 344 (1974) ("it is possible for fee splitting to offer incentives which actually improve patient welfare"). Dr. Arnold S. Relman, editor of the New England Journal of Medicine, would respond:

> The situation is different when physicians seek income beyond fee for service and make business arrangements with other providers of services to their patients. Such arrangements introduce a new and unnecessary conflict, which strains the physician's fiduciary commitment to the patient. Unlike the conflicts of interest in the fee-for-service system, these new arrangements are usually not fully disclosed to the patient, and therefore are more difficult to control.

Dealing with Conflicts of Interest, 313 New Eng. J. Med. 749, 750 (1985). Do the rule of necessity and the absence of disclosure justify felony imprisonment? For a rebuttal to Relman, see Mark A. Hall, Institutional Control of Physician Behavior, 137 U. Penn. L. Rev. 431, 493 (1988). For additional discussion of the proper role of financial incentives in medical decisionmaking, see Bradford Gray, Profit Motive and Patient Care: The Changing Accountability of Doctors and Hospitals (1991); Mark A. Hall, Making Medical Spending Decisions (1997); Marc Rodwin, Medicine, Money & Morals (1993); David Frankford, Managing Medical Clinicians' Work Through the Use of Financial Incentives, 29 Wake Forest L. Rev. 71 (1994).

4. *General Tests for Legality.* Following *Greber*, the First and Ninth Circuits adopted the same broad interpretation of the federal statute, dashing the hopes of those who initially read that decision as aberrational. United States v. Bay State Ambulance and Hospital Rental Service, 874 F.2d 20 (1st Cir. 1989); United States v. Kats, 871 F.2d 105 (9th Cir. 1989). However, the First Circuit made a conviction at least marginally more difficult by requiring a showing that there be a "primary" rather than merely an "incidental" purpose to induce referrals.

Under either test, aren't all hospital medical staffs inherently illegal, considering that the main reason hospitals grant admitting privileges is to generate patient admissions? In exchange, physicians receive the economic benefit of free access to the hospital, an implicit form of in-kind "remuneration." On the other hand, if physicians were charged for their hospital privileges, those who receive referrals from the hospital might be in violation of the statute.

Is it comforting that federal prosecutors simply overlook the fact that so many accepted and socially beneficial relationships in the health care industry potentially violate a felony statute? Federal officials maintain that the statute's overbreadth is not as threatening as the industry complains because prosecutorial discretion has been used to attack only truly abusive arrangements. Professor Blumstein provides a colorful metaphor for this legal state of affairs:

> [T]he modern American healthcare industry is akin to a speakeasy — conduct that is illegal is rampant and countenanced by law enforcement officials because the law is so out of sync with the conventional norms and realities of the marketplace. . . . This poses a formidable civil liberties concern as prosecutors exercise enormous prosecutorial discretion, which is subject to abuse.

The Fraud and Abuse Statute in an Evolving Healthcare Marketplace: Life in the Health Care Speakeasy, 22 Am. J.L. & Med. 205 (1996).

5. *Scienter*. Federal prosecutors, for their part, are frustrated with the *Hanlester* court's adoption of an extremely demanding scienter requirement, which will make it much harder to convict in cases of serious abuse. All the defendant has to do is establish reasonable doubt about his actual knowledge of the law.

Do you think the *Hanlester* court wanted to make prosecution difficult in order to counteract the statute's overbreadth? Realize that, under the statute, the government could have sought felony criminal convictions, not just exclusion from Medicare, and could have prosecuted the physician investors as well as the joint venture promoters.

As actually applied in *Hanlester*, was the scienter test as purely subjective as it sounds? What evidence was there about the actual state of mind of the various defendants? Could the court's holding be justified under the more objective test developed in Hall's article? Shouldn't it be enough to show knowledge and intent that a payment will induce a referral, without showing specific knowledge that such conduct is illegal? Further clarification comes from the Supreme Court's subsequent decision in Bryan v. United States, 524 U.S. 184 (1998). Although *Bryan* arose under a different criminal statute, the Court held that "as a general matter, when used in the criminal context, a 'willful' act is one undertaken with a 'bad purpose,'" which the Court defined to mean acting "with an evil-meaning mind" and "with knowledge that [the] conduct was unlawful." However, it is not necessary to show knowledge of the precise statutory provision in question. See generally Douglas Blair, The "Knowingly and Willfully" Continuum of the Anti-Kickback Statute's Scienter Requirement: Its Origins, Complexities, and Most Recent Judicial Developments, 8 Ann. Health L. 1 (1999); Note, 50 Vand. L. Rev. 1029 (1997); Note, 91 Nw. U. L. Rev. 413 (1996).

Highlighting the dilemma that lawyers face in giving advice under these ambiguous laws, in Kansas the U.S. Attorney prosecuted two lawyers who drafted agreements under which a hospital paid physicians to manage nursing home patients, an arrangement that was found to be a criminal violation of the anti-kickback statute. United States v. Lahue, 261 F.3d 993 (9th Cir. 2001). The prosecutor presented evidence that some of the physicians overbilled Medicare and solicited kickbacks for recruiting patients. However, in dismissing the case against the lawyers, the trial judge ruled (March 9, 1999) that they tried in good faith to structure an arrangement that they thought complied with the law, and they should not be faulted for technical failures or other people's hidden motivations, considering the complexity, ambiguity, and evolving nature of this law. See

Stuart M. Gerson & Jennifer E. Gladieux, Advice of Counsel: Eroding Confidentiality in Federal Health Care Law, 51 Ala. L. Rev. 163 (1999); Frances Makuch & Philip Pomerance, Counseling a Suspect Healthcare Client: Some Thoughts on a Lawyer's Ethical Duties in the Wake of US v. Anderson, 27(6) Health L. Dig. 3 (June 1999).

6. *Qui Tam Suits.* In addition to government enforcement through criminal or regulatory actions, the federal False Claims Act (enacted following the Civil War) authorizes what are known as "qui tam" actions, where private citizens act as deputized attorneys general to recoup losses caused by fraud against the government. These actions can be brought by anyone who knows about the fraud, even if they have not suffered injury. As a reward, they receive 15 to 25 percent of any recovery. In the view of one court, violations of the referral fee statutes give rise to a qui tam action even though the services billed to the government were medically appropriate. United States ex rel. Pogue v. American Healthcare, Inc., 914 F. Supp. 1507 (M.D. Tenn. 1996); *contra* United States ex rel. Thompson v. Columbia/HCA Healthcare Corp., 125 F.3d 899 (5th Cir. 1997) (the false claims statute requires a claim for payment that is literally false, not simply one that is technically illegal). Under the Stark law, the case for "false claims" is stronger since that statute explicitly disallows payment for services rendered in violation of the statute's terms. As a consequence, every disappointed business partner, disgruntled employee, patient or lawyer is a potential bounty hunter under the referral fee statutes. See Pamela Bucy, Civil Prosecution of Health Care Fraud, 30 Wake Forest L. Rev. 693 (1995); Dana Matthew, Tainted Prosecution of Tainted Claims, 73 Ind. L.J. 525 (2001); Patricia Meador & Elizabeth Warren, The False Claims Act: A Civil War Relic Evolves into a Modern Weapon, 65 Tenn. L. Rev. 455 (1998); T. O'Neil et al., The Buck Stops Here: Preemption of Third-party Claims by The False Claims Act, 12 J. Contemp. Health L. & Pol'y 41 (1995); John Ruhnka et al., Qui Tam Claims: Threat to Voluntary Compliance Programs in Health Care Organizations, 25 J. Health Pol. Pol'y & L. 283 (2000); Symposium, Health Care Fraud: Past, Present and Future, 51 Ala. L. Rev. 1 (1999); Comment, 18 J. Contemp. Health L. & Policy 543 (2002); Note, 9 J.L. & Health 163 (1994).

7. *Safe Harbors and Particular Transactions.* New safe harbors under the fraud and abuse statute are periodically adopted or proposed. 42 C.F.R. §1001.952. Among the more important ones not mentioned in the main readings are safe harbors covering physician recruitment, space rental, management contracts, price discounts, certain joint ventures, and physician investments in certain health care entities. These are very similar to the various exceptions contained in the Stark Bill. More fundamental is a 1999 safe harbor to protect providers who practice under capitation and other "at risk" incentives that discourage overutilization. Also, DHHS now is required to issue rulings on individual transactions under the anti-kickback statute (but not under the Stark law).

Two rulings that have caused considerable difficulty for contractual arrangements in widespread use question the legality of management services organizations (MSOs) or physician practice management companies (PPMCs) in which physicians pay a management fee for running their business operations, calculated as a percentage of net profits or revenues. Because of the incentive this creates to drum up business, the DHHS Office of Inspector General, and the Florida Board of Medicine, have each ruled these arrangements entail illegal referral fees or fee splitting. However, the Florida Board of Medicine issued a subsequent ruling in August 1999 that approved a practice management contract in which the management fee is capped at a reasonable ceiling calculated to reward the company for its office management efforts as opposed to being an open-ended incentive to bring in more business. See Richard O. Jacobs & Elizabeth Goodman, Splitting Fees or Splitting Hairs? Fee Splitting and Health Care — The Florida Experience, 8 Ann. Health L. 239 (1999).

Many of the advisory rulings under the federal anti-kickback statute have been equally conservative. For instance, in one ruling, DHHS stated that hospitals may not restock ambulance supplies for free since this might act as an inducement to bring patients to one emergency room rather than another, and in another ruling, it said that an ambulance company may not give nursing homes a discount on some of their patients for fear this might induce nursing homes to refer other, non-discounted patients to the ambulance company. Also, the DHHS ruled that it is potentially illegal for a hospice to offer free services to terminally ill patients who do not have insurance coverage. Some rulings have been more permissive. One approved a joint venture arrangement in which physicians own or invest in an outpatient surgery clinic. Nevertheless, this ruling was limited to surgery because the facility fee is only a small fraction of the procedure fee that surgeons earn regardless of their investment in the facility; therefore, having a stake in the facility fee creates very little added incentive to perform more surgeries. This contrasts with investments by primary care physicians in diagnostic facilities, in which the opposite is the case: the ordinary physician fee is much smaller than the facility fee.

The self-referral statute has some surprising effects that are not apparent from the portions quoted above. One is that, when hospitals buy physician practices, they may not pay the purchase price in installments because repeated payments create a prohibited "financial relationship" whereas a one-time payment does not, and there is no exception stated for practice buy-outs. The self-referral law creates the most complexity with respect to physicians' compensation within their own practice groups. Observe that the statute covers ordinary employment by a physician group. Although the employment exception is available, it does not allow for the "productivity bonuses" that are common forms of payment within a group. To the extent such productivity measures include ancillary services covered by the statute, they would be in direct proportion to the volume of referral services and therefore illegal — except for another special exception not quoted above that applies to group practices. This raises further complexities around the intricate definition of "group practice." The key question is whether physicians must all practice at one site, or instead whether the law authorizes the formation of so-called clinics without walls, that is, physicians in far flung locations who claim to practice as a group. As currently written and interpreted, there are few restrictions on these looser physician groups as long as most of each physician's billings go through a single group account and ancillary services are performed on premises under the member physicians' supervision. However, some types of productivity bonuses that were common within physician groups are now illegal. These issues are likely to receive further attention in the future.

Various technical clarifications and refinements to the Stark law are contained in a very large proposed rule, 63 Fed. Reg. 1659 (Jan. 9, 1998), and partial final rule, 66 Fed. Reg. 856 (Jan. 4, 2001). For a summary and analysis see Maria Morrison, An Analysis of the Stark II Proposed Rule, 67 UMKC L. Rev. 613 (1999); Albert Shay & Gary Francesconi, Proposed Stark II Rules: Clarification or More Confusion?, 31 Health Hosp. L. 95 (1998); Albert Shay & Gary Francesconi, Stark Final Rule (Phase I) Gets Mixed Reviews, 34 J. Health L. 187 (2001).

For additional description and analysis of the safe harbors and the exceptions to the self-referral statute, as well as the effect these statutes have on contemporary business arrangements, see Thomas Mayo, State Illegal-Remuneration and Self-Referral Laws (1996); Douglas A. Blair, The New Proposed Safe Harbors for Certain Managed Care Plans and Risk-Sharing Arrangements, 9 Health Matrix 37 (1999); Donn Herring, The ASC Safe Harbor: The Triumph of Public Policy over Legal Consistency, 33 J. Health L. 485 (2000); C.J. Williams, Toward a Comprehensive Health Care Anti-Kickback Statute, 64 UMKC L. Rev. 291 (1995); Note, 87 Geo. L.J. 499 (1998); Note, 19 J. Corp. L. 313 (1994); Note, 73 N.C. L. Rev. 293 (1994); Note, 81 Geo. L.J. 167 (1992); Comment, 30 San Diego L. Rev. 161 (1993); Comment, 13 J. Leg. Med. 521 (1992).

8. *Impact on Organizational Form.* Professor Frankford, supra, argues that the referral fee prohibition distorts health care institutional arrangements by concentrating more power within medical institutions. This is because "referrals" do not occur within institutions, only between them, and the safe harbors are more protective of larger than smaller institutions. In short, there is less legal exposure if health care institutions grow to absorb more physicians and sources of payment. 89 Colum. L. Rev. 1861. In this regard, referral fee laws might be seen as an unnatural stimulus for fully integrated delivery systems.

Observe, also, that the referral law's bias toward complete integration is at odds with the corporate practice of medicine doctrine, which prohibits physician employment, and it is in tension with tax exemption law that imposes greater scrutiny when doctors are "insiders." Also, the safe harbors protect physician ownership in for-profit entities, but have no equivalent protection for physicians who are insiders in nonprofits, which discourages adoption of the nonprofit form.

9. *Impact on Managed Care.* Professor Blumstein, supra, observes that these laws also threaten various contractual arrangements that are transitional states between no integration and full integration. Casting into doubt the financial relationships that exist in partially or "virtually" integrated models (such as hospital/physician joint ventures and physician office management contracts) makes the movement toward full integration more difficult. Health care lawyers and policy analysts complain, however, that the referral fee prohibition makes no sense in the context of prospective or capitated payment systems because it was meant only to address the abuses of fee-for-service reimbursement. In response, DHHS adopted additional safe harbors to protect providers who are subject to HMO-type incentive payments that discourage excess costs. Nevertheless, it is clear that these new payment systems create their own concerns about abuse in the opposite direction, that of underservice, which is addressed by related legislation discussed in Chapter 3.E.3.

10. *A Look Back.* Look back over this chapter as well as Chapter 3 to observe the many ways in which federal and state regulation of health care fail to achieve a coordinated and purposeful public policy. One searching for imperfections might justifiably assert that health care corporate and regulatory law suffers from each of the following pathologies:

- ERISA unthinkingly creates a regulatory vacuum that is only erratically filled by state insurance regulation.
- State corporate practice of medicine law is anachronistic and unpredictable.
- State insurance regulation fails to achieve a level playing field between traditional and innovative forms of health care delivery, and confuses consumer protection with provider protection.
- Tax exemption law discourages the formation of nonprofit HMOs and is too lenient on hospitals.
- Fraud and abuse law deters legitimate ventures and fails to see that incentives in a fee-for-service era are fundamentally different than those in a prepaid or capitation era.
- The details of each of these particular bodies of law point in inconsistent directions on fundamental questions such as how tightly integrated financing and delivery systems should be and the proper role of physicians in their ownership and management.

In your view, are these hypothetical criticisms valid?

Problem: Medicare/Medicaid Fraud and Abuse

You are outside counsel to the Marcus Welby Healthcare Corporation, which among its other operations owns a durable medical equipment (DME) subsidiary, which sells equipment for home use such as crutches, wheelchairs, and oxygen concentrators. You learn that the subsidiary has had certain business practices about which you have some question under the Medicare and Medicaid Anti-Fraud and Abuse provisions:

- Salesmen regularly offer home health agency employees a "premium" whenever their clients order DME from the subsidiary.
- The subsidiary offers "rebates" to patients who use its equipment.
- The subsidiary pays hospital and home health agency personnel for assisting its patients in learning how to use its products.
- Some arterial blood gas test results may have been "massaged a bit" by the DME in order to facilitate Medicare payment for oxygen concentrators.

What advice would you give?

Problem: Reverse Referral Fees

You are outside counsel to the Marcus Welby Healthcare Corporation (MWHC), which is concerned that expenses in some of its ancillary departments are causing it to lose money under Medicare and HMO insurance. It would like to start charging its hospital-based physicians for some of the costs of running their departments. Its current relationship with these physicians is one in which they have exclusive contracts to work in these departments, but no money changes hands between them. The hospital handles all billing, staffing, and overhead, but it bills separately for facility charges versus professional fees, and the physicians keep all the professional fees the hospital collects on their behalf. This is the standard practice in the industry. MWHC has the following suggestions for changing this arrangement:

- Have the radiology group pay for services, supplies, personnel, utilities, maintenance, and billing services furnished by the hospital. In a nonhospital, office-based setting, this package would normally cost about $100,000 to $150,000 per year. The hospital will charge the radiology group only $25,000 at first, but increase the charges to $100,000 over four years. Payments are due only if the hospital's gross revenue derived from radiology services exceeds $1,000,000 in the previous year.
- The hospital's clinical laboratory, under the direction of the pathology group, would pay the hospital a 20 percent fee for "specimen collection and handling services" when a physician on the MWHC medical staff orders a test from the clinical lab.

What advice would you give?

Comprehensive Review Problem: Forming an Integrated Delivery System

Review the introductory discussion at page 359 and the description of Marcus Welby Hospital at page 364. Now, consider the following methods the hospital might pursue for closer affiliation with physicians, in order to begin to form an integrated delivery system. Suppose this affiliation was undertaken either to market a comprehensive managed care insurance plan, or, less ambitiously, to establish an outpatient clinic. How would each of three possible integration/affiliation models fare under each of several business and legal factors that have been reviewed in this chapter? Fill in this chart by indicating whether each business or legal factor would view each arrangement favorably (+), negatively (−), or in neutral/mixed way (/).

	Physician Autonomy	Clinical and Financial Integration	Corporate Practice of Medicine	Antitrust	Referral Fee Law	Tax Exempt
Foundation Plan The hospital's corporate parent buys out physician practices and employs the physicians.						
Physician-Hospital Organization (PHO) Hospital and several physician groups form joint-venture partnership, contribute equal capital, and split the proceeds.						
Management Services Organization (MSO) Hospital contracts with independent physicians to provide office management services and to act as negotiating agent with insurers/employers.						

Glossary of Organizational Terms and Acronyms

In previous generations, it was necessary to learn a specialized vocabulary to study law and medicine. This is still true, but in the past that vocabulary was purely medical. Today, it includes many obscure organizational terms as well. This is a selected glossary of organizational terms and acronyms, adapted from Prospective Payment Assessment Commission, 1996 Report to Congress.

AFDC	Aid to Families with Dependent Children
AHA	American Hospital Association
AHRQ	Agency for Health Care Research and Quality
AMA	American Medical Association
CMS	Center for Medicare and Medicaid Services
COBRA	Consolidated Omnibus Budget Reconciliation Act of 1985
CON	Certificate of Need
DRG	Diagnosis-Related Group
DHHS	See HHS
ERISA	Employee Retirement Income Security Act of 1974
ESRD	End-Stage Renal Disease
FDA	Food and Drug Administration
HCFA	Health Care Financing Administration, now CMS
HHS	Health and Human Services, Department of
HIV	Human Immunodeficiency Virus
HRA *or* HSA	Healthcare Reimbursement or Health Savings Account (see also MSA)
HMO	Health Maintenance Organization

IDS	Integrated Delivery System
IPA	Independent Practice Association
JCAHO	Joint Commission on Accreditation of Healthcare Organizations
MSA	Medical Savings Account
MSO	Management Services Organization
NCQA	National Committee for Quality Assurance
OBRA	Omnibus Budget Reconciliation Act
PHO	Physician-Hospital Organization
POS	Point of Service
PPO	Preferred Provider Organization
PPS	Prospective Payment System
PRO	Peer Review Organization
RBRVS	Resource-Based Relative Value Scale
SNF	Skilled Nursing Facility
SSI	Supplemental Security Income
TEFRA	Tax Equity and Fiscal Responsibility Act of 1982
UR/UM	Utilization Review, or Utilization Management

Community Rating—A method of determining an insurance premium structure that reflects expected utilization by the population as a whole, rather than by specific groups.

Cost Shifting—Increasing revenues from some payers to offset uncompensated care losses and lower net payments from other payers.

Diagnosis-Related Groups (DRGs)—A system for determining case mix, used for payment under Medicare's PPS and by some other payers. The DRG system classifies patients into groups based on the principal diagnosis, type of surgical procedure, presence or absence of significant comorbidities or complications, and other relevant criteria. DRGs are intended to categorize patients into groups that are clinically meaningful and homogeneous with respect to resource use. Medicare's PPS currently uses 490 mutually exclusive DRGs, each of which is assigned a relative weight that compares its costlines to the average for all DRGs.

Fee-for-Service—A method of reimbursing health care providers in which payment is made for each unit of service rendered.

Health Maintenance Organization (HMO)—A managed care plan that integrates financing and delivery of a comprehensive set of health care services to an enrolled population. HMOs may contract with, directly employ, or own participating health care providers. Enrollees are usually required to choose from among these providers and in return have limited copayments. Providers may be paid through capitation, salary, per diem, or prenegotiated fee-for-service rates.

Integrated Delivery System (IDS)—Any number of different arrangements among doctors, hospitals, other medical facilities, and insurers in which a full range of medical services is offered to employers, subscribers, or insurers. Includes conventional arrangements such as HMOs, as well as more innovative arrangements known as PHOs, PSNs, or MSOs, which are discussed in Chapter 4.

Managed Care—Any system of health service payment or delivery arrangements in which the health plan or provider attempts to control or coordinate health service use to contain health expenditures, improve quality, or both. Arrangements often involve a defined delivery system of providers having some form of contractual relationship with the plan.

Medical (or Health) Savings Account (MSA/HSA)—A tax-sheltered account, similar to an IRA and also known as a Healthcare Reimbursement Account (HRA), used to pay for medical expenses. It is coupled with high-deductible or "catastrophic" insurance, such that the MSA can pay for most ordinary expenses and insurance is used only for very expensive treatment.

Peer Review Organization (PRO)—An organization that contracts with HCFA to investigate the quality of health care furnished to Medicare beneficiaries and to educate beneficiaries and providers. PROs also conduct limited review of medical records and claims to evaluate the appropriateness of care provided.

Physician-Hospital Organization (PHO)—A joint venture or affiliation among one or more hospitals and physicians or physician groups. The venture might encompass the full range of medical services, or only one or a few services.

Point-of-Service (POS)—A health plan allowing the enrollee to choose to receive a service from a participating or a nonparticipating provider, with different benefit levels associated with one or the other types of providers.

Preferred Provider Organization (PPO)—A health plan with a network of providers whose services are available to enrollees at lower cost than the services of nonnetwork providers. PPO enrollees may self-refer to any network provider at any time.

Prospective Payment—A method of paying health care providers in which rates are established in advance. Providers are paid these rates regardless of the costs they actually incur.

Prospective Payment System (PPS)—Medicare's acute care hospital payment method for inpatient care. Prospective per case payment rates are set at a level intended to cover operating costs for treating a typical inpatient in a given diagnosis-related group. Payments for each hospital are adjusted for differences in area wages, teaching activity, care to the poor, and other factors.

Relative Value Scale—An index that assigns weights to each medical service; the weights represent the relative amount to be paid for each service. The relative value scale used in the development of the Medicare Physician Fee Schedule consists of three cost components, physician work, practice expense, and malpractice expense.

Risk Adjustment—Increases or reductions in the amount of payment made to a health plan on behalf of a group of enrollees to compensate for health care expenditures that are expected to be higher or lower than average.

Uncompensated Care—Care rendered by hospitals or other providers without payment from the patient or a government-sponsored or private insurance program. It includes both charity care, which is provided without the expectation of payment, and bad debts, for which the provider has made an unsuccessful effort to collect payment due from the patient.

Utilization Review (UR)—The review of services delivered by a health care provider to evaluate the appropriateness, necessity, and quality of the prescribed services. The review can be performed on a prospective, concurrent, or retrospective basis.

Table of Cases

Principal cases are in italics. Cases cited in excerpted materials are not listed here.

573

Index